THE KOREAS

Titles in ABC-CLIO's *Asia in Focus* Series

China   Robert André LaFleur, Editor

Japan   Lucien Ellington

The Koreas   Mary E. Connor, Editor

THE KOREAS

Mary E. Connor, Editor

A B C • C L I O

Santa Barbara, California • Denver, Colorado • Oxford, England

Library of Congress Cataloging-in-Publication Data
The Koreas/Mary E. Connor, editor.
    p. cm.—(Asia in focus)
  Includes bibliographical references and index.
  ISBN 978-1-59884-160-2 (hardcopy : alk. paper) ISBN 978-1-59884-161-9 (eBook)
  1. Korea—Civilization. 2. Korea (South)—Civilization.
3. Korea (North)—Civilization. I. Connor, Mary E.
  DS904.K66   2009
  951.9—dc22   2009006299

13   12   11   10   2   3   4   5

This book is also available on the World Wide Web as an eBook.
Visit www.abc-clio.com for details.

ABC-CLIO, LLC
130 Cremona Drive, P.O. Box 1911
Santa Barbara, California 93116–1911

This book is printed on acid-free paper ∞

Manufactured in the United States of America

For my husband, Gerry Fallon, and America's teachers.

Contents

About the Editor
and the Contributors

Mary E. Connor taught U.S. history and Asian studies for 35 years and now serves as president of the Korea Academy for Educators. She is the author of *The Koreas: A Global Studies Handbook* (Santa Barbara, CA: ABC-CLIO, 2002) and the recipient of the Peace Corps Association's Global Educator Award and the Organization of American Historians Tachau Award.

Bruce Fulton holds a PhD in modern Korean literature from Seoul National University and is the inaugural holder of the Young-Bin Min Chair in Korean Literature and Literary Translation in the Department of Asian Studies at the University of British Columbia. He is the cotranslator, with Ju-Chan Fulton, of numerous works of modern Korean fiction, most recently *There a Petal Silently Falls: Three Stories by Ch'oe Yun* (New York: Columbia University Press, 2008); the editor of the Korean sections of *The Encyclopedia of Modern Asia* (Chicago: Berkshire, 2002) and *The Columbia Companion to Modern East Asian Literature* (New York: Columbia University Press, 2003); and the coeditor of *Modern Korean Fiction: An Anthology* (New York: Columbia University Press, 2005). He has received numerous awards and grants, including the first National Endowment for the Arts Translation Fellowship (1995) ever awarded for a work of Korean literature and the first Banff International Literary Translation Centre residency (2007) for a work translated from any Asian literature.

Dong Suk Kim is an assistant professor of the Department of Ethnomusicology at the University of California, Los Angeles; director of the Korean Classical Music and Dance Company; and recipient of the Durfee Award (2008). Dedicated to sustaining the rich traditions of Korean music and dance, he has conducted more than 5,000 school performances throughout California, averaging between 150 and 250 each year.

Doug Kim holds a master's degree in business administration from the University of California, Berkeley, and is currently a lecturer in the Asian American Studies Department of San Francisco State University. He is an advanced beginner in Korean martial arts, with more than 34 years of experience. Kim has published articles for the Smithsonian's Folklife Department on Korean culture and the martial arts.

Meher McArthur is a free-lance Asian art historian, author, and educator based in Los Angeles, California. She has a master's degree in Japanese studies from Cambridge University and a master's degree in Asian art history from London University's School of Oriental and African Studies. She worked for nine years at the Pacific Asia Museum as curator of East Asian art and still regularly guest curates exhibitions there. Her most recent publications are *Reading Buddhist Art: An Illustrated Guide to Buddhist Signs and Symbols* (London: Thames & Hudson, 2002) and *The Arts of Asia: Materials, Techniques, Styles* (London: Thames & Hudson, 2005).

John H. Song, dean of the Sejong Institute of Los Angeles and section head of the Korean Language Program of the Modern and Classical Languages and Literature at California State University, Northridge, is currently working on a PhD in intercultural education. He is a coauthor of *Beginning Korean 1* (Seoul: Korean Language Institute, 2008) and contributor to *Short-Term Missions Boom* (Ada, MI: Baker, 1994).

Preface

Asia in Focus: The Koreas is an attempt to meet the need for a comprehensive and up-to-date introduction to both North Korea and South Korea. What has been available is often too detailed for the general reader, especially the young. It is my hope that the book will serve those who are new to a study of Korea as well as those who have some knowledge of the nation's long and dramatic history, its distinctive culture, and the courage, perseverance, and accomplishments of its people. It is also my hope that educators will find it to be a very practical and engaging resource for bringing Korean history and culture into their classrooms. For those who plan to travel in Korea for pleasure or for conducting business, this book is intended to serve as a helpful guide.

My intellectual odyssey with Korea began in 1993. By that time I had taught history (United States, Europe, and China and Japan) for 22 years on the secondary level. I had the good fortune to meet Dr. Jon Covell, Fulbright scholar, art historian, author of five books on Korea, and a woman whose passion for that culture was passed on to me. In one of our first conversations about Asia, she said, "You know, Korea is the most interesting of the Asian cultures." I became captivated by Korea and incorporated its history and culture into my curriculum.

Since I began my own discovery, I have had the pleasure of communicating with many Koreans in the United States and abroad. Inevitably, my own passion delights and at times amazes them. As a result of numerous speaking engagements and the publication of articles on teaching about Asia, I received a Korea Society Fellowship in 2000 to study and travel in Korea. Since this fellowship and subsequent trips to South Korea and North Korea, the Korean peninsula has virtually become the center of my world. I am surprised that Americans still know so little about the Koreas.

Many of the Koreans who migrated to the United States want to forget the hardships of the past and create a more secure life for their families. The word *han*, living with great and sustained sorrow, expresses the anguish that most felt during the 20th century. From 1910 to 1945, the peninsula was under the harsh rule of the Japanese. Liberation came with the end of World War II, but the hopes of the indomitable Korean people were almost shattered. What followed was political division, occupation, and civil war. At the end of the Korean War in 1953, Korea remained divided, heavily fortified, and occupied again, but this time by two rival superpowers: the United States and the Soviet Union. Both North and South were devastated by the war and ranked among the poorest nations of the world. After the U.S. Congress adopted the Immigration Act of 1965, it was possible for many to come to the United States. They decided to leave their homeland because there might be yet another war.

In light of its turbulent history, strategic location, and the continual state of tension of the peninsula, Korea has often flashed across newspaper headlines and television screens for more than 50 years, only to disappear from view when the immediate crisis passes. The periodic attention of the world means that few people in most countries have any historical context for understanding a particular event or its significance for the stability of East Asia. After the attack on the World Trade Center and the Pentagon on September 11, 2001, I hoped Americans would feel a great need to become more interested in international affairs and our place in them; however, I remain very aware that Americans know little about Asia, especially the Koreas.

Whether the reader of *Asia in Focus: The Koreas* is a student, educator, business person, tourist, or someone who is simply curious, it will become clear just how closely involved the history of the United States is with that of Korea. The United States has been connected to this nation since 1882, when Admiral Robert Schufeldt opened the country to the West by a treaty that was designed to enlarge trading opportunities. While most people are aware that the United States provided the major support to defend South Korea when North Korea invaded in 1950, they are not aware that the United States divided the Korean peninsula without consulting any Koreans at the end of World War II. U.S. troops remain stationed in South Korea, and the peninsula remains one of the most heavily fortified regions in the world.

Few realize that while U.S. students demonstrated against the Vietnam War, 300,000 young South Koreans fought in it. And in 1994, the United States almost went to war with North Korea. Former U.S. president Jimmy Carter as a private citizen walked across the border with his wife, met with the leader of North Korea, and war did not happen. In the 21st century, the United States continues to be closely connected to Korea. Although the administration of George W. Bush was largely occupied by the war in Iraq and critical issues involving the Middle East, resolving the nuclear issue on the Korean peninsula became a high priority in the later months of his administration. The issue continues to be an area of serious concern for the administration of U.S. president Barack Obama.

ACKNOWLEDGMENTS

I have many people to thank for assisting me in writing this book. My husband, Gerry Fallon, made the completion of this book a reality because of his patience, advice, encouragement, and invaluable computer assistance. I want to thank the authors (Bruce Fulton, Don Kim, Doug Kim, Meher McArthur, and John Song) for their expertise and dedication to make this book a reality.

I wish to express gratitude to Joy Kim (curator, Korean Heritage Library, University of Southern California) and Tammy Chung (librarian, Korean Cultural Center, Los Angeles) for their guidance and support. Frank Shin (director of the Korean Tourism Organization, Los Angeles), Edward Chang, Jennifer Goger, and Helie Lee were very helpful in assisting me with photographs for the book. I also thank Mark Peterson (Korean studies, Brigham Young University) for reading parts of the manuscript and offering ideas to improve it. I also wish to thank Lynn Jurgensen and Kim Kennedy White at ABC-CLIO for their support along the way.

A NOTE ABOUT KOREAN SPELLING

And finally, I should comment on the Korean spelling in this book. Our alphabet does not have sufficient symbols to cover the Korean sound system. It is not possible to convey the exact Korean pronunciation by means of the English alphabet. Different systems of romanization have been devised over the years; however, Western authors prefer the McCune-Reischauer system that was adopted in 1984. For the most part, I have kept to this system.

Maps

Korean Peninsula, 2009

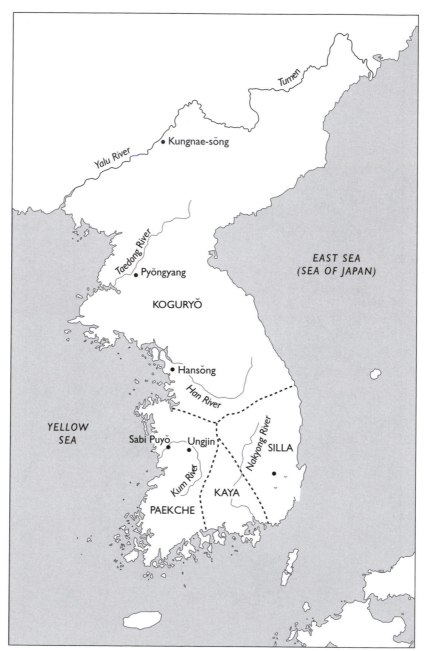

The Three Kingdoms, and Kaya Kingdom.

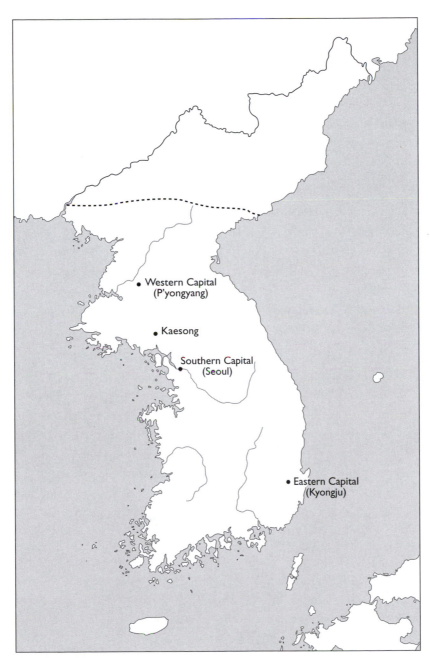

11th-Century Koryo.

Korea, Choson Dynasty.

Geography

Mary E. Connor

THE KOREAN PENINSULA

Situated in the northeastern corner of East Asia, the Korean Peninsula is bounded to the north by two giant neighbors, China and Russia. The peninsula was divided almost in half at the end of World War II in 1945, with the communist Democratic People's Republic of Korea (North Korea) occupying about 55 percent of the peninsula and the Republic of Korea (South Korea) occupying about 45 percent.

The length of the Korean Peninsula is approximately 625 miles from the northern border to the southern tip and extends southward from eastern Siberia and Manchuria to within 70 miles of Japan at the peninsula's southernmost point. While it may appear small (85,563 square miles) on a map of the Asian continent, the peninsula is half the size of California but smaller than the combined areas of England, Scotland, and Wales. It is considerably smaller than Japan (145,370 square miles). The combined population of North and South Korea is about 72 million, almost double that of California and more than half that of Japan. With its north-south elongation, the Korean Peninsula separates the Yellow Sea (which Koreans call the West Sea) from the Sea of Japan (which Koreans call the East Sea).

In spite of division, powerful neighbors, and periods of foreign occupation (China, the Mongols, Japan, and after World War II, the United States and Soviet Union), Korea remains essentially a homogeneous society. They have an evident identity long preserved by geographic isolation and resistance, warfare, and negotiation. In spite of the turbulent events of the past century, including Japan's 35-year military occupation, one of history's most brutal civil wars, and poverty levels

Ch'angdokkung Palace buildings in Seoul, South Korea. (Courtesy of the Korea Tourism Organization)

ranking among the worst in the world, Koreans have not abandoned their traditional traits of warmth and generosity. Those who travel to South Korea (visitors to North Korea are severely restricted) often remark that the people are among the most responsive and friendly anywhere.

Considering the peninsula's moderate size, the Koreas have a relatively large number of rivers and streams. These waterways played a significant role in shaping the way of life of the people and of economic development. Such cities as Seoul (South Korea's capital) and P'yongyang (North Korea's capital) developed along major rivers as ports. With the arrival of railroads and automobiles, the importance of rivers declined.

An important Korean river is the Imjin, which flows through both North and South Korea. The peninsula's major rivers flow north to south or east to west and empty into the Yellow Sea or the Korean Strait. Most Korean rivers are used extensively for irrigation. Because of the seasonal variations in precipitation, rivers are shallow most of the year except for the summer rainy season. This causes a great deal of variation in hydroelectric generation as well as in water supply. Coastal and inland plains provide fertile farmland and excellent locations for cities. Over the centuries, the Korean people developed a passion for nature that was fostered by the sheer beauty of the country and four very distinct seasons.

Most of the peninsula is mountainous; the eastern range is rugged and meets the ocean suddenly, making the eastern coast a very scenic one. Few peaks on the peninsula exceed 4,000 feet; however, the highest and most sacred place on the entire peninsula is Mount Paektu (9,003 feet), which straddles the North Korean–Chinese border. For most of Korea's history, the mountains and the sea made it more difficult for invading armies to occupy the peninsula. The mountain ranges of the Koreas run in two major directions, north to south and northeast to southwest. The ranges that stretch from north to south—the T'aebaek range in South Korea and the Nangnim range in North Korea—form the spine of the peninsula and create a watershed between the western and eastern mountain slopes.

The peninsula's coastline is long compared to its total land area because there is so much indentation along the south and west coasts. However, the east coast has a relatively smooth coastline.

Such high peaks as Kumgangsan (North Korea) and Soraksan (South Korea) are located along the dividing ridge of the two mountain ranges and are famous for their scenic beauty. Hiking in these mountains has been a passion for the Korean people for many centuries, and both mountains remain popular tourist attractions. Kumgangsan ("Diamond Mountain") is so named because its spectacular granite peaks glisten in the sunlight. Ancient sources reveal that this mountain has been considered a sacred place for thousands of years. Currently, Kumgangsan is one of the few places in North Korea where South Koreans can visit relatively freely. The area of Soraksan ("Snowy Crags Mountain") is known for its magnificent high craggy peaks, lush forests, huge waterfalls, white-water rivers, and ancient temples, some of which date back to the Silla era.

The peninsula is a fairly stable land mass in spite of its proximity to Japan. The Koreas do not have active volcanoes or strong earthquakes. The volcanic Mount Paektu has been worshipped for centuries as the place of Korea's ancestral origins. Lake Chonji ("Heavenly Lake"), one of the highest crater lakes in the world, is located at its summit.

Because the peninsula is adjacent to Japan by a short distance across the Korean Strait, its location has allowed Korean society to make contact with various civilizations throughout history. Thousands of years ago, Asian continental culture introduced Chinese characters, pottery, and Confucianism to Korea. These cultural influences were transformed and then transmitted to Japan. Today, Korea holds considerable economic and geopolitical importance in East Asia.

One cannot discuss the Korean Peninsula without mentioning the demilitarized zone (DMZ), which was created by the 1953 Korean Armistice Agreement that ended the Korean War in a stalemate. The DMZ, used for border protection, extends roughly 150 miles between the Koreas and is 2.5 miles wide (or 6 miles wide, if each country's buffer zones are included). The two Koreas have more than 1 million troops who face each other across the DMZ, a territory that has seen virtually no other human activity for more than 50 years.

The DMZ has become home to many species of plants and animals. It is now an important rest stop for birds as they migrate. Rare Manchurian cranes and Siberian herons are two of the many birds that use it as a resting place. According to figures compiled by environmentalists, the DMZ is home to about 2,900 different plant species as well as about 70 different types of mammals and 320 types of birds. Visitors who come to the DMZ can see trees completely full of birds. This area crosses mountains, prairies, swamps, lakes, and tidal marshes, giving the area a wide range of biological diversity. In its role as wildlife sanctuary, the DMZ is protected as long as the conflict between the Koreas officially continues. Ironically, peace is the one thing that threatens its existence. The land's incredible natural beauty and the fact that it is only 20 miles from Seoul could mean big profits for ambitious developers.

The Korean Peninsula sits at the vital center of East Asia, one of the world's most strategically important and dynamic regions. The geographic outlines on the map of the Korean Peninsula will not change, but with reunification, the dividing line at the 38th parallel will be a memory and no longer a political demarcation.

PHYSICAL GEOGRAPHY: NORTH KOREA

North Korea occupies slightly more than half of the peninsula and is bounded by the Yellow Sea (West Sea) to the west, the Sea of Japan (East Sea) to the east, and China and Russia to the north. Most of North Korea is mountainous and rugged, and the coastline is indented with numerous small islands, coves, and promontories. The land boundary between North Korea and China is mostly formed by the Yalu River and the Tumen River, the easternmost 10 miles of which serve as the border with Russia.

The Yalu (499 miles long) and the Tumen (323 miles long), which flow from Mount Paektu, are the two longest rivers in North Korea. The Tumen, the North's second-longest river, is one of the country's few rivers to flow into the East Sea (Sea of Japan). It is navigable for only 52 miles because of the mountainous topography. The North's third-largest river, the Taedong (280 miles long), flows through North Korea's capital and largest city, P'yongyang.

The weather in the North and the South is similar, but it is colder and drier in the North. In North Korea, the seasons are dry except for the rains that arrive during the time of the summer monsoons. More than half of P'yongyang's 37 inches of annual precipitation falls in July and August. Summers are hot and humid in the low-lying regions, and temperatures in July can reach 80°F. During the summer months, North Korea's temperatures are milder in the highlands. Occasionally, typhoons strike the coast, wreaking havoc on cities and farms. Fall features moderate temperatures and changing weather that leads into the bitterly cold, clear winter. During the winter months, continental high-pressure air masses develop over Siberia and bring strong winds and dry, frigid temperatures. The peninsula is located in the East Asian monsoon belt; thus, North Korea's monsoons—usually stronger in the winter than the summer—can cause great suffering. Winter temperatures in P'yongyang can plummet to −10°F. Spring brings another warm and mild season to the North before the summer monsoons begin.

Some 80 percent of North Korea's land area is composed of mountains and uplands. All of the peninsula's mountains with an elevation of more than 6,000 feet are in North Korea. Most North Koreans live in the plains and lowlands.

In North Korea, only 14 percent of land is arable, and most of that comprises fertile plains in the southwest and land scattered along the island-free east coast. North Korea's high mountain areas contain the majority of its forest resources, while the lower foothills provide grazing lands for livestock and orchard areas for fruit trees. Neat, one-story brick houses with traditional roofs or multistory, stark-looking concrete structures appear periodically among vast rice paddies or near hillsides covered with maize (a close relative of corn). Maize is grown on virtually every spare strip of land in the North Korean countryside and even in the cities. Flooding in 1995 and 1996, and drought in 1997 and 2000, severely affected all of the North's agricultural areas, creating continuing food shortages in the country. Rice cultivation is concentrated in the coastal lowlands, and such crops as corn, wheat, and soybeans are grown on dry field plateaus. North Korea's principal crops (aside from maize) include rice, potatoes, corn, cabbage, apples, soybeans, and sweet potatoes, and important livestock products include pork, eggs, dairy, veal, goat meat, and beef.

North Korea contains about 90 percent of the peninsula's mineral deposits, encompassing some 200 economically valuable resources. The country's main mineral resources are barite, copper, fluorspar, gold, graphite, iron ore, lead, limestone, magnesite, silver, tungsten, and zinc. Major deposits of iron ore lie in the provinces of North Hwanghae and South Hwanghae. North Korea's magnesite reserves, the world's largest, are located in Tanch'on, in the province of South Hamgyong. The country's main gold and silver mine is located in Unsan in the province of North Pyongan, while South Hamgyong produces most of North Korea's lead and zinc. Major deposits of anthracite coal can be found along the Taedong River—mostly at Anju, north of P'yongyang, in the province of Yanggang.

North Korea's hydroelectric power resources were originally developed along the Yalu River during the early-20th-century Japanese occupation. Today, hydroelectric power provides most of North Korea's electrical needs, although a 1996 flood damaged much of the country's hydropower infrastructure, and some facilities have not been repaired. In addition, thermal electricity from coal-fired generating plants is becoming increasingly important to North Korea because of lower costs and the difficulty of generating hydroelectricity during the dry season.

PHYSICAL GEOGRAPHY: SOUTH KOREA

In South Korea, the Naktong River (323 miles long) and the Han River (319 miles long) are the two major waterways. The Han flows through Seoul, which is not only South Korea's capital but also its largest city.

The South Korean spring is warm and long, summer is hot and humid, autumn is cool, and winter is cold. Summer's normal high temperature ranges between 80°F and 90°F, except for South Korea's northern interior. Autumn (especially late October and early November), with its crisp air, blue sky, and glorious fall colors, is the

View from Cheju Island. (Courtesy of the Korea Tourism Organization)

season most widely loved and the best time for visitors to travel in South Korea. Another good time to visit is in late March and early April to witness the blooming of beautiful pink cherry blossoms that cover the nation's mountains and fields. April, May, and June are considered good months before the summer monsoon rains. Winter, from November to March, can be bitterly cold due to the influence of Siberian air. Heavy snow in the northern and eastern parts of South Korea provides very favorable skiing conditions. Cheju Island, sometimes referred to as the Hawai'i of Korea, is located off the south coast and is the warmest place in South Korea—and also the wettest. Cheju Island is extraordinarily beautiful and a place that Koreans hold very dear, attracting honeymooners, families, and foreign tourists.

Approximately 3,400 islands lie off the Korean coast, and most are located in South Korea, off the southern and southwestern coastal areas. The largest of these is South Korea's Cheju Island, with an area of 706 square miles. Where the mountains are near the sea, the coast is rocky with few beaches. In areas where there are small streams running into the sea, there are beautiful lagoons and clean sandy beaches that are attractive to tourists in the summer months. The south and west coasts contrast with the east coast in that coastlines are very irregular with innumerable islands, small peninsulas, and bays. The length of the southern coastline is about eight times longer than its straight-line distance, and its indentation is far greater than that of the west coast. The tidal range of the southern coastline is relatively small, some 4.2 feet at Pusan on the eastern side. The west coast faces the Yellow Sea and has a large tidal range and a shallow offshore bottom.

Because the peninsula's terrain is predominantly mountainous, only a small percentage of each country's surface area is arable land that can be used for food production. Approximately 21 percent of the land in South Korea is suitable for cultivation. Rice is South Korea's principal crop and is grown on approximately 60 percent of the country's agricultural land. Barley, wheat, soybeans, potatoes, millet, and an assortment of vegetables are also grown in South Korea, with barley and rice commonly double-cropped (the crops grow interspersed with each other) in the country's southern provinces. Ginseng fields can also be seen throughout many parts of South Korea. And in recent years, South Korea has expanded its fruit production, particularly the cultivation of apples, oranges, grapes, persimmons, pears, and peaches. Cotton, silk, and hemp are also produced in South Korea, and the country's farmers raise such livestock as pigs, cattle, and goats.

For decades, South Korea has been home to one of the world's busiest fishing industries. The country's major ports are Ulsan and Masan, and its most important marine resources are seaweed, squid, mollusks, anchovies, tuna, pollock, and mackerel.

South Korea's natural resources are not plentiful. With the exception of graphite and tungsten deposits in the region around Sang Dong, which are some of the world's largest, the countryside offers relatively sparse mining resources. These reserves include anthracite coal, gold, silver, lead, iron ore, and zinc, with most South Korean mining activity focusing on the extraction of coal and iron ore. However, South Korea possesses a mere 10 percent of the peninsula's coal deposits.

While hydroelectric power accounts for only a small amount of South Korea's production of electricity—with most hydropower stations situated along the Han River near Seoul—thermal electric power totals more than 50 percent of the country's power generation. In recent years, South Korea has built an increasing number of nuclear power plants, with which the government hopes to fill almost half of South Korea's energy needs in the near future.

HUMAN GEOGRAPHY

The Korean people, unlike Americans, are racially and linguistically homogeneous. Except for approximately 20,000 Chinese, no sizable indigenous minorities exist on the peninsula. While early cultural contacts with China and Japan were extensive, the Korean peninsula's native population remained conscious of ethnic differences and cultural distinctions. Assimilation did not occur. Half a million Koreans live in Central Asia, and 2 million more reside in the vast area of Manchuria. Koreans physically resemble the peoples of Manchuria and Mongolia. They have almond-shaped eyes, black hair, and relatively high cheekbones. Like other Mongolian peoples, Korean babies are born with blue spots on the lower part of the back. Koreans have maintained their distinctive cultural and ethnic identity.

Kaesong, North Korea, once the capital city of the Koryo Dynasty, is some 4 miles north of the DMZ. It was exempt from carpet-bombing during the Korean War, but it was badly damaged from the ground war. The South Korean and North Korean governments have created an industrial zone in Kaesong to improve economic conditions. (Courtesy of Marsh Wong)

North Korea

The Democratic People's Republic of Korea (North Korea's official name) has for more than 50 years directed a society vastly different from South Korea, through the exercise of totalitarian control. The collapse of the Soviet Union and other European communist countries had a powerful impact in North Korea, as did China's shift to a "socialist market" economy. The North rejected market reforms and sought to bargain its way out of difficulties with a nuclear weapons program and buildup of conventional forces as its principal method of negotiation. Thus, it has raised fears throughout the world about the dangers of nuclear warfare and sparked ongoing political debate within the United States regarding national security.

North Korea is divided into nine provinces (*do* indicates a province): Chagang-do (Chagang), Hamgyong-bukto (North Hamgyong), Hamgyong-namdo (South Hamgyong), Hwanghae-bukto (North Hwanghae), Hwanghae-namdo (South Hwanghae), Kangwon-do (Kangwon), P'yongan-bukto (North P'yongan), P'yongan-namdo (South P'yongan), and Yanggang-do (Yanggang).

The estimated population of North Korea as of 2008 was 23 million, with a life expectancy of 72 years. The North's birthrates have been declining in recent years, leading to an annual population growth rate of 0.79 percent. Of the two countries, North Korea has a lower population density.

In the process of transforming a typical agricultural society into an industrial one, significant migration from rural areas has occurred in both the North and South. In North Korea, the estimated number of workers involved in agriculture is 37 percent—a much higher percentage than in South Korea. Agriculture contributes 23 percent to the gross domestic product (GDP) of North Korea. In the North, approximately 70 percent of the population lives in cities, significantly less than in the South.

North Korea's biggest metropolis, the capital of P'yongyang, has a population of approximately 2.7 million people. The capital is a well-ordered city carefully designed to glorify national founder Kim Il-Sung and promote socialism. It is also the political, cultural, and educational center of the nation. Huge sterile-looking buildings resembling Soviet architecture appear in P'yongyang and smaller cities throughout the country. The majority of the people live in austere, concrete, modern high-rise buildings. The streets are clean, and boulevards are lined with trees. Billboards with propaganda appear everywhere.

Air pollution is not a problem in North Korea because of its reliance on hydroelectric power rather than on fossil fuels, both for industry and for the heating of urban residences. Pollution is also limited because of the North's oil shortages, its very small number of automobiles, and its use of natural gas–powered vehicles. The lack of available consumer goods is evident in P'yongyang. There are very few stalls or vendors on the streets, and there is no litter because there is very little to throw away. North Korea is clearly not a consumer society. Current environmental issues include localized air pollution attributable to inadequate industrial controls, water pollution, and inadequate supplies of potable water.

In addition to its relative lack of automobiles, North Korea possesses only a small reserve of gasoline, and there are virtually no bicycles in the country. Most vehicles in North Korea are used exclusively by the military. Although rural bus service links most villages, and cities have bus and tram service, few public buses connect major cities or cities to rural areas. North Koreans must have official permission to travel within their country, and visitors must travel by bus or car accompanied by a government driver and guide.

In recent years, observers have estimated that the country has about 19,000 miles of roads, though they are not well maintained and only a small percentage of North Korean roads are paved. Of those paved roads, the country has only three multilane highways: a 124-mile east coast motorway linking P'yongyang and Wonsan; a 62-mile expressway connecting P'yongyang and Kaesong; and a 27-mile highway from P'yongyang to Namp'o, the capital's major port. North Korea's Choson Cul Minzuzui Inmingonghoagug is the country's only railway operator and is estimated to maintain about 3,000 miles of track.

One of North Korea's most notable landmarks—and a United Nations Educational, Scientific, and Cultural Organization (UNESCO) Cultural World Heritage Site—is the Koguryo Tombs complex, named for the feudal state of Koguryo (100 BCE–668 CE). Located in the Taedong River basin south of P'yongyang, the complex consists of more than 70 tombs decorated with murals—the oldest paintings on the peninsula—depicting a wide range of subjects including gods, kings, soldiers, and workers. Another important landmark is P'yongyang's 558-foot-tall

Juche Tower, which was built in 1972 and is today the world's loftiest stone tower. Juche Tower is an ever-present reminder of *juche*, North Korea's ruling principle, which emphasizes self-reliance. In addition, the cult of personality surrounding North Korean founder Kim Il-Sung is exemplified by the Mansudae Grand Monument, a colossal bronze statue of Kim unveiled in 1972 to honor the 60th birthday of the "Great Leader."

South Korea

Notwithstanding the utter devastation of the Korean War, South Korea's subsequent rapid economic growth was spectacular. Between 1953 and 1995, the Republic of Korea (South Korea's official name) progressed from being one of the world's poorest nations to becoming the world's 11th-largest economy, a development called the Miracle on the Han (the Han is one of South Korea's major rivers). However, it was talented and hard-working people who created the industrialized economy we see today. Another noteworthy advance in South Korea since the 1980s has been the transformation from political instability and autocratic rule toward stability and democracy.

South Korea is divided into nine provinces (*do* indicates a province): Cheju-do, Cholla-bukto (North Cholla), Cholla-namdo (South Cholla), Ch'ungch'ong-bukto (North Ch'ungch'ong), Ch'ungch'ong-namdo (South Ch'ungch'ong), Kangwon-do, Kyonggi-do, Kyongsang-bukto (North Kyongsang), and Kyongsang-namdo (South Kyongsang).

As of 2008, the estimated population of South Korea was 49 million, with a life expectancy of 77 years. Recently, birthrates in the South have been declining, and the country's annual population growth rate is at 0.39 percent. Population density is much greater in the South, where 2 million people migrated from the North following World War II. In contrast to the country's past, only 3 percent of South Korea's labor force is today involved in agriculture, and agriculture contributes only 7.5 percent to the South's GDP.

South Korea's urban population accounted for only 28 percent of the total in 1960. Today, nearly 90 percent of the population lives in urban areas. Metropolitan growth and urbanization have been most pronounced in the two largest cities, Seoul (11 million people) and Pusan (3.9 million people), where residents seem to live on top of each other. Employment opportunities, together with the best public and private institutions—ranging from financial and commercial to educational and cultural—have led to the rapid growth of cities in South Korea.

Seoul, the South's political, economic, and educational hub, is a city of incredible contrasts. It is a modern metropolis complete with skyscrapers, though the still-standing, centuries-old royal palaces, temples, and ancient gateways remain timeless. High-rise apartment buildings are stacked close to each other and numbered in bold figures to simplify the process of locating a residence. And there are the inevitable traffic jams and air pollution; air and water pollution in large South Korean cities is a significant problem.

Rice fields near Kyongju, South Korea, once the ancient capital of the Silla kingdom. (Courtesy of Mary Connor)

The streets are clean and free of litter. Other principal South Korean cities are Taegu, the center of the silk industry; Inch'on, the major port on the Yellow Sea; and Kyongju, the ancient capital of the Silla kingdom.

Unlike the North, South Korea has a modern, extensive transportation network, encompassing railways and other public transit, airlines, private automobiles, and multilane highways, which were mostly constructed since the 1980s. The country has more than 10 million passenger cars, which regularly clog South Korea's 63,000 miles of roads—almost 50,000 miles of which are paved. South Korean bus travel is safe, fast, and punctual, and bus routes are categorized as *Gosok* ("express") and *Shioe* ("intercity/suburban"), with the latter making more frequent stops. South Koreans can also travel by ferry to offshore islands and within interior lakes.

South Korea's rail system is operated by Korea National Railroad, and its trains are clean, safe, and on time. In addition to local trains, the country's railways feature a high-speed service called "KTX," which travels the length of South Korea. The nation's bullet trains can reach speeds exceeding 185 miles per hour. Such major cities as Seoul and Pusan (among others) are home to safe, efficient, inexpensive subway systems.

It is anticipated that further urbanization will continue in both Koreas, but that the rate will moderate. Public policy will be directed toward balancing regional development. In South Korea, the reduction of urban and rural disparities in socioeconomic conditions will be essential in alleviating the urbanization trend. Most of the rural population in the South is involved with agriculture and lives in the lowlands of the west and south coasts and along major river valleys. Clustered villages are common except in mountainous regions and reclaimed land on the west coast. Farm labor shortages have arisen primarily because of the excessive rural-to-urban migrations of South Korea's young people.

Two of South Korea's most exceptional landmarks are the Pulguksa Temple complex and the nearby Sokkuram grotto, which are UNESCO World Heritage sites. The Pulguksa Temple complex, completed in 752 CE during the Silla dynasty, features a series of stone pagodas and terraces on T'ohamsan Mountain. About 2 miles up the mountain overlooking the East Sea (Sea of Japan) is the temple grotto of Seokguram, which features a large white-granite sculpture of Sakyamuni Buddha. The grotto also contains other sculptures and relief carvings from the Silla period. Another notable landmark is Seoul's 40-acre Kyongbokkung Palace, which was completed in 1394. Some of the palace's highlights are the Kunjongjon (throne room), the Hyangwonjong pavilion and lotus pond, and the Kyongch'onsa Temple's 10-story pagoda.

REFERENCES

Adams, Edward B. 1986. *Korea's Guide: A Glimpse of Korea's Cultural Legacy.* Seoul: Seoul International Publishing House.

Cumings, Bruce. 1997. *Korea's Place in the Sun: A Modern History.* New York: W. W. Norton.

Korean Overseas Information Service. 1993. *Handbook of Korea.* 9th ed. Seoul: Korean Overseas Information Service, Ministry of Culture and Information.

————. 2003. *A Handbook of Korea.* 11th ed. Seoul: Korean Overseas Information Service, Ministry of Culture and Information.

Herskovitz, Jon. 2005. "CNN Founder Turner Wants Nature Park for Koreas' DMZ." Garden-Web. http://nature.gardenweb.com/forums/load/sustain/msg0818560613110.html (accessed March 28, 2008).

Neufield, Ann Nichole. 1997. "Case Study: The DMZ." *ICE Case Studies.* Inventory of Conflict & Environment. http://www.american.edu/ted/ice/dmz.htm (accessed March 28, 2008).

Oh, Kongdan, and Ralph Hassig. 2000. *North Korea through the Looking Glass.* Washington, DC: Brookings Institution Press.

Park, Young-Han, et al. 2003. *Atlas of Korea.* Seoul: Sung Ji Mun Hwa Co., Ltd.

Reitman, Valerie. 2000. "Amid Tears, Koreans Cross 50-year Divide." *Los Angeles Times,* August 16.

Shin, Ki-sop. 2003. *Korea Annual: 2003.* Seoul: Yonhap News Agency.

Sohn, Yong Taik, and Kwang Jaw Jim, eds. 1998. *Facts and Fallacies about Korea.* Seoul: Korean Educational Development Institute.

U.S. Department of State. 2008. "Background Note: North Korea." http://www.state.gov/p/eap/ci/kn (accessed March 27, 2008).

————. 2008. "Background Note: South Korea." http://www.state.gov/p/eap/ci/ks (accessed March 26, 2008).

Willoughby, Robert. 2005. *North Korea: The Bradt Travel Guide.* Guilford, CT: Bradt Travel Guides, Ltd.

History

Mary E. Connor

EARLY KOREA

Various tools from the Paleolithic age uncovered in all parts of Korea indicate that human beings have inhabited the area for half a million years. It is not clear when the ancestors of modern Koreans began to inhabit the peninsula, but most scholars agree that they are not the ethnic descendants of those Paleolithic people. They descended from Neolithic groups who entered the peninsula from areas north of Manchuria, probably in several successive migrations between 5500 and 2000 BCE.

The Koreans are Tungusic peoples, cousins of the Mongols, and their ethnic origins may be traced from those who lived in and around the Altai Mountains in Central Asia. Some of the strongest evidence for this origin is the fact that modern Korean is part of the language family of northeast Asia called "Altaic."

The early tribal peoples had a fishing, hunting, and gathering culture. They produced comb-patterned pottery similar to that found in northern Europe and Siberia, and later, after the emergence of agriculture, built large aboveground tomb chambers of stone blocks, often mounded over with earth. Evidence of rectangular huts and burial sites in the form of dolmen and stone cysts is widespread. The early Koreans believed in animism and thought all natural objects had spirits. Artifacts were closely connected to their religious practices.

Their Bronze Age began about the ninth or eighth century and lasted until the fourth century BCE. People lived in shallow pits on high ground above the flatlands where they grew their food. Agriculture during this age included rice cultivation. Clans came into contact, and advances in smelting bronze furnished powerful

13

weapons for the conquest of different clans and contributed to the rise of larger units of tribal society and even walled towns. Early artwork in the form of wall paintings reflects strong influences of Siberian and Manchurian traditions. Korean bronze daggers spread to Kyushu in Japan and greatly influenced the formation of the Japanese bronze culture.

Korea is one of the oldest countries in the world. The standard account of the origins of Ancient Choson is contained in the legend of the first great ruler, Tan'-gun, who was born of a union between the son of the divine creator and a female bear that had achieved human form. According to ancient Chinese historians, Tan'-gun made the walled city of P'yongyang the capital in 2333 BCE, called his country Choson ("Land of the Morning Calm"), and ruled for 1,000 years. No evidence supports this story, but over the centuries the legend has contributed to the Korean sense of identity as a distinct and proud race.

The walled-town state of Old Choson in time combined with others to form a single large confederation, the head of which came to be designated as its king. The use of iron hoes, plowshares, and sickles brought significant social changes. Food production increased, particularly benefiting the ruling elite. Artifacts from this period also include bronze and iron daggers and spears. Families still lived in pit dwellings, but the use of ondol devices (heating of flues under the floor) appeared.

Records indicate that the Han dynasty of China conquered Choson by 108 BCE. While the Chinese rulers allowed some political independence, the native population was forced to do whatever labor was demanded of them. Archaeological remains from this period reveal absorption of cultural influences from the Han and a remarkable degree of refinement and luxury; most likely, the people eagerly cultivated the technological advancements and artistry that came with Han occupation. With the fall of that dynasty in 220 CE, the military retreated, and the country was on its own.

The Three Kingdoms

With the end of Han dominance, three kingdoms gradually arose: Koguryo (pronounced ko-goo-rio), in the north (37 BCE–668 CE); Paekche (pronounced peck-chay), in the southwest (18 BCE–660 CE); and Silla (pronounced shil-la), in the southeast (57 BCE–935 CE). Each of the three kingdoms left records of the influence of Confucianism on government and society.

Throughout the Three Kingdoms period and afterward, Korea maintained a close relationship with China. The relationship was maintained through what was called "tributary diplomacy," the formal recognition that China's power was superior. Tribute was a gesture of friendship and involved commercial trade and cultural exchanges. It did not mean that the three kingdoms were colonies of China.

The Koguryo tribes lived in the mountainous region north of the Yalu River and maintained an aristocratic society of mounted warriors who demanded tribute from surrounding agricultural peoples. During the fourth century CE, Koguryo grew in strength and spread over the northern two-thirds of the peninsula. Meanwhile another centrally organized state, Paekche, appeared in the valley of the Han River. At the end of the fourth century, an independent kingdom named Silla appeared.

A hunting scene of Koguryo warriors that appears on the eastern wall of the Muyong Tomb located in T'ung-gu, Manchuria. The murals show that the Koguryo people hunted tigers, boars, deer, and pheasants on foot with spears, on horseback with bows, and with hawks. (Courtesy of the Institute of Culture, Art and Tourism, Sookmyung Women's University with the assistance of Jiseon Lee)

From the fourth to the second half of the seventh century CE, most of the peninsula was divided among these three states. Each kingdom eagerly sought cultural innovations from China yet retained distinct cultural elements unique to each kingdom. The three kingdoms also engaged in continuous warfare with each other.

Koguryo's proximity to China promoted continuous new influences. In 372 CE, a monk introduced Buddhism. Ultimately, this religion became the spiritual foundation of the nation. About the same time, a university was organized to teach the Confucian classics. Additional Chinese influences included a law code and a complex style of bureaucratic government. The artistic skills of Koguryo can be seen in royal tombs that contain some of the finest wall paintings of the fourth and fifth centuries. When Koguryo was defeated by Silla in the seventh century, part of it was incorporated into a state called Parhae in eastern Manchuria and northern Korea, which rose to its zenith of power and cultural achievement in the early ninth century. While Parhae is not considered one of the three early kingdoms, Koreans consider this state to be an integral part of their history.

Paekche, the second of the kingdoms, is not as well known in terms of its government and culture. Shortly after Buddhism was introduced to Koguryo, it arrived in Paekche through connections across the Yellow Sea. Beautiful tiles and other artifacts suggest that Chinese-style arts and crafts were becoming highly developed, but many objects, such as funerary urns, reveal characteristics that are unique to Korea. Several tombs of the kings of Paekche have been discovered, and artifacts

Kwaenung Tomb, the tomb of King Wonsong of Unified Silla, is in the area of Kyongju.
(Courtesy of Mary Connor)

demonstrate the impressive artistic ability and architectural skills of Paekche workers. At this time, Korea became a conduit for transmitting culture to Japan. The
people of Paekche sailed to Japan and introduced Chinese characters, Buddhism,
music, and art. In the fourth century, Paekche and Koguryo began nearly three centuries of war with one another.

Silla, the third native kingdom to emerge, was initially not as developed as
Koguryo or Paekche, it was less influenced by Chinese culture, and the arts retained
nomadic traditions. Silla ultimately became the longest dynasty in Korean history,
lasting from 57 BCE to 935 CE. Silla is also noteworthy for the position that women
held in government and society. Although Confucianism had started making inroads
into Silla, its teaching of inequality between men and women does not seem to have
had an impact. Two women occupied the throne of Silla, and one occupied the
throne of Unified Silla in the ninth century. However, they were the exceptions.

By the sixth century, the Chinese title of *wang* ("king") had been adopted, and
Buddhism was accepted as the state religion. Identifying the king with the new religion worked to consolidate authority, but the aristocrats retained power in the government on the basis of hereditary bone ranks, meaning bloodline. The top bone
ranks monopolized the bureaucracy. Bone ranks also conferred various privileges in
everyday life, including the size of the home, the color of dress, and even the orna-
mental decorations of horses. The aristocracy also dominated the military. The
hwarang were the young sons of aristocrats who followed a very strict code of conduct based on Confucian doctrines and Buddhist teaching of compassion.

Distinctive elements of Silla culture may be found in magnificent decorations, such
as the gold crowns, bracelets, and ear pendants that have been found in the tombs of the

The stone pagoda of the Punhwang Temple was built during the reign of Queen Sondak (r. 632–647) and is the only one surviving from the preunified Silla period. Originally the pagoda had nine stories, but only three remain. (Courtesy of Mary Connor)

royalty and nobility. All of these reveal a high level of artistry and testify to the wealth of the aristocracy. Earthenware technology was transmitted to Japan and became the basis for stoneware of the Japanese Kofun period. Ch'omsongdae (constructed between 632 and 647), one of the oldest astronomical observatories in the world, can be seen today in Kyongju and attests to the ingenuity of these early Koreans.

The rise of the Tang dynasty during the seventh century gave Silla an opportunity to extend its kingdom. An alliance between Silla and the Tang dynasty was arranged, and their combined forces defeated both Paekche and Koguryo; however, Paekche and Koguryo then allied with Silla against the Tang forces. Silla emerged as the unifying force on the peninsula. In Kyongju are burial mounds of those who accomplished this great feat.

Silla's unification in 668 CE did not include the entire peninsula, but this did not diminish the importance of its independence. Because Silla became independent from Tang political domination, the territory and people of Unified Silla were able to lay the groundwork for a long-lasting national culture. The historical significance of the unification of Silla cannot be overemphasized. Unified Silla laid the foundation for the historical development of the Korean people.

Unified Silla (668–935 CE)

Unified Silla survived for nearly three centuries and for a time, along with Tang China, was more advanced than probably any area of Europe except for the

Byzantine Empire. Freed from concerns of internal conflicts and foreign invasions, it achieved rapid development in the arts, religion, commerce, education, printing techniques, and other fields. Trade flourished with Tang China and Japan, and Silla ships came to dominate the maritime lanes in East Asia. The government was a powerful and strong state system under a single monarch. Educational institutions were well established and technology highly advanced. Present-day Kyongju, the capital of Silla, became the center of learning and creativity and grew into a large city with approximately 1 million people.

Monks traveled to China and India to study Mahayana Buddhism, which at this time had more appeal than Confucianism. Chinese political institutions did influence the development of government; however, hereditary bone rank continued to determine government positions. Slavery was prevalent and contributed significantly to the growing affluence of the hereditary aristocracy.

Travelers today still witness the achievements of the golden age of Silla. The craftsmanship and aesthetics of that period are thought to be among the finest in the world during that time. The objective of the artisans was to create a beauty of idealized harmony combined with refined artistic craftsmanship. Massive stone pagodas may be found throughout the South. Unlike Chinese and Japanese pagodas, which were built with bricks or wood, Silla's stone pagodas reveal incomparable technical superiority and harmonious beauty. Silla statues are considered as fine as those produced in Tang China. The famed Pulguksa Temple near Kyongju stands as a monument to Silla's ability to create a sense of harmony through superior artistry. The great Buddhist images of the Pulguksa and the large stone Buddha and bas-reliefs of the Sokkuram grotto convey a sense of spirituality even for the non-Buddhist and are among the finest works of Buddhist art in the Tang style. The Emille Bell, beautifully resonant and exquisitely wrought, is the largest surviving bronze bell from this period and is exhibited at the National Museum in Kyongju.

As religion and scholarship advanced, printing techniques were improved to print Buddhist and Confucian texts. When the Sakyamuni Pagoda (completed in 751 CE) from Pulguksa was dismantled in 1966 for repairs, the *Pure Light Dharani Sutra* and 70 cultural relics were found in the pagoda. The *Dharani Sutra* is the oldest example of printing with wooden blocks in the world.

One limitation on cultural development in Silla, as in early Japan, was the lack of a writing system suitable for transcribing the native language. Because Chinese characters were the only writing the early Koreans and Japanese knew, they adopted the script of an alien language. A method and set of rules were developed to represent a word either with a Chinese character having its sound or with one sharing its meaning. What developed was a full-fledged writing system called *idu*; later a more sophisticated system was developed called *hyangch'al*.

Silla began to decline by the late eighth century. Wealthy families challenged one other, the bone ranks system brought little unity, and the youthful *hwarang* warriors degenerated. The borrowed Chinese political institutions had not evolved into a government based on merit and so became increasingly costly and inefficient. After a king was assassinated in 780, political turmoil became constant, and succession by violent means was the norm for the next 150 years. By the end of the ninth century, peasant uprisings swept the country. In 918, General Wang Kon seized control, moved the capital to Kaesong, and reunified Korea. Kyongju faded into obscurity. Not until the 20th century were the magnificent achievements of Unified Silla rediscovered. If the treasures of Kyongju had been known over the centuries, they most likely would have been stolen, destroyed, and lost forever.

THE KORYO DYNASTY (918–1392)

Early Koryo

In 918, General Wang Kon founded a new unified dynasty that was to last almost five centuries. He named it Koryo, an abbreviation of Koguryo and the origin of the name Korea. Wang Kon implemented a policy of northern expansion, abolished the bone-rank system, and put in place a Chinese form of centralized government. Kaesong (located north of the mouth of the Han River) became the national capital. Wang Kon showed his diplomatic skills by treating his conquered subjects with compassion; he gave the former Silla king an important government position and large landholdings. He also married a woman from the Silla royal family and gave other grants of land to Silla and Paekche officials who pledged loyalty to him. The nobility became part of the Koryo bureaucracy; consequently, a tradition of aristocratic continuity was established that would continue to be part of the Korean political tradition into the 20th century.

The Koryo state incorporated elements of Confucianism. In 958, a civil service exam was set up on the Chinese model, schools were opened to teach the Confucian texts, and the central army was made powerful and permanent. Regional capitals were established in P'yongyang, Kyongju, and Seoul. By the 11th century, in spite of threats from Khitan armies to the north, Koryo had established a unified government over the entire peninsula to the Yalu River on the northwest, but it did not yet extend to the Tumen River to the northeast.

In spite of the adoption of Confucian political ideals, Koryo deference to aristocrats created a significant departure from Confucianism. Few commoners had opportunities in the government because of class prejudices and official restrictions. The sons of high aristocrats could hold important posts without taking the qualifying examinations. Military officers advanced by reason of family ancestry. Nobles received their own tax-free lands from the government in accordance with their rank; consequently, the tax base to support the government was reduced. The nobility chose not to live on their estates, left them in the hands of local aristocrats, and congregated in Kaesong. Most people were commoners or lower-class people: slaves, government workers, specialized artisans (such as those in porcelain factories), and peasants. The merchant class virtually disappeared. Most of the national wealth was located in the capital in the hands of the royal court and the aristocracy.

Buddhism, at its height in the 10th and 11th century in Koryo, played a major role in the social life and acted as a principal force in cultural achievements. Since it was believed that personal and national well-being could be assured through faith and pious acts, hundreds of temples throughout Korea, including more than 50 in the

---

WANG KON (877–943)

Wang Kon unified the three kingdoms after a period of intense warfare on the peninsula and established the Koryo dynasty (918–1392) with Kaesong as its capital. He named the dynasty Koryo, a shortened form of the name Koguryo, meaning "high mountains and sparkling waters." Once he had defeated his enemies, he was particularly adept in placating them through land grants, placement in government positions, and diplomatic marriages. Before his death, he drafted 10 injunctions for his successors to observe.

---

capital alone, were constructed. Many royal princes and aristocrats entered the clergy. Monasteries were exempted from taxes, grew affluent by sizable contributions from the wealthy, held large estates, and even conducted banking practices. Sons of the elite entered the clergy. Buddhist teachers served as advisers to government officials. One of the greatest achievements was the publication of the entire Buddhist Tripitaka (canonical scriptures) on woodblocks in 1087. These were later destroyed in the 1231–1232 Mongol invasions; however, more than 81,000 new blocks were completed in 1251, and these can be seen at Haeinsa, one of Korea's most beautiful temples. These wood-block carvings are the finest examples of some 20 Tripitaka carvings created in East Asia. By 1234, if not earlier, Koryo had also invented movable metal type, two centuries before Gutenberg. Koryo's use of this printing method is the earliest in the history of the world.

The Buddhist art of Koryo matched the artistic excellence of Silla, and landscape painting and porcelain became increasingly important. Celadon articles with delicate colors, graceful curves, elegant shapes, and exquisite inlaid designs of flowers or animals rank among the finest accomplishments in earthenware in the world and are considered the crowning glory of Koryo's artistic achievements.

There were also notable literary accomplishments during this period. A private Confucian school was founded in 1055, and Kim Pu-sik, a great scholar-statesman, compiled in 1145 the *History of the Three Kingdoms*, the oldest surviving history of Korea. A great concern was the establishment of libraries, the acquisition of books, and their duplication by a wood-block technique. Chinese as well as traditional Korean music (*hyang-ak*) flourished. The former was employed in Confucian ceremonies; the latter continued to be the music of the people. Many new instruments were either imported or invented. The hourglass-shaped drum, the *changgo*, became the most popular instrument in Korea.

Later Koryo

Centralized rule that had been patterned after China began to show signs of decay in the second half of the 11th century. Weak kings, aristocratic access to government taxes, incessant conflicts among noble families, military coups, peasant rebellions, and slave uprisings contributed to instability. Aristocrats held to the principle that civilian rulers were superior to the military, so officers experienced political and economic hardships. In 1196, an officer, Ch'oe Ch'unghon, rose to power, killed those who challenged his authority, established dictatorial rule, and brought stability for more than half a century. This military rule brought a new landed elite to the top and an end to the hereditary status system. Most likely, the presence of Mongolian and Manchurian armies to the north meant that a centralized force was needed for protection.

In the early 13th century, Genghis Khan, whose genius for leadership and power had united the normally independent Mongol tribes, was about to conquer half the known world. In 1215, he captured Beijing, and the rulers of northern China were defeated. In 1231, the Mongols with vastly superior forces invaded the peninsula, seized the capital of Kaesong, and demanded a huge tribute. Peasants and the low-born resisted and were mercilessly slaughtered. More than 200,000 people were taken captive, countless people were left dead, and an entire region was buried in ashes. Kings were forced to marry Mongolian princesses, the governmental structure was changed to signify subservience, and military garrisons and officials were stationed all over the peninsula. By 1271, the military leadership surrendered and was forced to accept Yuan (Mongol) suzerainty. The peasants were burdened with the responsibility of tribute obligations, and many were forced to build ships and furnish supplies for Mongolian expeditions against Japan. Tribute included gold, silver, horses, ginseng, hawks, artisans, women, and eunuchs. Intolerable suffering left deep scars. Koryo kings continued to rule but had to remain loyal to the Yuan.

Because of the vastness of the Mongolian Empire, Korea was now more open to cultural and technological influences. The cotton plant was introduced and largely replaced hemp, which led to a marked improvement in clothing and textile production. Other advances included a calendar, gunpowder, and astronomical and mathematical knowledge.

The firm hand of the Mongols served to sustain the Koryo dynasty for about a century, but beneath the surface the foundations of government were crumbling. Farmland continued to flow from public domain to the estates of the nobility. Invasions, repeated attacks by Japanese pirates, and reduced financial support led to increased reliance on Mongol power. As internal dissension and paralysis among Mongol leaders spread in the 14th century, Koryo attempted to reassert control, but rival factions supporting the Mongols and the successor Ming dynasty emerged. General Yi Songgye, ordered to support a mobilization against a Ming invasion, thought this unwise and resisted because he did not believe the smaller kingdom could hold out against the much larger force. Yi and his army attacked the Koryo capital instead. Seizing the throne in 1392, he brought the 474-year dynasty to an end.

THE CHOSON DYNASTY (1392–1910)

The Early Period: 1392 to the 17th Century

Yi Songgye (more commonly called T'aejo) founded Korea's longest dynasty, lasting until the 20th century. The new kingdom was renamed Choson. The capital was moved from Kaesong to Seoul, which became the political, economic, and cultural center of Korea and has remained so ever since. To protect the new capital, T'aejo ordered the construction of a great 10-mile wall with massive gates, parts of which remained into the 21st century. The Namdaemun Gate, once Seoul's principal city gate, survived until a great fire destroyed it in 2008.

T'aejo continued the traditional relationship with China. At least four missions per year visited the Chinese capital. The purpose of each mission was political but also allowed for cultural borrowing and economic exchange. Articles exported included horses, ginseng, furs, and hemp. In return, Korea received silk, medicines, books, and porcelain. During the next five centuries, Korea gave virtually unquestioned loyalty to Chinese political institutions and readily accepted cultural influences.

In spite of the fact that T'aejo was a devout Buddhist, he directed the dynasty to adopt Neo-Confucianism. While Confucianism had influenced Korea for centuries, the new approach was to create an ideal society in harmony with the particular attitudes and concerns of the Choson dynasty. The establishment of Confucian schools became a high priority. For the first 200 years, Choson experienced peace and prosperity under the guidance of enlightened kings. T'aejo and his successors built a strong foundation for the dynasty: they restructured society through the bureaucracy, strengthened national defense, and promoted the economy and culture of the kingdom. National boundaries were established along the Yalu and Tumen rivers.

T'aejo's son, T'aejong (1400–1418), dedicated himself to the completion of reforms that had begun under his father's rule. T'aejong's successor, Sejong (1418–1450), became Korea's greatest monarch by bringing stability and prosperity to his nation. In addition to mastering Confucian learning, he was able to successfully negotiate with the *yangban* (office-holding aristocrats). His rule was known for progressive government, the creation of a phonetic script, economic development, scientific discovery, and technological innovation. He showed great concern for the peasants, providing relief in times of drought and flood as well as tax reform. Scholars were instructed to draw on the knowledge of elderly peasants to publish a book on agriculture; this book became the classic book on Korean agriculture.

During the Choson dynasty, Korea became a model Confucian society and emphasized the importance of education, social stability, filial piety, and good government based on a hierarchical social order of the elite selected through competitive civil service examinations. Another dimension of Neo-Confucian principles related to male and female relationships. Women were raised to understand that they were inferior and should be submissive to men at all times; they should be obedient to their fathers, then later to their husbands and in-laws, and when widowed, to their sons. These ideas extended to the practice of ancestor worship, and the eldest male was the spiritual head of the family.

Neo-Confucianism had a strong impact. Prior to this time, Buddhist and Confucian beliefs basically coexisted, but now there were restrictions against the practice of Buddhism and limitations on the number of Buddhist monasteries. Neo-Confucianism condemned the reclusive life of Buddhist monks and rejected the Daoist search for immortality. The civil service examinations were essentially limited to the *yangban*. Consequently, the hereditary elite continued to serve as the majority of the high officials in government. A scholar during the time of King Sejong

Courtyard and pond at the Ch'angdokkung (Changdok Palace) in Seoul. In 1405 King Taejong, the third ruler of the Choson dynasty built the palace to serve as a royal villa. After 1615 the seat of the government was moved to this location and kings ruled Korea from this palace for about 300 years. (Courtesy of Mary Connor)

formulated the idea that rulers had a mandate from heaven, as in China. Ethical conduct was essential for preserving their rule. Bad conduct destroyed the right to rule, and the overthrow of a government was justified. This notion predated John Locke's theory of the right of revolution by 300 years.

The influence of Confucianism contributed to the stability of society and perpetuated for centuries the continuation of a very rigid class structure. Ten percent of the population was of the *yangban* class, whose goal was education in the Confucian classics and government or military service. They married within their class and lived apart from the rest of society. More than 50 percent of the population was known as *yangmin* ("good people"). They were the farmers, merchants, fisherman, and craftsmen. The next class was the *ch'onmin* ("the lowborn"). These people belonged to certain disdained hereditary professions, such as butchery, or were shamans, entertainers, or slaves. It is estimated that more than one-third of the population was enslaved in this system, which existed into the 20th century.

Confucianism also influenced the growth of the Chinese examination system that had been used during the Koryo dynasty; in the Choson dynasty, however, it was the principal means of attaining high government office. This system selected officials based on academic achievement as opposed to social status, military success, or wealth, and made professional service the most certain route to acquisition of wealth. The exam system initially produced an effective bureaucracy, but in time it deteriorated and finally ended with the overthrow of the Choson dynasty by the Japanese in 1910.

Confucianism also had an impact on economic development. Its beliefs helped to perpetuate a static agrarian society and promoted contempt for the development of commerce, an activity seen as self-serving and socially divisive. A road system was maintained, but trade within the country and with the outside world (except for China and Japan) remained limited. In spite of the continuous flow of goods and ideas from China, Korea remained culturally distinct. In social structure, economic development, character traits, language, homes, dress, and food, it was in no danger of being culturally absorbed. Items exported to Japan included rice, cotton, hemp, and porcelain ware. The Buddhist Tripitaka, Confucian writings, histories, temple bells, and Buddhist images were among the cultural exports to Japan. In exchange, the Japanese exported minerals not available in Korea and luxury items for the *yangban* class.

Despite the conservative tendencies of Confucianism, there were significant technological advances in early Choson. A rain gauge was invented in 1442, and accurate records were maintained some 200 years before Europe began such practices. Movable type was more prevalent in Korea in the 15th century than any other place in the world. King Sejong and the Academy of Scholars made one of the greatest cultural innovations: a writing system. Known today as *han'gul*, it allowed people to write in characters appropriate to their spoken language. The educated classes preferred Chinese characters and continued using them in important documents. Women and the lower class used *han'gul*. It was not until the end of Japanese occupation that *han'gul* was in wide use. Today it is considered to be the most scientific system of writing in the world.

The influence of Confucianism may also be seen in the arts. Chinese-style landscapes, shrines, and music were characteristic of Choson. Enormous palaces, such as the Ch'angdokkung in Seoul, were constructed and reflected the ambition of kings. In Seoul today, one can see a few buildings that were part of the palace built by the first Choson king. During this dynasty, green celadon gave way to white porcelain, and brownware appeared in the 16th century.

In spite of the early enlightened monarchs, there were signs of difficulties that ultimately weakened the Choson dynasty. The kings had limited power and for the most part were not highly respected by the *yangban*. To garner their support, the monarchs doled out generous grants of nontaxable land. For the peasants, this meant increasingly burdensome taxes. Since *yangban* were forbidden to participate in trade, their principal objective was to serve in the bureaucracy. Extreme competition for government posts led to the growth of hereditary groupings that could no longer marry or associate with rival families. Geographic rivalries between *yangban* resulted in systematic purges of hundreds of officials, even executions. Feuds among the nobility had existed in China, but it was a much greater problem in Korea because the kings did not have the power of a Chinese emperor.

As these intense factions grew, Japanese warlord Toyotomi Hideyoshi was crushing his rivals and reunifying Japan. In 1592 he launched an invasion against Korea in what was to be a step toward challenging the Ming dynasty in China. Since the Choson dynasty had been relatively free from foreign threats and the *yangban* aristocrats were accustomed to peace, they were ill prepared for a major invasion. Within a

HIDEYOSHI INVASIONS (1592–1598)

After Toyotomi Hideyoshi unified Japan, he planned to launch an invasion of Korea as a step toward conquering the Ming empire. In 1592, the Japanese invaded Korea and quickly proceeded to take control of most of the country. Admiral Yi Sun-sin and his famed turtle ships came to the rescue and began to destroy Hideyoshi's fleet. Meanwhile, armies of *yangban*, peasants, Buddhist monks, and slaves united and dealt severe blows to the Japanese. Ming armies arrived and helped to defeat the Japanese in 1593. After attempts were made to end the war, the Japanese launched a second campaign in 1597. This time, Admiral Yi trapped the Japanese fleet in a narrow channel and destroyed more than 300 ships. Hideyoshi died shortly thereafter, and the Japanese forces withdrew.

month the Japanese captured Seoul and nearly the entire peninsula. However, Admiral Yi Sun-sin rescued the nation. For a year, he had strengthened his naval forces, building warships and training the crews. He constructed "turtle boats" with a protective covering (probably the first use of iron plate) to ward off enemy arrows and shells. Spikes and cannons were placed around each ship. With the assistance of these formidable warships, Admiral Yi stopped Japanese advances and severed connections to their supply routes. Meanwhile, *yangban*, peasant farmers, and slaves united into guerrilla armies, and Ming forces arrived to support their tributary state. Peace negotiations were then attempted, but they failed. The Japanese launched another attack in

The Tongsipchagak (East Cross Tower) is a watchtower in Seoul built at the place where the outer wall of Kyongbokkung (Kyongbok Palace) bends northward to the East Palace Gate. Kyongbokkung, built in 1394–1395, was burned down during the Hideyoshi invasions (1592–1598). It is not known exactly how much was actually destroyed, but it was rebuilt in 1868 by Taewon'gun, King Kojong's father. (Courtesy of Mary Connor)

SAMYONGDANG (1544–1610)

At 13, Samyongdang decided to study Buddhism and become a monk. In his thirties, he was widely admired within the Son sect (Zen). When Hideyoshi invaded Korea in 1592, Samyongdang organized a Buddhist army and successfully repulsed the invaders; however, the Japanese managed to take many prisoners of war. The warrior monk sent a special envoy to Japan to negotiate their release. His efforts were very successful, and within a year more than 3,000 prisoners were released. Later, he moved to the Haeinsa Buddhist temple to restore his health but died within the year. There is a monument in his memory at this spot, one of the most famous and beautiful temples in all of Korea.

1597, but Admiral Yi and his fleet won a resounding victory. Hideyoshi soon died, and the Japanese completely withdrew.

This invasion has been emphasized in Korean literature and still contributes to bitterness against the Japanese. The fighting was disastrous. Nearly all the provinces suffered pillage and slaughter. The population decreased, and famine and disease became widespread. Buildings, works of art, and historical records were destroyed by fire. The government weakened, agricultural production decreased, and the tax yield declined enormously.

Korea had barely recovered from the invasions when the Manchus invaded from the north, seized land, and overthrew the Ming dynasty. Generally, this invasion was less destructive than those of the Japanese except in the northwest, where the Manchu forces inflicted almost total devastation. In 1637, Choson was forced to accept the suzerainty of the Qing (Manchu) dynasty and the leadership of the newly crowned emperor of China. The Koreans considered the Manchus to be barbarians, and for China to be ruled by them seemed like the end of civilization. Hostility toward the Qing lasted for a long time.

A Nation in Transition: The 17th, 18th, and 19th Centuries

The invasions of the Japanese and the Manchus were a turning point in Korean history. Devastated by what the outside world had wrought, monarchs adopted a policy of isolation. They remained weak, and the government lacked sufficient funding. To alleviate some of its financial difficulties, the government minted more coins. Tax reforms were also implemented. Upward social mobility, almost unknown before the war, began to take place. To raise revenue, rich peasants and merchants acquired *yangban* status by buying it; meanwhile, many of the latter lost their lands, status, and political power.

While the economy remained essentially agricultural, a mercantile economy was beginning to develop and significantly influenced the class structure. In the past, the government had restricted trade; now merchants were freer from government

Monument to Hendrick Hamel, Cheju Island, South Korea. In 1653 a Dutch ship was wrecked near Cheju Island on the southwestern coast. Hamel and his crew were rescued but held as spies for thirteen years. He escaped, returned to Holland, and published the first book on Korea in 1668, thereby introducing the country to Europe. (Courtesy of Mary Connor)

restrictions and began to be more active within and outside the country. This growth of wealth brought status to a class of people that had been previously treated with disdain and at the same time contributed to the decline of the *yangban*. Over time, some merchants in urban areas amassed fortunes through the control of trade and handcraft production, while many small merchants became bankrupt. In rural areas, some peasants became rich; many poor peasants had to give up their farms and became part of a growing population of landless vagrants. Social distinctions also began to fade between commoners and slaves. Many slaves received freedom in exchange for military service or simply bought their own freedom.

In spite of a policy of isolation, outside forces continued to have a significant impact. Koreans on tribute missions made contact with Jesuit scholars and brought back books on new scientific discoveries, maps, telescopes, and alarm clocks. Around the same time, a Dutch ship was wrecked near Cheju Island. While the sailors were rescued, the Dutchmen were held as spies for an extended period of time. One of them, Hendrick Hamel, escaped and returned to Holland to write a book on Korea. Because of these contacts with foreigners, Koreans began to have greater curiosity about the West, and Europeans acquired some knowledge about Korea.

Prior to the 17th century, a group of Confucian scholars suggested reforms and started the Sirhak ("Practical Learning") movement. They rejected Neo-Confucianism and recommended practical solutions to the problems of their time. Because of the dramatic influences of Western science and Chinese scholarship, these scholars continued to explore ways to resolve the problems of the common people through

Traditional thatch cottages at Hahoe Folk Village. The Korean people lived in thatched cottages for centuries. Hahoe is a genuine folk village with roots that can be traced back over 600 years. (Courtesy of Mary Connor)

land reform and promotion of social equality. The Japanese invasions and antagonism against the Qing dynasty ultimately fueled revolutionary ideas of cultural and political independence from China. The Sirhak movement, which also promoted revolutionary ideas of the rights of man and social equality, continued to grow during the 18th and early 19th centuries and contributed to the publication of books on politics, economics, health, and educational reform. The movement also influenced the growth of historical writing, fiction, poetry, and painting. The greatest change in the field of literature came with the large number of works written in *han'gul* (Korean script). Ultimately, the spirit of the Sirhak movement was to play a significant role in the reform movements of the late 19th century.

With the weakened position of the *yangban*, a popular folk culture grew rapidly. Greater realism and individualism were evident in the arts. Genre painting of ordinary events of everyday life became very popular. Folk music, including songs, dance, and mask plays, was performed. Shamanist beliefs were also evident in the musical and dramatic performances. A new form of dramatic narrative music (*p'ansori*) developed, enriching the lives of the Korean people.

Catholicism ultimately became a major force for change. When contacts were initially made with Jesuit missionaries in the early 17th century, Catholicism (known as "Western Learning") had little impact. When a Sirhak scholar was baptized by a Catholic priest in Beijing, the number of converts began to increase. What attracted many to Catholicism was the belief in the equality of the children of

God. For women in particular, Catholicism had great appeal. When the government learned that Christianity disagreed with Confucian tenets, such as ancestor worship, persecutions and executions followed; however, missionaries continued to spread their religion. The anti-Catholic policy was relaxed in 1849 but resumed in the 1860s with a vengeance and made Christian martyrs out of approximately 8,000 people, including several French missionaries.

In the 1860s, a new religion was established in reaction to Catholicism, government corruption, social injustice, and peasant poverty. It was called Tonghak ("Eastern Learning") and drew its support essentially from impoverished peasants. Frequent natural calamities were contributing factors to this movement: floods, famine, and epidemics occurred repeatedly and engendered major peasant uprisings. Ch'oe Ch'ue, the founder of Tonghak, combined concepts from Daoism, Buddhism, Neo-Confucianism, Catholicism, and Shamanism. Ch'oe also advocated political, social, and economic reforms to alleviate the suffering of the poor. Alarmed by Tonghak's growing popularity, the government decapitated its founder in 1864 on charges of subversion. Nevertheless, the movement continued to grow under the leadership of his successor.

In spite of these intellectual, social, and economic developments, the government resisted desperately needed reforms because powerful *yangban* officials feared change. National policy served their interests, not the welfare of the people. Yet the dynasty managed to remain in power until even greater challenges, the threat of Japan and Western nations, emerged in the late 19th and early 20th centuries.

The Opening of Korea, Attempts at Reform, and National Peril

The Korean people encountered additional problems in the 19th century as a result of the industrialization, nationalism, and imperialism of major world powers. Western nations, such as the United Kingdom, France, Russia, and the United States, and a modernized Japan actively pursued policies to secure wealth in Asian markets. These powers were able to take particular advantage of China. During the Qing dynasty, China suffered from a rapid increase in population, natural calamities, and ineffectual government.

The West referred to Korea as the "Hermit Kingdom" because it had for centuries essentially rejected all outside contact. Rejection of the West had been based on a general disdain for foreigners combined with the belief that Confucianism was the only valid belief; thus, any civilization that thought differently should be kept out. Until the 19th century, foreign relations consisted of annual tribute missions to Beijing and limited contact with Japan. In the 19th century, the West and Japan forced Korea to end its long-entrenched policies of isolation. Once opened to the world, it encountered a variety of challenges: exploitation, war, and the potential loss of national sovereignty.

During the late 19th century, Western nations exhibited an ever-growing interest in establishing contact with the Hermit Kingdom for commercial and other purposes. The French, in retaliation for the executions of French priests, attempted in 1866 to punish Korea for its actions by attacking Kanghwa Island, but Korean troops forced them to withdraw after a brief skirmish. In the same year, an American ship, the *General Sherman*, sailed up the Taedong River to P'yongyang to force the government to accept commercial relations with the United States. After it refused an order to leave, it was burned, and all aboard perished. As a result of this incident, U.S. secretary of state William Seward decided to punish the Koreans and to open Korean ports by force. When five U.S. warships entered Korean waters, they were met by cannons and newly strengthened fortifications. The U.S. Marines were forced to retreat. In 1871, in response to the threats from foreign powers, the staunchly isolationist Taewon'gun, regent to the future King Kojong, declared that the official policy was one of isolation. Five years later, Japanese warships invaded and demanded diplomatic and commercial relations. The Japanese said that if Korea refused, there would be war. Forced by what is now known as "gunboat diplomacy," the government signed the Kanghwa Treaty (1876), the first unequal treaty with an imperialist power. Within it was a clause that said Korea was a sovereign nation, paving the way for Japanese aggression without interference from China. Additional provisions opened ports with the condition that Japanese residents would be subject to Japanese laws in Japanese courts, business and trade would be conducted without interference, and business in the ports would take place under extraterritorial privileges. Korea gained no such privileges in Japan.

In 1873, King Kojong decided to deal more effectively with the outside world by promoting reforms in foreign trade, arms production, and foreign language education. He pursued a more open and flexible foreign policy than his regent Taewon'gun had followed. His hope was to establish diplomatic ties with the United States, a potential ally in helping to fend off growing threats from Japan and Russia. Officials in China, now believing that Korea needed to end its policies of seclusion to survive, offered to mediate a treaty between the United States and Korea. Consequently, in 1882 Commodore Robert W. Shufeldt of the United States signed the Korean-American Treaty of Amity and Commerce in In'chon. The treaty gave extraterritorial rights to U.S. citizens, fixed tariffs, and established port concessions and consular representation. When the terms of the treaty were explained to King Kojong, he was led to believe that the United States would guarantee the country's sovereign independence. This treaty was followed by similar agreements with the United Kingdom, Germany, Italy, Russia, France, and Austria-Hungary. All treaties were unequal in that they favored Western interests over national ones.

After the conclusion of these treaties, the government sent missions to Japan and the United States to learn more about these countries and to promote friendly relations. When the members returned, they brought back progressive ideas: modernization of the government, economic development, educational reform, social equality, and independence from China. Despite these would-be reformers, conservatives in government allowed only a few revisions, such as improved military training, the opening of a palace school staffed with American teachers, and the establishment of modern farming and a modern postal system.

With the influx of Protestant missionaries, Christianity spread and modern schools were established. In 1885 Presbyterians established a school for boys, and a year later Methodists established the first modern school, Ewha Womans University for girls. Protestant missionaries also established hospitals and gave lectures on agriculture, commerce, and industry. Their teachings fostered concepts of freedom and equality. In the late 19th century, nationalists also established schools, one of which is now Korea University.

While King Kojong and his officials promoted reforms to strengthen the nation, he was weak willed and easily manipulated by his wife, Queen Min. The queen, together with conservative Confucian officials, saw potential political threats in reform; consequently, serious conflicts developed. In 1882, the Chinese sent troops to Korea and crushed an antiqueen movement planned by the former regent, Taewon'gun, and progressives. The Chinese put Queen Min in charge, and thousands of Chinese troops were stationed in Seoul. Two years later, the queen was overthrown in a successful, but short-lived, coup supported by the Japanese. Shortly after this, King Kojong began again to implement reforms to make Korea a modern and progressive nation. The Chinese again sent troops to Korea, and with the support of the reactionaries the advisers to the king were replaced, but the government remained intact. Queen Min was again in charge with her conservative, pro-Chinese supporters. Hopes for a modernized, independent Korea vanished.

In addition to severe domestic problems, Korea became increasingly important to the rivalry among the United Kingdom, Russia, China, and Japan. The monarchy began to lean toward an anti-Qing, pro-Russian policy to curtail Chinese and Japanese involvement in Korea. As Russia advanced toward the Korean peninsula, the United Kingdom took over a strategic Korean island without the consent of the government. As rival powers positioned themselves around Korea, the conniving Queen Min and her supporters took greater control over a government that was notoriously incompetent and corrupt. The Japanese began to take increasing interest in the Korean rice and soybean markets to meet the demands of the rapid growth of Japan's population. At the same time, Japan increased its position in Korea's foreign trade and monopolized business in many port cities and elsewhere. Because of the challenges within and outside Korea, popular uprisings against the Min government began to break out in the 1890s, and banditry was everywhere.

The Tonghak Struggle, War, and the Kabo Reform

While Tonghak, or Eastern Learning, was a religious movement, it did respond to governmental corruption, foreign exploitation, and the desperate conditions of the peasants. Massive demonstrations took place in 1892 and 1893. In 1894, Chon Pong-jun, the leader of Tonghak, galvanized public discontent and ultimately began the largest peasant insurrection in Korean history. When initial protests led nowhere, the peasants resorted to violence. The government responded with mass executions. After another uprising, the Tonghak army defeated government forces. Meanwhile, King Kojong appealed to China to put down the rebellions. These uprisings now allowed Japan an opportunity to further involve itself in the national affairs.

In the summer of 1894, the Japanese attacked Chinese soldiers and warships in the area of Seoul, commencing the Sino-Japanese War. One victory followed another, demonstrating that Japan was now a formidable power. The Tonghaks organized an army to drive out the invaders; however, they suffered thousands of casualties. When Chon Pong-jun was captured and executed in Seoul, the rebellion

SINO-JAPANESE WAR (1894–1895)

At the time of the largest peasant uprising in Korean history, the Tonghak Rebellion, the Korean government asked China for help. After China sent in troops, Japan decided that only a war with China would remove Chinese influence in Korea. The combined forces of China and Japan defeated the Tonghak. China then proposed that both forces leave Korea, but Japan was determined to pursue its expansionist ambitions. The war began with the sudden seizure of the royal residence, Kyongbok Palace. Japanese troops fought the Chinese on land and sea and quickly won in impressive victories. A total victory culminated in the Shimonoseki Treaty, which recognized Korea's full independence from China and ceded Taiwan and the Liaotung Peninsula (part of Manchuria) to Japan.

ended, and China's vulnerability was evident to the world. It was now forced to accept Korea's independence. After many centuries of strong political and cultural ties to China, Korea was now on its own. But with China's defeat, Japan tightened controls over the country.

After the war, Japan hoped to modernize Korea and bring it into the Japanese sphere of influence. Japan demanded that the government carry out internal reforms, expel pro-Chinese officials, and appoint pro-Japanese ones in their place. This led to what are called the Kabo Reforms of the 1894–1896 period. The officials who undertook the Kabo Reforms had all studied or lived in Japan or the United States. With encouragement, these officials began to institute reforms that they felt would help the nation survive the challenges brought by the great powers. A council was created that acted independently of the king and queen and consisted of people who had supported progressive reforms. It abolished the Chinese-style bureaucracy, reformed local government, opened opportunities for talented people to serve in the government, introduced a modern court system, eliminated class distinctions, and freed slaves. An incidental result of the reforms led to Japan's even more dominant role in Korean markets.

As Japan tightened its grip, Queen Min secretly began to make overtures for Russian support to challenge Japan. In 1895, as part of an effort to maintain power, Japanese officials organized and carried out the murder of the queen. She was stabbed, doused with kerosene, and set afire to destroy the evidence. The king and the crown prince dressed themselves as court ladies, rode in sedan chairs, and fled to the Russian legation, where they stayed for a year. The country was run for the time being by the king under Russian supervision, and all reforms came to an end.

During King Kojong's residence at the Russian legation, he was apparently no prisoner but feared returning to his palace. In 1897, after hearing about growing unrest, he returned to his palace and declared himself emperor in the belief that he would have the power and the status of his counterparts in China and Japan. The nation's fate was now between Russia and Japan, which had already formulated some agreements regarding Korea. At one point, Russian and Japanese representatives contemplated dividing the peninsula between them, but they could not agree on the terms. Later, when Russia and Japan demanded concessions, the king relented. Kojong gave timber rights to Russia and commercial banking rights along with more than 200 business concessions to Japan. Gold mines, railroad, and electric power systems were granted to the United States.

The Independence Movement, Modernization, War, and Annexation

As Korea became a pawn in a world power struggle, many individuals and groups emerged to challenge the state of affairs. Now a more broadly based social movement than the Tonghak began to criticize the government's ineffective policies and fought aggressively for independence from foreign powers, particularly Japan. A group of reform-minded people in Seoul organized a political party called the Independence Club in 1896. The members, many of whom had formerly served in the government, demanded that Emperor Kojong implement the changes prescribed by the Kabo Reforms.

Several members of the Independence Club, including Syngman Rhee, who would later be South Korea's first president, became prominent leaders. The club began to publish *The Independent*, Korea's first newspaper in *han'gul* and in English. Their goals included protection of the country's independence from foreign aggression, revocation of all economic concessions, and adoption of a foreign policy that favored none of the rival powers trying to advance their interests on the peninsula. The club also sought to establish modern schools, develop industry, and create a defense system. Another objective was to support the growth of the democratic process.

As a result of the efforts of the Independence Club and the commitment of many dedicated people, modern schools were founded, and many Korean-language magazines and newspapers began to be published. The use of *han'gul* increased, as did literacy. Literary figures emerged and promoted a new cultural movement based on national independence and equality. Medical care improved, telegraph and telephone systems were established, and streetcar and railroad lines were installed. New banking institutions and Western architecture appeared. Korea appeared to be on its way to modernization.

The Independence Club frequently presented its grievances to the government. The club called for dismissal of corrupt officials and granting concessions to foreign powers. The public became increasingly supportive of change. Growing ever more resentful of the direct challenges to their authority, government officials began to arrest club leaders. In 1898, when Kojong ordered an end to the club, all opportunities for independence and modernization simply collapsed. Subsequently, the emperor destroyed the only group capable of reinvigorating the Choson dynasty.

With the growing power and rivalry of Russia and Japan, Korea was also threatened at its borders. The Russians had obtained rights from China to build the Trans-Siberian Railroad through Manchuria and to lease some Chinese ports. When the Chinese attempted to expel foreigners during the Boxer Rebellion in 1900, Russia moved troops into Manchuria and waited for an opportunity to invade. In 1902, an alarmed Japan negotiated a treaty with the United Kingdom, which agreed to Japan's aggressive policies. In return, Japan promised that it would check Russia's southern advances in the Far East.

In 1903, the Russo-Japanese rivalry reached a critical point when Japan gave an ultimatum to Russia to withdraw troops from Manchuria. When it refused, Japan declared war in 1904 and won a quick victory. In 1905, President Theodore Roosevelt negotiated the Portsmouth Treaty, in which Russia acknowledged Japan's rights in Korea. For this, Roosevelt received the Nobel Peace Prize. Since the United States had recently established the Philippines as a U.S. territory following the Spanish-American War (1898), Roosevelt accepted the Taft-Katsura Agreement (1905), which gave Japan a free hand in Korea with the promise that it would not interfere in the Philippines. As long as Japanese imperialism was directed toward Korea and Manchuria and away from American and British possessions, it had the support of the Western powers.

With this support, Japan moved quickly to establish a Korean protectorate. After publicly protesting the Protectorate Treaty, Kojong appealed without success to the United States and other world powers to support independence. The Japanese forced him to abdicate in 1907, and his mentally retarded son, Sunjong, became emperor of Korea and the puppet of Japan. More than 140,000 patriots joined guerrilla armies to resist the Japanese. Thousands of them died in their struggle, but even after annexation Korean emigrants in Manchuria continued to resist. By 1909, the powerful Japanese military had ended most resistance. A powerless emperor, Sunjong signed the Treaty of Annexation in 1910. The Choson dynasty, which had ruled Korea for 500 years, ceased to exist.

THE COLONIAL PERIOD (1910–1945)

The First Phase of Japanese Rule, 1910–1919

Annexation inaugurated a 35-year period of Japanese occupation that has left a bitter legacy. The experience heightened animosities that had existed ever since the Hideyoshi invasion of the late 16th century; however, no previous events could have ever prepared people for the catastrophic economic, political, and social changes that were to come. What happened between 1910 and 1945 is crucial for understanding the post–World War II attitudes toward the Japanese.

The Japanese were convinced that control over Korea was vital to their strategic and economic well-being. To justify the takeover, the Japanese convinced themselves that despite the fact that Koreans were the same race, they were inferior people. During the first years, citizens were controlled by a draconian police system that deprived them of basic freedoms. Japan moved quickly to pacify the country. All newspapers were suspended, political parties were abolished, and public gatherings were disallowed. Japan's close proximity made it easier to dominate all facets of life.

Authority was invested in the governor-general, who was appointed by the Emperor. He controlled the military and civil police force, made all laws, oversaw the judicial system, and had fiscal independence and total control of all appointments.

All officials, including teachers, were required to carry a sword as a symbol of authority. The colonial bureaucracy grew rapidly with Japanese officials dominating, especially in the upper and middle levels. Hiring practices eliminated even educated and experienced Koreans from governmental service.

The police had the power to judge, sentence, and execute even for minor offenses. They were the controlling agency in politics, education, religion, morals, health and public welfare, and tax collection. Even the large Korean contingent in the police force supplied the governor-general with information that set Korean against Korean.

The first decade of Japanese rule has been called the "dark period" because of the extensive repression of political and cultural life. The right of assembly was abolished. Police kept watch on intellectual, religious, and political leaders. In 1912 alone, there were more than 50,000 arrests. The occupiers created an educational system to train a labor force to serve the homeland's economic development and to educate in Japanese customs, culture, and language. The goal of education was to make Korean children loyal, useful, and obedient subjects of the Japanese emperor. Japanese was spoken, and Korean was taught as a second language. Because the Japanese limited access to colleges and universities, many bright Korean students traveled to Japan for higher education. There they were exposed to radical political ideas unavailable to students at home and ultimately established close contacts with a generation of political activists from around the world.

Another significant development during the first stage of the colonial period related to land laws. A Land Survey Bureau was created that required all owners to prove their land titles. The policies strengthened and codified the position of wealthy landowners and contributed to the deterioration of rural life. Large landowners had no difficulty reporting their holdings; however, many small landowners were unfamiliar with reporting regulations and lost their land. The widening gap between those who held land and those who did not caused tremendous social tension. In addition to the policies of the Land Survey Bureau, the government-general seized land that had belonged to the royal family and became the largest landowner in Korea.

The Japanese also consolidated their position in communications, public services, and economic activities throughout the peninsula. Railroads were particularly vital to Japan for military and economic reasons. The colonial government took control of mining, forestry, and fisheries. Japan was now free to exploit Korea's gold, silver, iron, tungsten, and coal. A law was passed requiring approval for the formation of public or private corporations. Few Koreans received such approval, making the number of Korean businesses insignificant compared to those of the occupiers. Japanese banks dominated the economy, and Korean businessmen were dependent on them.

The oppressive rule that accompanied the first phase of colonial rule contributed to a growing number of Koreans abroad, such as in Manchuria and Russia, who expressed opposition to colonial rule. Some became contract laborers in Hawaii; others settled in California. Many of the new activists were students who became radicalized by foreign contacts and by their own experience of ethnic discrimination. After 1914, the major powers were consumed by World War I. Although Koreans tried to get the attention of other nations, there was little interest in responding to their appeals.

The Second Phase of Colonial Rule, 1919–1931

The United States emerged as a world power after World War I. President Woodrow Wilson raised the hopes of colonized peoples around the globe with his commitment to the self-determination of peoples, national autonomy, and world peace. While most radical political leaders were in exile or in jail, Christian and Buddhist leaders in Korea now began to plan a national movement for independence. They wanted a nationwide demonstration on March 1, 1919. It was to be a nonviolent expression of their desire to be free and independent from Japan. Thirty-three nationalists signed the Korean Declaration of Independence as part of this movement. The death of the former emperor, Kojong, in January and subsequent rumors that the Japanese were involved in his death further inflamed anti-Japanese sentiments. Widespread demonstrations broke out in Seoul and elsewhere during the following months. The Japanese were caught by surprise, and the police responded with thousands of arrests, beatings, and the destruction of homes, churches, and even entire villages. A 17-year-old girl named Yu Kwansun was tortured by the police and died in prison.

Independence Monument, Seoul, South Korea. On March 1, 1919, the Korean people began a nationwide demonstration expressing their desire to be free and independent of Japan. The words of their Declaration of Independence are inscribed on this memorial. (Courtesy of Mary Connor)

AHN CHANG-HO (1878–1939)

Ahn Chang-Ho (pen name, Tosan) is sometimes called Korea's number one patriot. Born in a village outside P'yongyang, he became one of the most prominent orators and energetic independence fighters. After organizing a chapter of the Independence Club, he lived in the United States from 1902 to 1906 and dedicated himself to improving the lives of Koreans there. Upon his return to Korea, Ahn lifted the spirit of his people through his powerful oratory and raised funds for the independence movement.

The demonstrations failed to bring independence. What the March First movement did accomplish, however, was to unify the Korean people in a dramatic new way. The Japanese became more sensitive to world opinion. As a result, there were some alterations in Japanese policies, but there was no real letup on the domination of Korea.

The Japanese developed "cultural policy reforms" in hopes of improving world opinion of their colonial rule. These new policies included plans for greater efficiency of administration and police controls. The Japanese plotted ways to manipulate Koreans into supporting them. Whipping for minor offenses ended, but repression increased for militant nationalists and revolutionaries. Some minor adjustments were made to bring salaries more in line with those of Japanese civil servants. Promises were made to bring equality of education to the schools. Korean newspapers could be published again; however, they were subject to very strict censorship. The police no longer wore uniforms, but the size of the Japanese force was increased significantly. The objective was to create an army of informers so that no demonstration could catch the leaders by surprise as had the March First movement. Another dimension of their program was to increase rice production, but most of the rice was exported to Japan. Korean per capita rice consumption dropped throughout the period of colonial occupation.

While these reforms now seem somewhat insignificant, the period following the March First movement was a time of hope. Newspapers were published, and groups were formed throughout the colony. Koreans realized that direct confrontations with the Japanese would be met with force, so they developed a gradual approach to independence. Societies developed with the intention of fostering a national consciousness in literature, history, drama, music, and film. These activities were largely limited to the well-educated elite members of society. Their challenge was to find ways to harness the support of the vast majority of the Korean people who were peasants or members of the growing laboring class. The fact that the literacy rate was so low presented a major obstacle.

Many nationalists were forced to flee their homeland and join others in Shanghai and elsewhere. In 1919, nationalists in Shanghai established the Provisional Government of the Republic of Korea in exile and elected Dr. Syngman Rhee its

HAN YONGUN (1879–1944)

Han Yongun was a recognized poet, Buddhist monk, and independence fighter. In his youth, he became a follower of the Tonghak movement. His father and brother were executed by the government for their involvement in the Tonghak rebellion. At 16, he took refuge in a Buddhist temple, studied, and became a priest. He encouraged other monks to live among the poor to help improve their conditions. When Japan annexed Korea, he became a central figure in the independence movement.

first president. Other nationalists were attracted to communism because of the Russian Revolution and the emergence of the Soviet Union as a potential champion of oppressed peoples everywhere. Exiles were free to read and discuss radical ideas and join groups supporting Marxist-Leninist ideology and national liberation. Ultimately, the differing ideologies seriously divided the movement. Not only was it divided, but also no group was able to gather mass national support. In the 21st century, both North and South Korea continue to be influenced significantly by the class and ideological conflicts that developed during and after the period of colonial rule.

The Third Phase of Japanese Occupation and World War II (1931–1945)

For a variety of reasons, Japan's policies changed in the 1930s. As international trade shrank because of the worldwide depression, the Japanese realized that their new industrial economy was overextended beyond what the small empire could support. Chinese nationalist forces appeared to threaten Japanese interests on the continent. In response to these developments, Japan seized Manchuria in 1931, made it a puppet state, extracted its rich natural resources, and developed its industry. In Japan itself, the military took over the government. Korea was now to serve as the base for Japan's Asian plan. Newly instituted policies emphasized rural self-sufficiency and increased industrial production. As industry expanded, thousands of peasants took factory jobs.

Some resistance to the Japanese continued. Korean communists in the north organized underground peasant brigades that attacked their landlords and the police. Labor strikes were frequent. Some small guerrilla units managed to survive into the 1930s. One of the units was led by Kim Il-Sung.

By 1934, the Japanese began to be bolder, forcing the Koreans into the cultural and political life of the empire with the objective of eliminating the differences between them. Educational policies included a new curriculum that emphasized Japanese language instruction, ethics, and history. Although Japanese and Korean children originally attended separate schools, all children now attended school together. These new policies also included a pledge to the emperor, attendance at Shinto ceremonies, and the elimination of the study and use of the Korean language altogether. Koreans particularly objected to forced attendance at Shinto ceremonies.

When Japan invaded China in 1937, the colonial government began to shut down all Korean organizations. By 1940, virtually all Korean-language newspapers were closed. The Japanese created mass organizations to bring everybody into the war effort. They also reduced the number of Koreans in government and relegated those who remained to inferior positions. The colonial police recruited lower-class individuals for government service, creating great resentment among the general population and turning Koreans against one another.

In 1939, the oppressors struck at the most cherished source of family identity by forcing Koreans to adopt Japanese names. In a nation where reverence for ancestors and family lineage had been a way of life for thousands of years, this policy could create only a deep and lasting resentment on the part of the people. The Japanese believed that the very survival of the empire depended on their subjects acting and thinking like Japanese citizens. Their assimilation policies were doomed to fail, though, because they combined the belief that the Japanese and the Koreans could become one even though the Koreans were discriminated against on the basis of their ethnicity.

There were Koreans who attempted to succeed in the colonial system by collaborating. Ambitious educated men had very few choices unless they did work with the system. Rejection of the system would limit chances for a good job and lead to poverty, jail, or exile. Some of these collaborators profited enormously from the war effort. Many thought that by cooperating with Japan, Korea would become modernized.

After the United States entered the war in the Pacific, there were even greater hardships for the people. They now had to work in mines and factories in Manchuria and Japan, guard prison camps, build military facilities, and serve the troops in various capacities. The Japanese organized the entire colony into Neighborhood Patriotic Organizations, which were responsible for providing labor, collecting money for the war effort, security, and rationing. People were forced to donate gold and silver jewelry, brass, and other metals to the war effort. School hours were reduced so children could work as factory laborers or in the fields. One of the most shameful developments was the so-called Comfort Corps, made up of between 100,000 and 200,000 young Korean women who were forced to serve the sexual needs of Japanese troops. Thousands of Korean men served in the military, and approximately 4 million, some 16 percent of the population, lived outside the country or worked in factories and mines in Manchuria, northern Korea, and Japan.

The independence movement continued to grow through the involvement of exiled leaders, but divisions between nationalists and communists grew stronger throughout the 1930s. During the 1940s in China, the major Korean noncommunist resistance forces came together to form the Korean Restoration Army, which ultimately reached a membership of about 3,000 members. This army worked with Chiang Kai-Shek's Nationalist Peoples Party (Kuomintang, or KMT), developing close contacts with supporters of Chinese Nationalists and with U.S. military advisors. At the same time, the majority of Korean communists were working with their Chinese counterparts and gained invaluable military and organizational skills. Korean communist guerrillas in Manchuria went into hiding in the Soviet Union. Among them was Kim Il-Sung, who survived the Japanese extermination campaigns

The Mansudae Grand Monument. The towering 150-foot-tall statue of Kim Il-Sung was built for the leader's 60th birthday. Since his death in 1994, it has become a place of mourning and paying respects to the Great Leader. People visit the monument throughout the day and night to lay flowers and observe a moment of silence. (Courtesy of Mary Connor)

of the late 1930s. The Japanese considered him to be one of the most effective and dangerous of guerrillas. Overseas, Syngman Rhee worked tirelessly to become the leader of the government in exile. As the war was coming to a close, nationalists at home and abroad computed for the leadership of an independent Korea.

When the Emperor of Japan surrendered unofficially on August 15, 1945, it was a day of jubilation for Koreans. Flags that had been hidden by the Korean people now were unfurled on the streets, and the people celebrated freedom and national independence. It seemed that for the first time since early in the 20th century Koreans could shape their own destiny. However, Korea was soon to be divided after being unified for nearly 1,300 years.

LIBERATION, DIVISION, AND THE BEGINNINGS OF THE COLD WAR (1945–1950)

In 1943, Franklin Delano Roosevelt, Prime Minister Winston Churchill, and Generalissimo Chiang Kai-Shek issued the Cairo Agreement, which stated that "in due course Korea shall become free and independent." Joseph Stalin indicated support for this agreement in July 1945 by signing the Potsdam Declaration. In August, the Soviet Union, in accordance with the Yalta Agreement of February 1945, declared war on Japan and poured troops into Korea while U.S. troops were still fighting in Okinawa. Americans could not move quickly enough to stop Soviet occupation of the entire peninsula. Immediately after the second atomic bomb was dropped on

Nagasaki, officials in the United States proposed the division of Korea at the 38th parallel in an attempt to prevent a complete takeover by the Soviets. In their haste, they acted unilaterally. Their proposal involved a temporary division: The Soviet Union would establish a military zone north of the 38th parallel, and the United States would occupy a military zone to the south. Much to the surprise of U.S. military authorities, Stalin immediately accepted the proposal. U.S. forces began to arrive in South Korea the following month.

Although Korea was liberated from Japan, colonial policies continued to have a major impact on Korean politics and society. In 1945, Korea was a combination of old and new classes, political groups, and conflicting ideologies. About 80 percent of the population still lived on the land, but an assortment of businessmen, white-collar workers, factory laborers, and landless peasants who had been uprooted from their villages during the war were returning home. The colonial period had created nationalists with different ideologies and experiences who had remained within Korea or lived abroad. Rival groups had their own political agendas and supported different figures.

Two political factions developed in the liberation period. On the right were those who had collaborated enthusiastically with the Japanese and those who felt they had no choice but to collaborate in order to survive, support their families, and maintain their status in society. Others on the right were Koreans who had comprised 40 percent of the colonial police force and had limited education or no property. On the left was a broad spectrum of society (students, intellectuals, peasants, and laborers) politicized by the colonial experience. They condemned the inequities between classes that had prevailed for centuries and were attracted to the promises of Marxism and Leninism of bringing equality and justice to the poor and oppressed. Those attracted to communism desired a redistribution of wealth with an emphasis on land reform. Intense feelings existed between those who had collaborated and those who had not, between conservatives and the radical left, and between nationalists and communists.

Meanwhile tensions that had existed between the United States and the Soviet Union since the Russian Revolution increased during the war because of opposing strategies and conflicting ideologies. The U.S. War Department had anticipated a prolonged conflict in the Pacific and sought the support of the Soviet Union against Japan. Once the atomic bomb was developed, the United States knew the war would soon be over and wanted to keep the Soviet Union out of Japan. When the atomic bombs were dropped on August 6 and 9, 1945, the Soviet Union declared war on Japan, fulfilled its obligations from the Yalta Agreement, renewed its interests in Korea, and sent thousands of troops into areas that had been controlled by the Japanese: Manchuria and Korea.

Immediately after the unconditional surrender, a temporary peace-keeping organization, the Committee for the Preparation of Korean Independence (CPKI), was formed in August 1945 to assist in the transition, maintain order, and devise plans for a new national government. By September, there were committees in all of the major cities and even the smallest villages throughout all 13 provinces. In September, several hundred delegates met in Seoul and announced the formation of the

Korean People's Republic (KPR) and established a schedule for future national elections.

Scholars debate the political character of the KPR. The traditional American and South Korean view is that the KPR was a leftist organization with the objective of making Korea a communist state. Revisionist historians stress that the KPR was primarily a leftist organization but desired a coalition government as shown by the inclusion of such right-leaning nationalists as Syngman Rhee. The platform of the KPR was revolutionary; it called for the confiscation of land from the Japanese and all who had collaborated with them. Peasants would be given land, major industries nationalized, an eight-hour workday established, child labor prohibited, and a minimum wage determined. All men and women were to have the right to vote except those who had been collaborators. There was also to be freedom of speech, press, and religion. It seems at the time that the KPR was a reflection of the popular will of the majority of the people.

Japanese authorities in Seoul informed American leaders that local communists and independence supporters were plotting to subvert the peace process and warned of violence. Consequently, when the U.S. forces arrived in September, top officers were suspicious that the KPR was part of a Soviet communist conspiracy. Throughout the fall of 1945, Koreans dismantled the colonial administration at every level and expelled collaborators from positions of power. Communists played a significant part in the process, but they were not necessarily the leaders; there was always active participation by the local population.

General John Hodge, the leader of the U.S. occupation forces, under orders from Washington refused to recognize the KPR or any Korean government. He set up the United States Army Military Government in Korea (USAMGIK) and began to reestablish the colonial administrative government by appointing people who had served as collaborators. American leaders were unaware of the stigma associated with collaboration and felt it necessary to quickly create a government free of leftist influences. Many Koreans appointed to the new government were upper class, propertied, anticommunist, well educated, and English speaking. Hodge began to carry out policies to end all KPR committees south of the 38th parallel.

The Soviet occupation forces treated the KPR very differently. In the North, collaborators were thrown out of office and the colonial bureaucratic government destroyed. Large industries were nationalized. Japanese land was confiscated, and the majority of landlords lost most of their property. The objectives of the KPR were carried out with little violence since many northern landlords had already fled south.

In the final months of 1945, the foreign ministers of the Allies met in Moscow to establish an international solution to the Korean situation. The diplomats agreed to authorize the formation of a joint U.S.–Soviet commission to establish a government in consultation with its leaders to end the Allied occupation. The new administration would be put under a five-year trusteeship of the Allies. Koreans in both the Soviet- and U.S.-occupied zones reacted violently to the plan and carried out nationwide demonstrations. Many factors contributed to the response, but the main reason for protest was the right-left polarization of national politics that came with

Soviet and American occupation. In early 1946, Soviet pressure on Korean communists led to support of the Moscow Agreement; however, violence between Nationalists and Communists continued to occur throughout the peninsula.

Most of the turmoil was south of the 38th parallel. As a result of the trusteeship decision and subsequent American political and economic policies, people grew increasingly hostile to U.S. military rule. Strikes, mass demonstrations, and bloodshed occurred. From the American point of view, events in Korea seem to mirror fears at home. Labor strikes in both countries were all perceived as communist inspired.

Another important reason for the polarization of politics on the peninsula was the honor bestowed by the Americans and the Soviets on their favorite patriots who returned from years in exile. The Soviets gave their support to General Kim Il-Sung, the charismatic anti-Japanese guerrilla fighter who had established close contacts with communists in China and Russia while in exile. In February 1946, a provisional government, the Interim People's Committee, was inaugurated with Kim in control. He soon moved toward a dictatorship by eliminating nationalist and religious organizations, nationalizing businesses, and organizing an army. During this time, some 2 million Koreans fled to the South.

Almost simultaneously with the growth of autocratic government in the North, USAMGIK supported the development of a rightist, anticommunist government in the South. In October 1945, Syngman Rhee, a 70-year-old patriot who had been active in the independence movement, returned to his homeland. Educated in the United States, he had established close ties with governmental figures in Washington and with Nationalist Chinese leader Chiang Kai-Shek. An outspoken anticommunist, Rhee immediately condemned the Soviet Union, Korean communists, and the KPR.

Because of his personal dislike for Rhee and pressure from the U.S. State Department, General Hodge tried to form a coalition government acceptable to the Soviets. The plan was to exclude the extremes of the right (Syngman Rhee) and left (Kim Il-Sung) and form a trusteeship determined by the Moscow Agreement. Unfortunately, Koreans were too polarized to accept a coalition government. Relations had also deteriorated between the United States and the Soviet Union because of the continued Soviet occupation of Eastern Europe and the implementation of President Harry Truman's policy of containment.

Considering the international tensions of the time, it is understandable that two separate governments emerged on the peninsula. The final step came in May 1947 when the United States appealed to the newly created United Nations (UN) to resolve the Korea question. In November, despite protests from the Soviets, the UN General Assembly voted to send a commission to Korea to conduct national elections, establish a government, and end Allied occupation.

Most people wanted an immediate end to occupation and supported the UN plan. The Soviet Union disputed the UN's authority to conduct elections and rejected the resolution. Rhee and his supporters advocated elections in the South. Many opposed these elections for the obvious reason that they would lead to the permanent division of the peninsula. Members of the UN commission were determined to carry out elections, and on May 10, 1948, the first democratic elections were held in the South. Two months later a constitution was adopted, and on August 15 the Republic of Korea (ROK) was established with Syngman Rhee its first president. The ROK claimed that it was the only legitimate government on the peninsula. The United States and many other democratic nations promptly recognized the new government. In August, the North Korean communists had their own elections that were approved by the Soviet Union. A constitution was adopted for a separate state called the Democratic People's Republic of Korea (DPRK), and Kim Il-Sung was elected premier. Northern leaders claimed that theirs was the only legitimate government on the peninsula and that P'yongyang was to be the temporary capital. In late 1948, the Soviets withdrew their troops but left behind modern military equipment and advisers to train Kim Il-Sung's forces. The Americans left South Korea the following year, leaving poorly trained and inadequately supplied forces to defend with the South with the assistance of U.S. military advisers.

THE KOREAN WAR (1950–1953)

There has been much debate over the causes of the Korean War. The end of the Cold War era and research in Soviet archives have given further perspectives on the complexities of the war's origins. There is no doubt, however, that the northern troops actually crossed the 38th parallel on June 25, 1950. Yet this event has to be viewed within the context of important international developments and the polarization that existed on the peninsula. U.S. policy makers were strongly influenced by the lessons of the 1930s. They knew that "appeasement" of dictators simply encouraged them to escalate their demands, whereas decisive action to stop aggression would force them to withdraw.

With the end of World War II, the tenuous alliance between the Western powers and the Soviet Union deteriorated, and ideological competition ushered in economic and political instability throughout the world. The Soviet Union occupied Eastern Europe and successfully tested an atomic bomb, ending the U.S. nuclear monopoly. To stop Russian expansion and the threat of communism, the United States adopted the Truman Doctrine, the Marshall Plan, and the containment policy. To protect national security and maintain peace, the United States entered its first peacetime military alliance by joining the North Atlantic Treaty Organization. In 1949, Mao Zedong's army won the Chinese civil war, brought communism to the most populous country in the world, and proclaimed the People's Republic of China. Critics of the Truman administration claimed that the United States had "lost China." Senator Joseph McCarthy in February of 1950 further heightened U.S. security concerns by charging that the State Department was thoroughly infested with communists.

Meanwhile, there was continuous leftist guerrilla warfare throughout much of South Korea. Skirmishes between North and South Korean forces at the 38th parallel became frequent. Rhee and his generals spoke often of military operations to take over the North. Between 1945 and 1950, Kim Il-Sung repeatedly asked Soviet leader Joseph Stalin for permission to invade the South. As a result of the turbulence throughout South Korea and the frequent border skirmishes along the 38th

The East Gate and Seoul residences in the early 1950s. This photograph was taken by Cpl. Alfred (Bud) Hallam of the U.S. Army, who was killed during the Korean War. (Courtesy of Mary Connor/Alfred Hallam)

parallel, most historians now believe that the Korean War actually started as early as 1948 if not before.

In 1950, when Kim Il-Sung requested Soviet support to unify the country and promised a quick victory, Stalin reluctantly gave his permission as long as Mao would support the invasion. Mao agreed and released more than 60,000 battled-hardened Koreans from the People's Liberation Army for duty in North Korea.

Early Sunday, on June 25, 1950, North Korean troops opened fire and launched a well-planned attack against South Korea. Equipped with Soviet tanks and fighter planes, the North Korean Army crossed the 38th parallel and within three days captured Seoul and overran most of the peninsula within a short period of time. While the war began as a civil war, it became the first major power conflict since World War II. It was feared at the time to represent the beginnings of World War III.

Without a formal declaration of war, President Harry Truman tried to halt the invasion with U.S. air and naval forces, but the combined South Korean and U.S. forces could not stop the advances of the superior forces of the North Korean Army. Within a short time, it had captured all but the area around the port city of Pusan.

Realizing the grave danger to the ROK, Truman requested the assistance of the UN to support it. Stalin was apparently still lukewarm about Kim Il-Sung's war against South Korea. The UN Security Council, urged by the United States, adopted a resolution to condemn North Korea's actions. The Soviet Union delegate, who

P'yongyang Airport. The main airport is very small for a nation of 22 million people, but it services the nation adequately because few people travel to and from North Korea. (Courtesy of Mary Connor)

could have blocked the resolution with his veto power, had been boycotting the council to protest China's lack of representation in the UN. Soon afterward, a second resolution was adopted to go to war. Truman named General Douglas MacArthur the Commander of the UN forces, 90 percent of whom were American.

The U.S. Army, Navy, Air Force, and Marines arrived in Korea, and together with troops from the United Kingdom, France, Canada, and Australia, a counterattack was launched. MacArthur carried off a daring amphibious landing at Inch'on, several hundred miles behind North Korean lines. Eighteen thousand U.S. Marines landed on September 15, 1950, and quickly moved inland. The UN forces liberated Seoul and pushed the DPRK troops back to the 38th parallel. Even before Inch'on, Truman had redefined the objectives of the United States in fighting the war. He now believed that the whole peninsula should be liberated from communism and reunified by force.

In September, Truman authorized UN forces to cross the 38th parallel. Together with the ROK, they marched north; captured the capital, P'yongyang; and continued to move well into the North in pursuit of fleeing troops. U.S. aircraft also bombed bridges along the Yalu River, the border with China. Mao warned that he would not permit the continued attacks on transportation links with Korea. Although the collapse of their communist ally seemed imminent in mid-October, tens of thousands of

The Joint Security Area in the Demilitarized Zone. The buildings in the foreground are where armistice negotiations took place at the end of the Korean War. The building in the background, Panmungak, is located in North Korea. (Courtesy of Mary Connor)

Chinese soldiers poured into Korea from Manchuria and drove the UN forces back again. On January 4, 1951, Seoul fell a second time, but by March UN forces succeeded in recapturing the capital city. The front then stabilized around the 38th parallel.

The United States and the Soviet Union welcomed negotiations, but MacArthur had other ideas. The general wanted to extend the war into China, liberate it from communism, and restore Chiang Kai-Shek to power. In April, fed up with MacArthur's insubordination and backed by the Joint Chiefs of Staff, Truman fired him.

Armistice talks began in July 1951, but the fighting and dying continued for two more years. The most controversial issue in the negotiations was the fate of the prisoners of war (POWs). The United States maintained it would return only those North Korean and Chinese prisoners who wished to go home. The DPRK objected. Both sides were involved with brainwashing prisoners to resist repatriation.

As the POW issue continued to prolong negotiations, U.S. officials made vague public statements about the use of atomic weapons. American bombers devastated dams, rice fields, factories, airfields, and bridges. Casualties on both sides mounted. Finally, after two years of negotiations and the ultimate involvement of 21 countries, a truce was signed at P'anmunjom on July 27, 1953, and a 2.5-mile-wide demilitarized zone (DMZ) was established across the peninsula. China ultimately withdrew its forces in 1958, but more than 25,000 U.S. troops remain in South Korea.

Korean War Museum, Seoul. The museum, traces the history of war from the Three Kingdoms Period to the Korean War. (Courtesy of Mary Connor)

When the fighting finally ended, the two Koreas, for all they had suffered, would control essentially the same territory they held when the war erupted. It devastated both halves of a nation that had only begun to recover from four decades of Japanese occupation and political division. Around 3 million people, approximately one-tenth of the entire population, were killed, wounded, or missing. Another 5 million became refugees. It is estimated that 900,000 Chinese and 520,000 North Koreans were killed or wounded, as were about 400,000 UN Command troops, nearly two-thirds of them South Koreans. U.S. casualties were 54,000 dead and another 103,000 wounded. ROK property losses were put at $2 billion, the equivalent of its gross national product for 1949; DPRK losses were estimated at only slightly less. Fifty-five years after the war, an estimated 10 million people remain separated from their families by the 38th parallel. North and South Korea are technically still at war. Frequent notices appear over the Internet that the remains of those missing in action are still being found on the battlefields of the Korean War.

A DIVIDED KOREA: THE SOUTH KOREAN EXPERIENCE (1953–2008)

The First and Second Republics, 1948–1961

For South Korea, the next several decades would bring radical changes in government and tremendous economic growth. The war left the country with massive economic, social, and political problems. Showing a strong desire to hold onto power, President Syngman Rhee became increasingly domineering and autocratic. With the support of the Liberal Party, he revised the Constitution, gave unlimited tenure to his office, and suppressed the opposition Democratic Party. The spark that brought his administration to an end was the effort to rig the election of 1960.

Aware of his own unpopularity, Rhee and his supporters used every means to ensure victory for the Liberal Party. Massive demonstrations broke out, leading to police violence and the death of a student. As a result, nearly all of the students in the universities and high schools hit the streets. The government declared martial law, but shortly thereafter the National Assembly pressured Rhee to resign. He had no choice but to step down. Students had led the people into the first successful democratic revolution in the country's history.

The Second Republic (1960–1961), a liberal democratic regime with Premier Chang Myon at its helm, lasted only eight months. In May 1961, Major General Park Chung-Hee and young army officers overthrew the administration. For the first time since the 14th century, the military gained control of the government. Park was to be the key figure in a new arrangement of power that would last nearly two decades.

The Third and Fourth Republics, 1963–1979

Park Chung-Hee and army officers quickly put Seoul under military occupation, and stability was restored. The government promised that it would take a strong stand against communist infiltrators, develop stronger relations with the United States, establish a self-supporting economy, unify the nation, and hold elections the following year to establish a new civilian government. The election was held in 1963, and Park, who had resigned from the army, was elected president of the Third Republic, beginning a long era of authoritarian rule. Park was reelected to a second term (1967), and in his election to a third term (1971), he defeated Kim Dae-Jung.

Under President Park's leadership, the human and natural resources of the country were effectively organized for the first time in modern history. The economy began to grow rapidly, per capita income soared, and exports rose by more than 30 percent a year. Park managed to consolidate his power and manipulated the Constitution to remain in office indefinitely.

Park's foreign policy included normalization of relations with Japan in 1965 and the first formal dialogue with North Korea. His agreement to the normalization and to sending troops to aid the United States in Vietnam led to massive demonstrations on the part of opposition parties and students. His administration was destabilized by such changes on the international scene as Nixon's policy of détente with China and the withdrawal of 20,000 U.S. troops from South Korea. A slowdown in the economy together with the international situation led Park and his advisors to silence dissent. In 1972, he declared martial law, suspended the Constitution, and dissolved the National Assembly and all political parties. By the end of the year, he had transformed the presidency into a dictatorship. Park held power for seven more years. Finally, on October 26, 1979, the director of the Korea Central Intelligence Agency assassinated him. The prime minister Choi Kyu Hah, immediately became acting president.

KWANGJU UPRISING (MAY 1980)

On December 12, 1979, Maj. Gen. Chun Doo-Hwan took control over the military of the Republic of South Korea. In response to the Yusin Constitution (which removed restrictions on the term of office of a president) and Chun's declaration of martial law, students and citizens took to the streets of Kwangju. With the arrival of the army, hundreds if not thousands of citizens were killed. During the Kwangju demonstrations, citizens appealed in vain to the U.S. embassy to intervene. The United States took no action, and many South Koreans concluded that it supported Chun. The tragic developments led to increased opposition to the Chun regime and anti-American sentiments. Kwangju has become a symbol of the aspirations of the South Korean people for democracy.

The Fifth Republic, 1980–1988

During the next several months, the country was in turmoil. In December 1979, General Chun Doo-Hwan carried out a coup, became president of the Fifth Republic, declared martial law, and ruthlessly suppressed popular demonstrations. In the midst of this political crisis, the bloody Kwangju uprising of students and citizens occurred, resulting in possibly 2,000 casualties and causing antigovernment sentiment that lasted for years.

Although President Chun promised a new era, he continued to rule autocratically. The Fifth Republic did include the first-ever surplus in the international balance of payments. When student demonstrations led to a brutal murder of a Seoul National University student, riots broke out in major cities throughout Korea. Chun was subsequently forced to step down.

The Sixth Republic, 1988–1993

Roh Tae-Woo had served in both the Korean and Vietnam Wars and over the years rose through the ranks to become a general. After Chun became president, Roh resigned from the military and served in several posts in Chun's administration. After Chun chose Roh to be his party's candidate for president, massive protests broke out. In response, Roh proposed a broad program of democratic reforms, which led to the approval of a new constitution in October 1987. One of the main provisions was the direct election of the president by popular vote. Roh won the election in December because both major opposition candidates, Kim Young-Sam and Kim Dae-Jung, split the opposition vote.

As president, he committed himself to democratization. In foreign affairs, Roh cultivated new ties with the former Soviet Union, China, and many Eastern European countries. He obtained South Korea's admission into the UN and signed an agreement in 1991 calling for nonaggression between the two Koreas. In February 1993, Kim Young-Sam, whose anticorruption reforms targeted Roh and Chun, succeeded him.

In 1995, Roh publicly apologized for having illegally amassed $650,000 in secret political donations. He was tried, found guilty, and sentenced to prison. He was later pardoned by outgoing President Kim Young-Sam.

On February 25, 1993, Kim Young-Sam, who won the 1992 presidential election, was sworn in as the first civilian president of Korea. He defeated Kim Dae-Jung and another leading candidate. Once in power, Kim established civilian control over the military and tried to make the government more responsive to the electorate. He pursued reforms to eliminate political corruption and abuses of power. The economy continued to grow at a rapid rate, and the standard of living improved.

Kim was constitutionally barred from seeking a second term. His popularity declined rapidly in the last year of his five-year term as a result of corruption within his administration and the severe financial crisis that affected South Korea in 1997. The longtime opposition leader, Kim Dae-Jung, succeeded him as president.

Kim Dae-Jung's election, the first true opposition party victory in a presidential election, came at an extraordinarily difficult time: a new round of corruption scandals and the worst economic crisis in decades hit Korea and other parts of Asia. Kim vigorously pushed economic reform and restructuring recommended by the International Monetary Fund. The government's efforts for a fast economic recovery paid off when the nation completed repayment of bailout loans three years ahead of schedule. His government also carried out far-reaching restructuring of such conglomerates as Hyundai and Samsung.

The Kim administration is primarily remembered for its policy of engagement with North Korea, which is known as the Sunshine Policy. Between June 13 and 15, 2000, Kim Dae-Jung met in P'yongyang with Kim Jong-Il, the leader of the DPRK, the first meeting of the heads of North and South since the peninsula was divided in 1945. They agreed to allow visits of some of the 1.2 million family members separated since the Korean War and to address the gap between the two economies. After the summit, Kim Dae-Jung received the Nobel Peace Prize for his efforts of reconciliation. Needless to say, he was a hero at home and widely respected throughout the world.

In spite of his remarkable achievements, Kim's problems grew as the global economy weakened, joblessness increased, and his Sunshine Policy grew more unpopular. He came under fierce attack when his two sons were arrested for accepting bribes. His administration was also charged with secretly paying North Korea $100 million to get P'yongyang to agree to the historic summit. Kim defended his actions by saying it was for the sake of peace.

A human rights lawyer by profession, Roh Moo-Hyun entered politics in response to human rights abuses during the Chun administration. His presidency has been described as a roller-coaster ride. His administration was hurt by corruption scandals and hindered by a parliament dominated by opposition parties and fierce opposition to some of his policies, such as sending troops to Iraq and the continuation of a policy of engagement with North Korea. He was suspended in the first year of his presidency after the National Assembly voted to impeach him for violating an election law. The Constitutional Court later overturned this decision. Roh was also criticized for resisting pump-priming measures to stimulate the economy.

Roh and his advisors all shared the serious concerns that the United States might start a war to eliminate North Korea's nuclear programs at South Korea's expense. He was encouraged to strengthen the alliance with the United States to work toward a peaceful settlement of the nuclear issue through diplomacy. At the end of his presidency, he had a fairly successful summit with Kim Jung-Il.

Lee Myung-Bak, former mayor of Seoul, was sworn in on February 25, 2008. His presidency restored conservatives to office after a decade of liberal rule. In his inaugural address, he called for a renewed spirit of self-sacrifice and vowed to apply pragmatic solutions to governing a country where inequality of wealth has created "class conflict and animosity."

His early months in office were shadowed by an investigation of his business ties to an alleged felon, but a ruling early in his administration said there was no evidence to implicate him. He also assumed office amid a political storm over the appointees to his cabinet; some were forced to resign amid suspicions of corruption, and others had become very wealthy through real estate speculation. It appears that South Korea's bitter partisan politics will continue throughout his administration.

A DIVIDED KOREA: THE NORTH KOREAN EXPERIENCE (1953–2008)

The DPRK is a mystifying nation. It is described as being the most secretive and isolated nation in the world, and its government is characterized as one of the most authoritarian. Although it remains difficult to obtain reliable information about the country, much can be learned from examining the leadership and policies of Kim Il-Sung. The "Great Leader" was chief of state from 1948 until his death in 1994 when his son, Kim Jong-Il, took his place and became the "Dear Leader."

The Korean War left both sides socially and economically devastated, but the destruction was more extensive in the North as a result of the widespread use of napalm and incessant air campaigns on the part of the United States. During and after the war, Kim eliminated his enemies and rivals, and his supporters nurtured his personality cult, hailing him as a superhuman being. After 1953, Kim Il-Sung created a very strict, austere, militarized, and regimented existence for the people. While officially extolling *juche* (pronounced joó-chay), or self-reliance, North Korea in reality relied heavily on Soviet and Chinese economic and military support. It did receive substantial economic aid from China and the Soviet Union, but much less aid than the South received from the United States and Japan.

Kim Il-Sung stressed the reconstruction and development of major destroyed industries after the war, sacrificing the needs of consumers. The emphasis on industrialization, combined with unprecedented aid from the Soviet bloc, pushed the growth rate to 25 percent annually for the decade following the war, and for two

Triumphal Arch, P'yongyang. This is a photograph of the Kim Jong-Il and Kim Dae-Jung motorcade upon arrival in P'yongyang, the capital of North Korea, in June 2000. (Photographed by Cheong Wa Dae, Presidential Residence of the Republic of Korea, Photographer's Press Pool)

decades the North's growth outdistanced the South's. The achievements were so remarkable that some economists spoke of the "North Korean Miracle."

When the Soviet Union and China became unreliable allies in the 1960s, Kim Il-Sung promoted national self-reliance; people needed to count on their own national leaders and resources to solve problems. Kim felt no hesitation in proclaiming that under *juche* "man is the master of everything and decides everything." To prove that he had greater commitment and ability than anyone else, history was rewritten. It proclaimed Kim to be the originator of the Korean revolutionary movement, the founder of the People's Army, and the liberator of Korea from Japan. In order to perpetuate his legacy and prolong his revolutionary ideology, Kim Il-Sung took steps to establish his dynasty. In the early 1970s, he began to prepare his son, Kim Jong-Il, to succeed him.

North Korea was also affected by the policies of Park Chung-Hee, who proclaimed in 1961 that anticommunism was the most important principle of his administration. Park worked to develop strong ties with the United States and Japan, sent troops to support the United States in Vietnam, and received greater military and economic aid in exchange. Kim's response to these trends was to build up North Korea's military capabilities and to prepare for all-out war. Military spending rose from 4 percent to yearly averages ranging from 20 to 30 percent of the national budget. This represented a major drain on the country's resources and affected the government's ability to meet its economic objectives.

View outside the International Friendship Exhibition Hall, Myohyang, North Korea. No photo-graphs may be taken within the hall that contains over 71,000 gifts given to either Kim Il-Sung or Kim Jong-Il. One may view the gift that Madeleine Albright (former U.S. secretary of state) gave to Kim Jong-Il when she visited North Korea. (Courtesy of Mary Connor)

Aware of the rapid economic development of South Korea, North Korea attempted in the 1970s a large-scale modernization program through the importation of Western technology. In 1973, Kim introduced the Three-Revolution Team movement, a mass movement based on ideological indoctrination, technical innovation, and cultural education grounded in the *juche* ideal. The program involved teams of individuals traveling around the country to provide political, scientific, and technical training through mass meetings. The objective was to further educate everyone in the *juche* ideal and to improve productivity, technology, literacy, and cultural identity. Additional campaigns involved mass political movements within the military, such as the Three-Revolution Red Flag movement.

In spite of these efforts, the DPRK defaulted on its loans from free-market economies. In 1979, it was able to renegotiate much of its international debt, but in 1980 it defaulted again on most of its loans. Largely because of these debt problems, but also because of a prolonged drought and economic mismanagement, industrial growth slowed and per capita GNP was one-third of the South's by 1979.

North Korea's problems worsened in the 1980s and 1990s. Various initiatives were established to boost the country's economic situation. Trade was opened somewhat to the capitalist world. The government also tried mobilizing workers to work harder, better, and faster. Since the 1970s, the DPRK has been a major arms supplier to such countries as Libya, Iran, and Syria. The collapse of the Soviet Union forced it to aggressively pursue foreign investment, relations with capitalist firms, and new zones of free trade. In spite of the economic problems and the initiatives to deal with them, the country's basic economic structure and institutions have not changed.

In 1993, U.S. intelligence predicted that North Korea might have the capacity within two years to strike South Korea and Japan with nuclear missiles. When P'yongyang refused to allow inspectors from the International Atomic Energy Agency (IAEA) to inspect two facilities in North Korea, the IAEA turned the matter over to the UN Security Council. The United States hoped to get enough support in the Security Council to impose economic sanctions on P'yongyang, which North Korea regarded as a declaration of war. The crisis was eased in June 1994 when former U.S. president Jimmy Carter persuaded Kim to freeze the program in return for an easing of international sanctions and talks about ending North Korea's international isolation. Kim died on the eve of these talks at age 82.

Most experts predicted that the North Korean regime, struggling to reverse the country's economic decline, would not survive Kim's death. After two years of floods were followed by drought, a severe famine developed in the late 1990s that claimed an estimated 2 million people. Despite these disasters, Kim Jong-Il maintained complete control of the country. He built strong links with the army as the only sure foundation for his rule at a time of endemic food shortage and low public morale. Malnutrition and hunger continue to be a problem. Thousands of North Koreans have escaped to China or South Korea. Those who are caught attempting to flee face inhumane conditions in prison camps and execution.

In 1998, Kim Jong-Il seemed to justify the worst Western images of him when he test-fired a missile over Japan and raised suspicions regarding North Korea's nuclear ambitions. In 1999, North Korea agreed to allow the United States to conduct ongoing inspections of a suspected nuclear development site. In exchange, the United States promised to increase food aid and initiate a program to bring potato production to the country.

Tensions between North and South Korea improved dramatically in June 2000 when South Korea's president, Kim Dae-Jung, met with Kim Jong-Il in P'yongyang. The summit was the first meeting between leaders of the two countries since division in 1945. Hopes were high for reconciliation, reunification, and peace on the peninsula. North Korea agreed to freeze its existing nuclear program and to support the IAEA safeguards. The meetings included an agreement for visits between families separated since the Korean War, plans to close the gap between the two economies, and a policy to organize various cultural exchanges.

In January 2002, tensions escalated between the United States and North Korea as a result of President George Bush's "axis of evil" speech. His address marked a significant change from the policy of his predecessor, Bill Clinton, who supported a policy of engagement. In October 2002, North Korea admitted that it had violated the 1994 agreement to freeze its nuclear weapons program and was in the process of developing nuclear weapons. Two months later, North Korea forced UN

BAN KI-MOON (1944)

In 2007, Ban Ki-Moon became secretary-general of the UN, the first Asian in more than 30 years to serve in this capacity. He received his bachelor's degree from Seoul National University and his master's degree from Harvard. At the time of his selection as secretary-general, Ban was minister of foreign affairs and trade in South Korea. He has had long-standing ties with the UN and has been very actively involved in inter-Korean relations. In 2005, as foreign minister, he played a leading role in the adoption of the Six-Party Talks on resolving the North Korean nuclear issue.

weapons inspectors to leave the country and in January 2003 announced that it was withdrawing from the Nuclear Non-Proliferation Treaty. The United States refused to negotiate with North Korea until it agreed to dismantle its nuclear program. The Six-Party Talks in 2003, 2004, and 2005 among officials from China, Japan, North Korea, South Korea, Russia, and the United States to resolve the crisis ended in deadlock.

In 2006, North Korea launched seven missiles, the first major weapons test in eight years. Later in the year when the nation conducted an underground nuclear explosive test, Bush responded by labeling the test a threat to "international peace and security" and called for sanctions against the country. What was resolved was only a temporary solution to the problem. In early 2007, North Korea came to an understanding with the six-nation negotiators that it would shut down its nuclear program, including the Yongbyon reactor, and in return would receive approximately $400 million in heavy fuel oil and economic aid, among other diplomatic incentives. Since then, North Korea shut down its nuclear weapons reactor, and IAEA inspectors verified this action. North Korea reported that it would disable its nuclear facilities and would provide an accounting of all of its nuclear programs by the end of 2007. In October 2007, in the final months of Roh Moo-Hyun's presidency, he met with the North Korean leader, Kim Jong-Il. In this meeting, the second inter-Korean summit, the leaders agreed to collaborate on several economic projects and to move toward signing a treaty that would formally end the Korean War. However, North Korea did not fulfill its promise to give an accounting of its nuclear programs by the end of the year.

It was clear in early 2008 that the newly elected president of South Korea, Lee Myung-Bak, would use different strategies in dealing with North Korea. Lee vowed that he would not kowtow to North Korea and planned to limit inter-Korean cooperation unless the North abandoned its nuclear weapons. In May, a delayed nuclear declaration arrived in Washington, D.C.

In June 2008, in a gesture to indicate that it would now cooperate, North Korea destroyed the cooling tower at the Yongbyon nuclear facility. There was some reason to hope that this time North Korea might end its nuclear program. Three months later, however, P'yongyang announced that it was reassembling its main nuclear facility and blamed the United States because it had not yet removed North Korea from its list as a state sponsor of terrorism. In the same month, reports were rampant that the Dear Leader, Kim Jong-Il, might be seriously ill or even dead. Authorities speculated on the possible implications of a regime change and the huge risks and challenges that would come with it, such as the possibility of an out-of-control North Korean military, a flood of refugees into China and South Korea, and the overall humanitarian and economic consequences of the collapse of the DPRK.

North Korea's policy of self-reliance was a reaction to the prolonged sufferings of the 20th century and the desire to maintain a distinct Korean identity. After the extreme hardships of colonialism, poverty, and civil war, *juche* appeared to be the means by which the nation could protect itself from the agony of the past. When the Cold War ended, this policy appeared to be out of place. It was hoped that the summit meetings between the leaders of North and South Korea in 2000 and 2007 would be positive signs of the promise of a new century—the one that will bring reconciliation, reunification, and peace to the Korean peninsula and its people. After more than half a century, the tensions and the problems related to the Korean War remain. Many Koreans question whether reunification is necessary or even inevitable.

REFERENCES

Breen, Michael. 1998. *The Koreans: Who They Are, What They Want, Where Their Future Lies.* New York: St. Martin's Press.

Center for Defense Information. 2003. "Fact Sheet: North Korea's Nuclear Weapons Program." January 23. http://www.cdi.org/nuclear/nk-fact-sheet.cfm (accessed March 24, 2008).

Central Intelligence Agency. 2001. "North Korea." *The World Factbook.* http://www.odei.gov/cia/publications/factbook/geos/kn.html (accessed August 15, 2001).

Columbia Encyclopedia. 2008. "Roh Moo Hyun." http://www.encyclopedia.com/doc/1E1-RohMooHyn.html (accessed March 16, 2008).

Cumings, Bruce. 1997. *Korea's Place in the Sun: A Modern History.* New York: W. W. Norton.

———. 2004. "Korea: Forgotten Nuclear Threats." *Le Monde diplomatique,* December. http://mondediplo.com/2004/12/08/korea (accessed March 19, 2008).

Eckert, Carter, et al. 1990. *Korea Old and New: A History.* Seoul, Korea: Ilchokak Publishers.

Federation of American Scientists. 2006. "Nuclear Weapons Program—North Korea." November 16. http://www.fas.org/nuke/guide/dprk/nuke/index.html (accessed March 24, 2008).

Gunness, Christopher. 2002. "Kim Dae-jung's Tainted Legacy." *BBC News.* December 19. http://news.bbc.co.uk/2/hi/asia-pacific (accessed March 19, 2008).

Hart-Landsberg, Martin. 1998. *Korea: Division, Reunification, and U.S. Foreign Policy.* New York: Monthly Review Press.

JoongAng Daily. 2008. "DJ Plans U.S. Lecture Tour for April." March 24. http://joongangdaily.joins.com/article/print.asp (accessed March 24, 2008).

Korea Information Service. 1999. *Facts about Korea*. Seoul: Korea Information Service.

Korean Overseas Information Service. 1993. *A Handbook of Korea*. Seoul, Korea: Samhwa Printing Co.

Kim, Tong. 2008. "Irony of Roh Moo-Hyun." *Korea Times*, February 24. http://www.korea times.co.kr/www/news/opinion/2008 (accessed March 15, 2008).

Lee, Hyun-hee, Sung-soo Park, and Nae-hyun Yoon. 2005. *New History of Korea*. Seoul, Korea: Jimoondang Publishers.

Lee, Ka-baik. 1984. *A New History of Korea*. Seoul, Korea: Ilchokak Publishers.

Oberdorfer, Don. 1997. *The Two Koreas: A Contemporary History*. Reading, MA: Addison-Wesley.

Oh, Kongdan, ed. 2000. *Korea Briefing, 1997–1999: Challenges and Changes at the Turn of the Twentieth Century*. New York: M. E. Sharpe, Inc.

Oh, Kongdan, and Ralph C. Hassig. 2000. *North Korea through the Looking Glass*. Washington, DC: Brookings Institution Press.

Peterson, Mark. 2008. Personal communication.

Reitman, Valerie. 2000. "Amid Tears, Koreans Cross 50-Year Divide." *Los Angeles Times*, August 16.

Seth, Michael J. 2006. *A Concise History of Korea: From the Neolithic Period through the Nineteenth Century*. New York: Rowman & Littlefield Publishers, Inc.

Shin, In-seok. 2007. "Causes of Economic Slowdown." *Korea Focus* (Autumn). Seoul: Korea Foundation. Volume 15, No. 3, 30–32.

Suh, Dae-Sook. 1998. *Kim Il-Sung: The North Korean Leader*. New York: Columbia University Press.

U.S. Department of State. 2008. "Background Note: South Korea." October. http://www.state.gov/r/pa/bgn/index.cfin?docid=2800 (accessed August 15, 2001).

Wallace, Bruce. 2008. "New South Korea Leader Vows to Fix Economy." *Los Angeles Times*, February 25.

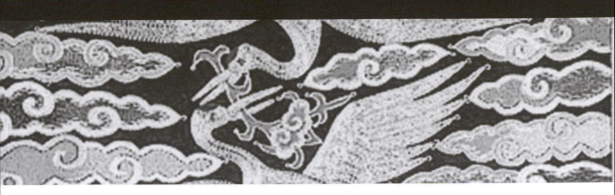

CHAPTER 3

Government and Politics

Mary E. Connor

Around midnight on August 10, 1945, the day after the second atomic bomb was dropped on Japan, the United States made a momentous decision about Korea. Fearing that the Soviet Union was going to take over the entire peninsula and establish a communist regime, the United States hurriedly urged the USSR to accept a division of the country at the 38th parallel. The agreement shattered nearly 1,300 years of unity. And since that day virtually every consideration on both sides of the division has essentially been connected to tensions emanating from the Cold War.

For 40 years, Korea had resisted Japanese oppression by holding on to the dream of independence. After liberation, the Democratic People's Republic of Korea (DPRK) and the Republic of Korea (ROK) promised, each in its own way, to give the Korean people what they wanted: stability on the peninsula and self-determination in their national destiny. Nonetheless, those people continued to endure hardships under authoritarian regimes both north and south of the 38th parallel.

In June 2000, the leaders of both sides met for the first time since the division. At that summit meeting, Presidents Kim Dae-Jung and Kim Jong-Il pledged to take concrete steps toward reunification. In the process, they attempted to redefine relations that had remained suspicious, if not hostile, for more than a decade after the Cold War ceased everywhere else. In spite of the hopes raised, major obstacles to unification remain. Political experts throughout the world continue to voice concern that problems on the peninsula pose a dangerous military threat to the stability of East Asia and even to the United States.

Kim Jong-Il and Kim Dae-Jung in P'yongyang, June 2000. (Photographed by Cheong Wa Dae Presidential Residence of the Republic of Korea, Photographer's Press Pool)

THE IMPACT OF TRADITION
ON POLITICAL DEVELOPMENT

Until the late 19th century, political and social traditions throughout the peninsula had not changed for centuries. Korea was an agrarian society until approximately two generations ago. Until 1910, it had a monarchical system of government. The centralized court and aristocracy monopolized wealth, power, and status, while the majority of people remained poor. During the Choson dynasty, eligibility for state examinations was limited to a small portion of society, the *yangban*, or aristocratic class. Because few other career paths existed, attaining a government post was the ultimate goal of the *yangban*. This fact tended to sanction any means, often including bribery, of securing positions.

Both the Koryo (918–1392) and the Choson (1392–1910) dynasties adopted Confucian principles of government. That system incorporated concepts of loyalty, filial duty, respect for age and status, and veneration for learning. Loyalty governed the relationship between ruler and subjects. The bonds were strictly hierarchical. Kings sometimes exercised power compassionately, but more often cruelly.

This tradition also incorporated the notion that the ruler and his officials must be virtuous to retain their mandate to rule. If they are no longer virtuous, people have the right to revolt. However, when a king was overthrown, reforms did not necessarily improve lives or change class structure. Periodic revolutions by the common people and slaves, usually triggered by their desperate economic circumstances, were brutally crushed. In the 19th century, followers of the Tonghak movement instigated the first nationwide peasant uprising in the country's history. Based on the Confucian notion of a justifiable revolution and beliefs borrowed from Catholicism, Buddhism, Taoism, and Shamanism, the Tonghaks dedicated themselves to improving the conditions of the people. They held the revolutionary notion that all human beings embody the divine, thus rejecting class distinctions that had for centuries condemned the majority of people to lives of poverty. Their call for equality between men and women and social and economic justice for all continues to have an enormous impact on the yearnings of the Korean people.

The Confucian legacy is still operative today. Most Koreans look to their leaders for major decisions. Family ties constitute the central element in people's lives and organizations. In the South, family-owned conglomerates dominate the economy. In the North, Kim Jong-Il was carefully groomed to carry on the ideological work of his father, Kim Il-Sung. Tradition dictates that each family member must be diligent in fulfilling his or her role. When something is done in the interest of the family, even misconduct may be overlooked.

THE IMPACT OF THE JAPANESE COLONIAL PERIOD ON CONTEMPORARY LIFE

From 1910 to 1945, Japanese colonial policies destroyed the foundations of a remarkably stable 19th-century hierarchical agrarian society. After overthrowing the Choson dynasty, the Japanese replaced it with their own strongly authoritarian regime, headed by a military governor-general who vigorously suppressed dissent. What resulted was a highly centralized colonial government that took control over every aspect of the cultural, political, and economic life of the nation. This authoritarian model was to manifest itself again in both Koreas during the post-1945 period.

One aspect from the Choson dynasty the Japanese did not destroy was the position of the aristocracy. They did remove most *yangban* from positions of authority in the colonial government, but landlords were allowed to maintain their estates, dominate the peasants, and export rice to Japan. The colonial period created a whole set of future political leaders, molded either by their resistance to or collaboration with the colonizers. Those on the right were the majority of propertied and educated citizens, many of whom cooperated with the regime. Those on the left came from varying backgrounds, including students, intellectuals, peasants, and workers who became politicized by negative experiences from occupation. They were attracted to communism because it opposed foreign rule and advocated justice for the poor. When the colonial system suddenly ended with liberation on August 15, 1945, they were committed to removing all collaborators from positions of power and influence.

MARCH FIRST MOVEMENT (MARCH 1, 1919)

Japan firmly established rule over Korea in 1910. President Woodrow Wilson's famous Fourteen Points (1918) raised the hopes of people throughout the world when he championed the concept of national autonomy and self-determination. The leaders of the Korean independence movement adopted a plan to have a nationwide demonstration on March 1, 1919, expressing the desire of the Korean people to be free and independent of Japan. Korean nationalists signed a Declaration of Independence, which was proclaimed at rallies throughout the country. The response of the Japanese was brutal. More than 500 demonstrators were killed, approximately 26,000 were arrested, and thousands of homes and churches were burned. It was not until August 15, 1945, that the hopes of the March First Movement were realized.

THE IMPACT OF U.S. AND SOVIET OCCUPATION AND THE KOREAN WAR ON POLITICAL DEVELOPMENT

After 1945 and the division of Korea at the 38th parallel, U.S. military authorities backed Syngman Rhee and other conservative politicians with ties to the *yangban* and former Japanese collaborators. Because of heightened fears particularly in the

The Government-General Building, the symbol of Japanese colonialism, was located in Seoul. It was torn down in 1996. (Courtesy of Steve Smith)

early Cold War years, the Americans, ignorant of Korean history, not prepared to speak the language, and lacking any knowledge of the culture, had difficulty distinguishing communists from persons with understandable demands for self-government and land reform. Although U.S. officials grew to thoroughly dislike Rhee's authoritarianism and the corruption in his government, he appeared to be their best hope of avoiding a communist government. Frustrated and prodded by communist agents, many turned to guerrilla warfare in the South prior to and during the civil war.

In the North, Soviet occupation forces supported Kim Il-Sung as interim ruler. Highly admired as a former anti-Japanese guerrilla leader, Kim redistributed land and raised the social status of the peasants, but his policies made life difficult for Christians, professionals, and landowners. He moved in ways that would eventually establish him as the absolute ruler of North Korea.

The most profound effect of the U.S.-USSR occupation of Korea was the institutionalization of the social and political divisions created after World War II. The DPRK's programs emphasized socialism, land reform, and independence from outside powers. The regime in South Korea was capitalist, pro-*yangban*, largely Japanese trained, and dependent on American aid, guidance, and approval.

Each of the Koreas has continually blamed the other as the sole aggressor in the Korean War. Kim Il-Sung survived politically, despite the fact that the Chinese had to rescue him and that he failed to reunify the nation as promised. He purged his critics and rivals and blamed others for the unsuccessful conclusion of the war. He presented himself as a hero. His revolutionary deeds were glorified and managed to generate a formidable personality cult. In South Korea, the 1948 Constitution made democracy the foundation of government, but within a short time the democratic principles were destroyed. The war provided Rhee with opportunities to demand absolute loyalty, remove potential rivals, and eliminate on a massive scale suspected leftists and their supporters.

The war, which ended in stalemate, resolved nothing and left a legacy of bitterness, fear, and mutual suspicion. What had begun as hostility between two governments and conflicting ideas about the economic and political direction of Korea now affected everyone throughout the peninsula. Most Koreans suffered greatly at the hands of those on the other side. The results contributed significantly to the growth of authoritarian rule and the suppression of civil and political rights both north and south of the demilitarized zone (DMZ).

A DIVIDED PEOPLE: THE SOUTH KOREAN EXPERIENCE (1948–2008)

The First Republic, 1948–1961

During U.S. occupation, General John R. Hodge established an interim government under the direction of U.S. authorities. A committee of prominent Koreans consulted widely among emerging leaders, such as Syngman Rhee, who favored a presidential system of government. On July 12, 1948, the National Assembly adopted the first formal constitution, which was definitely shaped by U.S. influence. The Constitution declared that the ROK "shall be a democratic republic" and that its "sovereignty shall reside in the people from whom all state authority shall emanate."

Certain provisions of the Constitution shed light on the future course of political development. Chapter I renounced all aggressive wars and charged the military with "the sacred duty of protecting the country." It stipulated that no officer should be appointed prime minister unless he resigned from active service. Chapter II enumerated basic rights, including equality before the law. Defined freedoms included speech, press, assembly, and private correspondence. The equality of men and women and equal opportunity of education were enunciated. Unlawful search was forbidden. These rights held great promise; however, other provisions paved the way for authoritarian rule, the violation of civil rights, and virtual government control of the economy.

Chapter II, Article 28, stated that restrictions on the rights of citizens could be enacted only when necessary for the maintenance of public order and the welfare of the community. Therefore, when the ruling authorities deemed it necessary for public order, all the above liberties could legally be restricted. Chapter II, Article 57, included an emergency clause that gave the president exclusive powers for convening the National Assembly to issue orders during civil war, dangerous situations arising with foreign powers, and natural calamities or financial crises. Chapter V stated that judges were to be free from executive and legislative interference. However, the president, with the approval of the National Assembly, appointed the chief justice, and judges of other courts were appointed for the relatively short term of five years. Procedures within this chapter made it difficult to declare any executive actions unconstitutional. Chapter VI provided for state or public management of such important enterprises as transportation, communication, banking, and insurance.

Notwithstanding the ideals of the Constitution, the growth of presidential power was understandable given political tensions on the peninsula. Provisions for immediate and decisive action were essential. Since the majority of people lived at a subsistence level, it also seemed natural that the Constitution should include an active governmental role in economic development.

Many people assumed that Syngman Rhee, who was educated at George Washington, Harvard, and Princeton universities, would model his own presidency on the U.S. Constitution. The early hopes for democratization now seem incredibly naïve given Korea's authoritarian traditions, Rhee's personality, and the international political and economic tensions of the time.

Although he spent most of his life in the United States, his conduct as president grew to resemble that of a Choson monarch. He initially impressed Americans because he was well educated, aristocratic, charismatic, and anticommunist; however, he established a police state. Throughout his administration, he frequently said that he hated the Japanese, but he appointed Koreans who had collaborated with the Japanese to serve in his government.

When Rhee was inaugurated, he was 73 years old. He assumed the presidency when South Korea was desperately poor and politically unstable. Within his first

---

SYNGMAN RHEE (1875–1965)

Syngman Rhee, patriot and first president of the ROK, led his country during some of the most turbulent years of its modern history. Prior to the presidency, he was active in the Independence Club, imprisoned and tortured for his revolutionary activities against the pro-Japanese government, and elected president of the Korean government in exile. At the age of 73, he was elected president of the First Republic (1948–1960). During the difficult years of the Korean War, Rhee became increasingly autocratic, and thousands of leftists were executed without trial. After being reelected several times, he became increasingly unpopular because of his oppressive tactics and ruthless suppression of the opposition. When it appeared to the public that the 1960 election was rigged, there were massive demonstrations that demanded his resignation. He resigned on April 27, 1960, and went into exile in Hawaii, where he died five years later.

---

three years, he was faced with overwhelming problems: severe economic hardship, civil unrest, and war. Even though he expressed sympathy for the plight of the people, he never proposed an official plan of economic development. His financial concerns primarily related to obtaining as much foreign aid and military assistance as possible.

In October 1948, a large-scale mutiny of two regiments of the Republic's army broke out at the port city of Yosu. The rebellion was suppressed by Korean officers under the direction of Americans, even though U.S. military occupation had ended. Rhee and his American supporters charged that North Korea had instigated the rebellion, but in effect, it was caused by the frustration of local leftists and resentment toward the U.S. occupation.

It was under these circumstances that the National Assembly adopted the National Security Law, which is still in force today, more than half a century later. Its purpose is to ensure "the national security and interests" by protecting the state from its enemies, defined as "any association, groups, or organizations" that conspire against the state. Harsh punishments were promised. The law restricted press freedom, criticism of the United States, and political activities of religious organizations and labor unions.

During the Korean War, the government became a military autocracy. Orders were given to execute leftists, and probably more than 100,000 people were killed without a trial. During the war, Rhee rammed through the assembly a constitutional amendment that established a precedent for manipulating the Constitution. In 1953, when the armistice was to be signed, Rhee refused. He was opposed to any agreements with the North because he believed the war should not end until United Nations (UN) forces achieved total victory. He never did sign the armistice.

A year after the war, he again amended the Constitution. By this time he had developed his own political party, the Liberal Party. It consisted of men who had

Syngman Rhee, first president of the Republic of Korea, poses with U.S. General Douglas MacArthur. (Library of Congress)

served in the colonial bureaucracy but were now intensely loyal to Rhee. With their support, he was able to get a constitutional amendment adopted to repeal the prohibition against a third four-year term of office. Rhee was now 79 years old, and his plan was to be president for life.

Public opposition grew. Although land reforms were carried out after the war, the farm population remained poor and politically inactive; however, criticism of the administration was growing in the cities. At the center of the urban discontent was a growing population of college and university students. They were South Korea's first postcolonial generation to come of age. They had been educated about constitutional democracy and hated the fraud and coercion of the administration.

In 1960, at the advanced age of 85, Rhee ran for another four-year term. The main opposition was the Democratic Party, which had emerged in 1955. Rhee's supporters were determined that he win a direct popular election according to the "democratic constitution." But instead of ensuring a democratic mandate, the president's principal supporters rigged the election. When the results were counted, the public was informed of a landslide victory.

Subsequently, a riot broke out in Masan. Even though voters were convinced that the election was stolen, they felt helpless against the police force. When a fisherman found the body of a 19-year-old high school student with a tear gas shell imbedded in one eye, the people lost all control. The resulting riot triggered massive student demonstrations in Seoul and other major cities.

On April 19, 1960, more than 3,000 students marched to the presidential mansion. The police initially fired tear gas shells, but when the students surmounted the barricades, the police began firing into the crowds. Within a few hours, more than 100,000 people were battling the police. Approximately 125 died, and more than 1,000 were wounded.

President Rhee declared martial law, sent heavily armed soldiers into Seoul, and blamed communists for the disturbances. Street demonstrations spread to all major cities. Although the president commanded the fourth-largest army in the world, he agreed to resign when informed that he would save lives if he did so. The uprising was a success. Rhee sought exile in the United States and spent the remainder of his life in Hawaii.

The Second Republic (1960–1961) and the Military Revolution

In the early months after Rhee's resignation, restrictions on the press and political activity were lifted. In reaction to abuses of power during Rhee's presidency, lawmakers made major revisions to the 1948 Constitution in order to eliminate the problems in the presidential system of government. The amended constitution created a parliamentary system centered on a prime minister and a cabinet that were responsible to the National Assembly. In 1960, the Democratic Party gained control of both houses of the National Assembly, and Chang Myon became the first prime minister.

From the beginning, Chang found himself in a very precarious situation. The economy was in decline. Partisan politics made long-range plans difficult. Widespread government corruption was exposed. When the won was devalued, prices soared, and within a year there occurred massive public demonstrations involving 1 million people. Unfortunately, the Chang administration began to practice tactics similar to those of Rhee.

On May 16, 1961, Major General Park Chung-Hee ordered tanks into Seoul and seized control of the government in the first successful military coup d'état since the late 14th century, and for the next 32 years, South Korea would be ruled by military governments. A 16-man junta declared martial law, dissolved the National Assembly and all political parties, outlawed demonstrations, and exercised strict censorship of the press. It moved swiftly to get U.S. support by claiming that the first purpose of the government was anticommunism. Although the United States initially resisted support of the coup, its opposition did not last for long.

Military Rule, 1961–1963, and the Third and Fourth Republics, 1963–1979

Park was similar to Rhee in his desire for personal power and the continuation of American military and economic support, his hostility toward North Korea, and his

---

PARK CHUNG-HEE (1917–1979)

Park Chung-Hee was the third president of the ROK. Park, whose father had fought with the Tonghak rebels, was raised in poverty. He trained at an officers' school in Japan during the Japanese occupation and graduated from the Korean Military Academy during U.S. occupation. On May 16, 1961, Major General Park Chung-Hee in a military coup seized control of the government of President Chang Myon and established military rule for the next 32 years. His term as president was marked by extraordinary economic development but also included political and social repression. He was assassinated in 1979 by one of his own men, the head of the KCIA.

---

desire to eliminate opposition. He stressed the dangers of the communist threat, made pledges to restore civilian government within two years, and implemented plans to bring about rapid economic development.

The Park era divides essentially into three periods. During the first two years (1961–1963), he ruled through a military junta called the Supreme Council for National Reconstruction (SCNR). He moved decisively to control the whole nation to an extent not seen since the colonial period. After thousands of arrests, trials, and forced resignations in the military, a new generation of officers was in Park's debt.

Park Chung-Hee. (Corbis)

The SCNR created the Korean Central Intelligence Agency (KCIA) with Kim Jong Pil as its head. The organization, established to include domestic and international surveillance, ultimately became one of the main symbols of the repression of the Park era.

In the second period (1963–1972), Park responded to domestic and international pressure to restore civilian rule. He was particularly concerned about pressures from the United States, whose aid programs counted for more than 50 percent of the national budget. In December 1962, after martial law was lifted, a constitutional referendum approved a third republic, promising a strong, popularly elected president and a party-centered unicameral legislature.

Nevertheless, Park and his officers were still determined to surrender as little power as possible. To make himself more appealing, Park declared that he was retiring from the military and would run for office as a civilian. To strengthen his position, laws were adopted to ban serious rivals from any political activity, and the KCIA created a highly centralized political organization, the Democratic Republican Party (DRP), to help maintain power. After the party was fully operational, the ban was lifted on political activity. A date was not announced until a month before the presidential election. Consequently, opposition parties had little time to organize. In subsequent elections, the DRP won and thus controlled the majority of the seats in the assembly. By the end of 1963, Park established what appeared to be a civilian government.

For a number of significant domestic and international reasons, Park would change his mind. Because party politics was becoming too disruptive and threatening to his agenda, he and the DRP developed new strategies. When he wanted an amendment passed to give him a third term, his party, the DRP, adopted one. His opponents joined forces to form a New Democratic Party (NDP). The party now had new leaders, such as Kim Young-Sam and Kim Dae-Jung, who were well-known critics of the Park regime. Popular support for the NDP grew, particularly in urban areas.

After successfully ending term limits on the presidency, Park was more determined than ever to win decisively in the election in 1971. To achieve this, the KCIA and additional progovernment organizations were effectively mobilized. Since big business had prospered enormously from Park's economic plans, it helped to finance his campaign, hoping to benefit directly from his reelection through defense and public works contracts, low-interest loans, and other special favors.

Park's biggest challenger in the election was Kim Dae-Jung, who attacked him for his military-dominated authoritarianism. With his enormous campaign war chest and all the resources of the government behind him, Park had a huge advantage in spite of mounting domestic problems and international concerns. He was reelected with 53.2 percent of the vote, a much smaller victory than anticipated.

International developments were a cause of growing concern before and after the election. Dramatic changes in U.S. foreign policy had recently shocked Seoul. President Richard Nixon announced the withdrawal of 20,000 troops that had been stationed in South Korea since the end of the Korean War. This came at a time when 50,000 Koreans were still fighting in Vietnam. Nixon's visit to China in 1972 ended U.S. support for Taiwan, a close anticommunist ally of South Korea. These developments and increased tensions between North and South Korea led Park to again consolidate power.

YUSIN (REVITALIZING REFORMS) (1972–1979)

In 1972, President Park announced what is known as the Yusin system that began the Fourth Republic. Citing domestic and international insecurity, Park proclaimed martial law. The Yusin Constitution made it possible for Park to remain in office indefinitely through well-controlled electoral procedures, to dismiss the cabinet and the prime minister, and to dominate the National Assembly. Through this system, he transformed the presidency into a legal dictatorship. All political parties were dissolved, and restrictions were placed on free speech and the press. By the end of 1972, Park was more firmly entrenched than ever. Although his control appeared total, the price was high. It ultimately led to civil unrest, betrayal, and death by assassination.

A recession in the early 1970s loomed as an additional threat to the regime. Citing domestic and international insecurity, Park suddenly declared a state of emergency in December 1971. The next year began what was to be the third and final stage of his rule. He imposed martial law, suspended the Constitution, and again dissolved the National Assembly and all political parties. Colleges and universities were closed. Political activity and civil liberties including free speech were restricted. The Constitution was amended yet again in order to prolong his presidency indefinitely—making Park a legal dictator—and to dissolve the assembly whenever he felt it necessary. The president was also empowered to appoint one-third of the National Assembly, enabling him to control the legislature more directly than ever before. The Yusin ("revitalizing") Constitution was approved by a national referendum when the country was still under martial law. By the end of 1972, Park was the head of the Fourth Republic and appeared to be more firmly in control than ever.

How was Park able to dominate politics for a total of 18 long years? His rule was solidified by a number of institutional, social, and international forces. He had the support of the national police, the bureaucracy, the KCIA, the military, and the DRP. Economic development also gave him continued support. Businesspeople grew rich and received favorable tax credits and low-interest loans. A fast-growing economy enriched the middle class, so they tolerated Park's tactics.

There were also many reasons for the continued international support for Park. Ongoing hostility between the Koreas led many people to accept political conditions that normally would be unacceptable. Two assassination attempts by North Koreans generated public sympathy for Park and gave credibility to his authoritarian rule. Park's commitment to send 300,000 Korean troops to Vietnam between 1965 and 1973 made it virtually impossible for the United States to condemn Park.

The third period of the Park regime (1972–1979) and the Yusin system witnessed growing animosity from the population at large. Kim Dae-Jung, Park's popular rival for the presidency in 1971, continued to criticize the government and became a symbol of the growing resistance. However, the most important group in the antigovernment movement was the students. The Yusin system stimulated a massive movement that included dissident writers, musicians, and other artists. Protest gradually came to include intellectuals, the middle class, urban workers, and Christian groups.

In May 1975, Emergency Measure No. 9 made any criticism of the president a crime. Anyone who took a stand against Park faced arrest, forced confession, imprisonment without trial, and execution. In spite of brutal measures to stop all opposition, the truth about the government spread throughout the nation and overseas. Victims became an inspiration to others to continue the fight. One of the most famous symbols was Kim Dae-Jung, whom Park detested. KCIA agents kidnapped him in 1973 from a Tokyo hotel in a murder plot designed to look as if North Koreans committed it. Fortunately, a former KCIA director, Kim Hyong-Wook, intervened to save him. The U.S. ambassador in Seoul rushed to the Blue House (the official residence and office of the president) and demanded that Kim Dae-Jung be returned alive. Five days later, a bruised and shaken Kim was dumped outside his home and barred from political activity for the rest of Park's term.

In spite of Park's effort to maintain command, political and economic problems continued to spin out of his control. They turned worse when the Organization for Petroleum Exporting Countries (OPEC) nearly doubled the price of crude oil. Low-paid workers expressed their frustrations in increasingly militant strikes. A short time later, Kim Young-Sam, a vocal opponent of Park from a faction of the NDP, gained control of the opposition. Park's DRP promptly expelled him from the National Assembly. A week later the opposition walked out of the National Assembly in protest, and in Park's hometown of Pusan, students, workers, and urban residents demanded his resignation and an end to the Yusin system. Within a short time, massive demonstrations broke out throughout the country.

On the evening of October 26, 1979, Park had a dinner meeting at the KCIA annex near the Blue House. At this meeting, an argument broke out about the demonstrations. Park's bodyguard lambasted Kim Jae-Kyu, the head of the KCIA, for not controlling the demonstrations. Kim argued that this would mean killing thousands of people. Park then argued that he would be willing to kill 30,000 people. Kim had been frustrated for some time about the politics of his job as KCIA director and Park's criticism of his performance. He left the room and returned with a pistol, shot the bodyguard, and then shot Park.

Park's death came as a shock to the Korean people, but not a cause for national mourning. His assassination was followed by at least a decade of condemnation. Since then, his place in history has been reassessed. Today, Park is generally recognized as South Korea's most effective leader for the remarkable economic progress that he personally engineered. Nevertheless, the nostalgia for Park represents the worst legacies of his era: the disregard for human rights, callousness toward human suffering, and aversion to solving problems through dialogue and compromise.

Political Turmoil, 1979–1981

After Park was killed, Choi Kyu Hah, a career diplomat and bureaucrat, became acting president of the interim government. Choi pledged that the Constitution would be amended "to promote democracy" and announced that elections would

CHUN DOO-HWAN (1931–)

Chun grew up during Japanese occupation, entered the Korean Military Academy during the Korean War, spent one year training in American schools at Fort Bragg and Fort Benning, and received the U.S. Bronze Star for his military service in the Vietnam War. Chun seized power in the "12.12" Coup (December 12, 1979). He was initially sentenced to death for abuses of power but was ultimately forgiven in an act of reconciliation and pardon by Kim Dae-Jung.

be held. He removed emergency decrees of the former regime and restored civil rights. These events helped create a sense of national well-being that was known as the Seoul Spring. Kim Young-Sam, the head of the NDP, called for the elimination of the Yusin system, and Kim Dae-Jung, who formed the National Coalition for Democracy and Unification, demanded rapid democratization.

Unfortunately, the high hopes of the people were quickly dashed. South Koreans were to experience the greatest violence since the Korean War and control by a military junta. The 12.12 Coup occurred on December 12, 1979. Major General Chun Doo-Hwan, a close friend of the murdered Park and the head of the Defense Security Command, led the coup with two key assistants, Major General Roh Tae-Woo and Major General Chong Ho-Yong. In order to pull off the coup, Chun had used the Ninth Army, which was part of the American-Korean Combined Forces Command (CFC). However, Roh had moved the division from the DMZ to Seoul without notifying General John A. Wickham, the commander of the CFC. The U.S. government delivered a strong warning to Chun for violating the CFC's operation control.

Chun's actions resulted in massive student demonstrations calling for his resignation and the immediate end of the Yusin system. Approximately 70,000 to 100,000 students voiced their opinions in the streets of Seoul. Chun, the new head of the KCIA, extended martial law, dissolved the National Assembly, closed colleges and universities, banned labor strikes, and prohibited all political discussion and activity. His seizure of power essentially complete, he had Kim Dae-Jung and Kim Young-Sam arrested.

The events of December 1979 brought U.S. officials face-to-face with the limits of their control over South Korea's political situation. The United States strongly advised Chun to refrain from interfering in the political process, which is exactly what he did. In mid-May 1980, the CFC commander, frustrated by the events, went to Washington, D.C., to discuss the situation. In his absence, the Chun forces quietly notified the CFC deputy commander, a Korean general, of their intent to move the Twentieth Division. The deputy commander immediately granted a notification of release.

The tumultuous events moved out of Seoul and into Kwangju in South Cholla. On the morning of May 18, about 500 students demanded Kim Dae-Jung's release

Chun Doo-Hwan, shown here reviewing troops, was the leader of a coup against interim President Choi Kyu Hah, bringing an end to a brief period of democratic reforms between authoritarian regimes. (Department of Defense)

and an end of martial law. They suddenly found themselves up against paratroopers who were told that North Korean communist agents were directing a rebellion. The paratroopers, who were outside of the U.S. Combined Command, began brutally clubbing protesters with riot gear and rifle butts. Citizens became outraged and poured into the streets to join the students.

General Chun grew impatient with the events in Kwangju and ordered tanks and armored personnel carriers to release their power on the protesters. Loudspeakers from helicopters warned that the ROK's Twentieth Division would enter the city and that people should return to their homes. When it was all over, probably 2,000 or more were killed. This event severely damaged the Chun government from its very inception. The Kwangju massacre became a pivotal event in the country's journey from dictatorship to democracy. Ultimately, both Chun Doo-Hwan and Roh Tae-Woo were arrested and prosecuted as leaders of the massacre. During the Kwangju demonstrations, residents of the city had appealed in vain to the U.S. Embassy to intervene. Since nothing happened, students concluded that the United States supported Chun and approved his dispatch of forces to the city, especially because the government-controlled media confirmed this fact.

President U.S. Jimmy Carter based his foreign policy on a commitment to global human rights. Uncomfortable with Chun's takeover and the subsequent massacre, U.S. authorities in Korea and the Carter administration could have used armed forces to intervene. Nevertheless, distraught by the simultaneous Iranian crisis and concerned about fictitious KCIA reports of North Korean troop movements, the United States feared taking any step that could weaken the stability of the existing South Korean regime and security on the peninsula.

In his last months in office, Carter took steps to save Kim Dae-Jung's life. After the Kwangju incident, Chun immediately arrested Kim and blamed him for planning the rebellion, despite the fact that Kim was in prison at the time. After a show trial, Kim was sentenced to death for sedition. Since Chun wanted to obtain legitimacy for his regime, he was eager to be invited to Washington, D.C. As a quid pro quo for an invitation to the White House to meet the newly inaugurated president, Ronald Reagan, Chun commuted Kim's death sentence to life imprisonment.

On May 31, Chun promoted himself to four-star general and discharged himself from the army. Operating under the procedures established under Park's Yusin Constitution, Chun had himself inaugurated president in February 1981.

The Fifth Republic, 1981–1988

There is consensus on the seven-year rule of Chun Doo-Hwan's military regime. It was essentially the most tyrannical period in the modern history of South Korea. Even though he denounced past corruption and promised a new age of growth, honesty in government, and justice, Chun was consistently more heavy-handed than Park, who could at least justifiably claim credit for rapid economic growth.

When Chun received notice that Seoul would host the 1988 Summer Olympics, he started major construction projects. He emphasized economic growth over any serious efforts toward democratization but did lift the ban on political activities by former politicians. Chun forged a strong political party in the National Assembly as a means of controlling the legislative process and allowing military personnel to serve as legislators. To stop criticism, he frequently said that he would turn over his position to an elected successor in February 1988. He hoped that time would allow him to gain public acceptance.

His strategy did not work. Although Park came into power with relatively little bloodshed, Chun's coup involved the death of soldiers and a savage attack on civilians. The fact that he refused to accept any responsibility for the tragedy in Kwangju created even greater public hostility. Students became increasingly hostile to Chun and anti-American because they believed the United States had backed him during the events in Kwangju.

As Chun continued to restrain civil unrest and antigovernment activities, students and workers became more militant. The middle class also demanded change. It had grown to expect that economic growth would continue. After the 1985 elections, a new political party, the New Korean Democratic Party (NKDP), became the largest opposition bloc in the National Assembly. The two leading members of the NKDP were Kim Dae-Jung and Kim Young-Sam, both Christians who championed democratic reforms. There was now a broad base for challenging the authoritarian regime of Chun.

Early in 1987, a 21-year-old student from Seoul National University died in police custody. The police had continually dunked his head in a bathtub and smashed his windpipe in the process. They allegedly tried to cover it up, but details leaked and inflamed the populace against the regime. In response to the protests, Chun appeared agreeable to a constitutional amendment to allow a direct popular election to choose his successor. However, on April 13, 1987, Chun announced that he had changed his mind. Two months later, he met with his key supporters from the ruling Democratic Justice Party (DJP) and announced his decision to appoint Roh Tae-Woo as his successor. On June 10, the ruling party held its convention, and 99 percent of the delegates rubber-stamped the Roh candidacy in an indirect election to the presidency.

Chun had a sense of urgency that Roh succeed him as president. He needed a loyal friend to succeed him, one who would not prosecute him for his illegal seizure of power before and after the Kwangju massacre. It was strongly suspected and later confirmed that Chun and Park had received huge political donations from the *chaebol* (conglomerates) as kickbacks for profitable contracts. Chun could pledge Roh all the money he needed to win the election.

In response to the Roh candidacy, dissenters organized a coalition of opposition called the People's Movement to Win a Democratic Constitution and demanded direct presidential elections and a series of reforms. Although there had been many demonstrations since the founding of the ROK in 1948, there had never been anything as large in size or scope as the ones in the summer of 1987. This massive protest became a watershed moment in the evolution of democracy in South Korea. The political crisis grabbed the attention of a U.S. administration that feared civil arrest might overthrow the regime. Consequently, President Reagan sent a letter to Chun expressing support for his previous commitments to a peaceful transfer of power and the release of political prisoners. At the end of the letter, Reagan held out the promise of a state visit to the United States after Chun peacefully left office in 1988.

On June 29, Roh surprised the nation by accepting the demand for a direct presidential election. His announcement included a program of reform that comprised amnesty for Kim Dae-Jung, freedom of the press, and autonomy for the colleges and universities. Two days later, Chun publicly accepted the recommended reforms. The crisis was over, and the country took a step further in the democratization process. No one knows exactly why Roh opted for reform or why Chun agreed to it, but the 1988 Seoul Olympics was a factor. This was South Korea's chance to gain international recognition and respect. The fact that the overwhelming majority of Koreans wanted reform, together with tremendous pressure from the United States to abstain from a military solution, made reform more tolerable.

After six months of constant political activity, on October 29, 1987, a national referendum accepted the new constitution that had been approved by both the opposition and the ruling parties. This was the eighth time since the founding of the ROK that the Constitution had been amended or rewritten. The revised document contained sweeping changes and remains the fundamental law of South Korea.

One of the most important elements of the 1987 Constitution was that the president be elected for a single term of five years by a universal, direct, and secret ballot of the citizens. The powers of the president were restricted in order to provide a greater balance between the executive branch and a unicameral National Assembly, with members holding four-year terms. The latter was given impeachment power over the president, the prime minister, judges of the court, and numerous other offices. The armed forces were charged solely with national defense and were forbidden to be politically active. Gone were the provisions from the 1948 Constitution that rights and freedoms could be taken away in order to maintain public order. Restrictions on free speech and the press were ended. Workers were given the right to form unions, bargain collectively, and strike. One clause that was retained continued the government right to regulate economic affairs in order to maintain proper distribution of income.

Given the long history of authoritarian rule, the course of democratization in South Korea would depend heavily on the character of future presidents, the composition of the National Assembly, sustained economic development, and stability on the peninsula. The December 1987 election, the first by direct popular vote in 16 years, was a particularly significant test of whether the country would have a civilian president or another retired general loyal to Chun. During his campaign, Roh portrayed himself as someone who would finally end military-backed rule.

Roh had the advantage of leading the incumbent party, massive funding, and extensive exposure in the media, which was still controlled by the government. The major factor in the election results was the political rivalry between the two main opposition leaders, Kim Young-Sam and Kim Dae-Jung, who split the Democratic Party and allowed Roh to win. There were numerous accusations of vote buying and fraud; however, the election results were generally accepted by a public weary

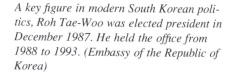

A key figure in modern South Korean politics, Roh Tae-Woo was elected president in December 1987. He held the office from 1988 to 1993. (Embassy of the Republic of Korea)

ROH TAE-WOO (1932–)

Roh Tae-Woo, president of South Korea (1988–1993), grew up during the final and most harsh years of Japanese occupation. A close friend of future president Chun Doo-Hwan, he became the head of South Korea's elite First Division during the Vietnam War. He supported Chun's military coup after the assassination of President Park in 1979 and served in varied cabinet posts. Growing opposition to repressive rule led to popular demands for democracy, and the public considered Chun's choice of Roh as his replacement just one more military dictator. But Roh surprised everyone by announcing his support for democratic reforms. In 1988, in the first peaceful transition of power in modern Korean history, he won a free election and began a five-year term as president. He took steps toward reconciliation with North Korea, established formal diplomatic relations with Moscow and Beijing, and allowed for more press freedoms. Since the Constitution prevented him from running for a second term, he supported Kim Young-Sam for president. In 1995, Roh was charged with accepting $654 million in secret political donations. In 1996, he was tried, along with Chun; convicted; and sentenced to serve 22.5 years in prison. President Kim Young-Sam pardoned him in 1997.

from tumultuous politics. Roh Tae-Woo, whose nomination had created civil disturbance and media attention throughout the world, was peacefully inaugurated as president in Seoul on February 25, 1988.

The Sixth Republic, 1988–1993

Roh Tae-Woo's inauguration in February 1988 was the first normal constitutional transfer of presidential power in Korea since 1948. Although he expressed eagerness to implement the new constitution, it would be a challenge for a man accustomed to giving orders and being obeyed. This challenge would become even more daunting because the DJP for the first time in 40 years did not get the majority of the votes in the National Assembly elections.

To convey to the public that a new era had dawned, Roh blamed Chun Doo-Hwan for the coup of December 12, 1979, and for the Kwangju uprising. However, Roh protected his longtime friend from punishment and jail by allowing Chun the opportunity to check into a remote Buddhist temple for meditation. Although Roh seemed to be more popular than Chun, his selection of cabinet members indicated that a true break with the past had not occurred. With the new checks-and-balances system, however, he lacked the power of previous presidents.

Another sign of change appeared in June 1988 when Roh announced efforts to improve relations with P'yongyang. His Northern Diplomacy efforts were geared toward improving communication and ending North Korea's isolation from the international community of capitalist nations. His policies reflected the immediate goal of creating an atmosphere conducive to a successful Summer Olympics and marked a significant departure from adversarial confrontation with the North, China, the Soviet Union, and other socialist nations. North Korea had attempted to pressure its communist allies to boycott the games. Two months after the North had rejected the final International Olympic Proposal and refused participation in the games, two highly trained DPRK espionage agents blew up a South Korean airliner.

An unprecedented political development occurred two years later, in January 1990, when three political parties merged. The parties of Kim Young-Sam and Kim Jong-Pil joined Roh's ruling DJP to form the Democratic Liberal Party and establish control over the National Assembly. This was good news for Roh because it would end the gridlock in the assembly, and it was a maneuver for Kim Young-Sam toward obtaining the presidency. After the three parties merged, Roh Tae-Woo had greater freedom to arrest dissidents under the National Security Law and to crush various labor strikes. More than 1,000 dissidents were arrested in one year.

With the end of the Cold War in 1989, Roh continued to make overtures to improve relations with North Korea. Relations with the former Soviet Union and China were normalized. In 1991, South and North Korea joined the UN simultaneously, a sign of the success of the Northern Diplomacy. Both Koreas pledged to avoid force against each other, reduce arms, and transform the armistice into an era of peace. They also pledged to develop economic, cultural, and scientific exchanges; to allow correspondence between divided families; and to reopen roads and railroads between the countries. Both sides agreed neither to produce, test, or deploy nuclear weapons, nor to possess nuclear reprocessing and uranium enrichment facilities. They also agreed to reciprocal inspections of facilities to be carried out by a Joint Nuclear Control Commission.

Despite Roh's achievements in diplomacy, the rate of economic growth slowed to the lowest point in decades. Anxiety about the economy clearly showed in the results of the March 1992 elections for the National Assembly. The Democratic Liberal Party created by the merger lost control over the assembly by one vote. The opposition party, the Democratic Party led by Kim Dae-Jung, made a strong showing.

As Roh's single-term presidency was ending in 1992, there was no question about duly electing the next president through a direct popular vote. The ruling Democratic Liberal Party had its convention and nominated Kim Young-Sam. As Kim celebrated his nomination, students led anti-Kim demonstrations in 22 urban centers, including Seoul, Pusan, and Kwangju. Students denounced the ruling party as being an illicit union of three parties. The government immediately called out the riot police and quickly ended the demonstrations. As expected, Kim Dae-Jung received the nomination from the opposition party.

The election was to be one of many firsts. Citizen groups organized on a massive scale to ensure a truly democratic election. Grassroots movements arose to oversee a fair election. They promised to expose any corrupt or coercive practices in electioneering, such as the distribution of gifts or pressure by local officials. Another first was that candidates were all civilians, with no military background or backing by the military.

Kim Young-Sam, president South Korea from 1993 to 1998, became the first civilian to hold the office since 1960. (Embassy of the Republic of Korea)

Throughout the campaign, Kim Dae-Jung proved to be an articulate and charismatic campaigner who stressed democratization and reunification. However, he did not have the financial resources of his rivals. Kim Young-Sam had abundant funds and could travel everywhere by helicopter. When the ballots were counted, Kim Young-Sam emerged the winner. The inauguration took place on February 25, 1993; it was the first peaceful transfer of power to a duly elected civilian president in 32 years.

Roh is not highly regarded in Korea today primarily because he served time in prison, as did Chun Doo-Hwan, for secretly accepting huge amounts of money from political supporters. Roh has since admitted that what he did was wrong and has apologized. In recent years, some have reassessed the leadership of Roh Tae-Woo by acknowledging his diplomatic achievements, such as his role in lowering military tensions in the region, improving relations between the Koreas, and establishing South Korea's diplomatic position in the world.

Civilian Government, Kim Young-Sam, 1993–1998

At the time of Kim Young-Sam's inauguration, his political career had already spanned four decades. The leader of the nation launched his regime by announcing that the Seventh Republic would open a civilian and democratic era for a new South Korea by rooting out corruption and misconduct. What was not revealed is that he owed considerable political debts to business for its part in the 1990 merger of the three parties.

Initially, Kim's presidency showed hopeful signs of change. Nearly all the members of his cabinet were reform-minded, and for the first time several women received cabinet posts. Kim took immediate steps to bring the military under the control of a civilian government by dismissals, early retirements, and demotions. Within two years, and for the first time in Korean history, nationwide mayoral and gubernatorial elections were held to elect city mayors and provincial governors.

In 1994, when the economy was the 11th largest in the world, President Kim declared his vision of *segyehwa* (globalization) to prepare for the monumental changes taking place throughout the world, to open South Korea in all fields (political, economic, and social), and to meet global standards of excellence, such as the protection of human rights, especially for workers.

At the same time that Kim was promoting his vision of globalization, a major crisis was building up on the peninsula. When the International Atomic Energy Agency was denied access to North Korea's nuclear sites, it turned the matter over to the UN Security Council, from which the United States hoped to get enough votes to impose sanctions on P'yongyang. North Korea denounced sanctions as a declaration of war and threatened to turn Seoul into "a sea of fire." In response, U.S. president Bill Clinton sent substantial reinforcements to South Korea. As developments seemed to be spinning out of control, former U.S. president Jimmy Carter offered to go to North Korea. In spite of Kim Young-Sam's belief that the visit was "ill-timed," Carter, as a private citizen, met with an ailing Kim Il-Sung and defused the crisis. His meeting paved the way for an agreement that became the October Framework; P'yongyang would freeze its graphite reactors and accept full inspections under the Nuclear Non-Proliferation Treaty (NPT), and in return, a consortium of nations would supply light-water reactors to help solve energy problems.

Several developments impaired the remainder of Kim's presidency. His detractors, knowing that he had risen to lead the ruling party during Roh's presidency, suspected that he was involved in some aspects of its corruption. A member of the National Assembly was able to prove that Roh had approximately $500 million deposited under false-name accounts while in office.

A huge rally, organized by Kim Dae-Jung, demanded that Kim Young-Sam prove that he did not receive money from Roh's accounts. The president then amazed everyone by announcing that legislation would be introduced to deal with the corruption and military activities of former administrations. The Constitutional Court ruled two days later that those involved in the Kwangju massacre could be prosecuted. This surprise development paved the way for criminal prosecution of those involved in the coup of December 12, 1979, and the massacre led by Chun and Roh. A special law to deal with political scandal and the massacre was quickly adopted by the National Assembly and paved the way for the indictment of Chun, Roh, and other former army officers on charges of mutiny, treason, and bribery.

Their trial began in December 1995 in a heavily guarded courthouse in Seoul. Chun admitted that he had received donations, but not bribes, and had provided some $240 million directly to Roh for his 1987 presidential campaign. Roh also said that he had received only donations and that they amounted to approximately $575 million from 35 of the nation's leading conglomerates. Roh evaded

P'anmunjom, the truce village between North and South Korea, is the only location along the DMZ where visitors are permitted. This is the truce village on the ceasefire line established at the end of the Korean War in 1953. (Courtesy of Mary Connor)

questions that related to the possible financial support of Kim Young-Sam's election. When Chun suggested that he might reveal recipients' names if he were treated harshly, the public trial was conveniently postponed, preventing any revelation embarrassing to President Kim or the ruling party from being made before the assembly elections. Kim knew that the election would be a test of his presidency and democratization.

As part of his drive to show that his party was creating a new South Korea, Kim changed its name to the New Korea Party. He warned that there would be no further reforms if the opposition got control of the seats in the National Assembly. Encouraged by the results of local elections, Kim Dae-Jung created a new political party, the National Congress for New Politics, and announced that he would run for the presidency for the fourth time. Immediately, nearly 100 members of the Democratic Party joined his new party, which made it the largest opposition party in the assembly.

Six days before the elections, hundreds of armed North Korean soldiers entered the northern sector of P'anmunjom in violation of the 1953 armistice agreement. President Kim placed the military on its highest level of readiness and capitalized on this crisis by urging the public to support his party in order to secure peace and stability on the peninsula. The election results clearly reflected the impact of the North's activities along the DMZ.

The New Korea Party, in spite of its strong showing, was 11 votes short of a majority. Nearly half of the elected assembly members were well-educated professionals new to politics, certainly a development that reflected voter disillusionment with traditional party politics.

Shortly after the elections, prosecutors in Chun's trial revealed that they had discovered some $8 million that Chun had not disclosed. This was known before the election, but the fact that it was not made public until afterward is a sign that the Kim government needed to protect itself. In August 1996, both Chun and Roh were charged with seizing power illegally, amassing illegal wealth by abusing their power, and murdering innocent citizens. The prosecutors demanded the death sentence for Chun and a life sentence for Roh for mutiny, treason, and corruption.

The trial made possible by Kim's civilian government stood as a lesson that former presidents could be punished for their actions. Newspapers reported that democracy was now stronger. Nevertheless, there was deep suspicion that Kim Young-Sam had probably received slush funds from Roh during his 1992 campaign. Another scandal shortly thereafter revealed that one of Kim's sons was involved in bribing high-level officials. Meanwhile, the country was beset by a worsening economic crisis.

As the economy took a sharp downturn in 1996, the mass media, some of which were owned or heavily dominated by the *chaebol*, appealed to citizens not to expect wage increases. Korean workers, known internationally for their hard toil and for working the longest workdays in the world, had seen little improvement in their wages over the years and resented the obvious extravagance of high-ranking government officials and the *chaebol* tycoons. Predictably, nationwide strikes ranged from assembly-line workers at Hyundai to subway engineers.

While the public was preoccupied with the declining economy and worker strikes, investigations involving the Hanbo Steel industry revealed that several of President Kim's closest friends and his other son were involved in corruption. The question of funds in the 1992 presidential campaign again surfaced at this inopportune time. Kim Young-Sam was now charged with receiving approximately $75 million from the Hanbo group and $375 million from Roh Tae-Woo. The National Assembly initiated televised hearings on the matter, but the results were inconclusive. Most witnesses denied the charges, and no one could produce any hard evidence. When the public demanded a thorough investigation by the prosecution, Kim's son was questioned for three days. As a result, he was charged with taking some $3.6 million in bribes from the business community.

With the beginning of his son's trial in July, the popularity of the president hit a low. When Kim took office, he had promised to clean up the so-called Korean disease of corruption, and his zeal for change led to the imprisonment of two former presidents. A public opinion poll indicated that he was now even less popular than the imprisoned Chun. As the economy continued to decline, it became evident that he was incapable of dealing with the nation's mounting problems.

Two former presidential aspirants declared themselves candidates. Both Kim Dae-Jung (National Congress for New Politics) and Kim Jong-Pil (United Liberal

Democratic Party) were in their seventies and thought they would try one last time. While the nation was preoccupied with the approaching December 18 presidential election, the public was shocked to learn that the government would apply for a bailout from the International Monetary Fund (IMF) to avoid national bankruptcy.

Prior to the election, Kim Dae-Jung and Kim Jong-Pil agreed to end their 36 years of political enmity and forged an alliance. Kim Dae-Jung would be the presidential candidate and Kim Jong-Pil the prime minister–designate. To counter this alliance, Lee Hoi-Chang, the ruling-party candidate, and Cho Soon, the Democratic Party candidate, whose popularity was lowest among the major candidates, also joined forces. Cho agreed to give up his candidacy and to accept the presidency of the ruling party, which was renamed the Grand National Party (GNP). As a result of these alliances, it appeared that the leading candidates were now Kim Dae-Jung, Lee Hoi-Chang, and Rhee In-Je, the candidate for the New Party for the People.

The presidential election of 1997 turned out to be the least violent and most inexpensive campaign ever and was closely monitored by civic groups. A new development was the broadcast of televised debates, which aroused voter interest and eliminated the expensive outdoor rallies of the past. Eighty percent of the qualified voters, more than 26 million people, turned out on Election Day. Kim Dae-Jung won by a very slim margin. Kim's victory was the result of his clever manipulation of existing regionalism and his alliance with Kim Jong-Pil.

Kim Dae-Jung, 1998–2003

Kim Dae-Jung's inauguration was particularly significant because it was the first peaceful transfer of power from an entrenched ruling party to an opposition leader since the founding of the republic. Kim called for reconciliation with the country's authoritarian past and for a strong national effort to overcome the disastrous economic crisis. It was also a very extraordinary event because Chun and Roh attended the ceremony. As a sign of Kim Dae-Jung's message of conciliation and forgiveness, he agreed to pardon the former presidents from their lifetime prison sentences for corruption.

In his inaugural address, Kim said: "Let us open a new age during which we will overcome the national crisis and make a new leap forward." He explained his Sunshine Policy by stating that he intended to work toward reunifying the Koreas. Part of his policy included the reunion of separated families, the expansion of cultural and academic exchanges, economic cooperation, and the exchange of special envoys.

In response to the severity of the economic crisis, Kim initiated structural reforms. Significant changes took place within a short period of time, a remarkable achievement considering the fact that he was a minority president. His political party had only 78 members in the National Assembly, as opposed to the GNP's total of 161 members. Kim was able to gain support in part because the public blamed the GNP for the economic problems that had surfaced. Because of the IMF bailout, the president could move toward resolving economic problems without major political risks. Before his inauguration, he managed to get major financial,

Kim Dae-Jung was president of South Korea from 1998 to 2003. In 2000 he received the Nobel Peace Prize for his lifelong struggle for democracy and his crusade for reconciliation with North Korea. (Corbis)

labor, and *chaebol* reform measures adopted. After his inauguration, intense partisan politics led to deadlock in the National Assembly.

Since 1948, South Korea upheld representative democracy as its ideal; however, political parties continued to be loose combinations of regional factions that coalesced around individuals rather than policy issues. The goal was to bring rival regional leaders into winning coalitions and to build electoral machines through the distribution of financial rewards and privileges to those who join together by bloodlines, school networks, or regional ties. Regional prejudices and money politics, not policy, have been the primary instruments for achieving mass support in electoral politics.

What Kim Dae-Jung inherited is a system that arose from Confucian familism. Korean regionalism is basically emotional and psychological and is based on loyalty to one's place of birth. Businesspeople contribute money to the campaigns with an implicit or explicit agreement for political and financial support. Recipients see these funds as a rightful reward for their efforts. Party leaders regard the distribution of funds as a manifestation of Confucianism or paternal benevolence to their loyal followers. As a result, corruption permeates politics, contributes to astronomical campaign funds, curtails reform, and diverts scarce resources from productive economic activity.

The impasse in the National Assembly prevented further reform and increased public disgust about politics, but it provided an opportunity for the Kim Dae-Jung

---

KIM DAE-JUNG (1924–)

Kim Dae-Jung was elected president in 1998 during the most severe economic crisis to grip South Korea in decades. He worked to restore economic stability, restructure the *chaebol*, promote greater democracy, and improve relations with North Korea. In 2000, he was the honored recipient of the Nobel Peace Prize for his lifelong struggle for democracy and his crusade for reconciliation with North Korea. He attributes his achievements to his Catholic faith, love for his country, and the dream of reconciliation between the Koreas. Born into a poor farm family of seven children in South Cholla province, Kim grew up with his father's passion for books and philosophy. He was an excellent student and graduated at the top of his high school class, ultimately completing a master's degree in economics at Kyunghee University in Seoul. During the Korean War, his future direction materialized as he saw "the suffering of the people caused by bad politics." Because of his tenacious efforts to assume leadership in Korean politics, he faced death five times, 6 years of imprisonment, and 10 years in exile or on house arrest.

---

administration. In the process of an investigation of the GNP, individuals were arrested for neglect of duty, violation of campaign laws, and conspiracy. Since corruption was so rampant, opposition politicians and independents feared for their careers and flocked to Kim's governing coalition. Finally, partisan realignments gave him a parliamentary majority and saved the president from becoming a target of political intimidation by the GNP.

Through this process of political realignment, Kim was able to build a network for devising viable reform strategies. In spite of all the partisan bickering and an all-time-high unemployment rate of 8.7 percent in his first year of office, Kim's public approval rating was 80.2 percent in early 1999. By the end of that year, the government announced the encouraging news that economic growth had hit 9 percent, compared with −5.8 percent in 1998. By October, the unemployment rate was down to 4.6 percent.

By February 2000, Kim had met with foreign officials and businesspeople more than 10 times a month, attended domestic events four times a day, and held nine state visits in order to overcome the economic crisis and improve foreign relations. In spite of this schedule, voter apathy and cynicism were pervasive during March and April, when the campaign for the National Assembly began. It was clear that the election results would be a test of his achievements. His successes in terms of economic recovery were respected and acknowledged even by the opposition party; however, his record on the Sunshine Policy was in question because P'yongyang had not responded in any significant way to Seoul's overtures.

In anticipation of the elections, he renamed his National Congress for New Politics the Millennium Democratic Party (MDP) and pledged that its members would reform themselves in an effort to improve the nation. When Seoul and P'yongyang jointly announced a summit to be held in June 2000, the initial reaction was mixed. Many people were suspicious about the timing of the announcement, only three days prior to the elections. After the election, the GNP was still in control of the National Assembly; consequently, there was continual political deadlock in the legislature. The outcome of the election also reflected the continuing role of regionalism in national politics.

A momentous and promising development occurred in the weeks following the elections. In June 2000, the leaders of North and South Korea met for the first time since the division. Relations between them were precarious during the Cold War because the ROK policy was based primarily on deterring P'yongyang's military and ideological threats. With the end of the Cold War, the collapse of the Soviet bloc, and deteriorating economic conditions in the North, it appeared that a more durable peace might in time become a reality.

In June 2000, the leaders of North and South Korea agreed to take specific steps toward reconciliation between the Koreas. Since the 1990s, the North had expressed hopes for the formation of a Korean confederacy consisting of "one nation, one state, two systems, and two governments." At the summit, President Kim Dae-Jung joined North Korean head of state Kim Jong-Il in support of the creation of a confederacy. They agreed that they would first lay a foundation for reunification through peaceful coexistence, reconciliation, and cooperation. They agreed that unification should be determined by North and South Korea and not by a foreign power. At the summit, they also agreed to provide an opportunity for some of the more than 1 million family members to visit one another after nearly half a century of separation. They further agreed to narrow the gap between their two economies, reopen the railway link between the Koreas, and speed cultural, athletic, medical, and environmental cooperation and exchanges. Kim Jong-Il pledged that he would visit Seoul at an appropriate time.

Although the summit was a positive step, the historic accord between the two Korean leaders did not address decreasing the size of the North Korean and South Korean armies, which comprised 1.7 million soldiers tensely eyeing their counterparts across the DMZ. The agreement also made no mention of North Korea's sales of advanced missiles to foreign countries, its nuclear weapons facilities, or its insistence that the U.S. military withdraw 37,000 troops from South Korean soil.

In October 2000, the Norwegian Nobel Prize Committee awarded Kim Dae-Jung the peace prize for his work for democracy and human rights in South Korea and East Asia in general, and for reconciliation with North Korea in particular. While the year 2000 held great promise and was the zenith of Kim Dae-Jung's political career, he continued to face formidable obstacles. In addition to relations with North Korea, major tasks included the deteriorating economic situation at home and growing public criticism. When new U.S. President George W. Bush announced early in 2001 that he needed to reexamine U.S. foreign policy with North Korea, an angry Kim Jong-Il called off several high-level contacts with the South and criticized the United States, raising fears that a fragile rapprochement between the Koreas could be derailed.

Bush's harder line against North Korea gave Kim Dae-Jung's critics further ammunition. When terrorists attacked the World Trade Center in New York and the

U.S. Pentagon on September 11, 2001, both Kim Dae-Jung and Kim Jong-Il condemned the attack. However, North Korea was one of the world's leading exporters of ballistic missiles and related technology to the volatile Middle East, and this worked against support within South Korea for the Sunshine Policy. In 2003, a special prosecutor revealed details of an illegal transfer of $500 million to the North just before the 2000 summit, evidently because Kim Jong-Il demanded it. Critics had even more reason to denounce Kim Dae-Jung and proponents of the Sunshine Policy for lacking principle in dealing with North Korea.

Kim Dae-Jung continues to be widely respected throughout the world; however, he remains the subject of constant controversy and is strongly criticized at home. Despite Kim's record as a lifelong campaigner for democracy, his own administration was not noticeably more open or less corrupt than that of immediate predecessor. Both of his sons were found guilty of corruption.

Roh Moo-Hyun, 2003–2008

The 2002 campaign between the MDP candidate Roh Moo-Hyun, a 56-year-old former activist and human rights lawyer, and the major GNP candidate, LeeHoi-Chang, was seen as a sign of fundamental change in Korean politics. Roh's reformist agenda appealed to the people, especially the younger generation, because it effectively captured the desire for change that had been building up in the South Korean voters.

During the campaign, Roh's supporters were particularly successful in making effective use of Internet technology to mobilize voters, especially those in their twenties and thirties. As a result of Roh's successful appeal to the reform-spirited younger generation, Lee Hoi-Chang's main supporters were people in their fifties and sixties and older, and it was more difficult to mobilize these older voters over the Internet. The results of the election signified a shift from regionalism and the domination of business interests to generational politics, greater diversity of opinion made possible by the Internet, and an increased number of women participating in politics.

The influence of young voters was also seen in the response to the 2004 attempt by the opposition to impeach Roh for establishing a new party (Uri Party) ahead of the April National Assembly elections. What transpired was an unusually high voter turnout (60 percent) for the general election together with a voter backlash mobilized by Roh's supporters. The Uri Party tripled its representation in the assembly and now held 152 of the total 299 seats, becoming the first liberal party to control a South Korean government. The Constitutional Court ultimately overturned the impeachment, stating that Roh's actions did not amount to an impeachable offense.

Roh initially studied law as a means of escaping poverty. After being one of the leaders of the 1987 demonstrations against the dictatorship of Chun, he entered politics and served in the National Assembly. When he campaigned for the presidency, he ran on a platform of change: End the corrupt ties between business and politics, reform the *chaebol*, reduce labor unrest, achieve unification by supporting the Sunshine Policy, and increase South Korean autonomy from the United States.

ROH MOO-HYUN (1946–)

In order to escape the poverty of his youth, Roh Moo-Hyun entered the legal profession. When exposed to human rights abuses in the 1980s, he defended antigovernment activists and became a leader in the struggle against the infamous Chun Doo-Hwan military regime. Deciding to enter politics, he was elected to the National Assembly in 1988 and served on a committee that investigated government corruption. After being elected to a second term, he served as a minister in Kim Dae-Jung's government. Running as a candidate who would root out political corruption on the MDP ticket, he became president (2003–2008). During his presidency, he strongly supported the Sunshine Policy of engagement with North Korea and a more independent stance from the United States. His administration has been described as a "rollercoaster ride" for charges of corruption and parliamentary opposition that led to Roh's impeachment. His impeachment was subsequently overturned, however in May, 2009, he committed suicide after being implicated in a bribery scandal.

However, after assuming the presidency, he failed to build public consensus on issues of vital interest and isolated himself from the people who essentially shared his views. Also, financial scandals surfaced regarding illegal campaign donations that involved Roh's inner circle.

The issues of North Korea and the U.S.-Korea alliance were reevaluated during his administration. Roh and his advisors expressed serious concerns that the United States might start a war to eliminate North Korea's nuclear programs at the peril of South Korea. Even though President Bush said that he would not invade North Korea, Roh's fear about possible military action was not alleviated by Bush's repeated statements, which included "all options [are] on the table."

His lack of experience, his uneven handling of economic policy, which resulted in creating a greater gap between the rich and poor, and such controversial decisions as supporting the United States with ground troops in Iraq and relocating the capital of Seoul, led to approval ratings of 31 percent at the end of his term. Yet he had a relatively successful summit meeting with Kim Jung-Il. The agreement at the P'yongyang summit contained a declaration that would hopefully lead to a formal peace accord to end the Korean War.

Lee Myung-Bak, 2008–

Lee Myung-Bak of the GNP won a landslide presidential victory on December 19, 2007, by dominating every region except the southwest and turned South Korea away from a decade of liberal governance. In the GNP primary for the presidency, Lee had defeated Park Geun-Hye, the daughter of Park Chung-Hee, a rising star in politics and one of the most prominent women in South Korea. However, the presidential campaign produced little public interest, especially from the younger generation, who had campaigned enthusiastically and turned out in droves to elect Roh in 2002. Aside from the fact that the candidates were not very exciting, the government's electoral commission enforced a strict code to ban online comments that were deemed negative.

The election did not produce much ideological conflict between leftists and conservatives, a possible reaction to the disappointing leadership of Roh and the fact that Lee Myung-Bak, a former top Hyundai executive and popular mayor of Seoul, had such a commanding lead. As a result, voter turnout was only 48 percent, the lowest in the country's history of democratic elections. The low turnout may also have reflected nagging doubts about Lee's ethics relating to his role in an investment company accused of stock manipulation. Two separate investigations later cleared him of wrongdoing. The overriding issue for the public was the widespread perception of a widening income gap and shrinking economic opportunities for the middle class. Voters essentially set aside doubts about Lee's character and elected a hard-working, pragmatic business executive whom they hoped would support tax cuts and stimulate foreign investment.

In his inaugural address on February 25, 2008, Lee vowed to boost economic growth, strengthen ties with the United States, and reward North Korea with massive investment if it gives up its nuclear ambitions and opens up to the outside world. Within days of his inauguration, Lee faced his first political showdown over his choice of prime minister and several of his cabinet nominees due to allegations of ethical lapses and acquisition of wealth through real estate speculation. While Lee's appointment of Han Seung-Soo was confirmed for prime minister, several of the cabinet appointees withdrew after accusations of corruption.

On April 9, the Lee Myung-Bak administration was able to secure a majority in the National Assembly elections, thereby ushering in a new era of conservative dominance in South Korea's domestic politics. A careful analysis of the assembly seats reveals that Lee holds only a slim majority. A sizeable group of assembly members within the GNP are supporters of Park Geun-Hye, who may well keep Lee's government in check. It has been said that one of the real victories of the 2008 assembly election is Park, who easily won her district in the city of Taegu.

In mid-April, Lee met with U.S. President George Bush. Lee's more aggressive approach toward North Korea was described as a welcome change for Bush, who was often at odds with Roh's support of the Sunshine Policy. The two leaders expressed hopes that North Korea would provide details of the nuclear weapons program and pledged to work together to resolve this issue through the multilateral Six-Party Talks. Lee previously expressed interest in helping to increase North Korea's per capita income to $3,000 within 10 years if it abandons its nuclear weapons program.

They also discussed the Korea-U.S. Free Trade Agreement, which faces opposition from both the U.S. Congress and the National Assembly. Lee agreed at the time to partially lift the ban on U.S. beef imports, a step that was taken in the belief that this would remove some of the obstacles to congressional approval of the Free Trade Agreement. Since then, many Koreans feel that Lee has betrayed them, and some even talk of impeaching him as the fears are rampant that American beef could cause an outbreak of mad cow disease.

LEE MYUNG-BAK (1941–)

Born in Japan during World War II and returning to Korea almost immediately after the war, Lee grew up in poverty and worked his way through school collecting garbage. After graduating from college, he went to work for Hyundai and earned the nickname of "the bulldozer" for his ability to carry out tough projects. Within 10 years, he was CEO. Lee served as the mayor of Seoul (2002–2006) and was known for his innovative policies that led to the restoration of a stream, the beautification of the center of Seoul, and reinvigoration of the capital's economy. He ran as a candidate for the conservative GNP in 2007 and became president in 2008. He has pledged to revitalize the economy, establish a firmer policy with North Korea, and improve ties with the United States.

South Korean President Lee Myung-Bak delivers a New Year's speech on December 31, 2008 at the presidential office Cheong Wa Dae. (Corbis)

Another controversial stance taken by Lee involved his views on Japan. He has called for South Korea and Japan to stop feuding over their history and build ties to bind the two neighboring countries. During Roh's administration, tension developed over Japan's Prime Minister Junichiro Koizumi's repeated visits to the war-related Yasukuni Shrine in Tokyo, the contents of Japanese history textbooks, the ongoing issue of compensation for the comfort women, and control over Dokko Island, which is claimed by both Japan and Korea.

In May 2008, Lee Myung-Bak apologized for the shortfalls in the early stages of his administration. It is hoped that he will develop a greater sensitivity to public opinion, and build coalitions within the National Assembly. It essentially depends above all on the exercise of his leadership and the art of the possible in dealing with the National Assembly and the public.

Meanwhile, it appears that politics in South Korea has not changed that much. Partisan conflict remains rife; it still involves overlapping personal networks involving regional, organizational, and educational underpinnings. The system also consists of intense rivalries that tend to induce paralysis in the decision-making process. Ongoing revelations of persistent political corruption have debilitated successive administrations and contributed to a widespread sense of public cynicism.

What has changed in South Korean politics represents a greater diversity of voice through a broader range of constituencies than in the past. Different interest groups, generations, and genders are all shaping the political climate. Greater diversity inevitably increases conflict, but reaching a compromise between conflicting voices is inevitably the challenge of a democracy. Jasper Kim in *Crisis and Change: South Korea in a Post-1997 New Era* writes that "this challenge is what Korea must tackle on its own in order to emerge as a significant and engaged nation within Northeast Asia" (2005, 134).

A DIVIDED PEOPLE: THE NORTH KOREAN EXPERIENCE (1945–2008)

Kim Il-Sung (1945–1994)

Accurate information on the DPRK (or North Korea) is difficult to obtain for many reasons. Entry into the country is closely regulated, minders accompany visitors everywhere, statistics vary, defectors' observations are not necessarily reliable, and propaganda is everywhere. Travel within North Korea is strictly controlled, so the visitor can see only what the authorities want him or her to see. It has been said that the only figures that are truly reliable on North Korea are dates. Additional challenges in analyzing North Korea are reflected in discarded opinions by some observers that it was destined to collapse in 1989 and 1994. Neither the disintegration of the Soviet Union nor the death of Kim Il-Sung triggered the collapse of the DPRK.

No nation in the 20th century has constructed an identity so associated with its founder and leader as North Korea. As Dae-Sook Suh expressed in *Kim Il-Sung: The North Korean Leader*, a study of Kim Il-Sung and his rule is the study of North Korea. Kim Il-Sung, former commander of anti-Japanese guerrilla units and senior

View of the capital city of North Korea, P'yongyang, and the Taedong River. The city is the political, economic, and cultural center of the DPRK, and is designed to impress visitors. (Courtesy of Mary Connor)

officer in the Soviet army, was Stalin's hand-picked candidate for head of state. He adopted Marxism-Leninism as its ruling philosophy when he established the DPRK in 1948. In the official history that was constructed after 1945, he became the embodiment of the regime's legitimacy and symbol of its virtue. His career as the leader of North Korea for almost half a century was remarkable for both longevity (longer than any other 20th-century national leader) and consistency of purpose. The political stability has to be viewed in terms of the means by which it was achieved: sustained ideological propaganda, punishment of dissenters, and periodic purges. Kim's beliefs live on even after his death; the 1998 Constitution clearly asserts that Kim Il-Sung is to be "the Eternal President of the Republic."

During his life, Kim overcame many hardships to reach and maintain the pinnacle of power, using both rewards and punishments to enforce his will. His absolute power was accepted by virtue of his long crusade against the Japanese, his belief in an independent and reunified Korea under socialism, and his charismatic personality. Endowed with boundless self-esteem, he fabricated his record, glorified his accomplishments, and built monument after monument to himself. Described as the personification of benevolence, he became known as the Great Leader and was truly loved and respected by the people.

Author Mary Connor and DPRK officer at DMZ, September 2007 in the area surrounding the DMZ. (Courtesy of Mary Connor)

When he was 7, his family moved from occupied Korea to Manchuria. When the Japanese took over Manchuria, Kim ended his formal education in the eighth grade and launched a political career. At 17, the Japanese imprisoned him for three months for organizing the Korean Communist Youth League. His military career began in his early twenties when he joined a group of guerrilla fighters called the Korean Revolutionary Army. In the early 1940s, he fled to the Soviet Union. There Kim received military training, married Kim Chongsuk, and fathered his first son, Kim Jong-Il. By the time the Japanese surrendered in August 1945, Kim was a captain in the Soviet army and a famous guerrilla fighter. In 1946, at the age of 34, he was selected by the Soviets to chair the North Korean Interim People's Committee. Telephone poles and billboards were soon adorned with pictures and posters expressing how wise and farsighted Kim was. By 1949, he had manipulated his way into the chairmanship of the Korean Workers' Party (KWP), a position he would hold until his death in 1994. Determined to reunify Korea by force, he started the Korean War with the reluctant support of Stalin and Mao Zedong. The entrance of 1 million Chinese into the war saved Kim from defeat. As soon as the armistice was signed in 1953, Kim began to eliminate all political opponents, took total control of the government, and proclaimed that he had defeated the Americans.

For the next 40 years, Kim Il-Sung rebuilt North Korea and moved systematically and ruthlessly to increase his power. He was relentless in his efforts to construct a socialist society. He became adept at dealing with leaders of the communist world and obtaining financial support from China and the Soviet Union. Under his leadership, the economy surpassed that of the South, and the standard of living improved enormously. By the 1960s, his hold on the nation was absolute. In 1972, when he turned 60 years old, the veneration of Kim knew no bounds. The party journal said that Comrade Kim Il-Sung, a genius of revolution and great Marxist-Leninist, had lived his entire life for the people's freedom and happiness. In the same year, he began to prepare his eldest son to succeed him; however, the formal announcement did not come until 1980. Until the day of his death by heart attack, he remained active. During his last years, North Korea was beset with economic problems and increased political isolation. When he died, people genuinely mourned for him in the belief that the Great Leader had liberated them from the Japanese, won the Korean War, and revitalized the economy.

The Constitution states that "The DPRK is an independent socialist state representing the interests of all the Korean people." Unlike orthodox socialist societies, however, the North's ruling principle is *juche* (self-reliance), an ideology created by the national founder and developed further by his son, Kim Jong-Il, into what is said to be "a man-centered philosophy." This claim has been a part of the DPRK rationale since the early 1970s and was used to justify a plan for Kim Jong-Il to be the indisputable successor to his father.

Juche is firmly rooted in the experience of Kim Il-Sung and his people. It is the most important idea of Kim's rule. He believed that people should adopt the principles of Marxism and Leninism; however, he took what he wanted from these principles and discarded the rest. His thought system was based on the idea that the master of revolution is the people; therefore, the people should be armed with self-reliant thought, problem-solving skills, and a determination to create a national consciousness unique to Korea. He stressed that self-reliance is essential for political independence, economic self-sustenance, and military defense. Last, but perhaps most important, is the role of the supreme leader in the idea of *juche*.

Although the masses are the masters of the revolution, they cannot play that role individually; someone must lead. Thus, the people must obey the instructions of the leader unconditionally. These ideas give insight into the behavior of the North Koreans: their xenophobia, regimentation, militarism, isolation, and complete devotion toward the personality cults of Kim Il-Sung and his son. In every city, town, and village, there are statues, and images of the supreme leader appear on billboards and subway and apartment walls. All citizens wear Kim buttons on the left breast. His portrait is hung in every home, workplace, and virtually every room in public buildings as well as on billboards throughout North Korea.

Kim adopted the values of Marxism-Leninism, which brought radical changes to society. Land reform led to confiscation of estates and redistribution of farm plots to peasants. Business enterprises were nationalized. In spite of the complete devastation that occurred during the Korean War, the nation used its abundant mineral and hydroelectric resources to develop military strength and heavy industry in the following decades. Despite the stress on self-reliance, Soviet and Chinese assistance and machinery were crucial to industrial growth. By 1972, 11 years of schooling became free and compulsory. Public health facilities were comprehensive and free, housing was available, and until the late 1980s and early 1990s food supplies were generally adequate. There is minimal unemployment, and compared to many Third World nations, the standard of living is high.

Of all the communist nations, North Korea has one of the most traditional, rigid, and tightly controlled totalitarian societies. It has been described as the closest thing to the Orwellian world described in *1984*. The commitment to "democratic centralism," by which all subordinate bodies submit to the decisions formulated by the Central Committee of the Workers' Party (the principal political institution), ensures the unity considered essential to a socialist society. When Kim Il-Sung was at the helm, the Central Committee made all the decisions on government policies and appointed government officials, including cabinet members.

The Constitution of the DPRK guarantees its citizens the usual political liberties: a free press; freedom of speech, petition, and religion; free elections; and safeguards against arbitrary arrest. Implementing these freedoms is under the auspices of the state authority, the KWP, which is controlled by the supreme leader. In reality, there are no civil rights. The press is strictly controlled, and the media offer only elaborate praise for the Kim regime and its policies. Any criticism of the leader, the party, or its policies is illegal and rewarded with imprisonment and hard labor.

The harsh reality of a dictatorship is softened by the way it is presented to the people. As in traditional Korean society, Kim Il-Sung's authority as ruler stemmed from his virtue and benevolence and was reinforced by the notion that he was not only a just ruler, but a loving father, a wise general, the sun of the world, and the greatest leader in 1,000 years. In spite of the fact that all religion was officially outlawed in North Korea, there are astonishing continuities from the Confucian authoritarianism of the past. That tradition of loyalty to one's family or lineage is extended to the nation as a whole. Such virtues as loyalty, obedience, industry, respect, and reciprocity between the leader and the led are highly valued in communist North Korea. The language used to describe Kim Il-Sung's virtues is essentially Confucian. According to that tradition, what makes people human is their acceptance of social roles that integrate them into the whole, a notion consistent with the collective spirit of communism. Family-based politics, authoritarian rule, the succession of the leader's son, and the extraordinary veneration of Kim Il-Sung are all extensions of ancient Confucian traditions.

Kim's vision of a socialist paradise became a massive failure. Although located in the heart of one of the most economically dynamic regions of the world, North Korea has, for a variety of reasons, recorded negative economic growth for 10 consecutive years starting in 1990. The totalitarian nature of the regime obstructs the innovation and creativity needed for sustained development. Because the 27 volumes of Kim Il-Sung's teachings form the core curriculum, education has not provided essential advanced technological and communication skills.

Since the division of Korea, the biggest economic problem has been the lack of farmland. The ideal of *juche* was impossible to achieve; therefore, the DPRK

Room in the Grand People's Study House, the State Library on Kim Il-Sung Square, P'yongyang, North Korea. Framed photographs of Kim Il-Sung and Kim Jong-Il appear everywhere, including in most rooms in public buildings. (Courtesy of Mary Connor)

supported itself by bartering raw materials, heavy manufacturing, and military hardware to other countries to pay for food and oil. However, the continuing U.S. trade embargo and the collapse of the socialist bloc deprived P'yongyang of major markets, leading to a steadily declining gross national product. The country has also experienced severe energy shortages exacerbated by a series of natural disasters: floods followed by drought. Since 1995, the nation has suffered famine and relies on international charities to feed its 23 million people. It has been estimated that between 2 million and 3 million people died of starvation and hunger-related illnesses.

Kim Jong-Il (1994–)

Storybooks in North Korea inform children that their Dear Leader, General Kim Jong-Il, was born on Mount Paektu and that he personifies the revolutionary spirit of Korea's sacred mountain and birthplace of Tan'gun, the legendary founder of Korea. Western media often describe Kim Jong-Il to their readers as eccentric, arrogant, self-centered, and even weird. He is compared by many as being markedly different from his father, who could be magnanimous, charismatic, and open to the opinion of others. When the U.S. secretary of state Madeleine Albright met him, she was amazed that he was in reality quite charming. No one doubts his cunning or intelligence.

Kim Jong-Il used to be called Dear Leader, but since his father's death he has been more frequently referred to as the respected and beloved general, a designation more appropriate for his father than for him. Born in a Russian military camp, he was given the name of Yuri, which he kept until he was in high school. As a child, he was known to be wild and constantly in trouble. After graduating from high school, he attended the Kim Il-Sung University. Upon graduation in 1964, he was put in charge of his father's bodyguard, taking a position on the KWP Central Committee. In 1973, the 31-year-old Kim was appointed to the Politburo and named director of the Organization and Guidance Department, the most powerful bureaucratic position in the party. It was clear that his father had chosen him to be his successor.

Kim Jong-Il immediately began to consolidate his power by lavishing gifts on his supporters and eliminating all who opposed him. By the mid-1980s, he was making most of the executive decisions (Lynn 2007, 103). In 1992, he was appointed supreme commander of the Korean People's Army (KPA), in spite of the fact that he had never served. To consolidate his position, Kim had himself named chairman of the National Defense Commission. During the 1990s, Kim Jong-Il assumed power and was determined to preserve a system that had been failing for some time. He replaced many of his father's stalwart supporters with individuals who would be loyal to him. His most trusted advisor, Kim Yong-Nam, president of the Presidium of the Supreme People's Assembly, became the de facto head of state and is frequently in the news for his state visits.

Between 1990 and 1998, the North Korean economy declined by approximately 55 percent, and more than 1 million people starved to death. Kim Jong-Il told his people to tighten their belts and eat two meals a day. By May 2001, international donors were feeding at least one-third of North Korea's 22 million people, but the government had not made any significant efforts to change economic policies or to reduce military expenditures, which were averaging 25 percent of the budget.

After his father's death in 1994, Kim Jong-Il kept a low profile until the June Summit of 2000 with Kim Dae-Jung. Prior to the summit, he never gave a public speech to a large audience nor traveled to any extent outside of North Korea. He was known to the world as a rogue dictator and described as being unpredictable, independent, arrogant, shy, disrespectful, impulsive, quick-tempered, and violent. At the June 2000 summit, he surprised the world with his wit, charm, and social graces.

It soon began to be clear that the DPRK was developing weapons of mass destruction. There were several near-crisis situations concerning the weapons program, particularly related to a suspected underground nuclear facility and the test-launch of a long-range ballistic missile over Japan. These incidents triggered loud protests from the United States and Japan and prompted hard-line responses toward the North. Nevertheless, Kim Dae-Jung pursued his policies of reconciliation as the principal means for bringing permanent peace and possible reunification.

Although Kim Il-Sung's legacy remains largely intact, there have been some significant changes since the mid-1990s that have helped Kim Jong-Il to consolidate his power. One example is the policy known as Military First Politics. Whereas under Kim Il-Sung the KWP had been above the KPA, the power of the KPA has been clearly ascendant since 1998. Some authorities attribute this development to a short-lived breakdown of law and order in 1995–1996, during the tragic famine. This policy has dramatically expanded the role of the military in North Korean society, economy, and politics. The KPA is not only the defender of the nation and the main guarantor of regime survival, it is also involved in virtually every part of life, including agriculture, arms sales, education, propaganda, youth groups, and veto power in all policy discussions.

A second development has been the increased control over information: radio, television, telephones, and the Internet. Responding to the tight security and secrecy in North Korea, U.S. Assistant Secretary of State Christopher Hill amused his audience by saying that even Kim Jong-Il's sweater size is a state secret (Ross 2008). The KPA actively works to suppress possible dissent within the intelligence and counterintelligence community. Foreign visitors give up their cell phones upon arrival and they are not returned until minutes before departure. Ordinary North Koreans are prevented from browsing the Web, as they are allowed to log onto only the official Intranet that carries only the allowed Web sites of the state and its institutions, particularly the universities. Information about the outside world is restricted, while classrooms and even restaurants reverberate with the revolutionary music and the greatness of Kim Il-Sung and Kim Jong-Il.

Because of heightened fears of outside forces, particularly the main enemy, the United States, Kim Jong-Il began a program to develop nuclear weapons. The strategy was to use constant anti-imperialist and anti-U.S. propaganda to shore up domestic control. Another tactic was to reframe how the public remembers the famine of the 1990s. As opposed to dwelling on the starvation and loss of life at the time, it is now systematically promoted as "the arduous march," and it was only because of their leader that North Koreans were able to survive. Publicity about the U.S. invasion of Iraq proved that their most feared enemy, the United States, might invade North Korea.

In 2002, responding to a small but developing amount of entrepreneurial activity, Kim Jong-Il implemented a limited number of economic reforms that liberalized wages and prices and allowed existing private markets to expand. These reforms, combined with increased efforts to enforce them, allowed the government to exert control over emerging quasi-market conditions.

Finally, in order to break away from international isolation, normalize relations with former enemies, and attract needed foreign aid, Kim Jong-Il began in the late 1990s to hold summit meetings with such leaders as China's Jiang Zemin, Russia's Vladimir Putin, Japan's Junichiro Koizumi, and ROK president Kim Dae-Jung. He also was host to U.S. secretary of state Madeleine Albright in P'yongyang.

Is life any better in North Korea? There are visible signs of improvement in people's lives. There are more electric lights in public places and in homes. More buildings have been repaired and repainted. There is more vehicular traffic, and there are more district markets than ever before. There are restaurants, bars, cafes, bowling centers, and golf courses for the well-to-do. Elegant women appear before visitors beautifully dressed in traditional attire. Some visitors are absolutely convinced that life is better than ever before. There is visible improvement, but everywhere are still signs of abject poverty, people scavenging for food in the countryside, and a very weak infrastructure outside of urban areas. Most of the people have lived and will continue to live very hard lives.

How long North Korea will continue to survive on its current course remains unknown. Nevertheless, both regime change and economic collapse are possibilities. Since Kim Jong-Il missed attending the celebration of the 60th anniversary of the founding of the DPRK on September 8, 2008, there have been mixed reports on the state of his health. No one really knows what will happen after Kim. The irony is that for all his eccentricities and threats, he may start to look more attractive than his successor, given the fact that he has not groomed anyone and that his leadership may turn out to be the lesser evil.

To stave off the current economic adversities that include serious food shortages, Kim Jong-Il was expected to expand cooperation with neighboring countries. The future will depend largely on how long Washington will keep its less antagonistic stance toward the North. And the key will depend on North Korea's sincerity to resolve the nuclear question once and for all.

REFERENCES

Armstrong, Charles K., ed. 2007. *Korean Society: Civil Society, Democracy, and the State.* New York: Routledge.

BBC News. 2007. "Profile: Roh Moo-hyun." August 8. http://news.bbc.co.uk/2/hi/asia-pacific/2535143.stm (accessed April 22, 2009)

Breen, Michael. 1998. *The Koreans: Who They Are, What They Want, Where Their Future Lies.* New York: St. Martin's Press.

Buzo, Adrian. 2007. *The Making of Modern Korea.* New York: Routledge.

Cumings, Bruce. 1997. *Korea's Place in the Sun: A Modern History.* New York: W.W. Norton and Co.

Eckert, Carter, et al. 1990. *Korea Old and New: A History.* Seoul: Ilchokak Publishers.

Gregg, Donald. 1999. "Despite a Dictatorial Streak, South Korea's Long-serving President Converted an Economic Basketcase into an Industrial Powerhouse." *Time* 154, no. 7/8 (August).

———. 2008. "South Korea's Emergence as a Significant World Power." *Korea Society Journal* (Winter): 15.

Kihl, Young Whan. 2008. "The Prospect of South Korean Domestic Politics under the New Lee Myong-Bak Administration." Paper presented at the Symposium on South Korea under New Administration: Past, Present and Future, Korea Studies Institute, University of Southern California, April 25.

Kihl, Young Whan, and Hong Nack Kim, eds. 2006. *North Korea: The Politics of Survival.* London: M.E. Sharpe.

Kim, Byung-Kook. 2000. "The Politics of Crisis and a Crisis of Politics: The Presidency of Kim Dae-Jung," in *Korea Briefing 1997–1999: Challenges and Change at the Turn of the Century*, edited by Kongdan Oh, 35–74. New York: Asia Society.

Kim, Hong Nack. 2000. "Foreign Relations under the Kim Dae-Jung Government," in *Korea Briefing 1997–1999: Challenges and Change at the Turn of the Century*, edited by Kongdan Oh, 170–172. New York: Asia Society.

Korea Times. 2001. "Five Upcoming Tests for Kim Dae-Jung's Leadership." http://hk.co.kr/kt_nation/2001 (accessed May 22, 2001)

Lynn, Hyung Gu. 2007. *Bipolar Orders: The Two Koreas since 1989*. London: Zed Books.

Oberdorfer, Don. 1997. *The Two Koreas: A Contemporary History*. Reading, MA: Addison-Wesley.

Oh, Kongdan, ed. *Korea Briefing 1997–1999: Challenges and Change at the Turn of the Century*. New York: M.E. Sharpe, Inc.

Ross, Nancy L. 2008. "Waiting for the Last Tulip." *Cosmos Club Bulletin* (April).

Suh, Dae-sook. 1988. *Kim Il-Sung: The North Korean Leader*. New York: Columbia University Press.

Wallace, Bruce. 2007. "The Excitement Doesn't Reach Voters in S. Korea." *Los Angeles Times*, December 15.

———. 2008. "South Korean Race Is a Liberal-Free Zone." *Los Angeles Times*, January 24.

Economy

Mary E. Connor

The recent economic history of the Koreas showcases some similarities but is largely a study in contrasts. North Korea is an impoverished country that has chosen to focus on self-reliance, leading to virtual isolation and insolvency. The economy is centrally planned and largely state-owned. The nation is something of an anachronism, living out the label of Hermit Kingdom. On the other hand, few countries in the world have matched South Korea's rapid economic progress and successful integration into the global economy. In slightly more than one generation, a country with few natural resources resurrected itself from profound poverty to become one of the world's foremost economic powers, achieving one of history's most rapid rates of economic growth. Though central planning and government involvement played a key role in the economic development of both countries, the trajectory of that involvement—and the subsequent development—was very different.

ECONOMIC DEVELOPMENT

In the 19th century, the West made forays into East Asia in order to benefit from new trade. Along with military muscle to force favorable treaty concessions, attempts were made to modernize the ancient cultures. Japan adopted the industrial and military techniques and technology of the Western powers and was eager to copy their dynamic expansionism as well. In 1876, Japan forced commercial relations on Korea, where a stagnant agrarian economy and weak government policies inhibited development, and similar agreements were soon made between Korea and such Western powers as the United States and Russia. Japan soon became the dominant foreign influence in Korea, however, and forced a protection treaty in 1905 that was followed by formal annexation as a Japanese colony in 1910. Investments in electricity, communication services, and railroad construction quickly facilitated a move toward modernization in Korea. Through collaboration with the Japanese, a small capitalist class emerged; however, development was largely enriching the Japanese, not the Koreans.

During the colonial period, Japanese needs and interests largely determined the country's development, and the chief beneficiary of Korean economic expansion was Japan. Exploitative policies forced the population to assimilate, mobilize, and support the Japanese war effort. Railroads, roads, rice mills, textile factories, hydro-electric plants, smelters, oil refineries, shipyards, and new cities were built. The economy actually grew very rapidly, but the income of the average Korean remained low. Still, the developmental investment brought to Korea by the Japanese was substantial and essential to the transformation of the Korean economy.

The Japanese developed and managed the industrial and agricultural sectors, but both worked primarily to support Japan at the expense of the Koreans. By 1936, more than half of all farm output was shipped to Japan, residents were deported to work in Japan and its Manchurian puppet state of Manchukuo, and some peasant farmers were forced to become urban factory workers. The exploitation was so severe that it led to "starvation exports," as Korean rice was sent to Japan despite the fact that the total output was not even sufficient to support the Korean population. During the war, most of the heavy industry and mineral extraction was located in the northern part of the peninsula, while the textile industry and much of the agricultural base was in the South.

During the postwar occupation (1945–1948), a struggle began between communism and capitalism on the peninsula. The Soviet Union actively promoted and assisted in the establishment of a planned socialist economy in its northern occupation zone, while the United States favored a market economy in the South and attempted to create an environment in which landowners and businessmen could thrive. However, the Korean people had become resistant to any economic system imposed from above that could be perceived as exploitative. Having suffered under the colonial administration, people were reluctant to again surrender their freedom to foreign occupiers. Unrest took hold across the peninsula—among the primary demands was comprehensive land reform to replace the Japanese tenancy system—but was dealt with in different ways on either side of the 38th parallel. The reforms and economic policies of North and South Korea quickly differentiated the two regimes.

South Korea

Despite early economic struggles and the devastation wrought by the Korean War, South Korea has achieved an incredible record of growth and integration into the world economy since the early 1960s. The monetary value of all goods and services produced in the country, or the gross domestic product (GDP), in 1961 was at the level of many poor developing countries. By 2004, South Korea had joined the wealthiest of the world's economies. In 2006, its per capita GDP was $20,045, equal to some economies in the European Union.

Resort hotel on Cheju Island in the Yellow Sea. Cheju Island, one of the most popular spots for Koreans and foreign travelers and is considered "the Hawaii of Korea." It includes geographic features similar to Hawaii, such as spectacular beaches, extinct volcanoes, waterfalls, and palm trees. (Courtesy of Mary Connor)

From 1945 to 1948, the United States Army Military Government in Korea (USAMGIK) established direct control over South Korea. Industrial development in the southern part of the Korean peninsula was not a high priority under Japanese administration, as factories were usually built closer to the primary mineral resources, which were in the North. Thus, USAMGIK was faced with stabilizing an under-developed economy and quickly building a necessary infrastructural and industrial base. Yet as a result of the Cold War and its global containment policy, political stabilization was a higher priority, and the United States utilized Japanese-trained police and favored existing landowners and businesspeople. Without this backing, the undeveloped capitalist class would most likely have been swept away in the political turmoil following the war, as they were in the North. The limited market system functioned mainly through aid and development programs. Land reform was initially very limited; only 16.5 percent of all farmers became full owners of the land they farmed despite massive calls for serious reform.

The dire situation facing the South led to a consolidation of power that extended to economic affairs. At the creation of the Republic of Korea (ROK), authoritarian president Syngman Rhee (1948–1961) attempted to create a stable, viable economy through extensive government involvement. Although reunification was his highest priority, he hoped to create a stable, viable economy at a time when imports were running at 20 times exports. As soon as Rhee came into power, the government adopted the Land Reform Act, which resulted in one of the most extensive and successful land reform measures in the world. Before this measure, ownership was extremely unequal. Now farm ownership was limited to three *chongbo* (about 7.35 acres), which created a much more equitable income distribution within the agricultural sector.

Two years after Rhee assumed the presidency, the Korean War broke out, and U.S. and South Korean resources went chiefly toward the military effort. By the end of the war, South Korea was one of the poorest countries in the world, devastated by the fighting. Nearly 50 percent of the industrial capacity and a third of the housing were destroyed along with much of the public infrastructure, and the war eliminated one-quarter of the entire wealth of the country. Agriculture remained inefficient, unmechanized, and subject to flood and drought. Unemployment was high after the war, and most industries were devastated. A period of reconstruction was necessary.

Rhee's policy during this period was one of import substitution industrialization (ISI), intended to limit dependency on foreign resources by increasing domestic production. Under the ISI system, lessened dependence on foreign imports was stressed through promotion of domestic industries. This was somewhat similar to the move toward *juche* in the North in its intent, though it was carried out quite differently. The ROK government did not directly control the means of production as the Democratic People's Republic of Korea (DPRK) government did; instead, South Korea utilized other means to encourage the growth of domestic firms. Small banks were set up to help nascent domestic industries grow, and favorable lending was provided to companies; tariffs were set up to protect South Korean industries and encourage growth while discouraging reliance on imports; and the South Korean currency was artificially overvalued to make imports more expensive. Despite the ISI program, though, heavy investment by the United States played an essential role in South Korean development, and U.S. development planners were important in guiding policy, though Rhee often clashed with them.

The ISI system continued after the war, but an increasingly corrupt political regime created major obstacles to its success. Business leaders commonly bribed government officials in exchange for favors and resources that were theoretically to be allocated according to ISI principles, and the cost of these bribes was sometimes passed on to consumers in the form of higher prices. Similarly, a number of Rhee's economic decisions were guided in part by his desire to shore up political support among certain sectors. This led to an increasingly inefficient and highly unstable system that was poorly suited to overall economic growth. The United States became increasingly dissatisfied but continued to provide economic aid, on which South Korea depended. The basic reasons for this generosity were diplomatic and military, stemming from a desire to contain communism and prop up the ostensibly democratic and capitalist ROK.

Following a massive uprising of students in 1960 that was provoked by the increasingly obvious corruption of the Rhee regime, the new government quickly moved to address the economy according to strict, rational planning. Economic ministries were streamlined and corruption was rooted out in an effort to stabilize the economy over the long term. In the short term, however, the situation was dire; an effort to devalue the South Korean currency and create a more reasonable exchange rate to promote future trade led to disaster as prices rose sharply and employment dropped. Ultimately, the new government was unable to hold power long enough to create lasting change.

The succeeding military regime was able to continue the economic refocusing but also took economic planning in a new direction. The new president, Park Chung-Hee (1961–1979), decided on a bold policy to drastically accelerate productivity in a short time by shifting from ISI to a focus on labor-intensive export industries. His strategy was to make the best use of industrial commodities, powerful private business groups known as *chaebol*, high population density, and an excess of eager, educated workers. The types of incentives that drove the ISI system were still utilized, but they were now dispensed to the companies that could transition best to the production of export goods. Park was a great admirer of the economic accomplishments of Japan, which were centered on government promotion of exports. For the new export-led industrialization, the *chaebol* would have to adapt to foreign market strategies and constraints. By fostering market competition between domestic and foreign firms instead of just among South Korean companies, technology and efficiency were encouraged.

In 1962, Park initiated the First Five-Year Economic Plan. To force rapid industrial growth and promote exports, the state assumed an entrepreneurial role in determining new products, new production processes, and new markets. It became a stockholder in corporations, most of which also had private stockholders. It also undertook financial service activities by obtaining foreign capital and providing low interest or negative interest loans. Park nationalized the banking system, which allowed the government to determine the allocation and cost of credit. By 1970, the state directly controlled 96.4 percent of the financial assets and thus controlled interest rates and exercised considerable influence over businesses through subsidies, preferential tariffs, and a monopoly on foreign exchange. The Economic Planning Board and the Ministry of Trade and Industry were created to monitor and regulate the investment, price, and trade activities of each firm. Specialized banks financed underdeveloped sectors and small and medium-sized enterprises (SMEs).

Because people could not survive with what they produced from their own land, agricultural policies were established to expand rice production through land clearing and the conversion of dry fields into rice paddies, which now achieved the legal designation of absolute arable land never to be used for other purposes. As a result of these regulations, the areas of rice production increased between 1970 and 1980, in spite of the rapid expansion of urban areas.

The expansion of industrial capacity was achieved through existing *chaebol*. Their rate of growth accelerated to the point that they became vertically integrated in the production and distribution of a huge array of goods and services; consequently, these large business combinations greatly reduced their dependence on small firms. At one point, monopolies or oligopolies supplied 87.8 percent of 2,257 major manufactured goods. When start-up companies developed new products or made large profits, they were bought up quickly by the *chaebol*. Among the

50 largest of them (ranked by sales in 1992), 70 percent were established during the period between 1945 and 1960.

Government encouragement of business produced spectacular results. It is estimated that exports were responsible for approximately 30 percent of manufacturing employment by 1966 and rose to about 45 percent by 1980. Although these programs led to impressive economic growth, they immediately revealed disparities in income between agricultural and urban areas. As the urban-rural income gap increased, poor rural people flocked to cities for greater economic opportunities. By the late 1960s, overconcentration in the largest cities, especially Seoul, became a major social problem.

Government pressure to increase production and export forced companies to rely on loans from banks, either state owned or controlled, in order to finance their expansion. The government encouraged them to borrow money and set interest rates at a low or negative level. So companies borrowed money, often more than they needed. Any surplus was frequently used for real estate speculation. Of course, by borrowing heavily from the banks, the businesses found themselves under tight governmental control.

The National Tax Office employed many incentives. Firms were exempt from indirect taxes on income earned through export sales. Constant surveillance brought about strict compliance. Tax fraud drew down penalties and criminal prosecution. Among other inducements, export firms were granted reduced rates on the purchase of land for new industrial sites. Government agencies also tampered with the exchange-rate system, adopted favorable monetary and fiscal policy, implemented a system of import privileges for exporting firms, and provided cash subsidies to successful trading companies.

The government virtually ordered goals for individual firms, and the managers were expected to maximize exports over profits. If they achieved these goals, they would receive such special favors as loans, tax benefits, and licenses to import restricted and highly demanded commodities or permits to purchase government properties at under-the-market prices. In exchange for these favors, businesses were obligated to give kickbacks to Park's party, but these transactions were inevitably very lucrative.

In order to be competitive in the international market, workers, managers, and businesspeople had to be increasingly efficient, innovative, and productive. However, it was low labor costs that consistently provided the competitive edge in international markets. A number of factors made this possible: a low standard of living in the early stages of economic development, a well-educated workforce, low pay relative to business profits, poor working conditions, a 54-hour workweek, workers' endurance in the face of hardships, and restrictions on unionization.

Labor and business were treated very differently by the Park regime. In the labor sector, the government worked to control wages and restrict union organization. For example, when workers demanded better pay and improved working conditions in the late 1960s and early 1970s, Park revised the labor laws to make unionization more difficult. The procedures for collective bargaining involved so many obstacles that union activity was virtually impossible. The police and other security forces ruthlessly suppressed workers, resulting in brutal violence and imprisonment.

In the business sector, the *chaebol* were given a monopoly or oligopoly of goods and services and received enormous favors. During this time, the relationship between the government and business changed. Rather than the dominant, and at times antagonistic, position of the state during the 1960s, it now developed a more symbiotic relationship. Park particularly wished to develop the metals industry, but the ROK faced many challenges, including a lack of natural resources and the need for huge amounts of capital and high levels of technology. In spite of these difficulties, it managed to construct, in a relatively short period of time, one of the largest and most competitive steel industries in the world. Park was also personally committed to the development of the semiconductor industry. In creating a steel industry, big business had the certainty of financial support from the government and access to the latest technology, and manufacturers were given extensive privileges, including tax reductions, exemption from bureaucratic red tape, and low-rent, state-built factories. Companies also obtained substantial investment from the Japanese semiconductor industry.

Economic stability did become an issue, however, due to international events. In 1971, President Nixon decided to correct the U.S. balance-of-payments problem by devaluing the dollar and allowing it to "float" in international money markets. The Korean economy was disrupted along with the economies of other nations throughout the world. When high inflation occurred as a result of the first oil crisis in 1973, the economy experienced another severe blow. Fortunately, it was able to recycle earnings by bidding on Middle East construction projects. The profits were used to buy oil. That construction boom began in the mid-1970s. The oil crisis also made giant tankers a necessity, so the country started from scratch to create a shipbuilding industry. Despite the various setbacks, the GDP rose significantly over the course of the 1970s, though the need to import oil and industrial materials led to large foreign debt.

The economy of the ROK faced its first major crisis in 1979. Massive foreign debt grew to more than $20 billion. The inflation rate shot up to 21.2 percent. Export earnings plummeted. The trade deficit reached $4,396 billion. Students joined workers in protests and strikes. When the demonstrators demanded his resignation, Park called out the police, who brutally silenced all protests. Within weeks, the head of the Korean Central Intelligence Agency (KCIA), who claimed that he was preventing the slaughter of innocent civilians, assassinated Park.

Under the succeeding presidency of Chun Doo-Hwan (1980–1988), there was a focus on market diversification, leading to a large current account surplus in 1986. Chun continued Park's top-down management style and promotion of exports, but he emphasized stability. The government lowered interest rates to reduce business costs. Concomitantly, pressure had to be put on businesses to keep prices down. The government also worked to keep foreign exchange rates within a narrow range, keep wages under control, and harness inflation. The government maintained tight monetary and fiscal policy, and inflation dropped precipitously over the course of the 1980s. Unemployment also decreased by more than half. Public enterprises, such as banks, were privatized, and regulations were trimmed or removed. The Chun regime also set out immediately to end the concentration of power of the *chaebol*. Nonetheless, the business community resisted Chun's reforms when they went against its interests.

By the mid-1980s, exports of heavy industrial goods exploded. Although foreign debt reached a high of $46.8 billion in 1985, the economy grew by more than 12 percent per year for three years. The largest employer in the service sector was retail, made up mostly of small merchants in towns and villages. Company assets and the stock market became more important sources of capital than loans from the government. The total value of the stock market increased 28-fold between 1980 and 1989. In the mid-1980s, South Korean companies began investing overseas. Labor-intensive industries like footwear and textiles were facing difficulties; consequently, management explored relocating to countries where labor costs were cheaper. Electronics firms were concerned that protective tariffs in developed nations would hurt the industry, so they established plants in Europe and North America to circumvent those tariffs.

Labor militancy was on the rise in the later 1980s, however, as workers began to demand better wages and treatment in light of the country's economic success. By 1987, widespread strikes broke out against the *chaebol*. The strikes were supported not only by employees of these conglomerates but also by those in small and medium-sized manufacturing firms and by white-collar workers in numerous occupations such as health, finance, research, education, transportation, and tourism. The government allowed one union per company, but some companies disallowed unions.

The next president, Roh Tae-Woo (1988–1993), introduced a revised economic plan, stating that democracy demanded a more equitable distribution of wealth. It was time to accommodate farmers, fishermen, and industrial workers. These policies, along with renewed labor union activity, caused wages to rise sharply, and consumer prices rose concomitantly. Roh's other interest was to advance economic relations with China. That goal was facilitated when South Korea normalized relations with China and abandoned Taiwan.

President Kim Young-Sam (1993–1998) continued to pursue worker-friendly policies and level the economic playing field. His plan was to eliminate tax evasion and tax exemption for preferred groups, to end regulations hostile to innovative economic activities, and to increase public support for housing and the environment. He started a drive toward globalization (*"segyehwa"*) by which strong international relationships would be made across economic, political, social, and cultural boundaries. The first step was an open trade policy. Financial transactions were to become transparent so that foreign investors could confidently supply the necessary capital. Speculation and the underground economy were to be greatly curtailed. The engine for the new advance was to be the innovative spirit of the Korean people.

Part of the impetus for these reforms was the strong desire to gain membership in the Organization for Economic Cooperation and Development (OECD). A $1.75 billion fund was created to assist SMEs, and regulations were reduced in order to encourage private initiative. Kim pledged to weaken the *chaebol* monopoly by allowing market forces to shape the labor situation, investment, and credit allocation decisions. He attempted to reduce or at least stabilize inflation. The merging of the Economic Planning Board with the larger Ministry of Finance weakened the former, which had been a relatively stronger and more independent ministry.

Kim's reforms proved somewhat unsuccessful, though, and the balance of trade went negative again. Widespread strikes and rapid wage increases occurred. Inflation was higher than it had been for some time. Overproduction by other Asian countries trying to outdo South Korea's export strategy resulted in increased competition and lower prices for such major exports as computer memory chips, steel, and petrochemicals. An economic correction was imminent.

A major collapse came in 1997. In the first six months of that year, thousands of companies declared bankruptcy. The proximate cause of the shocking downturn was a more widespread Asian crisis. The move toward financial liberalization had led to large short-term external debt. Foreign exchange obligations quickly drained $18 billion of the Bank of Korea's foreign exchange reserves, which finally fell far below outstanding debt. Drastically reduced import earnings forced devaluation of the currency, and frozen foreign capital made recovery difficult. The South Korean won lost 18 percent of its value. The stock market collapsed. In return for assistance, the International Monetary Fund (IMF) demanded a high interest rate policy to stabilize the exchange rate. Rates soared to 30 percent. This resulted in a tremendous number of bankruptcies and a rise in unemployment. The IMF moved to stabilize the currency, and this intervention restored stability to the stock and bond markets.

Still, structural change was necessary, and President Kim Dae-Jung (1998–2003) took on the long overdue task of reforming the system. The economy had to move away from the centrally planned, government-directed investment model toward a more market-oriented one. The central bank curbed capital outflows, reduced interest rates, restructured foreign obligations, and issued foreign currency–denominated bonds. The GDP plunged in 1998 but recovered over the course of the next few years, though government debt rose quickly.

Major initiatives were put forward to reduce indebtedness, bring governance practices in line with international standards, and renew competitiveness. In the public sector, the Planning and Budget Commission reined in waste and inefficiency. Kim downsized the government, and budgets received new controls and limits, particularly regarding long-term projects. The Regulation Reform Committee also abolished numerous government regulations.

South Korea had never been enthusiastic about foreign direct investment (FDI). From the end of the Korean War until the mid-1990s, it accounted for only about 0.2 percent of total investment. In order to catalyze economic recovery, however, the government now set a target of $16 billion in FDI by 2000. Restrictions were lifted on foreign mergers and acquisitions of businesses, ownership of land, securities trading, and insurance-related activities. These measures provoked great stress because they led to reduced local management control, but they did attract new FDI.

Growth fell somewhat in 2001 because of the slowing global economy, declining exports, and the perception that much-needed corporate and financial reforms had stalled. Led by consumer spending and exports, however, growth in 2002 was impressive, despite the anemic global economy. The ROK was able to fully repay its IMF loan, and officials declared that they had successfully overhauled the outdated financial system that had prevailed for the previous 40 years. The Financial Supervisory Commission was created and the Korea Deposit Insurance Corporation reorganized.

Among the positive results of all this liberalization was a net inflow of $15.3 billion dollars in foreign capital. The national budget dropped to 1.3 percent of the GDP. Foreign currency reserves amassed to $200 billion by 2005. Interest rates fell sharply. However, many private equity funds became interested only in short-term profit. And because many of their shares were now owned by foreign investors, corporate managers accumulated cash to protect against forced mergers and acquisitions.

Under the presidency of Roh Moo-Hyun (2003–2008), the average citizen's share in the GDP rose to $18,372, and the value of the Korean currency surged relative to the U.S. dollar. This made imports cheaper and exports more expensive. Consumers were happy because prices were dropping, but exports were hurt. Average working hours, birthrate, and ratio of investment to GDP were decreasing. The heretofore frugal Koreans were now taking on more credit card debt. Despite rising incomes, middle-class purchasing power was eroding, and the vaunted public spirit was beginning to deteriorate. The democratic process made it more difficult to reach consensus than in the 1970s under a state-controlled economy. Far-reaching reforms were proposed, but many expressed caution about overzealousness.

Yet economic growth surged in 2006. Robust exports fueled private spending, and the GDP rose 5 percent to about $887 billion. However, the pace of growth slowed at the end of the year, as consumers became cautious about spending in light of high unemployment among young people and government efforts to curtail real estate speculation. In 2007, exports rose as shipments to China and Europe helped the nation weather a slowdown in demand from the United States. When President Lee Myung-Bak came to power in 2008, he decried the fact that South Korea's economy had dropped to 13th largest because of slowing demand and foreign investment. Lee called for cuts in taxes and further deregulation. In response to the financial crisis in late 2008, Lee urged his government to aggressively expand fiscal spending to revitalize the weakening economy—even if it meant a budget deficit. He also stated that a top priority would be to create job opportunities through infrastructure construction projects nationwide.

North Korea

When World War II ended, the North had most of the advantages. About three-quarters of the peninsula's mining was located there. It also possessed nearly all of Korea's electricity-producing capability and the vast majority of its heavy industry. A provisional government favored the nationalization of major industries, railways, communication, shipping, and banking. In 1946, land reform ended a centuries-old agrarian system in which a few aristocratic landlords owned most of the land. All of the former Japanese property was redistributed to landless peasants.

The DPRK, under the leadership of Kim Il-Sung, stressed national self-reliance (*juche*). The *juche* ideology, first officially proposed by Kim in 1955, stressed self-sufficiency as essential to the prosperity of the Korean people. Though the *juche*

North Korean countryside and farm village. (Courtesy of Mary Connor)

ideology was closely knit with nationalistic and even isolationist connotations, it has provided the fundamental basis for all North Korean economic planning. *Juche* combines aspects of Marxist-Leninist ideology and Confucian philosophy but has been bolstered, clarified, and changed by various proclamations by both Kim Il-Sung and his son and successor Kim Jong-Il.

In its early history, North Korea achieved remarkable economic growth, particularly in the realm of industrial production. The presence of Japanese industrial operations in the region gave the North something of a head start, and planning intended to ramp up heavy industry, decentralize agriculture, and promote local light industrial development was largely effective and led to rapid, enviable economic expansion. Though the country was decimated during the Korean War, a postwar boom followed plans centered on state investment in heavy industry, collectivization of agriculture, rural electrification and irrigation projects, and localization of light industry. In the 1960s, however, North Korea largely jettisoned rapid economic expansion in favor of military development, and growth slowed considerably (though it did continue).

Industrial efforts were part of broad central planning strategies, similar to those of many communist countries. A series of increasingly ambitious plans were enacted, beginning with the One-Year plans of 1947 and 1948, progressing to a Two-Year Plan in 1949, a Three-Year Plan following the Korean War in 1954, a Five-Year Plan

P'yongyang, the capital of North Korea. The high-rise structures are condominiums. The city is the North Korean government's idea of a modern progressive city and a model communist capital. (Photographed by Cheong Wa Dae, Presidential Residence of the Republic of Korea, Photographer's Press Pool)

in 1957, and a Seven-Year Plan in 1961. These plans were largely effective at resurrecting a Korean economy that had long been exploited by the Japanese—national and individual incomes went up, and industry expanded in both scope and size. During the 1950s in particular, the plans were enacted quickly and efficiently. In the years immediately after the Korean War, foreign investment in the form of both capital and technology from the Soviet Union and China played an important role in reconstruction efforts, but such investment tapered off quickly, and North Korea was soon largely on its own. Among the reasons for the cessation of foreign investment was North Korea's insistence on developing industry and processing, and thus domestically utilizing the natural resources it extracted instead of sending them abroad.

There was to be a very limited role for market allocation, restricted mainly to rural areas where peasants could sell produce from private plots. Small business was not part of the plan. Because Kim inherited half an economy, he had to embark on a series of measures to create a more balanced self-sufficiency in a communal society. The state did, in fact, transform its economy within a short period of time. While the South struggled with recession and high rates of unemployment in the 1950s, the North achieved full employment and rapid growth. This pleased Kim Il-Sung and reinforced the idea that a policy of self-sufficiency would undermine what he considered Western economic imperialism and lead to Korean prosperity.

Rice fields outside P'yongyang. (Photographed by Cheong Wa Dae, Presidential Residence of the Republic of Korea, Photographer's Press Pool)

The Korean War (1950–1953) devastated the peninsula. Three years of internecine warfare destroyed both the North and the South. At the end of the war and as soon as the armistice was signed, North Korea began an impressive rebuilding program. It launched a centrally planned economy that was certainly the most radical in the world. All assets, including land, are under control of the state. Enterprises are either directly owned by the state or by cooperatives that are theoretically under the control of the workers themselves. In time, that control was divided among central, provincial, or local party officials. Capital and technology were provided by the Soviet Union and its Eastern European allies. Some Chinese soldiers remained to help with physical labor.

The Three-Year Plan of 1954 gave priority to the development of heavy industry. It was so successful that it achieved its goals six months ahead of schedule and laid the foundation for an independent economy. The Five-Year Plan of 1957 resulted in an annual growth rate of 41.5 percent. The First Seven-Year Plan in 1961 put the DPRK ahead of the ROK in per capita national output, though it was still behind the South in total national output. The divergence was in part due to North Korea's smaller population, even though 450,000 Koreans left Japan to permanently settle in the DPRK (and even though most of these migrants were originally from the South). Kim visited the Soviet bloc countries of Poland, East Germany, Czechoslovakia, Hungary, Yugoslavia, Bulgaria, and Romania. Combined with vast amounts of aid from the Soviet bloc, North Korean efforts pushed economic growth to 25 percent per year in the decade after the war. These achievements were so extraordinary that economists spoke of a North Korean Miracle.

The First Seven-Year Plan was originally intended to improve the standard of living for North Koreans by increasing and diversifying production of food and consumer goods while still investing large amounts in heavy industry and mining. Yet the plan was quickly superseded by an all-out militarization effort intended to arm the populace and form militias, modernize the military, and fortify the country to withstand any attack. It became more important to ensure that the economy could withstand and support an armed conflict than to improve the lives of the people. Investment in technological development was largely confined to weaponry, to the detriment of industry. Due to this and a set of largely unrealistic production goals, the Seven-Year Plan of 1961 was not actually completed until 1970, and even then some of the goals were not met.

The militarization effort drastically changed the North Korean economy. No longer would economic plans be completed before schedule, and most of the goals were never completely achieved at all. From 1962 on, the military was the main focus of government planning as Kim planned for an eventual renewal of conflict with the South. Material and resources that might otherwise have gone to industry or agriculture were diverted to military projects as North Korea was turned into a fortified state. During implementation of the Six-Year Plan of 1971, Kim was determined to further increase military resources, with expenditures up to 25 percent of the GDP.

During this period the economy began to slow, and by the mid-1970s the South had caught up with the North and even pulled ahead in per capita GDP. Because the DPRK supported China during the Sino-Soviet dispute in the early 1960s, the Soviets withdrew aid and technical support and later reduced trade between the two countries. The result was that at least 30 percent of the national budget went to the military. This represented a major drain on resources and prevented the achievement of the plan's other goal of increasing the national income by 80 percent by expanding foreign trade.

From the establishment of the DPRK until 1973, local governments—those at the provincial, county, and city levels—were dependent on state funds for their operation. These localities were provided for in the national budget, and local industries were subsidized directly by the state. In 1973, however, budgetary responsibility was decentralized, and the local governments became responsible for operations with the various localities. Under this system, local governments became fiscally self-reliant, and local industries and services were charged with providing necessary revenue to cover local expenditures. Surplus revenue was directed to the state, but the central government was not expected to subsidize revenue shortfalls. Essentially, the localities had to become self-sufficient entities with their own planned economies.

By 1974, North Korea was purchasing perhaps twice as much from capitalist countries as from its communist partners. It planned to pay for these imports with earnings from export goods, some of which were to be produced by local industries; however, an international recession hit, and exports proved difficult to market. The country could not pay its debts and was unwilling to accept money from the IMF because of that group's demand for structural changes in the economy. Without financial aid, the country's trade fell by a third. At the same time, there was a shift in the focus of military spending, from domestic fortification and the arming of peasants to the development of more potent offensive capabilities and special weapons systems. Though overtures were made to sign a proper peace treaty with the United States and peacefully unify Korea, little came of these attempts, and large-scale militarization continued throughout the 1970s. The military remained prioritized, to the detriment of industry and agriculture. In addition, from the early 1970s the actual military budget was withheld from the State Planning Commission, preventing planners from truly understanding the extent of the resource drain.

A series of massive construction ventures began in the 1980s that taxed the country's industrial capacity. Some of these ventures were actually industrial plants themselves, including a huge complex at Sunchon northeast of P'yongyang intended to produce large amounts of vinalon and chemical products. Among the other resource-heavy construction projects were massive dams and the enormous Ryugyong Hotel in P'yongyang. Many of these projects were notably intended to incorporate new and sometimes experimental North Korean techniques and processes, but confidence in the new ideas was frequently premature: The plants were unable to produce at intended levels, dam projects did not provide enough electricity or reclaimed land, and the great Ryugyong Hotel never even opened. Further resources were invested in creating sports facilities and visitor accommodations in preparation for the 1989 World Festival of Youth and Students, an irregularly held communist-bloc event, hosted in P'yongyang in response to the 1988 Olympic Games in Seoul.

Economic prospects continued to decline throughout the 1980s and even more rapidly in the 1990s. In 1984, the DPRK took some steps toward economic reform. The August Third People's Consumer Goods Movement brought a degree of market responsiveness to the production and sales of local goods. The movement decentralized distribution and retail sales much as earlier efforts to encourage local industry had decentralized the production of consumer goods. Additionally, cottage industries were promoted, particularly those that could make needed goods from industrial by-products and scrap. Local stores were able to sell locally produced goods without entering the state distribution network, and local officials could set the prices for those goods within ranges determined by central planners (whereas prices for major goods were uniformly set by the state). This allowed local officials to respond to market forces and thus better meet local demand and avoid unnecessary production. It was even possible to take orders for certain goods from individuals and families and pass them along to local producers. The success of the movement in allowing local industrial production to respond to local supply and demand conditions furthered three important state goals: It increased the self-sufficiency and responsiveness of local economies; increased the output of consumer goods at little or no expense to the central government; and increased local revenue, creating larger budget surpluses that were fed back into state coffers. Though the movement strayed from traditional socialist ideals, it furthered the *juche* cause.

Initially confined to the districts of P'yongyang, the August Third movement quickly spread across North Korea. Most of the local retail stores that directly sold locally produced goods were located in major cities, especially county seats. By the mid-1990s, however, the movement spread to most rural areas after cooperative farms were allowed to open such stores. Agricultural workers and their families could thus produce needed goods in the time not spent farming and could then sell these goods locally. Hence, workers already employed outside of industry and some underutilized laborers were able to engage in the formal production of goods. Though a variety of goods were produced in rural villages, food products were particularly important as so much of the rural resource base was agricultural.

The month after the August Third movement was launched, the Joint Venture Law was enacted in an effort to attract some foreign investment. Under this law, joint venture firms between the DPRK and foreign entities could be opened in select areas of North Korea. The offer was not an attractive one to foreign investors, though: While the foreign partner could gain majority representation on the board of directors of a joint company, North Korean law required unanimous consent of all board members, which effectively allowed the state representatives to veto any action they disapproved of. Combined with widespread concerns over the stability and openness of the North Korean regime, this made the country an unattractive target for foreign investment, particularly from capitalist countries. What little investment did come from the capitalist West came in the form of one-shot consignment deals, wherein the foreign company provided materials and North Korean firms produced and delivered a set number of finished goods at an agreed-upon price.

In the late 1980s, the DPRK began to sell military technology to foreign countries. Such weaponry as Scud missiles—Soviet tactical missiles that North Korea imported from Egypt in the late 1970s, reverse engineered, and then improved—was exported to countries like Syria and Iran, and in some cases development of the weapons came to be financed in part by these countries. For the first time, the massive military expenditures of the previous decades were able to create some revenue for the state. Following successful North Korean tests of nuclear weapons and intercontinental missiles in the 1990s, the weapons trade became even more lucrative (and even more dangerous). While geopolitical motivations played an important role in the move to peddle such weapons abroad—it was thought that marketing weapons of mass destruction to enemies of the United States could improve the DPRK's bargaining position in its efforts to secure a withdrawal of U.S. troops from the Korean peninsula—the potential for export revenue amid the catastrophic downturn in the economy was among the few available to isolated North Korea.

In the Third Seven-Year Plan (1987–1993), economic growth was set at 7.9 percent annually, lower than the previous plan. By 1988, both income and spending had plunged by half in just four years. With the collapse of the Soviet Union, the overall trade between the DPRK and the former Soviet bloc fell by approximately 67 percent. By the end of 1991, none of the planned targets had been met. That year, North Korea began to open parts of the country to foreign enterprise by establishing free trade zones. The first of these were set up around the far northeastern port towns of Rajin and Sonbong, located in the Tumen River delta region. The Rajin-Sonbong Special Economic Zone (now often simply called Rason) was encouraged by the United Nations Development Programme (UNDP) as part of a larger effort to open and develop the Tumen River to trade, benefitting all of Korea, China, Russia, and Japan. Yet, true to form, North Korea developed the Rajin-Sonbong area largely on its own and coordinated little with the other countries involved in the Tumen River project. Still, a series of laws were passed over the next few years that permitted but heavily regulated the operations of foreigners in the free trade zone. In fact, the regulations were so stringent and international confidence in the North Korean regime so weak that little foreign investment came to the Rajin-Sonbong zone. What little investment was made was skewed greatly toward infrastructure development, including transportation, communication, and finance—manufacturing did not take off in a serious way.

The efforts of the 1990s to attract export-oriented foreign investment generated little. Limited attempts by the DPRK to loosen its rigid control failed. The shortage of foreign exchange because of large trade deficits, unpaid foreign debt, and dwindling outside aid constrained economic development. The state could afford few imports. Chronic food shortage, famine, and international pressure over its nuclear program only exacerbated North Korea's policy to go it alone. The United States was blamed for all difficulties.

Manufacturing continued to center on heavy industry and military needs, with light industry lagging far behind. A high level of military outlays from shrinking economic resources caused a steady decline in the GDP. Shortages of raw materials, energy, and food were universal. The centralized system failed, leaving small private suppliers to provide what they could. Growth in the economy in the last years of the decade was partly driven by foreign aid. Agriculture did remain a rather high 25 percent of the total, but output had not recovered to the levels of the early 1990s. The low point of North Korea's economy was a GDP of $12.6 billion for 1998.

In 2002, the DPRK made a significant adjustment in its economic policy. It brought to a close its near-total reliance on the public distribution system for food and other essential goods and services, and private trading was allowed. Previously small peasant markets were expanded to provide goods and services that the state simply could not offer. It was a tacit admission of the breakdown of many industries and the public distribution system, but the extent to which the private market system will be allowed to expand remains to be seen. Some scholars view these developments more as a way of preserving the political status quo during a period of economic crisis. For example, Hyung Gu Lynn writes in *Bipolar Orders: The Two Koreas Since 1989* that the 2002 reforms were not intended to alter the existing economic system to any extent but rather to ensure long-term regime survival.

INDUSTRY

South Korea

In the early postwar years, manufacturing consisted of labor-intensive goods intended mainly for domestic markets. This was followed by an emphasis on heavy industries like steel production and shipbuilding, which were geared mostly toward foreign markets. The industrial sector included utilities, communications, fertilizers,

CHUNG CHU-YONG (1915–2001)

Chung Chu-Yong, the founder of the Hyundai Corporation, quit school and ran away from home at 19. He later worked in construction and acquired invaluable experience as a bookkeeper in a rice mill, before starting the Hyundai Auto Repair Company in the 1940s. After establishing the Hyundai Construction Company in 1947, he received major construction contracts during and after the Korean War. During the Park Chung-Hee administration, his company built dams, power stations, and major highways. After the Asian financial crisis, Kim Dae-Jung pressured Hyundai and other *chaebol* to lower their debt/equity ratio and to dismantle family domination of management. After restructuring, however, the family still had controlling interests in Hyundai Motors, Hyundai Electronics, Hyundai Construction, and Hyundai Securities.

and chemicals. The large, private *chaebol* conglomerates, many of which were established between 1945 and 1960, were responsible for most industrial expansion. Their managers faced various challenges, among them the lack of natural resources and the need for huge amounts of capital and, later, high levels of technology. The government put pressure on private industry to achieve various export and production targets but also provided significant assistance, and the *chaebol* were able to grow rapidly with the help of significant government intervention.

Much of the investment in industry initially came in the form of aid from the United States, offered in order to develop a vibrant market economy in the South and stabilize the government. By borrowing heavily from domestic banks instead of seeking FDI, the businesses found themselves under even tighter government control. Nevertheless, low-interest loans, tax credits, exemption from red tape, and low-rent, state-built factories did lead to increased profits. From 1962 on, the industrial sector grew at an amazing rate. Production multiplied at an overall annual average of more than 13 percent for the next three decades, contributing about one-third of the nation's GDP.

In the 1970s, there was a transition toward heavy machinery, chemicals, shipbuilding, and electronics, although light industry continued to contribute more to the national economy until the end of the decade. Increased capital and specialized labor skills were called for. This expansion of industrial capacity was achieved through existing *chaebol*. Their rate of growth accelerated to the point that enterprises became vertically integrated in the production and distribution of a huge array of goods and services. Monopolies or oligopolies supplied the vast majority of manufactured goods. Consequently, these large businesses greatly reduced their dependence on small firms. Many who wanted to establish their own business found it nearly impossible to do so, and when start-up companies did develop new products or made large profits, they were quickly bought up by the *chaebol*.

By 1979, Korea was a surplus producer and net exporter of steel, and the focus on technological modernization and reinvestment of profits back into the companies allowed the country to continue to develop the steel industry. The growing automobile, shipbuilding, and electronics industries increased the domestic demand for steel, and the rest of the steel output went to eager foreign markets, mainly in developing economies. The public Pohang Iron and Steel Company (POSCO) became one of the largest and most competitive steel mills in the world. In 1983, more than 40 percent of the country's GDP came from the industrial sector, almost equaling that of the service sector and 27 percent higher than the rapidly diminishing agricultural sector. Along with this rise in manufacturing, there was increased need for small subcontracting firms to supply necessary components and services.

The growth of South Korean industry depended on the development of the financial sector. Business financing was originally obtained primarily through government-backed loans from domestic banks and from financial institutions in the United States and Japan. Private lenders also came to play an increasingly important role. Very high interest rates generally compensated for weak collateral. The domestic savings rate rose dramatically in the late 1980s because the economy was booming, but greater GDP growth necessitated a large infusion of cash through equity markets and FDI. The Korean Stock Exchange expanded rapidly, coming to list more than 350 corporations.

Although some of the conglomerates directly competed with one another, there was frequently cooperation among them. Restructuring of the *chaebol* was intended to stop overinvestment, duplication, and the consequent fiscal burden on the public. However, correcting the system was difficult because the economy depended so heavily on the large companies that it was very difficult to modulate their activities. Also, they fought back. In late 1983, an assassination attempt against the president killed 16 members of his administration. The economic reform subsequently lost momentum. It would take another 15 years before the Asian crisis brought about any real change. Nevertheless, liberalization of imports and foreign investment promoted greater business efficiency. And outside pressure on conglomerates to keep prices down did enhance their international competitiveness.

Nonetheless, these conglomerates still had inordinate control over the economy and were guilty of price-fixing, unfair competition, and violation of antitrust legislation. Consequently, the Korean Fair Trade Commission (KFTC) was established in 1981 to resolve issues of unfair competition and consumer protection. Another charge was to help create a competitive environment for SMEs. The KFTC attempted to weaken the economic concentration of the *chaebol* and halt their price-fixing activities. Two years after its enactment, 258 conglomerates were cited for increasing horizontal integration by the acquisition of independent firms.

The KFTC received more power to deal with collusion among the *chaebol* to fix prices, restrict output, and allocate territories to sellers. It also attempted to stop mergers and abuses of dominant positions in any industry, defined as one company controlling more than 50 percent of a market or three firms combining to control more than 75 percent of a market. For the most part, however, the KFTC's decisions and judgments were not enforced. When ordered to take over troubled firms, the *chaebol* demanded more tax subsidies and money for helping independent businesses instead of taking them over.

In 1982, Samsung Electronics invested $25.5 million in a plant in New Jersey so as to mitigate the U.S. complaint about low-cost imports. Initial annual production was 400,000 color televisions. The firm also planned to produce 150,000 microwave ovens within three years. Despite the fact that the government tried to limit their credit in 1984, the conglomerates were now in a position to take advantage of the global economic expansion. Foreign investors and consumers regained confidence in the South Korean economy. Samsung was a model of high productivity, to a great extent prodded by the government's insistence on a move toward computerization and automation. Of course, that meant that jobs were also eliminated.

Over the course of the 1980s, it became clear that the banks and the *chaebol* were hindering economic growth. The debt/equity ratio of the *chaebol* was terrible, yet government protection of their debt made them a safe bet for lenders. Globalization shed light on inefficient allocation of resources, overleveraged finances, and almost three decades of collusion and corruption. The KFTC investigated more than 5,000 cases of conduct alleged to be in violation of the law. One way that the *chaebol* maintained their ties was to install their own people in the government. Vast sums of illegal political donations and funds strengthened the powerful and resilient ties between big business and the state. The "big four" *chaebol*—Daewoo, Hyundai, Lucky-Goldstar, and Samsung—were often denounced as greedy and unscrupulous. Familial ties were common between high-level government officials and the upper management of the *chaebol*. For example, President Roh Tae-Woo married two children into *chaebol*-owning families.

Although these practices created strong ties between business and government, they reflect well the Korean management style, which stresses the importance of family. In spite of the rapid changes that have taken place in recent years, the family remains the basic social organization and the model for behavior of entrepreneurs. Fathers are expected to provide not only for their own immediate families but also for their close relatives, more distant relatives, and members of the clan. But in the move toward responsive democracy in 1988, the public blamed the concentration of power and wealth within the *chaebol* for many of the social and economic problems.

By 1990, the amazing expansion of computer connectivity and information technology opened an important sector to South Korean manufacturing. The country would quickly become one of the world's largest producers of semiconductor integrated circuits, behind only Japan and the United States, the industry's chief early innovators. Three *chaebol* (Hyundai, Lucky-Goldstar, and Samsung) made substantial investments in new product development, which would pay dividends later. The country's industrial structure became highly developed and more closely resembled that of advanced countries. Certain areas of comparative advantage, including information storage and electronic data processing, were focused on an effort to compete globally. Memory chips became a mainstay of the South Korean semiconductor industry. Another important sphere of production focused on new technology, materials, and systems development.

Like the old Silk Road, the new Information Highway passed right through South Korea. The Internet and the rise of high-tech consumer electronics fueled a major consumer spending boom. By 2005, at least 72 percent of the households had a broadband Internet connection. Mobile phone use also increased rapidly, and South Koreans are now among the most frequent users on the planet. Phones are traded in regularly for new ones with more features. Compact digital cameras are also very popular. However, innovation, current fashion, and new competition have saturated the market, making it more difficult to maintain growth in the electronics sector. Joint projects and acquisitions are now quite common.

The value of the top 30 *chaebol* rose from 13.5 percent of the GDP in 1992 to 16.2 percent in 1995. The top five accounted for 55.7 percent of the combined assets and 66 percent of annual sales. To satisfy the requirements of OECD membership, the government began to liberalize industry to accommodate FDI and venture capital. Enthusiastic investor response to this invitation was a factor in the big crash of 1997. At the time of the crisis, the top 30 *chaebol* had an average debt/equity ratio of 519 percent compared to 193 percent in the United States. Today, the founding families of the *chaebol* continue to wield power over the companies. Interestingly, of the top 30 groups in 1997, only 18 remained on the list in 2001.

The manufacturing sector was slow to rebound from the 1997 crisis. The sector's contribution to the GDP has now fallen back to about what it was in 1991. Among the most important products still manufactured domestically are ships, automobiles, and electronic equipment. With China quickly becoming a global manufacturing hub, South Korea has encountered limits to its manufacturing growth, as the plentiful South Korean labor market is dwarfed by even more plentiful Chinese laborers, who will generally work for lower wages; for similar reasons, Vietnam has recently become an attractive locale for simple manufacturing. South Korean workers will no longer stand for poor treatment and low wages, but the manufacturing sector benefits from a high level of technology. Significant investment is put toward technological and process development since labor no longer provides the competitive advantage it once did.

As in other highly developed economies, services are playing an increasingly important role as manufacturing is outsourced. Much of the money was invested in the services sector. This sector accounts for some 55 percent of the GDP and 70 percent of the nation's workforce. The service industry includes insurance, health services, entertainment, restaurants, hotels, beauty shops, laundries, and bath houses. Chain stores, supermarkets, department stores, and thousands of small retail shops joined the traditional large marketplaces in the hearts of urban centers. Game rooms, tea rooms, massage parlors, and later, Internet cafes could be found on almost every downtown street.

In the increasingly interconnected global economy, foreign investment has also become very important. In an effort to attract foreign investment, South Korea has created free economic zones (FEZs) in Inch'on, Kwangyang, and Pusan-Chinhae. In 2002, the South Korean government cooperated with private corporations and the North Korean regime to create a special industrial region in Kaesong, North Korea. Manufacturing facilities there have attracted some SMEs because workers are paid much less than in the South and are even less prone to disruption than laborers in China or Vietnam. South Korean companies can thus outsource very basic manufacturing to North Korea, though this has yet to really take off.

KIM WOO-CHOONG (1936–)

Kim Woo-Choong was one of Korea's most legendary, hard-working, and inspiring entrepreneurs. At age 14, Kim was forced to go to work to help the family survive during the Korean War. When he was 30 he founded Daewoo, coinciding with President Park's drive to develop an export economy. He was known to work 15 hours a day, seven days a week. By 1978, Kim had reached his goal of exceeding Samsung Company in exports. Until 1999, Kim was revered as a man who transformed a small textile business into Korea's second-largest industrial conglomerate. Subsequently, however, he was found guilty in a $42 million fraud case, which led to the collapse of Daewoo. Kim received a 10-year prison sentence but was pardoned by Roh Moo-Hyun in 2007.

Foreign investors enjoy many incentives from the government: no tax on corporate income for seven years, tax reduction in land leasing costs, and straight cash grants on investments in factory construction or purchase of equipment for research and development. Still, the outflow of FDI in 2006 surpassed the inflow by $3.4 billion. In the increasingly interconnected world economy, however, South Korean investment and penetration into new markets has made the names of many of the *chaebol* and their products familiar throughout the world.

The government's notion that the *chaebol* were too big to fail has created many problems. The Hanbo group, 1 of the 10 largest *chaebol*, failed in 1997. Daewoo had 30 subsidiaries and had grown at an annual rate of 54 percent for 30 years, but it collapsed in 1999, with total debts of more than $80 billion and the chairman, Kim Woo Choong, a fugitive. Its motor company was sold to General Motors. In 2000, Hyundai Engineering and Construction Company nearly defaulted on its massive debt. Other affiliates were called to the rescue, and finally the Korea Exchange Bank agreed to a massive debt-for-equity swap. In 2001, a very large percentage of state-run Korea Development Bank's bonds were underwritten by Hyundai affiliates. In March of that year, Hyundai's founder, Chung Ju Yong, died after overseeing the breakup of the Hyundai group. Two years later, Mizuho Financial Group, Japan's second-largest bank, announced a partnership with Korea's Shinhan Financial Group. In 2004, Citigroup acquired a stake in KorAm Bank, and Lone Star sold its controlling stake in Korea Exchange Bank.

In February 2008, the newly inaugurated President Lee Myung-Bak, himself the former chief executive of Hyundai Construction for 15 years, stated that corporations are the primary source of national wealth and the major creator of jobs. Lee favors deregulation of businesses in an effort to spur private growth, a far cry from the heavy government involvement of the early industrialization years. Among the first such moves, the Financial Services Commission allowed conglomerates to breach the 4 percent limit on investing in banks and ended the restriction on *chaebol* with large assets that prevented them from making investments in an affiliated company.

Agriculture and Fishing   South Korea has numerous small streams, long rivers, and flat fertile plains, but with less rainfall than most neighboring rice-growing countries, only 22 percent of the land in the South is considered suitable for cultivation and only 1 percent of the land is in permanent pasture. This land also generally demands intense cultivation, crop variation, and the use of chemical fertilizers to achieve productivity high enough to feed the population. In 1997, rice production per acre was the highest in the world.

For Koreans, rice is the preferred staple food. Corn is the major feed grain. Root crops, barley, cabbage, peppers, and other vegetables are also harvested. The South is particularly notable for its fruit orchards—Korean pears are known around the world—and fruits constitute an important export crop. Other fruits grown for the domestic and export markets include oranges, apples, and grapes.

The agricultural industry has long been protected by the government. Because people could not survive with what they produced from their own land, agricultural policies were established to expand rice production through land clearing and the conversion of dry fields into rice paddies. In the early 1960s, South Korea was still a predominantly agrarian country, where a large majority of the population lived in rural areas and most people engaged in agricultural work. Though industry was stressed by the Rhee and Park regimes, the government announced that the country had achieved food self-sufficiency by the end of the 1960s.

As industrialization created new urban jobs in the 1970s, cities grew rapidly and available farmland decreased. Because of this and the fact that farmers influenced elections and government policies regarding price support, subsidies, and trade, Park emphasized agriculture in many of his economic reforms. A population increase and economic shift toward industry caused the demand for food to greatly outpace supply. Nonetheless, the prices of agricultural produce were tightly controlled, resulting in a relatively stable market. Rice production even increased. However, by the 1980s, the country had to import roughly half its food. Self-sufficiency in grains fell to 27 percent in 1995. In 2002, there was an effort to diversify grain crops. Farmers were encouraged to use rice fields for cultivation of corn and other feed crops. The total size of rice paddies was reduced, and rice production that year dropped to the lowest volume since 1996. Agriculture now accounts for only about 5 percent of the GDP.

Most marine fisheries are situated in the southern coastal area of the peninsula, followed by western and eastern coastal areas. The fishing industry is the seventh largest in the world with a catch of 2.9 million metric tons per year. Aquaculture has also developed significantly. Farmed fish include yellowtail, black rockfish, sea bass, and red sea bream. The last two are the most important of the cultured finfish. The rock bream is very popular for Japanese sashimi and thus fetches high prices in both Korea and Japan. Fleshy prawn, black rockfish, rock bream, red and black sea bream, sea bass, gray mullet, and rainbow trout are also popular. Of the total catch, roughly one-third comes from coastal fishing. Fish farming is very productive, accounting for a sizable piece of the industry.

The agricultural workforce accounted for more than 13 percent of all South Korean workers in 1994, but less than 7.5 percent of the labor force is now involved in agriculture. The food industry is protected by government quotas and other trade barriers in an effort to promote domestic production and stop the rapid decrease in agricultural endeavors; still, as the economy and labor pool grow, food production will likely constitute an ever-smaller sector. Import restrictions are the highest on produce, especially rice, vegetables, and fruit. Significant pressure from the agricultural sector was put on the government to block the sweeping bilateral trade agreement with the United States, signed in 2007 but not yet ratified by either country's legislature. It is thought that an influx of relatively cheap U.S. food products will hurt South Korean agriculture.

Mining   Although the South has far fewer mineral resources than the North, the mining and chemical industries have played an important role both in exports and in manufacturing. In 1987, South Korea mined 23.4 million tons of anthracite coal and approximately 4,000 tons of tungsten. Production expanded at an average annual growth rate of 10 percent between 1985 and 1996, but it currently stands at well under 1 percent of the GDP. Despite well-developed extraction techniques and this growth, South Korea remains a net importer of raw resources and will almost certainly continue so unless reunification is achieved. In 1996, the country produced about $1.2 billion worth of minerals but consumed about $4 billion worth.

Among the few metallic resources present in the South is tungsten. Because of its rigidity, tungsten is used for boring and grinding quills. Its low thermal expansion is useful for the heat sinks and transition spacers used in electronic components. It has a low melting temperature and thermal conductivity, and it is thus commonly used in welding tips and lightbulbs. Its density aids radiation shielding and vibration sensing devices.

Graphite is another important South Korean mineral resource. Refractory materials, brake linings, and foundry equipment use graphite. It is also used in nozzles and troughs to convey molten steel. Carbon magnesite bricks line electric arc furnaces to withstand extreme temperatures. Products made from lightweight carbon fiber graphite composites include golf clubs and bicycle frames.

The vast majority of metals and other resources used in the steel industry in South Korean manufacturing must be imported. Iron ore production dropped from 565,000 tons in 1987 to 272,000 tons in 1998, and to 188,000 tons in 2002. That output met only 1 percent of the demand for the domestic steel industry, which has always relied on imports. Zinc was down from 47,000 tons to 11,474 tons over the same period. The country also relies on imports to meet nearly its entire demand for coal, copper, lead, fluorite, gypsum, and magnesite. Since the latter part of the 1980s, the coal industry in the ROK has almost ceased because of a desire to use clean energy and increased coal production from countries like China that have far greater reserves. Most metal mines were also shut down owing to very poor production and the success of the export-oriented economic policies that allowed South Korean firms to rely on imported metal.

Nonetheless, South Korean mining companies are among the most prominent in the world. A priority of mining policy has been to establish environmentally friendly technologies and to ensure workers' safety. The development and marketing of nonmetallic minerals has also proved fairly successful, and such products account for 73 percent of domestic mineral production. A lot of South Korea's mining and quarrying activity focuses on a few industrial minerals used largely in metal processing. Other important resources that are extracted in large amounts include limestone, silica stone, clay, shale, and sandstone. These are mainly important for the construction industry due to their use in cement.

Energy   Soon after Thomas Edison connected the first electric lightbulb, the Korean government sent a delegation to visit Edison and view his invention. And in 1887, Kyongbok Palace received the first electric lighting. Electric power services were inaugurated in 1898 by Seoul Electric Company, capitalized jointly by Korea and the United States. In 1910, Japan took over and later invested 213 million yen in the electric power industry. In 1915, Kyungsung Electric Company was founded. In 1943, Chosun Electric Company started and was followed in three years by Namsun Electric.

In 1961, the South Korean government facilitated the merger of Kyungsung, Chosun, and Namsun into the Korea Electric Company (KECO). KECO was replaced in 1982 when it was taken over by the government and renamed Korea Electric Power Corporation (KEPCO). The LG Group (Lucky-Goldstar) operates an independent power plant near Asan Bay. In 1999, KEPCO was deregulated; two years later, its power generation operations were divided into six independently operating subsidiaries.

Coal supplies about 22 percent of the total energy requirements. Much of it is imported from Australia and China since there is little domestic coal mining. Because coal and oil are not extracted in South Korea and import costs have risen for both resources, nuclear power has been particularly attractive. With this in mind, the Export-Import Bank announced in 1977 that it would underwrite the construction of 21 nuclear plants by the year 2000, the most ambitious nuclear program in the world. The next year, the first nuclear-powered generator, located near Pusan, came online. Of the 54.9 billion kWh of electricity generated by 1985, 22 percent came from nuclear plants then in operation, 74 percent from thermal plants (plants that burn oil and coal), and 4 percent from hydroelectric sites. Eight plants were operational by 1987 when atomic power generation was an estimated 71.2 billion kWh, or 53.1 percent of total electric power. In 2002, electricity consumption surged 8 percent to 278.5 billion kWh.

South Korea has to import all of its crude oil. In 2003, it produced 52 percent of the country's energy needs. In 2005, the country consumed about 2.17 million barrels a day. South Korea is the ninth-largest oil consumer and fifth-largest net oil importer in the world. Consequently, energy conservation is vital to the economy. A strategic petroleum reserve is managed by the state-owned Korea National Oil Corporation (KNOC). This serves as a safety net against disruptions and is roughly equivalent to a 90-day supply. In the long term, KNOC is pursuing equity stakes in oil and gas exploration around the world. It currently has 17 overseas exploration and production projects in 13 different countries. South Korea began producing a small quantity of natural gas from one offshore field in early 2004, but this has had little real effect on the country's energy situation.

In mid-2007, the energy supplied by oil-burning plants dropped 23.2 percent from the previous year, but coal-power production was increased slightly. Hydroelectric production fell by more than 50 percent. Nuclear power accounted for more than 81 percent of total domestic energy production, the largest share since 1989. It is currently estimated that demand for electricity will rise at an average annual rate of around 4 percent per year through 2015, and nuclear and renewable energy sources will probably be utilized to meet much of the demand. Increased demand for coal in China since 2004 has raised coal prices sharply for Pacific Basin importers, including South Korea, and worldwide oil prices have skyrocketed in recent years, making expansion of thermal energy production costly.

Forest Products   A tree-planting program launched by Park Chung-Hee in the early 1960s has resulted in significant forest resources in South Korea. Thousands of people were mobilized to dig trenches and create terraces that could support trees even on barren mountains. The country not only reclaimed areas denuded of trees but also established forests for fuel wood. Forests now cover approximately two-thirds of the country.

Most trees are protective rather than productive, though. Coniferous trees include pine, juniper, spruce, and cedar. Flowering trees include Japanese apricot, sweet brier, cherry, hawthorn, gardenia, crape myrtle, rattan, silk, forsythia, camellia, and tea tree. Others include maple, zelkova, beech, gingko, and lacquer tree. Forestry did produce 1.1 million cubic meters of logs in 1993, but this accounted for just 13.6 percent of domestic demand. Total consumption of logs increased from 4 million cubic meters in 1970 to more than 8 million cubic meters in the early 1990s, and imports have long been necessary. Most of the lumber used in the production of high-quality furniture and musical instruments must be imported.

North Korea

In 1945, when Korea was divided, about 65 percent of the industries, most of which had been owned by the Japanese in one form or another, were located in the North. Skilled Korean technicians, who had gained experience working for the Japanese during occupation, moved to the forefront of the economy, whereas the South had to employ technicians with little or no industrial experience. North Korea also inherited a sizable network of resource extraction and processing operations. Coal, iron, and such metals as zinc and copper were mined and processed by the Japanese, and the North Korean state took control of the mines and plants and nationalized them.

The One-Year plans of 1947 and 1948 nationalized major industries and called for an increase in the production of basic necessities. Larger enterprises remained under the direct control of the state, but later, others were allowed to be managed by local party officials or committees. Heavy industrial production was ramped up very quickly in the post–World War II era, with huge increases in the production of machinery, agricultural and industrial equipment, coal, metals, cement and other construction materials, and chemicals. Machinery and equipment production was a particular target of early North Korean industrial planning because the Japanese had not developed such production during colonization. Light industry, which also was not promoted in the North under the Japanese, was ramped up, and the volume of produced textiles, clothing, shoes, paper, and similar goods increased by almost 300 percent during the first few years. Despite the growth of light industry, however, production was generally unable to meet total demand. In all, however, industrial output grew by some 340 percent from 1946 to 1949, and the Two-Year Plan of 1949 brought further industrial growth.

Much of North Korea's industrial base was decimated during the destructive Korean War. During the postwar period, only heavy industry was redeveloped in earnest. The Three-Year Plan of 1954 centered on rebuilding facilities that had been damaged during the war and resulted in the prewar level of industrial output, an average annual growth rate of 41.5 percent. The Korean War ended in an armistice, however, not a peace treaty, and renewed hostilities were a distinct possibility; thus, North Korea needed to rebuild its heavy industrial capacity first and foremost in order to support its military. Notably, new plants were built inland, out of the range of naval bombardment, while earlier operations were largely in coastal areas. Though reconstruction was rapid and successful, it was not until the middle of the Five-Year Plan of 1957 that North Korea reached prewar levels of production. This plan stressed heavy industry and brought about a large annual growth rate, and targets were met one year ahead of schedule.

Light industry was confined to local industrial operations that utilized local resources and materials and produced goods for generally local distribution. The items produced were often determined by the availability of particular resources and the ingenuity of local leaders and workers and thus varied from county to county. This was intended to promote self-sufficiency in consumer goods production on the part of the peasantry and free up state resources for heavy industry and military production. The establishment of local industry also decentralized consumer goods production much as agriculture had been decentralized prior to the war, creating a system that was less vulnerable in the event of renewed military conflict. The little light industry that was part of the government rebuilding effort was mainly confined to mass production of items useful to the military, including fabrics, shoes, and paper. Local industry received little if any state funding, and operations were generally small-scale, low-technology affairs. Some of the items most commonly produced by local industry were processed foods, beverages, furniture, basic clothing, and household items. The rise of local industry was responsible for much of the economic expansion of the late 1950s and the early success of the Five-Year Plan of 1957, but this expansion proved more limited in later years as local resources and labor reached a ceiling.

Despite plans to ramp up production of consumer goods in the early 1960s, militarization efforts took precedence. Massive resources were shifted from productive industries to the military as the government sought to fortify the country and promote militia organization and training. Industrial production was inflated by promoting a system of ideological rewards and competition among factory workers that resulted in greater output, though sometimes at the expense of quality. Machinery was sometimes overused until it broke down. Still, the Seven-Year Plan of 1961 continued to emphasize heavy industry and generated a 13 percent growth rate. During most of the 1950s and 1960s, more than 50 percent of national investment went to the industrial sector.

During the 1960s and 1970s, local industry was bolstered by a movement toward even greater local self-sufficiency. Textiles, processed food, and paper were among the targets of a call for increased local production and utilization of local resources in 1962. Despite efforts to increase reliance on local resources, significant state investment and planning was still necessary for the local industries. Since the militarization campaign was sapping state resources, such investment began to dwindle, and local industries felt the effects. With this in mind, in 1973 the state decentralized local industrial investment, putting some budgetary decisions in the hands of local planners. Local industry became the primary revenue generator for cities, counties, and provinces, and the income was expected to cover industrial operations as well as local education, health care, and government services, with any surplus profits going to the central government. If local industry was insufficient to provide this income, then it had to expand—somehow. Consumer goods and services were the primary focus of these expansion efforts, as they were able to create the greatest revenue. An increase in both local revenue and consumer goods production resulted during the 1970s due to the implementation of these policies.

Overall, though, local industry proved insufficient to create the kind of light industrial growth envisioned by North Korean planners. The siphoning of resources toward the military and heavy industry made it difficult to expand consumer goods production. In order to spur growth, the government orchestrated a series of deals with capitalist countries between 1970 and 1975 to import large amounts of light industrial equipment and other capital on credit. The DPRK planners, assuming that renewed war on the Korean peninsula was imminent, intended to ramp up production as quickly as possible. In addition to the immediate production boost, the imported equipment was to be reverse engineered so that similar equipment could be produced in North Korea and used to expand nonlocal light industry.

The emphasis of the Six-Year Plan of 1971 focused on improvements in technology, light industry, and the purchase of foreign plants but was hampered by the continued focus on the military. The Second Seven-Year Plan in 1978 called for conservation and frugality. The snags were beginning to appear in the system, and the growth rate dropped. With state resources dwindling, local industry was promoted through the August Third People's Consumer Goods Production Movement, which achieved remarkable results but was unable to truly solve the economic problems brought about by excessive spending on large construction projects and the military. The Third Seven-Year Plan in 1987 opened foreign trade zones in an attempt to attract some investment from countries outside the socialist sphere, but the plan did not work. Target goals for production in all sectors did not reach even 36 percent by 1989, and these were probably optimistic targets.

The structural weakness of the North Korean economic model became very evident in the early 1990s. As the regime hardened ideologically and the economy declined further, manufacturing continued to center on heavy industry and military needs, with light industry lagging far behind. A high level of military outlays from shrinking economic resources caused a steady decline in the GDP. While Kim

Il-Sung often concerned himself with agriculture and consumer goods production, believing that these were essential to keep the population content and able to work hard, Kim Jong-Il looked instead to ideology and military power as the keys to North Korean strength. Light industry was deemphasized greatly, and consumer goods increasingly came from local industry or were smuggled from other countries. During the famine years of the mid-1990s, many factories shut down or produced well below capacity. Shortages of raw materials, energy, and food were universal. The centralized distribution system failed, leaving small private suppliers to provide what they could. Growth in the economy in the last years of the decade was partly driven by foreign aid.

The low point of North Korea's economy was a GDP of $12.6 billion for 1998. The chain of production at every level of industry had missing links. Shortages were the norm. The 1999 state budget was 50 percent below that of 1994. The response to economic failure has been to conduct ideological rallies. North Korea has generally rejected outside technological help. Some economists were predicting the collapse of the regime, and neighboring countries are concerned that a collapse could lead to war, particularly since the military has long been the target of the most vigorous spending. The 2002 economic reforms were an effort to avoid a total collapse of the system, but these appear to have done little to halt the general decline of North Korean industry.

Agriculture and Fishing   As in the South, one of the first major reforms instituted by the new government after World War II was a land reform effort. This was aimed not at collectivization—the norm for communist states—but instead at decentralizing agriculture and allowing individual farmers to become self-sufficient in food production. To this end, large tracts of land consolidated by the Japanese and some Korean landowning families were divided into small plots and distributed to rural farmers. About two-thirds of all rural families received land under this program, and many of the Korean landowners fled to the South. So long as the farmers could suitably work the land, it remained under their control; if the land proved poor or the farmers proved unable to cultivate it, it reverted to state control. This system proved the first of Kim's efforts to promote a socialist model based on small-scale, localized self-sufficiency.

Yet the land reforms were aimed as much at South Korea as they were at the North. They were intended both as a model of land reform for propaganda purposes and as a method of creating an agricultural system that allowed for both quick cultivation and rapid agricultural expansion with relatively limited government investment. Since the farmers themselves were responsible for the investment and the labor involved, the state did not have to expend the resources that would have been required by collectivization. Further, decentralized, small-scale farming is more difficult to disrupt or destroy during war, which the North Korean government was stealthily but steadily preparing for. The reforms proved effective: From their inception in 1946 to the eve of the Korean War, grain production increased by 40 percent and livestock numbers grew even more rapidly.

Following the widespread destruction of the Korean War, however, new agricultural reforms were enacted that collectivized the land much like other communist nations had done. The government presented the collectivization as a program of cooperation, forcing farmers to pool their resources in order to achieve greater agricultural output. In fact, though, by the end of the 1950s North Korean farmers were almost all working collectivized lands from which the output was distributed in a socialist fashion on the basis of work done instead of land or equipment owned. Most of these were not, however, state-run operations; there were only a few state farms, and workers on state farms were paid wages and ate according to strict rations instead of sharing the produce, as the output of state farms was intended for state purposes. Similar rations were also required of farmers on collective farms—any food produced in excess of the defined rations had to be sold back to the state at a fixed price. Though this allowed the state to stockpile and distribute food (particularly to the military and industrial workers), it made it nearly impossible for farm families to store enough food to guard against famine in poor crop years.

In addition to the collectivization efforts, irrigation and crop selection played an important role in postwar agricultural policy. Irrigation was necessary to counteract the frequent droughts that plagued the mountainous North, and farms were converted from traditional crops to the highest-yield types—mainly corn and rice. The cultivation of different crops successively within the same year was also encouraged in an effort to increase overall production, although this had disastrous effects on soil fertility. Provinces were expected to pursue local food self-sufficiency—since the outbreak of the widely expected next war would make food distribution difficult, and surpluses from highly fertile areas were earmarked for the military and heavily populated urban areas—and this required the more mountainous and less fertile provinces to utilize any available land and plant any crops that could be cultivated in order to feed its people.

Diversification and expansion of agriculture and a modernization of farm equipment was a centerpiece of the Seven-Year Plan of 1961, but these efforts were soon subordinated to the massive militarization of the 1960s. Still, efforts were made to more efficiently work the land during the 1960s. Agricultural taxes were lifted, prices paid for some surplus foods were increased while prices of machinery and farm tools were decreased, and hard work was incentivized with bonuses for work units that put in extra time and labor. During this period, however, overcultivation of crops began to decrease the fertility of the soil, and chemical fertilizers—a major industrial product in the country—were used in greater amounts in an attempt to preserve crop levels.

Although agricultural production was very high at the beginning of the decade, the militarization policies and declining soil fertility combined to stall further increase. Irrigation and mechanization programs continued, though the latter made little progress as farm equipment was deprioritized in order to utilize available resources and industrial capacity for military equipment and weapons production. Although plans were made to greatly increase mechanization and the use of chemical fertilizers in order to boost production and improve the lives of farmers, competing military needs led the state to divert resources away from agriculture, and farm equipment was not produced or distributed in sufficient quantities. This halt in mechanization was a major reason for the stall in agricultural progress. Irrigation programs during the 1960s were more successful but ultimately did little to effectively boost agricultural output.

In the early 1970s, a renewed effort to mechanize and fertilize the cooperative farms was embarked on, directed largely by Kim Il-Sung himself. Though massive resources were still being put toward the military, agriculture was deemed important enough to warrant greater investment—after all, the growing military needed to be fed, and fed well, and the people could not be expected to sacrifice more of their own meager consumption to meet the new demand. Tractors and other agricultural equipment were produced in greater numbers and distributed among the farms, and chemical fertilizer production was ramped up and modernized. Fertilizers were particularly important, as overcultivation was necessary to produce increased crop yields, but the practice was rapidly stripping the soil of necessary nutrients. New fertilizer plants were built around the country, and mining operations to secure the necessary components of the fertilizers were expanded.

The agricultural improvement goals of the 1960s were quickly realized and then surpassed by the latter part of the decade. There was a tremendous increase in yields coinciding with the increased investment. From 1974 to 1977, production increased rapidly enough to produce a food surplus, which the state began to stockpile. However, once it seemed that the planned improvements had been successful and food stockpiles grew larger (even outgrowing the ability of the state to properly store them), investment began to drop off once again. Resources, particularly steel, that had been diverted from military production to create farm equipment were again put toward martial uses. Chemicals utilized for fertilizer production were increasingly put toward other uses in the late 1970s.

Still, state planners intended to continue to increase agricultural output in the late 1970s and early 1980s, and ambitious crop goals were part of the Seven-Year Plan of 1978. An entirely different approach was taken to achieve these goals, however, one that mainly centered on a terraforming campaign, often referred to as "nature remaking." Irrigation was again stressed, as was land reclamation. Huge construction projects were started to build dikes in order to make coastal tideland into useable agricultural land. Hillsides were terraced, creating a better foundation for crops in the more mountainous areas. Mass mobilizations of workers, including many that would normally not have performed such work, were used to quickly complete many of these projects. While this allowed projects to progress much faster than would otherwise have been possible, it also led to quality issues as construction was often performed hastily by relatively inexperienced workers.

While the growth in agricultural output continued in the late 1970s and early 1980s, the rate of increase was not nearly as great as during the previous mechanization and fertilization push. The drive toward investment in land instead of equipment and process innovation was not as successful as the planners had hoped. The West Sea Barrage, a massive water-control project at the outlet of the Taedong River near the western city of Namp'o, was built between 1981 and 1986 as part of a large-scale land reclamation and irrigation scheme. Another huge damming project, the Taechon Power Station, began the same year as the West Sea Barrage and also served to further irrigation and reclamation efforts by diverting and redistributing water in the northwest (although its primary task was to produce electricity). Other endeavors in the 1980s and 1990s to reclaim land along the western coast included the building of embankments between peninsular points or small islets to expose tidelands. Near Ullyul, a particularly novel project utilized waste from coal mine excavations carried by a long-distance conveyor belt in the construction of the embankments. Though far less coastal land was reclaimed than initially envisioned by planners, the gains were significant.

Unfortunately, the land reclaimed from the sea by these projects was low and prone to flooding in the event of a storm, protected only by the relatively meager dikes. In the event of a typhoon, surging waters could overcome the embankments and put the areas underwater once more. Higher areas were also at great flood risk, though, as efforts to clear and plow all available land denuded the terrain. Though planners intended agricultural increases to be permanent and progressive, the importance of meeting short-term goals outlined in the plans led to policies that created a setup for a future crash. Reclamation, irrigation, and overplanting allowed for greater output but amplified the potential effects of natural disasters.

Following several poor harvests and efforts to decrease food ration sizes, a series of such natural disasters devastated North Korean agriculture. In 1995, destructive storms and subsequent flooding destroyed crops. Ultimately, the agricultural yield was less than half of what it had been the previous year, which had already proved insufficient. Making matters worse, food distribution—which was carried out mainly via electric rail—was severely affected and even halted entirely in some cases. This created immediate food shortages that were then exacerbated due to the crop losses. The next year, similar storms wreaked further havoc and crop yields decreased even further, and a drought in 1997 delayed recovery. The resulting famine killed hundred of thousands, perhaps millions, of people according to widely varying estimates (no official numbers have been released), and North Korea was forced to appeal to the international community for assistance. This public failure of the *juche* system could not have been easy to stomach for North Korean leaders, but it did bring an influx of aid from foreign countries, including South Korea.

In addition to the food aid provided by foreign sources, a movement was promoted to utilize any and all unused or underutilized land for agricultural purposes—including urban balconies and gardens, roadside areas, and parks. The planting of multiple crops on agricultural land was another effort to utilize every last bit of available land for domestic food production. This type of excessive cultivation on the already overworked land may have led to a minor initial increase, but the long-term effect was simply to decrease soil fertility even further. Similarly, the overuse of nitrogenous chemical fertilizers in some areas has led to acidification, which further decreases soil fertility and necessitates the use of other types of fertilizer. Other survival mechanisms pushed by the government were widespread breeding of goats—which yield milk and meat products and can subsist on plants other animals will not eat, reducing the need for feed crops—and indoor and outdoor mushroom farming. However, the destructive goat herds and cultivation of previously nonagricultural land has denuded the mountainous landscape and made the country more prone to flooding.

Compounding the issue of decreasing soil fertility and increasing risk of natural disasters, investment in existing agriculture had been low for more than a decade as most resources went toward the military or the large reclamation and construction projects. Lack of investment in farm equipment and fertilizer production led to decreasing agricultural yields, even as the various provinces were exhorted to pursue local food self-sufficiency by any means necessary. Fertilizer in particular was necessary to counteract the effects of overcultivation. Though agricultural data from the 1980s and early 1990s was scarce, the DPRK was forced to present yield estimates in 1995 so that necessary aid amounts could be determined. These data indicated that yields had declined since at least the mid-1980s, consistent with reports of increasingly serious famine in the country.

In the late 1990s, agriculture remained a rather high 25 percent of the total, but output had not recovered to the levels of the early 1990s. In response to international appeals, hundreds of tons of humanitarian food aid were provided to the DPRK. About 350,000 metric tons of food were sent through the UN Food and Agricultural Organization and the World Food Programme in 2004. The next year, the country suffered another terrible food crisis in the wake of further flooding. It is highly likely that such floods will be an increasingly common occurrence in the future.

After the 2002 market reforms, the price of rice increased almost 50 times. However, food production has increased significantly since that time. Besides donated fertilizer from South Korea and humanitarian organizations, the reason for the increase may be linked to the profit motive. The agricultural sector constitutes a rather high 30 percent of total GDP, but crop production has still not recovered to the levels of the early 1990s. The high percentage is due in part to a generally declining economy. A report released by the UN in October 2008 stated that North Korea was facing its worst crisis since the famine of the mid-1990s. It noted that millions of people are suffering from severe food shortages and that more than three-quarters of all households had reduced their food consumption, with more than half of all households eating only two meals per day.

Korea's fish production depends on the sea because the lakes are small and the many streams swift and shallow, especially after the monsoon season. However, in the North the mountains often go straight into the water, and there are not many beaches. Herring and Alaska pollack are available in the East Sea. The freshwater seafood catch was 45,000 metric tons in 1990 and 20,000 in 2000. Freshwater aquaculture produced 5,000 metric tons in 1987 but declined to 3,530 in 1997. The DPRK now allows Chinese fishermen to fish off the coast of Wonsan, a port city on the east coast, in return for 25 percent of the catch.

Mining　Most of North Korea is mountainous and well endowed with natural resources, especially metallic minerals. Mineral deposits include iron ore, coal, limestone, tungsten, graphite, molybdenum, lead, and kaolinite. These relatively abundant industrial mineral resources have been used in the steel, cement, glass, and ceramic industries. Moderate amounts of bismuth, cadmium, copper, gold, lead, nickel, and zinc can also be found. The Mines Decree promulgated in 1915 by the Japanese exploited the mining of gold and silver for cash and tungsten, iron, and anthracite as war materials. Fluorite, pyrite, salt, and talc were also mined. Because of its mountainous topography, the area that formerly constituted Hamgyong province is still an important center of mining.

After independence, the economy of the DPRK relied on the extraction and processing of its many mineral resources. Mines provided such low-grade metals as copper, lead, magnesia, zinc, and other nonferrous metals. Ferrous metals and alloys included silicon-laden pig iron and ferrochromium. Aluminum alloys and copper scrap are also available.

Because there are no sources of natural gas or oil, the country depended on coal for heat and power. In 1979, mines produced 34.6 tons of anthracite coal, divided about equally among households, energy production, and industrial use. The coal industry also produces coke (used in the production of electricity and steel), coal tar, coal gas, chemicals, synthetics, and insulation. Coal is also a major input for vinalon, the "*juche* fiber," which has long been an important North Korean product. Coal production fell 44 percent from 1990 to 1998 as a result of the growing difficulty of extracting it, largely due to the use of inefficient and outdated extraction techniques by North Korean miners.

Iron ore production is crucial for industry. The country extracted about 16 million tons of iron in 1984. In the early days, the problem was to extract the ore quickly enough to meet the growing demands of the manufacturing sector. In 2003, mining grew by 3.2 percent. The iron mine at Musan is Asia's largest open-air mine and has an output capacity of 10 million metric tons per year. Since 2006, however, the DPRK has sold development rights to this and 10 other mines to Chinese firms for a 50-year period. Since 2002, China has also invested in copper and molybdenum mines and secured the rights to excavate the country's largest coal mine, at Yongdung in North P'yongan province. This shift toward outsourcing extraction is almost certainly a product of the North's failing economy.

In 2005, the Asia Pacific Economic Cooperation (APEC) ministers proposed to facilitate mineral exploration and expansion of mining projects. South Korea has now invested its capital and technological expertise in efforts to harvest North Korea's rich gold, iron, magnetite, and silver reserves, and two state-owned companies, the Korea Resources Corporation in South Korea and the Samchelli Corporation in North Korea, have formed a joint venture to mine graphite at Yongho. In late 2007, finished graphite products were sent from a joint venture factory near Haeju to South Korea. The graphite came from the nearby Jonchon mine, which may hold 6.25 million tons of crystalline graphite ore.

Energy   Early electrical generation depended on hydroelectric plants, which utilized one of the most abundant resources in northern Korea—swift-flowing rivers. During World War II, the Japanese authorities built several hydroelectric facilities, including the large Supung Dam on the Yalu River. The DPRK inherited these plants when the Japanese left (though the Supung plant was shared with China since it was on the border between the two countries), but they were largely destroyed by aerial bombardment during the Korean War. With significant Chinese and Soviet assistance, the plants were repaired and rebuilt as necessary.

After the rebuilding and industrial expansion phase of the late 1950s, however, electricity was required in ever-greater amounts in order to power heavy industry and the increasingly electrified countryside. Hydroelectric plants were very expensive to build and would have required resources that state planners wished to allocate to industry and the military; thus, most of the power plants built during the 1960s were coal-burning thermal plants. Coal was among the most plentiful mineral resources in the country, and since oil and natural gas were in short supply, coal was considered the best available energy source. Three major coal-burning plants—the P'yongyang, Pukchang, and Chongchongang power plants—were constructed by the late 1970s.

The only problem with the coal plants was that the DPRK could not mine enough coal to operate them at full capacity. Despite the presence of significant coal deposits in the country, there was a major shortage of coal for the plants. Mining operations were extensive, but North Korean mining technology was not advanced enough for efficient extraction. The average output of the mines was far lower than in more highly developed countries, and efforts to push miners to work harder did little to significantly increase production because the problem was rooted in outdated techniques and equipment. Further limiting the already inadequate supply of coal were the many other operations that required it, including steel, fertilizer, and vinalon production, for which coal was a vital component, and railroad transport. The *juche* ideal that stressed self-sufficiency had brought North Korea to rely far too heavily on coal, exacerbating the problems created by poor mine productivity.

The chronic coal shortage led planners in the 1970s to promote a new effort to build hydroelectric plants on rivers across the country, even those that were already dammed in other areas. Six hydroelectric plants were built in the country between the end of the Korean War and 1977, when the Six-Year Plan of 1971 was completed—including the Unbong plant on the Yalu River, a cooperative project with the Chinese—and three more plants were added on the Taedong River by the end of the Second Seven-Year Plan in 1984. Yet this was nowhere near the number of hydroelectric facilities called for in the plans. Construction took much longer than planners had anticipated—some of the plants initially slated to be built in just a few years were not completed for decades. The transport and upkeep of construction equipment in mountainous and difficult terrain made progress slow, and ambitious plant designs proved tricky to actually build. Efforts to divert and even redirect powerful rivers into systems of dams, reservoirs, and aqueducts were impractical but viewed by Kim Il-Sung and other planners as essential if North Korea was to achieve energy self-sufficiency. However, the 10 new hydropower plants that were constructed by 1984 failed to provide anywhere near the amount of power stipulated in the goals of the Second Seven-Year Plan. Smaller local hydropower generators were built all over the country, but these were chiefly intended to power the local industries.

Throughout the rest of the 1980s and the early 1990s, many of the delayed hydroelectric plants were finally finished, among them two large plants built in conjunction with the Chinese on the Yalu (the output of which was subsequently shared with China, as with the Supung and Unbong facilities previously built on the border river). Of the four plants built by North Korea alone, the Taechon power station in the northwest was the largest. The Taechon project involved the diversion of streams and the construction of huge dams. In the end, however, the Taechon plant and the other successful projects did not contribute enough electricity to achieve North Korean energy goals. Even worse, many of the facilities required expensive repairs and expansion projects in later years.

Unlike many developing countries, North Korea has made every effort to restrict its reliance on petroleum. There are few known deposits of oil in North Korea, and those that do exist in the country are mostly offshore and therefore expensive to extract. Because of this lack of accessible domestic oil, coal has been the preferred source of thermal power. Of course, some petroleum products are needed in North Korea—construction and mining equipment, tractors, trucks, tanks, and other vehicles require petroleum products for fuel and upkeep, and there is one thermal power plant near the border with Russia that relies on oil. Still, petroleum has long accounted for less than 10 percent of North Korea's total energy needs. Most oil imports came from the Soviet Union prior to its 1991 dissolution. After the breakup of the USSR, however, cheap oil imports from Russia could no longer be counted on. Interestingly, decreased oil availability actually made it more difficult to mine coal due to the reliance of mining equipment, transport vehicles, and explosives on petroleum products. Thus, the decrease of oil imports that followed the collapse of the Soviet Union proved disastrous, greatly hampering North Korea's electrical power production. Among the stipulations of the 1994 Agreed Framework between the United States and North Korea were annual U.S. deliveries of oil, but these proved difficult when the U.S. Congress took efforts to defund the agreed arrangements. When the agreement broke down completely in 2002, these oil shipments were stopped.

The most controversial of North Korea's energy production projects have certainly been its nuclear efforts. In the 1980s, the DPRK began its nuclear power production at its Yongbyon facility and later built another facility at Taechon. These reactors were gas cooled and graphite moderated and could be used to produce weapons-grade plutonium in addition to providing power. They contributed a significant amount of electricity but ultimately met only a small portion of the country's needs. As part of the 1994 Agreed Framework between the United States and North Korea, the DPRK pledged to shut down its graphite reactors, which could be used to create nuclear weapons, and replace them with light-water reactors (LWRs), which are water cooled and water moderated and make it more difficult to produce weapons-grade material and conceal tampering. The Agreed Framework ultimately fell apart, though, and the LWRs were never set up. As tensions have risen between North Korea and the United States in recent years, the use of the original reactors has been a key point of contention. It remains to be seen what role nuclear power will have in long-term North Korean energy production, but it is clearly an attractive option due to both its high output and its value as a geopolitical bargaining chip.

Forest Products   Although 97 percent of North Korea is estimated to have once been covered by forest, now only 36 percent of the land has tree cover, and much of that is on steep slopes because less hilly land has been used for farming. In the 1950s, national planting campaigns expanded forest area, and later a National Planting Day was celebrated on March 2. One sees trees in P'yongyang but also many women carrying small bundles of firewood, and there are fewer trees in the countryside. Trees have been planted along the roads, but as a whole there are not many. Because of the need to use as much land as possible for agriculture, deforestation continues at the edges of farms. This has increased soil erosion and is in large part responsible for the series of devastating floods during the last two decades.

Total forest products from 1996 to 1998 amounted to some 6.2 million cubic meters. Most of that (about 5,000 cubic meters) was used for fuel. The rest went to such industrial uses as paper and paperboard production. There is very little trade for forest products: The average value of imported forest products during the same period was $14,653, while exports were valued at $21,524.

LABOR

South Korea

The labor situation in the South changed radically after the Korean War. In 1953, most people worked on the farm, and about 5 percent of the total workforce was in manufacturing. As the urban–rural income gap increased in the 1970s, poor rural people flocked to cities for greater economic opportunities. Nearly half of the nation's 2.1 million factory workers were employed in Seoul alone. A higher number of women also found jobs. By the late 1980s, 25 percent of all workers were in the manufacturing sector; at the end of the next decade, they outnumbered farm workers 2–1.

Labor and business were treated very differently by the Park regime. In order to be competitive in the international market, workers, managers, and businessmen had to

Massive apartment structures in Seoul. The high cost of housing has been a major economic issue for city dwellers. (Courtesy of Mary Connor)

Panoramic photograph of Seoul, the capitol of South Korea. The city is a modern metropolis of 11 million people. The city is safe and clean, and its underground railways are convenient and inexpensive. (Courtesy of Mary Connor)

be increasingly efficient, innovative, and productive. However, it was low labor costs that consistently provided the competitive edge in international markets. The country had the world's longest working hours, still averaging about 54.7 hours a week in 1986. And worker safety was abysmal. Roh amended labor laws to favor unions. Labor militancy caused a large spike in strikes, rising from 276 in 1986 to 3,749 in 1987.

The government was determined to control wages and restrict labor union activities. The procedures for collective bargaining involved so many obstacles that union activity was highly curtailed. When workers did demand better pay and improved working conditions, the police and other security forces ruthlessly suppressed them, resulting in injury and imprisonment. Teachers defied the government and formed the National Teachers and Educational Workers Union. More than 1,600 lost their jobs in the union's first year, and hundreds of teachers were imprisoned for demonstrating. Despite many revisions in labor laws, union membership fell steadily, leading to very low numbers today.

Improved living standards created demand for foreign labor to perform menial jobs that many people no longer wanted. In 1991, there was a 20 percent labor shortage among unskilled workers. Illegal workers, especially ethnic Koreans from Manchuria, began to enter the country. Even highly educated foreign workers had difficulty obtaining desirable positions. Unemployment was only 1.1 percent for those with less than a junior high school education, but more than three times as much for those with some college background. Widespread strikes, a move toward greater democracy, and liberalization of trade unions led to an increase in wages by 15 percent a year until 1996, just before the Asian crisis.

The Tripartite Commission, created in 1998, was composed of representatives of labor, management, and government. Minimum wage legislation and both unemployment and industrial accident insurance followed. Job protection, which had been very strong, was modified according to strict formal criteria. Temporary workers were protected. Finally, an attempt at transparency of corporate policy mitigated

The waterway in Seoul. Cheonggyecheon Stream runs through the downtown financial and shopping districts of the city. (Courtesy of the Korea Tourism Organization)

corporate-labor strife. Kim Dae-Jung originally promised that he would avoid involvement in disputes; however, after Hyundai auto and ship workers went on strike, he sent out the riot police. Thousands were arrested. When Korea Telecom workers demonstrated for improved working conditions, the government arrested the union leaders. Kim warned that any action by a striking union member would be considered an attempt to overthrow the government.

Korea loses proportionally more workdays to strikes than any other OECD country. In heavy industry and transportation, labor unions are forceful and regularly demand higher wages, benefits, and a role in management decisions and policies. Korea's rigid labor laws make it hard to dismiss workers or hire new ones. Fears have been expressed over the power of organized labor to incite people to extreme measures. During the Roh Moo-Hyun administration (2003–2008), however, labor demands were initially supported.

In 2003, Hyundai, the country's biggest car manufacturer, agreed to introduce a five-day workweek of 40 hours. These concessions caused concern among investors. And the administration claimed that this contract would undermine competitiveness. A Hyundai affiliate, Kia Motors, was also hit by union demands. Roh abandoned his support of the unions and called in 5,400 troops to disperse striking railway employees. The strike ended without any concessions.

Union membership has dropped dramatically in recent years. The ratio peaked at 18.5 percent at the end of 1987 before it fell to 10.3 percent in 2005. The ratio of workers in the manufacturing sector has decreased from 43.1 percent to 27.6 percent, while that of the service sector, in which workers are less organized, surged from 11.9 percent to 30.4 percent. Until 1996, only 5 percent of companies with more than 100 employees adopted the annual salary system. After the financial crisis hit the nation, the ratio surged to 35 percent, with one out of five companies providing dividends based on job performance to their workers.

A new employer-sponsored pension plan established at the end of 2005 completed the public-employer individual retirement safety net found in most developed countries. Up to that time, some companies allowed their employees to receive their retirement benefits early and thus risk an unfunded retirement if they lived to old age. The new plan included outside fiduciary agencies that could offer different ways of allocating contributions and could protect the plan assets. These financial service providers had sizable pools of funds available for short- and long-term investments within certain limitations and appropriate disclosure.

The nation's job market has undergone significant change over the last 20 years. The employment rate has decreased most distinctly among young men. Young women have been relatively successful in joining the job market. There have also been changes in the wage system, which has weakened international competitiveness to some extent. Korean workers have the longest working hours in any developed country. In 2008, the OECD published a report showing that Koreans spent an average of 2,357 hours at work, 31 percent more than the average American worker. Yet President Lee Myung-Bak has stated that labor and management must learn to compromise with each other in this era of intense international competition. Others are calling for a crackdown on labor unions for not forcing their members to be more productive. Jobs in government are being reduced.

North Korea

At the beginning of its statehood, North Korea was very much an agricultural nation, with nearly two-thirds of its workforce employed in farm work. Following the Korean War, most North Koreans still worked in agriculture, with a smaller but sizable portion performing industrial tasks. Over the course of the 1950s, the percentage of industrial workers nearly doubled while the percentage of farmers decreased. Not all former farmers went to work in factories, however—some left the rural areas and went into office work. Regardless, there was a trend toward relocation for many agricultural workers during this period stemming from agricultural collectivization, mechanization programs, and a new focus on heavy and local industry.

In 1959, the Ch'ollima movement, one of the most important North Korean labor movements, was initiated. Tied with the overarching *juche* ideology, the Ch'ollima movement stressed that workers must sacrifice above and beyond their usual capacity and produce as much as possible for the good of the state. The movement led to remarkable production during the late 1950s, when investment from the Soviet Union and China was decreasing. The movement—named for the swift horse Ch'ollima of Korean mythology, on which the Korean people were said to be racing toward an ideal socialist state—was ideologically based and spurred both by nationalist sentiments and a spirit of competition. Work teams were organized that would compete with each other to produce the most. A team would be honored as a Ch'ollima Work Team and receive awards if it met certain production goals. The movement began among industrial workers but eventually spread to agricultural laborers as well. A spirit of competition similar to the driving force behind capitalist systems was thus fostered among workers in the North Korean system of socialism. Though production did rise dramatically, products were sometimes of low quality due to the workers' focus on quantity.

The increased production attributed to the Ch'ollima movement led in part to the idea that North Korean industry could expand forever at a similarly high rate if the people were properly motivated and well organized. In the 1960s, as massive militarization taxed the economy and hampered growth, ideological rewards were stressed even more. The Chongsan-ri movement—named for the Chongsan-ri cooperative farm, where it began—encouraged greater agricultural productivity through a series of incentives offered to farm workers and a more hands-on management style by farm managers. A similar movement began at the Taean Electric Machinery Plant, where party members were assigned to inspire plant managers and laborers to work ever harder toward production goals in the name of *juche*. In both cases, a committee of party members was responsible for collectively determining what production goals should be and was then responsible for inspiring their achievement. Of course, the party members charged with inspiring the workers also served as watchful eyes that would ensure that workers remained on task and performed efficiently. In addition, party members would gain an otherwise elusive understanding of the issues and conditions facing workers, important information both politically and economically. Like the Ch'ollima movement before them, however, the Chongsan-ri and Taean work systems often led to a situation in which the quantity of produced goods was more important than their quality or the sustainability of their production as managers and workers zealously targeted production goals.

Working conditions are often very difficult, and necessary equipment and machinery are sometimes lacking or in poor repair. Overworking, by Western standards, is commonplace. In addition, informal household work, which can be quite demanding due to a general lack of support services, takes place outside of these formal work hours, and as a result the average day for a laborer tends to be very long and busy. A six-day workweek is standard, and most workers put in eight hours of work and sometimes several additional hours of political study each workday.

A typical day for an urban laborer begins early in the morning, when household chores or morning exercises may be performed. The workday begins with political study and meetings as well as discussion of production or performance goals, followed by the beginning of actual work. Small breaks are provided every few hours, and a long break in the afternoon allows workers to go home to eat, nap, or finish household tasks. Work resumes in the late afternoon and continues through the evening. Self-improvement study and critique sessions are sometimes held in the later night.

There is a sharp contrast between the life and work of the vast majority of the population—which largely consists of very poor laborers, farmers, and office personnel—and the elite class. The elites live mainly in P'yongyang and are generally set apart from the rest of the populace: They attend special schools, are treated at special hospitals, shop at special stores, and spend their leisure time at recreation clubs not available to most North Koreans. Members of this privileged class include government and military officials, top scientists and engineers, important artists and musicians, renowned athletes, and top-ranking members of the ruling party. Great pains are taken to hide the privilege of the elite class from the rest of the populace, even in P'yongyang. Most workers in the capital take public transport to work, but the elite travel in private cars and limousines. Housing for an average family consists of a small one-bedroom apartment, but the elite live in more lavish executive apartments or, in certain cases, houses or mansions. Though education and health care are provided by the government, only the elite have access to the best medical technology and the finest schools. Perhaps most importantly, the elites are allowed greater food rations and have access to scarce foods.

These differences are much more pronounced than the differences in earned wages. There is a significant disparity in actual pay between the highest-level officials and the lowest unskilled workers, but the vast majority of the population earns nearly the same wages. Perhaps most interestingly, the wages of even the highest-paid North Koreans are meager, and savings are small (and frequently nonexistent). Yet in a socialist command economy like North Korea's, wages are of relatively minor importance because there is little market activity (although this has begun to change somewhat in recent years as the economy has broken down and market activity has increased). Since essential goods and services are provided and distributed by the government, wages earned go only toward clothing, food, and nonessential purchases like consumer goods. Additionally, because prices are largely determined by state planners, not by market value, items or services can be priced into or out of certain price ranges as necessary; indeed, the items and services deemed most important, including basic foodstuffs, clothing, and transportation, are priced relatively low. Thus, living standards are defined more by location and class status than by wages. The difference in lifestyle between a rural farmer and an urban laborer, or between a low-level office worker and a high government official, has much more to do with access to goods and services than it does with wages. Centrally set prices are uniform across the country (though the prices of locally produced goods vary a bit), but many goods and services are simply unavailable in some areas or to some sectors of society.

Because prices can be set artificially low for essential things like food, rations are imposed on all North Koreans in order to prevent personal stockpiling. Because the country has long suffered from a general scarcity of food due to inadequate domestic production and a lack of food imports, however, the rations have proved generally insufficient to produce a healthy, strong workforce. Staple grains have been rationed since 1957, with amounts based on the vigor of work performed. Rice, the traditional staple of Korean cuisine, is rationed even more heavily than other grains. Rank does not factor into determination of rations, and the type of work performed matters only as much as it defines the energy output necessary to complete tasks. Put more simply, rations are determined by the caloric needs of workers, not by status. Heavy laborers and soldiers have the highest ration levels, while desk workers and students receive the lowest levels. Yet rank and class do matter when determining how much of the rationed grain is rice; rice constitutes much more, if not all, of the grain allotment for elites, but it makes up a smaller portion of the grain rationed to less privileged North Koreans. Children receive higher rations relative to their size, which is deemed necessary for proper growth; during the famines of the mid-1990s and early 2000s, however, food scarcity prevented many children from getting enough food, and malnourishment became a serious problem. Nonrationed food, including meat and most vegetables, can be purchased but is enjoyed with any frequency only by the privileged class. A family's food supply can also be supplemented by such homegrown crops as beans or mushrooms, but these do not commonly provide much additional food.

Though the rations are low by international standards, they have been cut even lower in times of particular crisis and have not been raised during times of bounty. In the late 1960s, fears of renewed war brought a lowering of rations in order to stockpile food. When agricultural production increased dramatically in the 1970s and food stocks outgrew stockpile facilities, however, the rations were raised only to the earlier levels and then rather quickly cut once again in order to continue stockpiling and even export some food in an attempt to acquire money to pay off foreign debts. As agricultural yields decreased in the early 1990s, the government began to promote a two-meals-per-day diet, but once the great famine of the mid-1990s hit following the natural disasters of 1995 and 1996 and the drought of 1997, even this proved difficult to accommodate. Because farmers on collective farms are expected to provide their own food supplies, the crop destruction hit them the hardest; government officials and military personnel were affected the least. Industrial and office workers, whose food rations are distributed through the public distribution system, fared slightly better than rural farmers but were significantly affected by diminished state supplies, particularly in the years following the floods. The workers and farmers were thus forced to turn to markets selling imported food, usually from China, which was difficult to buy with their meager incomes.

One of the most interesting trends of the last two decades has been an increase in economic activity among women. Men, particularly heads of households, have long worked in agricultural or industrial jobs for the state, often in large factories or on cooperative farms. Prior to the 1990s, however, women were very often homemakers or employed in cottage industry operations. During the economic crumbling of the 1990s, men generally remained at their state-run jobs, yet many women began to engage in small-scale trade, especially after the 2002 reforms, operating market stalls and even smuggling goods from nearby countries like China. It is not uncommon today for a female businesswoman of this type to earn more income than her husband, and many families subsist largely on these earnings as state-run industry and agriculture have stagnated.

In contrast to more traditional Asian societies, most women in North Korea work outside the home in addition to their household work. This is due both to the influence of a communist ideology that stresses the importance of labor by those able to work and to the economic situation facing most North Korean families. It is quite difficult, if not impossible, for a family to survive on a single salary—food alone for a family would be difficult to purchase on the average worker's salary—and therefore many women must work in order to help provide for their families. For this reason, only the wives of the elite tend to be full-time homemakers. For similar reasons, family sizes in North Korea are generally small by Asian standards, as more children means more mouths to feed as well as more work around the house.

In the Rajin-Sonbong Special Economic Area, the first area opened to foreign trade and investment, labor is heavily regulated in order to minimize the influence of foreign capitalist enterprises. Foreign companies may utilize North Korean labor in the zone, but the workers allowed to work there are handpicked by the government and generally chosen for their ideological inflexibility; in effect, the government tries to ensure that only those laborers not inclined to be persuaded by the success of foreign companies will be working for those companies in North Korea. Further, foreign companies utilizing North Korean labor in the Rajin-Sonbong area are required to recognize and deal with labor unions that are associated with the ruling party; thus, party members are guaranteed a presence even in foreign-owned factories.

The reforms of 2002 allowed for an augmentation of North Korea's salary system through market activity, but such activity is generally conducted by family members and individuals who would otherwise not be working or would be working in local industry. In recent years, however, prices have skyrocketed, and any increase in household earnings is dwarfed by the inflation caused by de facto devaluation due to the market reforms. Workers and factory laborers have thus seen their living standards generally decline. Still, daily ideological indoctrination and a lack of information about the outside world make North Korean workers unlikely to seriously protest their conditions.

TRADE

South Korea

When the country gained independence, it relied on severe protectionism to bolster domestic industries, and in some industries it has never given up defending its domestic market against foreign products. In 1948, President Rhee's trade policy was based on import substitution, and quantitative restrictions on imports were meant to encourage domestic industries, especially producers of food and clothing.

In 1962, South Korea made a radical shift to an economy based on exports—the motto became "Exports First!" Machinery and manufactured goods replaced wigs and textiles. This was a bold jump because the country was very poor in terms of the mineral resources needed as inputs for these industries. Thus, tariffs were maintained on all imports except for raw materials. When new industries showed success, the government invested in infrastructure and incentives for them to sell their products abroad. Meeting exceedingly ambitious export targets was considered the pinnacle of success for both managers and public officials. Similarly, it became common to push employees in the large export industries to achieve or even surpass the almost unreasonable targets set by the government agencies.

Under the first Five-Year Economic Plan (1962–1966) exports grew from $55 million to $250 million, almost 45 percent a year. By 1972, exports were valued at $1.676 billion. The export-oriented policy was well adapted to the country's situation but necessitated some restrictions on domestic markets. The government's growth strategy initially restricted industries from selling many of their products in the domestic market in order to promote exports. For example, color television sets were exported but were not allowed to be sold in Korea until 1980. Portable telephones and stereo systems were also subject to these restrictions. This activity was in stark contrast to the policies pursued by Japan, where businesses generally marketed new products in the home country first.

The export-oriented development strategy was well suited to an increasingly globalized world economy, and the total value of exports has continued to grow at a high pace. Before 1960, they contributed less than 10 percent to the growth of GDP. This increased to 33 percent in the 1970s, and by 1980 the total value of exports was more than $17 billion. Exports also contributed to a rise in manufacturing employment from about 28 percent in 1968 to more than 52 percent in 1985. Korea depended very heavily on foreign trade with the United States and Japan—more than three-fourths of all shipments went to U.S. and Japanese markets in 1970.

The Ministry of Trade and Industry introduced general trading companies in 1975. Samsung was the first of 13 enterprises that by 1983 managed more than 51 percent of all exports. Daewoo, Hyundai, Koryo, and Kumho were later additions to the group. The export economy faced its first national economic crisis in 1979. Among the causes was South Korea's massive foreign debt, which grew to more than $20 billion. Another cause was a very high inflation rate, which rose to more than 21 percent. Export earnings plummeted, and the trade deficit rose dramatically. In the early 1980s, some import restrictions were loosened to promote more competition.

By the mid-1980s, South Korean electronics, automobiles, and computers had become increasingly competitive with those of U.S. and Japanese companies, and exports surged. In 1986, South Korea achieved its first trade surplus, and it recorded an even larger surplus the following year—becoming one of the five largest trade surplus countries in the world. The country's main trading partner during this period was the United States. Exports increased to 35 percent of the GDP but later dropped to 25 percent, a decrease that was blamed on the rising cost of labor, frequent strikes, a strong won, and high interest rates.

The high-technology proportion of the total bilateral trade between South Korea and the United States jumped from 44.2 percent to 64.8 percent between 1989 and 2006. To gain a foothold in the semiconductor industry, Samsung began mass producing what most U.S. firms had abandoned: small, solid-state computer memory devices. This step would prove important, as memory chip production became a mainstay of South Korean manufacturing. The emphasis on memory-device production and extensive broadband penetration were key factors in permitting the country to move to the forefront of the digital revolution. South Korean companies, such as LG Electronics and Pantech, accelerated replacement cycles and created many new products, allowing them to become component suppliers to big-brand home electronics and computer companies.

Influenced by the reforms in the former communist bloc, increasing protectionism in industrialized nations, and efforts to diversify markets, South Korea tried hard to expand trade with socialist countries. Delegations were sent to Eastern Europe and the Soviet Union, and later to China and Vietnam, and trade offices were subsequently established. The proportion of exports to nations of the former communist bloc rose, and South Koreans became economic advisers to some of the former Soviet republics.

By the early 1990s, the increasingly prosperous ROK had become the ninth-largest market in the world. Export dependence on a few large markets gradually decreased. The 30 percent of exports that were sent to the United States and the 15 percent to Japan represented a large drop from 20 years earlier. Exports to the United States amounted to more than $19 billion in 1990, a 6.3 percent decrease from the previous year. Exports to Japan stood at more than $12 billion, down 6.1 percent. Meanwhile, exports to European markets grew 19.7 percent to nearly $9 billion. Exports to Africa also expanded sharply, and trade with China reached $10 billion by 1992.

South Korea also benefitted from monetary conditions in neighboring Asian nations. From 1990 through the first three quarters of 1995, the value of the Japanese yen relative to the U.S. dollar rose by almost 40 percent. For an economy centered on growth of exports, a rising currency is dangerous because its products generally become more expensive relative to those of countries with weaker currencies. The strengthening of the yen thus gave a competitive advantage to exporters in South Korea. On the other hand, China's currency—which at the time was pegged to the U.S. dollar—was relatively weak, making its exports to South Korea relatively cheap; thus, neighboring China was well positioned to supply South Korean demand for imported raw materials.

Later in the 1990s, world economic conditions caused a slowdown in export growth, but the value of Korean exports and their growth rates remained relatively high, though not steady. They grew by 17 percent in 1994. The next year they jumped another 32 percent. Since 1960, they had gone from $100 million to $100 billion in the values of those years. They reached $129.7 billion in 1996. Partly as result of a reduction in tariffs and other barriers over eight years, the ROK now imported $150.3 billion worth of capital and consumer goods. This rapid growth led to significant trade deficits, and the negative balance of payments reached $20 billion by 1996.

Joining the OECD required allocation of financial aid to underdeveloped countries. In order to do so, Kim Dae-Jung had to lower trade barriers, thereby allowing Japanese and U.S. producers to increase exports to the ROK. However, South Korean manufacturing still required foreign capital, technology, and components, which caused a huge negative trade balance. From 1995 through 1997, South Korea had the only trade deficit it has ever had with the United States. The global decline in demand for some semiconductors and the fall in the price of steel coupled with declining productivity and the weakening of the Japanese yen negatively affected growth in the value of exports. For example, Samsung's profit fell 93 percent from 1995 to 1996. The situation has changed radically since that time, however—the export value of electronic products today accounts for more than $111 billion, up from $38 billion in 1995.

Import protectionism has had a long history in Korea because of its originally underdeveloped economy. In 1980, the average tariff was 24.9 percent. There were also quotas on imports, special taxes on expensive items like cars, and effectively uneven rates on items to protect certain domestic producers. Foreign rice has always been a target for protection. The United States is such a large and efficient producer of farm products that U.S. agricultural products are a threat to Korean farmers. They fear prices lower than their own. Because of the political structure, rural voting blocks can impede or at least stall free trade involving agriculture. Laws regarding agriculture have produced a number of stifling regulations regarding licenses, certification, testing, and inspections that may lead to quarantine; however, the future will probably favor the internationalization of trade.

Since 1948, the General Agreement on Tariffs and Trade (GATT) has endeavored to provide rules for international trade. The World Trade Organization (WTO) was created in January 1995 to assist members in dealing with any internal or external resistance they may face in trading with one other. It administers and monitors agreements, handles trade disputes, and offers assistance to developing countries. More recently, patents, trademarks, and copyright have been added to the list.

A series of WTO negotiations from 1986 to 1994, called the Uruguay Round, helped to reduce tariff rates and bring them in line with those of developed countries. In 2003, at talks in Cancún, Mexico, 15,000 farmers and indigenous people marched in protest of the large agricultural subsidies in the United States and the European Union. One of the leaders of the demonstration was Lee Kyung Hai, president of the Korean Federation of Advanced Farmers. When the march halted at a set of barricades, Lee climbed on top of them and committed suicide by stabbing himself in the heart. The negotiations collapsed three days later because members could not agree on farm subsidies and access to markets.

Growers, frightened that opening the agricultural market would have disastrous effects, continually petitioned the government to keep the tariffs high. However, in 2004 the ROK did agree to a gradual 10-year increase in rice import quotas from 4 percent to 8 percent of total consumption. In the past, imported rice was used primarily for processed foods, but by 2010 one-third of the imported rice will be made available directly to consumers. Nine rice-exporting countries agreed to this compromise because after 2014 the South Korean rice market will be fully opened. In 1993, the average tariff on all imports was 10.6 percent.

Bilateral trade with the United States includes a number of sectors. The relative value of these exports has obviously changed over time. The biggest drop was trade in the textile sector, and the biggest gain was in the high-tech sector. The ratio between those two sectors has changed by a factor of 10. This is because China, Indonesia, Thailand, and Latin American nations have become more competitive in the export of textiles. For the past few years, a major goal for clothing manufacturers has been to streamline the whole process of production and distribution in order to survive. With margins being squeezed, brand managers are constantly looking for ways to improve their supply chain. Innovative companies offer Web-based supply chain management to help wholesalers and manufacturers become more versatile.

Trade between the United States and South Korea continued to grow from 1989 to 2000. A global economic downturn and concomitant drop in exports led to lower growth rates in 2001, but the next year trade grew by 6.1 percent. South Korea's trade surplus with the United States jumped in the mid-2000s, and the balance of trade is now heavily skewed in favor of the ROK. Yet the United States has now fallen to the second-largest importer of Korean goods and services and is only the seventh-largest trading partner of the ROK.

China is now South Korea's primary trading partner and the largest target for exports: In 2006, almost one-quarter of the ROK's exports, valued at more than $46 billion, went to the Chinese market. Increasing trade with China is expected to boost South Korea to a leading position among Asia's developed economies. The ROK is also expected to lead the world in penetrating Japan's trade barriers. In 2006, total exports amounted to more than $325 billion. Among them were computers, motor vehicles, semiconductors, wireless telecommunications equipment, steel, ships, and petrochemicals. That same year, it imported about $260.6 billion worth of machinery, electronic equipment, oil, steel, transportation equipment, organic chemicals, and plastics.

During the 1990s, despite efforts to comply with the Uruguay Round commitments, South Korea has found a number of ways to frustrate importers. Among the nontariff barriers were special taxes, sanitary restrictions, quotas, complex percentage calculations, domestic trade organizations' control over certain imports and requirement to approve import documentation, sweetheart deals between buyers and producers, effective protection of certain products over their nominal rate of tariff, clearance delays at customs, and stringent testing, labeling, and certification requirements.

A move away from domestic trade barriers toward potential free trade agreements began in the mid-1980s as South Korean firms started to compete more successfully in the global marketplace. Discussion and negotiations over a free trade agreement with the United States took place over many years and were concluded in 2007 with the signing of the Korea-U.S. Free Trade Agreement (KORUS FTA). Though KORUS FTA has not been ratified, it may well greatly improve trade relations between the two countries. Still, remaining South Korean tariffs on such goods as automobiles have led to some opposition in the United States.

North Korea

Since the establishment of the DPRK, prices have been set by the State Planning Committee. Unlike in market economies, where prices are determined largely by supply and demand, prices in North Korea are determined as part of the central economic planning. The economy is set up for domestic distribution, and foreign trade has long been treated simply as a means to bring about outside investment in order to facilitate the continuation and diversification of domestic trade. A U.S. embargo and distrust among many Western nations stung by North Korea's inability to repay its debts in the 1970s has made foreign trade difficult, but limited trade within the Northeast Asian region has slowly grown in recent years. Still, North Korea has an inward-oriented economy and for the most part intentionally removes itself from global trade networks.

Prices for most goods in North Korea are set by the central government's Price Assessment Commission. This body sets uniform prices for all major goods and exercises control over the provincial committees that determine prices for more unique locally produced goods. Prices are the same in all areas, regardless of transportation costs, variable production costs, or local supply and demand conditions. However, for locally produced, directly sold goods like those promoted by the August Third movement, there is some localized price flexibility. County-level officials can set prices for these goods within ranges determined by state planners; thus, it is possible to take costs and local supply and demand into account when determining prices for these local goods. Still, both set prices and the price ranges for locally sold goods are artificial and essentially arbitrary, determined according to the wishes of state planners without necessarily taking economic conditions and consumer demand into account.

Nearly all retail commerce was state-run by 1958; the only exceptions were small, local farmers' markets where homemade handicrafts and surplus food were sold. The Ministry of Commerce presided over a system of distribution and sales whereby state-run industries went through the central ministry directly and local industries dealt with local branches at the district level. Goods were then delivered to the counties and distributed to retail stores where people could purchase them. What goods were produced and delivered by state industries were largely determined by central planners, while local industrial production was determined by local conditions and resources. What little direct selling (outside of the distribution system) occurred took place at factory stores that would sell goods produced with industrial by-products and scrap. These stores were associated with a particular industrial operation or government bureau, and the sales proceeds went directly to the overseeing entity instead of being funneled through the Ministry of Commerce. Under this system, trade was particularly unresponsive to consumers.

As part of the August Third People's Consumer Goods Production Movement in the 1980s, however, local retail stores were set up that directly sold locally produced goods. These stores cut out the government middlemen and sold local goods, providing revenue for localities as part of the drive toward local self-sufficiency. These were effectively very similar to the factory stores set up previously, but these directly benefitted counties, cities, and districts. This movement began in P'yongyang under the direction of Kim Jong-Il (who was increasingly involved in the government) but quickly spread across the country. Local retail operations and local production were combined in a way that responded to local consumer demands. If more of a particular good was needed, the local stores would sell more of it, prompting greater local production of that good if possible to meet the new demand. Thus, market principles were able to affect local economies to some extent under the August Third movement.

In the early 1990s, consumer responsiveness was expanded by the Chung Choon Sil movement, promoted by Kim Jong-Il. This movement was patterned after the practice of Chung Choon Sil, a rural store operator who kept track of the needs of all of the families in her area as a way of charting local demand. Using these records as a guide, Chung and other workers attempted to meet as many of the needs as possible through local production and small-scale agriculture. This sort of attempt at local self-sufficiency was in line with the *juche* ideal and was promoted heavily by the government. As state production declined during the 1990s, the ability to meet local demand increasingly fell on local industry and retail, and the efforts to utilize all available resources were essential. Traders were to be involved in both distribution and production of goods, as all citizens were tasked with doing their part.

Some domestic trade occurs outside of the state and local distribution networks, on a small but growing scale. By the 1980s, the farmers markets of earlier decades began to include foreign-produced goods (mainly from China) brought into the country by visitors or family members. Coinciding with a decline in the supply of some consumer goods, these items became a commodity brought from town to town by travelers. Such deliveries and purchases essentially constituted a black market, but authorities often looked the other way as the items were meeting local needs that domestic production and distribution were unable to adequately meet. Similar informal trade for food occurred during the widespread famine of the mid-1990s. In 2002, the government began to allow larger general markets where both food and goods can be purchased. The most notable of these markets is the Tongil Street Market in P'yongyang, where small vendors rent stalls and sell imported food and consumer goods from nearby countries. Similar urban markets can be found in most North Korean cities. Since banking is virtually nonexistent in North Korea, though, would-be merchants must turn to local moneylenders for initial funds. Lending of this type often involves tremendous interest rates that are enforced through criminal means since there is no real guarantee of a return on the investment and no government recourse for lenders.

North Korea was primarily dependent on the Soviet Union and China for its early foreign trade. The rift with the USSR in the late 1960s, brought about by a de-Stalinization of Korean socialism, resulted in diminished aid. The DPRK needed to turn to the West for credit, but it could never repay the loans because of its deteriorating economic situation. During the early 1970s, North Korea attempted a large-scale modernization program through the importation of Western technology, principally in the heavy industrial sectors. However, rapidly rising costs for importing oil further exacerbated the difficulties. It became the first communist country to default on its loans from free market countries. Nevertheless, there were imports of raw materials and industrial equipment, and foreign trade reached record levels in 1979.

In 1984, the DPRK tried again to promote joint ventures with Western nations, but its poor international financial standing and wariness on the part of potential foreign partners largely derailed the efforts. Some financial support did come from the General Federation of Korean Residents living in Japan, but it was not enough to allow the economy to move forward to any extent. Trading companies were set up, but as Eastern European nations were liberated and the Soviet Union collapsed, even trade between North Korea and the former Soviet bloc fell by approximately 67 percent.

The most obvious foreign trading partner is, of course, South Korea, but official DPRK policy has made trade between the two Koreas difficult. If trade is carried out through normal avenues and thus subjected to South Korean trade laws, the South Korean government would be legitimized. Additionally, if North Koreans were introduced to the far higher standard of living in the South, it could undermine the state's ideological efforts. As the DPRK has long been intent on reunifying Korea under the communist regime, both of these things are generally seen as unacceptable. For this reason, early trade between the North and the South in the late 1980s occurred through middlemen in Japan, Hong Kong, Singapore, or China; goods were sent from North Korea to these foreign intermediaries and then shipped to South Korea. This allowed the DPRK to avoid paying heed to any South Korean trade laws while still providing a trade route between the countries. Of course, this type of trade was impractically expensive. These expenses proved a major barrier to inter-Korean trade, and North Korean insistence on the practice limited such trade.

Beginning in the 1990s, some direct trade between the North and the South was allowed. Concurrently, trade through foreign intermediaries rose significantly as relations between the two Koreas inched toward improvement. Much of this trade was through consignment operations similar to those employed by Western companies. In the mid-1990s, some of these restrictions were dropped, and some direct trade has taken place since, though indirect exchange is still common. After China and Japan, South Korea is now the DPRK's third-largest trading partner, and some of the trade with Japan and China is also related to indirect trade with South Korea.

In 1996, the government partnered with the South Korean *chaebol* Daewoo in a joint venture to produce clothing and bags. The factories were set up in the port city of Namp'o, and the company was presented in the North as nationalist venture. At a time when most trade between the North and South was still indirect, this was a major step toward trade normalization (as well as perhaps a tacit admission that the North Korean economy was becoming increasingly weak). Two years later, a similar joint venture was set up with Hyundai in the southern port city of Haeju. These partnerships paved the way for the establishment of special economic zones (SEZs) with laws more conducive to foreign investment.

China is the DPRK's primary trading partner, and this relationship has been strengthened as the North Korean economy has declined in recent years. Since 2003, China has embarked on a historic effort to prop up the North Korean economy. The North Korean percentage of trade with China has fluctuated over the years from 75 to 40 percent. It stayed steady at 70 percent from 1960 to 1967, after which the ratio increased to around 90 percent in the wake of the upheaval of China's Cultural Revolution. In 1993, the DPRK shipped coal, steel, cement, and fish to China and imported oil, grain, and electronics. However, the value of trade fell from $899 million to $371 million in 1999. Then, due to the renormalization process underway since 1999, Sino-DPRK trade jumped to $488 million in 2000 and $738 million in 2001, a 51 percent increase. In 2005, trade between the countries rose to $1.58 billion.

Trade with Russia came alive in 2000 when Vladimir Putin and Kim Jong-Il realized that their interests might be closer than they had imagined in the 1990s. Each made breakthrough visits to the other's nation. Common suspicion of the

United States helped to bring them together. In the DPRK-Russia Declaration of August 4, 2001, Russia pledged to find financial resources for North Korea. After a long decline, North Korean exports to Russia grew every year from 2001 to 2005 to a total of $232 million.

Since early 2008, cargo trains have been making a short daily round trip to North Korea. The principal purpose of the new train service is to supply the Kaesong Industrial Complex with raw materials, which should help spark the zone's productivity. South Korean officials say their country has a financial interest in developing more train routes to the North, and there are plans to eventually connect the South Korean rail network to China, Russia, and Europe via the North. Such an expansion could help slash transport costs for producers in the South's export-heavy economy. Even if this takes place, though, the future of trade between the two Koreas, as well as North Korean trade with other Asian countries, remains unpredictable. For example, in late 2008 P'yongyang restricted and even closed traffic across the border because of what it called Lee Myung-Bak's hard-line policy. Yet most of North Korea's top trading partners have not scaled back economic ties, and an increased focus on foreign trade relations is likely given that the North Korean economy has not been able to achieve the self-sufficiency called for by the principles of *juche*.

REFERENCES

Albright, David, and Kevin O'Neill, eds. 2000. *Isis Reports: Solving the North Korean Nuclear Puzzle*. Washington, DC: Institute for Science and International Security Press. http://www.isis-online.org/publications/dprk/book/app3.html (accessed October 5, 2007).

Asianinfo.org. n.d. "Korean Mining and Manufacturing." http://www.asianinfo.org/asianinfo/korea/eco/mining_and_manufacturing.html (accessed November 1, 2007).

Central Intelligence Agency. *The World Factbook*. 2007. https://www.cia.gov/library/publications/the-world-factbook/index.html (accessed November 16, 2007).

Cha, Gi-tae. 2005. "Can a Market Economy Flourish in Korea?" *Korea Focus* 13, no. 1 (January–February): 25–26.

Chah, Eun Young. 2004. "Focus on Economic Growth, Rather than Income Distribution." *Korea Focus* 12, no. 4: 35–36.

Chase-Dunn, Christopher K. 1980. "Socialist States in the Capitalist World-Economy." *Social Problems* 27, no. 5: 505–525.

Chung, Joseph Sang-Hoon. 1972. "North Korea's 'Seven Year Plan' (1961–70): Economic Performance and Reforms." *Asian Survey* 12, no. 6: 527–545.

Chung, Young-Iob. 2007. *South Korea in the Fast Lane: Economic Development and Capital Formation*. New York: Oxford University Press.

Eberstadt, Nicholas. 2007. *The North Korean Economy: Between Crisis and Catastrophe*. New Brunswick, NJ: Transaction Publishers.

Glionna, John M. 2008. "N. Korea Halts Most Border Traffic." *Los Angeles Times*, December 1.

Haggard, Stephen. 1990. *The Pathways from Periphery: The Politics of Growth in the Newly Industrializing Countries*. Ithaca, NY: Cornell University Press.

————. 1991. "The Transition to Export-Led Growth in South Korea: 1954–1966." *Journal of Asian Studies* 50, no. 4: 850–873.

Harvie, Charles, and Hyun-Hoon Lee. 2003. *Korea's Economic Miracle: Fading or Reviving?* New York: Palgrave Macmillan.

Hattori, Tamio. 1999. "Economic Development and Technology Accumulation: Experience of South Korea." *Economic and Political Weekly* 34, no. 22: M78–M84.

Hunter, Helen-Louise. 1999. *Kim Il-Song's North Korea*. Westport, CT: Praeger.

Jang, Hasung. 2004. "Significance of the 'Korea Discount.'" *Korea Focus* 12, no. 6: 32–33.

Kim, Byoung-Lo Philo. 1992. *Two Koreas in Development: A Comparative Study of Principles and Strategies of Capitalist and Communist Third World Development*. New Brunswick, NJ: Transaction Publishers.

Kim, Do-hoon. 2008. "Direction for FTA Policy of the New Administration." *Korea Focus* 16, no. 2: 123–129.

Kim, Joungwan Alexander. 1965 "The 'Peak of Socialism' in North Korea: The Five and Seven Year Plans." *Asian Survey* 5, no. 5: 255–269.

Kim, Samuel S. 2000a. "Korea's *Segyehwa* Drive: Promise versus Performance" in *Korea's Globalization,* edited by Samuel S. Kim, 242–281. New York: Cambridge University Press.

————. 2000b. *North Korean Foreign Relations in the Post–Cold War World*. Carlisle, PA: Strategic Studies Institute. http://www.strategicstudiesinstitute.army.mil/pdffiles/PUB772.pdf (accessed November 16, 2007).

Kim, Young C. 1975. "North Korea in 1974." *Asian Survey* 15, no. 1: 43–52.

Kimura, Mitsuhiko. 1995. "The Economics of Japanese Imperialism in Korea." *Economic History Review* 48, no. 3: 555–574.

————. 1999. "From Fascism to Communism: Continuity and Development of Collectivist Policy in North Korea." *Economic History Review* 52, no. 1: 69–86.

Kiyota, Kozo, and Robert M. Stern. 2007. *Economic Effects of a Korea-U.S. Free Trade Agreement*. Washington, DC: Korea Economic Institute.

Koh, B. C. 1977. "North Korea 1976: Under Stress." *Asian Survey* 17, no. 1: 61–70.

————. "North Korea in 1987: Launching a New Seven-Year Plan." *Asian Survey* 28, no. 1: 62–70.

Korea Economic Institute and Korea Institute of International Economic Policy. 2007. *Korea's Economy 2007*. Washington, DC: Korea Economic Institute. http://www.keia.org/Publications/KoreasEconomy/2007/07Guerrero.pdf (accessed November 13, 2008).

Kuark, Yoon T. 1963. "North Korea's Industrial Development during the Post-War Period." *China Quarterly* 14 (April–June): 51–64.

Lankov, Andrei. 2006. "The Natural Death of North Korean Stalinism." *Asia Policy* 1: 95–121.

Lee, Dong-hwi. 2007. "Reforming and Opening North Korea's Economy: Evaluation and Prospects." *Korea Focus* 15, no. 2: 129–142.

Lee, Doowon. 2000. "South Korea's Financial Crisis and Economic Restructuring" in *Korea Briefing: 1997–1999, Challenges at the Turn of the Century*, edited by Kongdan Oh, 9–34. New York: Asia Society.

Lee, Ho-jin. 2007. "Economic Interdependence between Korea and the United States" in *Dynamic Forces on the Korean Peninsula: Strategic & Economic Implications*, edited by James M. Lister, 1–14. Washington, DC: Korea Economic Institute.

Lee, Hy-Sang. 2001. *North Korea: A Strange Socialist Fortress*. Westport, CT: Greenwood Publishing Group.

Lee, Moon-hyung. 2005. "Appreciation of Chinese Yuan Calls for Export Diversification." *Korea Focus* 13, no. 3: 42–43.

Lim, Hyun-Chin, and Chung Young Chul. 2004. "Is North Korea Moving toward a Market Economy?" *Korea Focus* 12, no. 4 (July–August): 49–79.

Lim, Wonhyuk. 2007. "Inter-Korean Economic Cooperation at a Crossroads" in *Dynamic Forces on the Korean Peninsula: Strategic & Economic Implications*, edited by James M. Lister, 139–164. Washington, DC: Korea Economic Institute.

Lynn, Hyung Gu. 2007. *Bipolar Orders: The Two Koreas Since 1989*. London: Zed Books.

Noland, Marcus. 2000. *Avoiding the Apocalypse: The Future of the Two Koreas*. Washington, DC: Institute for International Economics.

———. 2001. "Famine in North Korea: Causes and Cures." *Economic Development and Cultural Change* 49, no. 4: 741–767.

Oh, Kongdan, and Ralph Hassig. 2000. *North Korea through the Looking Glass*. Washington, DC: Brookings Institution Press.

Olsen, Edward A. 2005. *Korea, the Divided Nation*. Westport, CT: Praeger, 2005.

Roh, Jeong Seon, ed. 2000. *Korean Annual*. Seoul, Korea: Yonhap News Agency.

Smith, David A. 1997. "Technology, Commodity Chains and Global Inequality: South Korea in the 1990s." *Review of International Political Economy* 4, no. 4: 734–762.

Soh, Changrok. 1997. *From Investment to Innovation? The Korean Political Economy and Changes in Industrial Competitiveness*. Seoul: Global Research Institute, Korea University.

Song, Byung-Nak. 1997. *The Rise of the Korean Economy*. New York: Oxford University Press.

Steinberg, David I. 1993. "The Transformation of the South Korean Economy" in *Korea Briefing, 1993: Festival of Korea*, edited by Donald Clark, 31–54. New York: Asia Society.

Yoo, Byung Sam. 2005. "The Reality of the Current Economic Slump." *Korea Focus* 13, no. 4: 37–39.

Zhuang, Reana, and Won W. Koo. 2007. "Implications of the U.S.-Korea Free Trade Agreement: A General Equilibrium Approach" in *Static and Dynamic Consequences of a KORUS FTA*, edited by James M. Lister, 7–28. Washington, DC: Korea Economic Institute.

Society

Religion and Thought

Mary E. Connor

INTRODUCTION

Four main streams of religious and philosophical influences shaped Korean culture over time. Indigenous Shamanism prevailed in the spiritual life of the early Koreans. Buddhism entered Korea in the 4th century CE and provided the backbone of the intellectual and spiritual life until the 14th century. Confucianism came from China during the Three Kingdoms period and dominated nearly all aspects of life for 1,500 years. Christianity first entered Korea from China in the 18th century. A native Korean church called "Ch'ondogyo" inspired the Tonghak revolt of 1894 and still exists, though marginally.

Until 1945, there was little difference between religious beliefs and practices. What is said about Korea before 1945 applies to the entire peninsula. More is known about religion and thought in South Korea after 1945 because North Korea is one of the most isolated countries in the world.

In many countries, industrialization and urbanization have lessened formal religious affiliation, but this is not the case in South Korea. Despite rapid change and modernization, religion has become one of the most significant developments in modern times. Since 1945, there has been an upsurge in religious activity leading to the sustained and rapid growth of Buddhist and Christian communities along with new religions and the continuation of Shamanism, Daoism, and Confucian beliefs. In South Korea, spiritual forces touch every aspect of society and exert a powerful impact on the daily lives of citizens.

Buddhist temple in Myohyang, North Korea.
(Courtesy of Mary Connor)

In North Korea, very different forces operate to shape virtually every aspect of life for the people. From the time a visitor lands at the P'yongyang airport to the moment of departure, the visitor becomes aware of a belief system that appears almost religious, and it is deliberate. With the division of the peninsula and the subsequent creation of the communist Democratic People's Republic of Korea (DPRK), the government fostered an ideology of *juche* ("self-reliance"), Marxism, and Neo-Confucianism that suppressed nearly all religious activity. The belief in the infallibility and goodness of Kim Il-Sung is evident everywhere: city streets, monumental buildings, statues, walls of public buildings, billboards, and badges that are a required component of everyone's attire.

The contrasting belief systems of North and South Korea make the peninsula one of the most diverse places in the world in terms of religion and thought. These differences inevitably heighten interest in the Koreas, but they are very problematic for possible reunification.

SOUTH KOREA

Aside from the very evident contrasts between North and South, South Korea itself is one of the most religiously diverse countries in the world. Ancient religious practices and Confucian philosophy continue to have an enormous significance. Koreans, like other East Asians, are traditionally eclectic rather than exclusive in their religious commitments. Shamanism, Buddhism, Daoism, and Confucianism coexist with one another. Christians are somewhat of an exception. The combination of varied

Pulguksa, near Kyongju. This temple was originally built in 528 CE and enlarged in 751. The stone stairways and structures are original. The most magnificent example of Silla architecture, Pulguksa was reconstructed along its original lines during the Park regime. (Courtesy of Mary Connor)

religious and philosophical beliefs together with a practical secular view of the world characterizes contemporary society.

It is easy for foreigners to witness this religious diversity by simply walking the streets of Korea's cities and towns. They will see Confucian shrines, Buddhist temples, and Christian churches side by side. Signs of Shamanism also exist everywhere: homes, offices, apartment buildings, and storefronts make known that a fortune-teller, or Shaman, is inside. In the United States, religious diversity reflects ethnic diversity, but religious pluralism in South Korea exists in a country that is perhaps the most ethnically homogeneous place on Earth (Baker 2007). Unlike in the United States, where God is on the currency and in the legislature, South Korea has no civic religion.

Prior to the Korean War (1950–1953), two-thirds of the Korea's Christians lived in the North, but most subsequently fled to the South. It is not known how many Christians remain in the North. Since the end of the Korean War, the number of Koreans professing religious affiliation has increased significantly. From 1964 to 1994, the religious population jumped sixfold, while the total population expanded about one and one-half times (Connor 2002). This increase was particularly evident from the early 1960s to the end of the 1980s, the time of the most significant economic and urban development. Andrew Kim (2000) explains the sociohistorical factors that inspired such an increase in religious growth. He attributes this development to the painful legacy of Japanese colonial rule, the trauma of the Korean War, and the sense of isolation arising from rapid industrialization and urbanization. Churches provided a haven for refugees from the North and new urban dwellers who sought community and comfort. Churches in the United States do the same, providing a sense of community and refuge for the Korean immigrant.

Recent surveys in South Korea indicate that the trends toward association with a specific religion continue. According to a 2005 report of the National Statistical Office, 53.1 percent of the country's total population has a religious affiliation. Buddhism, Protestantism, and Catholicism represent 98.1 percent of the entire religious population. Of the entire population, however, 22.8 percent are Buddhist and 29.2 percent are Christian. There are more Protestants (18.3 percent) than Catholics (10.9 percent); however, the Catholic population has grown by 74.4 percent in the last decade, and Protestantism has declined slightly by 1.64 percent (K. Kim 2008).

Many of those who are unaffiliated with a religion may well have consulted Shamans or visited a Buddhist temple, a Christian church, or a Confucian shrine. Religious pluralism may also be seen in practices relating to the life cycle: There are Shamanist and Buddhist practices connected to pregnancy and childbirth, Confucian and Christian rituals in weddings, and Buddhist practices during funerals and ancestor memorial services.

The three major religious organizations (Protestant, Catholic, and Buddhist) support nationally broadcast cable television and radio networks. South Korea's Buddhist television network was the first of its kind in the world. Religious organizations publish more than 200 magazines and periodicals and operate daily newspapers of their own. In addition to numerous primary and secondary schools, more than one out of every five colleges and universities in Korea has a religious affiliation. Religious groups also own land, hospitals, publishing houses, and prayer and rehabilitation centers.

Shamanism

Shamanism is considered to be Korea's oldest religion. It encompasses a variety of beliefs and practices that have been influenced by Buddhism and Daoism and may include prayer, worship, and rituals that are considered signs of religious faith. Many of the gods who appear in Shamanic rituals are borrowed from Buddhism. Shamanist rock formations signifying wishes for good health and prosperity may regularly be seen adjacent to Buddhist temple structures.

Folk religion and Shamanistic influences are seen in folk art that has become increasingly popular in recent years. Decorations in South Korea's restaurants, hotels, government offices, and even the presidential Blue House use many-paneled folding screens painted with themes whose basic symbolism and meaning can be grasped best through knowledge of Shamanism or its emphasis on longevity as a goal of life. Symbols of longevity (the crane and the turtle) and good luck (dragons, phoenixes, and unicorns) are found everywhere.

While the first tribal kings of Silla were recorded as Shamans, evidence of Shamanism is found in the artwork in early burial tombs. Although Shamanism never developed a theological system, it never showed any hostility toward foreign religions that came to the peninsula; it mingled freely with them. For centuries, the Shamans were considered to be at the top of the social structure.

For centuries, Koreans worshipped many gods, such as the village god, the house master god, the fire god, the house site god, and the god of wealth. In the past, Shamanistic rites included agricultural rites, such as prayers for an abundant harvest. With a shift away from agriculture, this has been largely lost. Since many Koreans have moved from small rural villages to modern cities, most have left their household gods and rituals behind.

Many of their traditional beliefs have been challenged by Christianity and modernization, but Shamanism has survived. The majority of South Koreans who profess a religion consider themselves Buddhists or Christian, although many still turn to the old Shamanist folk traditions. In fact, Shamanism is thriving in Korea today. The Korea Worshipers Association, the organization that represents Shamans, reports that there are approximately 300,000 Shamans, or 1 for every 160 South Koreans (Choe 2007). When the Internet boom hit South Korea, Shamans were among the first to set up their own Web sites and offered online fortune-telling. Seeing a psychologist is considered a sign of serious mental weakness, but it is perfectly acceptable to visit a fortune-teller (E. Kim 2003).

In contemporary Korea, a Shaman is known as a *mudang*. The role of a *mudang*, usually a woman, is to act as an intercessor between a god or gods and human beings. Shamanism is centered on the *mudang*, who makes contact with spirits through special techniques. An individual will hire a *mudang* to perform a ceremony (*kut*) to communicate with the spirits. Through the Shaman's intercession, Koreans are able to appeal to spirits in the hope that they will solve their problems or bring good luck. Shamanistic rituals are also regularly held for the launch of a new business or the dedication of a new building. Some Shamans practice fortune-telling by reading the words of the spirits after throwing coins or grains of rice. They no longer perform elaborate rituals but sit in offices and wait to offer advice to their customers based on their interpretation of signs from the spirit world. Once established, a Shaman can usually make a good living.

The word "Shaman" is a Tungusic word for "to know," and the Shaman is believed to have direct contacts during a trance with the spirit world for the benefit of people in this world. On the strength of this ability to connect with spirits, the Shaman then acts as a spiritual healer, priest, and prophet to administer to those who seek help and peace of mind. Shamanism may be seen as a way to alleviate anxiety in the modern world within the traditional Korean culture, even though Shamanism itself is considered primitive and magical.

Daoism

Another ancient religion, Daoism failed to proliferate as an independent religion but has influenced Korean thought and society for centuries. Its belief in a multiplicity of gods was compatible with belief in the unseen spirits of nature. Daoism freely borrowed from Confucianism and Buddhism in its institutions, temples, ceremonies, and doctrines. There were no halls for the study of Daoism or Daoist temples in Korea's mountains. The only official Daoist temples in Korea were ones located in the capital for the use of the court and government.

Daoism was imported from China, and by the late fourth century Paekche scholars were well versed in Daoism and Confucianism and were sent to Japan to share their knowledge. In Silla, Daoism penetrated into the life of the Flowery Princes (*hwarang*) and hence the ruling class. King T'aejo of Koryo contributed greatly to the growth of Daoism and Shamanism during his reign. Neo-Confucianism during the Choson dynasty attempted to eradicate Daoism, but by then Daoist thoughts were so pervasive in the life of the nation—in religion, popular beliefs, art, politics, and folklore—that even the Neo-Confucian scholars succumbed to its influence without realizing it.

Daoism continues to manifest its influence on the Korean people, such as in their love for nature. It is also apparent in their search for blessings and longevity, two of its most prominent features. Everyday articles are adorned with symbols of prosperity and long life. The names of many mountains and valleys throughout the country indicate a strong influence of this religion. The influence of Daoism is most visible on the national flag with its *yin/yang* blue and red symbol representing the dualism of the universe.

Buddhism

Buddhism, which entered the peninsula in the fourth century, flourished throughout the Three Kingdoms period (57 BCE–668 CE) and became the state religion during the Koryo dynasty (918–1392) but suffered a long period of repression during the Choson dynasty (1392–1910). Its spectacular revival is a major development in modern Korean history. Approximately 11 million South Koreans are adherents of Buddhism.

When Buddhism entered during the Three Kingdoms period, it was introduced to the ruling class by monks from China and India who suggested that Buddhism had a greater capacity to heal diseases than the less powerful gods of folk religion. They conveyed the idea that royal families could live longer and that their kingdom would be protected if they practiced Buddhism. Within a few centuries, Buddhism became the dominant religion of the people. Over time, elements of Buddhism blended together with Daoism, Confucianism, and Shamanism.

Haeinsa Temple, founded by two monks in the ninth century, is located in the mountains of Kayasan National Park. The most famous attraction at the temple is the Tripitaka Koreana, the most complete and important set of Buddhist teachings in the world. It was carved during the 13th century on 81,340 woodblocks. (Courtesy of Mary Connor)

Korean Buddhism, like that of China and Japan, is mainly of the Mahayana ("Great Vehicle") school, emphasizing the attainment of eternity through faith. The idea of the Great Vehicle suggests a large ferryboat in which all types of people can be carried across a river to achieve enlightenment. Mahayana emphasizes that nirvana is not only attainable by monks but also possible for everyone. Mahayana also stresses that enlightenment is a call to compassion. In order to be saved, one must save others.

The historical Buddha Shakyamuni taught that the fate of all living beings is to suffer throughout their lives. The attainment of nirvana, or deliverance from life's suffering, is to be sought through the rejection of earthly desires, through many reincarnations, followed by enlightenment. The three main foundations of the Buddhist faith are the Buddha himself, his teaching, and the community of monks whose conduct is guided by an Eightfold Path—a daily guide for righteous living and right thinking. Ordinary people are expected to be considerate and selfless toward others and to improve themselves according to the standards of righteous life, but they cannot expect to attain nirvana within their lifetime. Salvation is an individual matter, and the emphasis is on withdrawal more than on social action. This does not mean that Buddhism has no social conscience; love and charity toward all living things are dominant parts of the belief system.

Mahayana Buddhism derives from the same East Asian tradition out of which Japanese Zen was born. In Korea, this tradition is called Son. One first studies the sutras and commentaries to comprehend the doctrine. Once this is accomplished, the Son Buddhist will seek to go beyond intellectual understanding through meditation. The goal is the abandonment of human attachments and the concentration of one's mind and thought in order to experience the Buddha-nature that is inherent in all things. In addition to the importance of understanding doctrine and practicing meditation, Mahayana Buddhism focuses on compassion. There are said to be a large number of Buddhas and Bodhisattvas ("enlightenment beings") who, out of compassion, offer help to those who are suffering.

Some of the best-known Buddhas in Korea are the Sakyamuni (the historical Buddha Gautama), Amitabha (the Buddha who helps the believer to be reborn in Western Paradise and achieve enlightenment), Maitreya (the Buddha of the future who helps believers to achieve health, wealth, and longevity for themselves and their families and who promises that a Buddhist paradise will ultimately be established on earth), and Kwanum (the goddess of compassion who is available to help solve problems anyone might face).

In Mahayana, wisdom remains an important objective, but the combination of wisdom and compassion is central to its teaching. The term for compassion is *karuna*, which may also be translated as "empathy" or "sympathy." For the Mahayana Buddhist, *karuna* implies that we are all part of an ever-changing universe. Individuals are all the same. To be kind to others is actually to be kind to oneself. All living beings, including animals, are interrelated, and one must be kind toward all living things. The Bodhisattva, the enlightened one, will not enter nirvana in order to remain on earth to help others until all are enlightened.

Rocks at Haeinsa Temple are piled on top of one another to signify wishes for good health and prosperity. (Courtesy of Mary Connor)

Until very recently, the majority of Koreans were Buddhist. The continuous influence of the West combined with the fact that the recent presidents of South Korea were Christian led to a temporary decline in the followers of Buddhism. Also, young people and those who wanted to be more modern were inclined to join Christian churches. During the 1960s and 1970s, the South Korean government supported the reconstruction of historic sites, including many Buddhist temples. Many people began to reclaim the faith as something to honor and revere as opposed to something that was old-fashioned. As a result, membership in Buddhist congregations grew and is now just about equal to that of Christian churches. Mountain monasteries still flourish today and are frequently visited by pilgrims and tourists in search of a traditional Buddhist experience. Urban temples offer Sunday morning services in addition to traditional rituals. Monks in some sects are permitted to marry. Buddha's birthday is a national holiday that includes parades, the lighting of lanterns, rituals, and festivities.

Buddhists recently became more involved in politics and society. After the tragedy in Kwangju, an incident in which government troops killed hundreds of pro-democracy demonstrators in 1980, Buddhists adopted an activist role and were known to be vocal about issues of poverty and justice. For the first time in modern history, Buddhist monks could be seen demonstrating in the streets for democratic reforms. Buddhists have also opened meditation halls in condominium complexes and office buildings to provide a place for urban followers to meet, meditate, and discuss Buddhist teachings.

Gate of Kyongbok Palace, Seoul. In 1972 President Park Chung-Hee announced the Yusin ("revitalizing") policy. This policy included martial law, suspension of the South Korean Constitution, and dissolution of the National Assembly. (Courtesy of Steve Smith)

Urban lay Buddhists have also modernized their music. They sing the words of their traditional rituals to well-known Christian hymns. In 1972, a Buddhist Bible was published. This Bible incorporates the most important and popular sections of the immense canon in a book of a few hundred pages. Buddhists may be seen reading their Bible on subways and buses as Christians do.

There are now 39 Buddhist orders. Congregations are involved in charitable activities, education, and missionary work. There are more than 11,000 temples, more than 26,000 monks, and Buddhist-run media outlets including television programs, radio networks, and newspapers (E. Kim 2003). The most famous Buddhist temples—such as Pulguksa and Haeinsa—are beautifully maintained, and tourists flock to these sites. It is common to see young monks, with closely shaven heads and garbed in gray robes, laughing and enjoying the companionship of their associates in the streets and restaurants of Seoul.

Confucianism

Nothing has shaped Korean society as much as Confucianism. Whether Confucianism is a religion or a philosophy is less important than the fact that it has formed the basis for ethical standards and for ideas about government, society, and family relationships for thousands of years. Even though Confucianism originated in China, the Koreans adopted it in a much stricter form than the Chinese.

HAEINSA (802)

This ninth-century Buddhist temple is among Korea's most beautiful and representative. The very famous attraction is the Tripitaka Koreana, which is the most complete and important set of Buddhist teachings in the world. It was carved during the 13th century on 81,340 woodblocks. There are approximately 320 Chinese characters magnificently carved on each side of each block. The blocks are housed in two large buildings complete with a simple but effective ventilation system to prevent their deterioration.

Today more than 200 shrines and numerous academies are scattered throughout the country (E. Kim 2003). While large numbers of people claim to be Buddhists or Christians, everyone in Korea, to one degree or another, is Confucian. The ideals recommended by Confucius and his followers continue to guide people in their social relations in the home, workplace, school, and government in Korea and wherever there are Koreans in the world. Even in North Korea, where the government has suppressed nearly all religious activity, Confucianism remains a significant component of the culture. Although many alterations were made by Confucian scholars over time, Confucianism can lay claim to being the most influential system of human thought ever devised.

Sokka Pagoda, Pulguksa, near Kyongju. The pagoda is 27 feet high and is regarded as the most elegant stone pagoda in Korea. A Buddhist text believed to have been printed before 751, the year the Sokka Pagoda was constructed, was discovered in 1966 inside the pagoda and is regarded as the oldest Buddhist text printed with wooden blocks in the world. (Courtesy of Mary Connor)

Pyongsan Sowon (Confucian Academy), near Andong. Young men studied at Confucian academies in preparation for the civil service. (Courtesy of Mary Connor)

Confucius, the Chinese sage who lived approximately 2,500 years ago, set up an ideal ethical-moral system intended to govern relationships within the family and the state in harmonious unity. His ideas first entered Korea in the fourth century along with Buddhism. Koguryo, Paekche, and Silla all left records that indicate the early existence of Confucian influence. Confucian philosophical ideas came to Korea from China primarily as a tool for government administration, and a guide to writing poetry and history, rather than as a religious tradition. Confucianism provided an ethical-moral system for this world and left questions about why we were here on earth for Buddhism to answer. Buddhism became the state religion of Unified Silla, but it was Confucianism that formed the philosophical and structural backbone of the state.

During the Koryo dynasty (918–1392), Confucianism was adopted as the basic rationale for government and, in 958, the government service examination system based on Confucianism was established and lasted for more than 900 years. Neo-Confucianism became dominant after 1392 with the creation of the Choson dynasty (1392–1910), which established a Neo-Confucian government that challenged Buddhism and increased support for Confucian social values. Neo-Confucian scholars re-examined and elaborated on the Confucian classics and incorporated elements of other philosophical and religious traditions into their system. Korea became the most Confucian nation in the world, and the impact of those five centuries of Neo-Confucian thinking during the Choson era is still felt today.

Neo-Confucians criticized Buddhist monks as being immoral because they abandoned their familial responsibilities and sought their own enlightenment in temples situated far away in the mountains. They were seen as selfish as their personal needs came before family and community, subsequently placing more responsibility, work, and taxes on those they left behind. Neo-Confucian scholars emphasized

YI I (1536–1584)

Yi I (pen name Yulgok) is one of the most famous sages and Confucian philosophers. He is widely respected for his interpretations of previous Confucian scholars and his own views on Confucianism. With the assistance of his educated and devoted mother Sin Saimdang, Yi I completed the basic studies in the classics by the age of 7, composed poetry at 8, and passed the literary civil service exams when he was 13. He continued his education by studying the Buddhist scriptures and the Daoist classics. When he was 29, he passed the civil service examination. Rising to the highest levels of government, he served as governor, vice director of the Royal Academy, minister of justice, and minister of defense. Two years before his early death at age 48, he completed one of his most important works, *A Key to Annihilating Ignorance* (*Kyongmong Yogyol*).

Traditional Confucian ceremony to express respect for one's ancestors. (Courtesy of the Korea Tourism Organization)

YI HWANG (1501–1570)

Yi Hwang, whose pen name was T'oegye, was Korea's foremost Confucian scholar. His portrait appears on the 1,000-won banknote. His writings contributed to the spread of Neo-Confucianism in Japan during the Tokugawa period and are known throughout the world. At the age of 12, he began his quest to understand philosophy. His motto was "Sincerity and Reverence." In 1515, he established the Tosan Sowon Confucian Institute in Andong, where he studied and lectured. For several hundred years, the institute was the most highly regarded school for those who aspired to be civil servants. The buildings have been converted to a museum containing nearly 5,000 of his works.

---

that people should work for what was best for society and cultivate through education one's inner goodness. Buddhism placed emphasis on love and distributing mercy and grace to all living things; Neo-Confucianism instructed morality and codes of behavior for the home, society, and the government.

The primary emphasis was laid on hierarchical norms, and the social order was reproduced at home. Confucianism made the family, and the roles and responsibilities of each member of the family, the foundation for morality. The young were to respect their elders, children their parents, wives their husbands, daughters-in-law their mothers-in-law, students their teachers, employees their employers, and friends their friends.

Confucianism also influenced the Korean concern for social rank. Koreans viewed the world as a hierarchical order in which everyone has a place. The young were subordinate to the elders, women to men, commoners to members of the upper class, and subjects to the ruler. In all of these relations, people were bound by moral obligations. Everyone was to pay respects to their ancestors. Leaders were to be moral. If they were not, the leader lost legitimacy.

Although modern times have brought revolutionary changes to the lives of people on the peninsula, Confucian beliefs persist. The belief persists that children should learn before the age of 10 that their lives are not their own but belong to their family. Decisions are to be familial, not personal. The Confucian tradition still may influence one's choice of a marital partner because spouses traditionally are not to have the same paternal ancestor. Korean parents continue to hope that their children will consider their advice on choice of college, careers, and marital decisions. Paternal grandparents are considered the real grandparents.

The Confucian system continues to guide Koreans throughout the world. One example is seen in the names used to address family members and relatives. Korean American mothers may still refer to their female friends not by name but as the wife of Jae or the mother of Benjamin. Korean American youth may think that the behavior of their parents is idiosyncratic, but once enrolled in an Asian Studies class they learn that Confucian values are operable within their very household. Another example may be found in Christian churches. Korean American associate pastors are to show marked deference to senior pastors who, steeped in hierarchal Confucian tradition, are accustomed to assistants who do not express contrary opinions. Confucian ethics continue to be operative in the roles men and women play in their families and their communities.

The emphasis on the collective over the individual reflects Confucian values. Koreans continue to use such terms as "filial piety" and place value on the Confucian virtues of duty, hard work, humility, loyalty, personal discipline, righteousness, and sincerity.

Traditional family rituals (a child's first birthday, marriage, a 60th birthday, ancestor worship, and funerals), though somewhat changed, continue to be celebrated with a degree of ritual elaboration worthy of the past.

Before Korea became an economic success in the mid-20th century, many felt that Confucianism had been one of the factors that had prevented prior economic development. It would be more accurate to say that industrialization in Korea and in other Asian economies has been aided by Confucian values. The emphasis on harmony and respect for authority contributes positively to the effectiveness of business operations. The value of loyalty promotes the individual's and the company's interests. This commitment is one of the principal reasons that Koreans were willing to endure the longest workdays in the world for little pay from the mid-1960s to the mid-1980s. Additional Confucian values of cooperation, duty, sacrifice, sincerity, and family as analogous to the company provided management with effective decision making and labor control, both of which have been central to industrialization.

The younger generations of Koreans are not necessarily observant or appreciative of the value of long-standing Confucian traditions. They have not experienced authoritarianism, economic hard times, or war. The young are prone to consider the family as a group of people united by affection and are more individualistic and independent in spite of being financially dependent on their families. Teens, especially those born after 1990, are regarded as the iGeneration (Internet generation).

Confucianism is being modified by modern life. The lesser status of the female is being altered gradually as women are demanding greater respect and equal opportunity. There is more flexibility in adjusting to individual needs and personalities. Rather than dying, Confucianism may well be entering a new stage in its long life. The core of Confucianism is unassailable. It is primarily an ethical system because it focuses on correct moral behavior. Yet it is more because it upholds a vision of harmony in human relationships and the universe.

Christianity

In spite of the fact that Korea is a country steeped in ancient beliefs, Christianity is becoming the dominant religion. Since the introduction of Catholic worship in the 18th century and the coming of Protestant missionaries in the late 19th century, Christianity has become a popular religion, and its influence is seen everywhere. Women have been central to its growth. Until Christianity arrived, most people did not think of themselves as Buddhists rather than Confucians, or of Buddhism and Shamanism as being mutually exclusive. It has been primarily in response to people claiming to be Christian that others have taken religious labels for themselves. Together, Protestants and Catholics make up close to a third of the entire South Korean population. They also appear to be among the most religious in terms of frequency of church attendance, praying, and scripture reading.

The fastest-growing denomination in the 1990s was Roman Catholicism, with 4 million followers. It came to Korea in 1784 when a Confucian scholar named Yi Sung-hun returned from Peking after being baptized by a French priest. Yi quickly converted other Confucian scholars to the new religion. In time, it became a problem. Authorities in Rome said that Catholics could not perform Confucian rituals because ancestor worship is a form of idolatry. When one of the converts refused to perform a Confucian mourning rite in the prescribed manner, he was sentenced to death and became Korea's first Christian martyr.

Since Catholics believe in only one God, they refused to participate in rituals honoring other gods. The government of Korea required all educated Korean men to honor their ancestors with Confucian rituals. It also supported the belief that the king was the Supreme Being. Catholics challenged this idea because they believed that only God was supreme. Catholics rejected the king's claim that he had the power to tell them what rituals they could or could not do. Since they refused to comply with the state-supported belief in ancestor worship and performed the Catholic mass without official permission, this new faith challenged not only the authority of the king but also ideas that were at the core of Confucianism and hundreds of years of tradition.

The number of Catholics executed by the Choson dynasty government reached into the thousands by the end of the 19th century. The effort to extinguish Catholicism was the first significant act of religious persecution in all of Korean history. When Pope John Paul II visited Korea in 1984, 93 of the Korean martyrs were canonized for their piety. As a result of the Pope's visit, citizens could boast that South Korea had more officially recognized Catholic saints than any other nation outside of Western Europe.

The first Protestant missionaries in Korea were American and arrived in 1884 at a time when religious persecution was coming to an end. One was Henry Appenzeller, a Methodist, and the other was Horace Underwood, a Presbyterian. Emphasizing the mass circulation of the Bible (which had been translated into Korean), the missionaries established the first modern educational institutions in Korea. One of the schools, the first to offer formal education for women, became Ewha Womans University, now regarded as one of the best universities. The schools facilitated the rapid expansion of Protestantism among the general populace and in time enabled the Protestant faith to overtake Catholicism.

Horace Allen (1858–1932), a physician-missionary attached to the U.S. legation, contributed to the acceptance of the missionaries by saving the life of Prince Min after an attempted coup. Allen opened the first hospital in Seoul in 1885. Protestant missionaries were allowed to proselytize and operate freely because the government felt their activities were helping the country to modernize. In 1898, in response to pressures from the West, the government acknowledged freedom of religion.

Protestantism expanded rapidly for four main reasons. First, Protestant services are conducted in vernacular Korean and not Latin as in the Catholic Church.

WESTERN LEARNING (CATHOLICISM)

Jesuit missionaries in Ming China introduced Catholicism to a visiting Korean scholar in the early 17th century. The Sirhak thinkers were the first group to take an intellectual interest in Catholicism, or Western Learning as they called it; however, they were not inclined to adopt it. Support for Western Learning grew after Yi Sung-hun (1756–1801), a scholar baptized by a Jesuit priest in Peking in 1783, returned to Korea with many religious books to establish Catholicism in Korea. The number of converts grew rapidly in spite of the opposition of the government and the *yangban* class. What Sirhak converts seemed to have found in Catholicism was a means to struggle against the social and political inequalities of the Choson dynasty. Catholicism brought renewed hope and the promise of creating a heavenly kingdom on earth. The government began to fight back by persecuting Catholics after 1791; however, it could not eradicate Western Learning's deep roots.

Second, worship in the Korean Protestant church is congregational, allowing for active participation on the part of laypeople. Third, the Christian belief in the essential equality of all human beings is a revolutionary and appealing notion. And fourth, the nation was rapidly losing its independence to Japanese imperialism. As a result, many Christians became involved in nationalistic, anti-Japanese politics, such as the March First movement, and demonstrated against the demands that they honor the emperor and the gods of Imperial Japan at Shinto shrines.

During the Japanese occupation of Korea in the first half of the 20th century, Christianity gathered strength and support from patriots who used church institutions as havens from Japanese oppression. When Korea was liberated and divided into a communist-controlled North and an anticommunist South, more than one out of three Catholics and three out of five Protestants lived north of the 38th parallel; subsequently, many Christians fled to the South.

After the Korean War, churches grew rapidly. Since the early 1960s, when there were fewer than a million Protestants in South Korea, their number has more than doubled every decade. One of the reasons for the spectacular growth is based on the fact that the Korean Protestant community was determined to "save" as many souls as it could in the shortest amount of time possible. Because it believed that Protestant Christianity offered the only sure route to salvation, believers would have to convert non-Christians. By 1997, there were approximately 100,000 ministers representing more than 160 Protestant denominations. It was also the nation's largest denomination, with more than 10 million followers. Presently, Protestant Christians make up a larger percentage of the population in South Korea than in any other Asian country (Connor 2002).

Each Sunday, about 68 percent of Catholics and 74 percent of Korean Protestants attend church. By 1998, South Koreans supplied the third-largest number of the world's missionaries. There are now approximately 60,000 Protestant churches and

---

KIM TAEGON (1821–1846)

Kim Taegon, also called Father Kim, was the first Christian martyr of Korea. He studied theology and other subjects in Macao, fled to the Philippines during the Opium War, and during a stay in China became the first Korean to become an ordained Catholic priest. When he attempted to return to Korea, he was imprisoned and later beheaded. A large bronze statue of Kim stands next to the Han River in western Seoul and serves as a testimonial to Father Kim's faith. Another tribute to Father Kim is contained in the one of the tapestries at the Cathedral of Our Lady of the Angels in Los Angeles, California.

1,100 Catholic churches in South Korea, making it the most Christianized non-Western country in the world, with the exception of the Philippines (E. Kim 2003).

In addition to the rapid growth has come division. The idea that people with similar religious beliefs should create their own churches has led to the significant growth of Protestant denominations. The major denominations in terms of membership are Presbyterian, Methodist, and the Holiness Church. Many of the larger denominations have splintered off into subdenominations, such as the Presbyterian Church, which has more than 50 subdenominations on the peninsula.

In spite of the development of numerous subdenominations, there are commonalities within Korean Protestant churches. Nearly all Korean churches are fundamentalist and evangelical. Church attendance is expected not only on Sunday, but also during the week. Members are also expected to contribute 10 percent of their income or more to their church.

Five of the 10 largest churches in the world are reportedly found in Seoul (E. Kim 2003). The most conspicuous example is Youido Full Gospel Church, which has more than 700,000 members and is the largest congregation of Christian adherents in the world and recognized as such by the *Guinness Book of World Records*. The church's evangelical message has attracted huge audiences and influenced other churches to adopt it. Its threefold blessing is simply stated: Christ brings health, prosperity, and salvation. This theology of prosperity rests on the acceptance of the Holy Spirit: health, materialistic success in this world, and salvation in the next. The doctrine also supports the notion that illness, poverty, and misfortune are due to sin and the failure to live according to one's spiritual calling (E. Kim 2003).

The story of the Youido Full Gospel Church is an impressive one. The church was founded by two pastors, David Yonggi Cho and his mother-in-law, Choi Jashil, in 1958. Their first worship service was held in a home, and only six people attended. They began a campaign of knocking on doors, providing spiritual and humanitarian help to the poor, and praying for the sick. In a few months, the membership grew to 50, and they outgrew their home. Worship services were then held in a tent in the backyard. Within two years, membership grew to 1,000, and the church purchased its first plot of land. Within a decade, the church had three Sunday services and a membership of 8,000. Overworked and frequently ill, Cho devised a plan to restructure the church by dividing Seoul into zones. Each zone would have a "cell" that would meet during the week for worship and Bible study in the home of a "cell leader." Each cell leader trained an assistant and worked to recruit new members. Membership continued to grow and by 1977 had reached 50,000. In the 1980s, the Full Gospel Church established satellite churches throughout the city of Seoul. Although many members joined satellite churches, the mother church recruited new members through a vast cell network; this made up for the losses, and membership stood at 780,000 by 1973. The church was renamed Youido Full Gospel Church in the 1990s. Membership is now more than 700,000, with nine Sunday services translated into 16 languages.

The "Newly Rising Religions"

Adding to the religious diversity of the nation are large numbers of independent churches, which make up about 10 percent of all the churches in Korea, and an estimated number of 200 new religions, including Ch'ondogyo, Taejonggyo, Tongilgyo (the Unification Church), and Won Buddhism. These religions hold Sunday worship services in structures that resemble churches, sing hymns, and pray, but the doctrines of each of these religions are distinct from each other. All began in particularly difficult times, such as the late 19th century, the Japanese occupation, and the Korean War. Most have small memberships and a connection in some way to the Tonghak movement of the 19th century. Many share certain characteristics, combining elements of Buddhism, Confucianism, Daoism, and Christianity with Shamanism. They promise a utopia following an apocalypse. They stress the arrival of a savior, who happens to be the founder of their particular sect, with the coming of a new world. Finally, these religions are nationalistic and express the belief that Korea is the chosen land and Koreans are God's chosen people.

The most famous new religion is Ch'ondogyo, which literally means the "heavenly way religion." It was founded by Ch'oe Ch'ue in 1860 in response to the plight of the peasants in the late 19th century. It was then called Tonghak or "Eastern Learning." Ch'oe Ch'ue felt that Tonghak embodied the best principles of Confucianism, Buddhism, and Daoism to oppose Western Learning (Catholicism); however, the Tonghak movement included elements of Catholicism and Shamanism. Ch'oe's ideas supported equality for all human beings and responded to the needs of the peasantry. Arrested on charges of misleading the people, he was executed in 1864, but the movement did not die. After the turn of the century, the name was changed to the Religion of the Heavenly Way, or Ch'ondogyo. During the March First Movement of 1919, it became the leading force to challenge Japanese occupation.

There are approximately 1.13 million people in South Korea who profess faith in Ch'ondogyo. It stresses that God resides in each of us and all human beings are equal before God. It strives to convert earthly society into a paradise on earth. It attempts to transform believers into intellectual-moral beings who will live in harmony with the universe. It is also recognized in North Korea as an authentic Korean religious tradition.

There are about 17 new religions that have organized their theories around the mythology of Tan'gun, the founder of the Korean people and nation. The most well-known new religion in this group is Taejonggyo, which was founded in Seoul in 1909, a time when Christian missionaries were challenging traditional beliefs and practices and Japan was threatening Korea's very existence. Taejonggyo arose as a nationalistic response to a political and spiritual crisis. The central belief is that Koreans need not worship any foreign gods such as Jesus or Buddha because they have their own god, the legendary ruler Tan'gun, who ruled Korea 5,000 years ago.

Taejonggyo claims to have half a million followers, but a government survey in 1995 found fewer than 10,000 Koreans who listed this religion as their religious affiliation.

The Unification Church was established by Reverend Moon Sun Myung in 1954. The word "unification" in Korean is the same word for national reunification, which gives the name of the Unification Church a special meaning for Koreans. The Reverend Moon believes that Jesus appeared to him when he was 16 and asked him to accomplish the work left unaccomplished because of the Crucifixion. Moon accepted the mission and established the Holy Spirit Association for the Unification of World Christianity. The name alludes to Moon's stated goal for his organization to be the unifying force for all Christian denominations. The idea of unification of the Christian world has become an almost mystical idea of a perfect world or Christian heaven and may well have influenced the rapid growth of the Unification Church along with its intensive missionary activities throughout the world. There are 750 Unification Churches and 300,000 believers in South Korea.

It should be mentioned that the Unification Church is considered to be one of the most controversial religious organizations in the world. Moon has been criticized by most Christians and considered a strange individual by most South Koreans. The Unification Church has been accused of being a cult, denounced for brainwashing young people, and investigated by the U.S. House of Representatives for alleged widespread fraud. After serving time in the federal penitentiary in the United States for tax evasion, Moon returned to South Korea. He continues to appear at mass weddings and to preach about the day when there will be unity and harmony in the world.

Won Buddhism is one of many new religions based on Buddhism. Won Buddhism literally means "Circular Buddhism" or "Consummate Buddhism." Its founder, Pak Chungbin, achieved enlightenment in 1916 and came to believe that the world was entering an era of advancing material civilization to which human beings would be enslaved. The only way to save the world was by expanding spiritual power through faith in genuine religion and training in sound morality. Its basic doctrines have much in common with what is taught in most mainstream Buddhist monasteries. Won Buddhists sing hymns, pray, practice Son meditation, seek enlightenment, and practice compassion. Today, there are approximately 681,000 believers in Won Buddhism. They are involved in education, social work, and such business enterprises as rice cleaning, agriculture, and pharmaceuticals.

Korean wall, monk's quarters, and television aerial at Haeinsa. Monks live a very austere existence in the temple; however, television and other modern conveniences are not unheard of. (Courtesy of Mary Connor)

This-Worldly Orientation of Korean Religions

In the past, many people would have turned to Shamanism in hopes of becoming rich or living a long life. Today, instead, they turn to Christianity, which they see as a more appropriate, effective, and modern means to the same end. Many followers of Shamanism and large numbers of Buddhists and Christians have faith in the belief that Buddha, God, or spirits can grant them such earthly wishes as health and wealth. Popular Buddhism does not focus solely on meditation or asceticism, but also on prayers for granting wishes. Andrew Kim (2000) notes that Korean Christianity has also been "Shamanized" to suit materialistic tendencies. Surveys support the strong this-worldly inclination of making sense and providing security in people's lives.

This "earthly" tendency of many Buddhists and Christians, especially Protestants, is also reflected in the way they associate the offering with secular blessings. Buddhists give their offerings together with a list of prayer items to the temple. Both Catholics and Protestants contribute money to their churches whenever good fortune occurs, such as the birth of a son or when sons or daughters pass the university examination. According to the 1997 Gallup Korea survey, nearly 40 percent of the Protestant community indicated the belief that those who contribute money to the church will be blessed by more prosperity in return for their giving.

NORTH KOREA

The belief system of North Korea is shaped by historical forces, ancient traditions, and the belief in Kim Il-Sung, the Great Leader. The DPRK was born in 1948 as a communist state backed by ideas of Marx and Lenin and adapted to North Korea by Kim

Il-Sung and his Soviet advisers. Kim Il-Sung's ties to the Soviet Union, the poverty and exploitation of the majority of the Korean people by the bourgeoisie, and Western imperialism led many to believe that a Marxist form of socialism would be in the best interest of the people. Over time, North Korea did not follow the Soviet model. It sought to adopt both socialism and nationalism in creating a distinctive system of its own. The revolutionary ideas of class struggle and "comrades" seem foreign to most Koreans, and age-old respect for lineage, bloodlines, and clan had more appeal.

Confucian beliefs of respect for authority, loyalty, obedience, and the importance of the group over the individual form the core beliefs. Confucianism gives the ruler exclusive rights to make decisions for the country, speak for the people, impose a strict hierarchical social order, and demand absolute loyalty. Ideology now flows from the allegedly omniscient authority of the founder and his son, Kim Jong-Il. In many ways, North Korea resembles the family state of prewar Japan in that it regards Korean people as one family sharing the same bloodline, with Kim Il-Sung as a father figure. Kim even called himself the present-day Tan'gun, the founder of the Korean nation.

During his life, Kim Il-Sung was believed to be infallible; he became known as the Great Leader, and billboards, statues, and huge monuments in his name convey the idea that he is present in their lives. Even in death, he is considered the head of the North Korean state. Kim is the people's father and savior. The underpinning of the entire belief system is *juche* ("self-reliance"), which claims the allegiance of the vast majority of the population. It teaches that the people are not to rely on gods since human beings are quite capable of making wise decisions. They know that they can rely on Kim Il-Sung and his son. *Juche* is a nationalistic belief that North Korea is independent in politics and foreign policy, not only from the United States, Japan, and Western nations, but also from China. This ideology means growing their own food, making their own goods, and not relying on the outside world, which from their ideological standpoint cannot be trusted anyway, especially the United States. It also means self-reliance in national defense.

The people of North Korea are indoctrinated to distrust the United States. They are told that the United States divided the peninsula, killed millions of their people, and leveled most of the country during the Korean War. They are educated to believe that it is primarily the United States that has prevented reunification. In fact, most of the country's problems are seen as a result of U.S. policy.

In addition to *juche* is the philosophy of the Red Banner, reportedly first announced by Kim Jong-Il in 1996. It calls for a stronger revolutionary spirit based on *juche* and more reliance on the military. The North Korean people were told to safeguard their leader even at the cost of their lives, the requirement that is the core element of the ideology of the Red Banner, army-first politics, and carrying out Kim Jong-Il's policies of independence, unity, and love for the nation.

Traditional religion has been replaced by the personality cult of Kim Il-Sung, which permeates all sectors of social and cultural life and, unlike traditional Korean religious expression, tolerates only a limited practice of other religions. Some people have called Kim the "messiah of North Korea," and *juche* is seen as a replacement for traditional religion. There are only a small number of people who are officially recognized as having a religious affiliation other than *juche*. According to

DPRK reports, there are about 10,000 Buddhists, 10,000 Protestants, a few hundred Catholics, and 15,000 followers of Korea's oldest native religion, Ch'ondogyo.

Religion and Thought and the Issue of Reunification

Since Koreans north and south of the Demilitarized Zone share a common religious tradition, some have argued that religion might serve as a unifying force in the reunification process. They mention the persistence of Confucianism and the fact that Buddhists and Christians from the South have provided food and needed services to the North. South Koreans hope that this assistance may provide a step toward ending decades of mistrust and helping to finally bring unity.

While this view expresses hope, it ignores the overwhelming differences between a totalitarian socialist state that is impoverished and a democratic and capitalist republic that is the 13th-largest economy in the world. In 1993, Kim Il-Sung spoke about his hopes for reunification. He recommended that the North and the South be drawn together into a federal state "on the condition that the north and the south recognize and tolerate each other's ideas and social systems, a government in which the two sides are represented on an equal footing and under which they exercise regional autonomy with equal rights and duties" (I.-S. Kim 2003, 28). Kim's suggestions may well be the only answer if Korea is to be reunified in the near or distant future.

REFERENCES

Baker, Don. 2007. "Introduction," in *Religions of Korea in Practice*, edited by Robert E. Buswell, Jr., 1–31. Princeton, NJ: Princeton University Press.

Choe, Sang-Hun. 2007. "Shamanism Enjoys Revival in Techno-Savvy South Korea," in *The Korean Wave: As Viewed through the Pages of the* New York Times *in 2007*, 110–112. New York: Korean Cultural Service.

Clark, Donald N. 1986. *Christianity in Modern Korea*. Lanham, MD: University Press of America.

———. 2000. *Culture and Customs of Korea*. Westpot, CT: Greenwood Press.

Covell, Jon Carter. 1981. *Korea's Cultural Roots*. Seoul: Hollym Publishers.

Lee, Kwang-kyu. 2003. *Korean Traditional Culture*. Seoul: Jimoondang Publishers.

Macdonald, Donald Stone. 1990. *The Koreans: Contemporary Politics and Society*. Boulder, CO: Westview Press.

Molloy, Michael. 2005. *Experiencing the World's Religions: Tradition, Challenge, and Change*. Boston: McGraw-Hill.

Oh, Kongdan, and Ralph C. Hassig. 2000. *North Korea through the Looking Glass*. Washington, DC: Brookings Institution Press.

Pew Forum on Religion and Public Life. 2006. "Religious Demographic Profile: South Korea." http://pewforum.org/world-affairs/countries/?CountryID=194 (accessed October 2, 2007).

Shin, Gi-Wook. 2006. *Ethnic Nationalism in Korea: Genealogy, Politics, and Legacy*. Stanford, CA: Stanford University Press.

Sohn, Yong-taek, ed. 2005. *Cultural Landscapes of Korea*. Academy of Korean Studies, Center for Information and Culture. Seoul: Jimoondang Publishers.

Social Classes and Ethnicity

Mary E. Connor

In ancient times, a number of peoples entered the peninsula, but gradually all merged into a single ethnic unit, sharing one language and later one political system until 1945. In modern times, there have been no significant ethnic minorities in either North or South Korea. What has bound Koreans together is their long history, language, geographic isolation, a shared culture based on Confucianism, and a strictly hierarchical social structure. Although the Koreas were divided more than 60 years ago and have very different economic and political systems, ancient traditions and beliefs continue to shape attitudes about class and ethnicity. The people remain one of the most homogeneous societies in the world.

EARLY KOREAN HISTORY

Scholars believe that today's Koreans descended from Neolithic families who came to the peninsula between 5500 and 2000 BCE. Their ancestors are believed to be from various Mongol tribes. Ancient sites provide evidence of clustered dwellings that indicate some form of communal life. The basic unit of society was the clan. These groupings were bound together by bloodline and headed by a tribal chieftain.

The people who lived during Korea's Bronze Age (ninth century BCE to about the fourth century BCE) lived in settlements of slightly increased size, and the surviving artifacts and dolmens provide information about the social structure. Bronze articles were rare and possessed by the privileged few. Some dolmens, created for the successors of the tribal chieftains and having capstones weighing more than 70 tons, demonstrate that these societies were highly stratified. Early people built walls around their communal villages and initiated a political culture.

By the beginning of the fourth century, Old Choson merged with other walled-town states to form a single large confederation headed by a king. Some walled-town states, such as Old Choson, grew large enough that they were known in China. Artifacts from this period include bronze and iron weapons and horse trappings for the privileged warrior class.

The principal activity was agriculture. Most of those who worked the fields held commoner status, though there is evidence that slavery existed. Peasants could own their own land, paid burdensome taxes, and were not allowed to possess arms, a privilege of the elite. The peasants carried out many tasks for the establishment of an early state, such as building public roads and castle walls. The king was at the apex of society, but the aristocratic class possessed the power.

Taeguki flag at a World Cup rally in Seoul, South Korea. (Courtesy of the Korea Tourism Organization)

THE THREE KINGDOMS PERIOD (57 BCE to 668 CE)

During the Three Kingdoms, the power of the king increased along with rapid centralization of the government. Power in all three of the kingdoms was held by those who lived in the capital and by the aristocratic families who dominated a very rigid and hereditary social status system. Members of the upper and lower classes were differentiated in almost every aspect of their lives, including clothing, food, housing, and occupation. The person one could marry was determined by his or her social class. The lifestyle of the aristocracy was supported by slaves, who led miserable lives.

In Koguryo, the rulers and the high-ranking nobility built elaborate tombs with beautiful wall paintings that provide some of the only known remains of this culture. Vivid examples of the class structure can be found in paintings in which elegantly dressed women in skirts are in conversation with upper-class men. Figures are enlarged or reduced in size according to their social status.

The bone-rank system of the Silla kingdom provides the most vivid example of the hierarchical structure of aristocratic society during the Three Kingdoms period. This was a system that granted special privileges, ranging from economic and political to social advantages in relationships, to one's bone rank, which meant hereditary bloodline. There were two levels of bone rank: holy bone and true bone. The holy-bone status related to the royal house of Kim, and those with this status could become king. Those of true-bone rank were royal family members and the highest-ranking government officials but lacked the qualifications for heading the kingdom.

There were six grades of head rank that ranged from the most prestigious position, which was six, to the lowest level, which was one. Head-rank six was just below true-bone rank and included former members of the royal family, capital-based aristocrats, and the second-highest-ranking government officials. Head-rank five included capital-based aristocrats and the third-highest-ranking government officials. Head-rank four consisted of local leaders and the fourth-highest-ranking government officials. Head-ranks three, two, and one were the commoners.

Only those with true-bone rank could head a governmental ministry or hold a high military position. Those who held head-rank four were limited to lower rungs in the governmental bureaucracy. Bone-rank privileges also related to the size of the home, the color of clothing, the use of certain utensils, and the trappings of horses.

Because warfare was constant throughout the period, it is understandable that a warrior aristocracy held considerable power in each of the Three Kingdoms. In Silla, the fortresses were commanded by men of true-bone status. Their military units were supported by the *hwarang*, young sons of the aristocrats, who followed a very strict code of conduct combining Confucian doctrines and Buddhist teachings.

Over time, the central government extended its authority over the countryside. The residents of the capital were superior to the people who lived outside the capital walls. Large grants of land and prisoners of war were awarded to commanders who had been victorious in battle. This led to the continuous increase of large estates and a slave labor force for the aristocracy. The population consisted primarily of freemen who were obligated to pay taxes and build irrigation projects and fortifications. Some of the farming continued to be on a communal basis, but most worked their own land independently. Those who lost their land fell into a lower class of landless tenant farmers.

UNIFIED SILLA (668–935 CE)

After years of conflict, Paekche and Koguryo allied with Silla against the Tang dynasty, and the three kingdoms were united in what is known as Unified Silla. One of the most significant developments was that the king could have true-bone lineage and not just holy-bone lineage. The power of the king also rose at the expense of the aristocratic families. The hierarchical nature of society did not change, but the less-privileged members of the aristocracy (head-rank six) began to ally with the monarch and subsequently increased the power of the throne and lessened the influence of those in the upper levels of the head-rank system. In spite of these changes, the majority of the aristocratic families resided in the capital at Kyongju and lived extravagantly.

In contrast to their wealth was the rapid growth of poverty among the common people and the slave population. The commoners lived in small villages and were required to perform compulsory labor service. Those who committed crimes or were prisoners of war were essentially slaves and were transported to special settlements where they performed farming tasks or manual labor. These settlements of enslaved people existed in every region and were a distinguishing feature of Silla society.

The aristocrats initially resisted the increased centralization of government and the power of the reigning monarch, but their original solidarity in opposition to the king disintegrated. Noble families organized their own military forces and fought other noble families to determine who led the kingdom. Powerful families in regions far away from the capital built fortifications around their population centers, became known as "castle lords," assembled their own private armies, and took control over the region. All this challenged the power of the central government and threatened the very existence of Unified Silla. Another force for change was the wider acceptance of Confucianism as a doctrine that would provide a moral basis for effective government. Scholars who belonged to head-rank six could not be appointed to any position of authority and began to challenge the hereditary nature of the bone-rank system. They proposed that Silla adopt the Tang dynasty's examination system whereby men of talent could advance in society.

The conditions for the peasants deteriorated further as the castle lords in addition to the central government now demanded taxes. Insurgent peasant revolts flared up throughout the country. Eventually, Wang Kon, a member of the noble class, achieved significant victories, maneuvered his way to become king in 918, and solidified his position with other aristocratic families in Kaesong, which would become the new capital.

SOCIAL CLASSES DURING THE KORYO DYNASTY (918–1392)

In order to reunify the country and appease ambitious and potentially troublesome nobles, Wang Kon treated the Silla nobility with extreme generosity and brought them into the Koryo bureaucracy, a move that continued the tradition of the aristocratic class dominating government. His son, King Kwangjong (949–975), brought reforms during his reign, including establishing the civil service examination to bring educated men into governmental service. In order to strengthen his monarchial rule, the king carried out bloody purges of officials who challenged his authority, thereby sending a clear message to the aristocracy in the capital to accept his authority.

After Kwangjong's death, Confucian scholars of Silla's head-rank system assumed considerable influence and subsequently solidified the position of the aristocracy within a system of centralized government. During Silla, the true-bone members of royal lineage had been at the center of government. Throughout Koryo, one's bloodline still mattered, but positions in government were open to more members of the aristocratic class. Most aristocrats lived in the capital at Kaesong.

The entire Koryo social structure was based on one's bloodline and relationship to the political system. Various orders were established based on heredity and occupation, such as civil official, soldier, clerical worker, and artisan. The majority of the population, the peasants and the slaves, were not eligible to hold government offices and were relegated to a life of poverty without any opportunity to move up.

Land ownership also played a major role in one's power and status. Land was allocated to governmental officials instead of a salary. The more important the position, the larger the land grant from the king. As the power of the aristocracy grew, so did their land holdings. The freeborn peasants were not eligible to receive land and were obligated to pay one-fourth of the harvest on land that belonged to the state or one-half of the yield on land that belonged to aristocrats.

The lowborn peasants were assigned to farm labor or the production of paper, pottery, and silk. At the bottom of society were the slaves, whose status was hereditary. Most worked on land in the countryside and paid rent to their masters for the land they cultivated. There was also an outcast population that consisted of butchers and entertainers, whose occupations were considered despicable, and as a result they were treated like slaves.

As certain aristocratic families gained more land and governmental positions than others, armed conflicts among the aristocratic ruling class erupted. Military officials were disgruntled because they were in an inferior social position. High-level offices in government were denied to them, and land grants that they were entitled to receive were kept from them.

As members of the military began to form their own armies to protect their interests, incessant warfare broke out. Meanwhile, landless peasants grew in numbers and began to rebel against their desperate circumstances. Insurrections erupted continuously and gave a clear signal that the very foundation of Koryo society was weak. Those at the top of the social structure, the military, and those at the bottom were all challenging the hereditary status system that had dominated the peninsula for centuries. Additional challenges for the people of Koryo came with the Mongol invasions in 1231. After years of countless deaths and destruction of vast regions of the country, Koryo agreed to make peace in 1259.

KORYO SOCIETY DURING THE YUAN DYNASTY

During the Yuan dynasty, Koryo kings were forced to take Mongol princesses as their wives, and their offspring would succeed to the throne. The king kept his title, but he was essentially powerless. The Mongols were primarily interested in acquiring wealth and demanded gold, silver, cloth, ginseng, women, and even eunuchs. These burdens had a particularly harmful impact on the peasants who had to respond to the demands of the Yuan as well as those of their own government. Although most social classes suffered under the Mongols, some Koreans collaborated with the invaders, became high-ranking officials, and assumed considerable power.

During the period of Mongol control, a new bureaucratic class appeared. These men were the literati, educated in the Confucian classics and knowledgeable about government management. Drawing from clerical positions and lower-level government, they sought to advance through the examination system on the basis of their achievement. Some of the literati owned land in rural areas and personally worked it. They detested the powerful landlords who acquired huge estates as a result of their position in society and by illegal means. The appearance of these Confucian scholars, experienced in the workings of government, would ultimately become a force for change.

The decline of the Yuan dynasty in the 14th century allowed King Kongmin (1352–1374) to restore Koryo's independence and challenge the powerful aristocrats who had collaborated with the Yuan. He sought to reform the government by conferring with the scholar-officials who, unlike the old aristocracy, passed the civil service exam and were determined to put Neo-Confucian ideology into practice. However, the powerful hereditary aristocracy rose up against the king and murdered him.

During the last quarter of a century, Koryo was plagued with many problems, particularly by the Japanese. Commander Yi Seonggye defeated the Japanese, ousted the king from power, and paved the way to bring the 474-year Koryo dynasty to an end. Yi Seonggye and his Neo-Confucian supporters immediately used their new power to carry out sweeping land reform that was supported by the newly established literati class. The literati opposed not only the powerful aristocratic families but also the Buddhist establishment for its accumulation of huge landholdings and its belief system. The large estates of the rich and powerful families were confiscated, and all land throughout the country belonged to the state. Yi Seonggye ascended the throne as King T'aejo in 1392. The king named his dynasty after ancient Choson and moved the capital to Seoul.

CHOSON DYNASTY (1392–1910)

The Early Period: 1392 to the 17th Century

The class structure during Choson was based on status with a clearly established vertical hierarchy that divided people into elites, commoners, and slaves. The state served as the preeminent institutional resource for maintaining social power. The uppermost social class of Choson was the *yangban* class, and its members served in either a civilian or military capacity. The *yangban* evolved toward the end of the Koryo dynasty and became a fixed social class. The core belief of the elite was based on Neo-Confucianism, which was a more rigorous commitment to Confucian ideals.

Elite status in Korea, unlike that in China, was hereditary. One had to prove that at least one ancestor in the previous four generations had been a *yangban*. Ancestry became the main basis of status, and the maintenance of genealogies was essential to prove and maintain status. Since this class dominated the government, economy, and culture of Choson, the society was appropriately called a *yangban* society. Members married only among themselves and served in either a civil or military capacity.

The *yangban* class was considerably larger in size than the ruling classes of Koryo. This situation increased pressure to pass the civil service exam, the principal means for gaining a position as a civil servant. Only the sons of officials of the second rank and above could serve in high office, which greatly limited the path to advancement and powerful positions. Their studies were devoted exclusively to Confucian doctrine. The *yangban* would not serve in certain positions, such as accounting, astrology, medicine, law clerkship, or government arts; these professions belonged to the middle people, the *chungin* class.

There were distinctions among members of this elite class. The literati were part of the *yangban* class and consisted of the scholars who aspired to serve in politics. Service in the military carried less prestige than civil service. Military officials were recruited on the same basis as civil officials and on their family background. Their exams would test their knowledge of the military texts, military arts, and Confucianism.

The land system of Choson was based on public and private land. It was the tradition that the king basically owned all of the land, but in actuality the state had the right to collect taxes on the land, but not ownership rights. *Yangban* who received private land grants found ways to collect the rent and obtain the right to actual land ownership. Subsequently, they were able to establish huge landed estates and collect tax revenues as Koryo aristocrats had in the past.

Peasants were restricted to the land with no freedom to move to any other location. Everyone had to wear an identification tag at all times with their name, date of birth, class, status, and county of residence. The tax levels ranged from a 10th to a 20th of the harvest, which seemed reasonable, but this did not include what a given landlord might demand from those who lived on his land.

Another class of Choson society below the free common class was a large population of lowborn people, primarily slaves. Their economic position was similar to that of tenant farmers, but their status was hereditary and they could be bought and sold like animals. It is estimated that nearly one-third of the population during the Choson dynasty was enslaved. In addition to the slaves in a lowborn status were the outcasts who were limited to such roles as butchers and tanners. There were also the *kisaeng*, female entertainers, who were often taken as concubines or secondary wives of the *yangban*, and the female shamans known as *mudang*.

By the 15th century, the majority of the *yangban* did not hold high office and resented the fact that those who held power violated Confucian principles in their pursuit of wealth at the expense of society. Their accumulation of large landed estates burdened peasant farmers with taxes to the point that many began a life of wandering and banditry. Subsequently, men steeped in the doctrines of Neo-Confucianism became involved in bloody purges to rid the government of high officials who were not upholding Confucian values.

In 1592, the Japanese invaded Korea. Whole villages were destroyed, and disease and starvation were everywhere. Forty years later, in 1637, Choson was forced to accept domination by China's newly established Qing dynasty.

LATER CHOSON DYNASTY: 1637–1910

The invasions by the Japanese and the Manchus were a turning point in Korean history and had a significant impact on society. The greatest challenge related to the serious financial problems facing the country. A land tax that liberated the peasants from their previous burdensome taxes was adopted. Because the peasants were no longer burdened by taxes, a ripple effect emerged in the economy. More capital was available for merchants, and commercial activity was stimulated. This led to the growth of artisans, who were now independent of the government. These developments combined to bring about a major transformation of the economy and society.

With the opening of Korea's ports in the late 19th century, landlords and commercial agents made fortunes in international trade and began to lay a foundation for capital investment and industrialization in the 20th century. These changes in the economy also led to the growth of the merchant class.

New developments also occurred with the *yangban* class. Many who were born into this class were unable to pass the civil service exams, acquire positions in government, or support themselves in the style associated with their elite status. On the other hand, the hereditary middle class, the *chungin*, improved their status. Some accumulated great wealth in private trading companies, and many in clerical posts in the government had dreams of improving their position so that it would be commensurate with their ability.

There were even major changes at the bottom of the social structure. The position of most peasants declined. Some became wage laborers, handcraft workers, or miners. Another development was the decline in the institution of slavery. Numbers of slaves dropped continuously throughout the 17th and 18th centuries in response to the need for more men to serve in the military. Government slaves were freed in 1801, but the institution of private slavery was not abolished until 1894.

In spite of substantial changes in the economy in the 18th and 19th centuries, the reality for the overwhelming majority of the peasants was a life of continuous poverty. In 1894, peasants rose up against the government in what is known as the Tonghak Revolution, but they were defeated. After China lost to Japan in the Sino-Japanese War the following year, Korea came under the domination of the Japanese, and a pro-Japanese reformist government was installed.

What evolved under increased Japanese control was the Kabo Reform movement that lasted from 1894 to 1895. The individuals who were involved in the movement had lived in either the United States or Japan and desired to bring economic, political, and social reforms to Korea. One of their main objectives was to end the dominant position of the *yangban*. Class distinctions between the *yangban* and the commoner ended, slavery was abolished, and those who had been considered low-born were freed from this status. These reforms were carried out at a time when the Korean people were overwhelmed by the defeat of the Tonghak armies and shocked by the brutal murder of Queen Min by the Japanese. In 1896, the Independence Club was founded in the attempt to safeguard Korea's independence and support the democratic reforms of the Kabo movement. In less than 15 years, Japan annexed Korea and ended the 518-year rule of the Choson dynasty.

JAPANESE COLONIAL RULE (1910–1945)

Japanese rule had an extraordinary impact on Korea during occupation, and the memories of this period remain vivid and painful for millions of Koreans throughout the world. Immediately after annexation, the Japanese created a powerful, intrusive state that affected every aspect of life. Although they penetrated every level of society, they did not substantially change traditional class structure. While colonialism removed the aristocratic class from political power, it sustained the class economically.

In order to gain support, the Japanese worked to ingratiate themselves with conservative ex-officials and aristocrats. Thousands of pensions were given to Choson officials of all ranks. The Japanese also adopted policies to increase the prosperity of upper-class landlords. Most landless peasants remained at subsistence level, land tenancy continued to be unstable, and rents were high.

With the advent of the world depression in the 1930s, the situation in rural Korea worsened, and peasant disputes with landlords increased. Although the Japanese generally supported policies that favored the landed class, rural unrest and the deterioration of the rural economy changed state policies. Consequently, the colonial administration promoted a series of tenant regulations to check the escalating power of the landlord class.

The Japanese also found ways to play on ingrained tensions between upper and lower classes by recruiting large numbers of lower-class Koreans to serve in the police force. It became a vast network of native informants who checked up on all levels of the population and caused rifts between rich and poor, conservatives and leftists.

Many Koreans chose to collaborate with their oppressors. An ambitious Korean had few choices because upward mobility meant working in Japanese-dominated institutions. There were those who held deeply ingrained beliefs in equating the bureaucracy with status and opted for status over loyalty to Korea.

In the 1930s and the war years, virtually everyone was forced in some way to participate in the system. Some of the landed elite transferred their wealth into commerce and industry and would pave the way for full-scale industrialization after 1945. For example, the founders of Hyundai and Samsung started their business careers during occupation.

In the final years of occupation and World War II, thousands of Korean men were forced into the military. Women, possibly as many as 200,000, were forced to become comfort women and served as sex slaves to Japanese troops. Shortages of food made life unbearable. In the final year of the war, all classes of society looked for relief from their circumstances and the arrival of a new age.

DIVISION AND THE KOREAN WAR (1945–1953)

The joy experienced with liberation and the conclusion of World War II was short-lived. The war's end brought the division of the country and continued conflicts relating to class, ideology, and politics. Eighty percent of the population consisted of tenants and landlords. The other 20 percent included capitalists, white-collar professionals, factory workers, and thousands of landless peasants who had been relocated from their villages as a result of wartime mobilization and now were returning home. Colonialism had created nationalists, collaborators, communists, heightened class conflicts, and disputes within all groups. The liberals were a diverse group: students, intellectuals, peasants, and factory workers. Some were communists; all supported redistribution of wealth, help for the poor, and the removal of all collaborators from positions of power. The conservatives were essentially upper-class, educated, owners of property, unreceptive to land reform, and wanted to maintain their position of privilege in society. Many of them had collaborated with the Japanese during occupation.

Soviet and U.S. security interests immediately influenced policy during occupation between 1945 and 1948. The U.S. authorities distrusted the Soviet Union, feared communism, and supported conservatives. With virtually no understanding of the experience of the Korean people under Japanese occupation, General John R.

Hodge, commander of the U.S. occupation forces, appointed Korean police chiefs who had collaborated with the Japanese to new positions in the military government. The Americans trusted upper-class Koreans because they were propertied, educated, English-speaking, and anticommunist. The policies that developed supported the political right.

While the American authorities reduced tenancy rates from one-half to one-third of the crop, it was only in the last month of occupation that any reforms were adopted. The measures that were adopted related to rental property formerly controlled by the Japanese and were approximately 20 percent of the total. The Americans viewed labor unions and strikes as being supported by communists and used rightist-controlled police to deprive Korean workers of basic rights that were guaranteed under the law in the United States.

The Soviet approach was the complete upheaval of the political structure of Japanese occupation and the social structure that had existed for centuries on the peninsula. Collaborators were removed from office, and land reform ended the system of landed wealth that had persisted for most of Korean history. All land that had belonged to the Japanese was confiscated, and the large landholders lost most of their holdings. Landlords who did not collaborate with the Japanese could own and work on approximately 12 acres of land. Major industries were nationalized. An eight-hour workday was established along with equal pay for equal work regardless of sex.

The Korean War (1950–1953) resolved nothing, killed at least 3 million Koreans, and destroyed most of the peninsula. It also contributed to a significant alteration of the hierarchical class structure that had existed for thousands of years.

SOUTH KOREA (1953–PRESENT)

In South Korea, land reform finally began to be carried out in the postwar period. Nevertheless, many landowners anticipated land reform and sold their property before any measures were enacted. Those who lost their property were usually well educated and had personal connections that assisted them in maintaining their position in society. Between 1945 and 1960, the population of the cities grew by 30 percent. Most of this growth was the result of the migration of rural people to urban areas for factory work. Ironically, a significant proportion of the owners of these factories were former landlords who had made the transition to owning businesses or becoming professionals. A study in 1976 concluded that the vast majority of the country's business leaders came from the former landed elite.

Since the end of the Korean War, rapid economic growth, industrialization, and urbanization was the result of foreign capital, probusiness governmental policies, the high level of literacy, a strong work ethic, and low wages. These developments caused a radical change in the class structure of Korean society. Social classes of traditional society have essentially disappeared, and more opportunities exist for social mobility.

One of the most significant changes is the formation of a new middle class consisting of civil servants, salaried white-collar workers, and professionals with specialized training, such as architects, engineers, journalists, and university professors. Between

1960 and 1980, the new middle class (excluding self-employed professionals) grew from 6.6 percent to 17.7 percent. During the same period of time, the old middle class consisting of shopkeepers, small business owners, self-employed professionals, and craftsmen grew slightly from 13 percent to 20.8 percent of the population; as one study noted, the existence of a new upper middle class consisting of South Korea's economic and social elites increased from 0.9 percent to 1.8 percent of the population. The proportion of industrial workers expanded from 8.9 percent to 22.6 percent of the labor force during the same period. Landowning farmers, members of the rural lower class, and agricultural laborers declined in numbers; they were 64 percent of the population in 1960, 31.3 percent in 1980, and approximately 25 percent in the 1990s (Savada and Shaw, 1990).

Ancestry no longer provides a basis for claiming high status; however, South Koreans continue to be very conscious of class distinctions, and many are determined to join the elite. This pursuit of status on the part of South Korean families has become a distinct feature of a new urban class.

Family or bureaucratic background still matters, but numerous other factors are significant, such as one's marital partner, region, university, and occupation. Conspicuous displays of wealth have grown in importance. Certain boundaries between the upper and middle classes have become less distinct in recent years; however, similar to Choson society, there are greater differentiations between the middle class and the poor. Many members of the upper and middle classes are contemptuous of those who do blue-collar work, and they refuse to associate with them on equal terms. Social classes have changed in modern-day Korea, but attitudes about the lower class have not in some cases. Values have also changed from traditional restraint; after 30 years of government proclamations to save, be frugal, and work hard for the cause of national development, South Korea has become a consumer society.

South Koreans have revived interest in keeping genealogies and in performing ancestor worship, acts customarily associated with privileged status. Families with commoner background have also published genealogies to substantiate that they too come from a good family background, signifying the importance that social class and the *yangban* heritage have in defining status even in the 21st century. Seeking leadership roles in Christian churches rather than participating in ancestor worship has become an alternate approach of asserting status for many Christians in South Korea.

Manual labor is unthinkable for members of the new middle class. Businesses that require manual labor from their owners are generally considered lower class. If companies have a large volume of business and support a middle-class lifestyle, they are considered middle class. Although the merchant class was held in contempt during most of Korean history, attitudes toward commerce have changed to fit the requirements of a modern capitalist economy.

Except for high-level government positions, the civil service and teaching positions that had once been reserved for the *yangban* class would now be considered middle class. Careers in government and academia have maintained the same level of prestige as in the past. Whether a white-collar worker is middle or upper middle class depends on such variables as the size and prestige of the company. For government employees and corporate-salaried men, status is often based on age and advancement up the career ladder. What also differentiates the middle and upper classes is the function of power. Therefore, individuals who have positions of power in government, the military, and large business conglomerates have greater status than the average governmental workers, business owners, or salaried people.

Women's work also relates to social standing. Lower-class women hold positions in factories or low-level jobs in the service sector. Many college-educated women do secretarial work before they marry, but opportunities for prestigious positions remain limited. The majority of women in middle- and upper-class families are not employed but are expected to bring prestige through their contacts and activities, such as visiting their child's teacher at school, arranging for private tutors, purchasing expensive consumer goods, attending neighborhood meetings, and participating in volunteer work.

During the Choson dynasty, mastery of the Confucian classics and passing the civil service exam were the determining factors in achieving high status. Now, mastery of English and passing the university entrance exam (especially for the most prestigious universities) pave the way for social mobility and high status. The pursuit of education is not necessarily to acquire knowledge, but sometimes to acquire status. The source of one's diploma more or less determines one's eligibility for the best occupations or employers in a manner quite similar to the relationship between birth and bureaucratic eligibility in the Choson dynasty.

As in the past, finding a suitable marriage partner is an important consideration for maintaining or improving social standing. In Choson, there were certain lineages at the very top of the social structure who married only among themselves. Today, this is also evident, with *chaebol* family members marrying other *chaebol* family members, and the same for the government elite. For the middle and upper classes in South Korea today, one's choice of spouse is an essential determinant of status. Members of the middle and upper classes still use matchmakers to find the right marital partner; however, today's young couples usually make their own decisions.

In spite of greater opportunities for upward mobility, some authorities believe that much of the character of social stratification has held constant. Many have obviously found themselves in new situations and with a higher standard of living as a result of a college education, industrialization, technological innovation, and the diversity of occupations. Another way of viewing contemporary Korean society is to consider the sources of social inequality and the limitations imposed on upward mobility. The inequality of people's chances for social mobility has changed very little, especially for women and for people who live in rural areas. In spite of land reform, tenancy has grown. Education remains the single most important factor affecting social mobility since the 1990s.

With the exception of the military, the postwar elites share one characteristic: they are graduates of the most prestigious universities. Ties with college classmates are increasingly necessary for advancement in a highly competitive society. At the bottom of the educational pyramid are the low-prestige colleges whose graduates have little chance of becoming members of the elite, yet graduation from even these institutions offers the possibility of middle-class status. For those who are unable to attend a college, social mobility is virtually impossible, and this situation has widened the gap between the income of the middle and lower classes.

The Asian financial crisis in 1997 fundamentally transformed the middle class in South Korea. During Roh Moo-Hyun's administration (2003–2008), the middle class was reported to have contracted by 10–15 percent (Song 2004, 32). Job prospects for the middle class remain unpredictable. Many of those who were among the ranks of the lower middle class have since plummeted into the lower class, with reports of people now below the poverty line. In spite of the fact that there are limits to social mobility, the desire for acquiring status leads many to hope that if they work hard enough, they will achieve it. The transformation of the class structure from being fixed according to one's ancestry to greater fluidity has contributed to the dream that status and power are attainable.

What is also new on the peninsula is the growing number of migrant workers in South Korea. As of October 2005, the total number of resident foreign nationals stood at 711,869 (Kim and the *Korean Herald* 2008, 108). They began to arrive in the 1980s to fill the jobs of the small and medium-sized companies suffering labor shortages. Another development has occurred in rural areas. Because women prefer to live in urban areas, many rural men are now marrying women primarily from Southeast Asia. However, the general public perception and current social system are not yet adjusted to living in harmony with non-Koreans. Young children of mixed race currently suffer from discrimination and feel isolated in school. The perception of ethnic purity is so strongly embedded that people make little effort to help foreigners integrate into the society. Government has yet to prepare policies to deal effectively with the presence of growing numbers of minorities in South Korea. According to a United Nations research report, Korea will have to receive 11 million foreign workers by 2050 in order to meet labor demands; the proportion of immigrants and their descendants will rise to 21.3 percent of the population by that year (Cho 2006).

Gi-Wook Shin, in *Ethnic Nationalism in Korea*, stated that "Koreans need an institutional framework to promote a democratic national identity that would allow for more diversity and flexibility among the populace." He urged Koreans to become more tolerant of diversity and to build democratic institutions that treat people as equal citizens. He concluded by stating that this task will be all the more important and urgent as "Korea becomes more democratic, globalizes, and also prepares for national unification" (2006, 235).

NORTH KOREA (1953–PRESENT)

When the Korean War finally ended on July 27, 1953, the North had been devastated by more than two years of American bombing. Approximately 80 percent of its productive capacity and all its major cities lay in ruins. In spite of the destruction, the North rebuilt its economy with surprising speed.

After the Korean War, Kim Il-Sung directed the rebuilding of the economy following the Soviet socialist model with an emphasis on building heavy industry. His vision of a nation was a combination of a Confucian kingdom and a 20th-century

Children of Kaesong, North Korea. (Courtesy of Marsh Wong)

totalitarian socialist state. Kim drew on Confucian traditions in implementing a strict hierarchical social order with the masses at the bottom, a small number of elite who were now party cadres instead of *yangban*, and himself at the top as the virtuous leader who rules with the Mandate of Heaven. In ways similar to Choson, only the sons and daughters of the ruling class can become the elite. He also incorporated the Confucian concept that he is the father of the nation and that his people are one large homogeneous family connected to him by the same bloodline. Kim even called himself the present-day Tan'gun, after the founder of old choson.

The traditional class structure that existed in Korea for centuries was dismantled in the name of socialism. Landowners, farmers, businessmen, and intellectual classes were ousted from their positions in society. To prevent the revival of the traditional class structure, everyone was investigated, classified, and watched. People were categorized according to their loyalty to the Kim regime and family background.

Based on loyalty, three groups have been identified: the core class, the wavering class, and the hostile class. Among the 12 subgroups in the core class are those who were workers, poor farmers, office clerks, and soldiers prior to 1945. Some examples of those who qualified to be in the core class were those who were anti-Japanese, laborers, and individuals who lost family members during the Korean

War. Current members of the Korean Workers' Party are also included in this category. Every member of the core group receives priority in promotions, housing, food, medical service, and special privileges (Oh and Hassing 2000, 133–135).

The elite population of the core class consists of several thousand high-ranking party, government, and military officials in P'yongyang who live a more affluent lifestyle than that of their fellow countrymen. They have access to foreign information, and some have the opportunity to travel outside the country for their official work. Most have the privilege of living in the capital as members of the elite have done for centuries.

The members of the wavering class are those who can be won over by political education. Their families were either merchants, farmers, or service workers prior to 1945. Included in this group are families who came from South Korea as well as those who have relatives who left North Korea for South Korea. This class is divided into 18 subgroups. Some examples are former street vendors, craftsmen, and those who stayed in North Korea when members of their family fled to South Korea. Most of the members can live a fairly typical life for a North Korean and have aspirations that they might advance to a certain degree in their assigned occupation. Few ever have the opportunity to attend the best schools or rise in the party or governmental hierarchy.

It is estimated that between 20 and 25 percent of the population belongs to the hostile class. It includes those who have actually or allegedly criticized the Kim regime or whose families prior to liberation were wealthy landlords, merchants, or prominent members of religious organizations. Those in this category have virtually no opportunity for social or political advancement. Subgroups in this category include individuals who collaborated with the Japanese and Protestants, Buddhists, Catholics, and Confucian scholars.

The members of the hostile class are analogous to the lowborn or outcasts in traditional Korea. They live very difficult lives, are assigned to the least desirable jobs, and live in the poorest housing, often in remote rural areas where they receive few government rations and have no hopes for betterment in the future. They cannot live in P'yongyang, enter good schools, join the Korean Workers' Party, or advance in their occupations. Further down the ladder are the estimated 200,000 Koreans who live in squalor in concentration camps.

Some recent accounts report that a middle class is evolving along with a market economy. According to these reports, the middle class consists of people who own medium-sized businesses or are engaged in wholesale trade. As a result of the grave food shortages of the 1990s, cracks in the socialist system appeared that allowed for individuals to rely on the black market in order to survive. Based on observations of recent travelers to North Korea, the state apparatus remains firmly entrenched, and emerging markets pose no real or effective challenge to the state.

No government in recent years has been as successful as the Kim government in exercising so much control over its people. More than a half-century of propaganda and social control has shaped the attitudes, values, and behavior of all classes. In spite of dire poverty, the success of Kim Il-Sung and Kim Jong-Il at exerting total control has created a society that on the surface is as remarkably stable as the

Housing for people in Kaesong, North Korea. (Courtesy of Marsh Wong)

Koryo and Choson dynasties were in the past. Kim Il-Sung is still venerated and worshipped as the country's "Eternal President," a modern extension of ancient ancestral worship.

CONCLUSION

Clearly, the two Koreas occupy very different positions in the world community in the 21st century. South Korea stands as an evolving democratic nation with an increasingly sophisticated postindustrial economy and is a major participant in the global economy. On the other hand, North Korea remains an impoverished totalitarian state that is diplomatically and economically isolated from the world community.

The possibility for reunification of the Koreas appears to be one of the great challenges of the era. Leaders of both North and South Korea have expressed a deep-rooted sense of ethnic national identity and unity shared by their long history and ancestry. A survey in the fall of 2000 in South Korea revealed that 93 percent of the respondents reported that their nation has a single bloodline, and 95 percent agreed that the North Korean people are of the same ethnic group (Shin 2006, 3). North Korean minders enthusiastically explain to visitors Kim Il-Sung's "Three Charters for National Unification," which emphasizes the importance of mutual understanding and trust between members of the same family. Ultimately, one of the great forces for unification will be the strong sense of unity of the Korean people based on a common bloodline and ancestry for thousands of years.

REFERENCES

Abelman, Nancy. 2005. *The Melodrama of Mobility: Women, Talk and Class in Contemporary South Korea.* Honolulu: University of Hawai'i Press.

Breen, Michael. 1998. *The Koreans: Who They Are, What They Want, Where Their Future Lies.* New York: St. Martin's Press.

Bunge, Frederica M., ed. 1981. *North Korea: A Country Study*. Washington, DC: The American University.

Cho, Joon-mo. 2006. "Foreign Workers Policy Requires Harmony of Humanitarianism and National Interests." *Korea Focus* 14, no. 3 (Autumn): 50–51.

Chun, Shin-yong. 1982. *Upper-Class Culture in Yi-Dynasty Korea*. Seoul, Korea: Sis-sa-yong-o-sa Publishers, Inc.

Cumings, Bruce. 1997. *Korea's Place in the Sun: A Modern History*. New York: W. W. Norton and Co.

Eckert, Carter, et al. 2006. *Korea Old and New: A History*. Seoul, Korea: Ilchokak Publishers, 1990.

"From Racial Purity to Ethnic Diversity," editorial, *JoongAng Ilbo*, February 10, 2006, in *Korea Focus* 1 (Spring): 40.

Hwang, Moon Kyung. 2004. *Beyond Birth: Social Status in the Emergence of Modern Korea*. Cambridge, MA: Harvard University Asia Center.

Joe, Wanne J. 2000. *A Cultural History of Modern Korea*. Elizabeth, NJ: Hollym.

Kim, Kyong-dong, and the *Korea Herald*, eds. 2008. *Social Change in Korea*. Vol. I. Seoul, Korea: Jimoondang Publishers.

Lee, Hyun-hee, ed. 2005. *New History of Korea*. Seoul, Korea: Jimoondang Publishers.

Lee, Kwang-kyu. 2003. *Korean Traditional Culture*. Seoul, Korea: Jimoondang Publishers.

Lett, Denise Potrzeba. 1998. *In Pursuit of Status: The Making of South Korea's "New" Urban Middle Class*. Cambridge, MA: Harvard University Asia Center.

Lewis, James, and Amadu Sesay, eds. 2002. *Korea and Globalization: Politics, Economics, and Culture*. New York: RoutledgeCurzon.

Savada, Andrea Matles, and William Shaw, eds. 1990. "Social Classes in Contemporary South Korea." Library of Congress Country Studies. http://lcweb2.loc.gov/cgi-bin/query/r?frd/cstdy:@field(DOCID+kr0065) (accessed October 7, 2007).

Oberdorfer, Don. 1997. *The Two Koreas: A Contemporary History*. Reading, MA: Addison-Wesley.

Oh, Kongdon, and Ralph C. Hassig. 2000. *North Korea through the Looking Glass*. Washington, DC: Brookings Institution Press.

Robinson, Michael E. 2007. *Korea's Twentieth-Century Odyssey: A Short History*. Honolulu: University of Hawai'i Press.

Shin, Gi-Wook. 2006. *Ethnic Nationalism in Korea: Genealogy, Politics, and Legacy*. Stanford, CA: Stanford University Press.

———. 1996. *Peasant Protest & Social Change in Colonial Korea*. Seattle: University of Washington.

Song, Ho-Keun. 2004. "The Collapse of Korea's Middle Class." *Korea Focus* 12, no. 1: 31–34.

Suh, Jae-Jean. 2005. "The Transformation of Class Structure and Class Conflict in North Korea." *International Journal of Korean Unification Studies* 14, no. 2: 52–84.

Zook, Darren. 2007. "North Korea between Hope and Despair: Ideology, Rhetoric, and Reality in the Juche State." Center for Korean Studies, University of California at Berkeley. http://ieas.berkeley.edu/events/2007.11.02a.html (accessed October 31, 2007).

Women and Marriage

Mary E. Connor

THE THREE KINGDOMS (57 BCE–668 CE)

Although it is difficult to know precisely what the prescribed norms were for women in ancient times, early records from the period of the Three Kingdoms indicate that women of all classes had considerable freedom. Chinese chroniclers noted that men and women of the Koguryo kingdom (37 BCE–668 CE) would sing and dance together well into the night. There was also some freedom of choice in marriage. If a man and a woman liked each other and people approved, they could marry. Until the seventh century, women of the Silla kingdom (57 BCE–935 CE) also had considerable freedom and were allowed to travel on their own. Female Shamans acted as ritual leaders, participated in public life, and merited great authority and respect.

From the time Buddhism entered the peninsula in the fourth century, women enjoyed relatively equal opportunities with men in religious practices. Many shaved their heads and became nuns, and others made donations for temple construction or provided the physical labor to help build them.

Women rose in Silla, and three became queens. Queen Sondak (reigned 632–647) became one of the most influential monarchs in all of Korean history. She paved the way for the unification of the peninsula, improved conditions for her people, and supported cultural advancement. When touring the ancient capital of Silla (Kyongju) and its environs, one can still witness the cultural legacy of this remarkable woman.

The Silla queens assumed their role as monarchs because of the "bone-rank" (bloodline) system. Only those who belonged to this system were eligible to sit on the throne. Sondak was selected to be queen because the male line had simply died out. No record indicates that there were any objections to being ruled by a woman. Gender did not matter, but bone rank did. Although Confucian beliefs were well established by the fourth century, they did not yet convey the idea of inequality between men and women. Queen mothers could also exert enormous political power when acting as regents for the young royal offspring.

In spite of the significant role some women played in public life, they were the exception to the rule. As Buddhism became associated with state affairs, the role of women became more limited. Because Shamans could make ominous predictions that would upset the reigning monarch, they could find themselves in big trouble and under state control. By the 14th century, their power and influence was curtailed significantly.

In Silla society, the matrilineal system existed side by side with the patrilineal system until the unification of the peninsula. As a result, the women had more legal rights (such as property inheritance) and relatively high social status compared to

QUEEN SONDAK (REIGNED 632–647)

Queen Sondak was one of the most influential queens in Korean history. In a period of more than 1,000 years, only two other queens achieved as much authority and influence. Known as a kind, respectful, wise, and farsighted leader, she ruled at a time when there was intense rivalry between Silla and the kingdoms of Koguryo and Paekche. By initiating a policy with Tang China, the queen paved the way for the eventual unification of Korea. She concerned herself not only with the defense and security of Silla and her throne but also with improving the conditions of her people and supporting cultural advancement. The famed Buddhist temple of Hwangnyongsa (a nine-story wooden pagoda) and Ch'omsongdae (one of the oldest astronomical observatories in the world) were built under her direction.

their counterparts in Koguryo. Equal importance was given to the mother's rank as to the father's in determining the status of the child. Royal succession during this period was limited to the holy-bone level that included the king's sons, daughters, brothers, and sons-in-law. A holy-bone–ranked woman therefore could assume the throne.

The importance of the maternal lines also affected the lives of commoners. A widow could be recognized as the head of a family. However, if she was still married, her husband was dominant. The inability to produce a son was not yet a valid basis for divorce. In matters of property inheritance and family succession, the women of Silla had more rights than women in Koguryo or Paekche.

Because status was determined by bloodline and family background, a marriage that was not approved was unacceptable. Most marriages were therefore arranged according to ritual and social considerations rather than on the desires of the couple. Records indicate that parents had the right to select the marriage partner and approve or disapprove of the marriage. Free marriages took place more frequently among commoners than with the nobility.

Numerous customs determined the matchmaking process. Marriage was an alliance with a woman's family line as well as a union between a man and a woman. For the most part, royal family marriages in Koguryo were a means of joining two tribes in allegiance, whereas in Silla it was meant to consolidate power into a single clan. There it was considered essential that the bone-rank system be maintained. Marriage outside of one's clan was quite rare.

It was the custom in Koguryo for the bride to stay with her family, while the groom visited her each night with parental consent. The newly wedded couple would live in a home built on the bride's parents' property until the wife bore a son and the husband matured. After this, she left her family and lived with her husband's clan. This custom of staying at the wife's family home for a certain length of time continued through the Choson dynasty.

In poor families, a girl would be taken to the home of the bridegroom until she was old enough to be married. After that, she was sent back to her parents and stayed there until the groom paid a "bride price" to get her back. This custom was not common but helpful for poor girls who found it difficult to marry.

Until the end of the Three Kingdoms period, a wife was the full partner of her husband. After their deaths, the burial ground was to hold the couple as one unit. The women of Silla essentially had more rights than the women of the two other kingdoms on the peninsula. In fact, the women of Silla possessed more rights and privileges than women were to ever hold again in Korea until the 20th century.

UNIFIED SILLA (668–935 CE)

With unification of the Three Kingdoms, rulers needed to firmly establish control over a vast territory and to solidify their power through the orderly succession of the royal line by a legitimate son. The hereditary succession of the royal line became so important that the king could even divorce the queen if she did not give birth to a son. The position of women within the family also began to deteriorate.

Although Confucianism entered the peninsula from China during the Three Kingdoms period, its values penetrated more deeply into the social and political fabric of Unified Silla. The position of men in the household was strengthened, and adjustments came about in the bone-rank system. Although Buddhism became the religion of Unified Silla, Confucianism still prevailed as the state philosophy. The Confucian doctrine of male dominance and female subservience provided the stimulus for social change regarding the norms for women. The conduct of upper-class women was established by what is known as the three obediences: obedience to the father in childhood, to the husband during marriage, and to the son in old age.

There were also changes in marriage customs in Unified Silla. With the collapse of the exclusive bone-rank system at the end of the Silla period, marriage as a means of elevating one's status became prevalent, and the wedding ceremony became more elaborate.

KORYO (918–1392)

In 918, Wang Kon overthrew Silla and became the founder of a new dynasty. The new king honored the deposed Silla monarch by awarding him with the highest post in his new government and selected a Silla woman to be his wife. In order to win over rival factions and consolidate his position, Wang Kon took 29 wives. Members of his family married their daughters to important landlords for the same purpose.

Women had almost equal rights with men in terms of inheritance regardless of whether they were single or married, and they could inherit property from their husbands or sons. Although women had property rights, the rules governing husband-wife relations were very rigid. From the age of seven, boys and girls were never to sit or play together, a custom that paved the way for their separate roles later in life.

There were definite rules relating to marriage. A woman could not marry someone with the same family name or a blood relative, and she had to marry a person from the same class. Laws forbade marriage during the mourning period for a parent or a spouse. The rule most violated was marriage between blood relations.

The bride's side of the family had the principal responsibility of financing the wedding. The bride was expected to bring household supplies and her wardrobe to her husband's home. A wedding usually was a great financial burden for a poor family. As a result, some fathers sent their daughters to the nunnery. Many poor women died single because they simply could not afford to marry. It was essential that a woman remain chaste. If her husband died, she was expected to be celibate for the rest of her life. Chastity was considered one of the most important virtues for a woman.

While men dominated public life, a woman was in charge of the family. She was responsible for managing the family finances and had the primary duty of educating the children. Mothers gave their daughters lessons in cooking, sewing, home management, and good manners. Women could be officially honored for their roles as mothers if a son passed the highly competitive civil service examinations. They also were permitted to participate in rituals relating to ancestor worship.

A *yangban* (upper-class) woman was confined to the domestic sphere. Within the realm of the home, she had some authority, but participating in the public sphere was out of the question. The only way she could be acknowledged was as the wife of a prominent man or the mother of a successful son. Her essential virtues were filial piety and fidelity. A woman could be severely punished for committing adultery or being jealous. If a woman committed either of these offenses, her name would be registered and none of her sons could receive a position in government.

Men could obtain a divorce if they had their parents' consent or for any of the "seven evils" spelled out in Confucian teachings, but women could not initiate a divorce under any circumstances. Confucian teachings included seven conditions for divorce: disobeying parents-in-law, bearing no son, committing adultery, jealousy, carrying a hereditary disease, larceny, or loquaciousness. A woman's principal role was to have children and to produce at least one son. It was common for men of means to have several wives who were all hoping to have sons. The women in the household were never to express any jealousy of each other.

The majority of women were commoners or lowborn. They were the backbone of the economy but lived in poverty and without status. Educational opportunities were limited. Their lives were spent in agricultural labor and caring for children, husband, and parents. Commoner and lowborn women probably had more equality with men than did upper-class women.

CHOSON DYNASTY (1392–1910)

In 1392, Yi Seonggye came to the throne and established a dynasty that was to last for the next 518 years. As the leader of this new dynasty, Yi Seonggye and his supporters planned to restore morality to Korean society through the rigorous application of Confucian beliefs (Neo-Confucianism). Over the course of the Choson dynasty, these updated Confucian values shaped family and society, particularly the lives of women, in profound ways. Such traditional Confucian values as social stability, filial piety, good government, and the importance of education were sustained, but the particular emphasis on restoring morality contributed significantly to the decline of women's position in society.

Early Choson officials, influenced by Confucian ideals, were dismayed by the lack of morality. As a result, regulations were established whereby women were to remain secluded in their homes. All women, regardless of their class, had to veil their faces when outside their homes. They were to be seen only by close relatives. All were instructed to achieve Confucian virtues and to be subservient to men. Women's subordination to men was to be a moral law similar to the relationship between subject and ruler. They were to be educated not as intellectuals with independent thoughts of their own, but to know how to manage their homes, be self-disciplined, be courteous to their husband's family, and rear and educate their children.

Women were not addressed by their own names. They were identified by their position in relationship to a man, such as the wife of Younghi or the mother of Byung Hyo. In her family registry, only the name of the son-in-law or husband was recorded. Her name never appeared. Only the paternal-line relatives were regarded as relatives. A wife could not carry on the family line nor perform the worship ceremonies even for her own ancestors. The sole authority in the family resided with the father, who had control over the children. Firstborn males held the right to lineal succession.

The persons who had the right to arrange marriages were, first, the grandparents and parents and, second, the uncles, aunts, older brothers or sisters, and maternal grandparents. Marriages could not be arranged between members of the same clan or between blood relatives. If individuals violated these rules, they could be beheaded or hanged. Marriage while people were in mourning or between people of different social classes was also prohibited. Marriages were prevented between commoners and the lowest level of society, the *ch'onmin*.

A woman was to remain chaste before marriage, after widowhood, and even during war. The Japanese Imjin War in the 16th century and the Manchu invasion of the early 17th century caused women miserable hardships. Many were assaulted and raped by Japanese soldiers or transported off to Manchuria. When faced with such horrors, some women chose suicide over submission because society would blame them for being raped.

The legal age for marriage was 14 for girls and 15 for boys. In practice, even younger children were married. On the day of the wedding ceremony, the bride and groom met for the first time in the bride's home. After the exchange of formal bows, they retired to separate parts of the house. The women went to their section of the house, and the men gathered together and celebrated the occasion. After the ceremony, the bride and groom went to the bridal chamber. As a result of an ancient custom, the female relatives peeped into the room through holes torn in the paper doors. Both the bride and groom had to be utterly quiet the first night of married life together. If she made any noise whatsoever, she became the object of teasing for those who stayed near the bridal room door. The day after the marriage, the groom's relatives and friends came to the bride's home to celebrate. Because weddings were costly, many young girls never married.

The wife belonged in the home, which had separate quarters for the men and the women. It was improper for males as well as females to enter one another's section except by invitation of the master of the house. A husband and wife had basically a

---

SIN SAIMDANG (1504–1551)

One of the most famous and respected women of Korean history, Sin Saimdang is admired for being the ideal mother, wife, and daughter. She was also a respected painter, embroiderer, and poet. Her son, Yi I (Yulgok), is one of the most celebrated Confucian scholars.

---

separate existence most of the time, even in the home. If a family was poor, there still were separate quarters in their thatched cottages for men and women. Out of necessity, commoner women could move about more freely outside their home because most were farm laborers.

By tradition, *yangban* men had several wives. Their widows were prohibited from remarrying. As a result, some young widows committed suicide rather than live life alone. These measures were originally established for the aristocracy, but the Confucian norms gradually permeated the entire society. The shame attached to remarriage was so prevalent that not only the woman suffered from such an act, but also the entire family was subjected to legal and social constraints. Consequently, few divorced.

Preference for male children was most evident in the laws for adoption. Each family had to have at least one son. If the family had none, a child had to be adopted from among the male children of the same clan. A son that was not a blood relative was rarely adopted. In spite of many restrictions, a woman still had the right to inherit her father's property. Inheritance laws were apparently separate from the rights of ancestor worship ceremonies or family-line succession. Husband and wife had joint ownership of their personal property. Because in reality all the power in the family belonged to the male, a woman seldom exercised her right of joint ownership. For example, her dowry was supposed to go back to her father after her death; however, the husband still had control over it.

Neo-Confucianism obviously had a tremendous impact on society. It may be assumed that not all women adhered strictly to its precepts and that personality, social status, and economic circumstances often came into play. Nevertheless, the legacy of Confucianism lived on and continued to have an impact throughout the 20th century and to the present day.

THE OPENING OF KOREA AND JAPANESE OCCUPATION (LATE 19TH CENTURY–1945)

The beginnings of formal education for women can be traced to the late 19th and early 20th centuries. After increased contact with Western nations and Japan, the government of Korea sent missions to Japan and the United States to learn about economic development, political modernization, educational reform, and social equality. At the turn of the century, some leaders began to speak of the importance of educating women, who were, after all, half of the population. To most Koreans,

YU KWANSUN (1904–1920)

Considered by many to be Korea's Joan of Arc, Yu Kwansun at the age of 16 became one of the most famous independence fighters. After she helped plan the March 1, 1919, demonstration against Japanese occupation, she continued to organize protests, was arrested and tortured, and died along with an estimated 7,500 Koreans who participated in demonstrations that swept the country. Since her death, she has become an important symbol of the patriotic spirit of Korean youth. In her lifetime, she represented something that was new, but common now: the participation of women in political activism.

however, schooling for women threatened both traditional Confucian views of women and the patriarchal social order.

Protestant missionaries not only tried to convert the people to Christianity but also supported the establishment of hospitals, schools, and churches. Korea's first school for women, the Ewha Girls School, was established in 1886 by American missionaries. Young women not only learned to read and write at Ewha but were also introduced to the concepts of political, religious, and personal freedom. In 1894, the government, as part of the Kabo Reforms, abolished the traditional class system, allowed widows to remarry, and modernized the government's examination system. The Independence Club, founded in 1898, announced its support of women's education. The club stressed equal opportunity for women and conveyed the notion that they were equal to men.

In 1910, Korea was annexed by Japan. Under Japanese rule, children were indoctrinated to become subjects of the empire. The Korean people realized that education was a way to modernize and ultimately free the nation from foreign domination. Consequently, more schools for girls were opened, and girls were encouraged to attend them; however, education was basically limited to the primary level. The Japanese approach to the education of girls was designed to create the "good wife," the "good mother," and obedience to her superiors. In spite of the fact that their education was limited compared to boys, the formal education of women had finally begun.

Christianity served to awaken nationalism among Koreans and contributed to the rise of organized resistance to colonization. Women took part in the independence movement with as much determination as did the men. Many were wounded, killed, or imprisoned. One of the most famous was Yu Kwansun, who was arrested for her involvement in the resistance movement. After a long period of torture and suffering, she died at age 16 in 1920.

A particularly shameful and tragic development during Japanese occupation and World War II was the creation of the so-called Comfort Corps, made up of young Korean women who were sent to the front to service the sexual needs of the Japanese troops. Perhaps as many as 200,000 women were forced into sexual slavery by the Japanese military between the early 1930s and 1945. Many of the women who survived this period were unable to bear children and never married. Only since the 1990s have some of the surviving comfort women overcome traditional taboos of chastity, defilement, and shame to speak out for the first time about their wartime experiences.

SOUTH KOREA (1945–PRESENT)

The Korean War (1950–1953) wrought devastation throughout the peninsula by displacing impoverished people and killing millions. More than 55 years after the armistice, approximately 10 million families remain separated from one another as a result of the political division of the country. This period also included rapid economic recovery, major industrialization, technological advancement, urbanization, democratization, and Western influences that have greatly affected family life, especially for women. Since 1948, the role of women in Korean society has continuously evolved and expanded to include the right to vote, hold political office, inherit property, and achieve fair employment. A woman today is better educated and more able to participate in all activities. But owing to enduring traditions, most women continue to suffer from inequality within the family, the workplace, the political sphere, and their sexual relations. The ethical basis for the restrictions on women remains rooted in Confucian traditions.

The pattern of family life in Korea, at least in appearance, has followed that of Western countries. The size of families has steadily declined from an average of 6.8 members in 1960 to 3.3 in 1995 (Connor 2002, 168). Most women today believe that two children are enough, and almost one-half of married women of childbearing age have said that they are not opposed to being childless. By 2006, South Korea's birthrate was 1.08, one of the lowest rates in the world (Cazzaniga 2006).

In the past, three generations lived under one roof. Now the pattern of family life has become more diverse: single-person households, single-parent households, and elderly couples living alone. Women are marrying later. Contemporary weddings are more elaborate and expensive in terms of gift exchanges and social display. Structural changes in families affect both roles and expectations. Since many married women work, they want their husbands to assume a greater share of the household responsibilities.

Men spend much of their time outside the home because society and employers expect them to work long hours. This obliges women to handle in a traditional way most of the family obligations, such as housekeeping, child rearing, and maintaining relations with their parents-in-law. However, women now desire greater warmth, kindness, and understanding from their spouse than were expected in the past. They want more assistance from their husbands in raising children and with household tasks. Men are helping more and are emotionally closer to their wives, but statistics indicate that women continue to perform most of the work in the home.

The overwhelming majority of married women who work outside the home support the idea of their freedom to make decisions. However, the gender divisions and attitudes from the past persist in modern families. A professional woman of high status still must subject herself in private to the ancient limits that define her as her father's daughter, her husband's wife, and her son's mother. While some

LEE TAEYONG (1914–1998)

Lee Taeyong, an advocate for women's rights, became the first female lawyer in South Korea. She graduated from Ewha College (today Ewha Womans University) in 1936, married an influential politician, became a devoted wife and mother, and crusaded for more legal rights for women. She created the Legal Aid Center, the first institution in South Korea that focused specifically on resolving women's problems, such as domestic violence and conflicts with in-laws. In order to improve women's legal rights, Lee successfully lobbied the government to create a family court to hear cases involving domestic abuse and divorce. Her efforts led to the passage of a family law that provided rights of inheritance and child custody, an essential step to guaranteeing greater equality for women.

may desire change, most women acquiesce to patriarchal traditions because notions of gender division are still respected within families.

A family law from 1991 permits a woman to head a household, recognizes a wife's right to a portion of the couple's property, and allows her to maintain greater contact with children after a divorce. Although the revisions help women who choose to divorce, the stigma of divorce remains strong. In 1980, the divorce rate per 100 marriages was 5.8 percent. By 2005, the divorce rate almost equaled that in the United States (Plate 2005). Most divorces are initiated by women, and personality conflict is the reason most cited. Women desire personal happiness, but divorced women find it difficult to support themselves and suffer from the strong social stigma of being divorced. Along with the increased divorce rate, domestic violence is known to be widespread. However, few victims take their problems to counselors or to the police.

Education for Korean women has come a long way since the Choson dynasty when women were denied that right. Opportunities for women have steadily expanded along with more education. The enrollment rate in primary schools reached 100 percent as early as the 1960s. As of the late 1990s, almost everyone was able to finish high school. The rate of high school graduates advancing to college has been increasing for both men and women. By 2004, 82.8 percent of male high school graduates and 79.7 percent of young women went to college or universities (Ministry of Education, 2008).

Gender inequality is also evident in terms of college majors. In 1998, female students continued to be enrolled in fields traditionally considered women's areas. For example, 73.1 percent of all students at teachers' colleges were women. In the area of natural sciences, the percentage of women earning advanced degrees was very low. In engineering, female students accounted for only 5 percent of all BS, 4 percent of MS, and 2 percent of PhD degrees (Connor 2002). By 2004, women accounted for 61.2 percent, 57.5 percent, and 53.0 percent of four-year university students majoring in teaching, humanities and arts, and sports disciplines, respectively. In the field of medicine and pharmaceuticals, women also have a much higher percentage (51.1 percent). However, women accounted for only for 37 percent, 43.2 percent, and 12.9 percent in the fields of social sciences, natural sciences, and engineering, respectively, which have traditionally had low rates of female enrollment (Ministry of Education, 2008).

Discrimination and inequality are sustained through separate curricula for men and women, with textbooks reflecting the gender division of work and traditional views of women. A study of elementary textbooks in Seoul revealed that men were described as leaders of families and women exclusively as housewives. As a result, the Seoul Metropolitan Education Office designed policies in 2007 to select textbooks and develop curricula to establish gender equality within the school system.

With educational and economic modernization, employment of women expanded. Since the 1960s, women's participation in the workforce grew from 26.8 percent in the 1960s to 42 percent in 2005 (*The Korea Herald* 2007). Various factors led to this steady expansion of women in the job market. Because of a labor shortage in the industrial sector, demand rose for women. They also wanted understandably to use their education in income-producing activity and sought employment in line with their level of education. Additional factors for the increasing numbers of women in the workforce are the high cost of living, fewer children, labor-saving devices in the home, and the general desire to live a more affluent life.

Although women's participation in economic activities has increased dramatically, the situation remains disappointing. Men dominate senior-level, high-paying, executive positions. According to a recent survey of the Korean Women's Development Institute (KWDI), women accounted for only 3 percent of the total number of executives in 546 large companies and state-invested corporations with more than 1,000 workers. As the Korean economy expanded during the 1980s, more and more educated women began to move up to white-collar jobs. Their attempts, however, to achieve professional advancement were often hindered by a glass ceiling. Efforts of various women's activist groups to eliminate discriminatory practices brought about the Equal Employment Act of 1987. In 2001, 67.5 percent of all service industry workers were women. Of those, 34.9 percent worked in retail, wholesale, food, and hotel businesses. This contrasts to the 22.7 percent ratio of male workers in the same industries. Women's earnings, on average, were 63.2 percent of what men earned for the same jobs in 2001 and 62.8 percent in 2003 (Ministry of Labor 2007).

The number of working women between the ages of 25 and 34 tends to be low in all jobs. A significant number of women in this age range quit their jobs when they get married, become pregnant, or take care of their children. Once they return to the labor market, they have less experience than their male counterparts and are hired at lower levels. Because of this phenomenon, employers hesitate to train their female employees, in the belief that they will not stay. In 2007, there were signs that more women were choosing work over marriage, and a much larger number of women are continuing to work even after having a family.

Between the 1980s and the early 21st century, a series of legal measures were adopted to promote the expansion of women's participation in economic activities. Under the 2006 Amendment to the Equal Employment Act, public corporations and large business enterprises are required each year to report their gender-disaggregated employment status for every rank within the organization. Those who fail to meet a certain level of female employment must create an action program to increase the ratio of women and report it to the government. These measures supposedly provide for gender equality; however, equality in the real world is a different matter.

Women have made considerable progress in education and other sectors of society, but less satisfactory has been their participation in national politics. As of June 2000, the number of women in the National Assembly was 17, or 6.2 percent of the total seats. The number increased to 41, or 13.7 percent, in the 2004–2008 sessions. As of August 2005, there were only two (11.1 percent) women ministers, the Ministry of Gender Equality and the Ministry of Legislation (National Election Commission 2007).

The average percentage of women in government and politics in Asia is approximately 13 percent; however, in South Korea it is approximately 3 percent. This fact is attributed to the Confucian philosophy that emphasizes the superior role of the male as the head of state and the head of household (Kirk 2000).

In the realm of sexuality, there is considerable tension between traditional and contemporary thought. The area where women's traditional values are best displayed is attitudes toward chastity. Female virtues were tied to chastity in traditional Korea, and this is true today. If women are sexually assaulted, they do not report such incidents to the police out of fear of being seen as unchaste. Men still place a high priority on virginity. Women alone are expected to maintain their chastity, while men's random sexual activities are tolerated. Consequently, prostitution and the sex industry are flourishing, while the denunciation of adultery is primarily limited to women alone. Heterosexuality is considered normal and homosexuality severely condemned.

While sexual violence was a hidden problem in the past, it has recently become a social issue. Beginning in the early 1990s, instances of workplace sexual harassment and stalking were reported. Rape remains a serious problem. Between January and August 2006, there were 4,917 reported cases of rape and 2,281 prosecutions. As a result of the stigma associated with rape, many are never reported (U.S. Department of State 2007). Abortion is widely practiced. In the past, married women have decided to have abortions because of the preference for sons, and unmarried women have had abortions as a result of the persistence of the tradition that a woman should be chaste.

Recently, the centuries-old preference for baby boys has been receding. This has led to what seems to be a decrease in the number of abortions performed after ultrasounds reveal that the fetus is a girl. Since parents now realize that daughters are more willing to provide emotional and financial support for elderly parents, couples are now deciding that having a daughter is a very important consideration for their overall well-being.

In 2006, the United Nations' Gender Empowerment Measure (GEM) survey ranked South Korea 53rd out of 177 nations in gender empowerment. The survey considered a wide range of women in various occupations and the ratio of female-to-male earned income. In the past, gender disparity was a result of inferior education for women, but the study concluded that sexual disparity still exists even if women obtain the same level of education as men (*Hankyoreh* 2006).

While there is no doubt that the contemporary family and Korea itself would collapse without them, women continue to be widely viewed as secondary and insignificant compared to men. The notion that men should work in the public sector and women stay in the private sector remains prevalent. The fact that the proportion of female legislators is the lowest among major Asian countries has inhibited reform. As late as 2005, the family headship system was abolished and ended the designation of the man as the head of the family and his children as the heirs of his name. And only in 2008 did a law go into effect that allows for a child to take the name of his mother and provides for more secure rights for adopted children and stepchildren in inheritance and certain rituals.

Clearly, patriarchal attitudes and practices can end only when men join women to end them. Disappointment and anger can eventually alter the culture and the institutions that perpetuate it. Hopefully this can come about without stigmatizing individual men whose behavior and attitudes reflect their own past oppression. Social change is fragile and fraught with difficulties, but women might find ways to make it happen. Inevitably, men need to be convinced that change will bring a better world for both men and women.

NORTH KOREA (1945–PRESENT)

In 1946, the Democratic People's Republic of Korea adopted a law that men and women are equal. Subsequent policy provisions support the equal status of women and uphold conditions to advance women in society. In theory, North Korea strongly supports sexual equality, but the Confucian tradition of male dominance remains strong. Sons are preferred to daughters for economic reasons and for

P'yongyang traffic policewoman. (Photograph courtesy of Cheong Wa Dae Presidential Residence of the Republic of Korea, Photographer's Press Pool)

KIM CHONGSUK (1919–1948)

Kim Chongsuk was a young communist who joined the guerrilla fighters in Manchuria during the Japanese occupation. She is said to have cooked, sewed, and washed for the guerrillas and supposedly saved Kim Il-Sung's life. She married Kim, who became the "Supreme Leader" of North Korea after World War II. In 1942, she bore him a son, Kim Jong-Il, who became the leader of North Korea after his father's death in 1994. Long ignored as a partisan who fought with Kim, she ultimately became enshrined in the history of North Korea as a great patriot, dutiful wife, and devoted mother.

continuing the family name. Women do most if not all of the housework in addition to working six days a week outside the home. There are usually four or five people in a family, and no more than two generations live together. Authorities discourage divorce, but it is easier for the husband to get a divorce than it is for the wife.

Because of work and a lengthy military service obligation, it is the norm for young couples to marry in their late twenties or early thirties. Traditional arranged marriages have basically disappeared, but the young still ask their parents for permission to marry. Weddings are simple but still include the traditional practices of meetings between families, gift exchanges, and wedding feasts.

Women are expected to fully participate in the labor force outside the home. The government views women's employment as essential because of the country's labor shortage. Women are expected to work six days a week and are required to leave their preschool-aged children in the care of elderly relatives or in state nurseries. Most women work in light industry and are paid less than their male counterparts in heavy industry. If they work in an office, they hold low-level positions. There is little information available on women's participation in politics as a whole, but few women have reached high levels of the Korean Worker's Party or the government. Nevertheless, North Korean guides will tell foreign visitors that women are well represented in the North Korean governmental apparatus.

There is considerable information relating to the trafficking of North Korean women along the Chinese–North Korean border. Some women are so desperate to leave North Korea that they knowingly take the risk of being sold into marriage with Chinese men in the hopes of being protected from the authorities. If caught, they risk being deported back to North Korea, where they face imprisonment and perhaps torture and death for having left their country.

REFERENCES

Bunge, Frederick M., ed. 1981. *North Korea: A Country Study*. Washington, DC: The American University.

Byun, Won-Lim. 2005. *The Lives of Korean Women*. Seoul: Iljisa Publishing House.

Cazzniga, Pina. 2006. "Low Birth Rate Data Released on Parents' Day." AsiaNews.it, May 10. http://www.asianews.it (accessed June 8, 2008).

Choe, Sang-Hun. 2007. "South Korea, Where Boys Were Kings, Revalues Its Girls." *The New York Times*, December 23.

Clark, Donald N. 2000. *Culture and Customs of Korea*. Westport, CT: Greenwood Press.

Eckert, Carter, et al. 1990. *Korea Old and New: A History*. Seoul: Ilchokak Publishers.

Gelb, Joyce, and Marian Lief Palley. 1994. *Women of Japan and Korea*. Philadelphia: Temple University Press, 1994.

Gluck, Caroline. 2003. "Koreans Learn to Live with Divorce." BBC News, May 8. http://news.bbc.co.uk/2/hi/asia-pacific/3011119.stm (accessed February 4, 2008).

Hicks, George. 1995. *Sex Slaves of the Japanese Imperial Forces*. St. Leonard's, Australia: Allen & Unwin.

Kendall, Laurel, and Mark Peterson, eds. 1983. *Korean Women: View from the Inner Room*. New Haven, CT: East Rock Press.

Kim, Doo-Sub, and Cheong-Seok Kim. 2004. *Creative Women in Korea: The Fifteenth through the Twentieth Centuries*. London: M. E. Sharpe.

Kim, Yung-Chung. 1976. *Women of Korea: A History from Ancient Times to 1945*. Seoul: Ewha Womans University Press.

Kirk, Don. 2000. "South Korean Women's Movement in Politics: How Big a Revolution?" *International Herald Tribune*, April 5.

The Korea Herald. 2007. "Women Account for 42 Percent of Total Workforce in Korea." April 24.

Korean Overseas Information Service. 1993. *A Handbook of Korea*. 9th ed. Seoul: Samhwa Printing Co., Ltd.

Hankyoreh. 2006. "Korea's Gender Divide Displayed by U.N. Figures." November 11.

Mantielli, Sandra, ed. 1977. *Virtues in Conflict: Tradition and the Korean Woman Today*. Seoul: Samhwa Publishing Co., Ltd.

Ministry of Education and Resources Development. 2006. "Economically Active Population and Labor Force Participation Rate." March 17. http://english.moe.go.kr/main (accessed January 24, 2008).

———. n.d. "Statistical Yearbook of Education (2002–2004)." http://www.moe.go.kr (accessed January 24, 2008).

Ministry of Gender Equality and Family. 2007. "World Women's Forum (2007)." September 12. http://www.mogef.go.kr (accessed February 5, 2008).

Park, Chung-a. 2006. "Career Jobs Elusive for Women." *The Korea Times*, July 20.

Peterson, Mark A. 1996. *Korean Adoption and Inheritance: Case Studies in the Creation of a Classic Confucian Society*. Ithaca, NY: Cornell University East Asia Program.

Plate, Tom. 2005. "For Asia's Desperate Housewives, Will It Truly Be a Happy Chinese New Year?" AsiaMedia, February 9. http://www.asiamedia.ucla.edu (accessed January 31, 2008).

Refugees International. 2003. "Trafficking of North Korean Women in China." July 28. http://www.refugeesinternational.org (accessed January 31, 2008).

Republic of Korea. National Statistical Office. 2007. "Women's Labor Force Participation." http://kosis.nso.go.kr (accessed February 4, 2008).

Ro, Hae-sook, ed. 1998. *Korean Women and Culture*. Seoul: Research Institute of Asian Women.

Savada, Andrea Matles, and William Shaw, eds. 1990. *South Korea: A Country Study*. Washington, DC: Government Printing Office.

Seth, Michael J. 2006. *A Concise History of Korea, from the Neolithic Period through the Nineteenth Century*. New York: Rowman & Littlefield Publishers, Inc.

Shin, Hae-in. 2007. "New Law Takes on Patriarchal Family System." *The Korea Herald*, June 4.

U.S. Department of State. 2007. "Country Reports on Human Rights Practices, 2006: Republic of Korea." March 6. http://www.state.gov/g/drl/rls/hrrpt/2006/78778.htm (accessed February 4, 2008).

Education

Mary E. Connor

Throughout their long history, the Korean people have attached great significance to education. This tradition has been sustained from the Three Kingdoms (Silla, Koguryo, and Paekche) period (57 BCE to 668 CE) until the present time. Historical records from the Silla kingdom (57 BCE–935 CE) document the existence of an advanced degree, basically equivalent to today's master's degree. The first formal institution was the Taehak (National Confucian Academy), established in 372 CE during the kingdom of Koguryo (37 BCE–668 CE). Little is known about the curriculum at Taehak, but it certainly included the classic Confucian texts, history, and literature, along with military arts. The tradition of male-only education in Korea began with the establishment of Taehak and continued well into the Choson dynasty.

It is assumed that the Paekche kingdom (18 BCE–660 CE) had some form of higher education and produced numerous scholars in various academic disciplines, many of whom made important contributions to the Japanese culture. According to the *Samguk sagi* (the oldest existing history of the Three Kingdoms), education involved learning Chinese thought and culture. Each kingdom essentially adopted the Chinese educational system, focused on the study of the Chinese classics, and carried out a policy of admitting aristocratic young men and preparing them for upper-level government posts.

The royal courts of Koguryo, Paekche, and Silla, the Unified Silla kingdom (668–935 CE), and the Koryo dynasty (918–1392) embraced Confucianism as the ideal ethical-moral system, by which youth study hard, memorize the classics, revere teachers, respect their elders, observe important rites, carry out appropriate ceremonies, and govern righteously. While Buddhism contributed to the development of a brilliant culture and reigned over the spiritual world of the Korean people,

Confucianism continued as the dominant force regulating education and government for the privileged class through formal academic institutes.

In 682, Unified Silla established its first national academy, Kukhak, modeled after the Chinese Tang dynasty's system of higher education and controlled by the state's Department of Education. The academy was headed by a rector who directed the faculty to educate young men in the instruction of the Confucian classics, Chinese history, and literature. This institution was open to sons of aristocratic families between 18 and 30 years of age.

KORYO

Throughout the Koryo period (918–1392), concern for education grew as a means of preparing men for the civil service examinations and of promoting Confucian learning and moral training. The sixth ruler of the dynasty, King Songjong, made education a high priority of his realm. He created the Kukchagam (national university) in Songdo (now Kaesong) in 992 and laid the foundation for Koryo's educational system. In his enthusiasm for education, King Songjong sent scholars of the classics, medicine, and other subjects to the countryside to teach.

When the reputation of Kukchagam declined in the 11th century, bright and ambitious young men began to attend private institutions of higher learning, the most famous of which was founded by Chung Choi in 1053 and named the School of Nine Halls. Choi, nicknamed the "Confucius of Korea," was considered a great scholar, and his students were known as the Disciples of Master Choi. His school produced many of the kingdom's leading officials and scholars.

In the 12th century, there were improvements in national higher education with the creation of seven halls of study that admitted 70 Confucian scholars and a limited number of warriors. The facilities of the Kukchagam were expanded, enrollment increased, additional systems of education were established, and the quality of education was perhaps at its highest level. It was at this time that three technical academies were created to teach law, calligraphy, and accounting.

There were basically two types of higher education in Koryo—one public and the other private. The public system, represented by Kukchagam, was the most important and prestigious. This institution, supported completely by the national government, continued the tradition of training students to be loyal civil servants through the study of Confucianism. The school was organized into six departments, and each department's structure related to the social standing of the students and reflected the hierarchical, aristocratic nature of society.

Regional schools and county schools in provincial areas served as local educational institutions that were also state run. Such private schools as the Sibi-do (Twelve Assemblies) and the Seowon were established during Koryo, and their level of education was generally comparable to those managed by the state. Many aristocrats considered it a great honor for their sons to attend the Sibi-do, which had great respect for Buddhism and Confucianism.

With the Mongolian invasion of the 13th century, the Koryo kingdom itself gradually declined. Some of the last Koryo kings made heroic efforts to improve the education system of the country. One went to the extent of collecting silver and cloth to fund the national university, and another supported the construction of a larger schoolhouse in the belief that this would help improve the quality of education. Despite their efforts, the kingdom ultimately did collapse and higher education along with it.

CHOSON

The Choson dynasty (1392–1910) was more than a change of dynasties; it was a 500-year effort to create a society that conformed to Confucian values and beliefs. Few developments in premodern Korean history are more important than this effort, which actually contributed in profound ways to create a characteristic cultural identity. Neo-Confucianism became the distinct ideology of Choson, with the goal of reforming society under the direction of an enlightened government based on Confucian belief.

The Neo-Confucian scholar was not so much interested in Confucian theories for their own sake but for the practical application of Confucian ethics to daily life. Buddhism was deliberately repressed by the regime and was seen by many scholars as an alien faith that interfered with harmonious relationships in society. They criticized Buddhist monks for their moral laxity, involvement in politics, the cost of supporting temples and elaborate rituals, and the Buddhist concept of abstract universal love, which was in conflict with the Confucian emphasis on the family.

Neo-Confucianism shaped the culture, educational system, government, and society. It subsequently became the measure of all things. Education was valued as a means of self-cultivation and an opportunity for social mobility, status, and power. The dynasty created a strictly authoritarian bureaucratic system by establishing Confucian academies and devising civil service examinations that essentially became the only route to high office.

As a result of the emphasis on Confucianism and the importance of passing exams, more schools were created. The national academy now became the Songgyungwan, and in time it became the highest center for Confucian education. The local school (*hyanggyo*) founded in each administrative district admitted boys between 14 and 20 years of age. The main purpose of *hyanggyo* was to prepare students for the exam.

A new development was the creation of the *sodong*, which was a private school for primary education. Eventually the *sodong* existed in every large village, supported either by a certain number of families or the entire village. In theory, it was open to all classes of children but was inevitably limited primarily to the *yangban* class. After a student learned all there was to learn at the *sodong*, he then attended the *hyanggyo*, from which he proceeded to the Songgyungwan.

The curricula of these schools were the Chinese classics. Teaching methods were essentially informal and individualistic. Students could move at their own rate. After years of study, the students traveled to Seoul and took the civil service examination, and their exam scores were the determining factor in their careers.

The educational system in Choson was similar to that of Koryo. The Songgyungwan continued to be the institution of higher education. Yi Seonggye, the founder of the dynasty, used land grants as a means of supporting the national academy. He built a shrine on the campus to honor Chinese and Korean Confucian scholars of the past. Another monarch, King T'aejong, increased the number of schools, produced thousands of pieces of copper type for the publication of books, and enlarged the land grant support for the Songgyungwan.

King Sejong (reign 1418–1450) is considered one of the greatest monarchs in Korean history for his contributions to Korean culture and the promotion of learning. His royal academy was built for scholars to devote themselves to creative endeavors. It was his academy that invented the Korean *han'gul* alphabet system. Given that literacy had been restricted to ruling elites, the invention of a writing system easily learned by the common people was a revolutionary idea. The curriculum at the academy included not only Confucian texts but also books on history, government, agriculture, medicine, and literature. Publishing flourished during Sejong's reign as a result of the remarkable improvement of metallic type and printing technology. Education was strongly promoted throughout the 15th century, and the culture at the time was at its peak.

As a result of internal strife and the invasions of the Japanese and Manchus in the 16th and 17th centuries, Korea retreated into hardship. The 18th century saw a revival of learning, and education was promoted. A group of scholars published an encyclopedia that encompassed nearly all aspects of life and culture. A royal library was established, and many books were published. Yet in spite of what appeared to be progress, scholars tended to engage in abstract discussions of Confucianism and did not pursue practical subjects or more scientific approaches in order to address the needs of the people and the nation.

The Role of the Songgyungwan (National Academy)

The Songgyungwan was the major educational institution throughout the Choson dynasty. Located in the capital, Seoul, the institution was essentially a training center for students (primarily sons of officials) who were preparing to take the higher-level civil service examination. The exam was divided into three stages, the first stage being given in provincial capitals and Seoul, the second in Seoul, and the third in the royal presence. Students were tested on their mastery of the Confucian classics, geography, history, literature, medicine, law, and military service. Those who were the most successful could expect careers at the highest level of the government.

The national academy was completely supported by the government yet had a high degree of autonomy. Students were admitted on the basis of their test scores on the preliminary civil service exams and teacher recommendations. These exams required years of study, so students whose families had the financial resources to pay for their education and hire tutors had an advantage.

When students assembled in the classroom, they were usually seated in order of their age. Student life was very regimented by strict rules of conduct. Examples of their ethical codes are as follows:

A scholar should have a definite goal in mind in pursuing the way to become a scholar, statesman, and promoter of world peace.

A scholar should always be well mannered.

A scholar should always devote himself to studying and learning.

A scholar should always practice filial piety (respect for parents) because a lack of respect for one's parents and elders is the root of all evil.

A scholar should always show respect to his teachers as the teacher is as important as the king and one's father. (Weidman and Park 2000, 19)

Failure to abide by the rules could lead to various degrees of punishment, from suspension and dismissal to prohibition from taking the civil service exam and losing the privilege of exemption from military service.

Student instruction involved listening to lectures; writing essays, eulogies, and poetry; and paying close attention to one's writing style and the art of calligraphy. Young scholars participated in student government, engaged in political discussions, and were free to organize demonstrations against policies of the government. It became the duty of the scholar to criticize the government and even the king. Confucianism was all about moral values and proper conduct, and improper conduct was seen as a threat to the order.

The curriculum was essentially based on the Confucian classics. Reading books on Daoism or Buddhism was prohibited. Instruction included a lecture, question and answer sessions, discussion, and exposition. The length of the course depended on the ability of each student to master the material. They took daily tests, and a lottery system was used as a means of selecting students to recite. More comprehensive exams occurred every 10 days and once a month. A major exam was imposed twice a year in the presence of high official examiners. The top three students were then selected to take a higher civil service exam. Evaluations were on a five-point scale from mastery to failure. Attendance was also factored into a point system. It became a requirement for each student to earn 300 points in order to take an exam. Various strategies were employed to encourage students to excel, such as publishing students' compositions and summoning an outstanding scholar to the royal palace.

Late Choson and the Beginning of Modern Education

Modern education began toward the end of the Choson dynasty. As a result of the major changes brought about by Japan and Western imperial powers, the government attempted, albeit unsystematically, to reform education. It experimented with a number of educational institutions in an attempt to introduce foreign ideas and technical skills. A group known as the Enlightenment Party advocated a Western-style system of state-supported schools and the addition of a modern curriculum to deal with changing times. The primary agents of these changes were missionaries. A Methodist from the United States, Mary R. Scranton, established the first school to offer formal education for women. It became Ewha Womans University, now regarded as one of the best universities. Many private schools were established in the belief that more schools would awaken the people to the dangers that lay ahead; however, the reforms were too late. Korea became increasingly dominated by imperial powers, and on August 28, 1910, the nation became part of the Japanese empire.

JAPANESE COLONIAL PERIOD

During the colonial period, Japanese imperialists designed the educational system and administrative structure to enforce a policy of Shinto-Confucian–centered instruction. Their method combined such Confucian ethical concepts and practices as loyalty, filial piety, ancestor worship, learning, and harmonious human relationships with Shinto, the state religion of Japan. The latter appealed to Japanese nationalists because it combined an ethical code of honor and valor with an emphasis on duty to Japan and belief in the divinity of the emperor. The Japanese used both ideologies to establish control over a nation that they believed was backward. The overall plan was to destroy the spirit of the people and to make them loyal subjects of the Japanese empire.

This period is generally discussed in terms of three stages. The first covered the time between 1910 and the independence movement in 1919. Korean children were segregated from the Japanese children, and the school curriculum emphasized practical learning and vocational training. Education was not intended to prepare Koreans for professional or administrative positions but to provide basic literacy and low-level tasks for men. For girls, the purpose was to foster feminine virtues and domesticity. The Japanese did not believe that higher education was necessary and developed policies to strictly regulate public and private schools.

In response to negative world opinion following Japan's brutal reaction to Korea's demonstrations for independence in the March First movement, policies became more moderate in the second period (1919–1934). Korean children could now attend school from 11 to 16 years, and the legal foundation for university education was established. In the belief that Koreans were intellectually inferior, policies limited their enrollment in science and engineering courses.

The third period (1934–1945) existed under wartime conditions. As World War II intensified, students were mobilized for military training, defense work, and public works projects. They were also forced to volunteer for military service. Students were required to worship at Japanese Shinto shrines and chant in unison the oath of loyal subjects in school assemblies. By 1941, only Japanese could be spoken in schools, and Korean history was replaced by Japanese history. People also had to abandon their Korean names and assume Japanese ones. By the spring of 1945, almost all classroom instruction was abandoned.

Overall Japanese objectives were to strengthen their control over how the Korean people were to think and behave. All schools were under the tight supervision and control of the government. Regulations involved textbook selection, curricula, teacher standards, and student quotas in higher education that gave preference to Japanese students. Thought control was maintained throughout the schools with the assistance of student police. The Japanese increased their police and surveillance

North Korean school girls in the Myohyang Mountain area north of P'yongyang. (Courtesy of Mary Connor)

system to the extent that it included 10 times as many people as the French needed to control Vietnam, a colony of similar size and population.

Despite the harshness of colonial educational policy, there were some positive outcomes in the long run. Public education was established regardless of social status and gender along with educational facilities and buildings. The Japanese emphasized regimentation, neat uniforms, and such student responsibilities as keeping classrooms and lavatories clean. This would contribute to the contemporary practice that schools serve as models of discipline, order, and cleanliness. The Japanese system established high standards for teacher training that served to augment traditional respect for teachers and enhance their authority in the classroom. Administratively, it was a uniform system of mass education to bring everyone up to a certain level. South Korean authorities continued this concern for creating a uniform basic education for everyone.

In 1945, when the 35-year Japanese colonial rule ended, it was estimated that two out of three adults were illiterate (Seth 2002, 91). Less than 5 percent of the adult population had more than an elementary school education. There was only one university, and most of the students were Japanese. The Japanese authorities regarded education as a tool for Japanese imperial objectives and humiliated the Korean people in ways that are not forgotten nor yet forgiven.

KIM SONGSU (1891–1955)

Kim was a well-known figure in the worlds of business, publishing, politics, and education. He is most famous for founding the *Dong-A Ilbo*, one of Korea's largest and most respected newspapers, and for being a major patron of Korea University. He used his newspaper to help keep the independence movement alive. The Japanese closed down the newspaper several times and closed it permanently in 1940. It began publishing again after liberation. Kim helped to establish Korea University and hired an architect to design the main building after Duke University in North Carolina. He also served in Syngman Rhee's administration for a time.

SOUTH KOREA

American Occupation and the Korean War (1945–1953)

Korea's liberation from Japan marked a turning point in the history of education. The principal objectives during American occupation (1945–1948) were to eliminate the totalitarian elements of Japanese influence and provide educational opportunities for all children. The hope was to promote ideas of progressive education, provide appropriate Korean-language textbooks and a Korean-oriented curriculum, and respond to the great demand for education that came with liberation.

The United States Army Military Government in Korea (USAMGIK) carried out policies based on those that the United States had created for the occupation of Japan and Germany. The underlying goal of policy was to create a system of democratic education in the belief that this would support the growth of a democratic society.

The educational system that was adopted followed the American model: six-year elementary schools, three-year middle schools, three-year high schools, and four-year colleges and universities, which include graduate programs leading to master's and doctorate degrees. Other educational reforms included coeducation at all levels, popularly elected school boards in local areas, and compulsory education up to the ninth grade. The most impressive achievement was the enormous expansion of schooling for millions of people. The percentage of children attending primary school doubled. As a result of promoting the use of *han'gul*, the rate of literacy rose to 71 percent by 1947.

During the Korean War (1950–1953), about 80 percent of all educational facilities were damaged or destroyed. In spite of widespread hunger, death, destruction, dislocation, and a shortage of teachers, textbooks, supplies, and buildings, efforts were made as early as 1951 to resume education. Korean parents were quick to do whatever was necessary to see that their children's education was not interrupted. They willingly sent their children to factories, refugee camps, tents, or even street schools if this was all that was available.

Children and their Confucian teachers during a festival in Yeongju, a South Korean city in an area known for Confucianism. Korean parents want their children to know about Confucianism and periodically hold festivals to sustain traditional beliefs. (Courtesy of Suk Tae Kim)

The Korean War increased the power of the South Korean government and the need to be alert to communist aggression and subversion. Education would promote this caution, giving the state the rationale for controlling educational development. In spite of 35 years of occupation, political division, and a disastrous civil war, people remained hopeful that somehow the lives of their children would be better. The basis of that conviction was the promise of universal education.

Post–Korean War to the Present

The most significant developments in South Korea following the Korean War were rapid economic growth and the expansion of education at all levels. Hundreds of public and private elementary and secondary schools and numerous colleges and universities were established within a decade, and schooling has continued to grow impressively ever since. In 1953, the majority of the population had no formal schooling at all, and there were few trained teachers and virtually no research facilities. By 1975, South Korea had one of the highest levels of education in the world, and literacy was almost 100 percent. In fact, South Korea had a higher level of educational achievement than any other nation of comparable per capita income. International tests revealed that the math and science scores of South Korean primary and secondary students were among the highest in the world.

Since 1945, the pattern of educational development in South Korea has remained basically consistent in spite of changes of governments and external and internal developments. The education administration consists of a strong centralized authority, the Ministry of Education and Human Resources Development, followed by the supervisors of education at the metropolitan and provincial levels and local boards of education. A prominent feature of South Korea's overall educational development has been the continual attempts to coordinate development with economic development needs.

On the national level, the public policies at first concentrated on achieving universal and uniform standards at the primary and then at the middle school levels before actively promoting the expansion of higher education. Relatively high standards were maintained for teachers, in spite of the great demand that coexisted with increased enrollment. A factor that has continued to contribute to the quality of those in the teaching profession is the tradition that teachers are more highly esteemed in South Korea than in the West. Many of the brightest students choose to enter the teaching profession.

A rigorous and uniform national curriculum was established in the mid-1950s and followed thereafter. The state emphasis on universal education eliminated the sharp disparities among regions and social classes that often exist in developing nations. It contributed to social cohesion and provided a literate workforce with the skills needed for a newly industrializing society. This caused strains between the demand for higher education and the state's policies to prevent an oversupply of advanced degree holders. The educational system was now open to a wide range of the nation's youth. However, competition became even greater than it was before and created what is commonly referred to as "examination hell."

At the present time, approximately 40 percent of the high schools in Seoul and 52 percent in the nation are coeducational. Some fees are charged in the middle and high schools, but 100 percent of the children attend middle school, and approximately 99 percent continue on to high school. Once students enroll in school, they stay and graduate on schedule. In 1995, the high school dropout rate was only 2.1 percent, one of the lowest dropout ratios in the world. Schools also have low incidences of absenteeism, tardiness, and on-campus violence. Eighty-two percent of high school graduates advance to the college or university level (Kim and Kwon 2008, 98–99). Among the Organization for Economic Co-operation and Development (OECD) countries, South Korea ranks first in the percentage of 25–34-year-olds who have completed secondary school (Ihm 2008, 244).

The school year covers 220 days, and students attend school 5.5 days per week. The calendar has two semesters; the first runs from March through July and the second from September through February. There are summer and winter breaks. High school students have 10 optional half-days before and after each break, which are attended by nearly every student.

The pressure to succeed begins in the primary grades and continues throughout the high school years. The primary school curriculum consists of 10 mandatory subjects: Korean language, etiquette and manners, social studies, arithmetic, natural science, practical skills, physical education, music, fine arts, and foreign language. The government has recently expanded foreign language instruction, enabling third graders and above to study English for two hours weekly. After completion of primary school, students advance to middle school for grades seven through nine. The curriculum consists of 12 basic or required subjects, electives, and extracurricular activities. It includes ethics, fine arts, mathematics, music, social studies, natural science, classical Chinese, English, practical skills (home economics), vocational skills, and physical education. After successful completion of middle school, all students desiring a high school education have to pass the state-administered qualifying examination. These tests are determining factors as to whether they will be on the college or vocational track.

High schools are classified into academic and vocational schools. In 1995, some 62 percent of students were enrolled in academic high schools and 38 percent in vocational high schools. The academic or college-bound courses of study include 13 general and several specialized subjects. Students may study another language in addition to English, such as Chinese, Japanese, French, or German, and in vocational schools they may study agriculture, engineering, or home economics.

College-bound students work so hard in high school that they see very little of their childhood. They typically arrive at 7:30 AM with boxed lunches and dinners. After a full day of classes that end in midafternoon, students continue their day with athletics, extracurricular activities, and study sessions until 5:00 PM. After a boxed dinner, the students go to study or work with tutors until 9:00 PM. They then come home to complete homework and stay awake with coffee. After four or five hours of sleep, the mother has breakfast prepared by 5:00 AM and two boxed meals to begin another day.

Even though Korea has many public and private colleges, mass education has created tremendous competition. In the past, a college education guaranteed a good job. Now there are so many college graduates that underemployment and unemployment have become major problems. Neither a high school diploma nor a college diploma is necessarily good enough. The reason for the intensive study and tutorial help is the university entrance exam. Attending the best universities is the only guarantee to move into the best employment opportunities and professions.

During the final year of high school, students take the College Scholastic Ability Test (CSAT). This examination measures the analytical abilities required to successfully complete postsecondary education. It has four sections: verbal (Korean language), math and inquiry (sections 1 and 2), and a foreign language section. The college admissions process factors in the student's high school academic record, extracurricular activities, and personal interviews.

The college examination is obviously critical to one's future. Only 15,000 of the approximately 875,000 persons taking the exam will be admitted to one of the top three universities. When students do not make it, they often spend the next year studying in private academies, hoping to better their score the next year. Mothers are known to go to Buddhist temples for 100 straight days to pray that their children will ace the most important test of their lives. Students study for months, getting little sleep, and parents shell out huge amounts of tutorial fees to have them coached. On the day of the exam, high school bands and cheering students meet test-takers at school gates to cheer them on. Landings and takeoffs at the airport are banned during the listening comprehension portion of the test. Even the U.S. military will halt activity at training bases for nine hours to respect the national day of testing.

Once in college, students find that life is easier. The great majority will have time to relax, perhaps the only time in their adult lives that they will not feel pressured. Many breathe a sigh of relief and do as little work as possible. No matter what grades they receive, they will become members of the college's alumni group, and their place in the network of graduates is guaranteed. Campus life is very social, and most students enjoy it to the fullest. Another dimension of college life in South Korean colleges and universities is political and social activism. Although only a small proportion of college students are actively involved in planning and carrying out political demonstrations, they are more politically alert and active than their U.S. counterparts. Since the 1960s, students on the campuses have the reputation of being the watchdogs of South Korean society.

The Need for Educational Reforms

In spite of the remarkable achievements in education, the Ministry of Education and the public at large are well aware that reform is necessary. Studies performed by the Korean Educational Development Institute (KEDI) and the OECD in the 1990s reported overcrowded classrooms, too much reliance on rote memorization, overly centralized school administration, methodologies that hinder creativity and independent thought, and insufficient funding on all levels, but particularly at the university level.

According to a 1995 study conducted by the KEDI, Korean families annually pay 17 trillion won ($21 billion) on such direct educational expenditures as tuition, mandatory fees, extracurricular activities sponsored by schools, transportation, and textbooks. The total government expenditures on education in 1994 amounted to 16.7 trillion won, which means that families privately paid for 51 percent of the total cost of education. In addition, an estimated 6 trillion won was spent on private tutoring. If the total costs were to be tabulated, 12 percent of the South Korean public's gross national product goes to education—considerably higher than in most industrialized nations. The most recent statistics available in 2008 indicate that South Korea spends a greater portion of national income on private education than any other country: 2.8 percent of the gross domestic product, compared with 2.3 percent in the United States. No other country is close (Seth 2002, 187).

Most students resent the emphasis on and the attendant pressures of the college exam that dominates high school education. The artistic but ill-disciplined student or the late bloomer may have nowhere to go. According to the Ministry of Education and Human Resources Development, a total of 35,144 primary and secondary school students left South Korea to study abroad in 2006. Korean parents are known to send their children to the United States for schooling. There, relatives or housekeepers supervise and care for them. A newly coined phrase, *jogi yuhak*, meaning "early study abroad," reflects the zeal for education among South Korean parents and the beliefs that the children will have a better education in the United States and that learning English is easier at a young age.

Teachers complain that their workday is too long and express dissatisfaction about their pay. A teaching day is long. For most, the day begins at 7:30 AM and ends at 5:00 PM. The regular workload consists of 5 classes that meet four times each week, with an additional 20 classes that meet once a week. Many teachers see between 250 and 500 students in their classrooms every week. Teachers express frustration that it is not possible to know all of their students by name. Because teachers have so many pupils, they rarely assign written work. English-language education is particularly flawed because the focus is on grammar and not conversation.

Many parents have become obsessed with getting their children into a good university, and as a result, corruption permeates the educational system from kindergarten upward. In a society where gift giving is a distinct part of the culture, many parents routinely give teachers money or gifts so that they will not ignore their children. A government investigation revealed that there are parents who pay enormous sums of money to buy a place in a university.

There are also serious problems in higher education. Scandals involving professors who plagiarize their theses or administrators who misappropriate school funds have raised questions about the integrity of faculty members and tarnished the reputation of numerous colleges and universities. Many college students are now more interested in preparing for the civil service examinations and entrance tests for large corporations as jobs are becoming increasingly scarce. The result is that students are not signing up for humanities and liberal arts courses (Cho 2006, 64).

The nation's most eminent institution of higher learning, Seoul National University, is not even ranked among the top 100 universities in the world. More than 90 percent of the university's faculty studied at that institution. Despite the fact that South Korea has one of the world's highest PhD-to-population ratios, a survey reveals that professors published the smallest number of research papers in international academic journals of the 29 member states of the OECD.

The Education Ministry has attempted to rectify the problems. One of the major objectives pointed to educating creative citizens in the knowledge-based society. The ministry's policies in the 21st century are targeted at increasing the budget for key educational policy items, removing rote memorization from the center of education, and giving more weight to the development of the individual student's creativity and ethics. Additional plans were announced to reduce class size, revise procedures for evaluating students, and revamp the university curriculum.

For thousands of years, education in Korea has been valued as a means of self-cultivation, status, and power. In modern times, the zeal for education has brought rapid economic growth, democratization, and social mobility. It remains the single most important factor in social mobility and status. As a result of the high cost of education—combined with the ever more competitive nature of college admission and the uncertainty of employment—increased antagonism among classes is developing.

In the 21st century, the government and public continue the debate about how to reform their system of schooling, reduce the existent pressures on children, and contain the obsessive zeal for prestigious degrees. Although advanced schooling is no longer a guarantee of economic security and social status, the financial and emotional costs remain constant. Desire for excellence and a drive to succeed have been characteristics of Koreans for centuries.

NORTH KOREA

With the end of Japanese occupation and political division, Kim Il-Sung (leader of North Korea from 1948 to 1994) expressed the desire that "we should open for the sons and daughters of the working people the opportunity of learning and train them to be splendid people shouldering the future of a new, prosperous Korea." After 1948, the leadership established an educational system that was modeled largely on that of the Soviet Union. There were serious challenges: Eighty percent of the population was illiterate, educational facilities were inadequate, and there were few trained teachers or administrators. The devastation caused by the Korean War curtailed virtually all attempts at educational development.

Reliable information on education in North Korea is limited. We do know that North Korean children attend school for 11 years: 1 year of preschool, 4 of primary school, and 6 of senior middle school. An estimated 14 percent go on to specialized

Chongam kindergarten in Chongam District, Chongjin City, North Hamgyong Province North Korea. (Democratic People's Republic of Korea)

technical and professional schools or to Kim Il-Sung University, the only comprehensive institution of higher education. The qualifications for admission are grades, performance on a college admission exam, political reliability, and connections. Competition for admission is intense.

Kim Il-Sung's guiding principles of education include the development of a party and working-class consciousness, establishment of the principle of *juche* ("self-reliance") in education, the combination of education and revolutionary practice, and the government's responsibility for education. Building on Confucian tradition, the Kims have taught that loyalty is the most important virtue. All schools emphasize political rectitude.

Young people learn about the life of Kim Il-Sung, listen to lectures on *juche* and communism, receive moral instruction, and study the full range of subjects, such as the Korean language, history, math, science, music, art, foreign language, and health education. Political education is approximately 25 percent of the curriculum for young children, and some estimates are as high as 40 percent for the university student. Readings about Kim Il-Sung and Kim Jong-Il take up a significant part of classroom time. Schoolbooks include readings about how much Kim Il-Sung loved children, optimistic statements about the future of *juche* socialism, and the evil deeds of Japan and the United States.

North Korea has maintained longer compulsory education than the South and has a younger age structure of the population, both of which would presumably contribute to high adult literacy. If one takes into account the reports of foreign business executives, it seems reasonable to believe that North Korea may well have achieved universal literacy (Noland 2000, 75).

In 2007, North Korea announced plans for educational reform that include early foreign language instruction and computer skills, creativity over rote memorization, programs for gifted students, and reeducating teachers. The plans are most likely in response to the realization that in an era of globalization, knowledge of foreign language and information technology is essential for economic advancement.

REFERENCES

Bunge, Frederica M. 1981. *North Korea: A Country Study*. Washington, DC: The American University.

Cho, Kuk. 2006. "Korean Universities Are in Need of Reform." *Korea Focus* 14, no. 4 (Winter): 64–66.

Eckert, Carter, et al. 1990. *Korea Old and New: A History*. Seoul: Ilchokak Publishers.

Korean Overseas Information Service. 1993. *A Handbook of Korea*. 9th ed. Seoul: Korean Overseas Information Service, Ministry of Culture and Information.

———. 2003. *A Handbook of Korea*. 11th ed. Seoul: Korean Overseas Information Service, Ministry of Culture and Information.

Han, Jun-sang. 2007. "Children Leaving Korea." *Korea Focus* 15, no. 1 (Spring): 59–61.

Ihm, Chon-sun. 2008. "The Political Economy of Educational Reform," in *Social Change in Korea*, edited by Kim Kyong-dong, 243–253. Seoul: Jimoondang Publishing Co.

Kim, Gyeong-hee. 2007. "Are Korean Youths Mentally Healthy?" *Korea Focus* 15, no. 2 (Summer): 46–48.

Kim, Joy, and Eun-Kyung Kwon. 2008. "Scholarly Communication in Korea," in *Scholarly Communication in China, Hong Kong, Japan, Korea, and Taiwan*, edited by Jingfeng Xia. Oxford, UK: Chandos Publishing.

Kim, Min Se. 2007. "North Korea: Education Reform in Progress." *Daily North Korea*, September 14. http://www.dailynk.com/english/read.php?cataID=nk (accessed March 7, 2008).

Lee, Jeong-kyu. 2002. *Korean Higher Education: A Confucian Perspective*. Seoul: Jimoon-dang Publishing Co.

Lee, Young Ho. 2004. "Urgent Need to Reform History Education." *Korea Focus* 12, no. 6 (November–December): 45–46.

Noland, Marcus. 2000. *Avoiding the Apocalypse: The Future of the Two Koreas*. Washington, DC: Institute for International Economics.

Oh, Kongdan, and Ralph Hassig. 2000. *North Korea through the Looking Glass*. Washington, DC: Brookings Institution Press.

Park, Kyung Mee. 2005. "Assessing Korea's Education System in a Positive Light." *Korea Focus* 13, no. 1 (January–February): 39–41.

Savada, Andrea Matles, and William Shaw, eds. 1990. "Education: South Korea," in *South Korea: A Country Study*. Washington, DC: Government Printing Office.

Seth, Michael J. 2002. *Education Fever: Society, Politics, and the Pursuit of Schooling in South Korea*. Honolulu: University of Hawai'i Press.

———. 2006. *A Concise History of Korea, from the Neolithic Period through the Nineteenth Century*. New York: Rowman & Littlefield Publishers, Inc.

Wallace, Bruce. 2008. "S. Koreans on Edge of Burnout." *Los Angeles Times*, April 19.

Weidman, John C., and Namgi Park, eds. 2000. *Higher Education in Korea: Tradition and Adaptation*. New York: Falmer Press.

Culture

Language

John Song

INTRODUCTION

Koreans are very proud of their language, especially their writing system known as *han'gul* (the script of Han). They are even eager to teach others how easy it is to learn Korean. They feel this way for good reason. *Han'gul* is considered one of the most well-designed and easy-to-learn alphabets in the world. In fact, the alphabet can usually be memorized in an hour or two by most people. *Han'gul*'s logical design is a testament to its creator, King Sejong the Great, who promoted widespread literacy by making the alphabet easy to learn.

HISTORY OF THE KOREAN LANGUAGE

King Sejong (1397–1450), one of the greatest kings in Korean history, is famous for his commitment to improving the quality of life for his people. In 1446, he perfected the phonetic writing system that was easier to learn than the complicated Chinese writing system. King Sejong was a scholar and considered the creation of *han'gul* his greatest accomplishment. Koreans today believe the *han'gul* alphabet is "the proudest cultural achievement of the Korean people" (Eckert 1990, 125).

Korean has been classified as part of the Altaic language family group related to Mongolian, Japanese, and Turkish. There were two forms of spoken Korean. In the North, Puyo was spoken, and in the South, Han. In the 7th century, under Unified Silla, major variations in the language began to disappear, and by the 10th century the Kaesong dialect became standard.

Calligraphy artist. (Corel)

Despite widespread belief, the language is not related to Chinese but has generously borrowed much of the vocabulary and initially all of its written characters from the Chinese system. Spoken languages are living and continuously evolve by usage and novelty. Over time, they gain a great degree of standardization by a codified writing system and widespread literacy. Korean has undergone the same process but stands out among other languages for its rather original and scientific design.

When not tending to the official duties of the state, King Sejong lived the life of a Neo-Confucian scholar, spending time reading and studying. Because of his intense interest in education, he established the Chiphyonjon, the Jade Hall of Scholars. In this academic research institute, scholars from every academic field came together to exchange ideas, conduct scientific research, and publish their results.

The king realized that the common citizens did not have the ability to read or write the intricate Chinese characters (*hanja*) used by the members of the noble class. This skill required many years of discipline to perfect. Also, because *hanja* is of foreign origin, people could not use it to fully express the meaning of spoken words.

Hunmin Chongum

What King Sejong envisioned for his citizens was a set of letters that was uniquely Korean and easy to learn for common use among his subjects. The Korean script,

KING SEJONG (1397–1450)

King Sejong (r. 1419–1450), one of the greatest kings in Korean history, is famous for his commitment to improving the quality of life for his people and for the invention of the Korean written language, *han'gul*. In his youth he was passionate about learning, and this quest for knowledge motivated him for the rest of his life. He was fascinated by the world of science, especially astronomy. During his reign, constellations were charted, rain gauges were refined, and sundials and water clocks were developed. Handbooks to improve agricultural production and medicine were completed. He sought out talented people to serve, trained them in the art of good government according to the Confucian classics, and made sure that their talents were utilized. His main goal was to find ways to improve literacy.

which is now called *han'gul*, was originally called *Hunmin Chongum*, or "proper sounds to instruct the people" (*Korean Overseas Information Service* 1993, 49). A manual was published under the same name in 1446 to explain the script. In the preface of that guide, King Sejong made this statement:

> Being of foreign origin, Chinese characters are incapable of capturing uniquely Korean meanings. Therefore, many common people have no way to express their thoughts and feelings. Out of my sympathy for their difficulties, I have created a set of twenty-eight letters. The letters are very easy to learn, and it is my fervent hope that they improve the quality of life of all people. (qtd. in Lee 1993, 516)

This statement captures the spirit of King Sejong's purpose, devotion to cultural independence, and dedication to the benefit of the Korean people. When first announced by King Sejong, the *Hunmin Chongum* originally had 28 letters. However, in modern Korean, only 24 letters are used. The term *han'gul* (Korean writing) came into use only during the 20th century (Seth 2006, 173).

The original *Hunmin Chongum* was 33 pages long. In the first 4 pages was the introduction written by King Sejong. The rest of the 29 pages of commentary was written by the scholars of the Jade Hall. For 500 years, the original version of the *Hunmin Chongum* was thought to have been lost; however, it was rediscovered in 1940. Today, it is stored in the Kansong Museum as National Treasure No. 70 (Diamond Sutra n.d., 90). It was included in the United Nations Educational, Scientific and Cultural Organization's (UNESCO) World Cultural Heritage in 1997. In recognition of its importance, September 10, the original date of its publication, has been designated as Han'gul Day by the government. Also, UNESCO has created an award called the King Sejong Literacy Prize as a part of its worldwide campaign against illiteracy.

Theory and Principles of Han'gul

There are approximately 6,000 languages in existence today. Only about 100 of them have their own alphabet made by an individual, for which the theory and motives behind their creation are well documented. For example, the Roman characters that we use today originated with the syllabic Phoenician alphabet. They have undergone a long process of gradual evolution. Similarly, the Chinese characters began as inscriptions on bones and tortoiseshells, and they also took thousands of years to reach their current form. King Sejong systematically analyzed the basic units of spoken Korean and alphabetized them. An entry in the *Sejong Sillok* on December 30, the 25th year of the king's reign, shows that the *Hunmin Chongum* was indeed Sejong's own invention: "This month the King has personally created 28 letters of the *Onmum* (the vernacular script). Though simple and concise, it is capable of infinite variations and is called *Hunmin Chongum*" (Diamond Sutra Recitation Group 2007, 91).

Han'gul incorporates philosophical elements of the Confucian worldview that dominated Korean thought in the Choson dynasty as well as scientific principles of language. It uses the concepts of *yin*, representing feminine, passive, dark, dry, and cold, and *yang*, the masculine, active, bright, wet, and hot. The interaction of *yin* and *yang* produces the five elements: wood, fire, earth, metal, and water. King Sejong and the scholars of the Chiphyonjon considered human sounds to be more than just physical phenomena. Corresponding to the principle of *yin-yang* and the five elements, each vowel and consonant in *han'gul* is assigned the properties of either *yin* or *yang*. There are five basic consonants, which represent the five elements, according to their place of articulation. Because Sejong and his scholars believed that there were unseen forces controlling observable phenomena, there must also be a common link between sounds and the changing of the seasons and between sounds and music (*Korean Overseas Information Service* 1995, 10).

A major innovation for the Korean alphabet was to symbolically represent the sounds based on the shape of the mouth when making certain sounds. Jared Diamond expressed in "Writing Right" that King Sejong's letters have been described as "the world's best alphabet" and "the most scientific system of writing." He was particularly impressed with the unique features of the *han'gul* alphabet, such as the fact that "*hangul* vowels can be distinguished at a glance from *hangul* consonants." Diamond felt that it was even more remarkable that "the shape of each consonant depicts the position in which the lips, mouth, or tongue is held to pronounce that letter" (1994).

According to the *Hunmin Chongum*, the basic consonant symbols were drawn from the shape of the mouth and position of the tongue and lips as the sounds were articulated. The other consonants were formed by adding strokes to these five basic shapes (see table A).

TABLE A. The Five Basic Shapes

ㄱ	ㄴ	ㄷ	ㅁ	ㅇ

TABLE B. Vowel Symbols

.	—	ǀ
Sky	Land	Man

The vowel symbols were based on the shapes of the sky, land, and man (see table B).

These three basic shapes are combined to form other vowels. The consonants and vowels each represent a phoneme, the basic unit of speech. When they are combined together, the letters make a syllable. With such elegance and compactness, *han'gul* is both an alphabetic and a syllabic language. G. K. Ledyard explains:

One of the most unique and interesting features of the Korean alphabet is the strict correspondence it shows between graphic shape and graphic function. Not only are the shapes of the consonants of a pattern different from those of the vowels, but even within these two main groups the shapes decided upon by Sejong clarify other important relationships.... It would be quite enough merely to have the systematic shapes within classes. But for those shapes themselves to be rationalized on the basis of the speech organs associated with their sounds—that is unparalleled grammatological luxury! (1966, 199–203)

Challenges in Introducing Han'gul

The development and spread of *han'gul* was a monumental achievement chiefly carried out by one person, Sejong, who later in life suffered from neuralgia, diabetes,

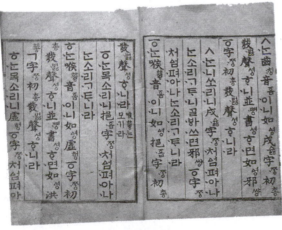

The original decree by Korean king Sejong establishing the Han'gul writing system. In 1446, Sejong promulgated a new writing system, intended to enable the common people to read and write. (Instructional Resources Corporation)

and poor eyesight. Consumed by his duty to his people, he devoted all his remaining energy to the creation of his writing system. Even when visiting the hot springs of Onyang and Chongju for medical treatment, he took his books on linguistics and continued his writing and research until he finished in the winter of 1443. Nevertheless, *han'gul* encountered strong opposition from members of the king's own court and the intelligentsia. Choi Manli, a senior scholar of the Jade Hall, wrote this criticism of the new alphabet:

> Since the new alphabet is so easily understood, I fear that the people will fall into laziness and never make efforts to learn. Those who do not use Chinese characters, but [use] other letters and alphabets, such as the Mongols, Sohans, Jurchens, Japanese and Tibetans, are all barbarians without exception. To use new letters would surely make us barbarians ourselves. . . . The new alphabet is in truth no more than an eccentric and ill-considered crudity, an obstruction to literary progress, and of no possible benefit to the government. (Diamond Sutra Recitation Group 2007, 94)

The concept of universal literacy was radical and revolutionary in King Sejong's day. Many even considered this concept undesirable. The scholars opposed universal literacy for the general population because they considered the public's ability to read and write to be dangerous. The creation of a new alphabet was further regarded as a challenge to the established culture, which had been under the influence of the long tradition and authority of Chinese script and to the Sinocentric world order. Knowing that there would be such opposition, King Sejong tried to persuade the noble class:

> Sol Chong of Silla created *Yidu* [a method of transcribing the Korean language based on sound and meaning of the Chinese characters] for the people, and now I too have made a new alphabet for them. Why do you agree that Sol Chong was in the right, while maintaining that your King is in the wrong? I myself take great delight in classical literature. Therefore it cannot be said that I am doing this simply because I prefer what is new to what is old. (Diamond Sutra Recitation Group 2007, 95)

King Sejong pursued a vigorous policy to promote the new alphabet and ordered the publishing of several literary works in the new Korean script; most notable among these were the *Yongbi Ochonga* (*Songs of Flying Dragons*), a eulogy of the royal ancestors, *Sokpo Sangjol* (*Episodes from the Life of Buddha*), and *Worin Chongang Chigok* (*Songs of the Moon's Reflection on a Thousand Rivers*) (Diamond Sutra Recitation Group 2007, 95). When giving his royal ordinance, King Sejong used both Chinese and the new Korean script. He gave public notices for the common citizens written in *han'gul*. To further institutionalize the new alphabet, knowledge and use of *han'gul* were requirements in the state examinations.

Paradoxically, the ease of learning *han'gul* was used as grounds for opposing it by its critics, who called it *Ach'imgul* (morning letters) as it could be learned in one morning. *Han'gul* was also called *Amk'ul* (women's letters) because it was perceived as so easy that even women, who were generally uneducated at the time, could learn it. For those scholars who had invested years learning the complex Chinese characters, *han'gul* did not appear to be worthy of study. At that time, education was the privilege of the noble (*yangban*) class and not considered suitable for commoners.

In spite of the brilliance of *han'gul* and the efforts of King Sejong and his supporters, centuries of tradition could not be changed quickly. For the next 400 years, the Korean civil servants and scholars would continue to use Chinese characters in both official and unofficial documents. However, eventually *han'gul* was accepted and strongly embraced by all segments of society. It has become the foundation of Korean culture, helping to preserve national identity.

Spoken Language

The language of the Korean people is relatively simple to pronounce because each syllable has equal value and the vowel sounds are distinct and regular. There are few stressed syllables and no sharp discrimination of gender in the personal pronouns. There are 10 vowels, 11 vowel blends, and 14 consonants.

For the late learner, matters are made much easier by the creation of a written system for reproducing Korean sounds. This system is called *han'gul*. Using a regular phonetic system of writing eventually produces widespread literacy that allows visual learners the opportunity to see the sounds they hear and in this way reinforces the learning process.

Words are made of a number of syllables that make different sounds. Each of the syllables has the value of one single note. So each is pronounced clearly and with the same stress. Every syllable must also be equal in length. When one pronounces the consonants *pp* (ㅃ), *tt* (ㄸ), *kk* (ㄲ), and *tch* (ㅉ), they require extra-strong emphasis. While the *s* (ㅅ) sounds very weak in Korean, the sound *ss* (ㅆ) is tensed and sounds like a very emphatic English *s*. There are many more pronunciation rules, but Table C gives some guidelines as to how to make the consonant sounds.

Written Language

The vocabulary of the modern Korean language is made up of about 40 percent indigenous words and 60 percent loan words, the vast majority of which are from Chinese, and an increasing number of which are from English. One result is a dual system of native (pure Korean) and Sino-Korean numerals. Another is that more formal or academic works are written in mixed script, using Chinese characters (*hanja*) and *han'gul*. In order to read the daily newspaper, the average person must know at least 1,800 *hanja*. College students must know twice as many. However, in recent years it has become less common to write Sino-Korean characters in newspapers, books, periodicals, and academic journals in South Korea. Many people express concern that the origins and meaning of the Chinese characters will ultimately be lost. North Korea abolished the use of *hanja* for purely nationalistic reasons, using *han'gul* exclusively.

While *han'gul* is described as a simple and scientific alphabet, learning how to use it may be considered difficult by Westerners because of the difference from the Roman-based writing system. Writing Korean syllables resembles writing Chinese characters (see Table D).

TABLE C. Pronunciation Guidelines for Consonants

Single Consonant	Sound Value	Aspirated Consonant (with air)	Sound Value	Double Consonant (tense)	Articulation Point (where these sounds are made)
ㄱ	[g/k]	ㅋ	[k]	ㄲ	Throat/soft palate
ㄴ	[n]				Gum ridge
ㄷ	[d/t]	ㅌ	[t]	ㄸ	Gum ridge
ㄹ	[l/r]				Gum ridge
ㅁ	[m]				Lips
ㅂ	[b/p]	ㅍ	[p]	ㅃ	Lips
ㅅ	[s] or [sh]			ㅆ	Hard palate
ㅇ	[-ng] or silent				Throat/soft palate
ㅈ	[j/ch]	ㅊ	[ch]	ㅉ	Hard palate
		ㅎ	[h]		Throat

Note: The shapes of the consonants ㄱ, ㄴ, ㅅ, ㅁ, and ㅇ are graphical representations of the speech organs used to pronounce them. Other consonants were created by adding extra lines to the basic shapes.

TABLE D. 6 Forms of Korean Consonants

가	소	뭐	한	국	왕

For example, the syllable *han* in the word *han'gul* is formed by an *h* in the top left corner, an *a* in the top right corner, and an *n* at the bottom, the whole syllabic group forming what looks like a Chinese character (see Table E).

It is possible to create more than 2,350 characters in this way. Spaces between written words are often deleted, causing considerable difficulty for those who are attempting to learn the written language. Another challenge is the fact that the pronunciation of Korean words has changed over time. Many words are not pronounced as they are spelled. Also, Korean adjectives have conjugations like verbs.

TABLE E. Example of Korean Syllable *han*

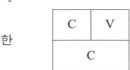

C	V
C	

In the *Hunmin Chongum*, there was a total of 28 letters. However, only 24 of the 28 letters are used in modern Korean. There are 14 simple consonants and 10 simple vowels.

TABLE F. Consonants

ㄱ	ㄴ	ㄷ	ㄹ	ㅁ	ㅂ	ㅅ	ㅇ	ㅈ	ㅊ	ㅋ	ㅌ	ㅍ	ㅎ
g/k	n	d/t	r/l	m	B	s	∅	j/ch	ch'	k'	t'	p'	h

TABLE G. Vowels

ㅏ	ㅑ	ㅓ	ㅕ	ㅗ	ㅛ	ㅜ	ㅠ	ㅡ	ㅣ
[a] bother	[ya] yacht	[o] awake	[yo] yawn	[o] coat	[yo] yolk	[u] boot	[yu] you	[u] put	[i] seed

Of the 28 letters in the *Hunmin Chongum*, 8 basic letters were used to create the rest of the letters. They were as follows:

TABLE H. Consonants

TABLE I. Vowels

Consonants, the initial sound letters, resemble the shape of the speaker's mouth. The shape of each letter is based on the form of different sound articulation units.

TABLE J. Pronunciation of the Consonants

ㄱ	(kiyok)	To pronounce this letter, part of the tongue touches the molar teeth and sticks near the uvula. The shape of the letter is based on the lateral form of this process.
ㄴ	(niun)	To pronounce this letter, the front of the tongue curves, and the tip of the tongue sticks to the upper gums. The shape of the letter is based on the lateral form of this process.
ㅁ	(mium)	To pronounce this letter, the upper and lower lips are joined. The shape of the letter is based on the form of the joined lips.
ㅅ	(shiot)	To pronounce this letter, the tip of the tongue and the upper teeth are brought close together, and sound is created by blowing through the narrowed passage. The shape of the letter is based on the form of the teeth during the process.
ㅇ	(iung)	To pronounce this letter that is created by stimulating the uvula, the throat assumes a round shape, hence, the form of the consonant.

Other consonants, excluding the five basic ones listed above, were created by adding strokes to those forms, based on the strength of the sounds.

Nine additional letters were made by adding strokes to the five basic consonants based on the strength of the sounds, as follows.

TABLE **K.** Additional Letters Made by the Five Basic Consonants

ㄱ	ㅋ
ㄴ	ㄷ, ㅌ
ㅁ	ㅂ, ㅍ
ㅅ	ㅈ, ㅊ
ㅇ	ㆆ, ㅎ

Note: "ㆆ" is no longer used.

The vowels, on the other hand, were created in the image of the sky, land, and man.

TABLE **L.** Meaning of the 3 Vowels

o	Resembles the roundness of the sky
—	Represents the flat land
ǀ	Is the image of a standing man

The other vowels are variations of these three basic vowels.

TABLE **M.** Other Vowels

ㅏ	ㅑ	ㅓ	ㅕ	ㅗ	ㅛ	ㅜ	ㅠ

Korean syllables are divided into three major parts:

TABLE **N.** The Parts of a Syllable

Ch'osong	Initial consonant
Chungsong	Peak vowel
Chongsong	Final consonant

The *Ch'osong* (initial consonant), *Chungsong* (peak vowel), and *Chongsong* (final consonant), which make up the basic structure, were used by the great King Sejong and his Chiphyonjon scholars as the foundation when creating the Korean letters. *Chongsong* (the final consonant) was not separately created. It was a repetition of the *Ch'osong* (the initial consonant). As a result, thousands of words can be created by combining the consonants and vowels.

TABLE O. Combinations of 14 Basic Korean Consonants and 10 Basic Korean Vowels

	ㅏ	ㅑ	ㅓ	ㅕ	ㅗ	ㅛ	ㅜ	ㅠ	ㅡ	ㅣ
ㄱ	가	갸	거	겨	고	교	구	규	그	기
ㄴ	나	냐	너	녀	노	뇨	누	뉴	느	니
ㄷ	다	댜	더	뎌	도	됴	두	듀	드	디
ㄹ	라	랴	러	려	로	료	루	류	르	리
ㅁ	마	먀	머	며	모	묘	무	뮤	므	미
ㅂ	바	뱌	버	벼	보	뵤	부	뷰	브	비
ㅅ	사	샤	서	셔	소	쇼	수	슈	스	시
ㅇ	아	야	어	여	오	요	우	유	으	이
ㅈ	자	쟈	저	져	조	죠	주	쥬	즈	지
ㅊ	차	챠	처	쳐	초	쵸	추	츄	츠	치
ㅋ	카	캬	커	켜	코	쿄	쿠	큐	크	키
ㅌ	타	탸	터	텨	토	툐	투	튜	트	티
ㅍ	파	퍄	퍼	펴	포	표	푸	퓨	프	피
ㅎ	하	햐	허	혀	호	효	후	휴	흐	히

TABLE P. Examples of Sounds Produced Using "ㄱ" and "ㄴ"

ㄱ + ㅏ = 가 (ga)	ㄱ + ㅑ = 갸 (gya)	ㄱ + ㅓ = 거 (go)	ㄱ + ㅕ = 겨 (gyo)	ㄱ + ㅗ = 고 (go)
ㄱ + ㅛ = 교 (gyo)	ㄱ + ㅜ = 구 (gu)	ㄱ + ㅠ = 규 (gyu)	ㄱ + ㅡ = 그 (gu)	ㄱ + ㅣ = 기 (gi)
ㄴ + ㅏ = 나 (na)	ㄴ + ㅑ = 냐 (nya)	ㄴ + ㅓ = 너 (no)	ㄴ + ㅕ = 녀 (nyo)	ㄴ + ㅗ = 노 (no)
ㄴ + ㅛ = 뇨 (nyo)	ㄴ + ㅜ = 누 (nu)	ㄴ + ㅠ = 뉴 (nyu)	ㄴ + ㅡ = 느 (nu)	ㄴ + ㅣ = 니 (ni)

Tables O and P are examples that clearly show *han'gul*, with only 14 consonants and 10 vowels, is capable of making just about any sound.

The Korean language is very detailed in sound and intonation. One can figure out differences, such as between bright and dark red, just by the sound of the word "red" in Korean. Therefore, when attempting to fully express Korean sounds using foreign alphabets, it is very difficult. However, due to its simple and scientific design, it is possible to approximate the sounds of foreign words using the Korean alphabet. Table Q shows some examples of English words expressed in *han'gul*.

TABLE Q. Some Sample English Words in *Han'gul*

English Word	Korean (Loan) Word
Coffee	커피
Banana	바나나
Hawaii	하와이
Hamburger	햄버거
Golf	골프
Web site	웹 사이트
Hello	헬로
I	아이
Am	엠
A	어
Man	맨
Good morning	굿 모닝

TABLE R. Example of a Korean Simple Sentence

저는	+	한국어를	+	좋아해요.
(Subject)	+	(Object)	+	(Verb)
I		*Korean*		*Like*

SOME MAJOR DIFFERENCES BETWEEN KOREAN AND WESTERN LANGUAGES

Syntax

The most commonly used order of words in a Korean sentence or clause is (1) subject, (2) object, and (3) verb; qualifying elements come before the objects qualified; dependent clauses also come before the independent clauses. In English, the usual word order is (1) subject, (2) verb, and then (3) object.

Honorific System

Because Confucian teaching and rules are reflected in all areas of Korean culture, a rigid hierarchical social structure is seen in the language as well. Each word must be chosen carefully depending on whom you are addressing (child, relative, adult, employer, or colleague). In reference to actual names, titles are often placed after the name.

In order to fit the Confucian philosophy, words come in various forms. Most of the nouns are regular for everyday use. However, there are other nouns that are

TABLE S. Example of Two Different Speaking Styles (Informal and Formal) in Three Different Hierarchical Forms

Speaker	Informal Form	Formal Form
You (speaker)	Honorific informal polite	Honorific formal
	Informal polite	Formal
	Informal (familiar)	

TABLE T. Example of Titles with Honorific Markers: "Mr. Kim is a Korean Professor."

김	선생님	께서는	한국어	교수님	이세요.
Kim (last name)	Teacher/Mr./Ms. (title)	Honorific subject marker	Korean language	Professor (honorific)	Is (to be) (honorific)

both humble, when referring to oneself or a subordinate, and honorific, when referring to someone older or of higher position. All verbs can be at three different levels of informality. Starting with the lowest level, a verb can be familiar and used among one's closest friends; informal, polite, and used for everyday casual conversation; and honorific informal polite, to be used with someone of higher position. Depending on the usage in either conversation or formal meetings, words can be either in the informal form or formal form. The formal form also comes in regular and honorific forms.

This is very different from American English, which really only has formal and informal speech. Due to the egalitarian nature of American society, there is very minimal honorific speech, making Korean's highly developed honorific system a challenge for Americans.

ROMANIZATION OF KOREAN

Another difficulty regarding the language is that over the years, the official romanized spelling has changed. In 2000, the Ministry of Culture and Tourism announced a new system of romanization and published a book containing all the changes. This completely replaces the system that had been used commonly in Korea and abroad since 1984. Tables U and V illustrate the new rules and examples of the changes that took place.

It is important that we are knowledgeable of the new rule changes and, especially when dealing with place names, understand enough *han'gul* to be able to arrive at the intended destination and not somewhere else!

TABLE U. New Romanization System (Simplified Chart)

ㅏ	ㅓ	ㅗ	ㅜ	ㅡ	ㅣ	ㅐ	ㅔ	ㅚ	ㅟ	ㅑ	ㅕ	ㅛ	ㅠ	ㅒ	ㅖ	ㅘ	ㅙ	ㅝ	ㅞ	ㅢ
a	ao	o	u	eu	i	ae	e	Oe	wi	Ya	yeo	yo	yu	yae	ye	wa	wae	wo	we	ui

TABLE V. Examples of Common Korean Words (Old and New Romanization Comparison)

	Old	New		Old	New
부산	*Pusan*	Busan	대구	*Taegu*	Daegu
광주	*Kwangju*	Gwangju	대전	*Taejon*	Daejeon
인천	*Inch'on*	Incheon	전주	*Chonju*	Jeonju
제주	*Cheju*	Jeju	청주	*Ch'ongju*	Cheongju
경주	*Kyongju*	Gyeongju	김포	*Kimp'o*	Gimpo
고구려	*Koguryo*	Goguryeo	동대구	*Tongdaegu*	Dongdaegu
부곡	*Pugok*	Bugok	정읍	*Chongup*	Jeongeup
울산	*Ulsan*	Ulsan	목호	*Muk'o*	Mukho

CONCLUSION

Through time, history has confirmed the importance and worth of King Sejong's *han'gul*. Now, linguists and scholars from all over the world are interested in *han'gul* and have come to cherish the language. *Han'gul* replaced Chinese characters as the dominant form of writing in all Korean books and newspapers, and Korea enjoys one of the highest literacy rates in the world.

Scholars remark that *han'gul* is the only alphabet that is completely native to East Asia and one that reveals an understanding of phonological science unequaled in the West until modern times (Diamond Sutra Recitation Group 2007, 97). Linguists have described it as "a star among alphabets" and comment on its simplicity and elegance (99). Another consequence of *han'gul*'s scientific and easy-to-learn design has been its adaptability to the changes in language. In the information age, it is no surprise that *han'gul* has been made so accessible on the Internet, much more so than Chinese and even Japanese. Yi Hwa-yong wrote in *Humanism, the Power of Korean Culture* that in the information age *han'gul* has a distinct advantage over other alphabets.

> On a computer keyboard, the consonants are arranged on the left, the vowels on the right, and words form as consonants and vowels are typed alternately. In terms of ergonomics, this allows for maximization of productivity by, inter alia, an efficient distribution of tiredness in the fingers. Moreover, the fact that each letter has one single sound is extremely advantageous. With *han'gul*, as the sound changes, the frequency also changes at a fixed rate, allowing speech recognition by computers to be done logically and easily. The sound and writing of *han'gul* therefore have a vast sphere of application, from the system of translation to the Internet. (98–99)

Linguists universally acknowledge the originality and philosophy behind *han'gul* and its logical and pragmatic basis. More valuable than the alphabet itself is the

TABLE **W.**   Everyday Expressions

"Hello?" / "How are you?" The following is appropriate anytime of the day and also means "Good morning," "Good afternoon," and "Good evening." (Note: The formal form is for the first meeting.)	
[an-ayng ha-sim-ni-kka?] (honorific formal) [an-anyong ha-se-yo?] (honorific informal polite)	안녕하십니까? 안녕하세요?
"Hello?" This greeting is used when on the phone.	
[ye-bo se-yo?] (honorific informal polite)	여보세요?
"My name is John Song." This statement follows the initial "Hello" greeting. When giving your name, it is always better to pronounce it clearly in your language. (Note: Use only once for the first meeting.)	
[je-i-rum-um John Song im-ni-da.] (formal)	제 이름은 John Song입니다.
"Nice to meet you." This expression follows the introduction of your name. (Note: Use only once for the first meeting.)	
[man-na-suh ban-gap-sum-ni-da.] (formal)	만나서 반갑습니다.
"Good bye." Said by the host when the guest is leaving his or her home.	
[an-nyong-hi gah-se-yo.] (informal polite)	안녕히 가세요.
"Good bye." Said by the guest when the guest is leaving the host's home.	
[an-ayong-hi geh-se-yo.] (informal polite)	안녕히 계세요.
"Thank you." Commonly used form of "thank you" (Chinese).	
[gam-sa ham-ni-da.] (formal) [gam-sa hae-yo.] (informal polite)	감사합니다. 감사해요.
"Thank you." Commonly used form of "thank you" (Korean).	
[go-mop ssum-ni-da.] (formal) [go-ma wah-yo.] (informal polite)	고맙습니다. 고마워요.
"I'm sorry." This form is used when apologizing to an older person (respectful form).	
[jeh-song ham-ni-da.] (formal) [jeh-song hae-yo.] (informal polite)	죄송합니다. 죄송해요.
"I'm sorry." This form is used when apologizing to your own generation and those who are younger (plain style).	
[me-an ham-ni-da.] (formal) [me-an hae-yo.] (informal polite)	미안합니다. 미안해요.
"Yes"	
[ne.] (proper) [ye.] (how people say it sometimes)	네. 예.
"No"	
[a-ni-o]	아니오.

legacy of King Sejong and his commitment to the Korean people so many centuries ago. His faith in the people and his wish that they could learn to express their thoughts are the main reasons why the Korean people remain very proud of their language and wish to share it with the world.

REFERENCES

Diamond, Jared. 1994. *Writing Right*. Discover, June 1. http://discovermagazine.com/1994/jun/writingright384

Diamond Sutra Recitation Group. 2007. *King Sejong the Great, the Everlasting Light of Korea*. Seoul: Korean Spirit and Culture Promotion Project.

Eckert, Carter, et al. 1990. *Korea Old and New: A History*. Seoul, Korea: Ilchokak Publishers.

Hangul—The Korean Alphabet. Korean Heritage Series. Seoul: Korean Overseas Information Service, 1995.

The Korean Alphabet—Hangeul. Seoul, Korea: Ministry of Culture and Tourism, 1995.

Korean Language Information Society. n.d. *Hangeul—Korean's Gift to the World*. Seoul, South Korea: Ministry of Culture and Tourism.

Ledyard, G. K. 1966. "The Korean Language Reform of 1446: The Origin, Background, and Early History of the Korean Alphabet." PhD diss., University of California, Berkeley.

Lee, Iksop, and Robert S. Ramsey. 2000. *The Korean Language: A Korean Cultural Perspective*. New York: SUNY Press.

Lee, Peter H., ed. 1993. *Sources of Korean Civilization: From Early Times to the Sixteenth Century*. Vol. I. New York: Columbia University Press.

Man, John. 2001. *Alpha Beta: How 26 Letters Shaped the Western World*. London: Headline Book Publishing Ltd.

National Institute of the Korean Language. 2006. *Korean Grammar 1 for Non-Koreans*. Seoul, South Korea: Communication Books.

———. 2006. *Korean Grammar 2 for Non-Koreans*. Seoul, Korea: Communication Books.

Our Beautiful Han-Gul. Seoul, South Korea: Hallyu Research Institute, 2006.

Sampson, Geoffrey. 1990. *Writing Systems: A Linguistic Introduction*. North Clarenton, VT: Tuttle Publishing.

Seth, Michael J. 2006. *A Concise History of Modern Korea: From the Neolithic Period through the Nineteenth Century*. New York: Rowman & Littlefield Publishers, Inc.

Yi, Hwa-Hyong. 2004. *Humanism: The Power of Korean Culture*. Seoul, South Korea: Kookhak.

Etiquette

Mary E. Connor

INTRODUCTION: HOW NOT TO SUCCEED IN KOREA

Walk through someone's home with your shoes on. Call a Korean by his or her given name. Refer to the wife of Mr. Kim as Mrs. Kim. Introduce yourself to a prominent person. Speak to a younger person before an elderly person. Make constant eye contact when in conversation. Invite someone to lunch Dutch treat. Pour your own drink. Bring up serious topics of conversation during a meal.

These behaviors are natural to many foreigners, but they are mistakes in Korea. Most Koreans are very forgiving of the blunders made by foreigners; however, by avoiding these behaviors a visitor will show sensitivity and respect. Most customs have served Koreans well for thousands of years, and traditional values are still strong.

CONFUCIAN CONCEPTS AND VALUES

Confucius lived more than 2,500 years ago, yet his beliefs continue to influence the behavior of Koreans. The behaviors and values described within this chapter are characteristic of traditional Korean culture and all socioeconomic groups. Although the older generation currently expresses concern that the young are not upholding the traditional principles of society, most of the described values persist wherever there are Koreans in the world.

Confucius believed that a perfect society could develop if people played their roles properly and Confucian literature, such as *The Analects*, served as a guide as to how one should live in social harmony with others. Confucius placed great importance on respect for superiors and parents, duty to family, loyalty to friends, humility, sincerity, and courtesy. Korean etiquette is strongly influenced by Confucian tradition, which values above all hierarchy, respect for one's elders, and harmonious relationships. One must be considerate of the other person through one's actions and words. For each situation, there are appropriate words to say, proper ways to dress, and correct actions (Hinton 1998).

Hierarchy By Confucian standards, age is one of the most important factors to consider. Elderly persons in Korea receive special treatment and are given more consideration than anyone else. When encountering a group of people, the elderly are to be acknowledged first. No one should ever question the wisdom of an elderly person. Respect is not limited to the elderly alone. Throughout life, one is to defer to anyone who is older. When greeting an elder with a bow, keep both legs together, put both arms by the side, keep the back straight, and bend from the waist. The head should be kept down to avoid looking at the elder. Do not offer a hand to shake if the person is older. Koreans always use the right hand when giving an object to a person of higher status. To show the most respect, both hands hold the object as it is given or received. When passing objects to people of lower status, either hand is acceptable, but using both hands is inappropriate.

Humility   Koreans are often demure about their accomplishments and allow others to give them praise. Modesty is considered a sign of good manners and breeding. In many countries, it is customary to say "thank you" to acknowledge a compliment. Koreans consider this too bold and often will deny the compliment. Rejecting praise is an indication of humility.

Harmonious Relations   Confucian principles continue to provide guidelines for conduct between individuals. Koreans wish to avoid conflict. If there are difficulties between two people, they prefer a third party to act as an intermediary to avoid open confrontation. This allows both parties to save face. If visitors encounter problems, they should be flexible. A Korean will likely concede changes to maintain harmony.

To admit that one does not know something can cause a person to lose face or, in other words, to be humiliated. As a result, Koreans may not admit ignorance or uncertainty and may well try to answer even though they know they could be wrong.

Most Koreans are proud of their heritage and their country and are very eager to ask visitors about their impressions; however, negative comments will not be well received. If one must say something negative, intersperse the negative with positive comments. It is best not to criticize anything Korean.

In many aspects of interpersonal communication, one must be sensitive to another's feelings to avoid giving pain. If people are invited to a drinking party, they are expected to drink. If they say no, it will ruin the general atmosphere of the party. It is considered bad form even when one does not drink alcoholic beverages. However, there are some possible acceptable excuses. A person can say that he or she is taking traditional Korean medicine and cannot drink or that his or her religion discourages drinking. With experience, one can gradually learn how to say "no" without giving offense.

One must also be aware that a "yes" does not mean that a Korean agrees or intends to comply. It simply means that the person understands the situation or that they will do their best to comply. The word "no" is seldom expressed. It is expressed indirectly. For example, a banker will not say "no" to a person wanting a loan but will make the terms so difficult that the person will reject the offer. If a Korean says "yes" but does not comply, he or she did not mean to deceive you. It simply means that it was not possible to carry out the action.

Kibun   Another concept that relates to the Confucian stress on harmonious relations is *kibun*. There is no exact equivalent in the English language. *Kibun* (feelings, mood, or state of mind) is of prime importance and valued in traditional Korean society. In essence, it is the person's inner sense, his or her very being. This invisible part of a person can be damaged by loss of face, disrespect, or unhappiness. All cultures value how people feel emotionally, but few cultures place as high a value on this as Koreans do. They are expert at sensing another person's emotional state and very helpful in getting one out of a bad mood by simple gestures. *Kibun* enters every aspect of life. To the Korean, harmonious relations are more important than efficiency, honesty, or truth. To foreigners, Koreans may seem too sensitive. For example, a Korean's *kibun* is damaged when someone does not show him or her proper respect by bowing soon enough or low enough, not using honorific words, or handing him or her something with the left hand. Koreans also believe that direct eye contact during conversation is rude and prefer to concentrate on what is being discussed and avoid eye-to-eye contact. These are rules of etiquette known by every Korean. While they may seem unimportant or foolish to the foreign visitor, they should be respected and observed.

Nunch'i A concept that is related to *kibun* is *nunch'i*. The concept of *nunch'i* relates to one's ability to assess nonverbal communication. In a society where being in harmony with others is vital, judging another person's state of mind is critical. If a person develops this ability, he or she will know when to ask delicate questions or to ask the boss for a favor. In Korea, communication requires people to focus on nonverbal behavior that provides clues to one's mood or inner feelings. What is most important is genuine friendship. Developing skills in assessing verbal and nonverbal communication is recognized as a means of developing good friendships, maintaining harmony in the home, and being able to negotiate successfully in business relations. Koreans are taught to control their emotions and to disguise their feelings. Therefore, determining the particular mood of a Korean may be a challenge, but it is a skill that could bring great satisfaction and reward in improved communication and international understanding.

HOW TO SUCCEED IN KOREA

Business Etiquette When involved in setting up meetings, it is important to consider many aspects of the culture and traditions. For example, many Koreans vacation from mid-July to mid-August, and it is wise to avoid trying to schedule business meetings during these times. Other inappropriate times are the Lunar New Year (January or February) or the Moon Festival (September or October). The best times for meetings are from 10:00 AM to noon and from 2:00 to 4:00 PM. Business hours are usually from 9:00 AM to 5:00 PM from Monday through Friday.

Another important consideration is the location of the meeting. One should use the largest meeting room available because the size of the room is a sign of the importance of the meeting and respect for the guests. If the room is warm, one should invite the guests to remove their jackets, but one should wait to remove one's own jacket until the guests remove theirs. It is the custom to offer seats to the guests according to their seniority. It is helpful to put name cards at each place. Green tea is preferred, but quality tea and coffee are also acceptable, and the coffee is often drunk without cream.

Since the guests will probably bring gifts, one should have gifts available to give them. Any small item representative of one's business or region is appropriate. The gifts should always be wrapped, but they will not be opened in your presence. This is to convey that the thought is more important than the gift.

Business cards are inevitably exchanged after introductions. The way an individual treats someone's business card is indicative of the way he or she will treat that person. It is considered proper to use both hands when presenting business cards and to be careful that the writing on the card is facing the recipient. If one side of the business card is translated into Korean, it will be a sign of respect and greatly appreciated. Cards should be received with both hands and placed on the table in front of the recipient. To immediately put the card in one's pocket or purse is considered rude. During the meeting, one should occasionally look at the card. Do not write comments on the other person's business card in his or her presence.

One must also be aware that Koreans prefer to do business with people with whom they have a personal connection. Relationships are developed through informal social gatherings and involvement in various organizations, and this process may take a considerable length of time. Legal agreements are viewed as loosely structured consensus statements that broadly define an agreement and leave room for flexibility and further deliberations. Once an agreement is signed, one should expect ongoing negotiations and the necessity to make additional adjustments to what has been determined previously. The contract is only the starting point for the development of the relationship. To avoid being in an unfavorable position, one should not concede everything before a contract is signed.

It is also considered very unwise to criticize someone in front of others or to boast about one's self. To maintain good relations, an intermediary is usually asked to help with delicate issues. Since it is critical to avoid putting individuals in a position where they might lose face, the way one asks a question is very important. It is better to ask, "When can you deliver the shipment?" than "Can I expect the shipment in two weeks?" since the second case requires a definite response. Another factor that is common to Confucian-oriented businesspeople is a definite reluctance to say no quickly and clearly to a proposal. It is customary for the meetings to drag on without any progress and without clear indications that the project is not going anywhere. One of the most common responses for shelving a proposal is to say, "*keul seh,*" meaning "We will think about it."

Men should wear conservative brown, black, and navy business suits with white shirts. Women should dress conservatively and wear subdued colors. The choice of dress should definitely be age appropriate for the wearer and modest. Women should also avoid tight dresses or skirts because meals are often eaten while sitting on the floor. Sleeveless outfits and very short skirts are considered unprofessional in the workplace and basically bad taste anywhere.

Many people cannot distinguish between the various Asian cultures. Korea is not Japan or China. Avoid making mistakes of confusing the cultures, or you will be seen as ignorant or rude. Be aware of Korean sensitivities about Japan. Koreans usually have an excellent grasp of written English but often lack conversational skills. Therefore, speak slowly and clearly and repeat any points that are particularly important. If they do not feel confident about their ability to express themselves correctly, they may be reticent about responding to e-mail messages or corresponding by letters. After a meeting, it may be worthwhile to exchange minutes to ensure that everything has been understood. After adjournment, the guests should be escorted to the reception area where it is appropriate for everyone to bow and to say farewell.

Clothes   Confucius reportedly said that clothes distinguished a cultured man from a barbarian. While notions of appropriate clothing are becoming more relaxed, Koreans take personal appearances seriously and are apt to be very conscientious of fashion. Foreign businesspeople are well advised to ensure that their appearance reflects the image they want to project. It is best to dress well and conservatively at all times. Avoid jeans, T-shirts, sleeveless blouses and dresses, and shorts unless told that it is acceptable to wear them.

Eating and Drinking in a Home   When invited to a Korean home, expect to be served a meal. Many homes now have tables and chairs, but it may be that guests will dine at a low table and sit on cushions. The whole meal will be served at one time, with rice and soup beside individual plates, and all side dishes will be spread out on the table. The food is not passed around the table. If it is a large table, there will be multiples of every dish at both ends of the table. Everyone waits to eat until the oldest person begins. One needs to be sensitive about conversation during dinner. If you are a daughter-in-law eating with a stern mother-in-law or if you are a Korean citizen and your host is a very prominent person, unnecessary conversation is not appreciated. If you are an American having dinner with Korean friends, you should speak, but you should not bring up serious topics of conversation during a meal. If you do, it will give the impression that you are dissatisfied with the hospitality of the host.

Koreans eat mainly with chopsticks, but rice and soup should be eaten with a spoon. It is considered impolite to pick up the rice or soup bowl in one's hand while eating. During the meal, leave the spoon and chopsticks, when not in use, on top of the rice or soup bowl. When you have finished eating, put them beside your plate. The hostess will encourage guests to eat more than they want, but this is an expression of concern. Since there is usually too much food, no one expects the guests to eat it all. It is the custom to decline the offer of more food. If you decline three times, your message will be clear to the host and the offer will not be made again. It is not the Korean custom to praise the cook for the delicious food; however, if guests say that the food is good, it will definitely be appreciated.

There are two particularly unacceptable behaviors at the meal table. Never eat with your fingers. Never blow your nose at the table. If one's nose is running from the spicy food, it is considered acceptable to wipe one's nose. It is also considered impolite to pass food or drink with the left hand or to pierce food with chopsticks.

In Korea, drinking alcohol after hours is considered by many to be essential for developing a sense of trust and building close relationships. Drinking to excess is expected, essential for bonding with other men, and proper for forging the relations conducive to business. Because of the influence of the West, it is important to realize that not all Koreans behave in the manner described. *Soju* is the popular drink of men, but at high-end hostess bars whiskey is purchased by the bottle. Most fine restaurants now offer wine, which has become very popular.

There are some simple, but very essential customs that any visitor should observe. It is important to use proper table manners. When drinking, offer to pour for the others at the table, starting with the eldest member of the party. To show respect when pouring, both hands should be used by holding the right arm or elbow with the left hand. Use both hands when accepting a drink. The eldest family member sits at the table first, and the others must not take up their chopsticks or spoon until he or she begins eating. When using the chopsticks, the spoon must not be placed back on the table until one is finished eating. When using the chopsticks, the spoon is placed in the rice or soup bowl or leaned against its edge. After picking up food in one's chopsticks, do not put it back in the dish. No one is excused from the table before the eldest is finished.

Eating and Drinking at a Restaurant   Korean restaurants are simple and functional. The service is quick and to the point. The turnover of seats in the average restaurant is fast, and guests are not expected to linger for a long time. Nevertheless, the servers are inevitably gracious and delighted that one has chosen to dine on Korean food. Most restaurants will have printed menus and may include helpful illustrations. The etiquette in restaurants is basically the same as when eating in someone's home.

Seating arrangements are different from Western restaurants. Most restaurants have conventional Western-style chairs and tables, but guests may have to sit on a cushion on a hard floor at a very low table. This could become very uncomfortable as one might be sitting in this position for quite a long time. If one arranges to sit in a private dining area, the shoes should be taken off outside the room. The shoes may be reversed in order to step into them easily when leaving the room. Metal chopsticks are used in most restaurants and require more practice than wooden ones. If a foreign guest expresses appreciation for the delicious meal, it will be graciously received.

When drinking or dining out in Korea, the rule is simple. The person who suggests going out pays. It is considered very impolite to go "Dutch treat." Usually people argue about who pays, but inevitably it is the person who initiates the get-together. People usually take turns paying for the meal. Always bring enough money with you and offer to pay at least once. The custom of Dutch treat can be very unsettling to older Koreans; however, it is becoming more common among the younger generation and in the workplace for each person to pay for his or her own meal. No tipping is required except occasionally at very high-class restaurants and/or after a large party has been served.

Forms of Address   Names are very personal. Westerners like to develop relationships by addressing another person by his or her first name. In Korea the first name is the family name, such as Park or Kim. If an individual refers to someone directly by his or her given name, it is an insult in most social situations. Refer to individuals as Mr. Kim or Miss Park. Positions or titles are very commonly included, such as Consul Park, Librarian Kim, or Reverend Lee. It is important to know that Korean women keep their family name when they marry; therefore, one should not assume that

Mr. Kim's wife is Mrs. Kim. She should be referred to as the wife of Mr. Kim. Many immigrant women will follow the U.S. tradition and take their husband's last name. In order to be safe, one should not address Mr. Kim's wife as Mrs. Kim, but as the wife of Mr. Kim or as a child's mother, for example, "Hello, Grace's mother."

Gestures   Some gestures in Korea will confuse the visitor. The Korean gesture for "come here" is similar to the Western wave of the hand to communicate "good-bye." Koreans always use the right hand when giving an object to a person of higher status. To show the most respect, both hands hold the object as it is given or received. When passing objects to people of lower status, either hand is acceptable, but using both hands is inappropriate. When Koreans are happy, they smile and laugh as other people do. However, Koreans may also smile when they are ashamed or uncomfortable. Avoid touching or backslapping a Korean who is not your relative or close friend.

Gift Giving   Gift giving is an important dimension of the culture. Koreans love to give gifts. It is impolite for a visitor not to bring a gift. It should be simple and personal. If it is extravagant, it will create a sense of obligation. The best gifts are ones that leave the recipient in good spirits and wanting to voluntarily reciprocate. In the world of business and government, elaborate gifts are often given. Westerners may consider it unethical, but until recently it has not been frowned on. If someone offers a gift, it is the custom to decline at least twice.

It is not uncommon for Korean parents to give gifts to teachers in hopes that educators will give special attention or better grades to their children. It is not a bribe, but an age-old custom. In the United States, some schools have established policies to redirect the gift-giving practice by suggesting that parents give donations to a charity in the name of a specific teacher. Many teachers welcome this policy.

Money may be given on special occasions to relatives, friends, and colleagues. Customarily, money is placed in an envelope with a greeting to the person together with the person's name. If one attends a wedding or a funeral, it is customary to bring a white envelope that contains money. Avoid writing a living person's name in red ink as a name written in ink means the person has died. Never give knives or scissors as gifts. Handing cash directly to someone is considered rude unless one is purchasing merchandise.

Humor   A visitor should avoid jokes, puns, and sarcasm. If one tells a joke, keep it simple, observe the appropriateness of your remark, and be sensitive to any comment that could be misinterpreted. Also, avoid using Korean slang and Japanese loan words. Do not compare Korea with Japan.

Introductions   Introductions are very important in Korea. Essentially, an introduction will affect how two people relate to each other in the future. One should wait to be introduced at a social gathering. Introducing a person of low status to a person of high status is not common. It is also unusual for Koreans to introduce themselves to someone with whom they have no connection. A third party will introduce two people to one another. When two people meet, a formal ritual follows. Each announces that it is the first time to see the other person. They will then face each other directly, bow, and say their names followed by *"man-na-so pan-gap-sum-ni-da* ("We meet for the first time" or "I am glad to meet you"). Foreigners are not expected to bow, but the foreigner who does will likely win respect. It is now quite common for Koreans to shake hands and bow at the same time. Business cards are then exchanged using both hands. Both people will glance briefly at the card to note the name and position. During the meeting, it should be left on the table next to you. Business cards help clarify status in relations. Knowing a person's status is critical since the proper language level to be used depends on the position of each person. When leaving a social gathering, it is considered good manners to say good-bye and to bow to each person individually.

It was customary in the past for Koreans to ask personal questions of a newcomer. They might have asked one's age, salary, education, or religion as a way to get to know a person, help with making conversation, and establish rapport. They did not perceive that these questions were intrusive. If one is asked personal questions that feel uncomfortable, try to sidestep them as gracefully as possible. Presently, Koreans are more sensitive to the privacy of individuals and probably will not ask someone personal questions as in the past.

It is the custom in Korea to place the family name first and the given name second. The family names are the traditional clan names, and each has a village from which it comes. The five most frequent names are Kim, Park (Pak), Lee (Rhee, Yi), Choi (Choe), and Oh. The spelling of these names varies because of the inconsistencies of translating names from *han'gul* to Roman characters. If staying at a hotel in Korea, be aware that your name may be listed under your given name, which may present difficulties for family members and friends contacting you.

Personal Space   The Korean concept of space is sometimes a source of frustration and misunderstanding among foreigners. If someone bumps into you in the United States, you expect an apology. However, Koreans live in one of the most densely populated countries in the world. For example, approximately 1,234 Koreans live in a square mile compared with approximately 73 Americans per square mile. Koreans are accustomed to congestion on streets, subways, buses, and marketplaces. Customarily, they do not apologize for coming too close to or jostling another person because they have not violated a rule of their culture.

Punctuality   Koreans are fairly relaxed about time and may be 5 to 20 minutes late for appointments. It is not uncommon for meetings, movies, and other public events to begin a little bit late. If one is invited to a function, it is perfectly acceptable to be 10 to 15 minutes late; however, being more than 30 minutes late is considered rude.

Shopping   When shopping in Korea, it is entirely acceptable to bargain in individually owned stores and booths. It can take more time, but it can become thoroughly enjoyable for most people. Department stores and chain supermarkets usually have fixed prices. When shoppers have done their research and know a good price when they see it, it will strengthen negotiating power and ultimate satisfaction. While

Woman watches over her stock at a market in South Korea. Bargaining is an accepted activity in individually owned shops and markets. (Corel)

bargaining is an old practice, many simply compare prices at different stores and purchase an item wherever the price is lowest.

Visiting a Korean Home   When visiting a Korean home, guests should always take off their shoes. Bare feet can be offensive, so it is best to wear socks or stockings. Many homes will offer slippers. It is appropriate to bring a gift, such as bakery items, fruit, quality chocolates, flowers, and wine. Koreans usually give a box of apples, Korean pears, or oranges. Gifts should be wrapped nicely. The number "four" is considered unlucky, so one should not give four gifts. Giving seven of an item is considered lucky.

The host will pour drinks for their guests in their presence. The hostess will not pour drinks. Wives and daughters can pour for their fathers and husbands but not for other men. Only hostess girls do this. The host may accompany the guests outside at the end of the visit because of the belief that it is insulting to say good-bye to guests indoors. Most will accompany their guests outside the door of their home or to the guests' car. After a visit, one should write a thank-you note the next day.

REFERENCES

Asia Pacific Management Forum. n.d. "Business Etiquette and Negotiating with Koreans." http://www.apmforum.com/columns/boyle46.htm (accessed January 4, 2008).

Associated Content. 2005. "South Korean Business Etiquette." October 31. http://www. associatedcontent.com/article/9626/south_korean_business_etiquette.html (accessed January 4, 2008).

Clark, Donald N. 2000. *Culture and Customs of Korea*. Westport, CT: Greenwood Press.

Cross Cultural Solutions. n.d. "Etiquette and Customs of South Korea." http://www. kwintessential.co.uk/resources/global-etiquette/south-korea-country-profile.html (accessed January 4, 2008).

Hinton, David, trans. 1988. *The Analects: Confucius*. Washington, DC: Counterpoint.

Hur, Sonia Vegdahl, and Ben Seunghwa Hur. 1997. *Culture Shock! A Guide to Customs and Etiquette*. Portland, OR: Graphic Arts Center Publishing Company.

Kim, Joungwong, ed. 1997. *Korean Cultural Heritage: Traditional Lifestyles* Vol. 4. Seoul: Samsung Moonhwa Printing Co.

Lee, Helie. 2008. Personal communication with the author, January 9.

Lee, Kwang-kyu. 2003. *Korean Traditional Culture*. Seoul: Jimoondang International.

Molloy, Michael. 2005. *Experiencing the World's Religions: Tradition, Challenge, and Change*. Boston: McGraw-Hill.

O'Brien, Betsy. 1997. *Let's Eat Korean Food*, Seoul, South Korea: Hollym.

One North East. n.d. "Meeting Etiquette." http://www.onenortheast.co.uk (accessed January 4, 2008).

Oracle Thinkquest Educational Foundation. n.d. "Korea's Etiquette." http://library.thinkquest. org (accessed January 4, 2008).

Seoul Searching. 2008. "Being Polite, Seoul Style." http://www.seoulseraching.com/culture/ etiquette.html

Shin, Frank. 2008. Interview with the author. Los Angeles, January 9.

Literature

Bruce Fulton

INTRODUCTION

Korean literature consists of oral literature; literature written in Chinese characters (termed *hanmun* if prose, *hansi* if poetry); and, after 1446, literature written in the Korean script (*han'gul*). Classical Chinese (or literary Sinitic) was the literary language of the scholar-officials who constituted the Korean elite from early times to the end of the Choson era. *Han'gul*, though officially announced to the people of Choson in 1446, did not gain widespread acceptance as a literary language until the 20th century. Korean literature is generally divided into the following periods:

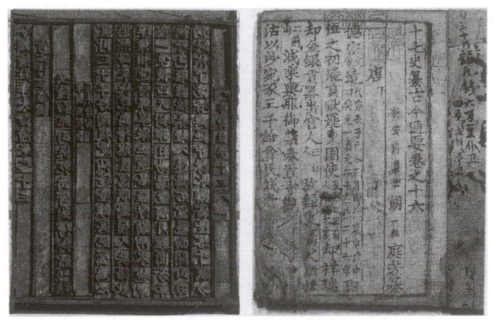

Sample movable type and a printed page from Korea. Movable metal type was first used in Korea 200 years before the first European printing press was made by Gutenberg. (Instructional Resources Corporation)

Three Kingdoms (57 BCE–667 CE), Unified Silla (667–935), Koryo (918–1392), early Choson (1392–1592), later Choson (1592–1910), and modern (1910–present).

Korean literature reflects Korean culture, itself a blend of a native tradition most probably originating in Siberia; Confucianism and a system of writing borrowed from China; and Buddhism. Modern literature, dating from the early 1900s, was initially influenced by Western models, especially realist fiction and image- and symbol-laden poetry, introduced to Korea by way of Japan. The Korean literary tradition has embodied two distinct characteristics: an emotional exuberance derived from the native tradition and intellectual rigor originating in Confucian tradition.

THE THREE KINGDOMS

Recorded Korean history begins with the three kingdoms of Silla (57 BCE–935 CE), Koguryo (37 BCE–668 CE), and Paekche (18 BCE–660 CE), which together occupied the Korean peninsula and part of Manchuria. Such Chinese records as the *Sanguo zhi* (third century CE; *History of the Three Kingdoms*) state that the Korean people were fond of song and dance, suggesting that a Korean tradition of oral literature was already established. This history contains fragments in Chinese translation of two of the ancient Korean songs known as *kodae kayo*: "Hwangjo ka" (17 BCE; "Song of the Yellow Warblers"), attributed to King Yuri of Koguryo, and "Kuji ka" (42 CE; "Song of the Turtle"). The former is a lyric of loneliness, the latter a religious invocation. Chinese sources also mention the titles of several other Korean poems.

The earliest surviving examples of literature appearing in Korean as opposed to Chinese sources are the *hyangga* ("songs of home," that is, songs indigenous to the Korean homelands rather than to China). This diverse group of songs, the majority of them from Silla times, includes works with oral origins as well as those composed and written down by individuals, primarily Buddhist monks and the Silla youth known as *hwarang*. Corresponding to Chinese Tang poetry and Sanskrit poetry, they have both religious and folk overtones. Many are Buddhist in spirit and content. At least 3 of the 25 surviving *hyangga* have come down to us from the Three Kingdoms period; the earliest, "Sodong yo," was composed during the reign of Silla king Chinp'yŏng (579–632). *Hyangga* were transcribed in *hyangch'al*, a writing system that used certain Chinese characters because their pronunciation was similar to Korean pronunciation, and other Chinese characters for their meaning.

UNIFIED SILLA

In 660, armies from Tang China, with assistance from Silla, defeated the Paekche kingdom; eight years later, the same alliance overcame Koguryo. When Silla then proceeded to expel the Tang forces, it had for the first time in Korean history unified the Korean peninsula under one ruling house. Over the next three centuries, the *hyangga* form continued to develop. One of the best-known *hyangga*, "Ch'oyong ka" (879; "Song of Ch'oyong"), is thought to be a Shaman chant, reflecting the influence of native spirituality in the Korean oral tradition and suggesting that *hyangga* represent a development of Shaman chants into Buddhist invocations. Buddhism, officially recognized by Silla in the sixth century, became the dominant system of thought and institutionalized spirituality in Unified Silla and exercised great influence over literature.

Hansi—poetry composed in classical Chinese but written by Koreans—became widespread among the literary men of Unified Silla. Contributing to the use of Chinese as a literary language was the rise of Confucianism, illustrated by such developments as the founding of the National Confucian College in 682 and the corresponding necessity of studying the Chinese classics. Ch'oe Ch'i-wŏn (857–?), a renowned official of Unified Silla who also served in the government bureaucracy of Tang China, is the first great Korean writer of *hansi* whose poems have survived.

In contrast with *hansi*, a poetry of the elite, was a rich oral tradition consisting of folksongs, Shaman chants, myths, legends, and folktales. The diverse genre of folksong comprises work songs; ceremonial songs; and—most numerous—love songs, both happy and sad.

KORYO

In 918 CE, General Wang Kon was proclaimed king of the new Koryo state. By 935, he had extended his control over the entire peninsula and founded the Koryo kingdom, which would survive until 1392. Koryo literature is distinguished by its folksongs, increased sophistication and diversity of poetry in Chinese, the collections called *sihwa*, and the appearance of *sijo* ("period tunes"), a concentrated, intensely personal song that would be composed in the vernacular (the spoken language) following the invention of *han'gul* early in the Choson era. Literature assumed increasing importance as the hereditary aristocratic bureaucrats who administered the nation early in the dynasty lost power during a period of military rule in the first half of the 12th century, to be replaced by a merit system of government whose civil servants were selected by a national examination that required mastery of literature among other subjects. Until the end of the Choson era early in the 20th century, Korea was thus assured of a steady supply of scholar-officials. The works of these men (women were prohibited from sitting for the civil service examination) constitute the great bulk of written Korean literature from Koryo and Choson times.

Koryo kayo is a general term for a diverse collection of Buddhist songs, Shaman chants, and songs composed by individuals. Many of them survive as court music from early Choson but originated in folksongs and thus combine folksong onomatopoeia and rhythms with refinements in diction and music. Outstanding examples are "Kasiri" ("Would You Now Leave Me?"), a song of parting that is echoed in Korea's best-loved modern poem, Kim Sowol's "Chindallae kkot" ("Azaleas"), and "Ch'ongsan pyolgok" ("Song of the Green Hills"), which has been variously interpreted as recording the realities of peasant life, the experiences of an exile, or the aftermath of a natural disaster.

Hansi reached an early zenith in the works of Yi Kyu-bo (1168–1241). Distinguished by the poet's ability to poke fun at himself and by penetrating glimpses of rural life, Yi's poems achieve a consummate balance of the universal and the particular:

A mountain monk coveted the moon;

he drew water, a whole jar full;

but when he reached his temple, he discovered

that tilting the jar meant spilling the moon.

(qtd. in O'Rourke 1988, 28)

The compactness, insights, and references to the speaker's life, thoughts, and feelings that we see in Yi's poems characterize many other *hansi* as well.

Prose writing achieved popularity with the emergence of *sihwa* ("talks on poetry"), collections of diary-like observations on life and poetry that are regarded by scholars as the earliest examples of literary criticism in Korea. Meant to entertain, these miscellanies combine the factuality of public records with the more poetic language of essays. A good example is *P'ahan chip* (1260; *Collection for Dispelling Idleness*), a posthumous compilation of writings by Yi Il-lo, one of the many scholar-officials who abandoned government service after the military takeover. This and other collections look ahead to the early Choson miscellanies known as *chapki*, which include more in the way of folktales and anecdotes.

Among the earliest examples of *sijo*, discussed below, are those of U T'ak (1262–1342). One of the best known of all *sijo* dates from the very end of Koryo.

YI KYU-BO

Yi Kyu-bo (1168–1241) is premodern Korea's finest poet. A brilliant young scholar who early came to the attention of the Ch'oe family of military rulers of the middle Koryo era, he kept a low profile at a politically sensitive time, perhaps using his fondness for alcohol to account for his lack of ambition for high office. He wrote essays and an epic poem about Chumong, founder of the great Koguryo state, but in his hands *hansi*, poetry in Chinese, reached an early zenith in the Koryo period. Distinguished by their self-referential humor and their keen glimpses of everyday life in the country, Yi's poems are both universal and particular. The brevity, revelation, and self-reference of his poems came to characterize the *hansi* of subsequent Korean men of letters as well.

Traditionally credited to Chong Mong-ju (1337–1392) just before his assassination by men loyal to Yi Seonggye, founder of the Choson kingdom, it sings of the writer's undying loyalty to the old regime:

Though my body die and die again,

though it die a hundred deaths,

my skeleton turn to dust, my soul

exist or not,

what could change

the red-blooded, undivided loyalty

of this heart toward my lord?

(qtd. in O'Rourke 1995, 117)

EARLY CHOSON

"Early Choson" designates the period extending from the founding of the kingdom in 1392 to the Japanese invasions of 1592–1597. The two most important historical developments affecting early Choson literature were the announcement of *han'gul* by King Sejong in 1446 and the adoption of Neo-Confucianism as the state ideology. The establishment of Neo-Confucianism, with its emphasis on classic Chinese texts, meant that Korean men of letters would continue to study and use classical Chinese. In fact, because mastery of classical Chinese ensured their monopoly on learning, these learned men continued for the most part to write in Chinese for centuries after the creation of *han'gul*. For its part, *han'gul* in theory gave all Koreans a literary language of their own; in all probability, though, until the 1900s it was used primarily by women and commoners, the vast majority of whom were not literate in classical Chinese.

One of the first works written in the new Korean script was "Yongbi och'on ka" (1445–1447; "Songs of Dragons Flying to Heaven"), an *akchang* (set of lyrics and chants accompanying court music) celebrating the virtues and moral authority of the Choson founder and his ancestors.

For recognition and advancement, Choson men of letters wrote in Chinese; to do so was to take part in *the* elite cultural tradition of East Asia, a tradition that by early Choson times had existed for a millennium already in its written form. But for their own pleasure and amusement, they wrote in Korean. Of the works they composed in *han'gul*, *sijo* are the most numerous. Most scholars believe that this short verse form is a native tradition that originated during Koryo times. *Sijo* were originally sung, and still are today. Three of the greatest *sijo* practitioners are Chong Ch'ol (1536–1593), Yun Son-do, and Kim Su-jang. Many of Chong's *sijo* offer symbolic commentary on court intrigue.

The other major vernacular (Korean-language) poetic tradition in Korea is the *kasa*. Appearing in the mid-1400s, *kasa* are generally longer than *sijo* and are variously narrative (telling a story) as well as lyric (songlike and emotionally expressive). Chong Ch'ol, in addition to his accomplishments with *sijo*, is considered by many to have perfected the *kasa* form, as seen in his "Kwandong pyolgok" (1580; "Song of Kangwon Scenes").

Women have until recently occupied a low profile in Korean literary history, yet considerations of language and sentiment suggest that they are responsible for some of the traditional folksongs that have survived, such as "Arirang," and they should be credited for that part of the oral tradition inspired by native Shaman beliefs and rituals (in Korea, Shamans are traditionally female). But not until early Choson do we have examples of literature by identifiable women writers. In Choson times and earlier, wellborn women were discouraged from acquiring knowledge of classical Chinese. And even after the creation of *han'gul* gave Korean women an accessible literary language, the Neo-Confucian emphasis on women's place in the home made them reluctant to attach their name to their writings or to circulate them outside the home. It was left to such aristocratic women as Ho Nansorhon (1563–1589) and to such *kisaeng* (professional entertaining women) as Hwang Chin-i (ca. 1506–1544) to lift the veil of anonymity that cloaked premodern women's literature. Their surviving poems—*sijo*, *kasa*, and a few *hansi*—offer eloquent echoes of this muted tradition.

It is also in early Choson that we see what is often considered the first example of Korean fiction: *Kumo sinhwa* (*New Stories from Golden Turtle Mountain*), by Kim Si-sup (1435–1493), consisting of five short romances written in Chinese. The *chapki*—a collection of such diverse writings as character sketches, poetry criticism, anecdotes, and folktales—developed around the same time. The *P'aegwan chapki* (*Storyteller's Miscellany*) of O Suk-kwon (fl. 1525–1544) is a good example.

Surviving examples of folk drama suggest that a rich variety of dramatic works existed by mid-Choson. The most important genre was the mask dance, a combination of song, speech, and dance that originated in local festivals. Like much folk literature, mask dances expose the failings of the privileged members of society. The masks, typically made of wood or gourd, were vivid, expressive, and meant for caricature. Masks for the Hahoe *pyolsin kut*, a mask dance probably inspired by a Shaman rite for expelling evil spirits, were fashioned as far back as Koryo times.

Also serving as comic relief for the common people was the puppet play, which, like the mask dances, was performed outdoors in spaces accessible to all classes of people. Thought by some scholars to have originated among Buddhist monks expelled from their monasteries by Neo-Confucianist kings, the plays provided commoners with a light-hearted alternative to the stern and highly structured Neo-Confucian society of Choson.

LATER CHOSON

Even to a people who had survived previous foreign depredations, the Japanese invasions of 1592 and 1597 proved especially destructive. It is the consensus of historians that the devastation also revealed the incompetence of the monarchy and the aristocratic bureaucracy. A backlash by the people was inevitable, and this reaction was felt in the world of literature. More people outside the *yangban* elite began to write, more Koreans began to write in *han'gul*, and women's voices were increasingly evident.

It was against the background of the Japanese invasions and the feeble Choson response that Ho Kyun (1569–1618) is thought to have written "Hong Kil-dong chon" (ca. 1610; "Tale of Hong Kil-dong"), usually cited as the first Korean fictional narrative written in *han'gul*. An account of a bandit leader with a popular following—a kind of Robin Hood figure—the work criticizes the injustice of a society that withheld privilege from illegitimate sons (of which Ho Kyun's childhood mentor was one) and implicitly censures a regime that fails to safeguard the welfare of its people.

A variety of fictional works in *han'gul* followed: morality tales where good is rewarded and evil punished, such as *Inhyon wanghu chon* (*Life of Queen Inhyon*) and *Hungbu chon* (*Tale of Hungbu*); accounts of military feats, such as *Imjin nok* (*The Japanese Invasions of 1592 and 1597*); and stories of love and conflicting virtues, such as *Ch'unhyang chon* (*Tale of Ch'unhyang*). Many of these fictional narratives originated in the oral tradition. These origins, together with the slight regard for fiction writing and a disregard for individual creativity, meant that authorship and date of composition are unknown in many cases. But even though the learned usually preferred poetry to fiction as a measure of their literary accomplishment, fictional works in *han'gul* had gained widespread popularity among commoners by the 18th and 19th centuries. Some 600 of these works survive, and more are coming to light.

A new fictional form that appeared late in the 1700s was the *kajok sa sosŏl*, or family saga, featuring several generations of family history and often dealing with life within the Choson court. These works are forerunners of the multivolume novels widely read in present-day Korea.

In contrast with the variety of fiction in *han'gul* that is solidly grounded in Korean soil are such romances as *Kuun mong* (ca. 1689; *A Nine-Cloud Dream*), by Kim Man-jung (1637–1692), which is situated in ninth-century Tang China. *Kuun mong* is often honored as the first Korean novel written in *han'gul*, but evidence increasingly suggests it was written in *hanmun* and that only *han'gul* translations have survived. The novel deals with the protagonist's contradictory desires for worldly success and escape from worldly affairs.

Among the comparatively small amount of fictional narratives written in Chinese, the works of Pak Chi-won (1737–1805), a *sirhak* (practical learning) scholar, stand out. "Ho Saeng chon" ("Tale of Master Ho") and "Yangban chon" ("Tale of a *Yangban*") are penetrating satires of Neo-Confucian society and economy, which were widely perceived by *sirhak* scholars as losing their vitality. In these tales, exemplary characters are often drawn from the lower classes and flawed characters from among the *yangban*. Though written in Chinese, these stories exhibit a more natural style than previous prose writing in Chinese by Koreans.

Writing by women continued to be little known outside the home, but in the mid-1900s scholars began to discover a large amount of writing in *han'gul* by later Choson women. This body of literature includes diaries, travelogues, memoirs, and biographies as well as great numbers of long instructive *kasa* passed down from mother to daughter and kept for generations within the family. *Sijo* by *kisaeng* and other women survive as well. Also dating from this period is *Hanjungnok* (*A Record of Sorrowful Days*), by Princess Hyegyŏng (1735–1815), a series of memoirs about her long life in court that is especially well known for its account of the death of her husband, Prince Sado, at the hands of his father, King Yongjo.

Hansi—poetry in Chinese—would be written until the end of the dynasty, but poetry in Korean continued to be favored for its greater expressive potential. Yun Son-do (1587–1671) and Kim Su-jang (1690–?), both mentioned earlier, are the great *sijo* poets of later Choson. Yun's *Obu sasi sa* (*A Fisherman's Calendar*), a series of 40 songs, is perhaps the finest example of the *sijo* form. Like most *sijo*, it portrays the poet and his subject—in this case the natural world and the changing seasons—in isolation from the uncertain world of court and capital. Kim's *sijo* are distinguished by the poet's wit. Kim himself was not a scholar-official of the elite but what we might call today a skilled worker, reflecting the increasing access of Korean commoners to the production of literature. It is perhaps mainly those common people who authored the great number of anonymous *sijo*—almost half of all surviving *sijo*.

Sasŏl (narrative) *sijo* is an expanded form of *sijo* that appeared in the 1700s. Like the standard *sijo*, it was meant to be sung. Unlike most *sijo* written until then, it was the work primarily of commoners. These longer *sijo* are often humorous, earthy in their language, and forthright in their expression of feeling. Most are anonymous.

As with *sijo*, more *kasa* were composed by women and commoners in later Choson than in early Choson. This increasing variety among writers led to a corresponding variety in the types of *kasa* they wrote: the *naebang* ("inner room," referring to the women's domain in the traditional Korean home) *kasa* previously mentioned, written primarily by women; accounts of journeys; *kasa* written in exile; and descriptions of everyday life.

Especially popular in the oral tradition was *p'ansori*, a narrative partly sung and partly spoken by an itinerant performer (*kwangdae*) accompanied by a lone drummer. The *p'ansori* performances, developing in the Cholla region in the late 17th century, appealed particularly to the common people, who were familiar, for example, with the Hungbu and Ch'unhyang stories, which became part of the *p'ansori* repertoire. That repertoire grew to include 13 works, most of which conformed to Neo-Confucian values on the surface but implicitly criticized the application of those values in real life.

MODERN LITERATURE

The development of a modern literature in Korea was influenced by two watershed events: (1) the enlightenment and modernization movement in East Asia at the turn of the 20th century and (2) the annexation of Korea by Japan in 1910. The first of these developments exposed young Koreans to such enlightenment ideals as literacy, education, equality, and women's rights. Annexation inspired a wave of nationalism that finally legitimized *han'gul* as the literary language of all Koreans and forced Korean writers to come to grips with the necessity of preserving their own language and literature in an increasingly repressive colonial environment. (In the last years of the Japanese occupation, before liberation in 1945, Koreans were forbidden to speak their own language in public gatherings, and it became virtually impossible to publish in Korean.)

Modern Korean literature is dated by some scholars to 1908, the year in which Ch'oe Nam-sŏn's poem "Hae egeso sonyon ege" ("From the Sea to the Youth") appeared, but the more common benchmark is 1917, the year that Yi Kwang-su's novel *Mujong* (*Heartlessness*) was published. But whereas *Mujong* is considered distinctly modern in its use of language and its psychological description, Ch'oe's poem was of a transitional type, traditional in its use of a rhyme scheme but innovative in terms of its optimistic enlightenment outlook. Corresponding to such transitional poetry was the *sin sosol* (new fiction), which flourished from 1906 to the early teens. Designed to appeal to a mass readership and distinguished from the more staid "old fiction," these new novels and novellas dealt with contemporary history, addressed real-life social problems, depicted intrafamily intrigues, or inspired patriotism through portraits of national heroes both domestic and foreign. Yi In-jik (1862–1916) is the best-known writer of the *sin sosol*, and the 1906 novel *Hyol ui nu* (*Tears of Blood*), his best-known work.

The first generation of writers of modern Korean literature were for the most part young men born around the turn of the century who studied in Japan and were there introduced, in Japanese translation, to literature from the West. There resulted an influx of Western literary models into Korea. The new generation of writers gravitated toward new, often short-lived literary journals in which they published poetry, short fiction, and essays (both critical and personal, the latter form termed *sup'il*). Novels maintained the mass readership they had enjoyed since late Choson times, and continued to be serialized in newspapers, but were considered lowbrow entertainment by the literary elite. Among the most important of this first generation of modern fiction writers were Yi Kwang-su for his enlightenment and cultural-nationalist agenda, Yom Sang-sop (1897–1963) for his psychological realism, Kim

---

HWANG SUN-WON

Hwang Sun-won (1915–2000) is modern Korea's most accomplished short-fiction writer. Hwang was born near P'yongyang and was educated there and at Waseda University in Tokyo. His first volume of stories was published in 1940. Almost 100 more stories would follow, including his best-known stories, "Hak" (1953; Cranes) and "Sonagi" (1959; The Cloudburst).

Hwang's literary career, spanning seven decades, has few parallels in Korean letters. As a craftsman, he is head and shoulders above most of his peers. His command of dialect, familiarity with both rural and urban settings, variety of storytelling techniques, vivid artistic imagination, diverse array of characters, sense of humor, and insights into human personality make Hwang at once a complete writer and one who is almost impossible to categorize.

Tong-in (1900–1951) for his modernization of the Korean language and his art-for-art's-sake views, and Hyon Chin-gon (1900–1943) for his fictional slices of life of colonial Korea.

Early-modern poetry ("early-modern," or *kundae*, refers to the period 1917–1945) is best represented by Kim Sowol (1902–1934), Chong Chi-yong (1903–?), and Han Yongun (1879–1944). Kim (known better by his pen name, Sowol, than his given name, Chong-sik) utilized traditional Korean folksong rhythms to produce poems that sound almost musical to the ear. His "Chindallae kkot" (1922/1980; "Azaleas") remains the best-loved poem of modern Korea. Chong was a master craftsman, drawing on both native and foreign sources for a rich bank of images in poems that often combines solitude, nostalgia, and nature. Han was a man of action, actively resisting the Japanese occupation of Korea, working to reform Buddhism, and attempting to instill in his readers a sense of their cultural identity. His best-known poem, "Nim ui ch'immuk" (1926; "Silence of the Beloved"), resounds on a number of levels.

Proletarian literature (literature describing the lives and struggles of the working class) was tolerated by the Japanese colonial authorities from the mid-1920s to 1935. After Japanese pressure put an end to the Korean proletarian literature movement in 1935, Korean fiction writers began looking to Korean tradition for inspiration, and often they found it in the countryside. A variety of new voices appeared: Hwang Sun-won (1915–2000), modern Korea's most accomplished short-fiction writer; Kim Tong-ni (1913–1995), considered by many Koreans to represent a distinctively Korean ethos; Ch'ae Man-sik (1902–1950), a writer of wit and irony who employed a direct, conversational style; Yi T'ae-jun (1904–?), a polished stylist; Kim Yu-jong (1908–1937), possessor of an earthy, colloquial voice that echoes the oral tradition; and the brilliant Yi Sang (1910–1937), an avant-garde poet as well as a modernist fiction writer. Their combined efforts led in the mid- to late 1930s to an early flowering of modern Korean short fiction.

Korean literature after 1945, termed *hyŏndae* ("contemporary") by Korean scholars, has to a large extent been thematically conditioned by Korea's turbulent modern history. Korean writers from premodern times to the present day have often felt a need to bear witness to the times, and authors from 1945 on have been no exception. The literature of the 1950s and 1960s is a good example. Reacting to the devastation inflicted on the peninsula by the Korean War (1950–1953), writers produced poems and stories portraying not just a shattered landscape but traumatized psyches and corrupted values. The stories of Son Ch'ang-sop (b. 1922) and the poems of Kim Su-yong (1921–1967) are excellent illustrations.

The late 1960s and early 1970s brought a new generation of writers, educated in their own language (their parents' generation had been educated in Japanese, and the literary language of their grandparents' generation was more often than not Chinese). With little or no memory of the Japanese occupation and a skeptical attitude toward the authoritarian rule that marked South Korean politics from 1948 to 1987, they produced fiction and poetry that display a more free-wheeling use of language and a powerful imagination. Fiction writers Kim Sung-ok (b. 1943) and Ch'oe In-ho (b. 1945) are good examples. Their contemporaries Ch'oe In-hun (b. 1936) and Yi Ch'ong-jun (b. 1939) are known for the intellectual rigor of their fiction.

The 1970s brought a chorus of powerful voices that exposed the social ills attending the economic development program of export-led industrialization pushed by South Korean president Park Chung-Hee. There is no better fictional treatment of this subject than Cho Se-hui's (b. 1942) *Nanjangi ka ssoaollin chagun kong* (1978; *The Dwarf*), perhaps the most important 1-volume novel of the post-1945 period. Yun Hung-gil (b. 1942) wrote of the scars of the civil war and of citizens subtly coerced by the authorities into keeping an eye on "subversive" neighbors. Hwang Sog-yong (b. 1943) depicted itinerant construction workers, urban squatters, and refugees from North Korea. Cho Chong-nae (b. 1943), in his 10-volume novel *T'aebaek sanmaek* (1989; *The T'aebaek Mountains*), took a revisionist approach to modern Korean history, challenging the official anti-Communist ideology that characterized South Korea from its birth in 1948 until the democratization of the political process in 1987. The 1970s also marked the debut of Yi Mun-yol (b. 1948), one of the heavyweights among contemporary Korean novelists.

Some of the most important works of modern Korean fiction are multivolume novels. These long fictional works have precedents in the family sagas of later Choson times and usually feature a historical background, a wealth of cultural information, and several generations of family life. In addition to Cho Chong-nae's *T'aebaek sanmaek*, the most important examples are Hong Myong-hui's (1888–1968) *Im Kkok-jong* (1939), about a Choson bandit leader of that name; Pak Kyong-ni's (1927–2008) *T'oji* (1994; *Land*); Hwang Sog-yong's *Chang Kil-san* (1984), also about a Choson bandit leader thus named; and Ch'oe Myong-hui's (1947–1999) *Honpul* (1996; *Spirit Fire*).

So Chong-ju, Sin Kyong-nim, Kim Chi-ha, Ko Un, and Kim Hye-sun stand out among poets of the post-1945 era. So (1915–2000) is Korea's most important modern poet, a master of the Korean language who mines Korean history and culture and the Buddhist worldview to produce short, revelatory lyrics and longer prose poems, all of them characterized by a sensuousness derived from the Korean soil and, earlier in his career, from French symbolism. Ko, Kim Chi-ha, and Sin have all exhibited a populist streak and have incorporated their own political activism in their poetry. Ko (b. 1933), a former Buddhist monk, is a passionate witness of the powerless. Sin (b. 1936) sings of farmers and workers in verse enlivened by folk rhythms. Kim's (b. 1941) "Ojok" (1970; "Five Bandits") was a courageous satire of dictatorship that along with other works, resulted in a jail term. Kim Hye-sun (b. 1955) is the most imaginative poet in contemporary Korea. Much of her poetry reads as if it comes directly from the subconscious; there is no one like her in contemporary Korean poetry.

Modern Korean drama, like fiction and poetry, was subject to considerable Western influence, especially in the first half of the 20th century. Among the earliest examples of modern drama is Kim U-jin's (1897–1926) *San twaeji* (1926; *Boar*). *T'omak* (1932; *Piece*), by Yu Ch'i-jin (1904–1973), marked the arrival of a new realist drama. The most important contemporary playwright, O T'ae-sok (b. 1940), blends an innovative, Western-influenced style with texts drawn from Korean history and folklore recent and past. A good example is *Sim Ch'ong-i nun woe tu pon Indangsu e mom ul tonjonnunga* (1994/ 1999; *Why Did Sim Ch'ong Plunge into the Sea Twice?*).

LITERATURE IN NORTH KOREA

Literature in the Democratic People's Republic of Korea (North Korea) appears to have followed the prescription of Soviet leader Joseph Stalin, adopted by North Korean president Kim Il-Sung, that writers are "engineers of the human soul." Writing in the early years of North Korea seems to have been spearheaded by such native northerners as Han Sorya, whose novel *Ryoksa* (*History*) helped to legitimize the regime of Kim Il-Sung, as well as by the hundred-odd established writers, such as Yi Ki-yong and Im Hwa, who migrated to northern Korea from southern Korea after liberation from Japanese colonial rule in 1945. By the 1960s, a variety of literary journals were being published in the north, perhaps the most prominent being *Choson munhak* (*Korean Literature*; North Koreans have retained the name Choson for Korea), a monthly publication featuring didactic, moralistic stories centered in the working masses and typically revolving around a sociopolitical problem and its resolution. More recently, the gradual warming of relations between the two Koreas has been reflected in the awarding in South Korea of the prestigious Manhae Prize (Manhae being the pen name of the distinguished early-modern poet Han Yongun) to North Korean writer Hong Sok-jung (grandson of *Im Kkok-jong* author Hong Myong-hui) for his novel about the celebrated early Choson *kisaeng* Hwang Chin-i.

RECENT DEVELOPMENTS

The most noteworthy trends in Korean literature at the outset of the new millennium are (1) the prominence achieved by women writers, (2) a watershed generational change in the culture of the South Korean publishing industry, (3) the literature of the Korean diaspora, and (4) the increasing visibility of Korean literature in translation. Long

Korean Novelist Ch'oe Yun, author of the acclaimed story "The Flower with Thirteen Fragrances." (Corbis)

marginalized by the overwhelmingly male literary establishment, Korean women writers, building on the pioneering efforts of such writers as Ch'oe Chong-hui (1912–1990), gained both critical and commercial success beginning in the 1970s through the narrative and thematic innovations of such writers as Pak Wan-so (b. 1931), O Chong-hui (b. 1947), and Ch'oe Yun (b. 1953). Thanks in large part to the defiant poetic voices of such women as Kim Hye-sun and Kim Sung-hui, contemporary women poets are finally beginning to earn recognition on a par with that accorded their fiction-writing sisters.

Modern literature in Korea is generally portrayed as a decidedly serious undertaking, one that is guided by a conservative, predominantly male literary establishment of scholars and literary critics (often one and the same) who have tended to prize historical consciousness, social relevance, and political correctness in both poetry and prose. Humor apart from satire is in short supply, and imagination has been constrained. The new millennium has brought a change to this literary culture, due in large part to the ascendance of the Munhak tongne (Literary Neighborhood) publishing house in Seoul. Munhak tongne has supplanted the Ch'angjak kwa pip'yong (Creation and Criticism) publishing company, the longtime conscience of the Korean publishing world, as the most successful publisher of literary fiction in

SO CHONG-JU

So Chong-ju (1915–2000) is modern Korea's most important poet, a master of the Korean language who draws on Korean history and culture and the Buddhist worldview to produce short, revelatory lyrics and longer prose poems, all of them characterized by the earthiness of the Korean soil and, earlier in his career, the sensuousness of French symbolism. Like many modern Korean writers, he has produced intertextual works, in his case poems inspired by, and sometimes containing, lyrics from premodern Korea. And like many Korean writers throughout the ages, he has been taken to task for his political views. But like Yi Kyu-bo before him, and Hwang Sun-won alongside him, he transcended the particularities of his time and place to create literature that resonates both inside and outside of his native land.

South Korea. The public image of Munhak tongne is the smiling face of a writer in his or her thirties (men and women are represented almost equally in the top ranks of the Munhak tongne list), colorful book covers, and imaginative works of literature. The future of Korean fiction, it could be argued, lies in the hands of such Munhak tongne writers as Kim Yong-ha, Pak Min-gyu, and Cho Kyong-nan.

Diaspora literature—works written in such languages as English, Japanese, Russian, and German by ethnic Koreans outside of Korea—is flourishing. Yi Miruk's German-language memoir, *Der Yalu Fliesst* (1946/1955; *The Yalu Flows*), and Richard Kim's English-language novel *The Martyred* (1964) are well known. In Japan, such writers of Korean descent as Yi Yang-ji and Yu Miri have captured the Akutagawa Award, that nation's most prestigious fiction prize. Such younger writers as Susan Choi, Heinz Insu Fenkl, Chang-rae Lee, and Helie Lee have achieved commercial and critical success in the United States, as have a number of Korean American writers of juvenile and young-adult fiction.

Thanks to a small group of dedicated translators, Korean literature has gained modest international visibility in recent decades. Poetry is better represented than fiction—though the gap is narrowing as contemporary Korean fiction writers, in some cases working through international literary agencies, are beginning to be published by mainstream presses in the West—and modern literature more than premodern. The short fiction of Hwang Sun-won and the poetry of So Chong-ju and Ko Un are especially well represented in the West, and the novels of Hwang Sogyong and Kim Yong-ha are drawing increasing attention abroad.

With the dawn of the 21st century, the hopes of many Koreans for unification of their divided peninsula remain strong. This long-awaited event will almost certainly give rise to a wave of literary expression of the lives and experiences of the millions of Korean family members who have been separated from one another since the Korean War cease-fire of 1953. In the meantime, fiction writers in South Korea have already begun to chronicle the experiences of northern defectors in the South.

REFERENCES

Cho, Se-hui. 2006. *Nanjangi ka ssoallin chagun kong* [*The Dwarf*]. Translated by Bruce Fulton and Ju-Chan Fulton. Honolulu: University of Hawai'i Press.

———. 1998. "Korean Novel," in *Encyclopedia of the Novel*, edited by Paul Schellinger, 674–678. Vol.1. Chicago: Fitzroy Dearborn.

———, ed. 2004a. "Korea," in *The Columbia Companion to Modern East Asian Literature*, edited by Joshua Mostow, 617–742. New York: Columbia University Press.

———. 2004b. "Place and Identity in Korean American Young-Adult Fiction," in *Diaspora in Korea (Immigrant) Literature*, edited by Seong-Kon Kim and So-Hee Lee, 2–19. Seoul: Seoul National University Press.

Fulton, Bruce, and Ju-Chan Fulton, trans. 1989. *Words of Farewell: Stories by Korean Women Writers*. Seattle: Seal Press.

Holman, Martin J., ed. 1990. *Shadows of a Sound: Stories by Hwang Sun-won*. San Francisco: Mercury House.

Kim, Chong-un, and Bruce Fulton, trans. 1998. *A Ready-Made Life: Early Masters of Modern Korean Fiction*. Honolulu: University of Hawai'i Press.

Kim, Kichung. 1996. *An Introduction to Classical Korean Literature*. Armonk, NY: M.E. Sharpe.

Myers, Brian. 1994. *Han Sorya and North Korean Literature: The Failure of Socialist Realism in the DPRK*. Ithaca, NY: Cornell University East Asia Program.

O'Rourke, Kevin. 1988. *Tilting the Jar, Spilling the Moon: Poems from Koryo, Choson, and Contemporary Korea*. Seoul: Universal Publishing.

———. 1995a. *Poems of a Wanderer: By Midang So Chong-ju*. Dublin: Daedalus.

———. 1995b. *Singing like a Cricket, Hooting like an Owl: Selected Poems by Yi Kyu-bo*. Ithaca, NY: Cornell University East Asia Program.

———. 1999. *Looking for the Cow: Modern Korean Poems*. Dublin: Daedalus.

———, trans. 2002. *The Book of Korean Sijo*. Cambridge, MA: Harvard University Press.

———. 2006. *The Book of Korean Poetry: Songs of Silla and Koryo*. Iowa City, IA: University of Iowa Press.

Pihl, Marshall R. 1977. "Engineers of the Human Soul: North Korean Literature Today." *Korean Studies* 1: 63–92.

Rutt, Richard, and Kim Chong-un, trans. 1974. *Virtuous Women: Three Classic Korean Novels*. Seoul: Royal Asiatic Society, Korea Branch.

Art and Architecture

Meher McArthur

INTRODUCTION

Around the middle of the fifth century when Europe was on the threshold of the Dark Ages, Korea enjoyed its first renaissance, a truly dynamic and rich period in the arts, evidenced by the exquisite treasures excavated from the royal tombs of the Three Kingdoms (57 BCE–668 CE) of Koguryo, Paekche, and Silla. These early kingdoms, influenced particularly by Chinese cultural features, reflect not only the Korean people's receptivity to Chinese civilization but also, and more importantly, their own ability to create powerful and distinctive art forms. As a result of historical developments and its geographic location, Korea was prepared from the very beginning to create art and architecture with uniquely Korean characteristics.

It is important to note that although outside forces did influence Korean artistic traditions, its art is as different from that of China and Japan as is the art of any Western country from that of its neighbors, even though all may have been influenced by similar traditions. Because Korea borders on China, its art was understandably more similar to that of China than to Japanese traditions. In the fine arts, where forms were often inspired by Chinese examples, Korean hands created art to respond to the aesthetic expectations of elite Korean patrons. Unlike the artwork of China and Japan, which have been collected and studied in the West for several centuries, Korean art has only recently become a subject of serious study among Western scholars and well represented in Western museums.

Following World War II and the Korean War (1950–1953), increased domestic stability stimulated research in archaeology and art history by Korean scholars. In the 1980s, the South Korean government and museums organized exhibitions of art that traveled to Europe and the United States, sparking new appreciation for Korean art. Western interest, coupled with a strong South Korean economy in the 1990s, resulted in the creation of new galleries devoted to Korean art in Western art museums, including the Metropolitan Museum in New York, the Asian Art Museum in San Francisco, the Los Angeles County Museum of Art, the Musée Guimet in Paris, and the British Museum in London. Now it is possible to see Korean art in many museums around the world, to read about it in several Western languages, and to study its history in numerous colleges and universities.

Korean art is as complex as that of any other culture. As will become clear in this brief chronological survey of the highlights of Korean art, there has been such a wide range of artistic productivity over the centuries—religious and secular, aristocratic and popular, foreign-inspired and indigenous—that it is impossible to identify one single artistic style or aesthetic running through Korean art.

THE PREHISTORIC PERIOD

The Koreans are an Altaic people of the Tungusic group from Manchuria and Siberia, and their language, their spiritual beliefs, and some of their early art bear similarities with those of other nomadic peoples of this group. It is not certain exactly when the first people inhabited the peninsula, but there is archaeological evidence of human sites dating to the early Paleolithic era (pre-10,000 BCE). The earliest examples of what we generally consider to be art—and not merely agricultural tools and weapons—date to the Neolithic period (ca. 6000–1000 BCE). At various sites throughout the peninsula, archaeologists have unearthed masks made of shell and clay; figurines modeled out of stone and clay; and necklaces, bracelets, and other ornaments made from shell, bone, and stone. The earliest pottery dates to the early Neolithic period and varies in form and decoration, depending on the region. One of the most common types is the *chulmun*, or "combed pattern" pottery, which features pointed or conical bottoms and herringbone patterns incised into the surface with a comblike tool. These early ceramics were found primarily in the central western area, including an important dwelling site at Amsa-dong on the outskirts of Seoul.

Late in the Neolithic period and into the Korean Bronze Age (ca. 1000–300 BCE), large numbers of dolmens (tombs covered with huge stone markers) and cists (tombs lined with stone slabs) were constructed throughout the region. Judging by the weapons, mirrors, curved beads (*kogo*), and other jewelry found in them, these were the tombs of clan chiefs and other members of the ruling classes. These tombs also held bronze vessels containing mirrors, daggers, axes, and chisels. The date of the earliest bronze production is disputed, but it seems likely that the first Korean bronzes date to around the seventh or eighth century BCE. The earliest are the so-called Liaoning daggers, which, with their bracket-like projections that create a violin-shaped outline, resemble bronze daggers found in Liaoning province in northeastern China. Early bronze mirrors also relate to their counterparts in Liaoning but have handles that are off center and uniquely Korean geometric patterns, which were likely carved into the clay molds from which the mirrors were cast. The pottery of the Bronze Age is generally referred to as *mumun*, or "no pattern," although some pieces feature incised and painted designs. Jars and other functional vessels were hand-built in a variety of different forms, depending on the region.

THE THREE KINGDOMS PERIOD

Koguryo (57 BCE–668 CE)

The period extending from 57 BCE to 668 CE is known as the Three Kingdoms period. Some of the most remarkable art from the Koguryo kingdom, located largely in modern North Korea and Manchuria, may be found in the paintings on the walls of the tombs of its nobility. These tombs date from the fourth to sixth centuries CE and were often constructed to resemble palaces, with pillars, corridors, corbeled ceilings, and multiple chambers, a structure that unfortunately made them accessible to tomb robbers, who removed the valuable burial goods housed within. However, paintings have survived on the walls of more than 70 Koguryo tombs. The painting style was marked by vitality and rhythmic movements. One of the most famous scenes is a hunting scene of Koguryo warriors from the Tomb of the Dancers that depicts the courageous and energetic spirit of the people. Another scene from the same tomb depicts a row of dancers wearing polka-dotted jackets and trousers. This image provides valuable information about the daily life and entertainment as well as ancient dress. Murals in Japanese imperial tombs from a slightly later period depict figures in similar clothing, suggesting a cultural link between the Korean and Japanese nobility of this period.

Mural of Dancers, from the Tomb of the Dancers, Tong'gou, Koguryo, 4th–6th century CE. (Courtesy of the Institute of Culture, Art and Tourism, Sookmyung Women's University with the assistance of Jiseon Lee)

Paekche (18 BCE–660 CE)

In the southwestern region, the kingdom of Paekche was also the source of outstanding examples of religious statuary and burial objects. Paekche had strong maritime ties to both southern China and to Japan, an important factor in the spread of Buddhism in the region. Monks from southern China introduced Buddhism to Paekche in 384 CE, bringing with them sacred texts and small votive images. Once the religion gained a foothold in Paekche, local artists produced figures of the Buddha, most notably out of stone, that combine Chinese stylistic elements and a local Paekche flavor. This "Paekche style" is most evident in the small (5.5 inches) soapstone figure of a seated Buddha from the second half of the sixth century. The image features the elaborately stylized drapery and the slightly large head and hands of earlier Chinese (and Koguryo) examples, but it also has a rounder face and a sweet smile, often called the "Paekche smile." (The king of Paekche may have sent such an image to the emperor of Japan in 552 CE when he encouraged the latter to embrace Buddhism.) It is worth noting that sculptors in Paekche also created the first rock-hewn Buddhist images in Korea, the most well known of which are the figures of the Buddha Amitabha and two attendants, dating to about 650 CE,

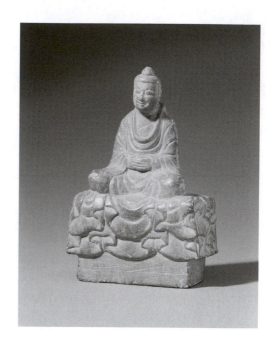

*Seated Buddha, sculpted from gray
soapstone, 2nd half of 6th century CE.
(National Museum of Korea)*

from Sosan in southwest Korea. Measuring more than 10 feet in height, the deities share the warm, welcoming features of the soapstone figure.

The Paekche rulers also built elaborate tombs, constructed with brick and similar to tombs found in southern China. As with the tombs of Koguryo, they were also easy to rob, so very little material from Paekche has survived. The most notable Paekche tomb is that of King Muryong (d. 525 CE) and his queen (d. 529 CE), excavated in the 1970s, which remained relatively intact. Its contents include ceramics and coins from China and locally made gold and silver ornaments, the most outstanding of which are the cut-gold floral decorations for royal crowns and elegant silver bracelets belonging to the queen.

Silla (57 BCE–935 CE)

Although Paekche is considered to have been the most artistically refined of the Three Kingdoms, more art from the Silla kingdom has survived. Silla tombs were constructed in a way that made tomb robbery difficult. After the burial of a king, the chamber containing the coffin and the burial goods was covered with gravel to create a mound and completely seal off the tomb. The Silla tombs contained many notable objects, including the famous birchbark saddle that bears the image of a flying horse, painted in white pigment. Dating to the fifth or sixth century, this is one of Korea's oldest surviving paintings and reflects early Siberian and Shamanistic influences. A similar image was discovered in the Gansu (Hexi) region in Central Asia, which was the Silk Road gateway to Asia and an indication of continuous cultural exchange along the Silk Road.

Gold Crown from Gold Crown Tomb, Kyongju, Silla, 5th–6th century CE. (National Museum of Korea, Seoul)

Silla was rich in gold, and by far the most spectacular objects found in Silla tombs are the royal crowns, constructed from sheets of gold, with a strip that went around the head and vertical projections in the form of trees and antlers. They are decorated with small spangles and jade *kogok* beads, attached with gold wire. Crowns with similar motifs (deer and trees) have been found in earlier tombs of the Scythians, Sarmatians, and Bactrians, in Central Asia and near the Black Sea, suggesting cultural links between the early Koreans and nomadic peoples. In all of these cultures, the crowns are believed to have been connected to shamanistic rituals. The Silla kings may have acted as shamans, creating a link between their people and the spiritual realm. In addition to these gold crowns, the tombs contained earrings, belts, and necklaces of gold, glass, and jade beads and many burial ceramics of note. Jars, bowls, and cups were typically constructed out of unglazed stoneware on tall bases with square and triangular perforations. Some remarkable examples from tombs of Silla and neighboring Kaya (absorbed by Silla in 562 CE) are in the shape of animals and birds, with small loops from which dangle leaflike forms, similar to the spangles on the crowns.

Although Buddhism came relatively late to Silla (528 CE), it soon took a strong hold and inspired outstanding artistry. Most well known are two gilt-bronze figures dating to around 600 CE of the Bodhisattva Maitreya, shown as a slender young man seated in a contemplative pose, with one leg crossed over the other and two fingers gently touching his right cheek. The tender facial expressions and the elegant fluidity of his posture have made these masterpieces of Korean sculpture. A similar figure in the Japanese nunnery of Chuguji (a subtemple of the Horyu-ji near Nara) was once considered a great Japanese masterpiece but is now thought to be either from Korea or made by Korean sculptors in Japan.

KYONGJU

For almost 1,000 years, Kyongju was the capital of the Silla dynasty. Today the city is an outdoor museum that includes tombs of the royalty, temples, shrines, palaces, gardens, and castles. Kyongju exemplifies the brilliance of the golden age of Silla culture. In 1979, the United Nations Educational, Scientific, and Cultural Organization (UNESCO) recognized the city as one of the world's 10 most historic sites.

THE UNIFIED SILLA PERIOD (668–935)

In the mid-seventh century, with the help of the Tang Chinese army, the kingdom of Silla overcame Paekche and Koguryo and established the Unified Silla kingdom in 668 CE. The Tang Chinese were initially intent on absorbing the peninsula into their empire, but the Silla armies successfully resisted them and for the following two centuries maintained peaceful diplomatic relations with Tang China. In fact, the Unified Silla period was influenced considerably by Chinese culture, as can be seen in the architecture, sculpture, metalwork, and literature of the period. The Silla capital of Kyongju thrived in part because of increased trade with China and Western Asian kingdoms along the Silk Road. Palaces and royal villas were constructed around the capital, some along the shores of an artificial lake known as Anap-chi (Lake of Wild Geese and Ducks). Excavations of the lake and four surrounding buildings in the 1970s yielded thousands of items including lacquered, ceramic, and metalwork objects for Buddhist rituals and daily use.

During this period, Buddhism flourished both among the rulers and the general populace, and the government spent considerable sums of money restoring and expanding older temples. Most famous is the Pulguksa (Temple of the Buddha Land), which was founded in Kyongju during the Silla kingdom in the mid-sixth century. The temple remained unaltered until the eighth century, when a dramatic expansion took place during Unified Silla. Largely modeled after Tang Chinese architecture, the buildings feature staircases (referred to as bridges) and wooden halls linked by corridors. The walls are filled with clay and painted in bright colors, and the hip-and-gable roofs are held up by complex wooden bracketing and surmounted with glazed ceramic tiles. The bridges are seen as gateways from the secular world to a Buddhist paradise. The two famous stone pagodas at Pulguksa are the original eighth-century structures, constructed out of local granite in several stories to house sacred relics, and are masterpieces of masonry, design, and exacting proportions. One of them, the Sokka-tap, contained a copy of a sacred Buddhist text, the *Dharani Sutra*, the world's oldest datable example of woodblock printing.

This period was particularly renowned for its metalwork, and such temples as the Pulguksa contained Buddhist figures cast in bronze and gilded, or cast in iron and coated with colored paint or plaster. Exquisite gold reliquaries, known as *sarira*, were crafted out of gold or gilt-bronze to hold the relics of the Buddha or

Pulguksa Temple (Temple of the Buddha Land) originally constructed in 528 CE, is considered the crowning glory of Silla temple architecture. (Courtesy of the Korea Tourism Organization)

sacred texts and then stored inside stone pagodas. Some of the most notable works in bronze are the large temple bells that sound the time and summon monks to prayer and services. Modeled after Chinese temple bells, Korean bells are unique in the elegant low-relief images of flying angelic beings that decorate the surface and the suspension loop in the form of a dragon.

Another architectural masterpiece is the cave temple at Sokkuram outside Kyongju. The temple was built between 751 and 774 out of granite in imitation of Indian, Central Asian, and Chinese stone Buddhist cave temples. The structure comprises a rectangular antechamber and a domed, round main chamber, in which is seated a magnificent stone carving of the Buddha measuring more than 11 feet in height. A lotus-shaped nimbus hovers on the wall behind the Buddha, giving the impression of a halo. This halolike nimbus is unique to Sokkuram. The figure features the fleshy face, sturdy physique, and full sensuous lips of Tang Chinese Buddha images, but its iconography is unique and the subject of great debate among art historians and Buddhists. Surrounded by images of monks and bodhisattvas carved in high relief on the walls of the chamber, the figure is considered by most scholars to be a masterpiece of Buddhist sculpture, and its spirituality is immediately recognized by the observer.

Sokkuram Cave Temple and Buddha was built between 751 and 774 CE in Kyongju. (Courtesy of the Korea Tourism Organization)

THE KORYO PERIOD (918–1392)

The Koryo period is often considered a golden age in Korean culture. The first Koryo ruler, King T'aejo, moved the capital north to Kaesong and enjoyed flourishing trade and cultural exchange with Song Dynasty (960–1179) China. However, this was also a period of great artistic innovations in Korea, with many artists gaining the enthusiastic patronage of both the royal court and the flourishing Buddhist temples.

In the Unified Silla period, wood-block printing had been developed in order to disseminate the teachings of Buddhism to a wider audience. In the 11th century, under the Koryo dynasty, the entire Buddhist canon was carved onto woodblocks, in part as a prayer to protect Korea against foreign invasions, but ironically these blocks were destroyed in the Mongol invasions in the early 13th century. In one of the most formidable creative endeavors in Korean history, a new set of 80,000 woodblocks was completed in 1251. The blocks were made of magnolia wood, carved with text on both sides, and finished with a protective coating of lacquer. This set managed to survive further invasions and is now kept in the Haeinsa

Buddhist monk at Haeinsa Temple holding one of the 13th-century Tripitaka Koreana *woodblocks. (Courtesy of the Korea Tourism Organization)*

Temple in South Korea. Around the same time, faced with a shortage of wood and blessed with advanced bronze casting technology, the Koreans invented metal movable type and by 1234 had begun printing both secular and religious books, some 200 years before Gutenberg's development of movable-type printing in Europe.

Despite these innovations in printing, handwritten texts were still highly valued, in particular among practitioners of Buddhism, who gained religious merit by hand-copying Buddhist texts or commissioning temple artists to write out and decorate texts. Some of the most exquisite works of art of the Koryo period are the illuminated Buddhist sutra manuscripts commissioned by wealthy aristocrats and written by monk-scribes in gold or silver ink on indigo-dyed blue paper. They are often decorated with elaborate scenes of Buddhist paradises, showing the Buddha preaching to other deities, monks, and devotees. Such fine detail is also apparent in the larger Buddhist paintings depicting such deities as the Buddha Amitabha (Buddha of the Afterlife) or the compassionate Bodhisattva Kwanum, which are finely executed in mineral pigments and gold on a silk ground and then mounted as hanging scrolls for use in temples and homes. Many of these Koryo manuscripts and paintings have been located in Japanese and other foreign collections for many years and have only recently been identified as Korean.

Fine attention to detail can also be seen in Koryo metalwork, lacquerwares, and ceramics. Bronze casting was already advanced in the Unified Silla period, and many outstanding Buddhist temple bells were produced during that period and into the Koryo period. However, the most remarkable Koryo bronze objects are those made for the Buddhist clergy and the royal court, most notably the incense burners, alms bowls, and water sprinklers. Such objects were often embellished with delicate silver and gold inlaid designs of scrolling lotuses, swirling clouds, and dragons. Similar inlaid decoration was also used in the Koryo lacquerwares made for the same patrons. Only a handful of examples remain of lacquered Buddhist sutra boxes and court ladies' cosmetic boxes. Typically, they feature a black lacquer ground decorated with lotus or chrysanthemum scrolls made of inlaid mother-of pearl, haliotis (abalone) shells, and tortoiseshell.

The most celebrated Koryo innovation is undoubtedly the celadon. The matchless celadons of Koryo possess natural warmth of color, shape, and decoration, setting them apart for the sheer perfection of Chinese wares and the informal character of Japanese ceramics. A ceramic with a greenish glaze originally invented in China, the Koryo celadon is famous for its elegant glaze, perfected in the 12th century and

Cup Stand in the Form of a Lotus with Chrysanthemum Sprays, Middle Koryo period, about 1100–1200 CE. *(Photograph © 2007 Museum Associates/LACMA)*

CH'ANGDOKKUNG PALACE (1405)

This palace, one of the most impressive and important palaces in Korea, was built as a royal villa in Seoul in 1405 by King T'aejong, the third ruler of the Choson dynasty. Kings ruled the country from this palace for about 300 years. It has been listed as a World Heritage Site because it is an outstanding example of Far Eastern palace architecture and garden design. The buildings and gardens blend harmoniously with the natural setting.

used until the end of the period. Inlaid decoration under a green celadon glaze is a Korean invention dating to the mid-12th century and may have been inspired by the inlay in metalwork and lacquer. Koryo potters incised designs of flowers, cranes in flight, mountains and streams, and weeping willow trees into the leather-hard clay and then filled the lines in carefully with black and white slip (liquid clay), covering the whole surface with the glaze to create delicate contrasting designs. Incense burners, water sprinklers, and other celadon vessels were made for use in Buddhist rituals, while wine ewers, wine cups, cosmetic jars, and cosmetic boxes were made for use in the homes and palaces of the upper classes.

THE CHOSON PERIOD (1392–1910)

Prior to the Choson period, architecture, books, textiles, painting, and calligraphy were certainly created in significant numbers, but regular attacks on the country by invaders and the fragility of many of these materials resulted in the loss of many early examples of these art forms. The Choson dynasty spanned five centuries and is the most recent of the historical periods, so a relatively large quantity and variety of its art still exists. This long period is usually divided by historians into an early and a late period, the latter beginning after the Japanese invasions of the late 16th century. Art historians generally agree that the 15th century and the 18th century were periods of the greatest cultural and artistic development, particularly under King Sejong (r. 1418–1450), King Yongjo (r. 1724–1776), and King Chongjo (r. 1776–1800). During these periods, Buddhism was largely replaced as the official faith by Neo-Confucianism, a form of Confucianism that was developed in Song (960–1179) China and blended aspects of Daoist cosmology and Buddhist spirituality with traditional Confucian concerns regarding society and government. As a result, although certain rulers privately followed Buddhism and much of the population remained Buddhist, the art and architecture of the upper classes were strongly informed by Confucian ideals and sensibilities.

Although many important Choson-period buildings were destroyed during the Japanese invasions of the late 16th century, the Japanese annexation in the early 20th century, and the Korean War, some original structures have survived, and 20th-century reconstructions are generally faithful to the original plans. As in earlier

Pavilion at Ch'angdokkung Palace, Seoul (Choson period). (Courtesy of the Korea Tourism Organization)

periods, Choson buildings were influenced by Chinese architecture, with palaces and temples typically built out of wood with curved roofs covered with ceramic tiles. However, in this period, buildings increasingly took on a native Korean flavor. For example, Chinese buildings traditionally face south and are laid out on a north-south axis, but several Choson-period royal palaces, including the Ch'angdokkung Palace in Seoul, were built facing east with no north-south axis. Buddhist temples, which were forced out of the cities due to the withdrawal of official support, were built to adapt to their mountainous surroundings instead of according to the traditional Chinese layout.

Details of Choson architecture also followed native styles. On the exterior, the beams and bracketing supporting the roofs of major buildings were painted with vivid designs in red, blue, yellow, white, and green, in an art form known as *tan-chong*. The interiors of Korean structures were also constructed in a unique manner. Koreans, unlike the Chinese, traditionally sit on the floor, and for centuries, they have heated their homes using an underfloor heating system called *ondol*, literally "warm stone," in which underground flues transport heated air from the kitchen to the rest of the building. Many Choson buildings incorporated this system, including vertical chimneys to create a draft.

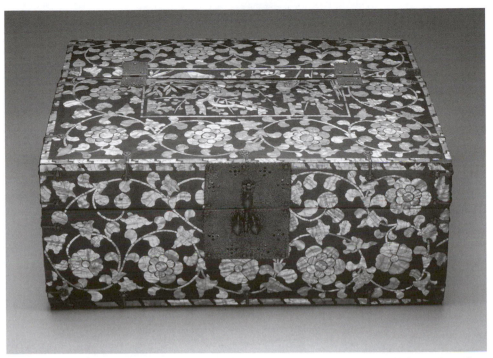

Lacquered wood box with floral scrolls and cartouche containing birds and blossoming plum from the Choson period, circa 1550–1700. (Photograph ©2007 Museum Associates/LACMA)

The homes of the wealthy were embellished with furniture and boxes decorated with lacquer, which also functioned as a protective coating. Storage chests, tables, cosmetic boxes, and document boxes were usually coated with black lacquer inlaid with designs in mother-of-pearl, tortoiseshell, and sharkskin, usually of floral scrolls but, later, increasingly of symbols of good luck and long life. Such lively decoration is also seen on the textiles that have survived from the Choson *dynasty*. The traditional Korean *hanbok*—a jacket and skirt for women, and a jacket and trousers for men—was well established by this period. For everyday wear, the *hanbok* was generally bold in color but reserved in decoration. However, robes created for formal occasions, weddings, and court ceremonies display spectacular woven, embroidered, and applied gold leaf designs. A princess's bridal robe, for example, was typically primarily red for celebration, with stripes on the sleeves of yellow, blue, and white, and was laden with auspicious symbols usually embroidered skillfully into the silk. Korean textile artists have long excelled at embroidery, and garments and accessories bearing embroidered details of birds, flowers, animals, and good luck symbols were favored by the aristocracy. Another noteworthy type of textile is the *pojagi*, a cloth traditionally made up of a patchwork of colorful scraps of cloth and made for wrapping and carrying objects.

In the realm of ceramics, green-glazed celadon was no longer produced for the court and the clergy after the end of the Koryo period, but a lower-quality variation

Wrapping cloth (pojagi) from the Choson period, circa 1800–1910. (Photograph ©2007 Museum Associates/LACMA)

of celadon was made and used by the lower classes. Known as *punch'ong* ware, these ceramics are made of grayish stoneware clay and are coated with a white slip and a bluish transparent glaze. These wares were often decorated with designs stamped into the slip or painted onto the slip with underglaze iron-brown pigment (see page 279). In the 15th century, these wares were exported to Japan, where practitioners of the tea ceremony admired their simple, humble beauty. By the time of the Japanese invasions, these wares were so highly coveted that not only the ceramics but also the ceramicists who made them were seized and taken to Japan, launching new ceramic traditions in Japan but contributing to their decline in Korea.

Porcelains, however, were made throughout the Choson period, both for use on the tables of the upper classes and for offerings on the ancestral altars. Because the Choson court embraced Neo-Confucian ideals of simplicity and austerity, porcelain ritual vessels in particular were left white with no decoration. However, some wine and food vessels were decorated with designs inspired by nature and by the 18th century were generally considered to be the artistic high point for Korean porcelains, bottles, vases, and jars. These objects featured delicate designs of autumn grasses, orchids, lotuses, and other floral motifs in underglaze cobalt blue. Copper

Punch'ong bowl with florets, early Choson period. (Photograph ©2007 Museum Associates/ LACMA)

red and iron-brown underglaze pigments were also used, particularly on the large storage jars that feature bolder, more dynamic designs of tigers, dragons, and other motifs borrowed from traditional folk painting (see photo on next page). Unlike Chinese and Japanese porcelains, Korean porcelains did not feature colorful over-glaze enameled decoration, and they were not exported.

Like the Chinese and Japanese, the Koreans have also used silk, along with pa-per, as a ground for painting and calligraphy, two of the country's most important art forms. Because of the fragility of these two materials, few examples of the "art of the brush" have survived from the Choson period, but many diverse styles of painting and calligraphy have remained from this era. Although official support for Buddhism was withdrawn in the Choson period, the religion continued to have many followers among the general populace (as well as with particular rulers who personally embraced the faith), so Buddhist paintings were still made during this period, most typically the cloth banners known as *taenghwa*, which were painted with Buddhist deities using vibrant mineral pigments. Hung both outside and inside the temple, these banners closely resemble Tibetan *thangka* paintings in their for-mat and function, though the selection and arrangement of the deities are very dif-ferent. Deities worshipped in the native shamanistic tradition were occasionally blended into Buddhist paintings, and although shamanism largely existed as an underground religion during this era, many paintings featured shamans; such

Glazed porcelain bottle with cranes and clouds, late Choson period, circa 1700–1800. (Photograph ©2007 Museum Associates/LACMA)

important nature spirits as the Mountain God, Sansin; and mystical landscapes containing auspicious symbols borrowed from Chinese Daoism. The official ideology of Confucianism was represented in art pictorially by portraits of rulers, nobles, and scholar-officials used to demonstrate family lineage and to enable descendants to honor these individuals after their death.

In secular painting, depictions of nature were extremely popular at all social levels. Court painters often specialized in Chinese-style paintings of nature, in particular depictions of bamboo, a plant that represents integrity and flexibility in the Chinese Confucian tradition that had been strongly embraced by the Choson court and scholar-officials. Birds, flowers, animals, and figures in gardens were also favorite subjects for artists, as were Chinese-style landscapes, usually depicted in black and grayish brushstrokes and ink washes on a white ground. Increasingly, Korean painters chose to use this style of painting to depict local landscapes, and by the 18th century, a Korean school of landscape painting had evolved. Around the same time, a vibrant folk painting tradition also emerged, capturing many similar motifs—birds, flowers, animals, and landscapes—on paper with a more vigorous, spontaneous brush. One of the most beloved types of folk paintings depicts a tiger being taunted by a magpie. The image was hung at New Year in order to protect homes from evil and bring good luck for the coming year. Typically rendered with bold brush strokes, vibrant colors, and much humor, these folk paintings were made for all levels of society and were often mounted onto folding screens and used to decorate rooms for special occasions.

Depiction of the bodhisattva Kshitigarbha (Chijang) and the Ten Kings of Hell, middle Choson period, circa 1700–1800 CE. (Photograph ©2007 Museum Associates/LACMA)

Many secular paintings depicted life during this period, including manuscripts and scroll paintings illustrating official court ceremonies and folding screens decorated with scenes of noblemen hunting wild animals. Some of the most revealing paintings of the period are the mildly erotic scenes of gentlemen and courtesans, or *kisaeng*, painted by Sin Yun-bok (b. 1758), or the scenes of daily life among the ordinary people by such artists as the celebrated Kim Hongdo (1745–1815?), who chose to depict merchants, entertainers, wrestlers, and farmers in his lively and often humorous genre paintings. These works are also known for their originality, artistry, and skill in the interplay of dark and light tones of ink that blend into the creation of a harmonious composition. One of his most famous paintings depicts a young student in a traditional Korean village school being scolded by his teacher as his classmates look on.

Beautiful writing, or calligraphy, has also been a highly regarded art form in Korea. Calligraphy from earlier periods has mostly remained in the form of the exquisitely handwritten sutra texts of the Koryo period. Under the

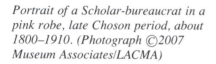

Portrait of a Scholar-bureaucrat in a pink robe, late Choson period, about 1800–1910. (Photograph ©2007 Museum Associates/LACMA)

influence of Confucian culture from China, skill in writing with the brush and mastery of Chinese characters were not solely the reserve of artists but also of scholars, courtiers, and priests. Calligraphic poems and inscriptions by masters were often featured alongside paintings to complement the subject matter of the painting. In addition, large bold calligraphic inscriptions or poems in Chinese characters were also mounted alone on scrolls and screens to be displayed on special occasions. In the early 15th century, under King Sejong, the Korean alphabet, or *han'gul*, was invented to help the lower classes to read, and the calligraphy in *han'gul* soon joined Chinese characters as a major artistic form.

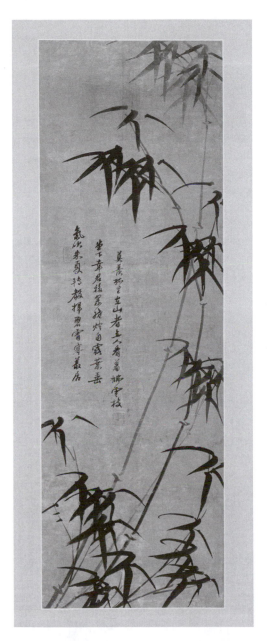

Painting of bamboo on paper scroll, late Choson period, circa 1800–1910. (Photograph ©2007 Museum Associates/LACMA)

THE MODERN PERIOD (1910–)

The century following the end of the Choson period has been one of great upheaval and change, and this is reflected in the various arts that have emerged over the last 100 years. The annexation of Korea by Japan in 1910 is considered the start of the modern period of Korean art, as it was then that Western-style oil painting was first introduced to Korea by the Japanese, and the word *misul*, meaning "fine art," was

KIM WHANKI (1913–1974)

Kim was a very famous artist who developed a style that was distinctly Korean in its liveliness and love of tradition. He was particularly drawn to the artistic traditions of the Choson dynasty. His paintings were not drawn from nature but combined stylized motifs from past works of art. His work changed dramatically in his final years. The heavy texture of his earlier work disappeared, and his canvases became reminiscent of Oriental ink paintings. At the end of life, his paintings became increasingly spiritual and conveyed the vitality and rhythmic quality characteristic of traditional Korean art.

coined for the first time. Art schools were established, and annual art exhibitions featured art by artists working in both traditional Korean and Western styles. In the realm of painting and calligraphy, some artists favored traditional ink painting on paper, while others combined traditional brush painting with such Western

Ink painting of a tiger, magpies, and pine, late Choson period, circa 1800–1910. (Photograph ©2007 Museum Associates/LACMA)

techniques as single-point perspective. Others still embraced Western-style painting and traveled to Japan to study under artists who had studied in Europe. They embraced classical oil painting, impressionism, and increasingly, new European artistic movements such as expressionism, abstract art, and fauvism, and they often produced works that were somewhat derivative of their European inspirations. Over the next few decades, Japanese militarism, World War II, and the Korean War plunged the Korean art world into a state of chaos, and artists used many different styles and techniques to express their despair at the fate of their country.

After the Korean War to the present, South Korea has experienced a period of peace and economic prosperity that has led to a great blossoming of art in many media and styles. In the realms of painting, printmaking, calligraphy, sculpture, and ceramics, many artists have looked to Western artistic styles for inspiration, studying in the United States and Europe and embracing such modern artistic movements as abstract expressionism, minimalism, conceptual art, and installation art. Many others still have sought to inject new energy into traditional Korean art forms, often resulting in such hybrid creations as abstract expressionistic brush paintings, such as the work of Suh Se-ok (b. 1927), and installations composed of ceramic sculptures with a celadon glaze, as in the work of Joo Ji Wan (b. 1965). At the turn of the 20th century, an increasing number of Korean artists, including video artist Paik Nam-June (b. 1932), have created art works that are global in their style and content and accessible to any contemporary audience. Paik's "Electronic Superhighway: Continental U.S., Alaska, Hawaii" (1995), on permanent display at the Smithsonian American Art Museum, is a stunning example of his exceptional vision and unique interpretation of American culture's obsession with television, the moving image, and bright shiny objects.

As more and more Westerners are becoming conscious of the quality and distinctiveness found in traditional Korean works of art, they are also witnessing the many innovations of new generations of highly creative contemporary artists who exemplify the dynamic spirit of the Korean people of the past.

REFERENCES

Choi, Sun-u. 1979. *Five Thousand Years of Korean Art*. Seoul: Hyonam Publishing.

Itoh, Ikutaro, and Mino Yutaka, eds. 1991. *The Radiance of Jade and the Clarity of Water: Korean Ceramics from the Ataka Collection*. Chicago: Art Institute of Chicago/Hudson Hills Press.

Kim, Chewon, and Lena Kim Lee. 1974. *Arts of Korea*. Tokyo: Kodansha International Ltd.

Kim, Hongnam, ed. 1994. *Korean Arts of the Eighteenth Century*. New York: Weatherhill/ Asian Society Galleries.

Kim, Won-yong. 1986. *Art and Archaeology of Ancient Korea*. Seoul: Taekwang Publishing Co.

McKillop, Beth. 1992. *Korean Art and Design*. London: Victoria & Albert Museum.

Moes, Robert. 1987. *Korean Art from the Brooklyn Museum Collection*. New York: Brooklyn Museum of Art.

Nelson, Sarah M. 1993. *The Archaeology of Korea*. Cambridge, UK: Cambridge University Press.

Portal, Jane. 2000. *Korea: Art and Archaeology*. London: British Museum Press.

Smith, Judith, ed. 1998. *Arts of Korea*. New York: Metropolitan Museum of Art.

Son, Chu-hwan, ed. 1994. *Korean Cultural Heritage: Fine Arts*. Vol. 1: *Painting/Handicrafts/Architecture*. Seoul: Sansung Moonhwa Publishing.

Whitfield, Roderick, ed. 1984. *Treasures from Korea*. Exhibition catalog. London: British Museum.

Yi, Kun Moon, ed. 1988. *National Museum of Korea*. Seoul: National Museum of Korea.

Music

Dong Suk Kim

INTRODUCTION

Music is one of the strongest expressions of any culture. Without it, life would be dry and our daily lives would lack that extra spark and inspiration that are often cultivated through the weaving of music into our social being. Every race of people has developed its own kind of music. It is a direct reflection of a people's beliefs, lifestyle, society, politics, and history. To know and understand a culture's music can often be a shortcut to understanding the people of that culture.

Asian culture is rich in musical traditions, yet the people of Korea have fostered an exceptional interest and passion for music and dance. In fact, the traditions of Korean music have often served as a spiritual and sociopolitical release for the people throughout its history. Although it is impossible to fully understand the entire scope of Korean music within a relatively short chapter, a better understanding of Korean culture can be attained by even a brief inspection of its musical arts. And as we strive toward a more global understanding of people, especially in our multicultural United States, an examination of the music of Korea will provide the reader with an understanding of the people and their culture.

Traditional Korean music today is diverse and lively. In contrast to many countries who lament the loss of interest in their traditional music, in Korea traditional music performers are heard everywhere. In the late 19th century, Western music was introduced into Korea, and it became solidly ingrained in the society. Many Koreans aspired to be Western professional musicians, and music from the West became more respectable than the traditional music of Korea. This began to change in the mid-1970s, and appreciation for the traditional Korean arts returned. Students began to learn the traditional mask dance (*talchum*) and farmers' music (*nongak*) and became aware that learning traditional music and dance was not a difficult task after all.

Children practing the ancient traditional instrument, the kayagum. (Democratic People's Republic of Korea)

In 1978, a musician named Kim Duk-soo started a percussion troupe, Samulnori, which revived and internationalized the farmers' bands of the past and contributed to the world's appreciation of Korean musical traditions. The revival of traditional music and dance became popular with the younger generation, and its growing popularity opened the door for students to explore more sophisticated traditional music. It is now common to hear the rhythms of gongs and drums of traditional folk music enriching the atmosphere of college campuses throughout Korea and elsewhere.

In the later 20th century, traditional *p'ansori* music had lost popularity because of its strenuous vocal projection and extremely raspy timbre, together with its past association with the low social status of the musicians. In 1993, the movie *Sopyongje*, directed by Im Kwon-taek, was a huge box office hit in South Korea and became an internationally recognized film. As a result, the general public suddenly became interested in *p'ansori*. The enthusiasm for this traditional music form spread widely to young and old, professionals and amateurs, and even Western classical music devotees.

These developments were also influenced by the emergence of nationalism and the general search for the cultural roots of Korea. The Ministry of Culture and Information and the Korean Culture and Arts Foundation actively supported research, preservation, documentation, and performances of traditional Korean music. The social status of musicians improved along with their financial security.

Drum Dance. (Courtesy of the Korea Tourism Organization)

NATIONAL MUSIC ORGANIZATIONS

Despite changes in ruling dynasties and ideologies, Korea's traditional performing arts have been passed down through national music organizations. The national music organizations—the Umsongso of the Three Kingdoms period (before the seventh century CE), Tae-ak-so of the Koryo dynasty (918–1392), Changagwon of the Choson dynasty (1392–1910), Yiwangjik A-akbu (Choson Dynasty Court Music Department) of the Japanese colonial period (1910–1945), and Kuknip-kuk-akwon (renamed the National Center for Korean Traditional Performing Arts in 1951)—not only preserved traditional music and dance but also developed and educated musicians from generation to generation.

In the past, the teaching of the music was intimately associated with governing the people. Music was a medium for guiding relationships between individuals, with the state, and between ancestors and posterity. The main roles of the early national music organizations were to oversee state Confucian rituals performed at the Munmyo and Chongmyo shrines as well as the rituals performed for the gods of heaven and earth and guardian deities of the country. They also performed at royal court ceremonies, banquets, and many national holidays. Court musicians were cultivated through a hereditary system, and were generally of a low social class. The system prevailed until the collapse of the Choson dynasty in the early 20th century.

The national music organizations also served as the main channel for musical exchanges with foreign countries. They used Korea's traditional musical instruments in foreign musical formats, integrated indigenous and foreign instruments, and adapted foreign musical formats to Korean styles. By assimilating the music of foreign countries, the early national music organizations played a significant role in the rich musical heritage that exists in Korea today.

The national music organization could have easily collapsed during Japanese occupation (1910–1945). During that time, the Japanese abolished the hereditary system among musicians, making it quite difficult to foster professional musicians. Yet a Japanese acoustics specialist, who fortunately believed that the traditional music of the Choson dynasty was like "music from heaven," convinced the authorities that this music had to be preserved. His convictions led to the creation of the Yiwangjik A-akbu, which established a school of music where students could study both traditional and modern music. Since then, the school has played an active role in preserving Korea's rich musical heritage. The Korean governments continue to play a role in preserving tradition by providing music scholarships and, in the case of North Korea, State sponsorship. Some argue that governmental support means political control of art forms; however, the efforts to preserve traditional music have saved and enriched Korea's music heritage.

HISTORY OF TRADITIONAL KOREAN MUSIC: ANCIENT TIMES TO 1945

Chinese sources referred to the early Koreans as a people who loved singing and dancing. The songs and dances of their ancient society were performed in close connection with religious rites and agricultural rituals in hopes of an abundant harvest, a common wish among ancient agricultural societies throughout the world.

Each of the Three Kingdoms (Koguryo, Paekche, and Silla), inherited the singing and dancing of the ancient tribal society; adopted imported instruments, and developed its own distinctive music, songs, and dances on the basis of its own practices. The music from this early period of Korean history had a strongly religious character, and ceremonial singing expressed prayers for the well-being of the kingdom.

Koguryo (37 BCE–668 CE), which was in the northern part of the Korean peninsula and the southern part of Manchuria, adopted the musical culture of China and the musical instruments of Central Asia that China had accepted along the Silk Road. The music of Koguryo is depicted in tombs, where dancing figures are moving to the accompaniment of a *komungo*, a six-stringed zither.

Paekche (18 BCE–660 CE), which adopted the *komungo* from the Koguryo kingdom along with such instruments from China as the *konghou* (harp), *chaeng* (long zither), and *chok* (flute), became the first of the Three Kingdoms to send musicians to Japan to introduce its own native music to the Japanese. A mask they used is presently preserved in the Horyuji Buddhist temple in Japan.

When the Kingdom of Kaya was defeated in 552 CE by Silla (57 BCE–935 CE), the people were introduced to the *kayagum*, a 12-stringed zither-type instrument

North Korean children attending music class. (Democratic People's Republic of Korea)

that has a softer and clearer sound than the masculine sounds of the *komungo*. A Kaya musician brought the indigenous music of Silla to a higher level by teaching singing, dancing, and the *kayagum* to functionaries of the government. As a result, the *kayagum* became the dominant musical instrument of the kingdom. The *komungo* and the *kayagum* remain the two main Korean stringed instruments today.

During Unified Silla (668–918), the music that was native to each of the Three Kingdoms was adopted and developed to a greater extent. Additional influences came from contact with the Tang dynasty of China. Chinese-derived music was introduced by way of the military music of its armies, the musical modes applied to three bamboo instruments, and the Tang style of Buddhist chanting.

The Koryo dynasty (918 CE–1392 CE) inherited and upgraded the Chinese-derived music and the native music of the Unified Silla kingdom. Emperor Hui-Tsung (1100–1125) sent a complete set of musical instruments, dance and music scores, costumes, and props for the performance of Confucian ceremonial music and dance to the king of Koryo and introduced a new musical genre, the *aak*. As a result, the elegant *aak* music was performed in Confucian and royal ancestral shrine ceremonies. Because of the strong influence of Buddhism, not much importance was attached to the Confucian ceremony. Consequently, by the late 12th century, this foreign ritual music had become mixed with the more familiar Korean music.

The Choson dynasty (1392–1910) was a very favorable period for dance and music. King Sejong (1418–1450) gave himself over to music and dance as much as he did to language, mathematics, astronomy, literature, and fine arts. With his chief court musician, Park Yeon, he classified all court music and dance into three primary divisions: *aak* (Confucian ritual), *tangak* (Chinese Tang and Sung dynasties), and *hyangak* (native Korean). He composed Korean songs that replaced Chinese versions of songs played in the royal ancestral shrines. Along with the invention of mensural notation (*chongganbo*), the theory of music was mastered, and a treatise on music was published. The method of mensural notation, describing both the pitch and the length of a note, was a truly significant event, not only in Korean music history: it was the first mensural notation ever invented on the continent of Asia.

After the Japanese invasions of the 16th century and the Manchurian invasions of the 17th century, the Korean people were confronted with many overwhelming challenges. The *aak*, *tangak*, and *hyangak* played at the court were in decline, but folk music and songs flourished. *P'ansori* (dramatic solo songs), a genre of vocal music developed by lower-class entertainers, and *sanjo* (instrumental solos) are two of the great developments of Choson. *P'ansori* may be described as the unique Korean style of folk dramatic song. *Sanjo* was taken from Shamanistic music and from *p'ansori*.

Western music arrived on the Korean peninsula in the late 19th century through the Christian hymns of missionaries and was augmented by military band music. American missionaries, including Horace N. Allen, Horace G. Underwood, and Henry Appenzeller, helped to bring Western music to Korea by teaching hymns that became the basis of popular music. From that time, music from the West began to permeate the culture. As Japan began to threaten Korean sovereignty, Korean patriotic songs were composed to Western melodies to lift the spirits of the people.

During the Japanese occupation (1910–1945), music education was essentially limited to Western hymns and Japanese-style music. As the occupation forces attempted to eliminate Korean culture—art, dance, film, language, music, and theater—they began to erode Korean cultural identity and confidence. When Korean nationalists fought back, the Japanese police repeatedly closed down performances that appeared in any way to be nationalistic. Subsequently, music had a very precarious existence, as did all of the arts.

The separation of Korea into two countries following World War II brought about two sets of musical practice demanding different aesthetic norms, among other differences. South Korea preserved traditional music and dance instead of reforming or assimilating foreign music. In contrast, North Korea abandoned many traditional styles, repertoires, and instruments. Therefore, the music of North and South Korea is no longer regarded as a single cultural manifestation.

CHARACTERISTICS OF TRADITIONAL MUSIC

Traditional Korean music is usually divided into two major categories, *chongak* (court music) and *minsogak* (folk music). The *chongak* is intellectual, solemn, calm, dignified, and contemplative, and the *minsogak* is emotional, unrestrained, direct, and exuberant. One might say that *chongak* music is the equivalent of classical music in the West, whereas *minsogak* corresponds to Western folk music and popular music. These two forms parallel Korean traditional culture, which had two very distinct representatives. One is the *sunbi* (scholar-aristocrat), who is upper class and considered elegant, refined, sedate, and contemplative. The other is the commoner, who is unbridled, unpretentious, robust, honest, and distinguished by humor and wit. Within the two major types of music are various subcategories that make up the whole of Korean traditional music, such as the music that relates to Buddhist and Shamanist traditions.

Both *chongak* and *minsogak* music conveys a gentle, warm timbre, in fact so gentle that even collision of tones and melodies results in harmony. The subtle tone color can be attributed to the fact that Korean musical instruments are made of natural materials. The *chongak* incorporates two main Asian philosophical theories based on ancient Chinese philosophy—*yin* and *yang* and the five elements—and instruments are played accordingly.

One of the important aspects of style in Korean music is the flexibility that permits personal deviation, variation, and improvisation in the process of performance. Korea is the only Asian nation that has such an improvisational music style. Folk music often occurs in such forms as *shinawi*, *sanjo*, and *p'ansori*. All three of these music forms are from the southern part of Korea and reflect the Shamanic rituals of the region. Because traditional Korean music is not rigidly codified, musicians may exercise a certain degree of freedom when interpreting rhythmic nuances and embellishing the basic melody. Therefore, the music (especially folk music) may vary with each performance.

A distinctive feature of the music relates to tempo. The leisurely pace of some of the music is due to the stress placed on breathing. Each beat relates to the musician's inhalation and exhalation. In Western music, the beat is similar to the heartbeat, which is active and progressive, whereas the *chongak* is based on breathing and is dignified and meditative. Another distinguishing aspect of the music is the fact that musical selections are frequently linked together when performed. This is illustrated by *gagok*, which consists of more than 20 long vocal pieces. The vocalist will sing all of the 20 selections without any clear break in the music. In the *p'ansori* epic, *Ch'unhyangga*, the vocalist takes on numerous roles while singing without stopping for more than eight hours! In the west, tempo varies from slow to fast movements. In Korean music, however, the tempo is slow in the beginning and gradually speeds up as the piece is performed.

Korean music is distinct from that of its neighbors in spite of the significant foreign influences, particularly from China. The triple rhythm or groups of three beats in Korean music is readily distinguishable from the duple (two beats to a measure) rhythm that is the particular feature of the music of China and Japan. Korean music also utilizes a unique mensural notation system that was designed to indicate the duration of a note.

Chongak: Court Music

Chongak music was considered appropriate for the ruling class in terms of Confucian philosophy, and its tradition includes both instrumental and vocal music.

It also refers to ensemble music for the upper class that existed outside of the court. *Chongak* literally translates as "correct" or "graceful" music and includes *aak*, *tangak*, and *hyangak*.

Aak is Confucian ritual temple music, and only one example (*Munmyoak*) survives to this day. The music traditions of *aak* are considered a unique and ancient heritage in East Asia today. When introduced from China in the 12th century, *aak* included 42 different types of instrument, comprising 575 individual instruments, in addition to elaborate clothing for all of the performers. Over time, *aak* has been scaled down. Now this ritual music is performed by two orchestras, one located on the terrace of the main temple and the other in the courtyard. The orchestras must use instruments that include eight materials (metal, stone, silk, bamboo, gourd, clay, leather, and wood). Some rare instruments, such as bronze bell chimes, stone chimes, a tiger scraper, a wooden box, and a baked clay jar, can also be heard. The ceremony also be includes more than 60 dancers.

Tangak literally means the music of Tang China, but it also includes the music from the Sung dynasty. It became court music when brought to Korea. Only two orchestra pieces and one dance have survived. Initially, the music was performed by vocalists and the orchestra, but contemporary *tangak* is purely instrumental. The orchestra consists of Chinese instruments but includes a Korean flute, the *taegum*.

Hyangak, indigenous to the Korean peninsula, is a traditional wind ensemble that may have been in existence for several thousand years. Most of the pieces in this category belong to banquet music. The *Sujech'on* is the most famous example in the *hyangak* repertoire; it may be the oldest of all court orchestral pieces and predates the first compilation of Gregorian chants. The main melody is carried by cylindrical oboes (*p'iri*) and large traverse flutes (*taegum*). The overall piece is very majestic.

Chongak: *Vocal Music*

There are three genres of classical vocal songs: long lyric songs (*kagok*), short lyric songs (*sijo*), and narrative songs (*kasa*). *Kagok* is considered the best vocal genre of the *chongak* tradition. No other vocal genre can compare with its beauty of form, instrumentation, and range of expressiveness. A *kagok* performer will sing slowly more than 20 long vocal pieces without a clear break and is accompanied by an instrumental ensemble that has to include five basic instruments: a *komungo* a *taegum*, a soft oboe (*sep'iri*), a two-stringed fiddle (*haegum*), and an hourglass drum (*changgo*).

Sijo, which is indigenous to Korea, is as slow as *kagok* and may be accompanied by the *changgo* drum or have no accompaniment at all. It employs only three notes. A single sustained tone makes any sense of rhythm indistinguishable. This genre is particularly popular among older Koreans and attracts the attention of the audience because of the subtle gradation of intensity and rapid changes of pitch combined with an unusually high-pitched singing voice.

The narrative songs of *kasa* are long and lack a strict structural framework or uniform singing style. Its songs were sung both by aristocracy and common people.

The *taegum* and the *changgo* drum were the most common instruments used to accompany the singer. The value of the *kasa* does not relate to melody but to its slow rhythm, high-pitched sounds, and an altogether quiet style.

Minsogak *Music*

Minsogak, the music of the commoners, includes Shamanic music, Buddhist music, folk songs, farmers' music (called *nong-ak*), dramatic *p'ansori*, and instrumental *sanjo*. The most important Shamanistic music is performed when instrumentalists accompany the female Shaman's ritual dance. The Shamanic dance music known as *shinawi* is improvised by the instrumentalists and played as long as the Shaman is engaged in the dance. A variety of rhythmic patterns is provided by such instruments as the *p'iri*, *taegum*, two-stringed fiddle (*haegum*), *changgo*, barrel drum (*buk*), and a large gong (*ching*). The basic musical elements of *shinawi* are also found in *p'ansori* and *sanjo*.

Buddhist ritual performing arts include chant, ritual dance, and outdoor band music. Of these, ritual chant is the most important in Buddhist rites. There are two

Farmers' music. (Courtesy of the Korea Tourism Organization)

types of Buddhist chants. One relates to praying to Buddha; it has a simple singing style and is sung by all Buddhist monks. The other is more complex, is sung by trained monks, and includes a wide range of tones and falsetto singing.

Korean folk songs may be those of the peasant as well as the highly trained professional folk singer and are characterized by their rhythmic structure. The majority of the folk songs are farmers' songs that related to the lifestyle of traditional agrarian society over the ages. Most are in the form of a call and response, in which a leader will sing an improvised solo tune and the chorus will answer with a repeated refrain. The rhythm of most of the songs is triple meter as opposed to the predominant duple meter of China and Japan.

Nongak (farmers' music) is an exciting kind of music that has been performed for centuries and has recently become very popular. *Nongak* varies from region to region but typically includes such percussion instruments as small gongs (*kkwaenggwari*), large *ching*, *changgo*, *buk*, and several hand drums (*sogo*). The performing group of four Korean percussionists known as Samulnori is directly related to *nongak* tradition.

Audiences who listen to the music of *nongak* are often inspired by the strongly accented rhythms and begin to clap their hands and move to the beat. Members of the audience are enthralled when dancers in colorful dress strike small drums and revolve a whiplike tail suspended from their hats. The dancers make the tails spin around in a circle by shaking their heads while striking the small drums. They perform numerous motions, sometimes running, sometimes sitting down, and sometimes standing up while the tail continues to swirl in circles. In the past, these performers provided not only music and dance for their village but also a great service by driving away the evil spirits.

P'ansori's birth and transformation into a musical art form was one of the greatest musical accomplishments of the late Choson dynasty. It was so widely popular in the late 19th century that its performers were the best-known musicians of the era. It remains an important cultural heritage that became increasingly popular in the late 20th century and continues to be widely appreciated. The five most popular productions are the stories of *Ch'unhyang-ga*, *Shimchong-ga*, *Heongbu-ga*, *Soogoong-ga*, and *Jeokbyuk-ga*.

A *p'ansori* performance is presented by two musicians, a solo singer and a barrel drum player. In order to achieve the skills necessary for *p'ansori*, a singer must go through exceedingly strenuous training by a master. When performing a long dramatic song, the *p'ansori* performer will sing, speak, and employ dramatic actions using gestures and carrying a fan and handkerchief as props and will make the audience laugh and weep. Meanwhile, the drummer creates rhythmic sounds.

Because this musical form is not written down, the singer begins with the phrase in the basic rhythmic pattern in order for the drummer to easily follow the singer. To fully appreciate *p'ansori*, one must pay particular attention to the beginning of every song. The long and continuous songs are relieved by speech that provides comic relief. Speech also is invaluable for the singer as it gives him or her time to take a breath. It also allows the audience to laugh and relax. The drummer beats his or her drum in recurring rhythmic patterns but will periodically shout out to the singer to encourage him or her to continue the long narrative songs of *p'ansori*.

Three Drums Dance (Samgomu). (Courtesy of Mary Connor)

The word *sanjo* literally means "scattered melodies" and is an instrumental version of *p'ansori. Sanjo* is highly emotional music that developed in the southwestern part of Korea in the second half of the 19th century. This type of music is performed by a solo instrument that is accompanied by the *changgo*. The characteristics include subtle melodic progressions and an extraordinary variation of rhythmic patterns. Because of the emotional content and skills necessary to perform *sanjo*, this musical form is widely appreciated.

CONTEMPORARY MUSIC (1945–2008)

South Korea

The creative environment for the development of Korean music from Japanese occupation (1910–1945) to the 1980s was impaired by Japanese policies to eliminate Korean musical traditions, the Korean War (1950–1953), and the successive military dictatorships that lasted until the 1980s. Composers were naturally affected by the pressures of politics and the sorrows of war. The first generation of postliberation composers of Western music adopted 19th-century Western techniques and theories to serve Korean purposes. This generation faced many hurdles but is recognized for the pioneering work in the development of *kagok*, short songs similar to the Germanic *Lieder*.

HONG NANP'A (1897–1941)

A brilliant composer, violinist, and patriot, Nanp'a, as he is known, inspired people with his music during the difficult times of Japanese occupation. When he was 13, he was encouraged by a music teacher to study the violin, an instrument that was unfamiliar in Korea. As he traveled back and forth from home to his lessons, the Japanese police, who were also unfamiliar with the unusual shape of a violin case, frequently stopped him. As he grew older, he became involved in the independence movement and composed inspiring nationalist music. His most famous song, "Pongsonhwa," became known as the song of the resistance. In 1937, Nanp'a was arrested for his support of Korean independence, interrogated, and imprisoned for three months. He was never the same again and died several years later.

The second generation sought to employ Western musical theories to attempt to rise above what they felt to be the backwardness of Korea. They focused on instrumental music rather than *kagok* and other genres of the first generation of composers. The third generation, including Lee Geonyong, became part of a group that opposed their predecessors' "futile" policies and sought to develop "Korean" musical theory. Ironically, the *kagok* of the first generation is the most widely known, while the modern works of the second and third generations have not drawn the attention of the average citizen.

Several developments prior to the outbreak of the Korean War provided hopes for broad-based music appreciation and the creation of new compositions, but the war brought a halt to any such aspirations. Korea's first symphony orchestra was established in 1945 under the name of the Korea Philharmonic Orchestra. In 1948, Chung Hoe-gap introduced his own string quartet at a concert commemorating the graduation of the first class from the Music College at Seoul National University. The same year, the first opera, Verdi's *La Traviata*, was performed. In early 1950, an opera composed by Hyon Che-myong called *Ch'unhyang-jon*, based on the famous love story of the same name, was enthusiastically received by the public.

As Korea began to recover from the devastation of the Korean War, composers became increasingly interested in techniques that were being introduced at the time. As a result, the composer Na Un-yong began to introduce the public to his music based on the 12-note system that was quite influential during the mid-20th century. About the same time, members of the Composition Department of the Music College at Seoul National University formed a composers club that facilitated the growth of new music. Yun Yi-sang and Ahn Ik-tae, the composer of the South Korean national anthem, won worldwide fame for their distinctive musical talents. The Seoul Philharmonic Orchestra and the Korean Broadcasting Symphony Orchestra were also formed in the 1950s.

In 1965, the National Opera Group opened with a performance of Puccini's *La Bohème*. Three years later, *La Traviata* introduced the Kim Cha-kyong Opera

---

CHUNG MYUNG-WHUN (1953–)

Chung is a world-renowned conductor. When he was 7, he made his debut as a pianist. He studied at the Juilliard School in New York and at 18 conducted the Korean Symphony Orchestra. In 1978, Carlo Maria Giulini appointed him assistant for the Los Angeles Philharmonic Orchestra. In 1970, he won the New York Times competition for his piano performance. Since that time, he has conducted in Germany, New York, and Paris. Since 2006, Chung has been the principal conductor of the Seoul Philharmonic Orchestra.

Group. Some of the most popular Korean operas performed since the 1960s are *Ch'unhyan-jon*, and *Shimchongjon*, by Kim Tong-jin. In the 1970s, increasing numbers of musicians were attracted to chamber music and adopted the techniques of their Western contemporaries. However, by far the form of classical music with the broadest appeal is opera. One of the most famous contemporary composers of Korean opera, Lee Young-jo, has recently staged operatic productions in Beijing, Tokyo, and Los Angeles with great acclaim.

An increasing number of Korean composers have explored innovative instrumental performance techniques by combining traditional and Western instruments. The term *changjak gugak* (newly composed Korean music) relates to the effort to express the spirit of time-honored music in new ways. The compositions are created for traditional instruments but use Western staff notations and various other devices, such as tempo indication. Kim Kisoo and Hwang Byungki are the two most influential contemporary composers of this type of music.

Kim Kisoo, known as a great master of composition, studied the *taegum* at the Yiwangjik A-akbu. In 1945, he wrote his first orchestral piece, celebrating the beauty of Korea and expressing the abject suffering of the Koreans during colonial rule. In 1952, he started to compose new music, *jeongbaikhon*, based on the traditional *chongak* style, such as "Songkwangbok," a song of Korean independence. He wrote more than 100 compositions in many different genres, exemplified by notable compositions that express his devotion to Korea, its people, and his hopes for reunification. Kim is recognized as a pioneer composer of a contemporary Korean music that reflects the spirit of the Korean people in a traditional way.

In 1962, the *kayagum* master Hwang Byungki composed a number of pieces including *Sup* (*Forest*), the first *kayagum* piece ever composed in a contemporary medium. His productions were groundbreaking in Korean music culture, a new role of the composer emerged, and greater experimentation with the fundamental sounds and rhythms of Korean music began. As a result, composers began to transform traditional musical practices, and their techniques became more daring and innovative. Hwang is now considered one of Korea's most celebrated composers and performers and received standing ovations during his tour of the United States in 2007.

AHN SOOK-SUN (1949–)

In 1997, Ahn was designated a "living cultural treasure" for her extraordinary gifts as a musician. Influenced by her mother's interest in traditional folk music, she learned to play the *kayagum* and *changgo* and to perform the *tan'ga* (a short solo song) at an early age. After years of special training, she came to Seoul at the age of 19 to study with one of the greatest music teachers in all of Korea. Since that time, she has mastered the musical styles of Korea's legendary musicians and dazzled audiences with her versatility, especially her improvised instrumental solos.

In recent times *Hallyu*, or the "Korean wave," has spread South Korean popular culture in East and Southeast Asia and beyond. The term originated in China, following the overwhelming success of Korean television dramas and pop music in China and Taiwan in the late 1990s. Since then, *Hallyu* has spread to the United States, Europe, and South America. Such pop music artists as Rain, HOT, NRG, and others reached the top of Chinese pop music charts while BOA's grand entrance into the Japanese market was a huge success.

The original Korean stage show *The Last Empress* was praised on Broadway as "the Korean *Evita*." The show *NANTA*, which launched a new era of percussion-based performance, is continuing the legacy of Korean musical traditions. Korean performing arts groups, such as Kim Duk-soo's Samulnori, are bringing to the world modern interpretations of traditional music drawn from Korea's long history and transformed into distinctive contemporary rhythms and melodies.

North Korea

As South Korean traditional, classical, and pop music have made their presence felt throughout most of the world, the music of the Democratic People's Republic of Korea is heard primarily by its own people and a limited number of foreign visitors. The music is strictly controlled by a government that encourages light, state-sponsored music or music with patriotic worker themes that praise Kim Il-Sung or Kim Jong-Il. Traditional Korean music and dance have essentially been abandoned. Propaganda songs sound quite similar to the patriotic music of China and the former Soviet Union. The men's choir run by the army is said to be world-class.

Music serves as a means for inculcating the *juche* philosophy of self-reliance and the need to continue the struggle for revolution and reunification of the Korean peninsula. The Japanese and the Americans are depicted as evil and imperialistic and the source of any great suffering past or present. On the other hand, the Korean revolutionary heroes and heroines are depicted as saintly figures who act for the purest of motives. The three most consistent themes in the arts are the ongoing revolutionary struggle, the happiness of the North Korean people, and the brilliance of both Kim Il-Sung and Kim Jong-Il.

KIM DUK-SOO (1951–)

Since Kim was 5 years old, traditional music was the center of his world. He is now the most renowned traditional percussionist in Korea and a major figure in an international renaissance of modern percussion music. From the time Kim was 13, he performed in other countries and became aware of differing cultural and artistic traditions. Although he recognized that Korean percussion music was not well known, he believed that it had a unique beauty from the natural energy of Korean rhythms and the immense power of the traditional percussion instruments. With three other musicians, he took farmer band music and created a modern form known as *samul nori,* which literally means "playing with four instruments."

Elaborate and beautiful operatic productions, such as *The Flower Girl,* serve as entertainment as well as nationalistic propaganda and include such predictable themes as suffering at the hands of greedy landlords and the Japanese. Foreign visitors are informed that Kim Il-Sung wrote the opera and that his son, Kim Jong-Il,

Kim Il-Sung's revolutionary opera, Flower Girl, *at the Grand Theater in P'yongyang. (Courtesy of Mary Connor)*

wrote the musical score. The most famous productions are the renowned mass games performed by as many as tens of thousands of performers singing, playing music, marching, and doing mass gymnastics and supported by pictures produced by thousands of card turners creating revolutionary images and portrayals of the Great Leader, Kim Il-Sung. For the foreign visitor, the performance is as strikingly beautiful as it is frightening. One particularly notes the disciplined performances of the young, who spend years training for the performance.

In February 2008, the New York Philharmonic performed a concert in P'yongyang at the invitation of the North Koreans, who opened the door to the largest delegation of Americans to visit the country since the Korean War ended. This time they arrived with violins and violas rather than the arms and armor that Americans brought the last time. The orchestra played pieces of Dvorak, Gershwin, and Wagner as well as the "Star-Spangled Banner." After the orchestra played its encore, "Arirang," a lilting folk song that inevitably touches the hearts of Koreans, the North Koreans were on their feet, applauding and waving at the musicians. A cellist from the New York Philharmonic said, "We felt such a connection with these people. They didn't want us to leave the stage and we didn't want to leave either. Some of us were crying we were so moved." (Demick 2008).

REFERENCES

Clark, Donald N. 2000. *Culture and Customs of Korea*. Westport, CT: Greenwood Press.

Demick, Barbara. 2008. "Mutual Standing Ovation in North Korea." *Los Angeles Times*, February 27.

Eckert, Carter, et al. 1990. *Korea: Old and New: A History*. Seoul: Ilchokak Publishers.

Korean Overseas Information Service. 1993. *A Handbook of Korea*. 9th ed. Seoul: Korean Overseas Information Service, Ministry of Culture and Information.

———. 2003. *A Handbook of Korea*. 11th ed. Seoul: Korean Overseas Information Service, Ministry of Culture and Information.

Han, Man-young. 1990. *Kukak: Studies in Korean Traditional Music*. Seoul: Korea Research Foundation.

Howard, Keith. 1988. *Korean Musical Instruments*. Seoul: Se-Kwang Music Publishing Co.

———. 2006. *Creating Korean Music: Tradition, Innovation, and the Discourse of Identity*. Aldershot, UK: Ashgate Publishing, Ltd.

Korean National Commission for UNESCO. 1983. *Traditional Korean Music*. Seoul: Si-sa-yong-o-sa Publishers.

Korean Spirit and Culture Project. 2007. *Fifty Wonders of Korea: Culture and Art*. Seoul: Samjung Munwhasa.

Korea Society. n.d. "Portrait of Hwang Byungki: Korean Traditional Music." http://www.koreasociety.org/arts/performing_arts/portrait_of_hwang_byungki (accessed January 14, 2008).

Lee, Byong Won. 1997. *Styles and Esthetics in Korean Traditional Music*. Seoul: National Center for Korean Traditional Performing Arts.

Lee, Byong Won, and Yong-Shik Lee, eds. 2007. *Music of Korea: Korean Musicology Series 1*. Seoul: National Center for Korean Performing Arts.

Song, Bang-song. 2000. *Korean Music: Historical and Other Aspects*. Seoul: Jimoondang Publishing Co.

Song, Hye-jin. 2000. *A Stroll through Korean Music History*. Seoul: National Center for Korean Traditional Performing Arts.

Underwood, Horace H., and Nancy K. Underwood, eds. 2002. *An Illustrated Guide to Korean Culture*. Seoul: Hakgojae Publishing Co.

Wakin, Daniel J. 2007. "Philharmonic Agrees to Play in North Korea: A Cultural First Amid Political Openings." *New York Times*, December 10.

Food

Mary E. Connor

INTRODUCTION

Food is a fundamental element in the Korean heritage, and Koreans take particular pleasure in their distinctive culinary art. Although their diet continues to change and develop over time, the basic diet pattern has remained the same for thousands of years. Many Koreans speak with pride in the belief that their food is a solution to the modern quest for a nutritious, low-fat, delicious diet.

Traditional dietary customs are evident in everyday foods, those eaten on special occasions, and those that are preserved for later use. Many Koreans are receptive to foreign food trends, but their indigenous dietary culture reflects ancient tradition. They take great satisfaction in preserving the recipes and cooking methods of their ancestors. Food plays an essential role in traditional rites of passage. Dietary customs reflect the great importance of Confucian values, family and community traditions, and the veneration of nature. The ancient ritual of drinking and singing after a meal persists. These customs serve as a foundation for the nutritious and distinctive flavor and color combinations particular to Korean cuisine.

Aside from the importance of tradition, food has a particular significance for members of the older generation. Those who lived during the Korean War and its aftermath vividly remember the hard times and starving people. There was also a preoccupation about health. Mothers and grandmothers spent considerable time making sure that family members, especially the children, got the nutrition they needed. Even though the standard of living has improved significantly, the older generation continues to value food as if it were rationed. Children grow up hearing "*mogo, mogo*," meaning "Eat! Eat!" Koreans insist that their guests eat more than they might want. This insistence is based on the host's desire to appear generous and concerned about the visitor's health.

Korean food can be sour, sweet, hot, burning hot, salty, bitter, or nutty. It is a remarkable combination of interesting flavors and aromas, and the variety of dishes reflects the seasons and time-honored traditions. The diet is largely based on rice, noodles, vegetables, and meats. Traditionally, main dishes are distinguished from a number of subsidiary dishes by larger quantities. Almost all meals are accompanied by steam-cooked short-grain rice, soup, and *kimch'i* (the national dish). The small dishes are served in a specific arrangement, alternated to highlight the shape and color of the ingredients. Fruit is often served as an after-meal refresher. In-season fresh vegetables are used at the peak of their ripeness and dried or preserved for out-of-season use later on.

Preparation is generally very labor intensive. Much consideration is given to such contrasting characteristics as warm and cold, hot and mild, rough and soft, solid and liquid, and a balance of presentation of colors. Food preparation methods are quite different from Western ones. The main tasks in preparing a Korean meal are the cutting, slicing, seasoning, and careful arrangement of the food. The cutting of foods is considered to be very important for appearance, convenient eating with chopsticks, and nutritional value. Vegetables, fish, and meat are cut or sliced into the same size, shape, and thickness so that they cook evenly. Cutting slits in the meat allows marinade to penetrate further and prevents it from curling up during cooking. Chopping the seasonings allows for better distribution of the flavor throughout a particular dish. Common seasonings include soy sauce, bean pastes, mustard, sesame, vinegar, garlic, green onions, ginger, red pepper, and wines. Various seasoned sauces are used for marinating meat or fish before broiling, grilling, or stir-frying. Sauces are also used in vegetable dishes. Different regions of Korea have their own seasoning combinations—some of which are very hot.

The final step in preparing most dishes is to carefully consider the arrangement of foods. Much thought is given to the color of the food and its arrangement in patterns of concentric circles, radial designs, or parallel linear columns. The food dishes are never set on a table without consideration of color and design. The arrangement is such that all diners can reach all dishes easily. These details exemplify the importance of aesthetics and tradition for the Korean people.

HISTORICAL BACKGROUND

Excavations from ancient sites tell us a great deal about the early Koreans and their dietary culture. Varied cereals were grown from the mid-Neolithic age. Rice was grown in some parts of the country as far back as 2000 BCE and became the staple of the Korean diet during the Three Kingdoms period (57 BCE–668 CE). Beans and cereals were also grown during this time. These became the staples of the diet. Because the peninsula has many large rivers, it boasts a plentiful supply of fish. The Yellow Sea and the East Sea continue to offer excellent seafood, seaweed, and shellfish for the Korean table. Fruit and vegetable cultivation also dates from ancient times. Pine nuts, chestnuts, pears, and peaches were popular. Yams, gourds, radishes, and eggplants comprised some of the many vegetables that were cultivated. Studies indicate that yams probably had the longest history, dating back to

Chapchae. (Courtesy of Helie Lee, author of "Still Life with Rice" and "In the Absence of Son.")

ancient times. Lettuce was apparently brought from China by a representative from Silla who reported that the lettuce was so expensive that it became known as a vegetable worth as much as thousands of pieces of gold.

Extreme seasonal changes demanded varied methods to process fermented foods. During the Three Kingdoms period, fermented foods became part of the basic diet. An interesting fact confirming the use of fermentation was the discovery of gifts sent to the bride of a Silla king in the 7th century. Such preserved foods as soy sauce, *kimch'i*, pickled cucumber, and fermented seafood have been eaten since ancient times. *Kimch'i* is thought to have originated from Chinese pickles brought to Korea some time during the Unified Silla period. The spicy red *kimch'i* that we know today has existed since the 17th century.

The people of ancient Koguryo, famous for their hunting skills in their largely mountainous regions, consumed deer and wild boar. Over time, hunting spread to all parts and established the tradition of meat dishes. An important development that influenced Korean food was the arrival of Buddhism from China around 400 CE. Meat eating gradually was abandoned in favor of a vegetarian diet. During the early years of the Koryo dynasty, nearly everyone from the lowest commoner to the king refrained from eating meat because of the influence of Buddhism. Korea's tea culture reached it peak during Koryo, and sweets and pastries began to be developed as part of what became a daily tea ritual. Dietary habits changed with the arrival of the Mongols in the mid-13th century. Eventually, the Mongols dominated the Koryo court and made demands that cattle be raised on the island of Cheju. From the Mongols, the Koreans again learned the pleasures of cooked meat. The Mongols were also responsible for introducing *soju* wine, distilled liquor made from fermented yeast and rice.

Agricultural techniques improved significantly during the Choson dynasty, and numerous texts were written that led to the advancement of farming methods specifically suited to the Korean peninsula. Irrigation was extended and improved rice planting techniques were promoted on a national basis. At this time corn, red peppers, peanuts, pumpkins, potatoes, sweet potatoes, tomatoes, and other foreign foods were introduced. The red peppers grown on the peninsula were uniquely sweet and hot, and their continued use is responsible for the unique taste of Korea's traditional food. Organized opposition to Buddhism came during the Choson period because the court espoused Confucianism. Additional dietary change came with the elimination of tea drinking, a not-too-subtle means of striking out against Buddhism. Boiled rice water took the place of tea, and only relatively recently has the practice of tea drinking been revived. Another eating habit that changed during Choson was the use of the spoon in addition to chopsticks at the table.

Over time the everyday diet of rice, soup, and side dishes evolved. Table settings showed a noticeable distinction between the main and auxiliary dishes. With four distinct seasons and significant climatic differences, the food of each region varied,

Galbi. (Courtesy of Helie Lee, author of "Still Life with Rice" and "In the Absence of Son.")

mostly in the side dishes consumed on a daily basis. Today almost all foods are available during every season of the year. Foreign foods are widely available, and food preparation techniques have been simplified. Time-consuming methods of fermenting foods have been largely replaced by mass production, and large freezers have been created to store foods that are essential to the daily diet, such as *kimch'i*.

DIETARY CUSTOMS

Although contemporary Koreans have accepted modern eating trends, their native dietary customs serve as a mirror of traditional culture. Rice, or *pap*, has been the principal staple for thousands of years. The traditional extended family had an average of 20 members, which meant food had to be prepared in large quantities. A process of rice preparation developed that produced two kinds of rice from the same kettle: soft watery rice and sticky, glutinous rice. This two-tiered approach took into consideration the needs of the elderly or infirm people who were living in the household. The daughter-in-law would carefully serve the softer rice to the honored family members first. No one could begin to eat until the elders were served.

Rice has always been served with subsidiary dishes that include vegetables, meat, fish, and seafood in the form of soup, casseroles, and steamed dishes. Seasoned vegetables with soy sauce, fermented seafood and vegetables, and *kimch'i* were inevitably served at most meals. In addition to rice, soup and *kimch'i* are also basic elements of Korean meals. Bowls of soup and rice are served individually, but the side dishes are shared by everyone at the table. Meals were served on low tables. Daughters learned to be good cooks, and if they were able to prepare particularly delicious food, it was said that they had developed a "tasty hand." Daughters were expected to master the art of good cooking from their mothers and their mothers-in-law and to pass on that knowledge to the next generation. Over the generations, passing down cooking methods and recipes contributed to the family's eating habits and tasty regional specialties.

The preparation of special holiday foods appears to have played a significant role in the lives of Koreans throughout the centuries. The preparation of these special foods fostered greater appreciation for the occasion itself and the importance of attending to farm tasks throughout the year. It also solidified the need for cooperation among members of a family and the surrounding farm community.

Rice cakes were the favorite special dish of traditional Korean society. When the harvest was completed and cold weather came, the preparation of rice cakes began. These delicious cakes (coated with sweet grain syrup or persimmons) were always shared with neighbors and were considered a vital step toward maintaining good relations with relatives and neighbors. Hot and cold noodles, grilled wheat cakes, pumpkin porridge, and red bean porridge were some of the favorite special dishes in addition to the rice cakes. The making of *kimch'i* in the winter was a major household event. When plentiful, cabbages and other vegetables were pickled, processed, and stored in order to provide essential nutrients throughout the winter season. Since making *kimch'i* required many hands, relatives and neighbors worked together to create what is considered to be the essential component of Korea's culinary heritage and an example of the people's belief in the importance of Confucianism and sustaining harmonious relations.

COMMON KOREAN DISHES

Rice   A discussion of food must start with rice, the basic food of the people. In fact, the Korean expression for "Have you had breakfast?" is "Have you eaten rice today?" A simple meal can be made of a bowl of rice and a few flavorful side dishes, such as *kimch'i* or soup. They grow many varieties. One is *tapkok*, rice that grows in lowland paddies everywhere. It is slightly sticky when served. The other main variety is upland rice, usually dried and milled for flour and beer brewing. In the past, rice meant wealth and was a tangible way for farming people to estimate their worth. In hard times, rice was equated with life itself.

Kimch'i   *Kimch'i* is the Korean national dish. It has been part of the diet for centuries, and cooks boast that there are more than 200 variations, depending on region, season, and personal preference. *Kimch'i* in South Korea is usually spicier than the *kimch'i* that is served in North Korea. It is the ubiquitous side dish and is made with a uniquely pungent mixture of fermented vegetables, usually cabbages

Kimch'i. (Courtesy of Helie Lee, author of "Still Life with Rice" and "In the Absence of Son.")

and radishes. Koreans are passionate about *kimch'i* and have been heard to say that it nourishes the soul as much as the body. Each autumn, there is a ritual in every household. It is the time when cabbage is particularly sweet and tender and the best time for making *kimch'i*. The cabbage is cut up; salted; seasoned with chili, salt, pepper, and garlic; and packed into large stone jars to ferment. Yet modern life is changing habits. *Kimch'i* can be found ready-made in chilled supermarket compartments, but the tradition is central to eating habits. A family of four eats about 20 heads of cabbage in the form of *kimch'i* during an average winter.

Soup   In addition to rice and *kimch'i*, every meal includes soup, the only liquid served with the meal. The variety of soups is very broad and can range from bland vegetable soup to an incredibly powerful stew made with tofu and red pepper paste. Koreans love a bowl of hot soup, particularly during the cold winter months. Meats, fish, and vegetables are the primary ingredients. *Kalbi-tang*, rich beef soup, is one of the favorites. *Mandu-guk* is meat dumpling soup that resembles Chinese wonton soup, but Korean dumplings are much bigger than Chinese ones. The dumplings are filled with beef, pork, garlic, green onions, and vegetables.

Beans   Koreans are also very fond of beans, an important source of protein in their diet. Mung beans are cooked whole or ground into a flour to make a popular

Manduguk. (Courtesy of Helie Lee, author of "Still Life with Rice" and "In the Absence of Son.")

snack, *pindaettok*, crunchy fried pancakes seasoned with chopped *kimch'i*. Soybeans are cooked whole or used to make bean curd. *Toenjang* is fermented bean paste used as a soup base and is also a condiment mixed with red pepper paste. A red bean, *p'at*, the same as Japanese *azuki*, is used in many desserts.

Noodles   Noodles are made from either buckwheat or regular wheat flour. The most popular are the brownish buckwheat noodles served in soups based on beef, poultry, or anchovy stock. *Mokkuksu* is the simplest of all noodle dishes and is cooked in either beef or chicken stock and served with *kimch'i*. *Kalguksu* is a hot and filling dish. The noodles are made from buckwheat and potato flour seasoned with a pepper paste. *Mullaengmyon* is cold noodle soup perfect for hot summer days. Diners particularly love *chapch'ae*, a noodle dish with mixed vegetables. If one has not eaten Korean food, trying *Chapchae* is a good place to start.

Pulgogi   One of the most popular dishes is *pulgogi*, broiled beef strips and ribs of beef, which exemplifies an age-old tradition of cooking on an iron hot plate at the table. Meats of all kinds, including mutton, pork, poultry, and seafood, are cooked in this way. One marinates the meat well in advance in a spicy mixture that includes soy sauce, sesame oil, garlic, ginger, pepper (or chili), toasted sesame seeds, and green

Pulgogi. (Courtesy of Helie Lee, author of "Still Life with Rice" and "In the Absence of Son.")

Pibimpap. (Courtesy of the Korean Tourism Organization)

onions. White rice, bowls of several *namul* (vegetable) dishes, and *kimch'i* complete the gamut of flavors that make *pulgogi* appreciated around the world.

Seafood   Seafood is plentiful and diverse. Abalone, crabs, crayfish, scallops, clams, and shrimp are used frequently. Octopus is stewed with strong seasonings into a delicious dish that is a particular favorite of fishermen. Kelp and seaweed provide extra nutrients and fresh-from-the-sea taste.

Galbi kui   *Galbi* is another well-known dish that is cooked in the same way as *pulgogi*, but it uses short ribs instead of beef slices. The beef short ribs are marinated in a mixture of green onions, garlic, sugar, sesame oil, and soy sauce.

Pibimpap   If you are visiting Korea, *pibimpap* is a must. A very simple but popular dish, *pibimpap* is piping hot rice served in a stoneware bowl with a variety of vegetables, cooked and raw, arranged on top.

Kujol-p'an   This is an interesting dish of pancakes that may include a choice of nine different fillings, such as shredded black mushrooms, grated carrots or radishes, diced green onions, eggs, chopped *kimch'i*, sautéed beef, and ground toasted sesame seeds.

Galbi Beef. (Courtesy of the Korean Tourism Organization)

Sinsullo   *Sinsullo*, a very popular dish, is a hot pot of meats, vegetables, and nuts simmered together and eaten with a tart vinegar and soy sauce dip.

Desserts   Seasonal fruit or rice cakes are usually served at the end of the meal. Sweets and desserts are generally eaten as snacks, not during main meals.

COMMON BEVERAGES

Alcoholic   The local wines are potent and vie with the strong flavors of the food. The lowliest wine for everyday consumption is *makkoli*. It is an unfiltered rice wine, sour in taste, and milky white. The quality varies by age and place, but it is very basic to village life. *Takchu* is a wheat-based wine that is low in alcohol and made from grain husks. *Yakchu* is another popular wine, but it is of a finer quality than *takchu* and has a higher alcohol content. *Chongjong*, also called *ch'ongju*, is a rice wine that is served warm like some Japanese *sake*. *Soju*, the most potent of all and something like vodka, is one of the most popular drinks. The most common form of *soju* is made from sweet potato starch and has an alcohol content of around 20 percent. Premium *sòju* (called Andong *soju*) is made from rice mash, has a higher alcohol content that runs between 20 and 35 percent, and is considered more flavorful. Koreans also enjoy beer, both domestic and imported.

Nonalcoholic   People drink rice or barley water after meals. The traditional teas are ginseng, ginger, and cinnamon tea. There is also a special tea called *Ssanghwa-tang*, containing such fruits as jujubes (dates), chestnuts, pine nuts, and honey water.

CEREMONIAL FOOD: LIFE'S MILESTONES

Koreans have placed great importance on celebrating life's milestones and have preserved meaningful rituals, some of which are based on ancient oral traditions. As a result, ceremonies have evolved that relate to birth, one's first birthday, coming of age, marriage, death, and memorial services after death. In all of these occasions, food plays a role in signifying the importance of the occasion itself. Many families continue to hold onto these traditions not only in Korea but also throughout the Korean diaspora.

Birth rituals begin prior to the birth. Just before a baby is born, three bowls of plain white rice and three bowls of seaweed soup are placed on a table. After the baby is delivered, the rice and the soup are served to the mother. Special ceremonies continue every 7 days up to the baby's 49th day of life. On each of these days, plain white rice, seaweed soup, and occasionally rice cakes are served. The relatives participate and bless the baby. Sometimes the food is shared with neighbors.

The first birthday includes a fascinating custom. A low table contains not only food but also a writing brush, inkstone, book, thread, money, and an archery bow, symbols to wish the baby success, longevity, and a happy future. If the child is a girl, a pair of scissors and a ruler take the place of the archery bow. The one-year-old is dressed in traditional attire and encouraged to select an item from the table. What the child selects will influence her or his future. If the child selects rice or money, it is a sign of future wealth. Thread symbolizes longevity, and books and the brush represent scholarship. The food connected with the celebration of a child's first birthday includes noodles, stuffed jujubes, sweet glutinous rice cakes, steamed rice cake, crescent-shaped rice cake, fruits, cookies, millet dumplings, rice cakes coated with bean flour, and plain rice.

The next milestone in a person's life is the coming-of-age ceremony that takes place for a boy between the ages of 15 and 20 and at age 15 for a girl. According to tradition, a man is not considered to be of age until he masters two Confucian classics, the *Analects of Confucius* and the *Book of Filial Piety*. This ceremony is rarely performed these days; however, when it is performed, the ceremonial table is quite simple and includes wine, dried meat, and marinated meat. Relatives and guests are served such additional food as noodles, rice cakes, other meat dishes, wine, and fruit.

The traditional wedding ceremony involved several steps, such as the formal agreement of both families to the marriage, the delivery of the wedding chest, the decision of a date for the wedding, and a final stage whereby the bride is received at the bridegroom's home. Immediately after the wedding ceremony, the new bride pays her respects to her in-laws in what is called a *pyebaek* ceremony. The bride performs a deep bow to her in-laws and then offers them gifts. The food service is very formal, consisting of wine and chicken or beef jerky, stuffed jujubes, broiled beef patties, chestnuts, and a nine-sectioned dish of such delicacies as nuts and dried foods. The mother-in-law then throws Chinese dates or chestnuts into the bride's skirt, wishing prosperity and many sons for the new couple.

The 60th birthday is a major event in the life of a Korean because all five revolutions of the Chinese zodiac have been completed. Much attention is given to a parent who has become 60 years old. The celebration of the event is usually organized by the person's children, who plan an outstanding banquet to celebrate and pay respects to their parent. The principal ceremonial table is placed in front of the person. Sometimes as many as 15 delicacies are served. The offspring pour a cup of wine, bow in pairs, and offer it to their parent. At the same time, there is singing and dancing.

A funeral is a very solemn occasion because it involves the spirit of the dead person. The funeral involves a long process that begins at the moment of death and continues for up to two years. Every morning and evening, food is laid out at the mourning shrine for the spirit of the dead person. During this period, the anniversary of the deceased's birthday calls for more elaborate ceremonies. Wine, fruit, meat, rice cakes, cold rice drink, white rice, soup, and greens are served. After two years of mourning, the family is expected to prepare annual memorial services for the deceased. Ritual food is prepared to honor the deceased, and a feast is organized for the relatives and neighbors who attend the rites. The temporary mourning shrine is then dismantled and a mortuary tablet placed in the ancestral shrine containing tablets of ancestors from four generations. Food offerings adhere to very strict rules and ancient traditions. For example, red fruits are placed to the east of the mortuary tablet and white ones to the west. A cold drink is placed to the east, and slices of dried marinated meat are placed to the west.

For ancestors from five generations or more, the descendants come together once a year and hold a memorial rite at the burial ground. When the rite has finished, family members eat the food that was used in the service and reminisce about their ancestors. Special services are performed at burial mounds on various festival days such as *Ch'usok* (the Harvest Moon Festival) and New Year's Day. Offerings are fairly limited and include fruits of three different colors, dried marinated meat, and rice cakes steamed on a layer of pine noodles for *Ch'usok* and rice cake soup on New Year's Day. After performing these memorial rites out of respect for the deceased, families will have a banquet to celebrate the particular festival. These ceremonies embody Confucian values and traditions extending through many centuries. They reflect the importance of family, respect for elders, and honoring ancestors. These values and traditions have significantly influenced the dietary culture of the Korean people.

HOLIDAY FESTIVALS AND FOOD

Each holiday has its own foods and customs based on ancient traditions, and their origins are essentially unknown. Rice cake soup is served on New Year's Day, glutinous rice or five-grain rice is served on *Taeborum* (first full moon of the year), rice flour and mugwort paste during the *Tano* festival (the fifth day of the fifth lunar month), and crescent-shaped stuffed rice cakes on *Ch'usok* (Harvest Moon Festival). On these four days, people take a rest and participate in special rituals and activities. People wear new clothes, eat delicious holiday foods, and visit elderly relatives and neighbors. The significance of these holidays is brought to life by the preparation of special foods.

New Year's Day is much celebrated as a time for honoring ancestors and for making a fresh start in one's own life. The food takes many days of preparation, and the main meal is always a full banquet. Some of the items on the traditional menu are rice cake dumplings, sesame cookies, sweet rice dish, sweet rice drink, skewered beef and vegetables, mung bean pancakes, steamed shrimp, fried rice cakes, *kimch'i*, hot radish *kimch'i*, glutinous rice cakes, boiled pork, a nine-sectioned dish containing nine different foods, red snapper casserole, broiled beef patties, wrapped-up *kimch'i*, jujube balls, chestnut balls, water *kimch'i*, whole cabbage *kimch'i*, coated sweet rice cakes, steamed shank of beef with soy sauce, vinegar soy sauce, and rice wine.

Ch'usok is also one of the biggest festivals of the year as the occasion celebrates the abundance that comes with the autumn harvest before the cold of winter sets in. New clothes are worn, and the best of the season's crop of fruits (such as persimmons, chestnuts, apples, and pears), cereals, and wine are offered to everyone. The much-anticipated foods include stuffed crescent-shaped rice cakes and a beef and mushroom soup. Family favorites and the specialties of the cook are also included at this time. A sample menu might include steamed rice cake with pine noodles, cooked seasonal vegetables, taro soup, chicken with vegetables, boiled ribs with vegetables, pear punch, and fresh fruits.

REFERENCES

Carter, David. n.d. *Food for Thought: Reflections on Korean Cuisine and Culture.* Seoul, Agricultural and Fishery Marketing Corp.

Chin-hwa, Noh. 1985. *Practical Korean Cooking.* Elizabeth, NJ: Hollym International Corp.

Choi (Yim), E. Soon, and Ki Yull Lee. 1976. *Practical Korean Recipes.* Seoul: Yonsei University Press.

Hepinstall, Hi Soo Shin. 2001. *Growing Up in a Korean Kitchen: A Cookbook.* Berkeley, CA: Ten Speed Press.

Hyun, Peter. 2002. *The Korean Cookbook: Quick and Easy Recipes.* Elizabeth, NJ: Hollym International Corp.

Kim, Joungwon, ed. 1997. *Koreana: Korean Cultural Heritage.* Vol. 4. *Traditional Lifestyles.* Seoul: Korea Foundation.

Kim, Man-Jo, Kyou-Tae Lee, and O-young Lee. 1997. *Kimch'i, Thousand Years.* Vol. 1. Seoul, Korea: Design House Publishers, Inc.

O'Brien, Betsy. 1997. *Let's Eat Korean Food.* Elizabeth, NJ: Hollym International Corp.

Leisure and Sports

Doug Kim

SOUTH KOREA: INTRODUCTION

As with most everything in South Korea, leisure activities and sports have become more contemporary and diverse as the country continues to modernize and is influenced by globalization. South Koreans treasure traditional activities and relish the latest computer games and online competition. Leisure time will increase in South Korea as the 44-hour workweek is being phased out in favor of a 40-hour workweek (with no work on Saturday). This change gives South Koreans more free time and allows weekend trips not possible under the old 44-hour regimen.

HOLIDAYS AND POPULATION MIGRATIONS

South Koreans have a number of holidays and special days. The two biggest holidays are Lunar New Year (*Sollal*) and Harvest Moon Festival (*Ch'usok*) on the 15th day of the eighth lunar month. These holidays are each celebrated for two or more days—enough time for Koreans to make customary and obligatory trips to their hometowns and relatives. Once home, gifts are exchanged, respects are paid to elders (by performing deep and formal bows) and ancestors (by visiting and often cleaning up family burial plots), and large family gatherings are common.

Some estimate that more than 75 percent of all South Koreans travel home for these holidays, putting 32 million people in transit. A consequence of these biannual mass migrations is that much of the holiday is spent in traffic. Although going home for the holidays is not unique to Korea, it is considered a duty far more so

Cheju Island attracts honeymooners, Korean families, and foreign tourists. (Courtesy of Mary Connor)

Buddha's Birthday Celebration, South Korea. (Courtesy of the Korea Tourism Organization)

than in the West. Koreans put up with the inconvenience and congestion, as traditional values remain intact despite modernization.

TRADITIONAL LEISURE

Public bathhouses, *Jjim Jil Bahng*, have long been a fixture in Northeast Asian culture. Commoners could not afford private baths due to the expense. Communal bathhouses proved a more cost-effective means of making a hot bath available to everyone. Individuals thoroughly clean and rinse themselves before entering a common soaking tub, where they often enjoy conversation and the company of others. In South Korea, the modest bathhouse has evolved into the modern *Jjim Jil Bahng* (which literally means a place to apply a hot poultice or compress, but has become the name for what the simple bathhouse is now), a favorite place to get clean, relax, and refresh. More than a bathhouse, these spa-like facilities offer amenities including swimming pools, restaurants, massages, saunas, steam rooms, sleeping areas, video rooms, showers, game rooms, and soaking pools of varying temperatures. Bathing and soaking are separated by gender, but eating and recreation areas are coed. Prices are generally reasonable, making a *Jjim Jil Bahng* retreat a luxury most everyone can afford.

BOARD AND CARD GAMES

Historical, space and resources were often limited in Korea. Compact, transportable, and engaging recreational activities were valued. Although modern housing and lifestyle provide more storage space and make it easier to transport items, three board games have enjoyed continued popularity in modern South Korea.

Yut   This quintessential Korean game traces its roots to the Three Kingdoms period (57 BCE–668 CE). The board (*mal-pan*) can be made of cloth, wood, or paper and has 29 "stations." These stations form a square with two diagonals (in an X pattern) connecting the four corners. Players use a token (*mal*) to represent them on the board and move according to the tosses of the *yut* sticks (*jang-jak*). There are four sticks, each flat on one side and rounded on back. This shape is traditional because originally small firewood pieces were cut and split down the middle to make them.

The sticks are tossed into the air, and the way they land determines how the player's token moves. Each of five possible landing combinations has a distinct name and point value. The team that brings all of their *mal* through the course back to the starting point wins.

Because there is no limit to the number of players, *yut* is a favorite at family gatherings and holidays. Players and onlookers shout out advice, hoping for a certain toss value or offering encouragement. *Yut* conjures up fond nostalgic memories for many Koreans of warm family reunions and happy times.

Baduk   Known as *Weiqi* in Chinese and *Go* in Japanese, Korean *baduk* was mentioned in texts as early as the fifth century BCE. *Baduk* is enjoyed for its complexity and endless strategies.

The game is for two opponents and is played by placing white and black stones on a 9 × 9, 13 × 13, or 19 × 19 grid. A board with fewer lines may be used to introduce the game to a beginner or to have an abbreviated game. Stones are placed on the intersections of the lines with the objective of capturing as many intersections as possible while not being surrounded by the opponent's stones. When one player's stone is surrounded, the surrounded stone is "captured" and replaced by the opponent's. The concomitant's need to be offensive and defensive *and* strategic and tactical give *baduk* its appeal. The game ends when both players can no longer gain more intersections nor capture more of the enemy's stones. The player holding the most intersections wins.

Janggi   *Janggi*, or Korean chess, is similar to Chinese *Xiangqi*. Each player has 5 pieces analogous to pawns in Western chess, 10 pieces analogous to the back row in chess, and 1 "general." Pieces are octagonal, but size varies according to importance. The two sides represent rival Chinese states Han and Cho, which were fighting for supremacy during the period after the Qin dynasty in China. The movement of the pieces is similar to how chess pieces move. The object of the game is to capture/kill the enemy's general.

Hwatu *Hwatu* is a popular game played with 48 cards. *Hwatu* means "flower card," as each card represents 1 of 12 different flowers. Games are played with two or more players in numerous variations. The variations make it impractical to enumerate them all here. Games are often associated with gambling and have roots that trace back to a 48-card deck of Portuguese playing cards introduced into Japan in the mid-16th century.

GAMES FOR GIRLS AND WOMEN

Neol Ttwigi Korean seesaw is traditionally played by females. Unlike Western seesaws, players jump on the ends of a board, which is six to eight feet long, two feet wide, and four to five inches thick. The board (*neol*) rests on a rice straw mat fulcrum. A third participant may sit on the center of the board, to maintain rhythm and keep the board centered and balanced. By jumping with knees slightly tensed and putting more pressure on the back of the foot than the front, players can launch each other into the air a yard or higher. The object of the game is to keep both players aloft for as long and high as possible. The game is one of cooperation—not competition.

The game traces its roots back to the days when women were cloistered behind walls of private residences. These walls were high enough to prevent occupants from seeing the outside world. To get fleeting glimpses of life beyond the walls, girls would play *neol twigi*. This game is now found mostly in folk villages and at cultural festivals.

Kune Ttwigi *Kune* is the Korean swing. Unlike its Western counterpart, the Korean swing is ridden with the feet on the crossbar. Korean swings are suspended on ropes that can be 20 feet or longer. The board that the player stands on is about a yard wide by about four inches across and made of wood or metal. Players need coordination, strength, and bravery, as the goal is to swing until the ropes are parallel to the ground. A bell may be hung in the swinger's path, and whoever touches it first wins.

Although no one is sure why, this game is traditionally played on Tano (the fifth day of the fifth lunar month). Although not restricted to females, this game is traditionally associated with them—perhaps because of the beautiful sight their skirts make as they rush back and forth. Ironically, *kune ttwigi* may have originated in the Koryo period (918–1392 CE) as an exercise for boys and men.

CHILDREN'S GAMES

Although Korean children enjoy many of the same games that children all over the world do, Korean shuttlecock-kicking and kite-flying are particularly noteworthy.

Jeigi A Korean shuttlecock *jeigi* can vary from a homemade version consisting of coins wrapped in a piece of cloth, to a factory-made version with feathers and a weighted rubber end. The important thing is that it be light enough to float

Jaegichagi, a traditional children's game. (Courtesy of the Korea Tourism Organization)

earthward after being kicked, and weighted so the base falls downward. *jeigi* resembles an American hacky sack or footbag. In play, the *Jeigi* behaves like a badminton shuttlecock.

There are different ways of playing *jeigi*, but as with soccer, contact with the hands is prohibited. Games can consist of seeing who can keep the *Jeigi* aloft for the longest time, passing it from person to person, or playing like badminton. Dexterity with all parts of one's body (except the hands), flexibility, and coordination are well tested when playing *Jeigi*.

Yeon Nalligi   Korean *yeon* (kites) come in a variety of shapes, but most famous is the rectangular "shield" kite. These kites are traditionally made of four bamboo sticks supporting a piece of rugged mulberry paper. A fifth stick is placed between the upper corners, creating a bow in the paper. The kite has a circular hole in the center and can be decorated according to the owner's taste. String is attached to the front of the kite at the top corners, the center, and halfway between the center and bottom of the middle stick. All strings are tied together in front of the center to form the "bridle." A tail may be used, but generally is not when kite-fighting.

Korean shield kites are used for fighting because they are highly maneuverable. In battles, the string may be coated with glue and ground glass or pottery filings to

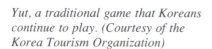

Yut, a traditional game that Koreans continue to play. (Courtesy of the Korea Tourism Organization)

cut an opponent's string. Kite strings may be made of blue silk, which is difficult for an opponent to see. In fights, the objective is to damage, disable, or cut loose an opponent's kite. In some areas, kites were used as a form of exorcism, whereby individuals listed their sins on the kite, flew it on New Year's Day, and cut the string once the kite was high in the sky. The freed kite supposedly carried away one's sins, leaving a clean slate to start the New Year.

CONTEMPORARY LEISURE

Billiards and Table Tennis   Before the country became a high-tech leader, most South Koreans could not afford expensive leisure activities. Two Western games that became popular were *danggu* (billiards) and *t'akgu* (table-tennis). Although neither is traditionally Korean, they have long been played by Koreans who valued their relative inexpensiveness, compactness, ease of mastery, and social nature. These games are often found in bars, recreation rooms, and other social places. In modern South Korea, these games hearken back to when economy was export-driven (and costly pastimes were few and far between) the nation's and they continue to be enjoyed as low-cost diversions, often by college students and young professionals.

*Spinning the top (pangyi), a popular
children's game. (Courtesy of the Korea
Tourism Organization)*

Video Games   More than any other modern development, the Internet and computer games have changed the way younger South Koreans spend leisure time. South Korea is one of the most wired countries in the world. By some estimates, 70 percent of all households have high-speed Internet. Sophisticated mobile phones are common. Technology has contributed to rapid and sometimes disturbing societal shifts. The Internet has spurred online chatting and Web-surfing and is changing access to news and entertainment. Thousands of PC *bahngs* (personal computer rooms) and Internet cafes can be found nationwide, providing online access outside the home.

Young South Koreans have taken to online video games with such fervor that new opportunities and problems abound. Addiction to game-playing has become common as gamers ignore sleep and food. A severe case involved a 24-year-old man who died after 96 hours of continuous play. Withdrawal symptoms similar to chemical addictions are seen in players who spend time away from video games, and a camp for video addicts has been opened to help cure addiction. There are three 24-hour cable channels dedicated to online game-playing, and top players can win $150,000 in sponsored competitions. Other countries are looking at South Korea to learn what to expect and avoid as Internet activity becomes widespread.

Norae Bahng   Long before the advent of karaoke machines, Koreans loved singing individually and in groups to celebrate friendships and create bonds with classmates, business associates, and family. So it is no surprise that the *Norae Bahng* (singing room) has become a staple in South Korea. Such rooms, often found in bars, nightclubs, and other social venues, come equipped with elaborate karaoke machines featuring a variety of songs with lyrics and accompanying imagery on large video screens. Friends or coworkers may go out for an evening of fun at the *Norae Bahng*. Even without karaoke accompaniment, Koreans love to sing a cappella around a campfire or while hiking a winding trail.

TRADITIONAL SPORTS

Hiking   Seventy percent of Korea is mountainous, restricting agriculture but making it a hiker's delight. The country is covered with hills, valleys, mountains, numerous Buddhist temples, shrines, and historic places. Koreans love to hike to these sites and the backcountry. Traditionally, dressing the part of a hiker was as important as the hike itself. A hike might be far shorter than the rest stop at a local tavern afterward, but it has always been important to look the part.

Archery   The ancient Chinese often referred to Koreans as "the big bow" people. Koreans have been skilled in archery since prehistoric times, and their expertise continues today as evidenced by 14 gold medals for archery in modern Olympic competition. South Korea is now tied with the United States in gold medals for archery.

The traditional Korean bow (*kuk kung*) is a relative of the Mongolian bow and consists of a bamboo spine supporting animal sinew with an outer facing of cow horn. The bamboo is covered with a tree-bark veneer that adds a beautiful appearance and organic feel. The *kuk kung* is profoundly resilient and able to bend back on itself into a "full recurve." This gives the bow a higher "draw weight" than most Western bows, while being lighter, more compact, and shorter from end to end (usually less than a yard at full draw). The resulting angle of the drawn string is more acute than on a Western bow, and a single thumb (protected by a thumb ring) and index finger are used to hold and draw the arrow back. The *kuk kung* is ideal for shooting from horseback. This was demonstrated by Genghis Khan and his equestrian archers, who used the same basic bow to great effect.

Although modern South Korean archers use high-tech bows, traditional Korean archery remains popular and revered. Perhaps what is most impressive is that Korean archers using the traditional *kuk kung* shoot with unerring accuracy at targets at a standard distance of 145 meters away.

MARTIAL ARTS AND MARTIAL SPORTS

Korea served as a transmitter of many martial arts migrating from China to Japan, as well as the recipient of various influences on indigenous Korean martial arts. During the 35-year occupation by Japan (1910–1945), as part of a general campaign of cultural genocide, the Japanese outlawed indigenous Korean fighting arts. Some went underground, and some disappeared entirely. Since the 1950s, South Koreans have rediscovered, preserved, and improved traditional martial arts, producing a variety of styles practiced internationally.

Establishing the origins of Korean martial arts is problematic. Some styles claim that prehistoric tomb paintings show evidence of their ancient precursors. Others hearken back to the *hwarang* of Silla (57 BCE–935 CE). The *hwarang* ("flower youth") were young men chosen from the best and brightest of their generation and educated in military and civil sciences to be leaders. Often compared to feudal European knights, the *hwarang* were celebrated for their prowess as fighters as well as for their bravery and loyalty. Less disputed than their origins is the goal that many styles espouse—namely, that while self-defense and fighting skills are a by-product of training the highest pursuit is union of mind, body, and spirit. In other words, the ultimate objective of the physical effort is spiritual development.

T'aekwondo   Korean *T'aekwondo* ("the way of the foot and hand") is arguably the most popular martial art in the world. Unlike Japanese karate, *t'aekwondo* places greater emphasis on kicking than punching and is known for high, aerial, and lightning-fast spin kicks. *T'aekwondo* has much in common with Northern Chinese styles that favor kicking. In addition to having a longer reach, kicks are preferred because damage to the hands could negatively affect one's ability to write. Good calligraphy was highly valued in Korea. Some believe that Korea's mountainous terrain strengthened legs, so kicks became superior to punches. Others hypothesize that Koreans view hands for creating and feet for baser pursuits.

T'aekwondo is a system of strikes, blocks, kicks, and stances optimally used when an opponent is a leg's distance away. There are no throws, grappling, breakfalls, or joint locks. While this style has effective applications in self-defense, it has gained the greatest popularity as a martial sport. Competition consists of *poomse* (prearranged kicks, punches, blocks, and stances designed to demonstrate balance, speed, strength, spirit, and memory) and *gyorugi* (sparring), in which one opponent is pitted against another. Through the efforts of many masters in the last decades of the last century, individual styles of *t'aekwondo* were unified into one. This Korean style has become an international phenomenon with millions of practitioners in more than 150 countries. *T'aekwondo*'s appeal was evidenced by its Olympic debut in 1988 and acceptance as an official Olympic event since 1992.

Yudo   Korea's form of judo is called *yudo*. While it is well documented that Japanese jujutsu was the basis for judo (in the early 1900s), it is less clear whether jujitsu was an independent invention in Japan, or if it was a variation of Chinese *Chin Na* and *Shuai Chiao* transmitted via Korea to Japan. Thus, the controversy over whether *yudo* or judo came first, or which is more original, has its basis. What is not disputed is that *yudo* enjoys great popularity in Korea and is taught in many South Korean public schools, often as the official sport.

Yudo does not have kicks, punches, or definite blocks. However, it does have a bewildering arsenal of throws, chokes, pins, and breakfalls. *Yudo* can be a very effective means of self-defense but requires that the opponent/assailant be within arm's length of the defender. *Yudo* is a sport that relies on leverage and momentum, which allows the defender to use the opponent's own momentum and power to the defender's advantage. Thus, a larger, stronger person does not necessarily have an advantage over a smaller, weaker person. *Yudo* competition is generally limited to sparring.

Yudo is renowned for its attention to technical detail and the use of power. South Korea has excelled in Olympic competition, amassing 33 medals, including 8 gold, making it the third-best in this sport.

Hapkido and **Kuk Sul Won**   Korea has a number of eclectic martial arts that combine percussive techniques with throws, falls, grappling, and joint locks. The resulting composite styles equip the practitioner with an arsenal of offensive and defensive options to deal with opponents who are as far as a leg's length away or as close as a few inches. Among these hybrid styles, two are perhaps best known: *hapkido* ("the way of coordinated power") and *Kuk Sul Won* ("national martial art"). Unlike *t'aekwondo*, these styles have throws, breakfalls, and rolls, and unlike *yudo*, they also make liberal use of kicks, punches, and strikes. Additionally, *hapkido* and *Kuk Sul Won* teach the use of such weapons as the cane, short stick, rope/belt, and staff, which are not allowed in *yudo* or *t'aekwondo*. There are some competitions, but the inherent lethality prevents these styles from being considered or practiced as sports.

T'aekkyeon   Often cited as a precursor to modern *t'aekwondo*, *t'aekkyeon* is a distinct ancient martial art whose origins are shrouded in the past. *t'aekkyeon* would have almost certainly disappeared had it not been for the efforts of Song Dok-ki. Song appears to have been the sole surviving *t'aekkyeon* practitioner after the Japanese occupation of Korea ended in 1945. He found a worthy successor in Shin Han-Seung, to whom he passed on the art. Shin was responsible for having *t'aekkyeon* classified as Intangible Cultural Asset No. 76 by the government in 1983. *T'aekkyeon* is the only Korean martial art to be so classified.

In practice, *t'aekkyeon* bears little resemblance to *t'aekwondo*. Although both make extensive use of the legs and feet, *t'aekkyeon* uses the foot to push an opponent more than to kick him or her. Movements are fluid and dancelike, and footwork and arm movements have a rhythmic, flowing quality. Feet move back and forth, and in and out, to allow the practitioner to quickly attack and move before a counterattack can be launched. *T'aekkyeon* kicks tend to be circular, and weapons used on the foot include not just the ball but also the heel, outsides of the heel, and outer edges of the foot. *T'aekkyeon* has sweeps, low kicks, and tripping techniques not found in *t'aekwondo*. Additionally, *t'aekkyeon* routinely targets the knee, which is considered illegal in *t'aekwondo*. *T'aekkyeon* does have some hand strikes, joint locks, and even head butts. However, the greatest emphasis is on using the legs and feet.

Ssirreum   Native Korean wrestling is called *ssirreum*. Evidence that this form of wrestling has been on the peninsula for a long time can be found in ancient

Koguryo tomb paintings. *Ssirreum* is conducted in a sand-filled arena, wherein two wrestlers each have a *satba* (a cloth of specified width, but varying length) wrapped around his waist and right thigh. Under the *satba*, each wrestler wears a *bokjang* (similar to bicycle shorts). Wrestlers hold on to each other's *satba* with one hand on the waist-level part of the sash while the other hand holds on to the sash that circles the thigh. Each takes a wide stance, forming a human triangle with heads resting on the opponent's shoulder. Thus, the center of gravity for the joined combatants is very low, which makes winning challenging. Success in *ssirreum* is a matter of strength, speed, skill, and leverage and participants may use tripping, lifting, pushing, pulling, twisting, and tackling to throw the opponent to the ground. Traditionally, matches are held at village festivals, and the champion would win a live ox.

Yong Mu Do   One of the most exciting developments in Korean martial arts is the synthesis of a new style called *Yong Mu Do*. This new martial art was developed at the start of the current millennium at Yong In University, well known in Korea for diverse and excellent martial arts curriculums. Experts from Yong In's programs (*t'aekkyeon*, *yudo*, *t'aekwondo*, *ssirreum*, and *hapkido*) joined to combine the most effective techniques into one comprehensive fighting style called *yong mu do* ("dragon fighting way"). *Yong mu do* is unique because of its genesis as a composite style deliberately developed by one of Korea's premier martial arts institutions.

YongMuDo, the newest Korean Martial art, includes kicks, punches, and throws (like the major-outer reap shown here) in its arsenal. (Photo shows and is courtesy of Doug Kim)

CONTEMPORARY SPORTS

Golf   There are more than 4 million golfers in South Korea, 30 percent of whom are women. This popularity is due in part to Pak Se Ri, who in 1998 led a wave of South Korean women into the sport. It is harder to say why golf has taken such a hold on the general population. There are more than 250 golf courses, and a round of golf can cost more than $200. Yet golf is increasingly popular. Two South Korean television channels are dedicated to golf. Some Koreans enjoy the game as an escape, while the demanding nature of the game appeals to the perfectionist. Motivations may vary, but fervor for the game shows no signs of diminishing.

Snow Skiing   Skiing is also increasingly popular in South Korea. In the 1970s, Yong Pyong Resort in Gangwon-do Province near Mount Sorak was the only ski resort in the country. While Yong Pyong remains the largest and most popular (and hosted the 1999 Winter Asian Games), South Korea now boasts 12 ski resorts. Snowboarding has also gained in popularity, and a number of ski areas now permit snowboarders on the slopes.

Baseball   South Korea's professional baseball league, the Korean Baseball Organization (KBO), was founded in 1982 with six teams. The league currently has

Golf course in South Korea. (Courtesy of the Korea Tourism Organization)

eight teams, named after the companies that own them. In 2007, each team played all other teams in the league a total of 18 times, making a regular season of 126 games. The KBO ends its year with the Korean Series, wherein the top four teams from the regular season compete.

Soccer   Soccer was first introduced to Koreans in 1882 by British sailors in Inch'on. The first national tournament was held in 1921. In 1933, the Joseon Football Association, which later became the Korean Football Association (KFA), was formed. In 1983, the Korean Professional Football League (K-League) was established along the lines of professional soccer leagues in Europe. The original five clubs have grown to 14 in the K-League, and they play each other at home and away during the regular season. The top six have a championship leading to the final, wherein the top two play each other. South Korea first sent a soccer team to Olympic competition in 1948. South Korea's national team, the Reds, has participated in seven World Cup tournaments and was the first Asian team to make it to the semifinals in 2002, while cohosting the Fédération Internationale de Football Association (FIFA) World Cup with Japan. The Reds lost to Germany in a spirited semifinal round watched by millions of Koreans worldwide. South Korean soccer remains extremely popular with amateurs, numerous nonprofessional leagues, and countless pickup games on the weekends.

PARTICIPATION IN THE OLYMPICS

Although South Korea began official participation in the modern Olympic Games in London in 1948, the Korean Sohn Kee-Chung won a gold medal at the 1936 Berlin Olympics. Sohn broke the existing Olympic record for the marathon. His teammate won a bronze medal. However, because Korea was forcibly occupied by Japan, and Japan was engaged in a policy of cultural genocide, Koreans were not allowed to use their real names. When asked his nationality by reporters, Sohn patriotically insisted that he was Korean, not Japanese. During the award ceremony, Sohn cried as Japan's flag was raised and the Japanese national anthem played. Although both men were Korean, due to political realities their medals were recorded as Japanese wins.

Since competing as an independent nation, South Korea has participated in all Summer Games except 1980. Teams have been sent to compete in all Winter Games except 1952. Prior to the 2008 Beijing Olympics, South Koreans demonstrated an almost genetic superiority in archery, winning 14 gold medals (tying the United States for the most gold in archery), seven silver, and four bronze. Strength has also been shown in wrestling, as 33 medals (10 gold) have been garnered. In the Winter Games, great ability in short-track speed skating has been demonstrated as 29 medals, including 17 gold, have been amassed. At the 2008 games, South Korea won five medals in archery (including two gold, surpassing the United States in total medals for archery), four gold medals in *t'aekwondo*, four medals in judo (including gold), and one gold medal in baseball.

SYDNEY OLYMPICS (2000)

On September 15, 2000, more than 110,000 fans at the Olympic opening ceremonies cheered as the athletes from North and South Korea marched together for the first time, waving a unification flag and holding hands before a standing ovation in Sydney, Australia. The marchers wore identical uniforms with a badge bearing a blue map of the Korean peninsula. Despite the joint march, the Koreas competed in the games as two different entities under their own flags and names.

KOREAN NATIONAL SPORTS FESTIVAL

South Korea hosts a weeklong sports competition each October. The festival has competitions at high school, collegiate, and nonschool levels. There are thousands of competitors (18,000 in 2007), and the venue rotates around the country. The festival traces its roots back to the All-Korea Basketball Series of 1920 and now includes competition in soccer, track and field, tennis, baseball, and *t'aekwondo*.

SPORTS IN NORTH KOREA

Obtaining accurate information about life in North Korea is problematic. Westerners visiting North Korea are closely monitored, and contact with typical North Koreans is restricted. Therefore, it is almost impossible to develop a clear picture of activities in North Korea. However, we can gain some perspective from North Koreans' participation in the Olympics, international soccer competitions, and the annual Arirang Festival.

A World Cup rally in 2002 in Seoul. (Courtesy of the Korea Tourism Organization)

BEIJING OLYMPICS (2008)

The North and South Korean teams marched separately in the Olympic opening ceremonies, essentially for political reasons. The principal cause was the recent shooting of a South Korean tourist who was in an area just north of the demilitarized zone. Since North Korea did not want to walk behind South Korea, the Beijing organizers had to rearrange the lineup so that there were several nations in between. They also had to make last minute seating changes so that North Korea's second in command, Kim Yong-Nam, would not have to sit near Lee Myung-Bak, the president of South Korea. In spite of these difficulties, the Beijing Olympics was a joyful event for South Korea, as the nation achieved its best performance by winning 7th place in the medal count with 13 gold, 10 silver, and 8 bronze. North Korea received 2 gold, 1 silver, and 3 bronze medals and was ranked 30th.

North Korean Participation in the Olympics   In the 2004 Summer and 2006 Winter Olympics, North and South Korea marched together under a unification flag for the opening and closing ceremonies. However, the two countries competed separately. Although North Korea did not take home any medals for the 2006 Winter

World Cup Soccer rally in Seoul, 2002. South Korea was a host country for the 2002 World Cup tournament. (Courtesy of the Korea Tourism Organization)

Olympics, they claimed four silver medals (in boxing, judo, table tennis, and weight lifting) and one bronze medal (in pistol shooting) in 2004.

North Korea first competed in the 1972 Summer Games. Since then, the country has participated in all Summer Olympics except for 1984 and 1988. When North Korea returned to competition in 1992, the team earned four gold and five bronze medals (in boxing, gymnastics, wrestling, and table tennis). Medal results in the Summer Olympics from 1972 to 2004 showed consistent strength in wrestling (nine out of 37 medals, including four gold medals), boxing (eight out of 37, including two gold medals), and weight lifting (seven out of 37). At the 2008 Olympics, North Korea garnered six medals, including one gold in weight lifting and one gold in gymnastics. Participation in the Winter Games has been inconsistent (with competitors at eight of the 12 games since 1964), and medals have been won only twice (a silver in 1964 and a bronze in 1992, both for speed skating).

North Korean Soccer   North Korean soccer is played by both men and women. In international competition, North Korea's national women's team has performed well and qualified for the FIFA Women's World Cup in 1999 and 2003. In 2003, the team won out over Nigeria, the African champions. The men's national team, the Chollima, advanced to the 1966 quarterfinals in the FIFA World Cup, upsetting Italy 1–0. To date, this is the most success Chollima has had in World Cup competition. Chollima continues to be active in international soccer competition (including the Asian Cup, the East Asian Cup, and the Asian Football Confederation Asian Cup) but has had limited success.

Arirang Festival   To celebrate the birthday of Kim Il-Sung, North Koreans traditionally start a two-month festival of synchronized gymnastics and mass games on April 15. This event is known as the Arirang Festival. The opening ceremonies feature giant mosaic pictures created by thousands of cards held up by highly trained schoolchildren. North Korea claims that this event includes more than 100,000 participants and is held in the world's largest stadium (Rungnado Stadium in P'yongyang).

REFERENCES

Baldry, Beth Ann. 2007. "Dispatch from South Korea." *Golfweek*, July 20. http://www.golfweek.com/business/retail/story/koreabusiness_feature_071907 (accessed July 20, 2007).

Cazaux, Jean-Louis. 2000. "Changgi: Korean Chess." March 10. http://www.chessvariants.com/oriental.dir/koreanchess.html (accessed June 30, 2008).

Culin, Stewart. 1958. *Korean Games (With Notes on the Corresponding Games of China and Japan)*. Mineola, NY: Dover.

Duvernay, Thomas. 2007. "Korean Traditional Archery." http://www.koreanarchery.org (accessed June 30, 2008).

Faiola, Anthony. 2006. "When Escape Seems Just a Mouse-Click Away: Stress-Driven Addiction to Online Games Spikes in S. Korea." *Washington Post*, May 27. http://www.washingtonpost.com/wp-dyn/content/article/2006/05/26/AR2006052601960.html (accessed May 27, 2006).

Gordon, Daniel. 2004. *A State of Mind*. Film. Sheffield, UK: VeryMuchSo Productions. http://www.astateofmind.co.uk (accessed June 30, 2008)

Ihlwan, Moon. 2007. "South Korea: Video Games' Crazed Capital." *BusinessWeek*, March 26. http://www.businessweek.com/globalbiz/content/mar2007/gb20070326_937184.htm (accessed March 26, 2007).

International Martial Arts Research Institute (IMARI). 2007. *Yongmudo: A Korean Martial Art*. Berkeley, CA: University of California Press.

Koh, Frances M. 1993. *Korean Games*. Manhattan Beach, CA: Eastwest Press.

Life in Korea. n.d. "Traditional Sports and Games." http://www.lifeinkorea.com/activities/traditional.cfm (accessed June 30, 2008)

Whang, Sung Chul, and Jun Chul Whang. 1999. *Taekwondo: The State of the Art*. New York: Bantam Dell.

Contemporary Issues

Mary E. Connor

SOUTH KOREA: THE YOUNGER GENERATION

Unlike their grandparents who suffered from Japanese occupation and the Korean War, the younger generation of South Koreans has been fortunate to grow up during a time of peace and prosperity. The young have only heard the older generations' stories of wartime devastation, family separations, and hard economic times. Their grandparents' attitude toward communism, North Korea, and the United States continues to be shaped by past experience. The majority of the older generation continues to distrust North Korea and is thankful to the United States for protecting them. They also have a great collective sense of shame that they have not been able to solve the problem of reunification.

The parents of the current younger generation are known as the "386 generation." This term was created for individuals who were in their thirties, born in the 1960s, and in college in the 1980s. In their youth, they were the activists who fought and succeeded in their efforts to reject military government and establish democracy. They found good jobs during the economic boom of the 1980s and now hold positions of authority and prestige.

Since the early 1990s, the youngest members of society have been identified by the name of *Shinsedae*, the "new generation" (S.-Y. Park 2007). They grew up at a time of the greatest economic growth in Korea's long history and were the first generation in Korea to grow up in a democracy. They are also the first generation to grow up on the Internet, travel widely, and study abroad. Recently, they were credited with having the most technologically advanced media habits in the world

Daeil Foreign Language High School, Seoul. The majority of schools in Seoul are now coeducational and most teachers no longer separate boys and girls. (Courtesy of Mary Connor)

(Shim, Kim, and Martin 2008a, 111). Because this generation is free of the ideological biases of the past and seems preoccupied with material possessions, the gap between them and their elders can be wide.

Three events have particularly defined the members of the new generation: the Asian financial crisis of 1997, the tragic deaths of two young girls in an accident blamed on U.S. military forces, and the South Korean soccer team reaching the semifinals of the World Cup in 2002 (S.-Y. Park 2007). The younger generation has been influenced in one way or another by Western culture and its individualistic values.

Most of the members of this generation were in high school or college when the Asian financial crisis hit. Severe economic problems evolved as a result of the loss of faith in Southeast Asian financial markets, which spread rapidly to South Korea. This development was similar in many respects to the financial panic that hit the United States in September 2008. Many young Koreans witnessed their fathers' humiliation in losing their jobs, some even committing suicide, and families falling apart. Since then, they have found that the job market is very competitive now that a college degree is no longer a guarantee of good employment. As a result, their concerns are primarily related to their economic well-being, not the ideological issues that absorbed their elders during the Cold War years.

They also have a different perspective about the role of the United States in Korea's history. While their grandparents have traditionally supported the United States, many of their parents grew disenchanted with its hegemonic role in South Korea, the Kwangju uprising of 1980, and troublesome interactions with American soldiers. Anti-Americanism grew so strong during the 1980s that the U.S. ambassador to South Korea, Donald Gregg, reported that he could never set foot on a college campus during that time because he feared for his safety.

The younger generation has been especially influenced by the tragic deaths of two young girls who were killed by a U.S. armored vehicle in 2002. Six years after this event, they still have vivid memories of candlelight vigils, the images of the young girls that were constantly appearing on television screens, and the accompanying anti-U.S. propaganda campaigns throughout the nation. With newspaper and television coverage, Internet Web sites, and text messaging, it became an enduring and tragic memory for which the United States never apologized. This generation is convinced that the United States dominates South Korea militarily and economically. They want their nation to be treated fairly and with respect. In a Gallup Korea survey taken in 2002, 76 percent of those in their twenties and 67 percent of those in their thirties had negative views of the United States (Stuehmke 2005).

They have also been influenced by the rise of nationalism, democratization, impressive technological achievements, and the 1988 Seoul Olympics. Shortly after the tragic deaths of the two young girls, the nation celebrated the stunning performance of the South Korean soccer team's winning its way to the 2002 World Cup semifinals. The spirited response was not so much about soccer as it was about national pride (Shim et al. 2008a, 106). In a June 2008 poll of Korean teenagers taken by the Ministry of Public Administration and Security, the overwhelming majority (80.7 percent) expressed pride and confidence in their country, compared to 19.1 percent who did not ("Teens Have Mixed Feelings about National Security" 2008). Most are ashamed of their nation's historical oppression by foreign powers and Japanese colonialism and have a strong desire to see Korea respected by other countries.

They have also been influenced by the Sunshine Policy, the mainstay of South Korea's policies toward North Korea to achieve peace on the Korean peninsula through reconciliation. Subsequently, the young have more positive views of North Korea than did their elders. Influenced by efforts to reduce tensions on the peninsula, the younger generation does not fear communism or a North Korean invasion of the South. When asked if they support reunification, their responses were essentially negative. Few felt it was an urgent matter and feared that it would bring economic hardship to South Korea. Eighty percent felt that reunification should be handled cautiously to avoid economic setbacks or preferred remaining divided (S.-Y. Park 2007).

They also believe that the tough policies of the George W. Bush administration only complicated North-South relations and that this led to increased negative attitudes toward the United States. However, a Pew poll in 2003 revealed that 72 percent of the entire population held negative views of the United States that went beyond criticism of the president (Pew Global Attitudes Project 2003). When teens were polled in 2008 about what country poses the greatest threat to South Korea's national security, 28.4 percent cited the United States, followed by 27.7 percent who cited Japan, and 24.5 percent who cited North Korea ("Teens Have Mixed Feelings about National Security" 2008).

Usually college students are expected to be liberal, but the younger generation in South Korea appears conservative, though inconsistently so. Of all the candidates in the 2007 presidential election, more than half of the polled college students supported the conservative candidate, Lee Myung-Bak, and the Grand National Party (Stuehmke 2005). A survey taken by the Federation of Korea Trade Unions reveals that these students value economic growth more than narrowing the growing economic gap between people. This attitude is very different from that of their parents, the 386 generation. Most young people are apathetic toward politics, but there are instances when they do get involved, such as in the candlelight vigils in 2008 over the change in their government's U.S. beef import policies. The young do not spend much time reading newspapers but connect with politicians and issues via the Internet. They see politicians as celebrities and do not necessarily vote, and the candidates' political affiliation and prior experience have minimal influence. Personal image appears to be paramount over political ideology (S.-Y. Park 2007).

Throughout their school years, the young experience intense pressure to excel in school and prepare for the exam that will determine university acceptance. They arrive at school by 7:30 AM, attend school all day, work with tutors in cram school until 9:00 PM, and finish off the day hopefully completing their homework by midnight. If lucky, they will get four or maybe five hours of sleep.

If a Korean son or daughter does not get accepted to a prestigious college, the entire family may be embarrassed. In order to regain "face," the son or daughter may have to continually retake entrance exams in hopes of eventual acceptance to one of the best universities. Because the reputation of the college they attend virtually determines the rest of their lives, the pressure is intense throughout the teen years. Once in college, students are able to relax, perhaps the only time in their adult lives they will not feel pressured. After graduation from college, the goal is to get a prestigious job and be successful. The avenue for achieving prestige seems to be acquiring wealth, and to a lesser degree education (Shim et al. 2008a, 64). A young woman said to this author that in Korea one is either a success or a failure. There is nothing in between.

Members of the younger generation are more individualistic than their predecessors, but they still value the family and have strong group ties. In fact, the family remains the basic unit in Korean society. In a country where Confucian thinking has been dominant for thousands of years, the paramount values of filial piety and paternalistic authority are still valid and are taken for granted within the family system. The young do not have quite the same sense of filial piety as in the past, but most respect their parents and grandparents and live out the traditional expectations of their proper role within their families. They possess more egalitarian views on women, such as their right to choose a career or to not be chaste.

The younger generation has not yet achieved full independence as Americans would view it. Koreans see themselves as individuals, but they are interdependent within the family and other groups. Many young Koreans protest against Confucian hierarchy in relations, but they cannot ignore them completely. Confucian values persist, such as the belief that children owe an unpayable debt to their parents for life. However, there are limits to individuality with the group. The young know that they have a familial obligation to perform well in school, respect their teachers, and contribute to their family's happiness and material success. When the young are successful, the reward is not a personal one but an achievement for the collective, the family as a whole.

What has changed is that family life is no longer centered on the traditional parent-child relationship but on the relationship between the spouses. Additional major changes include decisions in choosing one's mate and deciding whether to have children or not. In spite of these major changes, the Korean family still has a strong influence on the children's choice of schools, careers, and marriage partners. What is encouraged is based less on the parents' recognition of their child's abilities and aptitudes and more on society's norms that dictate what is and is not respected. The young may want to select their own paths in pursuing their interests and careers and in selecting their marriage partners, but the traditional Confucian value of harmonious relations persists. Young members of the family may have their own independent thoughts on the lives they wish to live, but the priority of the group, in this case the family, is more important than the individual. That person is expected to adjust. They may say that they have made their own decisions, but most likely the choices are subconsciously based on accepted norms. It has been said that what is decided or achieved "is meaningless unless related to the joy of family life" (Shim et al. 2008a, 79).

While South Korea is changing, it remains a very group-based society. Americans believe that society is a collection of individuals. In contrast, Koreans believe that society is a collection of groups. The group exists to promote its own solidarity, competitiveness, and self-reliance, rather than that of the individual. A young person in Korea might possess an independent spirit but must adjust to the group culture. Strong values are placed on human relationships within the family and all in-groups, such as a school group. A child is not automatically accepted into a group because he or she has the same school affiliation. One's acceptance is essentially determined by social status and wealth.

There is an intense fear of social isolation in South Korea, which exists in all Confucian cultures (Shim et al. 2008a, 87). Anxiety about being ostracized can force particularly the young to do what they might not want to do. They are obligated to go with the group's decisions. While harmonious relations are all important within the in-group, the same courteous behavior is not expected toward the out-group (a group that is disliked). Communication with an out-group is difficult to establish because such people are initially distrusted (Na 2008, 121). All cultures have distinctions between in-groups and out-groups, but the Korean culture is particularly rigid in its distinctions (Shim et al. 2008a, 87). The in-group may neglect and even shun those who are perceived to be in the out-group (Na 2008, 123). If one's in-group appears threatened, South Koreans may be hostile when dealing with the outsider (Shim et al. 2008a, 87).

What is changing on the part of the younger generation is that group formations are now becoming more based on common interests, and many are being drawn to communicating with people of similar interests through the Internet and making new friends at Internet cafés. These connections allow the younger generation to get a sense of personal space, join groups based on their own decisions, be in a stress-free environment, and have some fun. In the process, they are developing online relationships and strong group networks in the Confucian tradition, but now it is occurring in the much more open world of digital media and outside traditional in-group boundaries.

NORTH KOREA: THE YOUNGER GENERATION

It is an old saying that a picture is worth 1,000 words. One may never travel to North Korea, but current images and information on the Internet does provide a window into the life of the younger generation. YouTube images also reveal differing perspectives on what life is really like for North Korean children. The images range from the destitute, sickly, and those who may have died from starvation or suicide, to beautiful and talented children singing and dancing. Such compelling documentaries as Daniel Gordon's *A State of Mind* show the beauty of the mass games, the enthusiasm of the younger generation for training and performing in the games, the obvious delight of their parents in the astonishing skill of their children, and the intensity of their devotion to their "Dear Leader," Kim Jong-Il.

All children are involved in the Pioneers, a communist party organization for children, and wear red kerchiefs and Kim Il-Sung pins. They enter the organization in elementary school and stay until their teens. When not in school, they can roam the streets, but they remain with friends of their own age and gender. The quality of life is considerably better for children who live in P'yongyang than in rural areas. Those who grow up in the countryside have fewer options and are more vulnerable to the hardships that come with backbreaking labor, inclement weather, and food shortages.

Confucian respect for authority, family, and education is strong throughout society. One may see barefoot, poorly dressed children on dusty streets in Kaesong, the ancient capital of North Korea, but one can be certain that the vast majority can read, believe in socialism, and revere Kim Jong-Il. Individuals who have frequent contact with older students, such as those at the elite Kim Il-Sung University, report signs of possible change. These students want to learn about business, which is where children of the P'yongyang elite see their future (Oberdorfer 2005).

For those who defect to South Korea, life is not easy. The majority have great difficulties adjusting to the fast-paced, competitive, and materialistic elements of urban life. Although they are more secure economically, they miss the strong community life that exists in North Korea. Many South Koreans treat them as foreigners and feel that they come from a backward place (Lynn 2007, 167). Young defectors frequently say that "our classmates never shunned us" in North Korea (Corpun. com 2007).

In spite of diverse reports on the quality of life in North Korea, some visitors come away impressed by the younger generation. When Secretary of State Madeleine Albright visited P'yongyang in 2000, she said that the North Korean people should be proud of their children, who are so beautiful and talented and "who have the hope for a bright tomorrow in their eyes." She expressed hope that all children on the peninsula would have a future in which "every child is fed, and hunger is just a memory" (People's Korea 2000).

THE KOREAS IN THE INFORMATION ERA

South Korea

Within the last quarter of a century, South Korea has become the world's leader in broadband, wireless technology, and mobile phones, and is now the most digitally connected nation in the world (Chun 2008; Fitzpatrick 2008). Four out of five South Koreans own a mobile phone, and almost every home has a computer (Shim, Kim, and Martin 2008b). There are also free community access centers offering almost universal computer and Internet access for everyone, even at rest stops. The nation also leads in Internet and mobile gaming (Shim et al. 2008a, 112).

In response to the challenge of limited natural resources and global competition, the South Korean government decided 25 years ago to focus on high-tech development to modernize telecommunications. A facilitating fact in the nation's ability to become a digital powerhouse very rapidly was the fact that South Korea has such a highly educated populace (more than 80 percent of the population attends college), with perhaps one of the world's strongest work ethics (Kim and Kwon 2008, 98–99). Beginning in the 1980s, the government began to invest billions of dollars to modernize the telecommunications infrastructure and by the 1990s was promoting nationwide access to affordable broadband technologies. To make this a reality, the government directed computer manufacturers to make inexpensive personal computers and offered subsidies so that virtually everyone could buy them. Private business then focused on developing such digital technologies as mobile phones.

Unlike Americans, who use their cell phones primarily for talking and texting, Koreans use their phones for many activities: listening to music, checking traffic conditions, watching television, shopping, and performing bank transactions. More than 60 percent of elementary and high school students own cell phones and use their phones to talk, text message, check e-mail, and play games (Shim et al. 2008a, 117). One researcher commented that babies in South Korea seem to pick up cell phones earlier than spoons and chopsticks (Fitzpatrick 2008).

Since ancient times, the Korean people have been known to love music. Aside from using their mobile phones for voice and text communication, the next most-common use of phones is listening to music. Korean phone companies were the first to develop polyphonic ring tones to give a more musical and personal sound to the rings. Eighty percent of South Korean cell phones now play MP3 music files (Shim et al. 2008a, 117).

The nation leads the world in mobile phone banking and television. Nearly 300,000 mobile banking transactions take place daily (Shim et al. 2008a, 118). South Koreans can use their cell phones to pay for virtually everything from groceries to stocks, and even public transportation. A phone is recognized by a cash register or a scanner, the amount is recorded, and it is charged to an account. Mobile phones with television devices are seen everywhere and allow commuters to watch television as they travel to work and back each day.

South Korea is also the world leader in home broadband access (Chun 2008). The United States is in 24th place (Shim et al. 2008b). Ninety-nine percent of Koreans between the ages of 6 and 29 use the Internet; however, the rate of growth between 2005 and 2006 for people 60 and older was greater than any other age group (Shim et al. 2008a, 119). Although persons use the Internet to search for information, send e-mail, play games, and shop, they favor music, gaming, and video over e-mail compared to Internet users in the United States. There are more than 20,000 PC *Bahngs* (Internet cafes), where the young gather to play Internet games, e-mail, surf the Web, do schoolwork, and download music for only $1 per hour (Shim et al. 2008a, 122). Gaming and socializing with other young people are the primary reasons for participating in activities at the PC *Bahngs*. Almost all customers are young men who are drawn to online role-playing games and compete with many other players.

Online gaming has become such a fad that at least three television networks are devoted to gaming, and more than 3,000 video game companies are marketing their products throughout the world (Shim et al. 2008b; Schiesel 2007, 143). StarCraft, a game that pits humans against alien races, has become almost a national sport for men under the age of 40. Major banks and telecommunication companies sponsor StarCraft leagues and teams in the ways that major U.S. companies sponsor the National Football League (Schiesel 2007, 143–144).

Another major development is the growth of Internet community sites based on common interests, school ties, professional associations, and entertainment. The most popular Web community is Cyworld, and its Mini HP ("minihompy," or mini-home page) service includes a small home page that includes a three-dimensional room containing a user's blog, photo, and virtual items for sale. By 2005, one out of every four South Korean Internet users was using the Mini HP service (Shim et al. 2008a, 126a). By 2006, 90 percent of those in their twenties were using the Cyworld service (Taylor 2006).

The wide use of the Internet is having a tremendous impact not only on the young but also on all age groups for many different reasons, such as finding a mate; improving one's English via Skype, a free Internet telephony application (Strauch 2005); or participating in politics. Internet use is also seen as an agent of change, such as in Roh Moo-Hyun's election in 2002. During his presidential campaign, more than 300,000 people logged on to Roh's home page every day. *The New York Times* credited the Internet for his election and for more liberal policies for a period of time.

South Koreans do not "Google," they "Naver" (Choe 2007, 108). Naver.com is South Korea's leading Internet search engine and handles more than 77 percent of all Web searches originating in South Korea. Google, the top search engine in the world, is used for only 1.7 percent of South Korean Web searches because it offers limited Korean-language information. Naver has accumulated a user-generated database of 70 million entries (Choe 2007, 109).

In a nation where more than 70 percent of the 48 million people use the Internet, South Koreans want more than information when they log on; they want a sense of community, and Naver's "Knowledge iN," an interactive question-and-answer database, offers it (Choe 2008, 108). Each day, approximately 16 million people visit Naver to ask about 110 million questions (Choe 2007, 108). Naver's largest competitor, Daum, has 6.7 million virtual Internet cafés, which are not actual physical structures but online user groups built around hobbies or mutual concerns, such as the much-debated Free Trade Agreement.

North Korea

The leader of North Korea, Kim Jong-Il, has expressed support for the advancement of Internet technology. He has visited high-tech sites in China and Russia during his infrequent trips abroad and has enjoyed surfing the Internet (A. Shin 2005, 77). From a socialist perspective, the North sees the development of information technology in a capitalist society as benefiting only the elite; however, it believes that in a socialist society such technology liberates workers from hard labor, advances the economy of all the people, and guarantees "an independent, creative, and cultural lifestyle for the people" (A. Shin 2005, 70).

The North has established a college of computer sciences within the Kim Il-Sung University, launched information centers at several other universities, and upgraded computer training in all schools. Aside from a stated objective of increasing people's interest in information science and technology and the need for computer-related manpower, the leadership believes that Internet technology is also essential for reasons of national security.

Since North Korea is aware of its lack of available capital and technical know-how, a large share of its well-educated workforce is concentrating on software development. The North is also actively involved in international ventures to acquire knowledge of advanced technology. Its efforts have involved business partners in South Korea and ethnic Koreans who live in Japan and the United States. It has also sought out Korean-Japanese scientists and researchers and worked on collaborative software projects with Samsung Electronics, Hana Program Center, and P'yongyang IT Complex (A. Shin 2005, 73). Some of the software programs developed by North Korea include voice recognition, Japanese-Korean translation, and security-related programs. The nation recently succeeded in upgrading its Internet security program, "Neungra 88," to prevent interruption by hackers from outside the country and to stem the outflow of North Korean information (D. K. Kim 2008).

Because North Korea is the most closed society in the world, it is obviously fearful of the Internet's potential to open up the country to the outside world. It has built up its Intranet system in order to improve internal communication and information exchanges.

North Korea's response to information technology is a selective enterprise under which it adopts what it believes to be necessary while seeking to block out anything that might ultimately present a threat to its closed system. For example, cell phones are banned, and when tourists arrive in P'yongyang, they must give up their phones at the airport.

Vice Foreign Minister Kim Gye Gwan told American visitors during the New York Philharmonic's visit to P'yongyang that the Internet is "dangerous if allowed into the minds of the young. We need to be cautious," he said, "because we think they might be corrupted" (Woodruff 2008). This view will probably not change.

However, there is reason to be concerned about the future of the Internet in North Korea. A small group of elite students at the Kim Chaek University was allowed to use the Internet on a limited basis under the watchful eye of a state official. When foreign visitors had an opportunity to talk to members of the group, the North Korean students said they hoped that someday there would no longer be such restrictions. When a young woman was asked if she looked forward to a time when she could e-mail people outside of North Korea, she said she hoped that it would be possible. "Why not?" she asked. "All the big countries are using it" (Woodruff 2008).

THE KOREAN WAVE

Hallyu, or the Korean Wave, is the phenomenon of South Korean popular culture that has spread across the world. The Korean Wave includes television drama, film, pop music, movie stars, animation, and comics. Many consider mobile content (cell phones and iPods), video/computer games, and even the latest fashion, foods, home appliances, and cosmetics as part of the Wave.

The term was coined in the late 1990s by a journalist who was amazed at the sudden popularity of anything Korean, especially South Korean television dramas and pop music. Korean pop culture first became a sensation in China and Taiwan, spread to Southeast Asian countries and Japan, and then moved on to the Americas, Central and West Asia, Europe, and Africa (J. S. Park 2007, 272). As a result, the Wave has created "a generally positive and respectful sentiment towards the Korean people, their culture, and their products" (H. S. Kim 2008, 78).

How has South Korea been able to catch the attention of people throughout the world? One reason for its success is the fact that because of common cultural connections, it has offered broad appeal to Asian consumers of all ages. Some Asian nations welcome Korean dramas in reaction to the "Western (mostly American) cultural invasion" because they seek "the protection of 'Asian values'" (J. S. Park 2007, 276). South Korean dramas were seen as new, refreshingly different, and lower-priced than those of their competitors. A contributing factor to the success of the Korean Wave is the sheer numbers of Asian youth who have a passion for pop culture and the money to acquire it.

Of particular interest is the appeal of South Korean pop culture to differing age groups throughout Asia. The television drama *Winter Sonata* was a smash success in South Korea and China, but particularly in Japan. Bae Young Joon, the principal actor, appeals to middle-aged and older Japanese women not only for his good looks but also for the fact that he plays the role of a sweet gentleman, a welcomed change from the traditional roles that Japanese men play. Chinese fans come from

Hahoe Mask Dance Drama, Hahoe Village. The mask drama has been performed for centuries as a village ritual. Performances continue to delight modern-day audiences. (Courtesy of Mary Connor)

all age groups. They easily relate to the themes and situations, especially those concerning the family, which reveal enduring Confucian values and offer what was lost during the Cultural Revolution (Onishi 2006, 142). Another reason for *Winter Sonata's* appeal is that the Chinese see urban professionals prospering and enjoying their lives and hope that they can live like Koreans. Many report that American dramas are "too modern" or even "postmodern and difficult to appreciate" (Onishi 2006, 142).

Winter Sonata is an old-fashioned love story and arouses nostalgia for platonic love, which seems lacking in modern life. It contains a melodramatic story of true love, surprising twists of plot, excellent acting, unforgettable characters, and a heart-tugging soundtrack. The beautiful scenery (fall colors and dazzling winter snow scenes) touched the hearts of South Korean people, who are known to be particularly appreciative of the natural beauty of their country. It was reported that the drama became so popular that it spiked South Korean tourism by 40 percent (J. Shin 2007).

Another very popular television drama is *Dae Jang-geum* (*Jewel in the Palace*), a costume-drama series that portrays the true story of a Choson dynasty servant who raises herself up to become the only female physician to ever assist a Korean emperor. The main character is not only beautiful, smart, and courageous, but is also able to survive palace intrigue and challenge the dominant male hierarchy of her day. The show attracted a record-breaking audience in South Korea, and approximately 160 million viewers watched it in China alone (J. Shin 2007). Chinese children began to dress up in traditional Korean costumes, and *Dae Jang-geum* tours of shooting locations in South Korea were instantly popular. Thousands of consumer products and merchandise related to *Jewel in the Palace* were sold throughout Asia.

Aside from the popularity of the television dramas, the South Korean domestic film industry has been a driving force behind the Wave. A frequent theme has been existing tensions on the Korean peninsula. In 1999, *Shiri* (1999) electrified audiences in an action-packed thriller about a North Korean plan to attack South Korea. Because of the enthusiastic response to *Shiri*, the quality, artistic value, and marketability of South Korean films were acknowledged, and the number of films exported increased significantly (H. S. Kim 2008, 81). In 2000, *Joint Security Area* was recognized as another groundbreaking film involving ongoing tensions on the peninsula. This time, the plot focused on resolving the mystery surrounding a shooting in the Korean War truce village of P'anmunjom.

Silmido (2003) and *Tae Guk Gi* (2004) ranked as two of the most successful films in South Korean film history. *Silmido* (2003) portrays an actual attempt by a North Korean commando group to kill President Park Chung-Hee and a South Korean government plan to retaliate by killing Kim Il-Sung. *Tae Guk Gi* (2004), compared by some to *Saving Private Ryan* and *Platoon*, is a powerful, violent, and disturbing film about two brothers during the Korean War.

Hahoe Folk Village in Andong, which has preserved architecture and traditions from several hundred years ago. (Courtesy of Mary Connor)

Such films as *Old Boy*; *Spring, Summer, Fall, and Winter*; and *Ch'unhyang* have received international recognition. *Old Boy* (2003) caused a sensation at the Cannes Film Festival and wound up receiving the Grand Prix Award in 2004. A violent, suspenseful thriller, it tells a compelling story about an ordinary man who spends 15 years locked up in a hotel room without knowing why. Another film, *Spring, Summer, Fall, and Winter* (2003), captivates the viewer with the sheer beauty of the setting, a small Buddhist shrine near a remote mountain lake. Buddhist principles are woven into the tale of a child monk and how his life changes with the seasons. Another highly successful and memorable film, *Ch'unhyang* (2000), is a unique and visually beautiful remake of Korea's most famous folktale. It is a story of true love, long-suffering virtue, and the triumph of good over evil. It serves as a captivating introduction to Korean culture, particularly Confucianist values, and the way of life of the Korean people during the Choson dynasty.

The Way Home (2002) captured the hearts of audiences throughout the world. It is a touching account of a very spoiled seven-year-old city boy who visits his elderly grandmother, a deaf person who cannot speak, who has spent her life in a small rural village. Her selfless efforts to care for her grandson are rudely rebuffed. Another film, *The Host* (2006), received four awards at the first Asian Film Award Festival in Hong Kong and holds South Korea's box office record for domestic and foreign films. Described as "a satiric monster flick," the film tells the story of a family who runs a kiosk along Seoul's Han River. Their lives suddenly change when their daughter is lost to a monstrous creature that has been mutated by toxic wastes from a U.S. military base (Korea.net 2007).

South Korean films continue to make their way around the globe to vie for prizes and reach wider audiences. To make further headway into the competitive U.S. film market, Korean moviemakers are now filming in the United States. The recent film *Dragon Wars* (2007), a traditional story about a mythical creature called Imoogi, is actually a Hollywood film. Eighty percent of the movie was filmed in Los Angeles in English with an American cast (H. S. Kim 2008, 108–109).

Another highly creative and dynamic component of the Korean Wave includes the sounds of pop music, musicals, and performances by world-renowned artists. Described as being "dynamic and unique," pop music has been particularly successful in Southeast Asia. Such artists as Clon, Rain, HOT, NRG, Kangta, and Baby Vox reached the top of Chinese pop music charts. BoA's ("Beat of Angel," a female South Korean musical artist) entrance into the Japanese market caused a huge sensation. *The Last Empress*, praised as being the "Korean *Evita*," combines a lesson in Korean history—the story of the legendary Queen Min who tried to save her family and the nation from the Japanese—with traditional rhythms that distinguish the music of Korea from that of the West. The show *NANTA*, which launched a new era of percussion-based performance, combines the rhythms of Korean folk music with modern musical forms. One of the most famous South Korean performing arts groups is called Samulnori and is led by Kim Duk-soo. It revived and internationalized the music of farmers' bands and contributed to the world's appreciation of Korean musical traditions.

Another area of success is animation. South Korea is now the third-largest producer of animation in the world (Korea Center 2007). Such Korean-created

IM KWON-TAEK (1936–)

Im is internationally recognized as one of the most creative and gifted Korean film directors. His films have won every major South Korean film award and a host of prizes on the international film circuit. *Ch'unhyang* (2000) narrates the most beloved of all Korean folk tales. In the film, Im combines the story of Ch'unhyang, a beautiful courtesan's daughter, with his passion for *p'ansori*, an ancient operatic form. His film *Chihwaseon* (2002) captures the life of a 19th-century painter who influenced the direction of Korean art. Im's films have helped to preserve the rich cultural traditions of his homeland.

characters as Pucca, DIBO, Bumper King, and Pororo the Penguin are being marketed throughout the world. *Oseam* and *My Beautiful Girl, Mari* are two of the best-known films created by South Korean animators, who have developed a unique style that differs from American and Japanese animation in stories based on Koreans' lives and traditions. Based on a famous novel, *Oseam* (2003) tells the story of a blind girl and her younger brother who are adopted by Buddhist monks. The film *My Beautiful Girl, Mari* (2001), particularly impressive for the beauty of the animation, introduces us to Namoo, a 12-year-old boy who has lost his father and has only two friends, one his own age and Yoo, his cat.

Another dimension of the Korean Wave is *manhwa*, the Korean word for "comic book." According to one publisher, comics account for about 25 percent of all book sales in South Korea, and more than 3 million users pay to access comics online. Korean comics have become increasingly popular in the American market and are defined as "graphic novels," with lengthy stories that are usually serialized in more than two books. They have appeal because of their high quality, diversity (comedies, romance, science fiction, period dramas), engaging plots, and solid structures (Shin 2006).

In recent years, the success of the Korean Wave has been challenged in some areas. The Chinese government has grown concerned about the Wave's influence on youth and has reduced the amount of airtime for foreign broadcasts. The Japanese have also responded by reducing airtime. A Japanese comic book, *Hateful Hallyu*, was published in 2005 and reflected anti-Korean bias and local jealousy over the success of the Korean Wave. However, the Wave continues to be very popular in Southeast Asia, in India, and particularly among Asian-American youth in the United States (Chang 2008, 70; J. S. Park 2007, 281–283).

THE UNITED STATES AND SOUTH KOREA: ARE THEY DRIFTING APART?

The United States began formal relations with Korea 126 years ago, at a time of international rivalry among world powers. Japan's influence was on the rise in Asia,

Walls at the Hahoe Folk Village in South Korea. (Courtesy of Mary Connor)

and Western powers desired to establish spheres of influence throughout the world. Not wanting to be left out in the race for power, the United States established control over Cuba, Puerto Rico, Guam, Hawaii, and the Philippines.

In 1882, the United States established diplomatic relations with Korea in what is known as the Shufeldt Convention, or the Treaty of Peace, Amity, Commerce, and Navigation, and it was one of the first Asian treaties—an unequal one—with a Western nation. Article I of the treaty stated that "there shall be perpetual peace and friendship between the President of the United States and the King of Chosen and the citizens and subjects of their respective governments." Furthermore, Article X stipulated that "the two contracting parties hereby agree that should at any time the King of Chosen grant to any nation, or to the merchants or citizens of any nation, any right, privilege or favor connected either with navigation, commerce, political or other intercourse, which is not confined by this Treaty, such right privilege and favor shall at once freely inure to the benefit of the United States, its public officers, merchants and citizens" (USC-UCLA East Asian Studies n.d.).

Three of the provisions were related to Korean interests and needs. The United States suggested that it would provide its "good offices" to support Korea if threatened by another power. Koreans understood this to mean that in whatever circumstances arose, the United States would come to their aid. The treaty also established tariffs to protect Korea's new industries and to provide essential revenue. The third provision promised that the United States would abandon its extraterritorial rights when Korean laws and judicial procedures could be reformed to conform to those of the United States (Eckert 1990, 203–204). Between 1882 and 1910, the

North Korean children. (Courtesy of Mary Connor)

American presence in Korea was limited mostly to missionary activities, including the founding of schools and hospitals.

The next significant connection between the United States and Korea involved a strategic decision to negotiate a secret agreement with Japan regarding Korea. With the U.S. acquisition of the Philippines in the Spanish-American War (1898), the United States became concerned about its ability to protect this new territory. This concern led the secretary of war, William Howard Taft, to come to an agreement with the Japanese prime minister. In what is known as the Taft-Katsura Agreement, the Japanese recognized U.S. interests in the Philippines, and in return, Japanese interests in Korea were recognized by the United States. This action paved the way for the Japanese takeover of Korea, first as a protectorate in 1905 and five years later as a colony in 1910.

Since World War II and the end of the Japanese colonial period in 1945, the United States played an even more significant role in determining the course of Korean history. After the second atomic bomb was dropped on Nagasaki on August 9, 1945, the United States made a quick decision to divide Korea at the 38th parallel because policy makers feared the Soviet Union would take over the entire peninsula. In haste, the United States made an offer to the Soviet Union to accept the division and was surprised that the Soviets accepted it. In the rush to prevent a possible Soviet takeover of Korea, the Americans never consulted any Koreans.

There had been no specific plans for Korea after the war, but records indicate that U.S. president Franklin D. Roosevelt had thought that colonial-held countries would need a period of trusteeship in preparation for self-government and independence (Cumings 1997, 187). The division was to be temporary.

Before the Korean War (1950–1953), Korea still did not figure significantly in U.S. strategic thinking, but with the Cold War and the Korean War, that changed. Since the common experience of the Korean War and the ties created by the signing of the U.S.–South Korean Alliance (Mutual Defense Treaty) in 1953, the United States and the Republic of (South) Korea (ROK) established a much closer relationship. Since then, the alliance has provided "military aid and assistance to South Korea, security cooperation between the two countries, and the stationing of U.S. soldiers in South Korea" (U.S.–South Korean Relations 2008, 114). From 1945 to the present, the United States has played a much more active role in South Korea than perhaps any other nation in the world. For Koreans, the United States was very significant; however, Korea remains insignificant and virtually an unknown entity in the minds of most Americans.

For most of the Cold War years, the U.S.-ROK alliance was strong. Although there was tension from time to time, both South Korea and the United States felt that the alliance served both of their interests. Recently, however, there have been significant strains that are much more serious than in the past. Some scholars and policy experts have begun to question the future of the U.S.-ROK alliance. Don Oberdorfer, one of the leading authorities on Korea, expressed the belief in 2005 that "at the popular and leadership levels, the long-standing alliance is in trouble in both countries."

When the alliance was created, South Korea was a devastated, war-ravaged country under authoritarian rule. Now the ROK is highly industrialized, the 11th-largest economy in the world, the 7th-largest trading partner of the United States, and is democratized. How have these changes affected the alliance? What has caused the growth of anti-Americanism in South Korea and improved relations between the Koreas? Would reunification be more attainable if the alliance with the

Kyongbok Palace and modern buildings, Seoul. Visitors can see signs of both the very old and the new throughout the Korea Peninsula. (Courtesy of Mary Connor)

United States came to an end? All of these questions are of great concern to scholars and policy makers.

There are many causes of varying importance that are now having an effect on the U.S.-ROK alliance. One of them is generational. The older generation experienced the Korean War and has supported the alliance, but their numbers are diminishing. They have been grateful for American sacrifices to save them from communism. On the other hand, 85 percent of all South Koreans today were born after 1945 and do not have any experience of that war nor gratitude to the United States. In fact, more than 50 percent of South Korean teenagers in a recent poll did not know when the Korean War broke out or even that North Korea started the war by invading the South (Digital Choson 2008).

New trends in politics have also influenced South Korean attitudes toward the United States. First, democratization has meant less censorship and more freedom of expression. Second, the number of nongovernmental organizations has multiplied and become a significant force within politics (Lynn 2007, 44). And third, the Internet and the use of Web sites for lobbying and rallying supporters have at times galvanized the young in ways not seen since the highly politicized environment of the 1980s. These developments have also contributed significantly to increased intergenerational differences, particularly over South Korea's policies toward North Korea. Those who were born after 1960 generally favor a more conciliatory approach to the DPRK and question the presence of the U.S. military on their soil.

There are many long-term reasons for tension in the U.S.-ROK alliance, but the legacy of the tragedy in Kwangju is one that particularly stands out. Suspicions abound as to what the United States did and did not know during the Kwangju uprising (1980), which led to the government massacre of hundreds of student protesters. Another major reason for the growth of anti-American sentiment is resentment about the very fact that U.S. soldiers are still stationed in South Korea long after the end of the Korean War that brought them there.

Although there have been many instances of controversy involving U.S. troops over the years, the tragic accident of a U.S. armored vehicle that killed two young girls in 2002 brought the issue to a whole new level. This incident led to massive demonstrations, and that was only the beginning. The South Korean government wanted the U.S. Soldiers to be tried in Korean courts, but the United States disagreed on the basis of the U.S.-Korea Status of Forces Agreement (SOFA). The agreement states that the United States exercises jurisdiction over most criminal cases involving U.S. military personnel in South Korea (Lynn 2007, 155). When a U.S. military court found the soldiers not guilty of negligent homicide, there were candlelight vigils in most cities throughout South Korea. Those demonstrations included children and the elderly. People demanded a retrial, a public apology from President George W. Bush, and revision of the SOFA, which was described as an agreement that undermined the independence of South Korea (Asian Human Rights 2002). Part of the reaction was in response to the public's anger at Bush's 2002 State of the Union speech that described North Korea as part of an "axis of evil."

After South Korean president Kim Dae-Jung's inauguration in 1998 and implementation of his Sunshine Policy, relations steadily improved between North and South

Korea, culminating in the historic summit meeting between Kim Dae-Jung and Kim Jong-Il in June 2000. Decision making was difficult, but one of the points of agreement was that reunification would be determined by North and South Korea and not by foreign powers. Also, families separated since the Korean War were to be reunited. When U.S. President Bush assumed office in January 2001, he favored a hard-line policy toward North Korea that worsened anti-American feelings among Koreans.

Following the September 11, 2001, terrorist attacks, U.S. policies took a more nationalistic and unilateralist path, which became another source of anti-Americanism in Korea (Lee 2005, 95). The Bush administration viewed the nuclear issue as part of its war on terror and led efforts to prevent the proliferation of weapons of mass destruction.

Providing aid to North Korea was seen as a giveaway and a means of sustaining a regime that was dangerous, unpredictable, and abusive of the basic rights of its people. Meanwhile, the leader of North Korea, Kim Jong-Il, feared change and subsequently took steps to insure the survival of his regime. In 2002, North Korea admitted that it was developing nuclear weapons, expelled International Atomic Energy Agency inspectors, and withdrew from the Nonproliferation Treaty.

South Koreans saw the citizens of the North as part of the same nation and as their brothers and sisters. They felt that Bush's hard-line policies were undermining reconciliation with the North. They regarded the nuclear issue primarily as an issue of national security (Park 2005, 5). Toward the end of the Bush presidency, a more conciliatory approach to North Korea was in place. This change in policy, combined with the resumption of the Six-Party Talks (China, Japan, North Korea, South Korea, Russia, and the United States) began to show some signs of progress in convincing North Korea to shut down its nuclear program. On February 13, 2007, the Six-Party Talks finally produced an agreement in which North Korea agreed to shut down its nuclear reactor in exchange for fuel aid, and the United States agreed to start the process of normalizing relations. In June 2008, North Korea destroyed the cooling tower at its main nuclear plant in Yongbyon in a move to give up its nuclear program in return for an easing of international sanctions.

In April 2008, President Bush met with South Korean president Lee Myung-Bak. The two agreed to improve the relationship between their countries, which had obviously been strained during the past decade. Bush made clear that his administration would be patient with North Korea's nuclear issue but would not tolerate the state's nuclear arms. He also gave assurances to President Lee that the current level of U.S. troops stationed in South Korea would be maintained but indicated that the United States wanted South Korea to increase its share of the expense for stationing U.S. military forces there (Chung 2008, 20). Since his inauguration, Lee has received fierce criticism on a number of issues, such as his tough stance toward North Korea, which has increased tension between the Koreas.

How will the Barack Obama administration deal with the South Korean alliance? What will be the tenor of the U.S.-ROK alliance in the coming years? Many conservatives are uneasy about Bush's more conciliatory policies with North Korea and may put pressure on the Obama administration for a return to the former hard line after the election.

When the U.S.-ROK alliance was forged as a result of the Korean War and built on the continuing threat of North Korea and the Cold War, the alliance seemed necessary. Now there is growing negativity about the continued presence of U.S. troops and a sense that they infringe on national sovereignty. Antagonism toward North Korea was reduced under the South Korean government's Sunshine Policy, while anti-Americanism has emerged as a major social issue. Since the Cold War has not ended on the Korean peninsula and security concerns remain high under the threats of North Korea's weapons of mass destruction, many South Koreans still recognize the importance of a strong ally like the United States.

As long as North Korea has nuclear weapons, South Korea's relations with the North and with the United States will be intertwined. If North Korea does give up nuclear weapons, the U.S.-ROK alliance will undoubtedly change. If North Korea and the United States normalize diplomatic relations, peace will finally arrive on the peninsula. If this happens, South Korea will redefine its alliance with the United States (Kim 2007, 112).

CONTEMPORARY ISSUES WITH ANCIENT ROOTS

The Koguryo Kingdom

Since the beginning of the 21st century, there have been actions on the part of China and Japan that have greatly upset the Korean people. The issues themselves are not new. The controversy relating to China can be traced back thousands of years to the Three Kingdoms period (37 BCE–668 CE), and the particular issue with Japan may be traced back to the period following the Russo-Japanese War (1905) and Japanese occupation of Korea (1910–1945). Some might trace the roots of grievances against Japan to the 16th century and the havoc wrought by the Hideyoshi invasions. By themselves the issues may seem insignificant; however, each could seriously undermine stability in East Asia.

Chinese and South Korean scholars were essentially isolated from one another from 1945 until the late 1980s. On the other hand, North Korean scholars were able to hold conferences and communicate current scholarship with the Chinese as a result of the political alliance between the two countries. After the establishment of diplomatic ties between China and South Korea in 1992, South Korean scholars were able to conduct archaeological studies in Northeast China, particularly the sites related to the ancient Koguryo (Gaogouli in Chinese) kingdom (37 BCE–668 CE).

For a long time, Chinese scholars believed that the history of Koguryo was an integral part of Korea's history. History books published in China define Koguryo as "a minority regime that existed in northeastern China" (D.-B. Park 2004, 35). And Korean history books published in China begin with the history of Koguryo.

Recently, Chinese scholars have claimed Koguryo as a Chinese state. They stress that from the Han dynasty to the Tang, the "Gaogouli regime was an ethnic political power within their overall administration" (China.org 2003). They emphasize that the Koguryo people demonstrated their subordination to China by paying tribute to the central government. Archaeologists have unearthed ancient walls and artifacts that are distinctly Chinese (Han) in origin. Korean scholars acknowledge that part of Koguryo was located within ancient China but note that it also extended into the northern Korean peninsula. In South Korea, the people believe that nationalistic Chinese scholars are now distorting history. Korean historians comment that the people of Koguryo paid tribute to the emperor only as a sign of respect and that the kings of Koguryo were essentially free to govern and were left alone. They call attention to the ancient murals that are distinctly Korean.

Beginning with the withdrawal of Soviet power, Northeast China lost its political and economic prominence. Fearing that conditions would further deteriorate, local government officials appealed to the central government. Subsequently, the Northeast China Project was created. Historians of the Northeast region were particularly interested in the status of Koguryo and the artifacts and murals within its ancient tombs. The result was their redefinition of the kingdom within the framework of a unified, multiethnic history of China.

Initially, South Korea paid little attention to Chinese claims. Then both China and North Korea applied to UNESCO to have parts of Koguryo identified as World Heritage sites. When the Chinese leader of the UNESCO team found legitimate problems with the North Korean application, the South Koreans saw this as a Chinese attempt to claim Koguryo. In December 2003, South Korean scholars formed an ad hoc group to challenge China's distortions of Korean history and focused primarily on the treatment of Koguryo in Northeast China Project publications.

The project reported that over the seven centuries between the Han and Tang dynasties, successive dynastic rulers governed in different ways, but all the rulers considered Koguryo as part of ancient China. They assert that ancient Chinese texts prove that the kingdom is part of China's history and not Korea's (D.-B. Park 2004, 35).

Many Koreans saw this report as a sign that China is denying Korea part of its rich heritage. They fear that if North Korea collapses, China might absorb the northern area based on its claims to Koguryo. On the other side, some Chinese may speculate that a unified Korea could attempt to recover territory or that the thousands of ethnic Koreans who live in China will support a separatist movement (W.-J. Park 2004, 38).

Dokdo

Dokdo is a small group of barren islets off the east coast of South Korea. Virtually everything about them is controversial. The South Koreans refer to the islets as Dokdo and the surrounding sea as the East Sea. The Japanese call the islets Takeshima and the sea as the Sea of Japan. The total land mass is only 46 acres, most of it consisting of rough peaks, and essentially uninhabited except for a South Korean police garrison. The islets have symbolic importance to both Korea and Japan but are of themselves of little value. The surrounding areas do have significance in terms of fishing.

Occupying Korea after the Russo-Japanese War (1905), Japan claimed the islets and determined that they would be governed by the Shimane Prefecture. Since then,

Young North Korean men. (Courtesy of Mary Connor)

the Japanese government has considered the islets its territory. Following the occupation of Korea and Japan's defeat in World War II, the newly created South Korean government placed Dokdo under the jurisdiction of one of its provinces. Since the 1950s, Japan has attempted, without success, to bring its claim to the islets before the International Court of Justice. Only recently has the issue appeared in headlines throughout the world.

In 2000, the Japanese Foreign Ministry listed Dokdo as Japanese territory in its official documents. In 2004, the Japanese prime minister, Junichiro Koizumi, announced that Takeshima belonged to Japan. When the Shimane Prefecture passed a bill to claim its territorial sovereignty over Dokdo in 2005, South Koreans became outraged and staged anti-Japanese demonstrations throughout the country.

The controversy over Dokdo has not subsided and continues to make international headlines. When the Japanese minister of education, Tokai Kisaburo, announced a plan to define Dokdo as part of Japanese territory in a new manual for teachers and textbook publishers, South Korean president Lee Myung-Bak responded by recalling the South Korean ambassador to Japan and suggested that he might not return. The ruling Grand National Party followed with a statement that Japan's decision was an act of "encroaching on South Korea's territorial integrity." The opposition party went even further by saying that Japan's actions were "tantamount to pouring cold water on peace in Northeast Asia" ("S. Korea's Lee" 2008).

Even the *Rodong Sinmun*, North Korea's main state-run newspaper, said that Japan's new educational manual on Dokdo could "ignite a war around the Korean Peninsula" (Choe 2008).

About the same time, the U.S. Board on Geographic Names (BGN) changed the island's status from South Korean to "undesignated territory." This decision outraged South Koreans, who see this as yet another instance of their nation's fate being arbitrarily decided by a big power. The Bush administration became concerned that anti-American sentiments could only turn worse at a time that the president was planning to meet with Lee Myung-Bak. The BGN insisted that its decision was just technical, but the Bush administration intervened and gave orders that the old designation should be restored.

Koreans see the Japanese claim of Dokdo as symbolic of Japanese nationalism. The issue revives bitter memories of the colonial period. They feel that Japan has never apologized sufficiently for past injustices and continues to humiliate the Korean people. The potential for the situation into suddenly escalate into something more volatile remains a possibility. The South Korean Coast Guard reports that the number of Japanese patrol boats sailing around the islets has increased since the sovereignty issue has resurfaced (Choe 2008).

REFERENCES

Asian Human Rights Commission. 2002. "South Korea: Need Solidarity Action for Justice." http://www.ahrchk.net/ua/mainfile.php (accessed August 11, 2008).

Byington, Mark. 2004. "The War of Words between South Korea and China over an Ancient Kingdom: Why Both Sides Are Misguided." History News Network, George Mason University. http://hnn.us/articles/7077.html (accessed August 9, 2008).

Chang, Myung-ho. 2008. "The Korean Wave Hits India." *Korea Focus* 16, no.1 (Spring): 69–70.

China.org. 2003. "Gaogouli Role in Chinese History Traced." http://www.china.org.cn/english/2003/Jun/67908.htm (accessed August 17, 2008).

Choe, Sang-Hun. 2008. "Desolate Dots in the Sea Stir Deep Emotions as South Korea Resists a Japanese Claim." *The New York Times*, August 31.

———. 2008. "South Koreans Connect Through Search Engine," in *Korean Wave as Viewed through the Pages of the New York Times in 2007*. New York: Korean Cultural Service.

Chosun Ilbo. 2008a. "How Korea Got Its Way over Dokdo in the U.S." August 1. http://english.chosun.com/cgi-bin/printNews?id=200808010007 (accessed August 1, 2008).

———. 2008b. "How Japan Is Keeping Its Claim to Dokdo Alive." July 15. http://english.chosun.com/cgi-bin/printNews?id=200807150008 (accessed August 1, 2008).

———. 2008c. "Teens Have Mixed Feelings about National Security." June 24. http://english.chosun.com/w21data/html/news/200806/200806240019.html (accessed June 26, 2008).

Chung, In-young. 2008. "Korea-U.S. Strategic Alliance and Balance of National Interests." *Korea Focus* 16, no. 2 (Summer): 17–18.

Chun, Tae Ki. 2008. "Mobile Devices in Korean Daily Life." Lecture presented at the Changing Korea Conference, Loyola Marymount University, Center for Asian Business, Los Angeles, May 13.

Cumings, Bruce. 1997. *Korea's Place in the Sun: A Modern History*. New York: W. W. Norton & Co.

Demick, Barbara. 2008. "A Cluster of Rocks Erupts into a Mountain of Emotion." *Los Angeles Times*, November 9.

Eckert, Carter J., et al. 1990. *Korea Old and New: A History*. Seoul: Ilchokak Publishers.

Ericspresso. 2008. "Famine North Korea." June 15. YouTube. http://www.youtube.com/watch?v=K6JoK0-Yi3E (accessed April 22, 2009).

Fitzpatrick, Michael. 2008. "Robots Nag and Sofas Whine in the Land of Digital Natives." *Guardian*, April 17.

Gaoande. 2007. "P'yongyang Children's Palace Band." May 7. YouTube. http://www.youtube.com/watch?v=wuWx-YZF0I0 (accessed April 22, 2009).

Gregg, Donald. 2008. "Anti-Americanism in South Korea." Lecture presented at the Changing Korea Conference, Loyola Marymount University, Center for Asian Business, Los Angeles, May 13.

Japan Today. 2008. "S. Korea's Lee Orders Stern Response to Japan over Isles." July 15. http://www.japantoday.com/category/politics/views/s-koreas-lee (accessed July 25, 2008).

Journeymanpictures. 1997. "Famine North Korea." November 2. YouTube. http://www.youtube.com/watch?v=30-2sPGNGEw (accessed April 22, 2009).

Juchekorea. 2006a. "Education of the Child in North Korea 1." November 9. YouTube. http://www.youtube.com/watch?v=EM9oTF4x9WU (accessed May 15, 2009).

———. 2006b. "Education of the Child in North Korea 2." November 9. YouTube. http://www.youtube.com/watch?v=tDpAxpL0KLw (accessed May 15, 2009).

Kim, Do Kyung. 2008. "The Internet Comes to North Korea." *Daily NK*, August 7. http://www.dailynk.com/english/read.php? (accessed August 8, 2008).

Kim, Hak-sung. 2007. "Changing Perceptions of North Korea and the United States Forming a National Consensus." *Korea Focus* 15, no. 3 (Autumn): 104–113.

Kim, Hyun Sik. 2008. "Strategies for the Korean Film Industry: Focus on the Stimulations of Export to the U.S. Market." Master's thesis, Art Institute of Chicago.

Kim, Kyong-dong, and the *The Korea Herald*, eds. 2008. *Social Change in Korea*. Vol. 2. Seoul: Jimoondang Publishers.

KOCIS Archive. n.d. "The 1882 US and Korea Treaty: Draft and Final Versions." http://www.instrok.org/instrok/resources/draft%20and%20Final%20versions.pdf (accessed February 2, 2008).

Korean Cultural Center Los Angeles (KCCLA). 2007. *The Korean Wave: Korean Entertainment Phenomenon Captures Worldwide Attention*. Los Angeles: Korean Cultural Center Los Angeles.

Korean National Tourism Center. 2005. *Best of Hallyu (The Korean Wave): Open a New Era*. Seoul: Korea National Tourism Organization.

Kushner, Barak. 2008. "Whose Islands Are They?" *New Statesman*, July 21. http://www.newstatesman.com/print/200807210003 (accessed August 16, 2008).

Lee, Kang-ro. 2005. "Critical Analysis of Anti-Americanism in Korea." *Korea Focus* 13, no. 2 (March–April): 74–98.

Lynn, Hyung Gu. 2007. *Bipolar Orders: The Two Koreas since 1989*. Black Point, BC: Fernwood Publishing.

Na, Eun-yeong. 2008. "Collectivism vs. Individualism," in *Social Change in Korea*. Vol. 2. Seoul: Jimoondang Publishers.

Oberdorfer, Don. 2005. "The U.S. and South Korea: Can This Alliance Last?" Nautilus Institute. http://www.nautilus.org/fora/secutiry/0593oberdorfer.html (accessed August 9, 2008).

Onishi, Norimitsu. 2006. "China's Youth Now Looking to South Korea for Inspiration," in *The Korean Wave as Viewed through the Pages of the New Times in 2006*, 141–143. New York: Korean Cultural Service.

Park, Doo-Bok. 2004. "History of Goguryeo Calls for Fact-Based Approach." *Korea Focus* 12, no. 1 (January–February): 34–35.

Park, Jung-Sun. 2007. "Korean Pop Culture Spreads Beyond Asia," in *Insight into Korea: Understanding Challenges of the 21st Century*, edited by Yu Kun-Ha, 272–285. Seoul: Herald Media.

———. 2007. "What Is Hallyu, the 'Korean Wave'?" in *News and Reviews* (Summer): 3.

Park, Myoungo. 2005. "Seoul and Washington Maintain Divergent Views on Nuclear Issue." *Korea Focus* 13, no. 1 (January–February): 4–5.

Park, Sun-Young. 2007. *Shinsedae: Conservative Attitudes of a 'New Generation' in South Korea and the Impact on the Korean Presidential Election*. Honolulu: East-West Center.

Pew Global Attitudes Project. 2003. "International Public Concern about North Korea but Growing Anti-Americanism in South Korea." http://pewglobal.org/commentary (accessed August 1, 2008).

Radio Free Asia. 2007. "North Korean Defectors Face Huge Challenges." Corpun.com, March 21. http://www.corpun.com/krs00703.htm (accessed August 6, 2008).

Schiesel, Seth. 2007. "To the Glee of South Korean Fans, a Game's Sequel Is Announced," in *The Korean Wave as Viewed through the Pages of the New York Times in 2007*, 143–144. New York: Korean Cultural Service.

Shim, T. Youn-ja, Min-Sun Kim, and Judith N. Martin. 2008a. *Changing Korea: Understanding Culture and Communication*. New York: Peter Lane.

———. 2008b. Panel discussions at the Changing Korea Conference, Loyola Marymount University, Center for Asian Business, May 13.

Shin, Alex. 2007. "General Overview of Korean Entertainment Content." Lecture presented at the Conference on Korean Entertainment Content, Korean Cultural Center, Los Angeles, January 17.

Shin, Jiho. 2005. "North Korea's Response to the Globalization and Information Era." *Korea Focus* 13, no. 3 (May–June): 61–83.

Strauch, Joel. 2005. "Greetings from the Most Connected Place on Earth." *PCWorld*, February 21. http://www.pcworld.com/printable/article/id (accessed August 3, 2008).

Stuehmke, Dorothy. 2005. "Understanding South Korea's Younger Generation and Anti-Americanism." ISN (International Relations and Security Network). http://www.

isn.ethz.ch/isn/Digital-Library/Publications/Detail/?id=34935&lng=en (accessed July 31, 2008).

Taylor, Chris. 2008. "The Future is in South Korea." CNNMoney.com, June 14. http://money.cnn.com/2006/06/08/technology/business2 (accessed June 26, 2008).

UCLA Center for Korean Studies. 2007. Koguryo and Its Neighbors: International Relations in Early Northeast Asia. Conference, Korean Cultural Center, Los Angeles, February 24.

Welsh, David. 2007. "Forget Manga. Here's Manwha." *BusinessWeek*, April 23. http://www.netcomics.com/news/press_release.htm?uid (accessed August 8, 2008).

Woodruff, Bob. 2008. "Small, Elite Group of North Korea Students Experiment with the Internet." ABC News, February 25. http://abcnews.go.com/WN/Story?id=4353525 (accessed August 5, 2008).

Glossary

animism The belief that every object in nature is controlled by an independent spirit and that all human beings alive today have been influenced by the attribution of a human form, human characteristics, or human behavior to nonhuman things. In Korea, animism has not only had an impact on Shamanism but has also influenced many aspects of traditional and modern culture. It has affected Buddhist, Confucian, Daoist, and Christian beliefs. Animism is suppressed in North Korea.

"Arirang" This is known throughout the world as the quintessential Korean folk song. Most scholars detect its roots in folk ballads dating from the mid- to late Choson period, and some say that the song may have originated as far back as Unified Silla (668–935). Its status in contemporary Korea derives from its perceived role in strengthening Korean resolve to resist the Japanese during occupation from 1910 to 1945. Its theme of loss spoke to Koreans of their lost sovereignty. A moving rendition of "Arirang" was played by the New York Philharmonic in a performance in P'yongyang in 2008.

balance of payments A sum of payments for imports, exports, credits, debits, services, and financial transfers between two countries, expressed in national currency and averaged at an annual exchange rate with foreign currency.

bone rank A system that evolved during the Silla kingdom (57 BCE–935 CE). The bone rank system became the basis of a hierarchical social structure with sharply defined class distinctions established on hereditary bloodlines that ultimately characterized Korean society.

celadon A high-firing ash glaze that derives its color from a small quantity of iron oxide in the glaze mixture, which turns a cool bluish-green in a reduction (low-oxygen) kiln. Celadon earthenware is considered the crowning glory of the Koryo dynasty's artistic achievements.

chaebol These are interlinked South Korean conglomerates with close ties to the government. Some of the well-known *chaebol* are Daewoo, Hyundai, the LG Group, and Samsung.

Ch'angdokkung Palace Palace built in 1405 by King T'aejong to serve as a royal villa in Seoul. It is noted for its extraordinary architecture and gardens. After 1615, the seat of government was moved to its present location, and kings ruled from this palace for about 300 years.

changgo A drum shaped like an hourglass and one of the most popular instruments in all types of Korean music.

Ch'ondogyo A religion of 19th-century Korean origin, based on the premise that God lives in each of us with the objective of creating a paradise here on earth. Ch'ondogyo contributed to the Tonghak revolt at the end of the 19th century.

chongak A type of traditional court music in Korea. It may be described as solemn, calm, dignified, and meditative.

ch'onmin The lowest level in traditional Korean society during the 7th–19th centuries and often named the "mean people." The largest element within this class was slaves.

Choson dynasty (1392–1910) The longest and last 500-year Korean dynasty. Confucian values dominated the Choson social structure and attitudes.

chungin Korea's hereditary middle class, members of which had opportunities to improve their status.

Ch'usok The Korean Thanksgiving and the most important holiday of the year for visiting relatives and caring for ancestors' graves. *Ch'usok* is also a harvest festival, involving considerable feasting and celebration. The event stresses the Confucian values of family and respect for one's elders, ancestors, and superiors.

comfort women The term used to refer to the thousands of women who were conscripted throughout Asia to serve as sex slaves to the Japanese military during World War II.

Confucianism The philosophy of Confucius (551–479 BCE) and his followers that has deeply influenced East Asia for 20 centuries. Living in an uncertain time, Confucius recommended certain ideals based on proper social relationships that would help to restore order and bring harmony to the world. Loyalty to the ruler, piety toward one's parents, and the maintaining of a distinction between men and women were the main Confucian principles.

containment The policy of the United States from 1945 to 1989 to control the spread of communism. This strategy contributed to the U.S. decision to enter the Korean War.

current account balance The sum of the value of goods and services exchanged between two countries (usually positive for one country and negative for the other).

Daoism An ancient religion that has influenced Korean thought and culture for centuries. It combines many principles that offer a path or way to live, such as the concept of being in harmony with nature. It has contributed significantly to the Korean people's particular devotion to nature.

DMZ Acronym for the demilitarized zone established in 1953 as part of the armistice agreement that ended the Korean War in a stalemate. The DMZ is the buffer zone located on the 38th parallel that divides North and South Korea, which are still technically at war. The zone is 151 miles long and 2.5 miles wide.

DPRK Acronym for the Democratic People's Republic of Korea, the official name of communist North Korea.

East Sea The name preferred by Koreans for the sea between Korea and Japan, widely known as the Sea of Japan.

extraterritorial rights The practice whereby foreigners do not have to abide by the laws of the nation where they are residing. In the late 19th century, it was common for imperial powers to dictate these privileges in their treaties, which are now commonly referred to as unequal treaties.

familism A social pattern whereby the family maintains a position of ascendance over individual interests. As a result of family-centered Confucian ethics, Koreans place great value on the family and strive to maintain harmonious family ties. A child learns early in life that the family is more important than any member's individual needs. In North Korea, this concept is extended to the state.

filial piety A central Confucian virtue that children should be respectful toward their parents. It also means the devotion of all family members to one another's welfare. It includes the remembrance of ancestors, respect for all elders, and the importance of providing great care for children in the family.

free on board (FOB) Condition under which a seller must pay the costs to ship goods to their destination point. Once the goods are delivered, the buyer is responsible for any loss or damage.

Grand National Party The conservative party of South Korea, which since 2008 has been headed by President Lee Myung-Bak. This party wants to restore prosperity rights, supports free trade and the *chaebol* system, and desires strong U.S. ties. It is also anti–labor union and has taken a tough stance in dealing with North Korea.

gross domestic product (GDP) The value of final goods and services produced in a country, irrespective of the producer's nationality. It is best reported in constant dollars in order to compensate for inflation.

gross national income (GNI) The sum of all national income, domestic and foreign, earned in a year.

gunboat diplomacy A form of aggressive diplomacy backed by the use or threat of force.

Hallyu This is defined as the Korean Wave. This dynamic phenomenon of South Korean popular culture has spread across the world and includes television drama, film, pop music, movie stars, animation, and comic books.

hanbok Defined as Korean women's national dress, which consists of a wraparound skirt (*chima*) and a bolero-like jacket (*jeogori*). Men's clothing includes a short jacket (*jeogori)* and pants (*baji*). Korean clothing tends to be very colorful, pleasing to the eye, and comfortable to wear.

han'gul The name of the Korean written language. It was created to provide a writing system that would be accessible to the common people. *Han'gul* is one of the great cultural achievements of the Choson dynasty (1392–1910) during the reign of King Sejong.

Hermit Kingdom The name used in the West to describe Korea between the 17th and 19th centuries. After the devastating Japanese and Manchu invasions of the 16th and 17th centuries, Korea rejected all outside contact with the world until it was forced to open up by Japan and the West in the late 19th and early 20th centuries. North Korea is today commonly referred to as a hermit kingdom because it remains the most isolated nation in the world.

Hyundai Group This is South Korea's largest *chaebol* (family-owned conglomerate), which wields significant financial power in domestic and global markets.

juche The name for North Korea's ruling principle, based on self-reliance, an ideology created by Kim Il-Sung, the founder of the nation. Kim stressed that self-reliance is essential for political independence, economic self-sustenance, and military defense. *Juche* is a Korean word consisting of two syllables. *Ju* means "master" and *che* means "oneself," so translated literally it means "master of one's self."

galbi A Korean dish that includes beef short ribs that are marinated in a mixture of onion, garlic, sugar, sesame oil, and soy sauce.

Kaya A loose federation of small states that existed in the southern part of the Korean Peninsula from the forth to the sixth centuries CE. The people of Kaya had close connections with Japan, involving trade based on Kaya's supply of iron deposits. The Kaya states had a distinctive culture that influenced the development of Silla poetry and Japanese ware. The *kayagum*, a kind of zither, was developed in Kaya, and it continues to be one of the most popular musical instruments in Korea.

kayagum A Korean zither. It has 12 silk strings supported by 12 movable bridges. The tone quality is clear and delicate.

kibun The concept that relates to one's feelings, mood, or state of mind. There is no exact equivalent in the English language, but an example relates to "saving face." A Korean's *kibun* is damaged if someone does not pay him or her proper respect.

kimch'i The Korean national dish. Served at every meal as a side dish, it is made with a unique mixture of fermented vegetables, usually cabbages and radishes.

kisaeng A trained female entertainer, similar to the Japanese geisha. She was essentially a slave and was educated to be literate, appreciate poetry, play musical instruments, and entertain the *yangban* (aristocratic class). Although the *kisaeng* was not altogether respected, she could be greatly admired and loved by members of the aristocratic class.

Koguryo One of the ancient Three Kingdoms of Korea. Existing from 37 BCE to 668 CE, Koguryo extended from the northeastern part of China to the northern portion of the Korean peninsula and was dominated by a warrior aristocracy. Rulers and nobility built elaborate tombs during this time, which are one of the main sources of information about this ancient kingdom.

Korean Armistice Agreement Signed on July 27, 1953, the agreement ended the Korean War in a stalemate. It was signed by representatives from the United Nations (including delegates from the United States and South Korea) and by top communist officials from China and North Korea.

Korean peninsula The peninsula—encompassing North and South Korea—that extends southward from eastern Siberia and Manchuria to within 70 miles of Japan at its southern tip. The peninsula's area totals 85,563 square miles. Its northern half is occupied by the communist Democratic People's Republic of Korea (North Korea), while its southern half is occupied by the Republic of Korea (South Korea).

Korean Strait A sea passage that flows from the northwest Pacific Ocean and extends northeast from the East China Sea to the East Sea (Sea of Japan) between the Korean peninsula's southern coast and the Japanese islands of Kyushu and Honshu.

Korean War A conflict on the Korean peninsula that was fought from 1950 to 1953 between northern communist forces and southern noncommunist forces. The war began when North Korea invaded South Korea in June 1950 and quickly escalated, with U.S.-led United Nations forces fighting for the south, and Chinese forces fighting for the north. The conflict ended in a stalemate in July 1953 with the signing of the Korean Armistice Agreement.

Korean Workers' Party The communist party of North Korea, which has ruled the country and dominated its politics since 1949. The party, founded by

Kim Il-Sung (North Korea's leader from 1949 to 1994), espouses national self-reliance.

Koryo dynasty Dynasty founded in 918 by General Wang Kon; it lasted for almost 500 years. Wang Kon named it Koryo, an abbreviation of Koguryo and the origin of the name of Korea. Kaesong became the national capital, and by the 11th century the boundary of Korea extended to the Yalu River. Buddhism was at its height and played a significant role in cultural achievements, such as the famed Buddhist Tripitaka that may be seen at Haeinsa, one of Korea's most famous temples.

Kyongju The capital of the kingdom of Silla located in the southeastern part of South Korea.

kut A Korean Shaman ceremony. It is performed by a priestess for the purpose of securing good luck, curing a physical or mental illness, or pacifying a deceased spirit. It is an ancient practice that continues to be performed in South Korea. The ceremony is not allowed in North Korea.

literati Members of the *yangban* (aristocratic) class who were educated in the Confucian classics and were knowledgeable about government management.

Mahayana (Great Vehicle) Buddhism The form of Buddhism followed by most Koreans, which emphasizes the attainment of eternity through faith. The term "Great Vehicle" signifies a large boat in which all types of people can be carried across a river to achieve enlightenment. Mahayana Buddhism teaches that nirvana is attainable by everyone, not just by monks, and that in order to be saved, one must save others.

makkoli A sour, milky, unfiltered rice wine for everyday consumption. *Makkoli* is very important to Korean village life.

Millennium Democratic Party A liberal political party founded by former South Korean president Kim Dae-jung; it was originally the party of former president Roh Moo-hyun. The party supported the Sunshine Policy (which emphasized the reunification of the Koreas), pushed for economic reforms to revitalize the economy during the 1997 Asian crisis, and supported policies to check the power of the *chaebol*.

minsogak The name for traditional Korean folk music. It differs from the quiet, contemplative music of the court because it is emotional, lively, and expressive of the feelings of the common people. *Minsogak* vocal music includes *p'ansori*.

Mount Paektu The national symbol of the Korean people. The mountain is an extinct volcano located in North Korea near northeastern China. It is considered the location of the founding of the Korean race and is claimed as the birthplace of Kim Jong-Il, the leader of North Korea.

mudang The name for a female Korean Shaman.

Neo-Confucianism This philosophical movement offers a very strict interpretation of Confucian principles adopted during the Choson dynasty. Neo-Confucianism paved the way for Korea to become the most Confucian of all East Asian nations. It emphasized the importance of education, social stability, filial piety, and good government. The position of women declined with the adoption of Neo-Confucianism.

nong-ak A Korean farmer's percussion music.

nunch'i A concept that relates to one's ability to assess nonverbal communication. In Korea, communication necessitates focusing on nonverbal behavior to provide clues to another's mood or inner feelings. Developing one's skill with this concept is recognized as a means of developing harmonious relationships.

OECD Acronym for the Organization for Economic Co-operation and Development, a 30-member international organization that coordinates the economic and social policies of its industrialized members.

ondol **floor** The traditional heating system for Korean homes. It is a type of under-floor heating.

p'ansori A Korean dramatic musical form that developed in the late Choson period. In a *p'ansori* performance, a singer delivers a folk song while a drummer accompanies the vocalist. This form combines music, drama, and dance and has been revived for a variety of reasons, such as the success of the film *Chunhyang*.

Paekche One of the ancient Three Kingdoms of early Korea, which existed from 18 BCE to 660 CE. Not as much is known about this kingdom as of Koguryo and Silla, but people from Paekche sailed to Japan and introduced Chinese characters, Buddhism, music, and art.

P'anmunjom The truce village located in the demilitarized zone (DMZ), where the signing of the Korean War armistice agreement took place in 1953. P'anmunjom remains the symbol of a divided Korea.

pibimpap (bibimpap) A very hot rice served in a stoneware bowl with a variety of vegetables, cooked and raw, arranged on top.

pulgogi (bulgogi) A broiled beef dish and one of Korea's most popular dishes, which is usually cooked on an iron hot plate at the table.

Pulguksa (Bulguksa) One of the most famous Buddhist temples in South Korea, which has been described as the crowning glory of Silla temple architecture.

punch'ong The predominant grayish-green ceramic ware of the first half of the Choson dynasty (1392–1910). It was made of the same clay used in celadon but was coarser in texture, with white slip decoration. The simplicity of *punch'ong* ware appealed to the Japanese, and it has long been used in the Japanese tea ceremony.

P'yongyang The capital of North Korea since 1948, P'yongyang is also North Korea's largest city.

romanization The process of rendering Korean script in the English alphabet. Korean is a difficult language to romanize, given the variety of vowel and consonant sounds. There have been a number of romanization systems, but the McCune-Reischauer system (1939) has been the principal system used in the United States. In 2000, the South Korean government adopted a system made necessary by the widespread use of computers. Both systems are currently used in the United States, making it particularly confusing for the nonspecialist.

ROK Acronym for the Republic of Korea, the official name of South Korea.

Samguk sagi The oldest existing written history of Korea. It was written in 1145 by Kim Pu-sik, a court official, and covers the history of the Three Kingdoms to the end of the Silla period and the establishment of the Koryo state.

samul nori A type of traditional Korean musical performance that uses four percussion instruments and has recently become very popular throughout the world.

saving face A central belief in Asian cultures. In hierarchical societies, such as Korea, China, and Japan, the concepts of shame and honor are very important. Exposure to personal insults, disregard of one's status, or failure to achieve one's goals are examples of how one might lose face.

scholar-bureaucrats Officials who studied the Confucian classics and served in the Korean government.

Seoul The capital and largest city of South Korea. Seoul became the capital in the early Choson period and ever since has remained the political, economic, and cultural center of Korea.

Shamanism The name of one of the oldest religions in the world, characterized by belief in the unseen world of gods and ancestral spirits responsible only to a priestess (*mudang*), who makes contact with them through special techniques. Shamanism has played a strong role over the course of Korean history and continues to have a large number of followers.

Silla The name of one of Korea's ancient Three Kingdoms (57 BCE to 935 CE). It eventually became the longest dynasty in Korean history, lasting for nearly 1,000 years. It is particularly noteworthy for the status of women, the bone-rank system, magnificent gold pieces, and the burial grounds that visitors can see in the ancient capital, Kyongju.

Sirhak A movement that originated in the 17th century, also known as the Practical Learning movement. The followers rejected Neo-Confucianism, recommended practical solutions to the problems of their day, and advocated such ideas as the rights of man and social equality. It became very influential in the 18th and 19th centuries.

Sunshine Policy A South Korean diplomatic policy toward North Korea created by President Kim Dae-jung (1998–2003) and sustained by his successor, Roh Moo-hyun (2003–2008), designed to improve inter-Korean relations through reconciliation and cooperation. Kim's initiation of this policy led to the first North Korea–South Korea summit meeting in June 2000.

Taeborum The Korean name for the first full moon of the year.

T'aekwondo A self-defense martial art that has developed in Korea for more than 2,000 years. It stresses discipline, physical conditioning, and moral virtue.

talchum The Korean mask dance, a traditional folk dance that continues to be enjoyed by the Korean people. These dances originated many centuries ago as a Shamanist practice to eliminate evil spirits and to bring good luck to a people or their village. The wearing of a mask allowed for greater freedom for the entertainer to poke fun at the rich or annoying personality types and to ridicule powerful landlords and corrupt Buddhist priests.

Tan'gun The name of the mythical founder of the first Korean state, Choson, in 2333 BCE. In the 20th century, this myth was interpreted by some nationalist writers as supporting claims for the ancient origins of the Korean people and the distinctiveness of the Korean culture.

Thirty-eighth parallel The latitudinal dividing line between North and South Korea that was established at the end of World War II.

Three Kingdoms Collective name of ancient Korea's kingdoms of Koguryo (37 BCE–668 CE) in the north, Paekche (18 BCE–60 CE) in the southwest, and Silla (57 BCE–35 CE) in the southeast. Each of the three kingdoms left records of the influence of Confucianism on government and society.

Tonghak (Eastern Learning) The religious and social movement introduced to Korea in the mid-19th century to fight against corrupt government, social injustice, the *yangban* aristocratic class, and Catholicism. Most of its support came from poor peasants, and ultimately the movement had a major impact on modern Korean history.

UNESCO Acronym for the United Nations Educational, Scientific, and Cultural Organization. Korea has taken pride in the many world-famous cultural assets that UNESCO has designated on its World Heritage List, such as the Ch'angdokkung Palace, Pulguksa Temple, the Hwaseong fortress, the Sokkurum Buddha, and the Tripitaka Koreana woodblocks.

Unified Silla The dynasty that established the foundation for the historical development of the Korean people. Unified Silla (668–935 CE) was probably more advanced than any area of Europe at the time except for the Byzantine Empire. During this time, trade flourished with China and Japan, and Korean traders were actively involved in exchanging goods along the Silk Road. The famous Pulguksa temple, the Buddha at the Sokkurum Grotto, and the Emille Bell are all examples of the magnificent achievements of this period. Buddhism flourished and printing techniques became more sophisticated.

Unification Church The cultlike church (known as Tongil-gyo in Korean) founded by Reverend Sun Myung Moon in 1954. Moon claims that Jesus Christ appeared to him when Moon was 16 and asked him to accomplish the work left undone because of the Crucifixion. The church's name alludes to Moon's goal of being the unifying force for all Christian denominations. Because the Korean word for unification is the same as the word for national reunification, the church's name has a special meaning for Koreans. Today there are approximately 750 Unification churches and 300,000 believers in South Korea alone. The church is one of the world's most controversial religious organizations.

vinalon ("juche fiber") The leading textile produced in North Korea, vinalon (sometimes referred to as "juche fiber") is a synthetic fiber made from polyvinyl alcohol, anthracite coal, and limestone. Although it is inexpensive to produce, vinalon is made only in North Korea, possibly because it has been described as an extremely uncomfortable material to wear, is difficult to dye, and is prone to shrinking.

won The name of South Korea's currency. Won is also the name of North Korean currency, though U.S. citizens cannot legally convert their dollars into won in North Korea. They must exchange euros or Chinese yuan or renminbi.

yangban Korea's aristocratic class, particularly during the Choson dynasty (1392–1910). The status of the aristocrats was based on ancestry and wealth that was measured in land and slaves. The *yangban* were not part of the military but could be eligible for governmental service after completing competitive examinations.

yangmin The name for commoners in traditional Korean society.

Yut A traditional Korean board game that originated in ancient times and is still enjoyed in the computer age. The game is particularly popular with families on holidays because there are no limits to the number of people who can play. The game involves tossing four half-round sticks, which determine how the players' markers will move on the board. The individual or team that gets the markers to the home base first is the winner.

Facts and Figures

The following tables compare facts and figures for South Korea and, when available, for North Korea. These statistics begin with basic facts about each country and continue with each country's demographics (including population, ethnicity, and religion), geography, economy, communications and transportation, and military. Tables and graphs presenting enhanced statistics on the Korean people, political leaders, grain and rice production, average workweek hours, imports and exports, foreign investment, and other economic figures are also included.

TABLE A.1. Basic Facts and Figures, a Comparison of the Koreas

	Democratic People's Republic of Korea (North Korea)	Republic of Korea (South Korea)
Location	Korean Peninsula, north of demilitarized zone, bounded by China to the north and South Korea to the south	Korean Peninsula, south of demilitarized zone, bordered only by North Korea
Abbreviation	DPRK	ROK
Local long name	Choson-minjujuui-in' min-konghwaguk	Daehan-minguk
Local short name	Choson	Hanguk

(Continued)

TABLE A.1. Basic Facts and Figures, a Comparison of the Koreas (*Continued*)

	Democratic People's Republic of Korea (North Korea)	Republic of Korea (South Korea)
Government	Authoritarian socialist dictatorship	Republic with powers shared between the president and the legislature
Capital	P'yongyang	Seoul
Head of state	Chairman Kim Yong-Nam	President Lee Myung-Bak
Head of government	Premier Kim Yong-Il (Though he is officially neither head of state nor head of government, Kim Jong-Il acts as supreme authority and governmental leader.)	Prime Minister Han Seung-Soo
National holiday	Founding of DPRK, September 9 (1948)	Liberation Day, August 15 (1945)
Major political parties	Workers' Party of Korea (WPK—Choson Rodondang)	Grand National Party (GNP—Hannara-dang), Democratic Party (DEP—Han'guk Minjudang), Liberty Forward Party (LFP—Jayou Seonjin-dang), Democratic Labor Party (DLP—Minju Nodong-dang), Renewal of Korea Party (RKP—Changjo Hanguk-dang)

Sources: The CIA World Factbook (www.odci.gov/cia), the U.S. Department of State (www.state.gov), and the Korean National Statistical Office (www.nso.go.kr) (accessed 2008).

DEMOGRAPHICS

Table A.2 features information about the people of the Koreas, encompassing statistics on population, religion, language, and voting, among others.

TABLE A.2. Basic Facts and Figures, a Comparison of the Koreas

	Democratic People's Republic of Korea (North Korea)	Republic of Korea (South Korea)
Population	23,479,089 (2008 est.)	49,232,844 (2008 est.)
Population by age		
0-14	22.9%	17.7%
15-64	68.2%	72.3%
65+	8.8%	9.9%

TABLE A.2. Basic Facts and Figures, a Comparison of the Koreas (*Continued*)

	Democratic People's Republic of Korea (North Korea)	Republic of Korea (South Korea)
Population growth rate	0.732 (2008 est.)	0.371 (2008 est.)
Population density	495 people per sq. mile	1,285 people per sq. mile
Infant mortality rate	21.86 deaths per 1,000 live births	5.94 deaths per 1,000 live births
Ethnic groups	Korean	Korean, Chinese, Southeast Asian
Religions	Overt religious activity is nonexistent, but Buddhism, Christianity, and Confucianism have been traditionally practiced	46.5% nonreligious, 23.1% Buddhist, 18.3% Protestant, 10.9% Roman Catholic, 0.2% Confucian, 0.1% Ch'ondoist
Language	Korean	Korean; English widely taught at all levels
Voting age	17 years	19 years
Voter participation	n/a	70.8% in 2002 presidential election; 63% in 2007 presidential election
Literacy	99%	98%
Life expectancy (average)	72.2 years	77.4 years
Fertility rate	2.0 children per woman (2008 est.)	1.2 children per woman (2008 est.)

Sources: The CIA World Factbook (www.odci.gov/cia), the U.S. Department of State (www.state.gov), and the Korean National Statistical Office (www.nso.go.kr) (accessed 2008).

GEOGRAPHY

Table A.3 provides general facts and figures on Korean geography. More detailed information on Korean agricultural production is provided in another table below.

TABLE A.3. Basic Facts and Figures, a Comparison of the Koreas

	Democratic People's Republic of Korea (North Korea)	Republic of Korea (South Korea)
Land area	46,500 sq. miles	38,000 sq. miles
Arable land	14%	21%
Irrigated land	5,637 sq. miles (2003)	3,389 sq. miles (2003)

(*Continued*)

TABLE A.3.   Basic Facts and Figures, a Comparison of the Koreas (*Continued*)

	Democratic People's Republic of Korea (North Korea)	Republic of Korea (South Korea)
Natural hazards	drought, flooding, typhoons	typhoons, flooding; seismic activity in the southwest
Environmental problems	water pollution, waterborne diseases, deforestation, soil erosion	air pollution in big cities, acid rain, water pollution (sewage, industrial waste)
Major agricultural products	rice, corn, potatoes, soybeans, cattle, pigs, pork, eggs	rice, vegetables, fruit, barley, ginseng
Natural resources	coal, lead, tungsten, zinc, magnesite, iron ore, copper, gold, pyrites, salt, fluorspar, swift rivers	limited coal and tungsten, iron ore, limestone, kaolinite, graphite

Sources: The CIA World Factbook (www.odci.gov/cia), the U.S. Department of State (www.state.gov), and the Korean National Statistical Office (www.nso.go.kr) (accessed 2008).

ECONOMY

Table A.4 offers basic economic information on the Koreas, including financial, labor, trade, and industrial statistics.

TABLE A.4.   Basic Facts and Figures, a Comparison of the Koreas

	Democratic People's Republic of Korea (North Korea)	Republic of Korea (South Korea)
GDP	$26.7 billion (2007 est.)	$969.9 billion (2008)
GDP per capita	$1,146 (2007 est.)	$19,700 (2008 est.)
GDP by sector	agriculture, forestry, and fishing: 23.4%; industry: 43.1%; services: 33.6% (2002)	agriculture, forestry, and fishing: 3.0%; industry: 39.4%; services: 57.6% (2007 est.)
Exchange rate	140 won = US$1 (North Korea will not exchange for U.S. dollars but will exchange for EU euros and Chinese yuan)	931.5 won = US$1
Labor force	agriculture: 37%; industry/services: 63% (2004 est.)	agriculture: 7.5%; industry: 17.3%; services: 75.2% (2008)
Unemployment	n/a	3.3% (2007 est.)
People below poverty line	n/a	15% (2003 est.)

TABLE A.4.   Basic Facts and Figures, a Comparison of the Koreas (*Continued*)

	Democratic People's Republic of Korea (North Korea)	Republic of Korea (South Korea)
Major industries	textiles, chemicals, military products, mining, machinery	electronics, telecommunications, shipbuilding, petrochemicals, steel, minerals and mining
Leading companies	Korea Ferrous Metals Export and Import, Korea General Zinc, Korea General Chemicals, Korea General Machinery, Korea Ponghwa General, Korea Unha General Trading, Korea Kwang-myong Trading, Korean Ocean Shipping Agency, SEK Studio	Samsung Group, Hyundai, LG Group (formerly Lucky-Goldstar), Hanjin Group, POSCO (Pohang Iron and Steel Company), KT (formerly Korea Telecom), SK Group (formerly Sunkyung), Kia Motors, Hynix Semiconductor
Total value of trade	$2.9 billion (2007)	$728.3 billion (2007)
Exports	$1.5 billion, FOB (2006)	$371.5 billion (2007)
Imports	Petroleum, machinery and equipment, coal, grain, sugar, soybean oil, rubber	Petroleum and petroleum products, organic chemicals, iron, steel, foodstuffs, livestock, textiles, metals, electronic equipment, machinery and transportation equipment, grains

Sources: The CIA World Factbook (www.odci.gov/cia), the U.S. Department of State (www.state.gov), and the Korean National Statistical Office (www.nso.go.kr) (accessed 2008).

COMMUNICATIONS AND TRANSPORTATION

Table A.5 features facts and figures on the Koreas' communications networks (such as telephone users) along with the countries' transportation statistics (such as roads).

TABLE A.5.   Basic Facts and Figures, a Comparison of the Koreas

	Democratic People's Republic of Korea (North Korea)	Republic of Korea (South Korea)
Electricity production	33.4 billion kWh (2007 est.)	403.2 billion kWh (2007)
Electricity consumption	18.57 billion kWh (2005 est.)	368.6 billion kWh (2007)
Telephone lines	1.2 million (2007)	23.9 million (2007)
Mobile phones	n/a	43.5 million (2007)
Internet users	n/a	34.1 million (2006)
Roads	15,878 miles (2006)	63,418 miles (2006)
Railroads	3,252 miles (2006)	2,157 miles (2006)
Airports	77 (2007)	105 (2007)

Sources: The CIA World Factbook (www.odci.gov/cia), the U.S. Department of State (www.state.gov), and the Korean National Statistical Office (www.nso.go.kr) (accessed 2008).

MILITARY

Since the devastating Korean War, North and South Korea have built two of the world's largest militaries. Table A.6 outlines some basic statistics on each country's military situation.

TABLE A.6. Basic Facts and Figures, a Comparison of the Koreas

	Democratic People's Republic of Korea (North Korea)	Republic of Korea (South Korea)
Defense spending (% of GDP)	22.9% (2003 est.)	2.7% (2006)
Armed forces	1.2 million active; 7.7 million reserve (2008 est.)	687,000 active; 4.5 million reserve (2008)
Manpower fit for military service	5,142,240 males; 5,139,447 females (2008)	11,282,699 males; 10,683,668 females (2008)

Sources: The CIA World Factbook (www.odci.gov/cia), the U.S. Department of State (www.state.gov), and the Korean National Statistical Office (www.nso.go.kr) (accessed 2008).

POLITICAL LEADERS

Table B and C provide a chronological list of North and South Korea's political leaders since the countries were divided after World War II. Note that North Korea's table is considerably shorter as it has had only two leaders since the 1940s.

South Korea

TABLE B. South Korean Presidents

President	Beginning of Presidency	End of Presidency	Political Party
Syngman Rhee	July 20, 1948	May 3, 1960	Liberal Party
Ho Chong (as acting president)	May 3, 1960	June 15, 1960	Liberal Party
Kwak Sang Hoon (as acting president)	June 15, 1960	June 26, 1960	Democratic Party
Ho Chong (as acting president)	June 26, 1960	August 13, 1960	Liberal Party
Yun Po-Sun	August 13, 1960	March 24, 1962	New Democratic Party
Park Chung-Hee (as acting president)	March 24, 1962	December 16, 1963	Military

TABLE B. South Korean Presidents (*Continued*)

President	Beginning of Presidency	End of Presidency	Political Party
Park Chung-Hee (as president)	December 17, 1963	October 25, 1979	Democratic Republican Party
Choi Kyu Hah (as acting president)	October 26, 1979	December 7, 1979	Democratic Republican Party
Choi Kyu Hah (as president)	December 8, 1979	August 16, 1980	Democratic Republican Party
Park Choong-Hoon (as acting president)	August 16, 1980	September 1, 1980	Military
Chun Doo-Hwan	September 1, 1980	February 25, 1988	Military, Democratic Justice Party
Roh Tae-Woo	February 25, 1988	February 25, 1993	Democratic Justice Party, Democratic Liberal Party
Kim Young-Sam	February 25, 2993	February 25, 1998	Democratic Liberal Party, New Korea Party
Kim Dae-Jung	February 25, 1998	February 25, 2003	National Congress for New Politics, New Millennium Democratic Party
Roh Moo-Hyun	February 25, 2003	March 12, 2004	New Millennium Democratic Party, Open Uri Party
Goh Kun (as acting president)	March 12, 2004	May 14, 2004	None
Roh Moo-Hyun (restored as president)	May 14, 2004	February 25, 2008	Open Uri Party
Lee Myung-Bak	February 25, 2008	n/a	Grand National Party

North Korea

TABLE C. North Korean Leaders

General Secretary of the Korean Workers' Party	Beginning of Rule	End of Rule	Party
Kim Il-Sung	June 30, 1949	July 8, 1994	Korean Workers' Party
Kim Jong-Il	July 8, 1994	n/a	Korean Workers' Party

SOUTH KOREA: TABLES AND GRAPHS
RICE SUPPLY, 1980–2003

Table D details the supply of South Korea's most important agricultural product—rice—which is key to the diet, economy, and religious practices of the Koreas (as well as many other East Asian cultures). Total supply, the amount produced, the carry-in stock (the unused remainder of the previous year's supply), and imports are included.

TABLE D. South Korea Rice Supply (in thousands of metric tons)

	Total supply	Carry-in	Production	Imports	Other
1980	6,468	752	5,136	580	–
1981	6,861	1,066	3,550	2,245	–
1982	6,827	1,495	5,063	269	–
1983	6,814	1,423	5,175	216	–
1984	6,922	1,511	5,404	–	7
1985	6,929	1,247	5,682	–	–
1986	7,054	1,428	5,626	–	–
1987	6,856	1,249	5,607	–	–
1988	6,732	1,239	5,493	–	–
1989	7,174	1,121	6,053	–	–
1990	7,470	1,572	5,898	–	–
1991	7,631	2,025	5,606	–	–
1992	7,525	2,141	5,384	–	–
1993	7,330	1,999	5,331	–	–
1994	6,570	1,820	4,750	–	–
1995	6,216	1,156	5,060	–	–
1996	5,469	659	4,695	115	–
1997	5,567	244	5,323	–	–
1998	6,022	497	5,450	75	–
1999	6,000	806	5,097	97	–
2000	6,092	722	5,263	107	–

Table D. South Korea Rice Supply (in thousands of metric tons) (*Continued*)

	Total supply	Carry-in	Production	Imports	Other
2001	6,486	978	5,291	217	–
2002	7,004	1,335	5,515	154	–
2003	6,554	1,447	4,927	180	–

Source: Korean Statistical Information Service (accessed 2008).

GRAIN SUPPLY (EXCLUDING RICE), 1980–2003

Table E breaks down South Korea's grain production by year (excluding rice, which is featured in the table above), including total supply, carry-in, total production, and imports.

Table E. South Korean Grain Supply (Excluding Rice) (in thousands of metric tons)

	Supply	Carry-in	Production	Imports	Others
1980	8,307	1,924	1,912	4,471	–
1981	8,063	1,113	1,824	4,988	–
1982	8,467	975	1,762	5,677	53
1983	9,777	992	1,744	7,027	14
1984	10,130	1,370	1,620	7,140	–
1985	10,018	1,262	1,420	7,336	–
1986	10,526	852	1,240	8,434	–
1987	12,327	909	1,206	10,212	–
1988	13,263	1,320	1,229	10,714	–
1989	12,664	1,894	1,234	9,536	–
1990	12,469	1,332	1,115	10,022	–
1991	13,667	1,632	957	11,078	–
1992	14,665	1,690	872	12,103	–
1993	15,017	1,869	874	12,274	–
1994	15,979	2,191	715	13,073	–
1995	16,877	1,863	756	14,258	–
1996	17,432	2,460	809	14,163	–
1997	16,665	1,790	708	14,167	–
1998	15,659	1,921	672	13,066	–
1999	15,889	1,392	734	13,763	–
2000	16,494	1,309	668	14,517	–
2001	15,842	1,647	703	13,492	–
2002	16,814	1,745	647	14,422	–
2003	16,563	1,740	593	14,239	–

Source: Korean Statistical Information Service (accessed 2008).

IMPORTS AND EXPORTS, 1971–2007

Table F and Figure F chart South Korea's increasing trade activity—one indicator of the country's economic progress—over almost four decades.

TABLE F.   South Korea, Imports and Exports (in thousands USD)

	Exports	Imports
1971	1,067,607	2,394,320
1972	1,624,088	2,522,022
1973	3,225,025	4,240,277
1974	4,460,370	6,851,848
1975	5,081,016	7,274,434
1976	7,715,343	8,773,632
1977	10,046,457	10,810,538
1978	12,710,642	14,971,930
1979	15,055,453	20,338,611
1980	17,504,862	22,291,663
1981	21,253,757	26,131,421
1982	21,853,394	24,250,840
1983	24,445,054	26,192,221
1984	29,244,861	30,631,441
1985	30,283,122	31,135,655
1986	34,714,470	31,583,900
1987	47,280,927	41,019,812
1988	60,696,388	51,810,632
1989	62,377,174	61,464,772
1990	65,015,731	69,843,678
1991	71,870,122	81,524,858
1992	76,631,515	81,775,257
1993	82,235,866	83,800,142
1994	96,013,237	102,348,175
1995	125,057,988	135,118,933
1996	129,715,137	150,339,100
1997	136,164,204	144,616,374
1998	132,313,143	93,281,754
1999	143,685,459	119,752,282
2000	172,267,510	160,481,018
2001	150,439,144	141,097,821
2002	162,470,528	152,126,153
2003	193,817,443	178,826,657

TABLE F.   South Korea, Imports and Exports (in thousands USD) (*Continued*)

	Exports	Imports
2004	253,844,672	224,462,687
2005	284,418,743	261,238,264
2006	325,464,848	309,382,632
2007	371,489,086	356,845,733

Source: Korean Statistical Information Service.

FIGURE F.   South Korea: Imports and Exports, 1971–2007

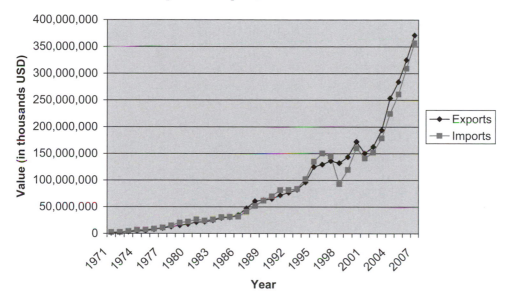

SOUTH KOREAN INFLATION, 1980–2007

South Korea's relative economic stability since the 1980s is reflected in Table G and Figure G, which chart the country's average percentage of change in consumer prices over more than a quarter-century.

TABLE G. South Korea Inflation, Annual Percentage of Change in Consumer Prices

1980	28.70
1981	21.35
1982	7.19
1983	3.42
1984	2.27
1985	2.46
1986	2.75
1987	3.05
1988	7.15
1989	5.70
1990	8.57
1991	9.33
1992	6.21
1993	4.80
1994	6.27
1995	4.48
1996	4.93
1997	4.44
1998	7.51
1999	0.81
2000	2.26
2001	4.07
2002	2.76
2003	3.52
2004	3.59
2005	2.75
2006	2.24
2007	2.54

Source: *World Economic Outlook, October 2008* (Washington, DC: IMF, 2008).

FIGURE G. South Korean Inflation, 1980–2007

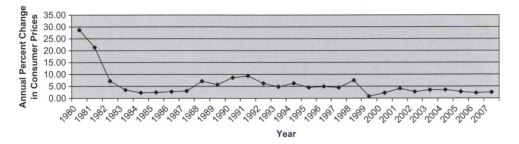

WORKFORCE BREAKDOWNS

South Korea's workforce has undergone dramatic changes since 1970, which is reflected in this series of tables on pages 382–390 that break down the country's labor force from 1970 to 2007 by such categories as total workforce, professional and technical, administration and management, clerical, and agricultural work, among others.

TABLE **H.** South Korea, Workforce Breakdowns, 1970

Unit in thousands	Total Workforce	Professional, Technical, and Related Occupations	Administration and Management	Clerical and Related Occupations	Sales	Service	Agriculture, Animal Husbandry, Forestry, Fishing, and Hunting	Production and Related Occupations, Transport Equipment, and Labor	Not Classifiable	Armed Forces	Unemployed, Seeking First Job	Unemployed, Previously Employed	Unemployed
All sectors	10,378	323	96	594	1,028	679	5,148	2,198	89		...		225
Agriculture, hunting, forestry, and fishing	5,157	2	1	4	1	1	5,134	15	0				...
Mining and quarrying	100	1	2	7	0	2	8	79	0				...
Manufacturing	1,448	16	47	144	28	23	1	1,188	1				...
Electricity, gas, and water	31	1	1	14	0	1	0	14	0				...
Construction	462	8	6	22	1	4	0	420	0				...
Wholesale and retail trade, hotels, and restaurants	1,280	12	5	34	961	228	2	38	0				...
Transport, storage, and communication	329	3	13	89	4	7	1	213	0				...
Finance, insurance, real estate, and business services	97	10	5	52	22	4	0	4	0				...
Community, social, and personal services	1,222	269	16	227	10	410	3	226	61				...
Other activities	28	0	0	1	0	0	0	0	26				...
Unemployed	225	...	...	...	...	...	...	...	...		...		225

Source: ILO LABORSTA Statistical Database (http://laborsta.ilo.org) (accessed 2008).

TABLE I. South Korea, Workforce Breakdowns, 1975

	Total Workforce	Professional, Technical, and Related Occupations	Administration and Management	Clerical and Related Occupations	Sales	Service	Agriculture, Animal Husbandry, Forestry, Fishing, and Hunting	Production and Related Occupations, Transport Equipment, and Labor	Not Classifiable	Armed Forces	Unemployed, Seeking First Job	Unemployed, Previously Employed	Unemployed
All sectors	13,595	581	134	1,203	1,531	895	4,768	3,570	1		...		913
Agriculture, hunting, forestry, and fishing	4,795	3	1	4	2	1	4,762	22	...				...
Mining and quarrying	91	1	2	6	0	2		81	...				...
Manufacturing	2,797	45	70	356	69	50	1	2,207	0				...
Electricity, gas, and water	37	4	0	16	0	2	0	15	...				...
Construction	664	23	13	57	0	8	0	563	0				...
Wholesale and retail trade, hotels, and restaurants	2,059	22	13	111	1,391	458	1	63	0				...
Transport, storage, and communication	551	9	13	151	0	20	0	359	0				...
Finance, insurance, real estate, and business services	286	27	10	144	69	19	0	16	...				...
Community, social, and personal services	1,403	447	13	358	0	335	4	245	0				...
Other activities	0	...	...	...	...	...	...	0	0				...
Unemployed	913	...	...	...	...	...	...	...	...		...		913

Source: ILO LABORSTA Statistical Database (http://laborsta.ilo.org) (accessed 2008).

TABLE J. South Korea, Workforce Breakdowns, 1980

	Total Workforce	Professional, Technical, and Related Occupations	Administration and Management	Clerical and Related Occupations	Sales	Service	Agriculture, Animal Husbandry, Forestry, Fishing, and Hunting	Production and Related Occupations, Transport Equipment, and Labor	Not Classifiable	Armed Forces	Unemployed, Seeking First Job	Unemployed, Previously Employed	Unemployed
All sectors	14,454	548	182	1,266	1,983	1,085	4,652	3,990			208		541
Agriculture, hunting, forestry, and fishing	4,658	2	1	4	1	1	4,634	15					19
Mining and quarrying	124	–	2	8	–	2	3	108					4
Manufacturing	2,972	20	95	366	37	65	2	2,386					188
Electricity, gas, and water	43	1	1	16	3	2		21					3
Construction	841	11	11	53	1	8	1	756					125
Wholesale and retail trade, hotels, and restaurants	2,625	20	15	127	1,832	549	1	82					107
Transport, storage, and communication	618	14	18	146	3	16	1	420					35
Finance, insurance, real estate, and business services	332	19	9	174	91	23	–	16					15
Community, social, and personal services	1,493	460	31	371	14	418	11	186					44
Unemployed, seeking first job	208										208		
Unemployed, previously employed	541												541

Source: ILO LABORSTA Statistical Database (http://laborsta.ilo.org) (accessed 2008).

TABLE K. South Korea, Workforce Breakdowns, 1985

	Total Workforce	Professional, Technical, and Related Occupations	Administration and Management	Clerical and Related Occupations	Sales	Service	Agriculture, Animal Husbandry, Forestry, Fishing, and Hunting	Production and Related Occupations, Transport Equipment, and Labor	Not Classifiable	Armed Forces	Unemployed, Seeking First Job	Unemployed, Previously Employed	Unemployed
All sectors	15,592	872	218	1,729	2,313	1,622	3,686	4,530			206		416
Agriculture, hunting, forestry, and fishing	3,733	9	3	13	1	2	3,680	26					11
Mining and quarrying	155	2	3	10	–	3	–	137					5
Manufacturing	3,504	78	103	466	44	63	1	2,749					123
Electricity, gas, and water	40	5	1	16	–	5	–	14					–
Construction	911	35	34	74	1	10	–	757					109
Wholesale and retail trade, hotels, and restaurants	3,377	45	14	235	2,107	874	1	102					91
Transport, storage, and communication	701	16	22	200	1	19	–	443					30
Finance, insurance, real estate, and business services	563	49	20	262	153	48	1	30					14
Community, social, and personal services	1,984	632	19	452	6	598	3	273					33
Unemployed, seeking first job	206										206		
Unemployed, previously employed	416	19	10	53	64	34	10	228					416

Source: ILO LABORSTA Statistical Database (http://laborsta.ilo.org) (accessed 2008).

TABLE L. South Korea, Workforce Breakdowns, 1990

	Total Workforce	Professional, Technical, and Related Occupations	Administration and Management	Clerical and Related Occupations	Sales	Service	Agriculture, Animal Husbandry, Forestry, Fishing, and Hunting	Production and Related Occupations, Transport Equipment, and Labor	Not Classifiable	Armed Forces	Unemployed, Seeking First Job	Unemployed, Previously Employed	Unemployed
All sectors	18,487	1,301	267	2,336	2,616	2,007	3,270	6,238			214		237
Agriculture, hunting, forestry, and fishing	3,292	7	3	8	–	2	3,260	12					...
Mining and quarrying	81	–	3	6	–	4	–	68					...
Manufacturing	4,847	116	117	640	61	93	1	3,819					...
Electricity, gas, and water	71	4	1	29	–	10	–	27					...
Construction	1,339	46	36	117	4	21	1	1,115					...
Wholesale and retail trade, hotels, and restaurants	3,920	50	22	346	2,288	1,050	2	162					...
Transport, storage, and communication	922	23	26	207	4	24	–	638					...
Finance, insurance, real estate, and business services	935	76	37	405	249	95	–	73					...
Community, social, and personal services	2,630	977	23	580	11	708	6	325					...
Unemployed, seeking first job	214										214		
Unemployed, previously employed	237	...	...	...	...	...	...	...	...				237

Source: ILO LABORSTA Statistical Database (http://laborsta.ilo.org) (accessed 2008).

TABLE M. South Korea, Workforce Breakdowns, 1995

	Total Workforce	Legislative, Administrative, and Managerial Occupations	Professional Occupations	Technical and Associate Professional Occupations	Clerical	Service and Retail Sales	Skilled Agriculture and Fishing	Crafts and Trades	Plant and Machinery Operations and Assembly	Elementary Occupations	Not Classifiable	Unemployed, Seeking First Job	Unemployed, Previously Employed	Unemployed
All sectors	20,855	524	972	1,841	2,520	4,485	2,382	3,227	2,187	2,296		166	255	421
Agriculture, hunting, and forestry	2,420	2	1	2	6	1	2,294		3	109			2	
Fishing	117	3		5	2	1	85	7	5	15			1	
Mining and quarrying	25	3			3				8	4				
Manufacturing	4,864	157	80	309	691	54	1	1,853	1,152	499			68	
Electricity, gas, and water	71	1	5	9	27	2		8	10	8			1	
Construction	1,944	107	49	77	190	9		962	138	374			38	
Wholesale and retail trade; repair of motor vehicles, motorcycles, and personal and household goods	3,835	78	32	242	408	2,212		240	111	451			61	
Hotels and restaurants	1,631	19	2	17	54	1,434		17	6	56			26	
Transport, storage, and communications	1,081	35	9	55	204	16		55	600	94			13	
Financial intermediation	724	36	5	126	345	7		1	6	194			4	
Real estate, renting, and business activities	931	30	123	226	178	77		46	23	212			16	
Public administration and defense, compulsory social security	646	16	12	253	158	106	1	12	25	61			2	
Education	1,019	19	485	331	90	28		3	22	35			6	
Health and social work	305	15	88	75	44	71		4	7	13			3	
Other community, social, and personal services	857	15	77	108	116	363		17	66	83			12	
Households with employed persons	193			2	1	103			4	82			1	
Extraterritorial organizations and bodies	15		1	2	4	1		2	1	4				
Unemployed, seeking first job	166										166			
Unemployed, previously employed	256	6	4	24	41	67	1	47	32	34				

Source: ILO LABORSTA Statistical Database (http://laborsta.ilo.org) (accessed 2008).

TABLE N. South Korea, Workforce Breakdowns, 2000

	Total Workforce	Legislative, Administrative, and Managerial Occupations	Professional Occupations	Technical and Associate Professional Occupations	Clerical	Service and Retail Sales	Skilled Agriculture and Fishing	Crafts and Trades	Plant and Machinery Operations and Assembly	Elementary Occupations	Not Classifiable	Unemployed, Seeking First Job	Unemployed, Previously Employed	Unemployed
All sectors	21,951	485	1,369	2,028	2,409	5,506	2,155	2,666	2,284	2,159		58	832	890
Agriculture, hunting, and forestry	2,214	2	1	3	3	2	2,083		2	108			10	
Fishing	87	3					61	9	3	13			2	
Mining and quarrying	18	1			1				5	2				
Manufacturing	4,380	126	135	343	486	54	1	1,378	1,157	562			138	
Electricity, gas, and water	64	1	3	15	18	1		9	5	11			1	
Construction	1,704	92	47	82	158	5		768	142	285			124	
Wholesale and retail trade; repair of motor vehicles, motorcycles, and personal and household goods	3,931	75	29	362	373	2,526	1	102	81	257			126	
Hotels and restaurants	2,010	14	2	23	43	1,722		24	8	87			87	
Transport, storage, and communications	1,302	30	11	65	228	25	1	70	713	123			36	
Financial intermediation	745	25	17	106	312	249		1	6	12			17	
Real estate, renting, and business activities	1,403	48	221	339	217	91	1	83	40	314			49	
Public administration and defense, compulsory social security	789	21	28	122	265	130	2	6	19	159			37	
Education	1,187	29	582	321	109	52		8	30	32			24	
Health and social work	420	3	167	117	56	43		4	6	17			7	
Other community, social, and personal services	1,285	15	124	120	136	483	4	199	65	101			38	
Households with employed persons	199			3		121				70			4	
Extraterritorial organizations and bodies	20		1	4	3	2		3	1	6				
Not classifiable	132												132	
Unemployed, seeking first job	58										58			
Unemployed, previously employed	832	9	18	58	86	184	7	121	75	143	131			

Source: ILO LABORSTA Statistical Database (http://laborsta.ilo.org) (accessed 2008).

TABLE O. South Korea, Workforce Breakdowns, 2005

	Total Workforce	Legislative, Administrative, and Managerial Occupations	Professional Occupations	Technical and Associate Professional Occupations	Clerical	Service and Retail Sales	Skilled Agriculture and Fishing	Crafts and Trades	Plant and Machinery Operations and Assembly	Elementary Occupations	Not Classifiable	Unemployed, Seeking First Job	Unemployed, Previously Employed	Unemployed
All sectors	23,743	574	1,839	2,363	3,269	5,625	1,708	2,436	2,563	2,479		42	845	887
Agriculture, hunting, and forestry	1,747	1	1	2	5	1	1,641	–	2	95				
Fishing	68	2	–	1	1	–	54	1	–	10				
Mining and quarrying	17	1	–	1	2	1	–	6	5	1				
Manufacturing	4,234	147	175	381	682	60	1	958	1,290	541				
Electricity, gas, and water	71	3	4	11	29	3	–	7	8	7				
Construction	1,814	110	48	121	191	5	4	898	141	298				
Wholesale and retail trade; repair of motor vehicles, motorcycles, and personal and household goods	3,748	74	46	312	463	2,383	–	63	78	329				
Hotels and restaurants	2,058	26	5	15	61	1,772	–	25	6	150				
Transport, storage, and communications	1,429	30	13	55	292	26	–	62	790	159				
Financial intermediation	746	37	20	84	368	221	–	2	3	11				
Real estate, renting, and business activities	2,037	58	348	478	356	115	4	93	79	506				
Public administration and defense, compulsory social security	791	12	21	107	364	158	2	11	20	97				
Education	1,568	40	773	465	157	78	–	3	21	31				
Health and social work	646	7	235	190	84	96	–	3	8	23				
Other community, social, and personal services	1,727	28	149	137	204	657	3	300	110	140				
Households with employed persons	130	–	–	1	1	49	–	–	1	78				
Extraterritorial organizations and bodies	24	–	1	3	9	2	–	5	1	4				
Unemployed, seeking first job	42											42		
Unemployed, previously employed	845												845	
Unemployed	887													887

Source: ILO LABORSTA Statistical Database (http://laborsta.ilo.org) (accessed 2008).

TABLE P. South Korea, Workforce Breakdowns, 2007

	Total Workforce	Legislative, Administrative, and Managerial Occupations	Professional Occupations	Technical and Associate Professional Occupations	Clerical	Service and Retail Sales	Skilled Agriculture and Fishing	Crafts and Trades	Plant and Machinery Operations and Assembly	Elementary Occupations	Not Classifiable	Unemployed, Seeking First Job	Unemployed, Previously Employed	Unemployed
All sectors	23,433	556	2,032	2,609	3,309	5,567	1,624	2,423	2,588	2,725		41	742	783
Agriculture, hunting, and forestry	1,670	1	0	2	7	3	1,563	1	5	89				
Fishing	56	0	0	1	1	0	41	0	0	11				
Mining and quarrying	18	0	0	1	3	0		7	6	1				
Manufacturing	4,119	159	206	393	665	50	0	866	1,235	546				
Electricity, gas, and water	86	3	7	21	28	3	5	11	8	6				
Construction	1,850	107	47	132	195	4	2	893	143	325				
Wholesale and retail trade; repair of motor vehicles, motorcycles, and personal and household goods	3,677	70	39	318	456	2,314		82	87	310				
Hotels and restaurants	2,049	23	9	16	77	1,696	0	23	4	202				
Transport, storage, and communications	1,498	26	14	83	279	31	1	66	834	165				
Financial intermediation	809	32	30	105	351	266		2	6	17				
Real estate, renting, and business activities	2,350	50	410	493	438	134	2	122	77	624				
Public administration and defense, compulsory social security	797	7	34	128	340	147	6	12	18	106				
Education	1,687	38	813	518	163	85	0	5	34	31				
Health and social work	745	9	257	235	79	103	0	12	11	39				
Other community, social, and personal services	1,845	32	165	163	218	667	4	322	119	155				
Households with employed persons	161	0	0	1	0	63		0	1	96				
Extraterritorial organizations and bodies	15	0	1	1	9	2	1	1	0	2				
Unemployed, seeking first job	41											41		
Unemployed, previously employed	742												742	
Unemployed	783													783

Source: ILO LABORSTA Statistical Database (http://laborsta.ilo.org) (accessed 2008).

AVERAGE WORKWEEK HOURS,
BY INDUSTRY, 1970–2007

Table Q and Figure Q show that the length of a South Korean employee's work-week varies depending on the industry in which the worker is employed—though for most industries, this generally exceeds the 40-hour week that has become standard in the United States.

392 | *Facts and Figures*

TABLE Q. South Korea, Average Hours Worked Per Week, by Industry

	Total	Mining and quarrying	Manufacturing	Electricity, gas, and water	Construction	Wholesale and retail trade, restaurants, and hotels	Transport, storage, and communication	Finance, insurance, real estate, and business services	Community, social, and personal services
1970	51.6	45.1	52.3		47.3		53.7		
1971	50.6	45.4	51.9		51.2		55.5		
1972	50.9	42.7	51.6		48.8		50.8		
1973	50.7	43.6	51.4		48.1		51.5		
1974	49.6	43.0	49.9		48.1		51.9		
1975	50.0	43.1	50.5		48.9		51.0		
1976	50.7	41.5	52.5		46.9		50.5		
1977	51.4	41.7	52.9		49.0		49.5		
1978	51.3	41.1	53.0		48.5		49.4		
1979	50.5	40.2	52.0		49.4		49.5		
1980	51.6	42.0	53.1	48.6	50.4	50.5	50.4	45.4	47.2
1981	51.9	41.3	53.7	48.9	49.9	50.3	50.8	45.5	46.9
1982	52.1	42.7	53.7	48.4	50.3	51.0	51.8	46.3	47.4
1983	52.5	42.7	54.4	48.5	48.6	50.9	52.4	45.8	47.3
1984	52.4	42.4	54.3	49.4	49.1	49.9	53.4	45.9	46.8
1985	51.9	41.4	53.8	50.0	49.0	50.0	53.2	45.8	46.6
1986	52.5	40.8	54.7	50.4	48.6	49.7	52.8	45.2	46.2
1987	51.9	39.3	54.0	50.0	48.1	49.5	51.9	45.3	46.1
1988	51.1	39.4	52.6	50.9	47.9	49.6	51.6	45.9	46.6
1989	49.2	37.9	50.7	48.1	46.6	48.0	50.3	44.6	45.0
1990	48.2	36.2	49.8	47.8	45.8	47.5	48.8	43.6	44.5
1991	47.9	39.5	49.3	48.6	45.6	47.8	48.7	44.2	44.6
1992	47.5	39.5	48.7	49.2	46.0	47.5	48.3	44.4	44.8
1993	47.5	40.7	48.9	48.0	46.6	46.5	47.2	45.6	44.7
1994	47.4	41.8	48.7	47.7	45.8	46.6	47.0	45.9	44.2
1995	47.7	43.9	49.2	48.9	45.8	46.3	47.7	45.6	44.4
1996	47.3	43.8	48.4	49.7	45.0	45.5	49.3	46.2	44.5
1997	46.7	43.9	47.8	49.2	44.5	44.9	48.4	45.9	44.3
1998	45.9	43.8	46.1	49.0	44.3	44.8	47.7	45.7	44.4
1999	47.9	44.4	50.1	48.7	45.1	45.8	50.0	45.5	45.3
2000	47.5	44.6	49.3	48.3	44.4	45.6	49.5	45.2	45.2
2001	47.0	43.8	48.3	49.1	44.4	45.9	49.1	45.0	45.0
2002	46.2	44.9	47.7	47.7	43.9	45.1	47.9	44.5	43.6
2003	45.9	45.0	47.6	47.9	43.3	44.6	47.4	43.6	43.2
2004	45.7	43.2	47.4	45.7	43.4	44.6	47.3	43.0	43.0
2005	45.1	43.7	46.9	42.4	42.7	45.2	45.8	42.6	42.6
2006	44.2	43.4	46.0	42.0	41.6	44.4	45.1	41.5	41.9
2007	43.4	43.4	45.5	41.6	41.2	43.8	44.6	39.1	40.5

Source: ILO LABORSTA Statistical Database (http://laborsta.ilo.org) (accessed 2008).

FIGURE Q. South Korea: Average Workweek Hours, by Industry

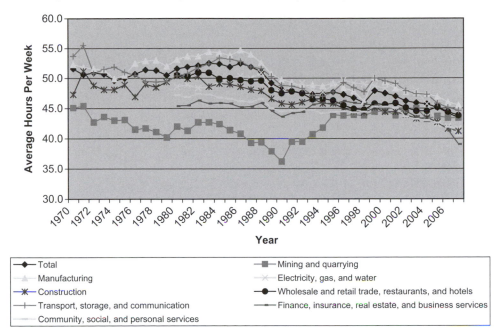

FOREIGN DIRECT INVESTMENT, 1962–2006

Another indicator of the "Miracle on the Han"—which refers not only to Seoul's major river but also to South Korea's increasing economic success over the past five decades—is foreign direct investment, which is listed by year in Table R and Figure R on the following pages.

TABLE R. South Korea, Foreign Direct Investment (in thousands USD)

	Total	United States	Japan	Germany	Hong Kong	Netherlands	Switzerland	United Kingdom	France	China	Others
1962	3,575	3,575	–	–	–	–	–	–	–	–	–
1963	5,737	5,114	–	–	623	–	–	–	–	–	–
1964	654	211	–	219	–	–	–	–	–	–	224
1965	21,824	10,722	500	–	–	–	–	10,500	–	–	102
1966	15,621	5,362	7,829	20	2,145	–	–	–	–	–	265
1967	28,272	14,869	9,751	556	–	–	–	–	–	–	3,096
1968	25,631	8,487	11,170	123	800	–	–	98	–	–	4,953
1969	48,579	14,761	21,338	30	821	5,205	–	–	–	–	6,424
1970	75,892	45,193	21,335	1,184	417	945	–	60	–	–	6,758
1971	40,246	12,030	26,094	630	967	–	–	–	450	–	75
1972	121,973	33,092	77,021	3,800	1,596	–	54	–	150	–	6,260
1973	318,151	16,630	294,320	152	3,576	–	28	50	2,600	–	795
1974	152,830	35,906	94,795	683	5,100	1,201	72	–	825	–	14,248
1975	207,317	34,944	111,771	665	400	19,636	49	–	1,250	–	38,602
1976	79,154	14,383	49,152	3,948	2,854	–	–	2,643	200	–	5,974
1977	83,626	19,560	40,135	523	4,124	1,088	1,245	4,744	3,727	–	8,480
1978	149,426	39,246	75,992	6,802	3,400	–	10,223	2,665	3,417	–	7,681
1979	191,300	46,689	104,494	5,214	5,247	2,516	4,640	7,967	1,091	–	13,442
1980	143,136	70,629	42,518	8,587	501	1,793	2,127	2,297	–	–	14,684
1981	153,161	59,536	37,712	3,512	33,865	1,320	12,652	–	1,121	–	3,443
1982	189,026	101,027	40,281	3,920	27,133	5,126	3,207	1,758	–	–	6,574
1983	269,424	54,135	168,136	2,510	6,897	9,500	5,866	792	1,573	–	20,015
1984	422,346	193,326	164,870	3,644	4,195	–	18,371	4,149	22,155	–	11,636
1985	532,197	108,007	364,253	11,255	13,447	504	6,962	12,289	5,072	–	10,408
1986	354,736	125,128	138,650	5,771	12,807	4,357	31,515	15,400	200	–	20,908
1987	1,063,327	249,140	497,014	47,493	45,880	45,861	55,615	48,329	11,309	–	62,686

TABLE R. South Korea, Foreign Direct Investment (in thousands USD) (*Continued*)

	Total	United States	Japan	Germany	Hong Kong	Netherlands	Switzerland	United Kingdom	France	China	Others
1988	1,283,757	284,401	697,269	74,040	13,835	48,897	24,439	21,781	50,355	–	68,740
1989	1,090,279	319,447	465,973	48,932	32,322	19,518	46,801	46,124	39,380	2,800	68,982
1990	802,635	317,830	235,530	62,330	2,977	36,315	18,990	44,841	22,439	100	61,283
1991	1,395,996	296,620	225,918	67,940	9,717	598,889	74,313	18,834	28,834	690	74,241
1992	894,505	379,182	155,190	120,485	9,538	43,785	36,684	23,694	29,202	1,056	95,689
1993	1,044,274	340,669	286,006	35,929	74,966	131,223	7,054	70,823	39,674	6,864	51,066
1994	1,316,505	311,016	428,407	60,230	43,058	67,271	10,949	24,988	56,358	6,145	308,083
1995	1,947,868	642,776	424,733	44,644	57,998	170,131	9,846	86,725	35,192	10,892	464,931
1996	3,202,580	875,004	254,676	94,861	228,536	204,891	161,970	78,986	90,317	5,578	1,207,761
1997	6,971,138	3,188,916	265,602	398,067	84,585	830,835	102,952	258,873	411,357	6,518	1,423,433
1998	8,858,025	2,970,279	509,613	785,241	38,379	1,323,249	76,390	60,667	369,421	8,381	2,716,405
1999	15,544,618	3,738,999	1,762,408	959,547	460,226	3,321,848	140,325	479,719	750,239	26,585	3,904,723
2000	15,256,009	2,921,330	2,451,886	1,627,003	123,459	1,775,172	24,725	86,481	607,470	76,288	5,562,195
2001	11,286,297	3,881,503	776,104	459,407	167,442	1,233,524	50,371	433,238	425,547	70,362	3,788,799
2002	9,092,517	4,490,730	1,403,531	283,663	234,147	450,516	30,648	115,441	110,824	249,380	1,723,638
2003	6,470,503	1,242,234	541,860	370,018	54,799	161,576	20,882	870,505	150,316	50,206	3,008,108
2004	12,792,006	4,717,126	2,262,485	487,030	90,136	1,309,083	70,354	641,971	179,962	1,164,760	1,869,099
2005	11,563,488	2,689,764	1,878,835	704,812	819,715	1,149,595	40,254	2,307,791	85,179	68,414	1,819,128
2006	11,233,077	1,701,014	2,108,032	483,907	165,055	800,061	228,713	705,266	1,174,434	39,595	3,827,000

Source: Korean Statistical Information Service.

FIGURE R.   Foreign Direct Investment in South Korea

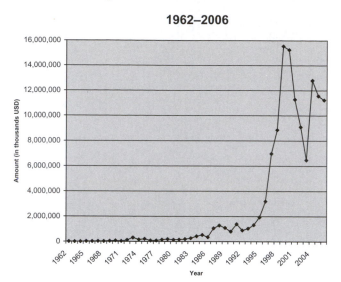

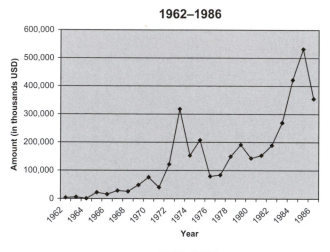

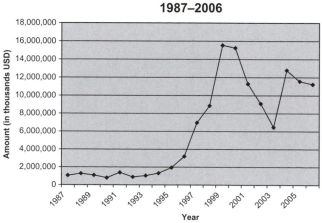

FISHING AND AQUACULTURE, 1970–2006

A staple of most South Koreans' diet is fish, and the catch of the country's fishing industry over almost four decades is detailed in Table S and Figure S.

TABLE S.   South Korean Fishing Catch (in metric tons)

	Total	Fishing	Aquaculture
1970	935,462	–	–
1971	1,073,733	–	–
1972	1,343,569	–	–
1973	1,686,484	–	–
1974	2,026,221	–	–
1975	2,134,979	–	–
1976	2,406,896	–	–
1977	2,421,273	–	–
1978	2,353,518	31,065	1,831
1979	2,422,163	39,882	1,418
1980	2,410,346	38,232	994
1981	2,811,914	39,297	838
1982	2,644,074	43,670	882
1983	2,793,023	45,442	1,554
1984	2,909,811	48,645	1,476
1985	3,102,605	50,400	2,664
1986	3,659,724	51,779	5,274
1987	3,331,825	47,598	9,505
1988	3,209,135	24,681	11,128
1989	3,319,395	18,958	11,596
1990	3,198,234	18,562	15,819
1991	2,906,131	16,146	14,254
1992	3,200,852	14,145	20,031
1993	3,335,718	11,834	18,353
1994	3,476,476	10,008	20,849
1995	3,348,178	8,878	20,350
1996	3,247,225	7,858	22,390
1997	3,243,675	6,932	24,864
1998	2,835,015	6,850	20,002
1999	2,910,569	6,317	11,529
2000	2,514,225	7,142	13,443
2001	2,665,124	5,971	12,170
2002	2,476,188	5,690	12,821

(Continued)

TABLE S. South Korean Fishing Catch (in metric tons) (*Continued*)

	Total	Fishing	Aquaculture
2003	2,487,042	6,080	13,600
2004	2,519,101	10,302	14,997
2005	2,714,050	7,500	16,339
2006	3,032,116	7,139	17,704

Source: Korean Statistical Information Service.

FIGURE S. South Korean Fishing, 1970–2006

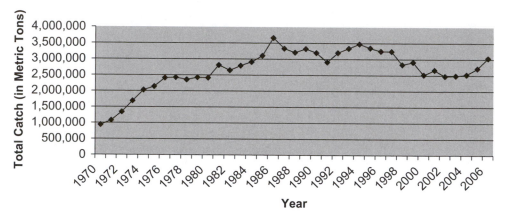

STRIKES AND LOCKOUTS, 1969–2007

Labor relations in South Korea have always been punctuated by passionate—sometimes violent—conflicts, a history reflected in Table T and Figure T, which detail the number of employee strikes and managements lockouts over the course of almost 30 years.

TABLE T. South Korea, Strikes and Lockouts, by Year

	Total	Agriculture, hunting, forestry, and fishing	Mining and quarrying	Manufacturing	Electricity, gas, and water	Construction	Wholesale and retail trade, restaurants, and hotels	Transport, storage, and communication	Finance, insurance, real estate, and business services	Community, social, and personal services	Other activities
1969	7	0	0	...	...	...	0	0	0	...	...
1970	4	0	0	...	...	...	0	0	0	...	...
1971	10	0	0	...	...	...	0	0	0	...	...
1972	0	0	0	0	0	0	0	0	0	0	0
1973	0	0	0	0	0	0	0	0	0	0	0
1974	58	0	6	47	0	0	0	4	0	1	0
1975	52	0	0	43	0	1	0	6	0	2	0
1976	49	0	1	32	0	1	0	11	0	4	0
1977	58	0	0	41	0	0	0	17	0	0	0
1978	102	0	3	63	0	7	2	20	0	0	7
1979	105	0	4	61	0	12	0	22	0	0	6
1980	206	0	17	149	0	4	3	27	0	0	6
1981	186	0	7	125	0	13	2	28	0	0	11
1982	88	0	10	45	0	1	1	25	2	0	4
1983	98	0	16	33	0	8	2	35	2	0	2
1984	114	0	9	54	0	2	1	37	8	0	3
1985	265	0	10	144	0	9	0	84	0	0	18
1986	276	0	13	134	0	10	5	99	8	0	7
1987	3,749	0	135	1,955	11	19	81	1,365	92	91	0
1988	1,873	0	44	801	1	19	25	811	40	57	75
1989	1,616	0	65	927	1	25	29	428	51	45	45
1990	322	0	14	230	1	1	2	47	5	22	0
1991	234	0	5	163	0	0	4	42	9	11	0
1992	235	0	11	135	0	2	5	40	21	21	0
1993	144	0	0	93	0	2	7	21	12	9	0
1994	121	0	3	60	0	2	7	34	7	10	0
1995	88	0	0	57	0	0	5	8	9	9	0
1996	85	0	0	56	0	2	4	8	3	12	0
1997	78	0	0	42	1	0	4	14	5	12	...
1998	129	0	0	72	0	1	2	37	8	8	...
1999	198	0	0	116	0	5	7	26	24	20	...
2000	250	0	1	121	2	4	12	27	33	50	...
2001	235	1	0	117	4	6	10	38	20	43	...
2002	322	...	...	...	...	...	...	...	...	...	...
2003	320	...	...	...	...	...	...	...	...	...	...
2004	462	...	...	...	...	...	...	...	...	...	...
2005	287	...	...	...	...	...	...	...	...	...	...
2006	138	...	...	...	...	...	...	...	...	...	...
2007	115	...	...	...	...	...	...	...	...	...	...

FIGURE T.   South Korean: Strikes and Lockouts, by Year, 1969–2007

SUPPLY AND DEMAND FOR GRAIN, 1973–1980

Though reliable statistics from North Korea have been rare in recent decades, earlier statistics can provide insight into many situations facing the country. Table U lists the supply and demand for grain in the country at a pivotal time in its agricultural development. Since this time, the agricultural situation has worsened considerably, with demand far outpacing supply.

TABLE U.   North Korea, Supply and Demand for Grain, 1973–1980

Year	Rate of Change (%)	Supply (million tons)	Population (thousands)	Per Capita Need (kg)	Demand (million tons)	Surplus (+) or Shortage (−) (million tons)
1973	3.8	4.95	15,759	345	5.44	−0.51
1974	15.5	5.79	16,140	350	5.65	0.14
1975	9.8	6.36	16,480	355	5.85	0.51
1976	3.9	6.61	16,788	360	6.04	0.57
1977	6.2	7.02	17,084	365	6.24	0.78
1978	−7.1	6.52	17,379	370	6.43	0.09
1979	14.1	7.44	17,682	375	6.63	0.81
1980	0	7.44	17,999	380	6.84	0.60

Source: For population, Nicholas Eberstadt and Judith Banister, "Military Buildup in the DPRK: Some New Indications from North Korean Data," *Asian Survey* 31, no. 11 (November 1991): 1103 (extrapolations for 1991–1993).

COAL AND ELECTRICITY PRODUCTION, 1960–1984

Like Table U, Table V presents data from an important growth period in North Korea. Electrical production has been generally insufficient in the North for most of its history, but the situation has become increasingly dire since the mid-1980s. The failure to meet the 1984 goals noted below was the beginning of a long period of difficulties.

TABLE V.   North Korea, Coal and Electricity Production, 1960–1984

	Unit	1960	1970	1976	1984 Plan
Coal	Million tons	10.6	27.5	50.0	70.0
Electric power	Billion kWh	9.1	16.5	28.0	56.0

Source: For 1960, Korean Central News Agency, *Korean Central Yearbook* (P'yongyang, North Korea: Author, 1963), 338; for 1970, *Korean Central Yearbook* (1971), 227–228; for 1976, *Korean Central Yearbook* (1997), 281–282; for 1984, Kim Il-Sung, "On the Second Seven-Year Plan (1978–1984) for the Development of the National Economy of the People's Republic of Korea," Ordinance of the Supreme People's Assembly of the Democratic People's Republic of Korea, adopted at the First Session of the Sixth Supreme People's Assembly, December 17, 1977, *Chojakchip* (*Works*) 32 (1986): 548–549.

STATE REVENUE, 1956–2000

Table W lists the revenue collected by the North Korean government over the course of nearly five decades. Note that revenue initially grows rapidly but grows at generally decreasing rates after the mid-1970s.

TABLE W. North Korean State Revenue, 1956–2000

Year	Revenue (1,000 won)	Annual Growth Rate	Period Growth Rate	Year	Revenue (1,000 won)	Growth Rate	Period Growth Rate
1956	992,540			1978	15,657,300	13.5	9.8
1957	1,251,160	32.5*	23.4	1979	17,301,320	11.5	9.8
1958	1,529,140	33.6*	23.4	1980	18,139,230	4.8	9.8
1959	1,715,700	16.9*	23.4	1981	20,684,000	14.0	9.8
1960	2,019,310	17.7	23.4	1982	22,680,000	9.6	9.8
1961	2,400,000	18.8	23.4	1983	24,383,600	7.5	9.8
1962	2,896,360	20.7	23.4	1984	26,307,764	7.9	9.8
1963	3,144,820	8.6	8.3	1985	27,438,870	4.3	4.7
1964	3,498,780	11.1	8.3	1986	28,538,500	4.0	4.7
1965	3,573,840	2.1	8.3	1987	30,337,200	6.3	4.7
1966	3,720,210	4.1	8.3	1988	31,905,800	5.1	4.7
1967	4,106,630	12.0	8.3	1989	33,608,100	5.3	4.7
1968	5,023,700	22.3	8.3	1990	35,690,410	6.2	4.7
1969	5,319,030	6.0	8.3	1991	37,194,840	4.2	4.7
1970	6,232,200	17.0	8.3	1992	39,540,420	6.3	4.7
1971	6,357,350	2.0	12.6	1993	40,571,200	2.6	4.7
1972	7,430,300	16.9	12.6	1994	41,525,190	2.4	4.7
1973	8,599,310	15.7	12.6	1995	withheld	–	−17.5
1974	10,015,250	16.5	12.6	1996	withheld	–	−17.5
1975	11,586,300	5.7	12.6	1997	19,711,952	–	−17.5
1976	12,625,830	9.0	12.6	1998	19,790,800	0.4	1.2
1977	13,789,000	9.2	9.8	1999	19,801,030	0.1	1.2
				2000	20,405,320	3.1	1.2

*Revenues for 1956 through 1958 are reduced by foreign aid receipts in computing the growth rates. The share of foreign aid in state revenue is 16.5 percent, 12.2 percent, and 4.0 percent in 1956, 1957, and 1958, respectively. See Kim Il-Sung University Faculty, ed., *Uri Nara ui Inmin Kyongje Palchon 1948–1958* (P'yongyang, North Korea: National Publishing House, 1958), 293; Philip Rudolph, *North Korea's Political and Economic Structure* (New York: Institute of Pacific Relations, 1959), 41–42.

Source: Korean Central News Agency, *Korean Central Yearbook* (P'yongyang, North Korea: Author, yearly issues for years through the 1980s); *The People's Korea,* April 20, 1991, April 18, 1992, April 17, 1993, and April 16, 1994, for years 1990 through 1994; *Rodong Sinmun,* April 8, 1999, for 1997 and 1998; *Rodong Sinmun,* April 5, 2000, for 1999 and 2000. Revenue and expenditure totals as well as economic, social, defense, and administrative expenditures up to 1993 are presented in Eui-Gak Hwang, *The Korean Economies: A Comparison of North and South* (Oxford, UK: Clarendon Press, 1993), 150–151.

INTER-KOREAN TRADE, 1989–1996

In 1989, North Korea began trading on a small scale with South Korea through indirect methods. This inter-Korean trade, which came to include some direct transactions, marked a turning point in relations between the North and South and was among North Korea's most prominent reforms of the later 20th century. Table X documents the evolution of inter-Korean trade through the early 1990s. Table Y shows the value and nature of North Korean exports to the South during this period.

TABLE **X.** Inter-Korean Trade, Customs Clearance, 1988–1996

	Exports of North to South (in $ millions)			Imports of North from South (in $ millions)		Total Excl. Gold and Inputs for Consignment Production
	Gold	Goods on Consignment Production	Regular Merchandise	Inputs for Consignment Production	Regular Merchandise	
1988	0	0	0	0	0	0
1989	0	0	18.7	0	0.7	19.4
1990	0	0	12.3	0	1.2	13.5
1991	17.5	0.02	148.5	0.01	26.2	174.7
1992	63.4	0.6	136.7	0.4	12.4	149.7
1993	75.5	4.4	108.6	3.6	10.0	123.0
1994	65.6	16.6	121.3	12.0	13.4	151.3
1995	74.9	26.5	134.6	20.7	53.1	214.2 (259.2)*
1996	55.4	29.5	97.5	30.9	30.8	127.0

*The number in parentheses includes a $45 million approximation for the 150,000 tons of rice provided free in 1995.

Source: The National Unification Board, *Monthly Movement of North-South Interaction and Cooperation* (in Korean) 67 (January 1996): 58 for gold, 66 for consignment production, 58–59 for regular merchandise.

TABLE Y. North Korea, Direct Exports to South Korea, 1989–1996 (approval basis)

	No. of Direct Transactions (A)	No. of Total Transac- tions* (B)	A/B (%)	Value of Direct Exports* (C) ($)	Value of Total Exports* (D) ($)	C/D (%)
1989	0	57	0	0	22,235,000	0
1990	0	75	0	0	20,235,000	0
1991	3	328	0.9	8,550,000	165,996,000	5.2
1992	11	365	3.0	7,987,000	200,685,000	4.0
1993	14	478	2.9	3,447,000	188,528,000	1.8
1994	22	601	3.7	6,978,000	203,521,000	3.4
1995	46	755	6.0	21,063,000	236,075,000	8.9
1996	73	956	7.6	18,052,000	182,444,000	9.9

*Includes gold and goods produced on consignment.

Sources: The National Unification Board, *White Paper on Unification 1995* (Seoul, Korea: Author, 1995), 305 for (A); *Monthly Movement of North-South Interaction and Cooperation* (in Korean) 55 (January 1996): 54 for (B), 79 for (C) and (D); 67 (January 1997): 70–71 for (A) and (C), 48 for (B) and (D).

INTER-KOREAN TRADE, 2000–2005

In the early 21st century, the two Koreas have developed closer trade relations, marked by an increase in direct trade. Table Z shows the value of North to South and South to North trade. Note that South Korea exports significantly more to the North than the North exports to the South.

TABLE Z. Inter-Korean Trade Volume, 2000–2005

	2000	2001	2002	2003	2004	2005
North to South	152,373	176,170	271,575	289,252	258,039	340,281
(49.4)	(25.3)	(54.2)	(6.5)	(−10.8)	(31.9)	
South to North	272,775	226,787	370,155	434,965	439,001	715,472
(28.8)	(−16.9)	(63.2)	(17.5)	(0.9)	(63.0)	
Total	425,148	402,957	641,730	724,217	697,040	1,055,753
(27.5)	(−5.2)	(59.3)	(12.9)	(−3.8)	(51.5)	

Note: Units are in thousands USD. ( ) = year-on-year growth rate.

Source: South Korean Ministry of Unification (http://www.unikorea.go.kr/english/ENK/ENK0301R. jsp).

Holidays

SOUTH KOREA

Ancient agricultural holidays follow phases of the moon in the traditional lunar cycle. The official government holidays are celebrated according to the more modern solar calendar and commemorate national events.

January 1

New Year's Day (*Sinjeong*) The day is usually spent visiting family and friends, and gifts may be exchanged. Business and schools are closed.

Lunar New Year (*Sollal*) The celebration is more elaborate than the New Year's celebration, and the occasion is celebrated over a period of three days according to the lunar calendar. *Sollal*, together with *Ch'usok* (the autumn festival), are among the most important holidays. The Lunar New Year holiday is everyone's birthday, since everyone says that they are a year older with the beginning of a new year. Families prepare and serve special foods and perform memorial ceremonies to honor their ancestors. During this time, the young visit their elders and offer their formal bows of respect. Some favorite New Year's games include kiteflying and *yutnori*, a backgammon-like game, and seesawing on large seesaws (*Neol Ttwigi*).

407

March 1

Independence Movement Day (*Samil*) This day commemorates the March First Movement of 1919. On March 1, 1919, the Korean people declared their nation's independence from Japan. It was the event that led to the creation of the Provisional Government of the Republic of Korea. Special ceremonies are performed in places particularly associated with the independence movement, such as Tapgok Park in downtown Seoul.

Buddha's Birthday (*Seokgatansinil*) Buddha's birthday is celebrated on the eighth day of the fourth lunar month. On this day, there are ceremonies in Buddhist temples all over South Korea, and colorful paper lotus lanterns are hung in courtyard temples. The Sunday before Buddha's birthday, people light the lanterns and carry them as they walk in parades. The lanterns are believed to symbolize wisdom and mercy and to remove the dark spots in one's heart.

May 5

Children's Day (*Eorininal*) This day is dedicated to children. For years, it was a national holiday during which schools closed and parents devoted their day to their children by taking them to amusement parks, zoos, and other places of interest. It is no longer a national holiday, but it remains a day that is committed to the well-being of children. The founder of Children's Day was Pang Chong Hwan (1899–1931), who was an advocate for children and an independence fighter.

June 6

Memorial Day (*Hyeonchung-il*) This is a day dedicated to the men and women who died during their military service, particularly in the Korean War. Memorial services are held on this day at the National Cemetery in Seoul.

July 17

Constitution Day (*Jeheonjeol*) This day commemorates the adoption of the Constitution of the Republic of Korea in 1948 and is a holiday that now celebrates democracy in South Korea.

August 15

Liberation Day (*Gwangbokjeol*) On this day in 1945, Korea was liberated from Japan after 36 years of colonial rule. The word *Gwangbok* means "the restoration of light." There are parades and speeches that recall the difficulties of the struggle against Japan and the importance of Korean nationhood.

Harvest Moon Festival (*Ch'usok*) This is Korea's Thanksgiving Day and is held on the 15th day of the eighth lunar month. It is a two-day holiday and is the second-most-celebrated holiday next to Lunar New Year's Day. The ceremonies begin with families honoring the graves of their ancestors or holding memorial services within the home. If they are able to visit the graves, they bow before the graves and clean the area before the onset of the winter months. Older family members tell stories to the younger family members so that they will not only remember those who are deceased but also conduct themselves in a way that will honor ancestors and show respect for their parents. After the service, the family members eat together and celebrate. Traditional food that is prepared for the occasion includes crescent-shaped rice cakes (*songpyon*) stuffed with sesame seeds, chestnut paste, or beans. Other meals usually include grilled foods, broth, cooked vegetables, fermented cabbage (*kimch'i*), and fruit. *Ch'usok* is a time to pay respect to one's ancestors, honor one's elders, and have a thankful heart.

October 3

Foundation Day (*Gaecheonjeol*) National Foundation Day is a public holiday that commemorates the foundation of the Korean nation in 2333 BCE by the legendary founder of the nation, Tan'gun. *Gaecheonjeol* means "Heaven-Opened Day." On this holiday, government officials celebrate the occasion by hosting receptions, and foreign dignitaries and heads of state send messages of congratulations to them.

October 9

Han'gul Day (*Han'geullal*) This day recognizes the creation of *han'gul*, the native alphabet of the Korean language, in 1446. It is also a day when Koreans are reminded of their greatest king, King Sejong, the creator of *han'gul*. This holiday provides a break from work and regular school routines.

December 25

Christmas This is a special day for Christians in South Korea, but it is also a day of celebration for those who are not members of that faith. It is enjoyed as a winter holiday and one that involves gift giving and the receiving of gifts.

NORTH KOREA

The Democratic People's Republic of Korea (DPRK) continues to celebrate the Lunar New Year, Liberation Day, Foundation Day, and the Harvest Moon Festival. These holidays provide opportunities for the North Korean people to visit family members and eat special foods. Other holidays or special occasions for celebration are essentially political and involve huge parades and gymnastic performances.

February 16

Kim Jong-Il's Birthday "Dear Leader" Kim Jong-Il's birthday, also called the "Day of the Sun," has been decreed by the Central People's Committee as the "most festive national holiday." At times, Kim's birthday has been combined with the celebration of the Lunar New Year, and is one of North Korea's most celebrated events of the year.

March 8

International Women's Day According to North Korea's official KCNA News Agency, International Women's Day "is a significant day which brings pride and happiness, pleasure and glory to the Korean women pushing vigorously one of the wheels of revolution." Around the time of this holiday, the local media agencies produce works celebrating the role of women in North Korean society. As part of the festivities, North Korean men traditionally present gifts to women. In addition, female teachers at all levels of primary and advanced education are presented with bouquets by their students.

April 15

Kim Il-Sung's Birthday The birthday of North Korea's founding communist "Great Leader" is the country's most important celebration. Many people visit Kim's boyhood home in Manyongdae as well as the site of his public mausoleum, the Kumsusan Memorial Palace, in the capital, P'yongyang. In advance of the celebration, everyone from government workers to schoolchildren prepare songs, poetry, and other performances, which must follow a fixed format emphasizing Kim's historic importance. In addition, all children younger than 12 are given cookies and candy.

May 1

International Workers Day North Korea honors this global celebration of the world labor movement with spectacles performed by vast numbers of entertainers, soldiers, and athletes at P'yongyang's May Day Stadium—similar to October celebrations honoring the creation of the country's ruling Korean Workers' Party—along with parades of workers. In addition, senior party and government officials visit industrial plants to congratulate workers on their successes.

September 9

Foundation Day Foundation Day celebrates the anniversary of the September 9, 1948 establishment of the Democratic People's Republic of Korea. National pride is celebrated on this day each year with a major parade in the capital, P'yongyang, highlighted by dancing and the singing of patriotic songs.

October 10

Korean Workers' Party Anniversary The honoring of the October 1945 creation of North Korea's ruling communist party frequently coincides with the Arirang Festival, celebrated by hundreds of thousands of citizens in P'yongyang's May Day Stadium, who watch or participate in a spectacle performed by vast numbers of loyal North Koreans. In recent years, the celebration has featured displays of coordinated gymnastics, airborne acrobatics, traditional Korean dancing, and military T'aekwondo exercises, synchronized to a huge video and laser light show.

Organizations

GOVERNMENT ORGANIZATIONS

Embassy of the Republic of Korea
2450 Massachusetts Ave. NW
Washington, DC 20008
Telephone: (202) 939-5600
Fax: (202) 797-0595
E-mail: (general) usa@mofat.go.kr
Internet: http://www.koreaembassy.org

The South Korean embassy and consulates in the United States are an excellent source of information on U.S.-South Korean relations. The embassy Web site features news items, business and sports articles, a multimedia library, and topical information on South Korea that may be of interest to U.S. visitors and recent immigrants from Korea. There is even a section on Korean cuisine. The consulates and embassy provide consular services, including visa and passport applications and various services for immigrants.

SOUTH KOREAN CONSULATES GENERAL

Atlanta

229 Peachtree St., Suite 500
International Tower
Atlanta, GA 30303
Telephone: (404) 522-1611
Fax: (404) 521-3169
E-mail: atlanta@mofat.go.kr
Internet: https://www.koreanconsul.org/jsp/eng/aboutus.htm

Boston

One Gateway Center, Second Floor
Newton, MA 02458
Telephone: (617) 641-2830
Fax: (617) 641-2831
E-mail: kcgnoston@mofat.go.kr
Internet: http://usa-boston.mofat.go.kr/eng/am/usa-boston/main/index.jsp

Chicago

NBC Tower, Suite 2700
455 N. Cityfront Plaza Dr.
Chicago, IL 60611
Telephone: (312) 822-9485
Fax: (312) 822-9849
E-mail: chicago@mofat.go.kr
Internet: http://www.chicagoconsulate.org/en/index.php

Hagatna (Guam)

125 C Tun Jose Camacho St.
Tamuning, Guam 96931
Telephone: (671) 647-6488
Fax: (671) 649-1336
E-mail: kcongen@kuentos.guam.net
Internet: http://usa-hagatna.mofat.go.kr/eng/am/usa-hagatna/main/index.jsp

Honolulu

2756 Pali Highway
Honolulu, HI 96817
Telephone: (808) 595-6109
Fax: (808) 595-3046
E-mail: cghi@mofat.go.kr
Internet: http://usa-honolulu.mofat.go.kr/eng/am/usa-honolulu/main/index.jsp

Houston

1990 Post Oak Blvd. #1250
Houston, TX 77056
Telephone: (713) 961-0186
Fax: (713) 961-3340
E-mail: kbshon73@mofat.go.kr
Internet: http://www.koreahouston.org/english/index.htm

Los Angeles

3243 Wilshire Blvd.
Los Angeles, CA 90010
Telephone: (213) 385-9300
Fax: (213) 385-1849
E-mail: korea@koreanconsulatela.org
Internet: http://www.koreanconsulatela.org/english/index.htm

New York

335 E. 45th St.
New York, NY 10017
Telephone: (212) 752-1700
Fax: (212) 888-6320
E-mail: info@koreanconsulate.org
Internet: http://www.koreanconsulate.org

San Francisco

3500 Clay St.
San Francisco, CA 94118
Telephone: (415) 921-2251
Fax: (415) 921-5946
E-mail: consularsf@mofat.go.kr
Internet: http://usa-sanfrancisco.mofat.go.kr/eng/am/usa-sanfrancisco/main/index.jsp

Seattle

2033 Sixth Ave. #1125
Seattle, WA 98121
Telephone: (206) 441-1011
Fax: (206) 441-7912
E-mail: shhong86@mofat.go.kr
Internet: http://usa-seattle.mofat.go.kr/eng/am/usa-seattle/main/index.jsp

Washington, D.C.
Consulate of the Embassy
2320 Massachusetts Ave. NW
Washington, DC 20008
Telephone: (202) 939-5654
Fax: (202) 342-1597
E-mail: consular_usa@mofat.go.kr
Internet: http://www.koreaembassy.org

Ministry of Foreign Affairs and Trade
37 Sejongno
Doryeom-dong
Jongno-gu
Seoul 110-787
Republic of Korea
Telephone: (82-2)2100-2114
Fax: 02-2100-7999
E-mail: web@mofat.go.kr
Internet: http://www.mofat.go.kr/english/main/index.jsp?lang=eng

The Ministry of Foreign Affairs and Trade is responsible for South Korean foreign policy, foreign trade, cultural cooperation, and services for Koreans living abroad. It is the overarching ministry in charge of the embassies and consulates. The Web site provides information on ministry activities and other items relevant to South Korean missions abroad.

BUSINESS AND ECONOMIC ORGANIZATIONS

American Chamber of Commerce in Korea
#4501, Trade Tower 159-1
Samseong-dong
Gangnam-gu
Seoul 135-729
Republic of Korea
Telephone: (82-2) 564-2040
Fax: (82-2) 564-2050
E-mail: amchamrsvp@amchamkorea.org
Internet: http://www.amchamkorea.org

The American Chamber of Commerce in South Korea (AMCHAM Korea), founded in 1953, works to promote trade and business relations between South Korea and the United States and to represent the interests of its members in Korea. The organization's Web site features news items and a variety of resources related to business and investment in South Korea. AMCHAM Korea also offers seminars and regular briefings on conducting business in South Korea.

Convention and Exhibition Center
COEX, World Trade Center
Samseong-dong
Gangnam-gu
Seoul 135-731
Republic of Korea
Telephone: (82-2) 6000-0114
Fax: (82-2) 6000-1301
E-mail: pipi@coex.co.kr
Internet: http://www.coex.co.kr

The Seoul Convention and Exhibition Center (COEX), located in the Korean World Trade Center, hosts various trade fairs, conferences, and exhibitions. The largest such center in Asia, COEX is among the world's premier venues for trade shows and conventions. The site also includes a huge shopping mall, numerous restaurants and bars, and a variety of entertainment offerings.

Federation of Korean Industries
28-1 Yeouido-dong
Yeongdeungpo-gu
Seoul 150-010
Republic of Korea
Telephone: (82-2) 3771-0114
Fax: (82-2) 3771-0110
E-mail: webmaster@fki.or.kr
Internet: http://www.fki.or.kr/en

The Federation of Korean Industries (FKI) is an organization of major South Korean business conglomerates and industrial groups. The main objectives of the organization are to promote sound economic policies, internationalize the economy to further develop the free market system, facilitate the growth of the Korean economy, and respond to the challenges of globalization in the 21st century.

Korea Chamber of Commerce and Industry
45 Namdaemunno 4-ga
Jung-gu
Seoul 100-743
Republic of Korea
Telephone: (82-2) 6050-3114
Fax: (82-2) 6050-3400
E-mail: webmaster@korcham.net
Internet: http://english.korcham.net

The Korea Chamber of Commerce and Industry (KCCI), established in 1884, is the largest South Korean economic organization. It is made up of 71 local chambers and various other business conglomerates. The basic goal of the KCCI is to promote Korean trade, business, industry, and development.

Korea Economic Institute
1800 K St. NW, Suite 1010
Washington, DC 20006
Telephone: (202) 464-1982
Fax: (202) 464-1987
E-mail: info@keia.org
Internet: http://www.keia.org

The Korea Economic Institute (KEI) is an educational organization affiliated with the Korea Institute for International Economic Policy (KIEP) in Seoul that focuses on economic and trade relations between the United States and South Korea. Through programs, publications, and research, the KEI endeavors to educate Americans about U.S.–South Korean economic ties. The group's Web site includes some excellent resources, including economic data on both South Korea and North Korea.

Korea Institute for International Economic Policy
108 Yangjaedaero
Seocho-gu
Seoul 137-747
Republic of Korea
Internet: http://www.kiep.go.kr/eng

KIEP is a South Korean research and advocacy organization (think tank) that specializes in the role of Korea in the international economy. In addition to its advisory role with the South Korean government, KIEP puts on seminars and produces publications dealing with international and regional trade, business, and investment.

Korea International Trade Association
460 Park Ave., Suite 1101
New York, NY 10022
Telephone: (212) 421-8804 (ext. 26)
Fax: (212) 223-3827
E-mail: kitany@kita.net
Internet: http://us.kita.net

The Korea International Trade Association (KITA) is a trade promotion agency representing South Korea. The group assists with business arrangements, researches and consults on trade issues, and resolves grievances. Its mission is to promote South Korea's commercial potential in the global community.

Korean Federation of Small and Medium Business
16-2 Yeouido-dong
Yeongdeungpo-gu
Seoul 150-740
Republic of Korea
Telephone: (82-2) 2124-3114
Fax: (82-2) 3775-1981
E-mail: webmaster@kbiz.or.kr
Internet: http://www.kfsb.or.kr/english

The Korean Federation of Small and Medium Business (Kbiz) is an organization that promotes and supports small and medium-sized enterprises (SMEs) in South Korea. The group engages in research, organizational development, management consultation, bargaining, and many other efforts in order to help South Korean SMEs remain competitive in Korea and the wider global economy.

Korea Trade-Investment Promotion Agency
300-9 Yomgok-dong
Seocho-gu
Seoul 137-749
Republic of Korea
Telephone: (82-2) 3460-7114
Fax: (82-2) 3460-7777
Internet: http://www.english.kotra.co.kr

The Korea Trade-Investment Promotion Agency (KOTRA) is a South Korean national agency dedicated to promoting global trade and investment in South Korea. KOTRA has 115 offices in more than 101 countries, including the Trade Center in Los Angeles. The organization assists foreign countries in locating business partners in South Korea, organizes trade fairs and trade missions in the United States and Korea, provides investment and technology services, sponsors seminars, and provides information on the South Korean economy and business practices. KOTRA also operates a network of localized Korea Trade Centers around the world.

KOTRA Trade Centers

Chicago
111 E. Wacker Dr., Suite 2229
Chicago, IL 60601
Telephone: (312) 644-4323
Fax: (312) 644-4879
E-mail: info@kotrachicago.com

Dallas

3030 LBJ Freeway, Suite 1150
Dallas, TX 75234
Telephone: (972) 243-9300
Fax: (972) 243-9301
E-mail: ktcdfw@kotradallas.com
Internet: http://www.kotradallas.com

Detroit

2000 Town Center, Suite 2850
Southfield, MI 48075
Telephone: (248) 355-4911
Fax: (248) 355-9002
E-mail: detroit@kotradtt.com

Los Angeles

4801 Wilshire Blvd., Suite 104
Los Angeles, CA 90010
Telephone: (323) 954-9500
Fax: (323) 954-1707
E-mail: jaktc@hanmail.net

Miami

One Biscayne Tower, Suite 3770
Miami, FL 33131
Telephone: (305) 374-4648
Fax: (305) 375-9332
E-mail: ktcmiami@aol.com

New York

460 Park Ave., Suite 402
New York, NY 10022
Telephone: (212) 826-0900
Fax: (212) 888-4930
E-mail: kotrany@hotmail.com

Silicon Valley

1875 S. Grant St., Suite 640
San Mateo, CA 94402
Telephone: (650) 571-8483
Fax: (650) 571-8065
E-mail: info@kotrasf.org
Internet: http://www.kotrasf.org

Washington, D.C.

1225 Eye St. NW, Suite 920
Washington, DC 20005
Telephone: (202) 857-7919
Fax: (202) 857-7923
E-mail: washington@kotra.or.kr

CULTURAL AND EDUCATIONAL ORGANIZATIONS

Asia Foundation
465 California St. #9
San Francisco, CA 94104
Telephone: (415) 982-4640
Fax: (415) 392-8863
E-mail: info@asiafound.org
Internet: http://www.asiafoundation.org

Founded in 1954, the Asia Foundation is a nongovernmental organization that works with public and private partners around the world to promote development in the Asia-Pacific region. Among the organization's primary focuses are good governance and economic reform. The Asia Foundation is headquartered in San Francisco and has numerous Asian branch offices, including a Korean office based in Seoul.

Branch Offices

South Korea

Seventh Floor, Yi Yangwon Building
63-7 Gyeongun-dong
Jongno-gu
Seoul 110-310
Republic of Korea
E-mail: tafkorea@asiafound.org
Internet: http://www.asiafoundation.or.kr/e_home/index.php

Washington, D.C.

1779 Massachusetts Ave. NW, Suite 815
Washington, DC 20036
Telephone: (202) 588-9420
E-mail: info@asiafound-dc.org
Internet: http://www.asiafoundation.org

New York Asia Society

725 Park Ave.
New York, NY 10021

Telephone: (212) 288-6400
Fax: (212) 517-8315
E-mail: info@asiasoc.org
Internet: http://www.asiasociety.org

The Asia Society is an international organization based in the United States that strives to bolster cultural ties between Asia and the United States. A nonprofit group founded in 1956, the organization primarily supports artistic and academic efforts, sponsoring art exhibitions, film screenings, lectures, and seminars and producing publications on Asian art, culture, and history.

Association for Asian Studies
1021 E. Huron St.
Ann Arbor, MI 48104
Telephone: (734) 665-2490
Fax: (734) 665-3801
Internet: http://www.aasianst.org

The Association of Asian Studies (AAS) is a scholarly association dedicated to the study of the peoples, culture, and history of Asia. The various efforts of the AAS include the publication of the *Journal of Asian Studies* and *Education About Asia* periodicals and the *Asia Past and Present* and *Key Issues in Asian Studies* book series, seminars and lectures, and communication facilitation among those interested in the study of Asia. The AAS includes four regional councils; endeavors concerning the Koreas are presided over by the Northeast Asia Council.

Council for International Exchange of Scholars
3007 Tilden St. NW, Suite 5L
Washington, DC 20008-3009
Telephone: (202) 686-4000
Fax: (202) 362-3442
E-mail: cieswebmaster@cies.iie.org
Internet: http://www.cies.org

The Council for International Exchange of Scholars (CIES) is a division of the Institute of International Education (IIE) based in New York City. IIE is a private nonprofit organization that assists the Department of State in administering Fulbright grants for graduate study. College graduates, graduate students, and PhD candidates in Korean studies may apply for Fulbright grants.

Korea Academy for Educators
505 Plymouth Rd.
San Marino, CA 91108
Internet: http://www.koreaacademy.org

The mission of the Korea Academy for Educators (KAFE) is to provide opportunities for educators to learn about Korean history and culture and the Korean-American experience. This is accomplished through five-day seminars, weekend workshops, and presentations for school districts and individual schools. Since 2004, more than 1,000 educators from throughout the United States have participated in KAFE programs. A limited number of fellowships are available for educators to participate in the summer seminar program.

Korea Foundation
Diplomatic Center Building, 10th Floor
2558 Nambusunhwanno
Seocho-gu
Seoul 137-072
Republic of Korea
Telephone: (82-2) 2046-8500
Fax: (82-2) 3463-6076
E-mail: webmaster@kf.or.kr
Internet: http://www.kf.or.kr

The Korea Foundation provides financial support to students in Korean Studies in the form of fellowships and organizes educational events on Korea, including workshops, conferences, and Korean language classes. It also publishes books on Korean culture, current events, and history. The foundation's Korea Studies Workshops, which bring educators to South Korea to participate in a 12-day program, are available to full-time social studies teachers and administrators at the high school and junior high school levels.

Korean-American Association
1229 Somerset Palace
85 Susong-dong
Jongno-gu
Seoul 110-885
Republic of Korea
Telephone: (82-2) 6730-8881 ext. 2
Fax: (82-2) 6730-8883
E-mail: koram@koram.or.kr
Internet: http://www.i-kaa.org

The objective of the Korean-American Association is to promote friendship and understanding between peoples of the Republic of Korea and the United States and to strengthen economic, social, and cultural relations between the two countries. Established in 1962, it is a nonprofit, nongovernmental organization with binational membership. The association offers seminars and musical concerts, holds exhibitions, arranges tours to visit U.S. military bases in Korea, and organizes American Korean associations in cities in the United States.

Korean Cultural Center of Los Angeles
5505 Wilshire Blvd.
Los Angeles, CA 90036
Telephone: (323) 936-7141
Fax: (323) 936-5712
Internet: http://www.kccla.org

The Korean Cultural Center actively serves the Los Angeles area by providing information on Korea. The center contains an extensive library of more than 15,000 volumes in both English and Korean and a video collection. The library furnishes information on the arts, history, language, philosophy, and contemporary affairs. Galleries exhibit traditional and modern art. Additional activities include a film night, cultural performances, workshops, and Korean language classes. The museum displays a permanent collection of historical and contemporary Korean artifacts along with a variety of replicas of historical pieces from Korea's dynastic kingdoms.

Korean Cultural Service of New York
460 Park Ave., Sixth Floor
New York, NY 10022
Telephone: (212) 759-9550
Fax: (212) 688-8640
E-mail: info@koreanculture.org
Internet: http://www.koreanculture.org

The Korean Cultural Service is an information resource for students of Korean culture and U.S.-Korean relations. In addition to guiding students hoping to study through exchange programs, the service is home to a gallery and a library housing more than 16,000 volumes and multimedia resources. The service also hosts performing arts events and lectures and seminars on Korea.

Korean Culture and Content Agency
5505 Wilshire Blvd.
Korea Center Building
Los Angeles, CA 90036
Telephone: (323) 935-5001
Fax: (323) 935-1101
E-mail: la@kocca.or.kr
Internet: http://www.koreacontent.org/officelan/frontus/index.html

The Korea Culture and Content Agency (KOCCA) was created by the Ministry of Korean Culture and Tourism in 2001 with the goal of developing Korean cultural products and promoting them abroad. KOCCA acts as a link between South Korean producers of such cultural products as comics, music, and games and their international distributors.

Korean Culture and Information Service
3-4 Floors, FNC
Kolon Corp.
15 Hyojaro
Jongno-gu
Seoul 110-040
Republic of Korea
Telephone: (82-2) 3981-800
Fax: (82-2) 3981-882
E-mail: webmaster@korea.net
Internet: http://www.kois.go.kr/kois_main_en.asp

The Korean Information Service administers the news and information Web site Korea.net. It provides support to international media in their coverage of Korea and disseminates educational media materials about Korea overseas.

Korean National Commission for UNESCO
3F 50-14 Myong-dong 2-ga
Jung-gu
Seoul 100-810
Republic of Korea
Telephone: (82-2) 755-1105
Fax: (82-2) 755-6667
Internet: http://www.unesco.or.kr/eng

The Korean National Commission for UNESCO (KNCU) is the agency tasked with carrying out the goals of the United Nations Educational, Scientific, and Cultural Organization (UNESCO) in the Republic of Korea. Among its many programs, KNCU organizes the annual International Youth Camp, which gathers together young adults (ages 18–27) to promote international cooperation on projects in human rights and the preservation of historic Korean cultural sites and the environment.

The Korea Society
950 Third Ave., Eighth Floor
New York, NY 10022
Telephone: (212) 759-7525
Fax: (212) 759-7530
Internet: http://www.koreasociety.org

The Korea Society is a nonprofit organization whose mission is promoting dialogue and cooperation between South Korea and the United States. It partners with the Korea Foundation in providing fellowships to K–12 educators, and via its Web site, it makes available extensive lesson plans on Korea that are developed by its former fellows. It also supports Project Bridge in Los Angeles and New York, an intercultural youth leadership program that annually takes students to Korea.

Overseas Koreans Foundation
Sixth Floor, Diplomatic Center 2558
Nambusunhwan-ro
Seocho-gu
Seoul 137-072
Republic of Korea
Telephone: (82-2) 3463-6500
Fax: (82-2) 3463-3999
E-mail: pr@okf.or.kr
Internet: http://www.okf.or.kr

The main objectives of the Overseas Koreans Foundation are to help overseas Koreans maintain a sense of identity and their social status in the countries of residence and to find an effective way to develop their potential as part of the Korean population throughout the world.

Pacific Century Institute
8944 Mason Ave.
Chatsworth, CA 91311-6107
Telephone: (818) 227-6620
Fax: (818) 704-4336
E-mail: pci@pacificcenturyinst.org
Internet: http://www.pacificcenturyinst.org

The Pacific Century Institute (PCI) is dedicated to providing greater communication between the nations of the Pacific Rim. Headquartered in the greater Los Angeles area, PCI has overseas offices in Korea and Japan. It hosts conferences and seminars, sponsors fellowships, and coordinates the Project Bridge program with New York's Korea Society.

Branch Offices

Japan

c/o Ko Shioya
Seta 2-19-1
Setagaya-ku
Tokyo 158-0095
Japan
Telephone/Fax: 813-03707-0369

Kentucky

c/o Kenneth J. Tuggle, Esq.
Frost Brown Todd, LLC
400 W. Market St., 32nd Floor
Louisville, KY 40202-3363
Telephone: (502) 568-0269
Fax: (502) 581-1087

South Korea

c/o Chung-in Moon

Yonsei University

134 Sinchon-dong

Seodaemun-gu

Seoul, 120-740

Republic of Korea

Telephone: (82-2) 2123-3542

Fax: (82-2) 362-1915

TOURISM ORGANIZATIONS

Korea Tourism Organization

40 Cheongyecheonno

Jung-gu

Seoul 100-180

Republic of Korea

Telephone: (82-2) 7299-497 ext. 499

Fax: (82-2) 319-0086

E-mail: webmaster@mail.knto.or.kr

Internet: http://www.knto.or.kr

The function of the Korea National Tourism Organization (KNTO) is to promote and facilitate tourism. Firsthand information and free brochures are provided to assist with trip planning. While in South Korea, travelers should seek the assistance of the KNTO Tourist Information Center, which provides numerous in-country services, including the services of a team of guides that can provide on-site translation and interpretation.

Toll-free number for U.S. offices: (800) 868-7567

Branch Offices

Chicago

737 N. Michigan Ave., Suite 910

Chicago, IL 60611

Telephone: (312) 981-1717

Fax: (312) 981-1721

E-mail: chicago@kntoamerica.com

Internet: http://www.tour2korea.com

Los Angeles

5509 Wilshire Blvd.

Korea Center Building

Los Angeles, CA 90036
Telephone: (323) 634-0280
Fax: (323) 634-0281
E-mail: la@kntoamerica.com
Internet: http://www.tour2korea.com

New York

2 Executive Dr., Suite 750
Fort Lee, NJ 07024
Telephone: (201) 585-0909
Fax: (201) 585-9041
E-mail: ny@kntoamerica.com
Internet: http://www.tour2korea.com

KOREAN AMERICAN ORGANIZATIONS

Korean American Adoptee Adoptive Family Network
P.O. Box 5585
El Dorado Hills, CA 95762
Telephone: (916) 933-1447
E-mail: kaanet@kaanet.com
Internet: http://www.kaanet.com

The Korean American Adoptee Adoptive Family Network is a group dedicated to building contacts and encouraging conversation among the 100,000 Koreans adopted into the United States, their adoptive families, and the broader Korean community. The network holds yearly conferences.

Korean American Coalition
3727 W. Sixth St., Suite 515
Los Angeles, CA 90020
Telephone: (213) 365-5999
Fax: (213) 380-7990
E-mail: info@kacla.org
Internet: http://www.kacla.org

The Korean American Coalition (KAC) is headquartered in Los Angeles and has numerous active chapters scattered across the United States. A nonprofit and non-partisan organization, KAC operates as a bilingual advocate for Korean Americans in the public sphere, promoting their civil rights and serving as a resource for information both for and about their communities.

Chapter Offices

Georgia

P.O. Box 920745
Norcross, GA 30010
Internet: http://www.kacatl.org

Illinois

5903 N. Campbell Ave., Unit 2
Chicago, IL 60659
E-mail: kachicago@gmail.com
Internet: http://www.kac-chicago.org

Colorado

P.O. Box 111111
Aurora, CO 80111
Telephone: (303) 555-1532
E-mail: brucegjohnson@hotmail.com
Internet: http://www.kacco.org

Texas

11422 Harry Hines Blvd., #125
Dallas, TX 75229
Telephone: (469) 235-1633
Fax: (214) 884-0555
E-mail: info@kacdfw.org
Internet: http://www.kacdfw.org

Washington, D.C.

1001 Connecticut Ave. NW, Suite 730
Washington, DC 20036
Telephone: (202) 296-9560
Fax: (202) 296-9568
E-mail: kacdc@kacdc.org
Internet: http://www.kacdc.org

Washington

1611 116th Ave. NE, #225
Bellevue, WA 98004
Telephone: (866) 399-5277
E-mail: info@kacwashington.org
Internet: http://www.kacwashington.org

Korean American Resource and Cultural Center
6146 N. Lincoln Ave.
Chicago, IL 60659
Telephone: (773) 588-9158
Fax: (773) 588-9159
E-mail: krcc@chicagokrcc.org
Internet: http://www.chicagokrcc.org

The Korean American Resource and Cultural Center (KRCC) is a Korean empowerment organization founded by low-income Korean American immigrant youth in 1994. It advocates for Korean American communities in the greater Chicago area and provides social services.

Korean Resource Center of Los Angeles
900 S. Crenshaw Blvd.
Los Angeles, CA 90019
Telephone: (323) 937-3718
Fax: (323) 937-3526
E-mail: krcla@krcla.org
Internet: http://www.krcla.org

A nonprofit organization founded in 1983, the Korean Resource Center of Los Angeles serves the Korean American community with programs in health access, education, and voter empowerment.

Koreatown Youth and Community Center
3727 W. Sixth St., Suite 300
Los Angeles, CA 90020
Telephone: (213) 365-7400
Fax: (213) 927-0017
E-mail: info@kyccla.org
Internet: http://www.kyccla.org

Established in 1975, the nonprofit Koreatown Youth and Community Center (KYCC) serves the residents of Los Angeles's multiethnic Koreatown neighborhood. The KYCC's programs include housing assistance, early childhood education, and academic support projects. The organization aims to support recent Korean immigrants and economically struggling youth.

National Korean American Service and Education Consortium, Inc.
900 S. Crenshaw Blvd.
Los Angeles, CA 90019
Telephone: (323) 937-3703
Fax: (323) 937-3753
E-mail: nakasec@nakasec.org
Internet: http://www.nakasec.org

Founded in 1994, the National Korean American Service and Education Consortium (NAKASEC) is a Korean American advocacy group that works in areas including immigrant rights, education, and research. NAKASEC's programs work to protect the most vulnerable segments of the Korean American community, including seniors, youth, and new immigrants.

Women's Organization Reaching Koreans
6105 Harvard Blvd., #220
Los Angeles, CA 90004
Telephone: (213) 239-0784

Women's Organization Reaching Koreans (WORK) provides resources to Korean American women to advance professionally and personally. Operating bilingually, WORK serves as a voice for Korean American women in the public arena.

Young Korean American Service and Education Center
136-19 41st Ave., Third Floor
Flushing, NY 11355
Telephone: (718) 460-5600
Fax: (718) 445-0032
E-mail: ykasec@ykasec.org
Internet: http://www.ykasec.org

The Young Korean American Service and Education Center (YKASEC) is a grass-roots Korean American organization dedicated to encouraging Korean Americans participation in civic life, protecting the rights of Korean immigrants, and providing services to more vulnerable members of the Korean American community, including the elderly, those with low income, and those without English proficiency.

Annotated Bibliography of Recommended Works on Korea

The book titles listed below are organized into categories that correspond to the chronology of this book's chapters. Considerable thought has been given to include the most highly regarded, current, and readable sources. For additional resources, consult the references at the end of each chapter.

In the following sections, a few books and Web sites are mentioned more than once. The purpose of this is to assist readers with interests in specific areas—for example, South Korea's economy—and to guide students who are seeking a particular focus.

Periodicals, literature, and Internet sites are listed after the book resources.

BOOK RESOURCES

Geography and History

Bird, Isabella Lucy. *Korea and Her Neighbors*. Boston: Adamant Media Corp., 2004.
   The author was a famous traveler and writer in the late 19th century who visited Korea four times between 1894 and 1897. Her book is a fascinating record of the Korean people, their customs, and their way of life just after the Sino-Japanese War (1894–1895). Bird's account includes her observations about Queen Min as well as the Liancourt Rocks (two islets and 35 smaller rocks in the East Sea [Sea of Japan]). The dispute over the Liancourt Rocks continues to be a diplomatic issue between South Korea and Japan to the present day.

Breen, Michael. *The Koreans: Who They Are, What They Want, Where Their Future Lies.* New York: Saint Martin's Press, 1998.
This is an informative, personal account of the Koreas and the Korean people today.

Cumings, Bruce. *Korea's Place in the Sun: A Modern History.* New York: W. W. Norton, 1997.
Cumings's work is an engaging and informative history that focuses on the 20th century. The author devotes a chapter to Korean Americans.

Eckert, Carter, et al. *Korea Old and New: A History.* Seoul, Korea: Ilchokak Publishers, 1990.
This source is one of the most widely consulted and acclaimed books about Korea. It is used as a basic text in Korean Studies courses.

Hamel, Hendrik. *Hamel's Journal and a Description of the Kingdom of Korea (1653–1666).* Seoul, Korea: Royal Asiatic Society, 1994.
Hamel's fascinating account is the earliest report in a Western language about Korea, its people, and their customs.

Korea Overseas Information Service. *A Handbook of Korea.* Seoul: Korea Overseas Information Service, 2003.
This volume is a very helpful introductory resource on information about the Koreas. The book includes history, geography, government, foreign policy, the economy, society, beliefs and religion, culture and the arts, and sports and tourism.

Hart-Landsberg, Martin. *Korea: Division, Reunification, and U.S. Foreign Policy.* New York: Monthly Review Press, 1998.
This work is an excellent introduction to the causes and consequences of the Korean War. The author evaluates U.S. foreign policy and sees North-South reunification as the optimal solution for Korea.

Kim, Yung-Chung, ed. *Women of Korea: A History from Ancient Times to 1945.* Seoul, Korea: Ewha Womans University Press, 1976.
This is one of the most thorough studies to date of the status, role, and activities of Korean women through the once-united country's long history.

Korean Spirit & Culture Promotion Project. *Admiral Yi Sun-sin.* Seoul, Korea: Diamond Sutra Recitation Group (Chungwoo Buddhist Foundation), n.d.
The book introduces the reader to the life and achievements of one of Korea's great military heroes. The entire book may be found at the following Web site: http://www.kscpp.net.

Lee, Ki-baik. *A New History of Korea.* Seoul, Korea: Ilchokak Publishers, 1984.
Lee's book is considered one of the most detailed, scholarly, and reliable sources available on Korean history.

Lee, Peter H., ed. *Sourcebook of Korean Civilization.* Vol. I: *From Early Times to the Sixteenth Century.* New York: Columbia University Press, 1993.
This book is one of the most comprehensive English-language anthologies of primary source material on Korean civilization ever assembled. It incorporates documents related to economic, political, social, and cultural developments in Korea from ancient times to the 16th century.

Lee, Peter H., ed. *Sourcebook of Korean Civilization.* Vol. II: *From the Seventeenth Century to the Modern Period.* New York: Columbia University Press, 1996.
This volume includes primary source materials related to economic, political, social, and cultural developments in Korea from the 17th century to 1945.

Lynn, Hyung Gu. *Bipolar Orders: The Two Koreas since 1989*. Black Point, NS, Canada: Fernwood Publishing, 2007.

Carter Eckert, Harvard University professor of Korean history, states that "among the plethora of recent books on Korea, this is one that truly stands out" as an essential book for anyone interested in contemporary Korea. While the author says he is not against reunification, he examines whether it is a "necessary or inevitable process."

Macdonald, Donald Stone. *The Koreans: Contemporary Politics and Society*. Boulder, CO: Westview Press, 1990.

This is an eminently readable, accurate, and balanced account of the Korean people today. The book covers Korean society and culture, economic and political development in North and South Korea, foreign relations, and the challenges of reunification.

Nahm, Andrew. *A Panorama of 5,000 Years: A Korean History*. Seoul, Korea: Hollym Publishers, 1987.

This book is a reliable, concise introduction to Korean history and culture that contains beautiful illustrations.

Oberdorfer, Don. *The Two Koreas: A Contemporary History*. Reading, MA: Addison-Wesley, 1997.

Oberdorfer, a highly regarded authority on modern Korean history, provides the reader with an enlightening and balanced account of historical and political developments on the Korean peninsula since 1945. Particularly noteworthy is Oberdorfer's account of how close the United States came to war with North Korea in 1994.

Oh, Kongdan, and Ralph C. Hessig. *North Korea through the Looking Glass*. Washington, DC: Brookings Institution Press, 2000.

This book will become basic reading for those interested in understanding why North Korea has survived in spite of the fall of the global socialist system. It is a fascinating (and disturbing) account of a mystifying nation. The book provides insight into the extraordinary challenges of North-South reunification.

Saccone, Richard. *Fifty Famous People Who Helped Shape Korea*. Seoul, Korea: Hollym Corp., 1993.

Saccone's book is the only English-language edition that focuses extensively on bibliographical information on Korean monarchs, politicians, military figures, philosophers, religious figures, businesspersons, scholars, artists, writers, composers, publishers, and patriots.

Seth, Michael J. *A Concise History of Korea: From the Neolithic Period through the Nineteenth Century*. New York: Rowman & Littlefield Publishers, 2006.

Seth's survey is one of the most engaging, well-written, and insightful books on premodern Korean history. It is a detailed chronological narrative that emphasizes early social, cultural, and political events. Throughout the book, comparisons are drawn between developments in Korea, China, and Japan.

Suh, Dae-Sook. *Kim Il Sung: The North Korean Leader*. New York: Columbia University Press, 1998.

Suh's book is considered one of the most definitive sources on Kim Il-Sung and his impact on the history and politics of North Korea.

Government and Politics

Eckert, Carter, et al. *Korea Old and New: A History*. Seoul, Korea: Ilchokak Publishers, 1990.

This book is an invaluable resource for understanding the political development of Korea from ancient times to the 1990s. The work is particularly strong in its coverage of political developments from the colonial period to modern times.

Kim, Byoung-Lo Philo. *Two Koreas in Development: A Comparative Study of Principles and Strategies of Capitalist and Communist Third World Development*. New Brunswick, NJ: Transaction Publishers, 1992.
The book provides comparisons of the economic, political, and social development of both North and South Korea since 1945. One chapter is devoted exclusively to political development.

Oh, John Kie-chian. *Korean Politics: The Quest for Democratization and Economic Development*. Ithaca, NY: Cornell University Press, 1999.
This is one of the finest books available on the evolution of democracy in South Korea. The author enlightens the reader about the impact of tradition on contemporary politics. It is an invaluable and engaging resource.

Oh, Kongdan, and Ralph C. Hessig. *North Korea through the Looking Glass*. Washington, DC: Brookings Institution Press, 2000.
The book is a very informative (though disturbing) commentary on the ideology, leadership, politics, and foreign policy of North Korea during the 1990s.

Yun, Phillip, and Gi-Wook Shin, eds. *North Korea: 2005 and Beyond*. Washington, DC: Brookings Institution Press, 2006.
In this work, leading authorities provide an understanding of contemporary North Korea and recommend various diplomatic approaches to solve difficulties in dealing with North Korea and a divided peninsula. It encourages thoughtful, pragmatic discussion about a very mysterious nation.

Economy

Eckert, Carter, et al. *Korea Old and New: A History*. Seoul, Korea: Ilchokak Publishers, 1990.
This resource provides a clear explanation of the economic development of South Korea from 1945 to 1990.

Harvie, Charles, and Hyun-Hoon Lee. *Korea's Economic Miracle: Fading of Reviving*. New York: Palgrave Macmillan, 2003.
This is a very useful book, especially on the topic of South Korea's *chaebol* and needed reforms.

Kim, Byoung-Lo Philo. *Two Koreas in Development: A Comparative Study of Principles and Strategies of Capitalist and Communist Third World Development*. New Brunswick, NJ: Transaction Publishers, 1990.
Kim describes the economic, political, and social development of both North and South Korea since 1945. An entire chapter is devoted to economic development.

Kim, Samuel S., ed. *Koreas Globalization*. New York: Cambridge University Press, 2000.
Twelve scholars tackle various aspects of President Kim Young-Sam's bold move toward globalization in 1994. Charts, footnotes, and an extensive bibliography are included. The book is available in paperback.

Noland, Marcus. *Avoiding the Apocalypse: The Future of the Two Koreas*. Washington, DC: Institute for International Economics, 2000.

Noland provides the reader with a very thorough description of the development of two diverse economies and takes into account the difficulties of making any detailed statements about the secretive North Korean economy. The opinions of others are weighed and charted. There is much detailed information throughout the book, and it includes extensive footnotes and a bibliography (available in paperback).

Song, Byung-Nak. *The Rise of the Korean Economy*. New York: Oxford University Press, 1997.
A detailed account of South Korea's economic transformation from an impoverished third world country to one of the world's leading industrialized nations. Song makes interesting comparisons with the Japanese economy. There are 60 useful tables along with a chronology. This is a very readable book that is available in paperback.

Religion and Thought

Buswell, Robert E., Jr., ed. *Religions of Korea in Practice*. Princeton, NJ: Princeton University Press, 2007.
This publication is the first anthology to bring together a comprehensive selection of original sources covering the whole range of religious practices in both premodern and contemporary Korea.

Clark, Donald N. *Christianity in Modern Korea*. Lanham, MD: University Press of America, 1986.
This is considered one of the most highly regarded books on Christianity in Korea and its role from the late 18th century to recent times.

Social Classes and Ethnicity

Lett, Denise Potrzeba. *In Pursuit of Status: The Making of South Korea's "New" Urban Middle Class*. Cambridge, MA: Harvard University Asia Center, 1998.
The author argues that South Korea's contemporary urban middle class exhibits upper-class characteristics that reflect a culturally inherited tendency to seek high status. She believes that the legacy of Confucianism has been the driving force behind the development of a new middle class in South Korea.

Shin, Gi-Wook. *Ethnic Nationalism in Korea: Genealogy, Politics, and Legacy*. Stanford, CA: Stanford University Press, 2006.
This book explains the roots, politics, and legacy of Korean ethnic nationalism, which is based on the sense of a shared bloodline and ancestry. Shin examines how this notion of a blood-based nation has become a dominant source of Korean identity from the 20th century to the present.

Women and Marriage

Clark, Donald N. *Culture and Customs of Korea*. Westport, CT: Greenwood Press, 2000.
This book provides an excellent introduction to the Korean people and their religion, arts, literature, daily life, and customs. It includes a concise history of Korea, information on life in North Korea today, and a chapter titled "Gender, Marriage, and the Lives of Korean Women."

Kim, Yung-Chung. *Women of Korea: A History from Ancient Times to 1945*. Seoul, Korea: Ewha Womans University Press, 1976.

Kim provides one of the most comprehensive studies to date of the status, activities, and role of Korean women through the long history of Korea.

Education

Korea Overseas Information Service. *A Handbook of Korea*. Seoul: Korea Overseas Information Service, 2003.

This volume includes Korean history, government, foreign policy, economy, society, religion and thought, culture and the arts, and sports and tourism. A section devoted to Korean education provides information on that subject from the fourth century to current times.

Kim, Yung-Chung. *Women of Korea: A History from Ancient Times to 1945*. Seoul, Korea: Ewha Womans University Press, 1976.

This is one of the most comprehensive studies to date of the status, role, and activities of Korean women through the once-united country's long history. The author includes information on the role of women in bringing about needed changes in many areas, but particularly in the field of education.

Seth, Michael J. *Education Fever: Society, Politics, and the Pursuit of Schooling in South Korea*. Honolulu: University of Hawai'i Press, 2002.

The author provides a fascinating account of the social demand for education and how it has shaped nearly every aspect of South Korean society. Seth also explores the problems of the South Korean educational system.

CULTURE

General

Kim, Joungwon, ed. *Koreana: Korean Cultural Heritage*. Vol. 4: *Traditional Lifestyles*. Seoul, Korea: Samsung Moonhwa Press, 1997.

This is the fourth volume in a series created by the Korean Foundation to foster a better understanding of Korean Studies abroad. It examines such aspects as clothing, food, housing, family systems, rites of passage, regional traditions, and folk culture. A wealth of beautiful photographs augments the text, bringing traditional Korean culture alive.

Koo, John H., and Andrew C. Nahm, eds. *An Introduction to Korean Culture*. Elizabeth, NJ: Hollym Corp., 1997.

This work provides a thorough introduction to Korean culture.

Lee, O-Young. *Things Korean*. Rutland, VT: Charles E. Tuttle Co., 1994.

O-Young Lee, a former South Korean minister of culture, provides a useful guide to traditional culture with more than 100 memorable photographs and illustrations.

Language (also see "Korean Language" under Web Sites)

Cho, Young-Mee, et al. *Integrated Korean Textbook* and *Workbook* (*Beginning, Intermediate, Advanced Intermediate, Advanced*, and *High Advanced 1* and *2*). KLEAR Textbooks in Korean Language. Honolulu: University of Hawai'i Press, 2000.

There are 10 books included in this series along with workbooks. The series has been developed to enhance speaking, listening, reading, writing, and culture. *Integrated Korean* is a project of the Korean Language Education and Research Center (KLEAR) with the support of the Korea Foundation.

Korean Spirit & Culture Promotion Project. *King Sejong the Great: The Everlasting Light of Korea*. Seoul, Korea: Diamond Sutra Recitation Group (Chungwoo Buddhist Foundation), n.d.
This booklet is an engaging and well-written account of King Sejong's achievements, especially the coverage of the invention of *han'gul* (Korean written language). The entire book can be found at http://www.kscpp.net.

National Institute of the Korean Language. *Korean Grammar 1 for Non-Koreans*. Seoul, Korea: Communication Books, 2006.
This is one of the most extensive Korean grammar handbooks published in the Korean language for teaching grammar to non-Koreans.

Etiquette

Hur, Sonja Vegdahl, and Ben Seunghwa Hur. *Culture Shock! A Guide to Customs and Etiquette*. Portland, OR: Graphic Arts Center Publishing Co., 1997.
This is a very helpful guide for understanding Korean culture and customs. It is essential reading for businesspeople and travelers.

Saccone, Richard. *The Business of Korean Culture*. Seoul, Korea: Hollym Corp., 1994.
This work is an extraordinarily helpful and interesting guide to Korean customs and etiquette.

Literature

Fulton, Bruce, and Youngmin Kwon, ed. *Modern Korean Fiction: An Anthology*. New York: Columbia University Press, 2005.
This is the only anthology of short fiction currently in print that covers the 1920s through the 1990s. The book includes a short story from North Korea.

Korean Spirit & Culture Promotion Project. *Chung Hyo Ye: Tales of Filial Devotion, Loyalty, Respect and Benevolence from the History and Folklore of Korea*. Seoul, Korea: Diamond Sutra Recitation Group (Chungwoo Buddhist Foundation), n.d.
The booklet contains some of Korea's most famous folktales and conveys many of the culture's most important values in the process. The entire booklet is available by accessing the following Web site: http://www.kscpp.net.

O'Rourke, Kevin, trans. *Looking for the Cow: Modern Korean Poems*. Dublin, Ireland: Dedalus Press, 1999.
This book contains a comprehensive selection of 20th-century poetry, translated by a poet who is one of the finest translators of Korean literature.

O'Rourke, Kevin, trans. *Singing like a Cricket, Hooting like an Owl: Selected Poems by Yi Kyu-bo*. Ithaca, NY: Cornell University East Asia Program, 1995.
Yi Kyu-bo, a Koryo literatus, is the most accomplished Korean writer of poetry in Chinese.

Art

Asian Art Museum of San Francisco. *5,000 Years of Korean Art*. San Francisco: Asian Art Museum, 1979.
The catalogue includes color plates and text for a major exhibit that traveled to leading museums in the United States. The exhibit was organized by the National Museum of Korea. Paperback copies are available on Amazon.com.

Chung, Yang-mo, et al. *Arts of Korea*. New York: Metropolitan Museum of Art, 1998.
The book covers the most significant developments in the history of Korean art from the Neolithic period to the 19th century and includes essays written by leading Korean art scholars who include information based on the latest research in Korean art studies.

Covell, Jon Carter. *Korea's Colorful Heritage*. Seoul, Korea: Hollym Corp., 1985.
The author, a highly regarded art historian, provides background on varied elements of Korean culture, especially the arts and religion. The book includes beautiful illustrations.

Korean Spirit & Culture Promotion Project. *Fifty Wonders of Korea*. Vol. 1: *Culture and Art*. Seoul, Korea: Diamond Sutra Recitation Group (Chungwoo Buddhist Foundation), 2007.
In addition to a section on printing, language, and history, the second part of this well-written book describes some of the great treasures of Korean art, architecture, ceramics, and sculpture. The booklet contains many impressive illustrations. The complete book can be found at this Web site: http://www.kscpp.net.

Yi, Kun Moon. *The National Museum of Korea*. Seoul: National Museum of Korea, 1998.
The catalogue includes clearly written text and photographs of Korean art from ancient times through the Choson dynasty.

Yoon, Yeolsu, and Wonjun Nam. *Handbook of Korean Art*. Vol 4: *Folk Painting*. Seoul, Korea: Yekyong Publishing Co., 2002.
This handbook is part of a five-volume series designed to provide the reader with a comprehensive, up-to-date, and readable introduction to major aspects of Korea's rich artistic traditions. This book provides essential information about folk painting, along with its varied styles and symbols. It also includes hundreds of colorful illustrations.

Music

Lee, Byong Won, and Yong-Shik Lee, eds. *Music of Korea: Korean Musicology Series 1*. Seoul: National Center for Korean Performing Arts, 2007.
This edition, written by leading authorities, is one of the most complete, current, and authoritative guides on Korean music. It includes a helpful timetable and covers both vocal and instrumental court, classical, folk, and religious music (Buddhist and shaman) along with professional and contemporary music.

Song, Bang-song. *Korean Music: Historical and Other Aspects*. Seoul, Korea: Jimoondang Publishing Co., 2000.
Song, one of the leading authorities on Korean traditional music, provides one of the most extensive and authoritative accounts written to date on Korean music in English.

Food

Kim, Joungwon, ed. *Koreana: Korean Cultural Heritage*. Vol. 4: *Traditional Lifestyles*. Seoul: Korea Foundation, 1997.

This beautifully illustrated book contains chapters on Korea's dietary culture, traditions, ceremonies, holiday customs, and food. It also includes information on traditional foods and table settings, *kimch'i*, traditional alcoholic drinks, and drinking practices.

Korean Spirit & Culture Promotion Project. *Taste of Korea*: *Korean Cuisine Full of Wisdom and Nature*. Seoul, Korea: Diamond Sutra Recitation Group (Chungwoo Buddhist Foundation), 2008.

This beautifully illustrated little booklet is a very handy introduction to the health benefits of Korean food and includes more than 25 recipes. The booklet is available on this Web site: http://www.kscpp.net.

Leisure and Sports

Culin, Stewart. *Korean Games with Notes on the Corresponding Games of China and Japan*. Mineola, NY: Dover Publications, 1991.

The book surveys Korean games and serves as a very helpful introduction to the study of games in East Asia. It includes 173 illustrations by native artists.

A Handbook of Korea. Seoul: Korea Overseas Information Service, 2003.

This volume is a helpful introductory resource for information on Korea. It includes history, geography, government, foreign policy, economy, society, beliefs and religion, culture and the arts, and sports and tourism. The section on sports includes organizations, major sports facilities, national events, traditional sports, and popular sports in Korea today.

Kim, H. Edward. *Taekwondo: The Spirit of Korea*. Seoul, Korea: Ministry of Culture and Tourism, 2000.

The text includes the history and philosophy of *T'aekwondo* and the place of this martial art in the modern world. The book also includes beautiful photographs.

PERIODICALS

Education About Asia. Published three times a year.

This 70-page illustrated magazine includes articles, book reviews, and lessons about Korea and other nations. For subscriptions: Association for Asian Studies, 1021 E. Huron St., Ann Arbor, MI 48104-9876. Order by phone: (734) 665-2490.

Korea Focus. Published quarterly by the Korea Foundation.

This publication provides timely articles on recent events and current issues and is an invaluable resource for keeping up to date with developments in Korea. *Korea Focus* is available as a monthly webzine: http://koreafocus.or.kr. For subscriptions: Korea Foundation, Seocho P.O. Box 227, Seoul, Korea, or http://Koryobooks.com.

Korea Journal. Published quarterly by the Korean National Commission for UNESCO.

The *Korea Journal* publishes scholarly papers, book reviews and book notes, and translations of Korean literary works including short stories, poetry, and drama. Articles include information on ancient, traditional, and contemporary Korea. For further information, e-mail kj@mail.unesco.or.kr.

KoreAm Journal. Published monthly.

KoreAm Journal provides a forum for English-speaking Korean Americans and includes feature stories, poetry, fiction, artwork, and photographs. For further information: info@koreamjournal.com. KoreAm Journal, 17000 S. Vermont Ave., Ste. A, Gardena, CA 90247.

Koreana: Korean Art and Culture. Published quarterly by the Korea Foundation.

This magazine includes articles on Korea past and present, people, travel, the Internet, events, and exhibits. Beautiful photographs of Korea are included in every issue. The foundation provides online access to abstracts of *Koreana* articles and their accompanying photos. For subscriptions: The Korea Foundation, C.P.O. Box 2147, Seoul, Korea, or http://www.koreana.or.kr.

Korean Studies. Published semi-annually by the University of Hawai'i Center for Korean Studies.

This publication's Web site states that the journal "seeks to further scholarship on Korea by providing a forum for discourse on timely subjects, and addresses a variety of scholarly topics through interdisciplinary and multicultural articles, book reviews, and essays in the humanities and social sciences." *Korean Studies* is now available in the Project MUSE electronic database. Web site: http://muse.jhu.edu/journals/ks.

Korea Observer. Published quarterly by the Institute of Korean Studies, a private, nonprofit research institute founded in 1968.

The institute was created for the purpose of encouraging Korean studies, especially in the fields of the humanities and the social sciences, and for promoting cultural exchanges with other nations. E-mail: INST68@chollian.net.

RECOMMENDED LITERATURE

Buck, Pearl S. *The Living Reed*. Wakefield, RI: Moyer Bell, 1996.

The famous author of *The Good Earth* also wrote a fine novel about Korea. *The Living Reed* is a poignant story based on factual material ranging from the 1860s to the division of Korea in 1945. There are memorable accounts of the experience of families during the Japanese colonial period.

Choi, Sook Nyul. *The Year of Impossible Goodbyes*. New York: Bantam, 1991.

Choi provides the reader with a moving account of the experiences of individuals during Japanese occupation, their high hopes after liberation in 1945, their fears as Russian troops took control of North Korea, and their dangerous escape to U.S.-controlled South Korea.

Fulton, Bruce, and Youngmin Kwon. *Modern Korean Fiction: An Anthology*. New York: Columbia University Press, 2005.

An outstanding collection of stories written by major authors and a very welcome publication for anyone interested in 20th-century Korea.

Kim, Richard. *Lost Names: Scenes from a Korean Childhood*. Berkeley, CA: University of California Press, 1988.

Kim recounts his own childhood and the suffering and insults inflicted on his village during Japanese occupation of Korea. The writing is simple, but poetic. The story is very touching and one of the most well-written and memorable books the author has read.

Lee, Helie. *In the Absence of Sun*. New York: Harmony Books, 2002.
This tells the exciting and inspiring true story of the author's dramatic rescue of her relatives from North Korea.

Lee, Helie. *Still Life with Rice*. New York: Scribner, 1996.
This is the captivating story of the author's discovery of her own identity and the inspiring story of her Korean grandmother's life during Japanese occupation and the Korean War years.

O'Brien, Anne Sibley. *The Legend of Hong Kil Dong: The Robin Hood of Korea*. Watertown, MA: Charlesbridge Publishers, 2006.
The legendary Hong Kil Dong of early 17th-century Korea stood as a champion of the poor. He gained knowledge and power denied to him by class and led an army of peasants against corruption and injustice. The book is beautifully illustrated and presented in cartoon form.

Park, Linda Sue. *Bee-bim Bop!* Hawesville, KY: Clarion, 2005.
This is a delightful storybook that will engage all readers but is particularly well-suited for very young children. It includes upbeat verse with charming illustrations, humor, and a recipe for a very popular Korean dish.

Park, Linda Sue. *A Single Shard*. New York: Yearling Press, 2001.
A Newbery Award–winning book, Park's story is alive with fascinating· information about life and art in ancient (12th-century) Korea. It is a tale of courage and devotion. A single shard from a celadon vase will change the life of a young boy and his master.

Park, Linda Sue. *Seesaw Girl*. Boston: Houghton Mifflin, 1999.
Impatient with the constraints on her as an aristocratic girl living in the 17th century (Choson dynasty), 12-year-old Jade Blossom determines to see beyond her small world. The author tells a charming story full of lively action and vivid descriptions, which is enhanced by appealing black-and-white paintings to give a clear sense of the period.

Park, Linda Sue. *When My Name Was Keoko*. New York: Yearling Press, 2002.
Inspired by her own family's stories of living in South Korea during the Japanese occupation, Newbery Medal–winning author Linda Sue Park chronicles the compelling story of two siblings, 10-year-old Sunhee and 13-year-old Taeyul, and their battle to maintain their identity and dignity during one of Korea's most difficult and turbulent times.

Potok, Chaim. *I Am the Clay*. New York: Ballantine Books, 1992.
A moving story by the acclaimed author of *The Chosen* (and veteran of the Korean War) about the experience of a family during the war.

INTERNET SITES

Art / Architecture

Asian Art Museum, San Francisco. http://www.asianart.org
Search the museum's Web site to view its extensive collection of Korean art, and see "The New Asian" in particular.

Asian Historical Architecture. http://www.orientalarchitecture.com
This is a photographic survey of Asia's architectural heritage, featuring nearly 6,000 photographs of 404 sites in 15 countries.

Cultural Heritage Administration, Republic of Korea. http://english.cha.go.kr
According to the Web site, this South Korean government agency is responsible for preserving and maintaining Korean cultural heritage in its original condition, cultivating tourism through promoting the value of South Korea's cultural properties, and expanding people's enjoyment of cultural heritage by disseminating information about Korean traditional culture throughout the world.

Freer Sackler Gallery. http://www.asia.si.edu/collections/KoreanHome.htm
This Washington, D.C., museum, located on the National Mall, has a substantial collection of Asian art, including an extensive array of Korean art.

Gyeongju Museum. http://gyeongju.museum.go.kr/eng/index.php
This is the Web site of one of South Korea's major museums.

Ho-Am Art Museum. http://hoam.samsungfoundation.org/eng/index.asp
This is the Web site of one of South Korea's leading art museums, managed by the Samsung Foundation.

Korean Pottery. http://www.koreafolkart.com/eindex.asp
This site provides photographs of different types of Korean pottery as well as information on important artists.

Korean Spirit and Culture Promotion Project. http://www.kscpp.net
This site includes entire books that are beautifully illustrated. One of the newest entries is *Fifty Wonders of Korean Art*.

Life in Korea. http://www.lifeinkorea.com
This Web site offers articles on Korean art, architecture, culture, society, and customs.

Metropolitan Museum of Art. http://www.metmuseum.org/explore/Korea/koreaonline/index.htm
The legendary New York City museum has an extensive collection of Korean art. The Web site includes ceramics, metalwork, decorative arts, Buddhist sculpture, and painting. Enjoy two activities: "Discover a Korean Dragon" and "What Color Is Celadon?"

National Museum of Korea. http://www.museum.go.kr/eng/index.jsp
This is the Web site of South Korea's biggest and best repository of Korean history and culture.

Peabody Essex Museum. http://www.pem.org
This museum, located in Salem, Massachusetts, maintains an extensive collection of Korean art, much of it viewable on its Web site.

Philadelphia Museum of Art. http://www.philamuseum.org
This is one of the largest museums in the United States, and by accessing its Web site, viewers can explore its renowned collections, including its array of Korean art.

Republic of Korea's Official Web Site. http://www.korea.net
The South Korean government's official English-language home page offers information about contemporary and traditional arts.

Royal Ontario Museum, Gallery of Korean Art. http://www.rom.on.ca/exhibitions/wculture/korea.php

This is Canada's only permanent Korean art gallery, and it illustrates Korean history and culture through a collection that comprises about 260 objects.

Civics and Government

Central Intelligence Agency World Factbook. http://www.cia.gov
   The CIA maintains an extensive public database on countries of the world. Select World Factbook and then click on North Korea or South Korea.

Republic of Korea. http://www.korea.net
   This is the official Web site of the government of South Korea.

Republic of Korea Embassy in the United States. http://www.dynamic-korea.com
   This embassy site includes information on politics, economics, news, science, Internet technology, culture, and heritage and also features a photo gallery.

U.S. Department of State. http://www.state.gov
   Click on South Korea or North Korea to access the State Department's information on the two countries.

Community Service

Liberty in North Korea (LINK). http://www.linkglobal.org
   LINK is a nonprofit, nonpartisan, nonethnic group whose mission is to educate the world about North Korea. It also acts as an advocate for human rights and humanitarian aid. Students can become involved by learning about conditions in North Korea and support projects that will assist in LINK's mission.

World Vision Korea. http://www.worldvision.or.kr/eng/index.asp
   World Vision International is a Christian relief organization that helps poor communities, and especially children, all over the world. The group provides aid to North Korea.

Economy

Asian Information. http://asianinfo.org/asianinfo/korea/pro-economy.htm
   This site provides information on many Asian and Korean topics in addition to economics.

Bank of Korea. http://ecos.bok.or.kr/EIndex_en.jsp
   The Web site of South Korea's central bank provides extensive economic statistics related to the country.

Buy USA/U.S. Department of Commerce. http://www.BuyUSA.gov/korea/en/investment climate.html
   This U.S. commercial service Web site provides information on doing business in South Korea.

Korea Economics Institute. http://www.keia.org
   The institute focuses on the importance of the U.S.–South Korea relationship as well as developments in South Korea.

National Statistical Office of South Korea. http://www.nso.go.kr/eng2006/emain/index.html
   This official government site provides a wide variety of statistics about South Korea.

North Korea Economy Watch. http://www.nkeconwatch.com/category/statistics/foreign-aid-statistics
This site offers news, analysis, and statistics related to North Korea's economy.

Environment

DMZ Forum: For Peace and Nature Conservation. http://www.dmzforum.org
This site provides information about conservationists' efforts toward establishing a peace park and environmental laboratory in the Korean demilitarized zone.

Green Korea United. http://greenkorea.org/english
The mission of Green Korea United is to help protect ecosystems and promote public awareness of work toward preserving the environment so people can live in harmony with nature.

Korea Environment Institute. http://www.kei.re.kr/index_eng.jsp
This site offers South Korean environmental policy papers and other publications, in addition to news and research information, in an effort to prevent and resolve the country's environmental problems.

International Crane Foundation. http://www.savingcranes.org/koreadecember52007.html
This international organization works to save the world's cranes, including those that reside in the demilitarized zone between North and South Korea.

Ministry of the Environment, Republic of South Korea. http://eng.me.go.kr/docs/index.html
The Web site of the South Korean government's environmental agency provides extensive information on the government's environmental policies and initiatives.

Films

iFilm Connections. http://www.asianfilms.org
This site provides an understanding of the Asian and Pacific Island film cultures.

Korean Films. http://koreanfilm.org
Extensive information is provided on Korean films, including movie reviews, interviews with actors and filmmakers, and reports on festivals.

Korean Wave. http://www.korea.net/korea/G08.asp
This Web site offers information on films that are part of the Korean Wave, a term that refers to the increasing popularity of South Korean culture throughout Asia and other continents.

Geography

Education Place. http://www.koreanembassyusa.org
This educational site features outline maps for personal use and for use in the classroom.

Korean Culture and Information Service. http://www.kois.go.kr/kois_main_en.asp
An outstanding site provides accurate and up-to-date information on Korea.

History and Culture

Amnesty International/North Korea. http://www.amnesty.org/en/region/north-korea

Amnesty International's North Korea Web page offers extensive information on the human rights situation in that country.

Asian Education Media Service. http://www.aems.uiuc.edu
This site assists educators in locating outstanding multimedia resources on Asia.

East Rock Institute. http://www.instrok.org
This Web site provides excellent lessons on such topics as cultural values of the Choson dynasty, different cultural values reflected in the 1882 U.S.-Korea Treaty, Korea's landscape, and the *P'ungsu* (feng shui) model.

Foreign Policy Research Institute. http://www.fpri.org/education/koreas
This site offers lectures, audio presentations, and PowerPoint presentations by major historians on such topics as "Dealing with the Nuclear Threat," "Why Americans Need to Know about Korea," "Modern Korean History," and "Korean Religion."

KCET/PBS: *Hidden Korea.* http://www.pbs.org/hiddenkorea
The Web site of Los Angeles's public TV station features *Hidden Korea*, which provides extensive information on Korean history, food, religion, ancestral traditions, holidays, and village life.

Korea Focus. http://www.koreafocus.or.kr
This Web site created by the Korea Foundation offers a wide variety of excellent articles on culture, economics, politics, and society.

Korean Cultural Center Los Angeles. http://www.kccla.org
The Los Angeles–based Korean Cultural Center's Web site includes extensive information about Korean culture, economics, government, history, the Korean language, and life in Korea.

Korean Cultural Service New York. http://www.koreanculture.org
Founded in 1979 by the South Korean Consulate General in New York City, the Korean Cultural Service attempts to expand international understanding of South Korea and its relations with the United States through a variety of cultural and academic activities.

Korean Culture and Information Service. http://www.kois.go.kr/kois_main_en.asp
This South Korean government site provides facts about South Korean culture and tourism as well as government policies.

Korean Culture and Information Service. http://www.korea.net
Korea.net, billed as "The Gateway to Korea," is a South Korean government site that falls under the auspices of the Korean Culture and Information Service. The site includes facts and figures on the country's government, culture, history, economy, and society.

Korean Spirit and Culture Promotion Project. http://www.kscpp.net
This site includes entire downloadable books, such as *King Sejong*, *Admiral Yi Sunsin*, *Fifty Wonders of Korea*, and *Chung Hyo Ye* (folktales). The material is outstanding for middle and high school classroom use.

Republic of Korea Embassy in the United States. http://www.dynamic-korea.com
This site, based in Washington, D.C., includes information on Korean culture and heritage.

Institutes and Fellowships for Teachers

Foreign Policy Research Institute. http://www.fpri.org

By accessing this site, users can download an outstanding PowerPoint lecture, "What You Need to Know about Korea," by Professor Edward Shultz, director of Korean Studies at the University of Hawai'i.

Institute of International Education. http://www.iie.org/ksw
The institute provides an opportunity for secondary social studies teachers and administrators to study and travel for 12 days in Korea. The program is funded by the Korea Foundation.

The Korea Society New York. http://koreasociety.org
The New York City–based Korea Society offers an outstanding fellowship program for elementary and secondary English/language arts and history/social studies teachers to study and travel in Korea.

Korean Americans

Arirang: An Interactive Classroom DVD on Korean American History. http://arirangeducation.com/main
This excellent documentary on Korean American history includes the soundtrack of Korea's most famous folk song, "Arirang," in addition to photographs, text, and lessons for teachers and their students.

Committee on Asian Pacific American Affairs. http://www.capaa.wa.gov
The committee's mission is to improve the quality of life for Asian-Pacific Americans by insuring their access to participation in government, business, education, and other areas.

Korean American Adoptee Network. http://www.kaanet.com
More than 100,000 Korean children have been adopted in the United States. The organization works to build understanding among adoptees, adoptive families, and Koreans and Korean Americans. The site maintains a monthly newsletter and provides information on its annual conference, books, and birth family searches.

Korean American Museum, Los Angeles. http://www.kamuseum.org
According to its Web site, "The Korean American community has established the Korean American Museum to interpret and preserve its history, culture, and achievements; to examine and discuss issues currently facing the community; and to explore new and innovative ways to communicate the Korean American experience to other American communities."

National Association of Korean Americans. http://www.naka.org
The site was established to help carry out the mission to protect Korean American civil rights, improve understanding between Korean Americans and other racial and ethnic groups, and develop better communication among the various generations of Korean Americans.

Korean Language

An Introduction to the Korean Language. http://langintro.com/kintro
This Web site offers a basic tutorial on speaking the Korean language.

Korean Cultural Center Los Angeles. http://www.kccla.org
The Korean Cultural Center's site provides information on learning the Korean language as well as classes offered at the Los Angeles facility.

KOSNET. http://www.interedu.go.kr
  The educational site offers Korean language study over the Internet.

Omniglot. http://www.omniglot.com/writing/korean.htm
  This site provides extensive information on the Koreas' written language.

Korean Tourism

Korean Tourism Organization. http://www.tour2korea.com
  This tourism site includes beautiful photographs of South Korea and facts about travel opportunities to Seoul and other regions of the country.

Life in Korea. http://www.lifeinkorea.com/Culture/spotlight.cfm
  This is an outstanding travel and cultural site that includes extensive information on various dimensions of life today in South Korea. The site's images are large enough to be useful for bulletin boards, PowerPoint presentations, and research papers.

Korean War

Discovery Education. http://school.discovery.com/lessonplans/programs/koreanwar
  The Discovery Channel's Web site provides a lesson plan on the Korean War for students in grades 9–12 and includes a link to interesting recollections from Korean War veterans.

Harry S. Truman Library and Museum. http://www.trumanlibrary.org/whistlestop/study_collections/korea/large/index.htm
  This presidential library site examines the Korean War from the perspective of participants in policy, participants in combat, and those affected by the tragedy of the war.

Korean War Children's Memorial. http://www.koreanchildren.org
  This site, based in Bellingham, Washington, features postings of more than 1,000 stories and photos relating to U.S. soldiers in the Korean War and the children of Korea during 1950–1954.

Korean War FAQ. http://www.centurychina.com/history/krwarfaq.html
  This Web site answers frequently asked questions about the Korean War.

Korean War National Museum. http://www.theforgottenvictory.org
  The Illinois-based museum's site includes resources, photographs, and links to other Web sites that provide information on the Korean War.

Korea War Project. http://www.koreanwar.org
  This Texas-based site focuses on those who are still missing from the Korean War as well as a DNA project to identify the remains of individuals who continue to be found on the Korean peninsula.

Lesson Plans / Resources for the Classroom

Association for Asian Studies. http://www.aasianst.org/EAA/about.htm
  This site provides sample articles and lessons from the association's outstanding journal for educators, *Education about Asia*.

Korea Society. http://koreasociety.org

The Korea Society has one of the best Web sites for obtaining carefully developed Korea-related lesson plans, PowerPoint lectures, digital information, and recordings for the classroom (click on "Korean Studies"). The site offers lessons for grades K–12 in nearly all disciplines and on the following topics: art, architecture, culture, dance, economy, education, geography, history, Korean War, language, music, North/South issues, religion, and women's issues.

National Consortium for Teaching about Asia (NCTA). http://ncta.osu.edu
The NCTA, described on its Web site as "a multiyear initiative to foster a permanent place for the teaching and study of East Asia at the middle and secondary school levels," is coordinated by the East Asian Studies Center at the Ohio State University.

News

Choson Ilbo. http://english.chosun.com
Choson Ilbo is one of South Korea's major newspapers, whose name is translated as the *Korean Daily News.*

Korean Broadcasting System (KBS). http://world.kbs.co.kr/english/news
KBS is one of South Korea's three major broadcast networks. This site provides world and domestic news stories.

The Korea Herald. http://www.koreaherald.co.kr
The *Korea Herald* is one of South Korea's largest English-language newspapers.

Korea Times. http://www.koreatimes.co.kr
The *Korea Times* is South Korea's oldest English-language newspaper.

North Korean Central News Agency. http://www.kcna.co.jp/index-e.htm
This is the English-language Web page of North Korea's official government news agency.

Yonhap News Agency. http://english.yonhapnews.co.kr
This Web site belongs to one of South Korea's major news agencies.

North Korea

BBC News. http://news.bbc.co.uk/1/shared/spl/hi/picture_gallery/05/asia_pac_unseen_north_korea/html/1.stm
The BBC News site features photos taken by an anonymous Western businessperson who was given the rare opportunity to travel throughout North Korea.

Council on Foreign Relations. http://www.cfr.org/publication/17322/north_korea
The U.S. nonpartisan foreign policy organization's site includes information on issues relating to North Korea, such as who will lead the nation after Kim Jung-Il.

Democratic People's Republic of Korea (North Korea). http://www.korea-dpr.com
This is the official North Korean government Web site. The site provides information on the Korean Friendship Association, which attempts to build international ties with North Korea.

Kim's Nuclear Gamble (PBS). http://www.pbs.org/wgbh/pages/frontline/shows/kim
This public broadcasting site features a *Frontline* program that examines North Korea's nuclear development issue and includes interviews with such U.S. government figures as Madeleine Albright, Stephen Bosworth, Jimmy Carter, Donald Gregg, and William Perry.

Marsh Wong. http://www.marshwong.com/200709_DPRK
> Photographer Marsh Wong's site features hundreds of images of North Korea. They include photographs of the North Korean people, P'yongyang, Kaesong, the DMZ, and rural areas. The photographs are excellent for classroom use.

National Public Radio (NPR): *Life in North Korea*. http://www.npr.org/templates/story/story.php?storyId=4657702
> An NPR broadcast by P'yongyang resident Richard Ragan describes his life in North Korea. His is the only U.S. family authorized to live there. Ragan heads the United Nations' World Food Programme in North Korea's capital.

North Korean Human Rights Act. http://www.internationalrelations.house.gov/nkhra.htm
> The U.S. House of Representatives site provides information on Congress's North Korean Human Rights Act and also covers such issues as North Korean refugees, humanitarian aid, and international abduction.

U.S. Committee for Human Rights in North Korea. http://www.hrnk.org
> The committee is a bipartisan, not-for-profit organization dedicated to promoting human rights for the people of North Korea.

U.S. Department of Energy/Energy Information Administration. http://www.eia.doe.gov/cabs/North_Korea/Background.html
> This U.S. government site provides information on North Korean energy, economic, and diplomatic issues.

Woodrow Wilson International Center for Scholars/North Korean International Documentary Project. http://www.wilsoncenter.org/index.cfm?fuseaction=topics.home&topic_id=230972
> The Wilson Center site offers an information-rich clearinghouse on North Korea.

North-South Reunification

Center for Strategic and International Studies. http://www.csis.org
> The center is a nonprofit bipartisan organization that recommends policy for government, international institutions, the private sector, and civil society (search for "Korea").

Korea Scope. http://www.koreascope.org
> This Web site provides information on North Korea and South Korea, reunification policy, and inter-Korean exchange and cooperation.

Ministry of Unification. http://unikorea.go.kr/english
> This is the South Korean government's official site for its Ministry of Unification, which is charged with the task of spearheading North-South reunification.

Workshops on Korean History and Culture for Educators

Korea Academy for Educators. http://www.KoreaAcademy.org
> The academy's site offers information on resources and programs for educators on Korean history and culture and the Korean American experience to administrators and teachers throughout the United States.

The Korea Society. http://www.KoreaSociety.org
> The society offers workshops for educators in New York City.

Thematic Index

Index

Tables are indicated with a *t*.